ESSAYS ON MORAL DEVELOPMENT

VOLUME II

The Psychology of Moral Development

ESSAYS ON MORAL DEVELOPMENT

Volume II

The Psychology of Moral Development

The Nature and Validity of Moral Stages

LAWRENCE KOHLBERG

1817

HARPER & ROW, PUBLISHERS, SAN FRANCISCO

Cambridge, Hagerstown, New York, Philadelphia
London, Mexico City, São Paulo, Singapore, Sydney

 For information address Harper & Row, Publishers, Inc., 10 East 53rd Street, New York, NY 10022. Published simultaneously in Canada by Fitzhenry & Whiteside, Limited, Toronto.

FIRST EDITION

Library of Congress Cataloging in Publication Data

Kohlberg, Lawrence, 1927–
THE PSYCHOLOGY OF MORAL DEVELOPMENT.

(Essays on moral development ; v. 2)
Bibliography: p.
Includes index.
1. Moral development. 2. Developmental-psychology.
I.Title. II. Series: Kohlberg, Lawrence, 1927–
Essays on moral development ; v. 2.
BF723.M54K62 vol. 2 155.2s [155.2] 83-47726
ISBN 0-06-064761-2

84 85 86 87 88 10 9 8 7 6 5 4 3 2 1

Contents

Acknowledgments

BECAUSE this book represents a line of work that started with my dissertation proposal in 1955, I would like to acknowledge my University of Chicago mentors and dissertation committee, Helen Koch, Anselm Strauss, and William Stephenson. Helen Koch, now dead, was an extraordinary mentor, and any mentorship I have been able to offer students has come from her example. Anselm Strauss, a sociologist, is perhaps the first American scholar to attempt to integrate the structuralist theory of Piaget with the symbolic interactionism of George Herbert Mead, a recurring theme of this volume. The latest scholar to attempt this task, Jürgen Habermas, is someone to whom I am also deeply intellectually indebted, as Part Two of this volume indicates. Unusual among writers about dialogue, now a trendy topic, Jürgen actually has a capacity to engage deeply in intellectual dialogue, a capacity from which I have greatly benefited. I have had an opportunity to acknowledge my indebtedness to Will Stephenson, still brilliant and prolific in his writing in his eighties, in another place (Kohlberg 1970). I would like to also acknowledge my lifelong friendship with Jack Gewirtz, who introduced me to the actual doing of child psychology research and who invented the experimental social learning paradigm as a young teacher at Chicago in the fifties. While I chose Anselm Strauss's paradigm rather than Jack's, our lifelong dialogue about the relation of communication across paradigms continues. It is difficult to imagine that this book could have been written by anyone who did not intellectually grow up at Chicago where, as an undergraduate with teachers like Henry Sams (Kohlberg, 1973e) and Alan Gerwith, I learned something of the great moral tradition from Aristotle to Kant, Mill and Dewey and its expression both in philosophy and literature. As a psychology graduate student, I had the good fortune to learn clinical theory and practice from Bruno Bettelheim, Carl Rogers, Bill Henry, and Sam Beck; philosophy from Charles Morris; and adult human development from Bernice Neugarten and Bob Havighurst.

Having acknowledged what I have learned from my former teachers, I also want to acknowledge what I have learned from my former students. Their work continually appears in this volume, the work of Jim Rest, Dick Kramer, Mordecai Nisan, Dick Krebs, and Moshe Blatt at Chicago; Eliot Turiel and Jim Fishkin at Yale; and Bob Selman, John Broughton, Dwight Boyd, Bob Kegan, Bill Puka, Peter Scharf, Joe Reimer, Al Erdynast, Betsy Speicher, Sally Powers, Laura Rogers, Alexandra Hewer, Dan Hart, John Snarey, Rich Shulik, and Clark Power at Harvard. All have long since ceased to be students and have become intellectual colleagues and friends from whom I continue to learn. All have gracefully helped me to make the stormy transition from mentor to colleague and friend less stormy and more rewarding than I could have imagined as possible. Among my current students at Harvard, Mark Tappan, Dawn Schrader, Cheryl Armon, and Bob Ryncarz have contributed to the book and to the ongoing life of the Center of Moral Education.

Among working colleagues, Anne Colby, Ann Higgins, Dan Candee, John Gibbs, Marc Liberman, and Chuck Levine have been central to this book and to Harvard's Center for Moral Education. Anne Colby (Colby et al., 1983, 1984) is lead author of the technical book and monograph on the longitudinal measurement of moral stages to which these theoretical essays are parallel. Without Anne's leadership and work on the ten-year project, it could not have been successfully completed. Her deep friendship continues to mean much to me. Her career in developmental psychology has continued to progress as Director of the Henry Murray Center for the Study of Lives at Radcliffe College. Her current work reminds me of my intellectual indebtedness to Henry Murray, the grandfather of all our work in personality development.

Dan Candee has been a friend who has kept alive the study of the relation of moral stages to moral action of which the chapter in this book is just one report. John Gibbs appears in these pages as a friendly critic, but was a second backbone to the longitudinal project as well as the creator of a valuable measure of his own.

The devotion of a chapter in the book to a comparison of my work with that of Jane Loevinger indicates the respect and colleagueship I feel toward her. While differing on many issues, I feel with her (Loevinger, 1979) that there is an "invisible college" of developmentalists facing new assessment problems together, a "college" that includes not only Jane and myself but many of the people already mentioned. Carol Gilligan is another psychologist whose approach is perhaps more divergent than Jane Loevinger's from my own, but who is also a member of this "invisible college," joining in discussion and debate about the frontiers of thinking about moral development.

Ann Higgins has been central to the book both as chapter contributor and overall editor of the book. More importantly, her company and support have been central to my life in the years this book was written, as it will be in the years to come. In Volume I, I acknowledged my mother's encouragement of my writing since adolescence. In this volume, I want to reaffirm this acknowledgment even though she thinks my best writing is "Beds for Bananas," which I wrote at age nineteen (Kohlberg, 1949).

The theoretical work in these essays was largely made possible by released time from teaching provided first by an N.I.M.H. career scientist award from 1969 to 1974, and then by a Danforth Foundation award from 1974 to 1980. I am deeply grateful to Gerri Bagby, vice-president of the Danforth Foundation, for her advice, support, and friendly role as "official needler" to get things in writing during this period. I myself view writing as having a largely dialogic function. This book like its predecessor was written for my students, my colleagues, and my friends, the people with whom one can carry on a dialogue about an ongoing research program.

Imre Lakatos (1978), the historian and philosopher of science, has had the sense to see that a scientific theory is not an axiomatic hypothetical-deductive system but an evolving research program. Critics like Phillips and Nicolayev (1978) have argued that my theory is a "regressive" program, adding epicycles to epicycles like Ptolmaic astronomy. Lapley and Serlin (1983) and Puka (1979) have answered Philips and Nicolayev, claiming that my theory is a progressive program. The reader may judge, but at least can judge based on the presentation of the evolution of the theory. When I started the work reported in this volume, Piagetian structualism was "out" in American psychology. When the earlier essays of this volume were written, structuralism was "in"; now it is "out" again. Research programs, however, do not, or should not, follow the fads of American psychology, though serious critics deserve the courtesy of a response, which I have tried to provide in this volume.

In this volume, I have not responded to much important and informed criticism like that of Richard Peters, since criticism related to moral education will be dealt with in the next volume. The next volume will find a more eclectic "Kohlberg's theory," since as we claim in the Preface moral education must not make the "psychologists' fallacy" of trying to derive educational practice from some one psychological theory. It will also acknowledge another group of important teachers, students, and colleagues whom I have not mentioned in this note.

In addition, I want to acknowledge the help of Carole Lee, who not only was responsible for the typing of this book but has been the mainstay of the Center for Moral Education in the years in which most of this book was written.

Finally, I wish to express my appreciation to the men whose development this book records, men who have cooperated every three years for twenty-one years in another go at the Heinz dilemma. Over the years they have become friends, not just research subjects.

Preface to *Essays on Moral Development*

YOU ARE reading one of three volumes on moral development, as follows:

Volume I. The Philosophy of Moral Development: Moral Stages and the Idea of Justice
Volume II. The Psychology of Moral Development: The Nature and Validity of Moral Stages
Volume III. Education and Moral Development: Moral Stages and Practice

Each volume is intended to stand independently of the others, but the flow of ideas and arguments logically suggests reading the volumes in the order listed.

Audience and Purpose of the Three Volumes

The three volumes are aimed at the same general audience and have the same general purpose. In writing, I have partly had in mind a special audience, the graduate students in psychology, philosophy (theology), and education whom I teach and who attend a course called "Moral Development and Moral Education." I have also had in mind a more general audience, all those potentially interested in a theory of moral education that combines (1) a philosophical theory of justice with (2) a psychological theory of the process of moral development to produce (3) an educational theory prescribing a reasonable practice of moral education in the schools.

In thinking of the more general audience, I have viewed moral education as of interest to more than a few specialists and graduate students. The major required readings for my graduate course (which these volumes supplement) are Plato's *Republic,* Emile Durkheim's *Moral Education,* Jean Piaget's *Moral Judgment of the Child,* and John Dewey's *Democracy and Education.* These books on moral education were not written for professional researchers or graduate students but for literate people interested in the great questions of society. Although my writings enter into the realm of technical research more than do these great books, and lack their grandeur of thought or style, I have tried to write them in a way that would be understandable to any literate person who might read these other books.

In writing and organizing these essays, I have also tried to keep in mind the awareness these great writers had that moral education is "interdisciplinary" and that it requires an integration of psychological, philosophical, and sociological (or political) perspectives.

Order in the Writing of the Three Volumes

Volume II, on psychology, represents both my earliest thinking and writing and my latest. The basic conception of six psychological stages of moral development goes back to my 1958 doctoral dissertation. It took, however, twenty years of longitudinal study to validate empirically the conception of the stages. This twenty-year period was not simply a matter of collecting dilemma interviews from my original subjects every three years. Rather, it was a period of revising and refining the stage definitions and the method of assessing them, a process just completed in the year of the first volume's publication. In addition to the longitudinal data themselves, Volume II reflects revisions of ideas in response to the discussions with my psychologist colleagues.

Volume III, on practice, represents the next set of ideas I worked on. When I started my dissertation in moral psychology, I was aware of a tradition of thought about moral education originating with Plato. In the contemporary world, however, it seemed as if only optimistic Sunday school educators and Boy Scout leaders thought or wrote about moral education. In 1958, that stereotype was not far from the mark. It was not until 1971 that an academically serious journal on the topic was started, *The Journal of Moral Education.* In writing in the early 1960s, I speculated on some implications of moral stage development for education. In 1969, I was galvanized into deeper reflection when to my surprise a graduate student, Moshe Blatt, engaged intermediate and high school students in a semester of Socratic classroom dilemma discussions and found that a third of the students moved up a stage, in contrast to control students, who remained unchanged (Volume III, Chapter 13). My first response to this evidence of stage change as a result of Socratic teaching was a lecture (published as Chapter 2 in Volume I, on philosophy) reasserting the ideas of Socrates about teaching about the knowledge of the good. My second response was to write a systematic treatise called "Moral Stages as the Basis for Moral Education" (1971).

These early educational writings were done before I personally attempted to engage in moral education, first in the Niantic prison in Niantic, Connecticut, starting in 1971, and then in the Cluster School, the alternative public high school in Cambridge, Massachusetts, beginning in 1974. Both the preface to Volume III and the chapters themselves make clear how my ideas about moral education changed through my experience of educational practice.

Volume I, on philosophy, presents essays written after my initial psychological and educational writing. The prod to writing was primarily educational. If an aim of education is stage growth, as I believe, then one must give a philosophic rationale for why a higher stage is a better stage. "Later" does not automatically mean "better," or senescence and death would be best of all. My answer focused on the idea of justice; later I became aware of moral philosophic issues not answered by the idea of rational justice but dealt with profoundly by literature and theology.

In summary, the volumes span a ten-year period of continued elaboration and revision of ideas. I have not attempted to present a single final statement, because my thinking, like that of my colleagues, is changing and growing.

Order in the Reading of the Three Volumes

Although my writings started first as psychology, psychology should not be our first concern as writers or readers about moral development. The key chapter in Volume I, Chapter 4, "From *Is* to *Ought,*" clearly indicates why some hard philosophic reflection on moral development is required before beginning empirical psychological research on the topic.

For this reason, I have placed Volume I, on moral, political, and educational philosophy, before the volumes on moral psychology and its applications to education. The reader is likely to start with Meno's psychological question to Socrates (in Plato's *Meno*): "Can you tell me, Socrates, is virtue something than can be taught? Or does it come by practice? Or is it neither teaching nor practice but natural aptitude or instinct?" For the psychologist, it is wiser not instantly to respond with a favored theory of conditioning, instinct, or cognitive development but to recognize the prior philosophic question and to reply, like Socrates, "You must think I am singularly fortunate to know whether virtue can be taught or how it is acquired. The fact is that far from knowing whether it can be taught, I have no idea what virtue itself is."

Once the psychologist recognizes that the psychology of moral development and learning cannot be discussed without addressing the philosophic questions What is virtue? and What is justice? the only path to be taken is that taken by Plato and Dewey, which ends with the writing of a treatise describing moral development in a school and society that to the philosopher seems just.

Although I initially approached moral development and education as a research psychologist, I have attempted to avoid "the psychologist's fallacy": that which makes a theory good for assembling and organizing psychological research data is what makes it good for defining the aims and methods of education. An example of this fallacy, in my opinion, is the belief that, because Skinner's theory of operant conditioning—behavior modification—is good for accumulating and ordering psychological data on animal and sometimes human learning, it must therefore be a good theory for prescribing to teachers the methods and aims of classroom learning.

Skinner's theory commits the psychologist's fallacy insofar as it claims that because a psychologist can go "beyond freedom and dignity" in the ideas ordering and interpreting research data on children's learning, the ideas of freedom and dignity are therefore not necessary ideas for teachers and citizens engaged in moral education. This claim of Skinner's is examined in Chapter 3 of Volume I, "Development as the Aim of Education." In contrast, Rochelle Mayer and I claim that concepts of justice, or of the right of each child and adult to liberty and human dignity, are the starting point of psychological research and educational practice rather than psychological hypotheses emerging from quantitative research data.

In moral philosophy, the "psychologist's fallacy" is called the "naturalistic fallacy." It is the fallacy that the philosophic question, Why is some action really right or good? can be directly answered by social scientific statements about the causation or motivation of the action. The central chapter in Volume I, "From *Is* to *Ought:* How to Commit the Naturalistic Fallacy and Get Away with It in the Study of Moral Development," is a discussion of the uses of moral stage psychology in answering philosophic questions while avoiding the psychologist's "naturalistic fallacy."

Order of the Contents of Volume I, on Philosophy

Volume I addresses the question posed by Socrates: "What is a virtuous man, and what is a virtuous school and society which educates virtuous men?" The answers given in Volume I are not new. They are the answers given by Socrates (Chapter 2); next by Kant, as interpreted by John Rawls's *A Theory of Justice* (Chapter 5); then by John Dewey, in *Democracy and Education* (Chapter 3); and most recently by Piaget, in *The Moral Judgment of the Child* (Chapter 4). Following Socrates, Kant, and Piaget, the answer I and my colleagues offer says that the first virtue of a person, school, or society is justice—interpreted in a democratic way as equity or equal respect for all people.

Democratic justice is an answer to the deontological question, What are the rights of people, and what duties do these rights entail? Given the democratic justice answer to the deontological question, we still need to answer the teleological question What is the purpose of a person's life or of a school or society's existence? Our answer is John Dewey's answer (and, in a sense, Aristotle's): the aim of education and of civic life is intellectual, moral, and personal development (Chapter 3).

What is new in our answers to these questions is the systematic stage framework with which we approach them. Basic to the cognitive-developmental theory of moral psychology presented in these volumes is the framework of *structuralism* (the analysis of invariant systems of relations among ideas), which underlies any attempt to define stages. On the philosophic side, this framework of structuralism gives rise to a theory of virtue as *justice.* Although Plato, Dewey, and Piaget each meant different things by *justice,* each recognized justice as the first virtue of a person because it is the first virtue of society. Each recognized justice as a *structure,* a pattern of equilibrium or harmony in a group or society. The interface between my psychological theory and structural theories of moral philosophy is the subject of the first volume.

Volume I is divided into four parts. Part One uses the moral stages to approach the problems of educational philosophy. Like Socrates and Dewey, I and my colleagues feel that the question of moral philosophy (the question What is virtue?), is both first and finally a question of education, which is the practice of philosophy.

Part Two focuses directly on issues of moral philosophy. Thus, the heart of Volume I is this part, containing two chapters, "From *Is* to *Ought*" (Chapter 4) and "Justice as Reversibility" (Chapter 5). These chapters argue that there are stages of moral reasoning and judgment, that the core of each stage is an underlying conception of justice, and that each higher stage is better for resolving justice problems.

The two remaining parts of Volume I apply the stage theory developed in Parts One and Two to problems in the humanities. Part Three applies the moral stages and the ideal of justice they imply to questions of political philosophy and the philosophy of law. It focuses on two U.S. Supreme Court decisions.

The first Supreme Court decision, considered in Chapter 7, is the *Furman* decision, prohibiting many uses of capital punishment as a violation of the Eighth Amendment prohibiting "cruel and unusual punishment." Chapter 7 supports this decision on the grounds (1) that, very slowly, public and individual sentiment is moving toward viewing capital punishment as cruel and unusual, and (2) that capital punishment violates Rawlsian justice and other Stage 6 justice principles.

In Chapter 8, I consider a second decision, the *Schempp* decision, making religious observation and teaching in the school a violation of the First Amendment and of the separation of church and state. This decision has been interpreted as prohibiting moral education in the schools on the grounds that such education is the propagation of a creed of secular humanism. In the chapter, I argue that the teaching of justice in the schools is not a violation of the right of religious minorities or majorities but is, in fact, a part of the Founding Fathers' vision of the mission of the public schools. I offer a developmental conception of the teaching of justice.

Part Four reaches into areas of the humanities that deal with questions beyond justice, the humanities of theology and literature. Justice is the first virtue of law and of political and personal action, so it is the first virtue of a person. But life is not just, so what is one to think or feel when one's sense of justice does not fit one's actions or the actions of others? This is the central issue raised for the reader or writer of tragedies. It is the central issue theologians face when talking about religion or faith. Chapters 9 and 10 do not try to answer these deep questions; they only attempt to point to the justice element presupposed by these questions and by answers to them.

Volume I, then, includes the following chapters:

PART ONE. MORAL STAGES AND THE AIMS OF EDUCATION

Chapter 1. "Indoctrination Versus Relativity in Value Education" (1971)

Can moral educators escape indoctrinating students with their own arbitrary and relative values or do more than simply clarify the student's own arbitrary values? I propose moral education through stimulating moral development as a way out of this dilemma.

Chapter 2. "Education for Justice: A Modern Statement of the Socratic View" (1970)

Can "a bag of virtues" guide moral education? I use the moral stages as a basis for restating Socrates' claim that virtue is justice, that it rests on knowledge of the good, and that moral education is a drawing out from within through dialogue.

Chapter 3. "Development as the Aim of Education: The Dewey View" (1972), with Rochelle Mayer

We clarify the relation between psychological and philosophical ethical theories in formulating educational aims and present Dewey's progressive educational theory, which combines a cognitive-developmental psychology with a philosophic ethic of liberalism.

PART TWO. MORAL STAGES AND THE IDEA OF JUSTICE

Chapter 4. "From Is to Ought: How to Commit the Naturalistic Fallacy and Get Away with It in the Study of Moral Development" (1971)

In this chapter, I present a culturally universal or nonrelative concept of morality and justice, outline the moral stages as justice structures, claim that a higher stage is a better stage, and give an account of the relation between psychology and philosophy in studying moral development.

Chapter 5. "Justice as Reversibility: The Claim to Adequacy of a Highest Stage of Moral Development" (1978)

Here I give an elaboration of the principles and process of judgment at Stage 6 and discuss Rawls's theory as a justification of Stage 6 moral judgments.

PART THREE. MORAL STAGES AND LEGAL AND POLITICAL ISSUES

Chapter 6. "The Future of Liberalism as the Dominant Ideology of the Western World" (1977)

My introductory structural analysis of liberal or progressive political philosophies leads to a statement of moral evolution at the societal level and places Rawls's Stage 6 concept of justice in the context of contemporary problems.

Chapter 7. "Capital Punishment, Moral Development, and the Constitution" (1975), with Donald Elfenbein

Here we work out in detail the philosophic and psychological aspects of one moral problem, capital punishment. Our explanations of why capital punishment is uniformly rejected at the highest stage but accepted at the lower stages indicate the relation between the content and structure of moral thought.

Chapter 8. "Moral and Religious Education in the Public Schools: A Developmental View (1967)

In this chapter, I assert that the teaching of justice in the public schools is not a violation of children's liberties or of the separation of church and state.

PART FOUR. MORAL STAGES AND PROBLEMS BEYOND JUSTICE

Chapter 9. "Moral Development, Religious Thinking, and the Question of a Seventh Stage" (1979), with Clark Power

We explore the relation between the moral stages and religious thinking. In this chapter, we postulate a stage of religious orientation to deal with issues unresolved by the highest stage of moral judgment (Stage 6).

Chapter 10. "Moral Development and the Theory of Tragedy" (1973)

As in the chapter on religion, in this chapter I use stages of justice to illuminate the form and experience of tragedy, a "postraditional" experience that involves the limits of Stage 6 rational human morality.

Epilogue. "Education for Justice: The Vocation of Janusz Korczak"

The life of a martyred Polish educator illuminates the centrality of education for justice in a "Stage 7" person's commitment to serving children.

Order of the Contents of Volume II, on Psychology

Volume II is divided into three parts. Parts One and Two trace the psychological theory of moral stages from earlier formulations to the present; Part Two includes a response to critics. Part Three presents the longitudinal data, and the method of scoring it, that justify the theory.

Although the oldest chapter in Volume II, Chapter I, was published in 1969, it was preceded by ten years of research and writing on the psychology of moral development, commencing with my doctoral dissertation (Kohlberg, 1958). I started the dissertation as an effort to replicate Piaget's (1948) description of moral judgment stages, to extend them to adolescence, and to examine the relation of stage growth to opportunities to take the role of others in the social environment. These goals led to my revision and elaboration of Piaget's two-stage model into six stages of moral judgment, at first cautiously labeled as "developmental ideal types." One thread running through Volume II is the progressive refining of my stage definitions and assessing of them through a twenty-year longitudinal study designed to clarify whether my ideal types were "really" stages, that is, whether they formed an invariant sequence through which all human beings move although at varying rates and end points of development. This longitudinal work is presented in Part Three of Volume II.

Without waiting for clear longitudinal results on this invariant sequence assumption of the stage hypothesis, I began to sketch its theoretical implications for the process of moral development and its relation to moral behavior. These implications define a cognitive-developmental theory or paradigm for the study of the child's moralization that is basically different from that offered by behavioristic learning theories or psychoanalytic accounts of superego formation. I explicated these differences in the first chapter of Part One by comparing some of the research findings from each paradigm. The second theoretical chapter presents a fairly recent statement of the nature of the moral judgment stages and their implications for the moralization process.

My most recent thinking about stages in the moral domain is contained in Part Two of Volume II. Part Two is divided into two chapters. The first discusses revisions in our theory of what we now label "justice stages," distinguishing "hard" justice stages from levels of development of social cognition and clarifying our theoretical enterprise as one which, following Habermas (1983), is a hermeneutic rational reconstruction of ontogenesis. The second chapter responds to a number of critics whose positions represent the range of social-scientific questions and criticisms that have been raised.

Volume II, then, includes the following essays:

Part One. Moral Development Theory

Chapter 1. "Stage and Sequence: The Cognitive-Developmental Approach to Socialization" (1969)

Here I clearly distinguish the cognitive-developmental research paradigm grounded in stages from other approaches to socialization and social learning. I extend the paradigm from moral stage growth to processes of imitation, identification, and sex-role development.

Chapter 2. "Moral Stages and Moralization: The Cognitive Developmental Approach" (1976)

This chapter presents a fairly recent summary of my cognitive-developmental theory of moralization, of the nature of each of the six stages, and of methods for assessing stages.

Part Two. Moral Stages: a Current Statement of the Theory and a Response to Critics

Chapter 3. The Current Formulation of the Theory (1983) with Charles Levine and Alexandra Hewer

This chapter summarizes the current statement of the theory, including revised claims and status of a sixth moral stage, the domain of moral judgment covered by the theory, revised claims as to the relation between moral philosophy and the stage theory, and conceptions of moral substage or moral types.

Chapter 4. Synopses and Detailed Replies to Critics (1983) with Charles Levine and Alexandra Hewer

This chapter summarizes and responds to criticisms of the stage theory made by Jürgen Habermas, Elizabeth Leone Simpson, Rick Schweder, Edmund Sullivan, Carol Gilligan, and John Gibbs.

Part Three. Empirical Methods and Results

Chapter 5. "The Meaning and Measurement of Moral Development" (1981)

This chapter reports on test reliability and on the longitudinal results validating the invariant sequence and structured wholeness of the first five stages in our American male longitudinal data. It compares the assumptions about theory and method of Jane Loevinger's test of ego development with our test of moral development.

Chapter 6. "Continuities and Discontinuities in Childhood and Adult Development Revisited—Again" (1983) with Ann Higgins

We report and integrate clinical longitudinal data on relativistic "retrogression" as a transition from conventional to postconventional morality and the reconstruction of what was earlier thought to be postconventional moral judgment in high school students as substage or moral type B. We discuss experiences of moral conflict related to service in the Vietnam War and experiences of work responsibilities in young adulthood (age 25 to age

35) as stimulating the development and consolidation of postconventional Stage 5 morality.

Chapter 7. "The Relationship of Moral Judgment to Moral Action" (1983) with Daniel Candee

In a review of studies relating moral judgment stage to actual moral behavior, we posit that a stage of judgments of justice is a necessary but not a sufficient condition for moral action, which also requires a second phase judgment of responsibility and a third phase of execution related to "will" or ego controls. We discuss philosophic issues in defining action as "moral."

Chapter 8. "Cultural Universality of Moral Judgment Stages: A Longitudinal Study in Turkey" (1982) with Mordecai Nisan

In this chapter we discuss the results of a ten-year longitudinal study of males in a Turkish village and city. Invariant sequence of the first four stages is documented in the village and the presence of some Stage 5 in the city subjects.

Chapter 9. "Cultural Universality of Moral Judgment Stages: A Longitudinal Study in Israel" (1983) with John Snarey and Joseph Reimer

Here we report results of a ten-year longitudinal study of kibbutz-born and city-born, but kibbutz placed, adolescents and youths, both male and female. Invariant sequence and structured wholeness through the first five stages were found in this sample. Females and males were found to go through the same stages and no differences in moral maturity between males and females were found.

Appendix A. The Six Stages of Moral Judgment

Appendix B. The Nine Hypothetical Dilemmas

Appendix C. "From Substages to Moral Types: Heteronomous and Autonomous Morality, with Ann Higgins, Mark Tappan, and Dawn Schrader

Here we present theory and data on a heteronomous moral type (or substage) A and an autonomous moral type B. The types show both stability over longitudinal testings and developmental movement from A to B. The types are related to the theories of Piaget, J. M. Baldwin, and Kant. They differentiate cultures and peer- and adult-centered social relationships, and they differentially relate to moral action.

Order of the Contents in Volume III, on Education

As noted earlier, the prod to my thinking and writing about moral education was Blatt's (1969) finding of upward stage change through classroom discussion of hypothetical dilemmas (reported in Chapter 13 of Volume III). My reaction to the finding was mixed. On the one hand, such an approach to moral education seemed almost like "teaching to the test" in order to raise scores on verbal interviews about hypothetical dilemmas. On the other hand, it seemed a modern reaffirmation of the Socratic vision of moral education as dialogue about knowledge of the good (Chapter 2 in Volume I).

My first paper for teachers, written with Elliot Turiel in 1971, tried to justify and explain Socratic moral discussion as a method for dealing with both hypothetical dilemmas and real classroom conflicts (Chapter 2 in Volume III).

My next paper for teachers elaborated the broader implications of John Dewey's view of development as the aim of moral education (Chapter 3 in Volume III). The first practical result of this line of thought was to bring dilemma discussion into the curriculum. I first accomplished this in collaboration with Edwin Fenton, an outstanding "new social studies" curriculum writer. I elaborated the justification of this marriage of dilemma discussion with social studies objectives in Chapter 5 of Volume III, "Moral Development and the New Social Studies."

By 1970, while continuing work on strategies for combining moral dilemma discussion with the academic curriculum of the school, I had become aware of the fact that moral education needed to deal with the "hidden curriculum" or the "moral atmosphere" of the school (Chapter 7 in Volume III). The most melodramatic statement of the need to attend to the moral atmosphere or hidden curriculum of an institution came out of work on moral reeducation in the prison (Chapter 9 in Volume III). This chapter notes that reformatory inmates seriously engaged in Socratic discussion of hypothetical moral dilemmas but lived in a prison environment of real moral dilemmas punctuated by inmates, and occasionally also guards, beating inmates. This conflict led us to attempt to create in one prison unit the moral atmosphere of a just community. The just community would be the heart of an enterprise that would also engage in dilemma discussion (Chapter 10 in Volume III). At the time when I was struggling hardest for an approach to explicate the concept of moral atmosphere, I paid a research visit to Kibbutz Sassa in Israel (Chapter 8, Volume III). In addition to operating as a direct democracy in most areas of decision, the kibbutz enlisted the authority of the group in the name of community.

Although I as well as the kibbutz teachers worried about the implications of conformity to the group, the teachers and some of the older students clearly were principled people, not conformists. The visit led to a serious effort by myself and my colleagues to clarify the idea of community we were trying to implement and add to the democratic justice practices in the prison unit. The result was a growing and changing theory of a just community, first developed in the prison setting (Chapters 9 and 10 in Volume III), and then in the Cambridge Cluster alternative public school and the Scarsdale Alternative School (Chapters 11, 12, and 15 in Volume III). Both the theory and the school and prison experiments are changing, in flux. Both, however, have sufficient viability to make writing about them worthwhile.

The chapters in Volume III, then, are as follows:

Chapter 1: Historical Introduction: "The Relation between Theory and Teachers Is a Two-Way Street" (1978)

The history of my education efforts reveals my growing awareness of the "psychologist's fallacy" and my resulting effort to build a theory meaningful to teachers through collaboration in an evolving alternative school.

PART ONE. MORAL STAGES AND THE CURRICULUM—STATEMENTS OF THEORY FOR EDUCATORS

Chapter 2. "What the Classroom Teacher Can Do to Stimulate Moral Development" (1971), with Elliot Turiel

How classroom moral discussion of both real classroom conflicts and hypothetical dilemmas can become a means for the moral stage development of students.

Chapter 3. "The Cognitive-Developmental Approach to Moral Education: A Current Statement of the Dewey View" (1975)

This overview of moral stage theory in psychology and philosophy stresses its roots in Dewey's thought, in relating theory to current experimental work in moral education.

Chapter 4. "Early Social and Moral Education" (1980), with Thomas Lickona

Socratic discussions and classroom community are viable and exciting strategies for moral development and education in the early grades.

Chapter 5. "Moral Development and the New Social Studies" (1973)

Here I discuss developmental moral discussion as part of the goals and methods of "the new social studies." Difficulties and failures of "the new social studies" arise from its neglect of the stage characteristics of adolescents.

Chapter 6. "Should the College Stimulate Moral Development?" (1976)

This chapter is a brief statement of the place of moral discussion in liberal education and a report on a pilot undergraduate course in ethics.

Part Two. The Hidden Curriculum and Moral Education

Chapter 7. "The Unstudied Curriculum: the Moral Atmosphere of the School" (1970)

Here I argue for the necessity of conscious moral education as preferable to the unconscious inculcation of values that characterizes the "hidden curriculum." I analyze the "hidden curriculum" in terms of the stage of moral atmosphere implicitly generated by teachers and administrators by modeling and by methods of creating and enforcing rules.

Chapter 8. "Cognitive-Developmental Theory and the Practice of Collective Moral Education" (1971)

This chapter is my report on the effects of kibbutz moral atmosphere and practices of moral education, stressing community and collective responsibility in moral stage development. Together with Chapter 7, on the moral atmosphere of the American school, this analysis laid the groundwork for my own experimental work.

Chapter 9. "The Justice Structure of the Prison—A Theory and an Intervention" (1972), with Peter Scharf and Joseph Hickey

Analyzing and trying to improve the moral atmosphere of the prison were the beginnings of the "just community interventions."

Part Three. The Theory of the Just Community

Chapter 10. "The Just Community Approach to Correction: A Theory" (1975), with Kelsey Kaufmann, Peter Scharf, and Joseph Hickey

Our first intensive experiment in moral education was the creation of a participatory democracy stressing moral discussion in a woman's prison. We here present the theory behind that intervention.

Chapter 11. "The Just Community in Theory and Practice" (1984)

In this chapter, I trace my thinking about education from (1) an initial focus on Socratic dialogue (ultimately leading to Stage 6) to (2) a focus on helping create high school just communities in Cambridge and Scarsdale.

Chapter 12. "The Moral Atmosphere of High Schools: A Comparative Study (1984) with Ann Higgins and Clark Power

Here we elaborate and integrate Durkheim's concept of group morality with our moral stage theory for assessing moral value change in the school group.

Part Four. Reports of Experimental Moral Education Practice

Chapter 13. "The Effects of Classroom Moral Discussion upon Children's Level of Moral Judgment" (written 1969, published 1975), with Moshe Blatt

This report of the first systematic experiments in moral education demonstrates that developmental moral discussion of hypothetical dilemmas leads to stage change. We give examples of such discussions.

Chapter 14. "The Effects of Secondary School Moral Discussion on Development of Moral Reasoning" (1976), with Anne Colby, Edwin Fenton, and Betsy Speicher-Dubin

A Stone Foundation–sponsored project incorporated moral dilemma discussion into Fenton's high school "new social studies" curriculum in twenty classrooms in Boston and Pittsburgh. The 1975 Blatt and Kohlberg findings were replicated when discussions were led by "average" high school teachers within the context of social studies curriculum goals and content. Methods of leading discussions are illustrated with transcripts from some typical classes.

Chapter 15. "The Just Community Approach in Practice at the Scarsdale Alternative School: A Student's View" (1979), by Edward Zalaznick

The other chapters in this volume reflect the perspective of the theorist and researcher. It seems important to include, in this volume on practice, a participating high school student's perception of the theory and its meaning to himself and his peers. He discusses both the value of the just community approach and some of the unresolved complications the theory presents to students.

Volume III, on eduction, most explicitly represents a stance that characterizes the earlier volumes. The chapters represent, not a fixed system attempting to be invulnerable to criticism, but an open "approach" that recognizes that the phenomena of a field such as moral education cannot be fully encompassed by any single theory. At the same time, conceptual growth requires pushing a theory to its limits and then revising it, rather than accepting a bland eclecticism. In Volume III, I move to thinking through the philosophic issues of Volume I and then expand and revise the theory in light of continuing experience in classrooms and community meetings in a "just community school." Of the three volumes, Volume III (on education) is the most unfinished, but its publication at this point seems warranted as a means for suggesting the practical import of the first two volumes.

The central practice to which psychology is relevant is education. Following Dewey, I believe that theory and research in psychology that do not directly address issues of practice are more than sterile—they are misleading or vague in their real meaning. The "operations" of a psychology dedicated to constructs with operational meaning are eventually the operations of an ongoing practice. I follow Dewey in making a similar claim about philosophy. Modern philosophy is primarily the logical analysis and criticism of underlying concepts and methods of thought in such basic areas as morality. The concepts and methods to be ultimately analyzed by philosophy are basically not those of other professional philosophers but of those engaged in the everyday practice of philosophy. The everyday practice of philosophy is primarily education, because teachers (and students) necessarily undertake to understand, evaluate, and transmit the core concepts of world culture, philosophy, and science, including the concepts of morality and justice. In this sense, the importance of moral education for scholars is not so much that it is a field of application of theory to enlighten ignorant teachers as that it is the arena of practice in which moral theory should be worked out.

It is gratifying, therefore, to see a revival of scholarly interest in moral education in the last five years. Some reasons for this revival are discussed in Volume III, reasons deeper than reactions to such contemporary events as Watergate and Vietnam. This revival is primarily due to the weakening of the American faith in conventional morality (discussed in Volumes II and III), a weakening of faith that leads parents and educators to seek guidance from scholars rather than from tradition. This is not the first time in which the weakening of traditional morality has lead to serious dialogue about moral education. The first time was the Athens of Socrates, Plato, and Aristotle. I hope that these volumes serve some purpose in reviving the dialogue in contemporary North America and Great Britain.

Introduction

THIS VOLUME is divided into the following sections:

Part One. Moral Development Theory
Part Two. Moral Stages: A Current Statement and Response to Critics
Part Three. Empirical Methods and Results

The order of the articles in each section is generally the order in which they were written. In this introduction I shall review some of the intellectual history of twenty-five years of research on moral stages, a history that runs through the different sections of the book.

My own involvement in this research dates from 1955, when I commenced work on my dissertation (Kohlberg, 1958). The purpose of this dissertation was to carry forward into adolescence Piaget's (1932) pioneering investigation of the development of moral judgment in children.

In studying moral development in adolescence, I decided to use Piaget's general assumptions and method. This meant first a focus on moral judgment and a definition of moral judgment in terms of judgments of justice. Like Piaget, I assumed that the child's active moral constructions, as distinct from passively learned assertions of adult moral cliches, would center on the child's sense of justice.

Like Piaget, in focusing upon reasoning about justice, I assumed that the developing child was a philosopher, constructing meanings around universal categories or questions such as the question of fairness. So I chose as cases for eliciting reasoning hypothetical dilemmas of ancient vintage discussed by philosophers.

The assumption of the child as philosopher is the assumption that the child's mind has its own structure. This is the first assumption of the cognitive-developmental approach to morality. I was drawn to the assumption of structure before discovering Piaget and had spent some years doing diagnostic and research work examining unconscious and affective structures from within a psychoanalytic framework. I eventually found it frustrating to look for unconscious mental structures beneath culturally conforming responses through "signs," since I was seldom entirely convinced by my own interpretations. In contrast, the Piagetian study of moral reasoning seemed to reveal mental structures quite directly. The responses of children and adolescents to my hypothetical dilemmas were clearly structurally patterned and clearly their own. Though often attempting to conform and give "the right answer," students gave reasons far from what I or the adult culture expected, reasons with their own clear inner logic.

These constructions of my subjects convinced me of the second major assumption of Piaget's cognitive-developmental approach, the stage assumption. If Piaget's first assumption was that of cognitive structure, the child as philosopher constructing his world, his second assumption was that these constructions were qualitatively unique and proceeded through an invariant sequence or order.

My dissertation, then, was primarily an elaboration and reassertion of Piaget's stage approach to moral development. It added tentatively described fourth, fifth, and sixth stages to the three stages of moral judgment described by Piaget (1932). For theoretical guidance in interpreting my material on these later stages, I turned to McDougall (1908), to Dewey (1934), to Mead (1934), and especially, to J. M. Baldwin (1906). Not only did my thesis add stages to Piaget's three early stages, but it led me to question Piaget's own construction of these stages. The earliest stages of development, as well as the most advanced or highest stages of development, in any stage schema are always the most problematic for definition or interpretation. In the case of moral development, the earliest stage and the final stage reflect the basic assumptions of a stage theorist about what the basic nature of morality is, a basic nature first seen in the definition of a first stage and finally seen in its pure form in a final stage. Piaget grounded his first moral stage, the heteronomous stage, in respect for parental and adult authority and respect for the rules emanating from parental authority, with subsequent stages showing a reduction in such unilateral respect in favor of a more utilitarian view of rules centered in mutual respect between peers. My own data did not strike me as reflecting respect for rules as the first stage of moral judgment and turned me to an account of moral levels more indebted to J. M. Baldwin (1906) than to Piaget. This debt is elaborated in a recent article on Baldwin's theory of moral development (Kohlberg, 1982) and in Appendix C. My questions about the adequacy of Piaget's account of moral judgment stages are elaborated in Kohlberg (1963b), Kohlberg (1964), Kohlberg and Helkama (1985), and in Appendix C. Essentially, my own data and my review of the data of others convinced me that Piaget had defined a series of cognitive-developmental dimensions of moral development, for example, judgment by intentions as opposed to judgment by consequences. Some of these divisions were culturally universal and related to cognitive-moral development, and others were not. These dimensions, however, did not define qualitative levels and did not cluster together to define a "structured whole" as the stage concept would imply. Piaget himself was cautious about claiming invariant sequential stages in moral judgment, stressing, rather, that his heteronomous and autonomous stages were Weberian ideal types, with individuals showing different balances of these ideal types. Many years after my thesis, I was led to define Piagetian heteronomy and autonomy as substages in each stage, as described in Chapter 6 and in Appendix C.

Though differing from Piaget in the definition of moral stages, my dissertation (Kohlberg, 1958) and subsequent early publications of it (Kohlberg, 1963a) showed equal caution by talking about my data as defining ideal types rather than strict sequential stages; this distinction is clarified in Chapters 3, 5, and Appendix C.

The six developmental types of stages defined in my dissertation were divided into three major levels of development:

Level A. Premoral:
- Stage 1—Punishment and obedience orientation.
- Stage 2—Naive instrumental hedonism.

Level B. Morality of conventional role conformity:
- Stage 3—Good-boy morality of maintaining good relations, approval by others.
- Stage 4—Authority-maintaining morality.

Level C. Morality of self-accepted moral principles:
- Stage 5—Morality of contract, of individual rights and democratically accepted law.
- Stage 6—Morality of individual principles of conscience.

The data used to define the stages was from a cross-sectional sample of seventy-two Chicago-area males aged 10, 13, and 16—with an added group of twelve delinquent boys (Kohlberg, 1963a and Chapter 5). The stages were defined by ideal-type grouping of cases. Besides order in the age-trends for usage of each stage, a simplex pattern of intercorrelations among the stages of thought was reported as indication that the types had at least some of the characteristics of hierarchical sequence expected of stages (Kohlberg, 1963a).

The stages just listed I write about now as structural stages. In my dissertation and early reports of it, I referred to them not as stages but only as developmental ideal types. Following Piaget's work on cognitive stages, I assumed that certain empirical findings were necessary to define or verify a set of developmental types as stages. These characteristics include

1. invariant sequence
2. structured wholeness or cross-task or cross-situational consistency
3. hierarchical integration or displacement of lower stages by higher stages

Claims for stages, then, rest upon (*a*) longitudinal and cross-cultural, cross-sex data and (*b*) a method of assessment revealing invariant sequence in such data.

Chapters 5 through 9 report the method and the longitudinal data in the U.S., Turkey, and Israel that, twenty-five years after my dissertation, now finally justify calling the types "stages."

Although my dissertation stayed quite close to my data in young American males, I was from the start convinced that defining moral stages required making some philosophic or metaethical assumptions about the nature of moral judgment and other normative philosophic assumptions that in some way would support the claim that a later stage was a better or more adequate stage of moral reasoning and judgment. These assumptions as they became more refined are the focus of Volume I of this series. We discuss these assumptions again in Part Two, but more briefly and with some modification and restriction of claims made in Volume I. In Part Two, we are clearer about defining the domain we study as the domain of justice reasoning rather than that of moral judgment and reasoning in general.

Though initially cautious about speaking of stages, I did not wait for twenty-five years to start talking about the theoretical implications of my developmental types as stages and started collecting data on some of these implications.

From the point of view of theory, the developmental types I talked about were similar to developmental types independently arrived at by others, notably Peck and Havighurst (1960), as well as Dewey and Tufts (1932) and McDougall (1908). In my earlier writing, I was less interested in making specific claims of results achieved with my own stages than I was in spelling out the cognitive-developmental perspective on theory and research on moralization that *any* of the above-mentioned developmental stage theories implied.

The first chapter of this book is a good example of the reviews I wrote from that more general perspective (Kohlberg, 1963b, 1964). A focus of Chapter 1 is that of placing cognitive-developmental work on stages of moral judgment in a comparative perspective with other approaches. These other approaches are the behavioristic approach, commencing with the work of Hartshorne and May, the psychoanalytic approach, and the cultural or sociological approaches identified with the thinking of Durkheim. None of these other approaches takes conscious moral judgment and its development seriously; they are instead "reductionistic," that is, they reduce moral phenomena to unconscious or nonmoral factors in the human personality or society and assume moral development to be a direct result of socialization. As I claim in Volume I and in the preface to Part One of this volume, in this reductionism they make a philosophic mistake. In Chapter 1, however, I do not stress the philosophic mistake so much as the empirical difficulties each of the other approaches has run into in trying to define or explain moral development itself.

The chapter "Stage and Sequence" is also a review of research with a more programmatic statement about stages, as its title suggests. It does talk about stages, primarily because group data indicated the hierarchical characteristics of our developmental types that the stage construct predicted. Three pieces of research led to the sense of confidence in our moral stages.

The first was Turiel's (1966) dissertation, an experimental documentation that the amount of assimilation of reasoning at other stages than the subject's own was predicted by the stage-order hypothesis; that is, groups of adolescents exposed to the next stage up would assimilate judgments to which they were exposed more than groups exposed to a stage either two above or one below their own, a study recently replicated by Walker (1982).

The second was the work of Turiel and others (L. K. Grimley, 1973; Turiel, Edwards, and Kohlberg, 1978) replicating my dissertation in other cultures, including Taiwan, Turkey, and Yucatan.

These replications indicated that, according to group age trends, the stages developed in the same order in all the cultures studied.

These studies, like many dissertation, were deficient as studies validating stages because they relied on group data or group averages. These group averages could be predicted better than chance by the stage hierarchy hypothesis, but the stage hypothesis demanded internal order and invariant sequential change in the individual longitudinally. Rest's thesis (1973) provided clear evidence of internal order supporting the stage hierarchy hypothesis. It indicated an almost errorless hierarchical Guttman scale (cf. Chapter 1) in comprehension of each stage and clear evidence that comprehension never went more than one stage beyond spontaneous production or usage of the stage. Rest's study and the cross-cultural data were the data featured for the optimistic 1969 statement of "Stage and Sequence." The statement advised caution until individual longitudinal data were shown in group data, but its spirit was one of confident steady advance in an established paradigm.

Confidence in the paradigm slowly generated efforts to implement it in practice. Blatt (1969) demonstrated that classroom dilemma discussion led to moral judgment advances in line with the stage-sequence model. Accordingly, immediately after the programmatic Kohlberg (1969) statement on developmental research I wrote an equally programmatic statement on stages of moral development as a basis for moral education. This programmatic vision brought to Harvard Rest, Blatt, and myself from Chicago and Turiel from Columbia, in what eventually became the Harvard School of Education's Center for Moral Education.

The first order of business for the group at Harvard was not programmatic advance, however. The first order of business was attending to some major cracks in the paradigm, cracks that could be viewed as cracks in the theory, cracks in the methodology, or cracks in both. These cracks were the anomalies of sequence in the results of the longitudinal data on my dissertation subjects who had been reinterviewed every three years for twelve years (Kramer, 1968; Kohlberg and Kramer, 1969). Our first interpretation, reported in Chapter 6, was to accept our stage scoring system as valid and to interpret the anomalies as evidence of genuine retrogression in the college years. Our second interpretation (Kohlberg, 1973, summarized in Chapter 6 of this volume) viewed the apparent retrogression of some of our college students to Stage 2 as a transitional "Stage 4½," the rejection of conventional morality without consolidation of a more principled morality. This "Stage 4½" hypothesis is reassessed in light of current findings in Chapter 6. The 1973 interpretation amounted to a reassertion of the sequence hypothesis in longitudinal data but was an acknowledgment of failure in the details of both stage definition and measurement.

I had, in fact, never thought my method of stage assignment was adequate. As noted, my thesis described stages not as true stages but only as ideal-type moral orientations. Longitudinal study, I thought, was necessary, not only to validate, but to define, an invariant sequence of stages. I did not think my dissertation provided a "test" or "scale" of moral judgment development. I thought, rather, my method was an exploratory assessment method, composed of two alternatives, sentence scoring and global story rating. In terms of reliability, my thesis data indicated that the method led to consensus between raters or between dilemmas sufficient for research comparing age (or other) group averages in terms of theoretical hypotheses. The data did not justify the method as a test locating individual subjects in terms of test-retest and other criteria of test reliability.

Some years after I had concluded that the dissertation method was inadequate, Kurtines and Grief (1974) wrote a critical review of our method and theory concluding the same. They were, however, led to recommend throwing out the theoretical stage "baby" with the assessment method "bath water." Anomalies in the data, they concluded, at the same time invalidated both the theory and the assessment method. Logically one cannot, as they did, question both the theory and the method simultaneously. My colleagues and I questioned the method prior to fundamentally questioning the theory.

Before worrying about developing a reliable method or "test," our concern was to revise the stage definitions using a clinical rating level and see whether such ratings were valid in terms of capturing invariant sequence in our longitudinal subjects. This rating method was what we called the intuitive issue-rating method, in use from 1972 to 1975. Longitudinal results with this clinical method were reported in a 1975 essay by Kohlberg and Elfenbein reprinted as Chapter 7 of Volume I. They indicated adequate conformity to the sequence hypothesis by this relatively subjective method.

Although issue-rating was a subjective method, it rested on a very important differentiation we had come to make in assessment. My dissertation method had obtained stage scores by clarifying reasoning content that we thought were signs of stage structure. Issue-rating attempted to directly infer to stage structure, holding issue content constant. Central to the structure of each stage, we thought, was its sociomoral perspective.

This more directly structural conception of the moral stages is at the heart of the theoretical chapter, "Moral Stages and Moralization" written in 1976. A brief discussion of "standardized issue scoring" in this chapter foreshadows the extensive discussion of this method in Chapter 5, "The Meaning and Measurement of Moral Development." Chapter 2, "Moral Stages and Moralization," then, is in a sense an updating of Chapter 1, "Stage and Sequence."

Like the earlier essay "Stage and Sequence," "Moral Stages and Moralization" contrasts the cognitive-developmental and socialization perspectives on moral development. It includes the revised structural statement of stages in terms of sociomoral perspective. The essay also adds a new theme to the way in which environments stimulate moral development. "Stage and Sequence" stresses the sense in which varying environments provide differential "role-taking opportunities" as stimulation for moral development. Chapter 2 introduces a new concept emerging from our educational work, the concept of moral atmosphere of schools and other institutions. The essay suggests that collective norms and institutional structures themselves could be defined as representing a given stage of moral atmosphere and as stimulating moral judgment and action accordingly.

This theoretical sociological theme is picked up more empirically in Volume III. In that volume we see moral atmosphere as a bridge between judgment and action. A more individual psychological approach is presented in Chapter 7 of this volume "The Relationship of Moral Judgment to Moral Action." As the chapter points out, the issue of the relation of judgment to action is not only a question of psychological theory and empirical conclusions but a philosophic question as to what we mean by moral action.

Underneath the chronology of the various essays in the volume, then, are what might be termed either three shifts in thinking or three phases of research. The first, lasting from 1958 until 1970, was an elaboration of the implications of the cognitive-developmental view to order moral differences between age and other groupings of subjects. The second phase of thinking and research took Piagetian structuralism more seriously as it applied to individual longitudinal development. Reflected in Part Three of this volume, it can be looked at as both clinical individual case study and as the construction and validation of a test of individuals.

The third, and the least finished shift of focus (or phase of research), has been a shift to the naturalistic study of moral action in the context of group or institutional moral atmosphere. Foreshadowed in theory by Chapter 2 ("Moral Stages and Moralization"), it is empirically clarified only in Volume III. It is only in our work on moral atmosphere that we have begun to work seriously with a sociological perspective. Our first chapter dismisses Durkheim's sociological perspective as reducing individual rational moral judgment to irrational shared norms of a group. Volume III quotes Durkheim as a source of our own thinking about moral atmosphere as stages of group structure or of collective norms.

My earlier writing was, in part, an overstatement of the case for rational individual moral development because it had been largely ignored by modern social science. Chapter 7 ("Relationship of Moral Judgment to Moral Action") like Chapter 1 ("Stage and Sequence") is a statement of the importance of individual moral development that, once recognized, allows return in Volume III to the analysis of group factors, acknowledging their importance and their "*sui generis*" nature. The social and moral climate of groups and organizations has been studied in a myriad of ways, all looking at the content aspects of social climate. Volume III proposes to study group moral atmosphere in terms of structure, rather than content. It proposes that we can look at collective or shared norms as having stagelike structure, as we have previously done for individual reasoning. This study (or phase of research) is still in its infancy. This is partly due to its difficulty, but it is also due to its being very closely tied to the thinking and research about education presented in the third volume. Research on moral atmosphere depends upon in-depth ethnographic study. Such study depends upon a variety of informal or tacit sensitivities and knowledge about the groups or institutions studied. No one can study the moral atmosphere of the classroom or school without lengthy participant-observer experience in schools. Therefore, our concept of moral atmosphere may better be looked at in our next volume on education than it could be in this volume as a third phase of psychological theory and research.

ESSAYS ON MORAL DEVELOPMENT

VOLUME II

The Psychology of Moral Development

PART ONE

Moral Development Theory

In the Introduction to this volume, I have traced the evolution of my theorizing about stages from Chapter 1, published in 1969, to its later statement in Chapters 2, 3, and 4, published in 1976 and 1983. This evolution, with its growing clarification of what was content and what was structure in my earlier formulation, is traced in detail in Part Three. The 1969 chapter presents descriptions and examples of the six stages as they were defined by the now obsolete Kohlberg (1958) concepts and assessment method, descriptions quite different from the conceptions elaborated in Chapters 2, 3, 5, and 6 and Chapters 8 and 9. In Chapter 1, over 10 percent of the moral judgments of middle class 16-year-olds in the United States and Mexico are reported to be at the sixth and highest stage, and Stage 5 is reported as the most used stage among American 16-year-olds, accounting for over 30 percent of their moral judgments. Chapters 5, 6, and 9 report no usage of Stage 5 thinking before the twenties and report that Stage 6 is a theoretical construction not identified even by the age of 35 in our longitudinal study of a quite representative sample of sixty American males.

Although there are large differences in the stage descriptions, methods, and reports of "age-normative" data in Chapter 1 and those of later chapters, these do not mean correspondingly large differences in the cognitive-developmental theory of moralization.

Accordingly, in this preface I shall try to pick out the underlying thread of argument in Part One and fill in the philosophic component of the argument discussed in depth in Volume I.

The fundamental issue discussed in Part One is the nature of human morality and its development. Two fundamental conceptions are contrasted in the first and second chapters. The first is the conception that moral development is socialization, that it is the learning or internalization by the child or adolescent of the norms of family and culture. Within this general conception of socialization very different theoretical explorations may still be advanced. The two most prevalent are the social learning theories, which equate moral socialization with situational learning through modeling and reinforcement, and the psychoanalytic theory, which postulates the early formation of a guilt-inducing superego or conscience through identification with, or incorporation of, parental authority and standards. Both theories agree, however, that moral development is the internalization of the standards of parents and culture. In contrasting cognitive-developmental theory to both kinds of socialization theory, we need to briefly review some philosophic issues from Volume I.

The volume of essays on philosophy explicitly treats two issues of which the reader of this volume must be aware. These two issues are value relativity in defining morality, and the relation between a scientific definition of morality and the philosophic definition of the moral. In the general preface I termed it "the psychologists' fallacy" to think that a definition of morality could be made purely in terms of effectiveness in ordering research data without dealing with the philosophic concern about what truly should be.

In Chapter 3 of the first volume, we cited as an example of the psychologists' fallacy Skinner's statement "Good things are positive reinforcers. The reinforcing effects of things are the province of behavioral science which to the extent that it concerns itself with operant reinforcement is a science of values. The effective reinforcers are matters of observation and no one can dispute them."

In this statement Skinner equates with or derives from a value word, "good," a fact word, "positive reinforcement." This equation is questionable. We may wonder whether obtaining positive reinforcement really is an intrinsic moral good. No one may be able to dispute observations as to what is an effective reinforcer, but someone can certainly dispute whether the positive reinforcer is really "good" in a philosophic sense. Skinner goes on to take a socially relativistic conception of good. He says, "What a given group of people call *good* is a fact. Each culture has it own set of *goods* and what may be *good* in one culture may not be *good* in another."

In Volume I we were concerned about relativism and about the psychologists' fallacy because we were concerned about elaborating a conception of justice that would stand up to philosophic questioning. In this volume, we are concerned about these matters from the standpoint of psychologists as scientists predicting and explaining moral behavior. In Chapters 1, 3, and 7 of this volume, we attempt to show that socially relativistic definitions of morality like Skinner's are inadequate, not only to the moral philosopher, but also to the moral actor, and therefore to the psychologist trying to order and explain research observations of moral behavior. The psychologists trying to keep their own moral philosophies out of the definition of what they study have been prone, like Skinner, to be social relativists. An example is Berkowitz's (1964) definition: "Moral values are evaluations of actions generally believed by the members of a given society to be either 'right' or 'wrong.'"

The social relativist ignores the fact that individual moral actors have their own points of view. Student civil disobedience is an example of a behavior studied by psychologists that may be wrong by the standard of the majority but right by the moral actors' own moral standards. Socially relativistic studies of moral values and behavior that neglect the actors' own standpoint soon lead into inconsistencies and lack the ability to order the research data gathered. Agreement with majority standards does not distinguish moral behavior from matters of manners, convention, or practicality. Typically, the social relativist has looked for something in the form and not just the content of a behavior or activity that distinguishes it as moral. This formal aspect has been the "internalized" nature of the moral, its being governed by internal factors independent of situational expediency. When social relativists study moral behavior by *their* definition, they do not find much internally governed or conscientious behavior. They find, as Hartshorne and May found, that adolescents (and by extension, adults) are not divided into groups, the conscientiously honest and the dishonest. They find instead that situational factors independent of conscience appear to be the determinants of honest behavior.

I and my colleagues advocate, instead, starting by studying the moral judgments of the actor. Such study can lead us out of the problem of both individual and cultural relativity, because there appear to be culturally universal moral values developing through an invariant sequence of stages. The higher stages of judgment have formal features making them moral that are more precise than the vague concept of conscientiousness or internalization. Insofar as an individual's action corresponds to his or her judgment and insofar as this judgment is distinctively moral, as it is at the higher stages, we can define an action as "moral" apart from cultural variations or views of the right and independent of factors of situational expediency. Chapters 2 and 8 offer a positive definition of moral action as action in correspondence with mature forms or stages of moral judgment.

We have revised the philosophic assumptions underlying Part One. It is not until Part Two that we add the necessary qualifications and cautions about our philosophic conceptions. The first qualification we draw from Habermas's interpretation of our work as a "rational reconstruction of ontogenesis." In this interpretation, philosophic claims about the greater adequacy of higher stages can be disconfirmed empirically, but empirical confirmation of the stages does not directly allow a claim for greater adequacy for higher stages that gives special philosophic privilege to the developmentalist.

The second qualification follows the philosophic distinction made by Boyd (1977) and others between three domains of moral reasoning: first, the deontic domain of the right and obligatory; second, the aretaic domain of the of the worthy and approvable in human action and character; and third, the domain of ideals of the good life. Only from the standpoint of deontic justice do Stages 5 and 6 have claim to ultimate adequacy. This, together with weak empirical data on Stage 6, leads us to modify but not relinquish our claim that Stage 6 is the defining telos of the rational reconstruction of development.

Using these three domains of moral reasoning, we interpret Carol Gilligan's (1982) empirical work on broadening the study of moral reasoning to what we see as aretaic judgments of personal worth and of special responsibilities for other persons with whom one has particular ties, as well as possibly including ideals of the good life, a focus of study by Armon (1984). Classifying the deontic justice domain as only one of three domains of moral reasoning, we call our stages "stages of justice reasoning" and suggest that it is only the deontic justice domain that is amenable to definition in terms of "hard" sequential hierarchical stages such as are defined by Piaget.

Looking ahead to Part Three, relativism is not a problem only for psychologists and philosophers studying morality, it is a problem for the developing person. The discontinuities in moral development discussed in Chapter 6 largely arise from the relativity problem as youth become aware of it. In that chapter we report college students sometimes asserting an instrumental and relativistic egoism, students who were at the fourth or, as we thought, fifth stage in high school. In that chapter we distinguish the nature of this college-age relativistic emotivism and egoism from Stage 2 egoism. We conclude that this relativistic moral egoism is not a return to the second stage but rather a transitional step from conventional to principled morality. Underneath the moral skepticism of college relativists is a dawning awareness of one principle, the principle of tolerance, or liberty of conscience. Fundamentally, then, these students are making a transition from conventional to principled morality. The transition is reflected in an awareness of the cultural relativity of definitions of values which may grow into a skepticism about morality in general. If the norms and laws of our society may be seen to be culturally relative, youth can question the validity or obligatory quality of all moral norms and see the egoistic or hedonistic self as having a point of view as valid or more valid than that of social (or conventional) morality. In Chapter 6 we review our cases showing radical relativism and then relinquishing this relativism as they define principles of justice and tolerance as having potentially universal validity. In Chapters 8 and 9 we present empirical data on the cultural universality of the stages and of the moral values they define.

Chapters 5 and 6 reflect a growing awareness of the need to more sharply distinguish content and structure (or form) in the definition and assessment of the moral stages. This awareness was not present in the programmatic statement in "Stage and Sequence," Chapter 1 of this volume. The description of the stages themselves in that chapter is out of date and is replaced by the theoretical statements in Chapters 2, 4, and 5 and appendix A. The current standard method of assessing moral stages that arose out of the theoretical statements of Chapter 3 is described and justified in Chapter 5, "The Meaning and Measurement of Moral Judgment."

The growing clarification of the distinction between form and content and the issue of youthful relativism discussed in Part Three led to a redefinition of principled, or Stage 5, reasoning as something first appearing in the postcollege years rather than as something found in earlier adolescence, and it leaves Stage 6 as a theoretical ideal rather than an actual stage of moral judgment found in longitudinal subjects. These changes in the definition of the stages have not altered the basic statement in "Stage and Sequence" as a theory of how interaction with the social environment and role-taking opportunities determine movement through the sequence of stages. Chapter 2 adds to this statement the notion that social environments themselves can be seen as having a dominant stage of justice and community that influences individual moral development. This topic is taken up again in Volume III: In that volume we begin a rapprochement between the sociological theory of Durkheim discussed in Chapter 1 and our emphasis on the development of the moral autonomy of the individual stressed in the present volume.

1. Stage and Sequence: The Cognitive-Developmental Approach to Socialization

FOR A NUMBER of years, I have been engaged in research on moral and psycho-sexual development, guided not by a theory, but by an approach labeled cognitive-developmental. The label cognitive-developmental refers to a set of assumptions and research strategies common to a variety of specific theories of social and cognitive development, including the theories of J. M. Baldwin (1906), J. Dewey (1930), G. H. Mead (1934), Piaget (1948), Loevinger (1966), and myself (Kohlberg, 1966b, 1968).

In this chapter, I shall attempt first to present and justify the general assumptions of the cognitive-developmental approach. Next I shall consider their application to the phenomena of moral socialization, contrasting this approach with social-learning and psychoanalytic approaches. Finally, I shall consider processes of imitation and identification from this point of view, since these processes are held to be basic in cognitive-developmental theories as well as in social-learning and psychoanalytic theories of social development.

Theories of Cognitive Development and the Origins of Mental Structure

Before considering the application of cognitive-developmental theories to socialization, we shall outline the basic characteristics of these theories in the cognitive area. Cognitive-developmental theories presuppose the assumptions of A. L. Baldwin (1969) on cognitive theory but share a number of basic further assumptions as well. Baldwin defines as "cognitive" theories which postulate a

---

Much of the author's research reported here has been supported by N.I.C.H.D. Grant HD 02469-01. The first half of the chapter is a revision of a paper prepared for the Social Science Research Council, Committee on Socialization and Social Structure, Conference on Moral Development, Arden House, November, 1963, supported by MH 4160 of N.I.M.H.

representational or coding process intervening between stimulus and response. This representation is applicable to a variety of proximal stimuli and may elicit a variety of responses depending upon "noncognitive" motivational and situational factors. In Baldwin's version of cognitive theory, it is assumed that such representations are learned, but that such learning does not depend upon making an overt response to any of the stimulus elements in the environment being learned, nor does it depend upon any definite reinforcement for learning (though such reinforcement may be necessary for performance as opposed to learning). As Baldwin points out, his conception of cognitive theory embraces most theories giving attention to cognitive phenomena, including mentalistic-associationistic theories like S-R mediation theories. (Aronfreed's [1969] and Bandura's [1969] social-learning theories recognize cognitive principles of learning in Baldwin's sense, although Gewirtz's [1969] does not.)

In contrast to associationistic theories of cognitive learning, cognitive-developmental theories make the following assumptions:

1. Basic development involves basic transformations of cognitive *structure* which cannot be defined or explained by the parameters of associationistic learning (contiguity, repetition, reinforcement, etc.), and which must be explained by parameters of organizational wholes or systems of internal relations.

2. Development of cognitive structure is the result of processes of *interaction* between the structure of the organism and the structure of the environment, rather than being the direct result of maturation or the direct result of learning (in the sense of a direct shaping of the organism's responses to accord with environmental structures).

3. Cognitive structures are always structures (schemata) of *action.* While cognitive activities move from the sensorimotor to the symbolic to verbal-propositional modes, the organization of these modes is always an organization of actions upon objects.

4. The direction of development of cognitive structure is toward greater *equilibrium* in this organism-environment interaction, that is, of greater balance of *reciprocity* between the action of the organism upon the (perceived) object (or situation) and the action of the (perceived) object upon the organism. This balance in interaction, rather than a static correspondence of a concept to an object, represents "truth," "logic," "knowledge," or "adaptation" in their general forms. This balance is reflected in the underlying *stability* (conserva-

tion) of a cognitive act under apparent transformation, with development representing a widened system of transformations maintaining such *conservation.*

The assumptions just listed are assumptions which hold for cognitive development in general, that is, for the development of ways of thinking about both physical and social objects. Their application to social development is made more concrete by the following additional assumptions about social-emotional development, assumptions whose explanation is left to a section on moral development later in the chapter:

5. Affective development and functioning and cognitive development and functioning are not distinct realms. "Affective" and "cognitive" development are *parallel;* they represent different perspectives and contexts in defining structural change.

6. There is a fundamental unity of personality organization and development termed the ego, or the self. While there are various strands of social development (psychosexual development, moral development, etc.), these strands are united by their common reference to a *single concept of self* in a *single social world.* Social development is, in essence, the restructuring of the *(a)* concept of self, *(b)* in its relationship to concepts of other people, *(c)* conceived as being in a common social world with social standards. In addition to the unity of level of social development due to general cognitive development (the *g* factor in mental maturity tests), there is a further unity of development due to a common factor of ego maturity.

7. All the basic processes involved in "physical" cognitions, and in stimulating developmental changes in these cognitions, are also basic to social development. In addition, however, social cognition always involves *role-taking,* that is, awareness that the other is in some way like the self and that the other knows or is responsive to the self in a system of complementary expectations. Accordingly, developmental changes in the social self reflect parallel changes in conceptions of the social world.

8. The direction of social or ego development is also toward an equilibrium or *reciprocity* between the self's actions and those of others toward the self. In its generalized form this equilibrium is the end point or definer of morality, conceived as principles of justice, that is, of reciprocity or equality. In its individualized form it defines relationships of "love," that is, of mutuality and reciprocal intimacy. The social analogy to logical and physical conservations is the maintenance of an *ego-identity* throughout the transformations of

various role relationships. (A concrete early developing example discussed later is a child's belief in his or her own unchangeable gender identity, which develops at the same age as physical conservations.)

The statement listed first presupposes a distinction between behavior changes or learning in general and *changes in mental structure.* Structure refers to the general characteristics of shape, pattern, or organization of response rather than to the rate or intensity of response or its pairing with particular stimuli. Cognitive structure refers to rules for processing information or for connecting experienced events. Cognition (as most clearly reflected in thinking) means putting things together or relating events, and this relating is an active connecting process, not a passive connecting of events through external association and repetition. In part this means that connections are formed by selective and active processes of attention, information-gathering strategies, motivated thinking, and so forth. More basically, it means that the process of relating particular events depends upon prior general modes of relating developed by the organism. The most general modes of relating are termed "categories of experience." These categories are modes of relating applicable to any experienced event, and include the relations of causality, substantiality, space, time, quantity, and logic (the latter referring to relations of inclusion or implication between classes or propositions).

The awareness that the child's behavior has a cognitive structure or organizational pattern of its own which needs description independently of the degree of its correspondence to the adult culture is as old as Rousseau, but this awareness has only recently pervaded the actual study of cognitive development. Two examples of the revolution resulting from defining the structure of the child's mind in its own terms may be cited. The first is that of Piaget (1928), whose first psychological effort was to classify types of wrong answers on the Binet test. By moving beyond an analysis of intellectual development in terms of number of right answers to an analysis in terms of differences in structure, Piaget transformed the study of cognitive development. The second example comes from the study of children's language (Chomsky, 1968) based for a generation on counting frequency and correctness of nouns and verbs as defined by conventional adult grammar. In the last decade, psychologists have approached children's grammar with the methods of structural linguistics, as if the child's language were that of an exotic tribe with its own structure. While the implications of the Piagetian revolution in cognition and the Chomskian revolution in language are far from clear, they have made the conception of mental structure a reality accepted even by associationistic theories of cognition (cf. Berlyne, 1965), though not by most associationistic theories of social learning.

Our second statement suggested that cognitive-developmental theories are "interactional," that is, they assume that basic mental structure is the product of the patterning of the interaction between the organism and the environment rather than a direct reflection of either innate patterns in the organism or patterns of events (stimulus contingencies) in the environment. The distinction between theories stressing the innate and theories stressing the acquired has often been thought of as a contrast in quantitative emphasis on hereditary biological factors as opposed to environmental stimulation factors in causing individual differences. When the problem is posed in such a fashion, one can be led to nothing but a piously eclectic "interactionism" which asserts that all concrete behavior is quantitatively affected empirically by both hereditary and environmental factors. The theoretical issues are quite different, however. They are issues as to the location of the principles producing basic mental structure within or without the organism.

It is evident that general questions about the origins and development of mental structure are not the same as questions about the origins of individual differences in behavior. As an example, while the fact that one 6-year-old child may pass all the 6-year items on the Binet test and another fail them all might be attributed purely to hereditary differences in general intelligence, the patterns of behavior involved in the child's actual Binet performance (e.g., knowing the word "envelope") may be purely culturally learned behavior. Because many American psychologists have been particularly concerned with individual differences rather than developmental universals, and because they have failed to understand the distinction between behavior differences in general and behavior structure, they have frequently misinterpreted European theories of development. For example, some American writers have misinterpreted Piaget's stages as "maturational" and have thought that he claimed intelligence is unaffected by environment. Others (like J. McV. Hunt, 1961, 1963) have correctly interpreted Piaget's stages as being based on the assumption of organism-environment interactions, but take this assumption as indicating that individual differences in intellectual performance as less hereditary than was long believed. In fact, there is nothing in Piaget's theory which suggests that individual differences in speed of development through his stages are not primarily due to hereditary factors.

Distinctions between environmental, maturational, and interactional theories or the origins of mental structure, then, are not distinctions based upon quantitative assumptions about the role of heredity in the formation of individual differences. In terms of quantitative role, maturational or nativistic theories, like those of Lorenz (1965), or Gesell (1954), recognize the importance of environmental stimulation in modifying genetically grounded behavior patterns. In a similar sense, associationistic-learning theorists like Pavlov (1928) or Hull (1943) recognize the quantative role of hereditary traits of temperament and ability in causing individual differences in personality and in rate and the type of learning. The difference between the two types of theories is not in the recognition of both innate and environmental causal factors in development but in which set of factors is seen as the source of basic patterning.

The contrast between *modifying* and *structuring* roles awarded to experience becomes clear with regard to the issue of critical periods. Most research on the effects of experience upon development has postulated "critical periods" in which the individual is especially sensitive to environmental influence in a given domain. Yet this notion of extreme quantitative sensitivity depends upon a maturational or nativistic theory.

The existence of a fixed time period during which a certain amount of stimulation is required to avoid irreversible developmental deficits presupposes an innate process of growth with an inner time schedule and an inner pattern which can be arrested or distorted by deficits of stimulation.

In the nativistic view, stimulation may be needed to elicit, support, and maintain behavior patterns, but the stimulation does not create these patterns, which are given by templates in the genotype. In fact, learning or environmental influence itself is seen as basically patterned by genetically determined structures. Learning occurs in certain interstices or open places in the genetic pattern, and the structuring of what is learned is given by these patterns (Lorenz, 1965). As an example, ethological "imprinting" or Freudian "libidinal fixation" represents a type of learning, a determination of response by environmental stimulation. However, the "learning" involved represents a specific sensitivity or open spot in a genetically patterned social-sexual response. As another example, an insect or bird may learn a specific "map" of the geography of its home place, but ethologists view this map as structured by an innate organization of space in general (Lorenz, 1965).

In dealing with developmental changes, nativistic theories such as Gesell's (1954) have stressed the notion of unfolding maturational stages. The patterning of these age-specific behavioral forms, their order and timing, is believed to be wired into the organism. The organism grows as a whole so that the effort to teach or force early maturation in one area either will be ineffective or will disrupt the child's total pattern and equilibrium of growth.

In contrast to nativistic theories, learning theories may allow for genetic factors in personality and in ease of learning of a complex response, but they assume that the basic structure of complex responses results from the structure of the child's environment. Both specific concepts and general cognitive structures, like the categories of space, time, and causality, are believed to be the reflections of structures existing outside the child, structurings given by the physical and social world.

Almost of necessity, the view that structure of the external world is the source of the child's cognitive structure has led to an account of the development of structure in associationistic terms. From John Locke to J. B. Watson and B. F. Skinner (Kessen, 1965), environmentalists have viewed the structure of behavior as the result of the association of discrete stimuli with one another, with responses of the child, and with experiences of pleasure and pain.

We have contrasted the maturationist assumption that basic mental structure results from an innate patterning with the learning-theory assumption that basic mental structure is the result of the patterning or association of events in the outside world. In contrast, the cognitive-developmental assumption is that basic mental structure is the result of an interaction between certain organismic structuring tendencies and the structure of the outside world, rather than a reflection of either one directly.

This interaction leads to cognitive *stages* which represent the *transformations* of simple early cognitive structures as these are applied to (or assimilate) the external world and as they are accommodated to or restructured by the external world in the course of being applied to it.

The core of the cognitive-developmental position, then, is the doctrine of cognitive stages. Cognitive stages have the following general characteristics (Piaget, 1960):

1. Stages imply distinct or *qualitative* differences in children's modes of thinking or of solving the same problem at different ages.

2. These different modes of thought form an *invariant sequence,* order, or succession in individual development. While cultural factors may speed up, slow down, or stop development, they do not change its sequence.

3. Each of these different and sequential modes of thought forms a *"structured whole."* A given stage-response on a task does not just represent a specific response determined by knowledge of and familiarity with that task or tasks similar to it. Rather it represents an underlying thought-organization, for example, "the level of concrete operations," which determines responses to tasks which are not manifestly similar. According to Piaget, at the stage of concrete operations, the child has a general tendency to maintain that a physical object conserves its properties on various physical dimensions in spite of apparent perceptual changes. This tendency is structural, it is not a specific belief about a specific object. The implication is that both conservation and other aspects of logical operations should appear as a logically and empirically related cluster of responses in development.

4. Cognitive stages are *hierarchical integrations.* Stages form an order of increasingly differentiated and integrated structures to fulfill a common function. The general adaptational functions of cognitive structures are always the same (for Piaget, the maintenance of an equilibrium between the organism and the environment, defined as a balance of assimilation and accommodation). Accordingly, higher stages displace (or rather reintegrate) the structures found at lower stages. As an example, formal operational thought includes all the structural features of concrete operational thought but at a new level of organization. Concrete operational thought or even sensorimotor thought does not disappear when formal thought arises, but continues to be used in concrete situations where it is adequate or when efforts at solution by formal thought have failed. However, there is a hierarchical preference within individuals, that is, a disposition to prefer a solution of a problem at the highest level available to them. It is this disposition which partially accounts for the consistency postulated as our third criterion. "Hierarchical" and structural cognitive stages may be contrasted with "embryologi-

cal," motivational, or content stages (Loevinger, 1966). The latter represent new interests or functions rather than new structures for old functions; for example, anal interests are not transformations of oral interests, they are new interests. While to some extent higher psychosexual stages are believed to typically include and dominate lower stages (e.g., genital interests dominate or include pregenital interests), this integration is not a necessary feature of the higher stage (e.g., lower stage interests may be totally repressed or be in conflict with higher stage interests).

The question of whether cognitive stages "exist" in the sense just defined is an empirically testable question. It has been held by B. Kaplan (1966) and others that stages are theoretical constructions, and that their theoretical value holds independently of whether or not they define empirical sequences in ontogeny. One cannot hold this to be true for embryological stages because there is no clear logical reason why an "anal" content is higher than an "oral" content. In the case of structural stages, however, their conceptual definition is based on a hierarchy of differentiation and integration. Every theoretical set of structural stages is defined in such a way that a higher stage is more differentiated and integrated than a lower stage. In this sense, a set of structural stages forms a valid hierarchy regardless of whether or not they define an ontogenetic sequence.

In spite of this fact, it is extremely important to test whether a set of theoretical stages does meet the empirical criteria just listed. If a logical developmental hierarchy of levels did not define an empirical sequence, the hierarchy would neither tell us much about the process of development nor justify our notion that the sequence is interactional in nature. If an empirical sequence were not found, one would argue that the "stages" simply constituted alternative types of organization of varying complexity, each of which might develop independently of the other. In such a case, the "stages" simply constituted alternative types of organization of varying complexity, each of which might develop independently of the other. In such a case, the "stages" could represent alternative expressions of maturation or they could equally well represent alternative cultures to which the child is exposed. It would hardly be surprising to find that adult physical concepts are more complex, more differentiated and integrated, in educated Western culture than in a jungle tribe. The fact that the Western and tribal patterns can be ordered at different levels of structural organization, however, would tell us little about onotogenesis in either culture, and would leave open the possibility that it was simply a process of learning cultural content.

In contrast, if structural stages do define general ontogenetic sequences, then an interactional kind of theory of developmental process must be used to explain ontogeny. If children go through qualitatively different stages of thought, their basic modes of organizing experience cannot be the direct result of adult teaching, or they would be copies of adult thought from the start. If children's cognitive responses differed from adults only in revealing less information and less complication of structure, it would be possible to view them as incomplete learnings of the external structure of the world, whether that structure is defined in terms of the adult culture or in terms of the laws of the physical world. If the child's responses indicate a different structure or organization than the adult's, rather than a less complete one, and if this structure is similar in all children, it is extremely difficult to view the child's mental structure as a direct learning of the external structure. Furthermore, if the adult's mental structure depends upon sequential transformations of the child's mental structure, it too cannot directly reflect the current structure of the outer cultural or physical world.

If stages cannot be accounted for by direct learning of the structure of the outer world, neither can they be explained as the result of innate patterning. If children have their own logic, adult or mental structure cannot be derived from innate neurological patterning, because such patterning should hold also in childhood. It is hardly plausible to view a whole succession of logics as an evolutionary and functional program of innate wiring.

It has just been claimed that it is implausible to view a succession of cognitive stages as innate. This claim is based on an epistemological assumption, the assumption that there is a reality to which psychology may and must refer, that is, that cognition or knowing must be studied in relation to an object known. The claim does not hold for postural or other stages which are not directly defined by reference to an outer reality. The invariant sequences found in motor development (Shirley, 1933) may well be directly wired into the nervous system. The fact that the postural-motor development of chimpanzees and man proceed through the same sequence suggests such a maturational base (Riesen and Kinder, 1952). The existence of invariant sequence in cognition is quite a different matter, however, since cognitions are defined by reference to a world. One cannot speak of the development of a child's conception of an animal without assuming that the child has had experiences with animals. Things become somewhat more complicated when we are dealing with the development of categories, that is, the most general modes of relating objects, such as causality, substance, space, time, quantity, and logic. These categories differ from more specific concepts, for example, the concept of "animal," in that they are not defined by specific objects to which they refer but by modes of relating any object to any other object. Every experienced event is located in space and time, implies or causes other events, and so on. Because these categories or structures are independent of specific experiences with specific objects, it has been plausible for philosophers like Kant to assume that they are innate molds into which specific experiences are fitted. If structures or categories like space and time are Kantian innate forms, it is difficult to understand how these structures could undergo transformation in development, however.

The interactional account assumes that structural change in these categories depends upon experience, then. The effects of experience, however, are not conceived of as learning in the ordinary sense in which learning implies training by pairing of specific objects and specific responses, by instruction, by remodeling, or by specific practice of responses. Indeed, the effects of training are determined by the child's cognitive categories rather than the reverse. If two events which follow one another in time are cognitively connected in the child's mind, it implies that the child relates them by means of a category such as causality, the child perceives his or her operant behavior as causing the reinforcer to occur. A program of reinforcement, then, cannot directly change the child's causal structures, since it is assimilated to it.

An understanding of the effect of experience upon cognitive stages presupposes three types of conceptual analysis customarily omitted in discussions of learning.

In the first place, it depends on analysis of universal structural features of the environment. While depending on structural and functional invariants of the nervous system, cognitive stages also depend upon universal structures of experience for their shape. Stages of physical concepts depend upon a universal structure of experience in the physical world, a structure which underlies the diversity of physical arrangements in which people live and which underlies the diversities of formal physical theories held in various cultures at various periods.

In the second place, understanding cognitive stages upon a logical analysis of orderings inherent in given concepts. The invariance of sequence in the development of a concept or category is not dependent upon a prepatterned unfolding of neural patterns; it must depend upon a logical analysis of the concept itself. For example, Piaget (1947) postulates a sequence of spaces or geometries moving from the topological to the projective to the Euclidean. This sequence is plausible in terms of a logical analysis of the mathematical structures involved.

In the third place, an understanding of sequential stages depends upon analysis of the relation of the structure of a specific experience of the child to the behavior structure. Piaget (1964) has termed such an analysis an "equilibration" rather than a "learning" analysis. Such an analysis employs such notions as "optimal match," "cognitive conflict," "assimilation," and "accommodation." Whatever terms are used, such analyses focus upon discrepancies between the child's action system or expectancies and the experienced events, and hypothesize some moderate or optimal degree of discrepancy as constituting the most effective experience for structural change in the organism.

In summary, an interactional conception of stages differs from a maturational one in that it assumes that experience is necessary for the stages to take the shape they do as well as that generally more or richer stimulation will lead to faster advance through the series involved. It proposes that an understanding of the role of experience requires: (1) analyses of universal features of experienced objects (physical or social), (2) analysis of logical sequences of differentiation and integration in concepts of such objects, and (3) analysis of structural relations between experience-inputs and the relevant behavior organizations. While these three modes of analysis are foreign to the habits of associationistic-learning theorists, they are not totally incompatible in principle with them. While associationistic concepts are clumsy to apply to universal objects of experience or to the logical structures of concepts and to the problem of match, it can be done, as Berlyne (1961, 1965) has demonstrated. As yet, such associationistic analyses have not led to the formulation of new hypotheses going beyond translations of cognitive-developmental concepts into a different language.

The preceding presentation of the cognitive-developmental approach has been rather abstract. Accordingly it may be useful to present an empirical example of a cognitive-stage sequence and elaborate why it requires an interactional theory of process for its explanation. The dream concept, studied by Piaget (1928), Pinard and Laurendeau (1964), and myself (Kohlberg, 1966a) presents a simple example. The dream is a good example of an object or experience with which the child is familiar from an early age, but which is restructured in markedly different ways in later development. One of the general categories of experience is that of substantiality or reality. Any experience must be defined as either subjective or objective. As the child's structuring of this category develops, the child's experience of the dream changes. According to Piaget, the young child thinks of the dream as a set of real events, rather than as mental imagining. This represents the young child's "realism," a failure to differentiate subjective appearance from objective reality.

Table 1.1 indicates the actual steps of development which are found in children's beliefs about dreams. The first step (achieved by about 4 years, 10 months by American middle class children) is the recognition that dreams are not real events; the next step (achieved soon thereafter), that dreams cannot be seen by others. By age 6, children are clearly aware that dreams take place inside them and by seven, they are clearly aware that dreams are thoughts caused by themselves.

The concept of stages implies an invariant order or sequence of development. Cultural and environmental factors or innate capabilities may make one child or group of children reach a given step of development at a much earlier point of time than another child. All children, however, should still go through the same order of steps, regardless of environmental teaching or lack of teaching.

Table 1.1 shows a series of patterns of pluses or minuses called Guttman scale types, suggesting that the steps we have mentioned form an invariant order or sequence in development. If there is an invariant order in development, then children who have passed a more difficult step in the sequence, indicated by a plus, should also have passed all the easier steps in the sequence and get pluses on all the easier items. This means that all children should fit one of the patterns on Table 1.1. For instance, all children who pass or get a plus on Step 3, recognizing the dream's internal origin, should also pass Step 2 and Step 1. The fact that only 18 out of 90 children do not fit one of these patterns is evidence for the exis-

Table 1.1. **Sequence in Development of Dream Concept in American and Atayal Children**

	Scale Pattern Types						
Step	*0*	*1*	*2*	*3*	*4*	*5*	*6*
1. *Not Real*—Recognize that objects or actions in the dream are not real or are not really there in the room.	–	+	+	+	+	+	+
2. *Invisible*—Recognize that other people cannot see their dreams.	–	–	+	+	+	+	+
3. *Internal Origin*—Recognize that the dream *comes from* inside them.	–	–	–	+	+	+	+
4. *Internal Location*—Recognize that the dream *goes on* inside them.	–	–	–	–	+	+	+
5. *Immaterial*—Recognize that the dream is not a material substance but is a thought.	–	–	–	–	–	+	+
6. *Self-caused*—Reconize that dreams are not caused by God or other agencies but are caused by the self's thought processes.	–	–	–	–	–	–	+
Median age of American children in given pattern or stage (Range=4 to 8)	4,6	4,10	5,0	5,4	6,4	6,5	7,10
Median age of Atayal of given pattern. (Range=7 to 18)	8	8	10	16	12	11	

Number of American children fitting scale types=72; not fitting=18.
Number of Atayal children fitting scale types=12; not fitting=3.

tence of invariant sequence in the development of the dream concept. (This is more precisely indicated by a coefficient of reproducibility of .96 and an index of consistency of .83, calculated following Green [1956].)

The importance of this issue of sequence becomes apparent when we ask, How do children move from a view of dreams as real to a view of dreams as subjective or mental? The simplest answer to this question is that older children have learned the cultural definition of words like *dream* and *real.* Children are frequently told by parents that their dreams are not real, that they shouldn't be upset by them, that dreams are in one's mind, and so on. In the learning view, this verbal teaching eventually leads children from ignorance to knowledge of the culture's definition of the dream. It is a little hard for this verbal-learning view to account for invariant sequence in the development of the dream concept, since it seems unlikely that children are taught Step 3 later than Step 2 or Step 1.

The issue of sequence becomes more critical when sequence can be examined in cultures with adult cognitive beliefs different from our own (Kohlberg, 1966a). The Atayal, a Malaysian aboriginal group on Formosa, believe in the reality of dreams. Most adult Atayal interviewed on the dream equated the soul, the dream, and ghosts. Dreams, like ghosts, are neither thoughts nor things; dreams are caused by ghosts and during the dream the soul leaves the body and experiences things in far places.

Interviews of Atayal boys and young men of various ages indicated a very interesting pattern of age development. The youngest Atayal boys were much like the youngest American boys in their responses. Up until the age of 11, the Atayal boys seemed to develop toward a subjective conception of the dream through much the same steps as American children, though more slowly. As the table shows, the Atayal boys' answers fell into the same sequential scale pattern as the American boys'. This suggests that the Atayal children tend to develop naturally toward a subjective concept of the dream up to age 11, even though their elders do not believe dreams are subjective and hence are giving them no teaching to this effect. Both the youngest child's conception of the dream as real and the school age child's view of the dream as subjective are their own; they are products of the general state of the child's cognitive development rather than the learning of adult teachings (though the adolescent's later "regression" to concepts like those held by the younger children does represent such direct cultural learning).

The apparent invariant universal sequence in the development of the dream concept in the absence of adult cultural support cannot be interpreted as being the direct result of maturational unfolding, since the culture can "reverse" it by specific training, a reversal presumably very difficult to teach for maturational postural-motor sequences. A maturational interpretation is also contradicted by the fact that the Atayal children go through the same sequence more slowly than do their Taiwanese and American age-mates, presumably because the Atayal exist in a somewhat cognitively impoverished general culture; that is, they have less *general* experience. In this regard the Atayal children are like culturally deprived American black ghetto children who also appear to go through the dream sequence more slowly than middle class black controls, even when the two groups are matched on psychometric intelligence (Kohn, 1969).

The culturally universal invariance of sequence found in the dream concept can be adequately understood through a logical analysis of the stages themselves. The steps represent progressive differentiations of the subjective and objective which logically could not have a different order. The first step involves a differentiation of the *unreality* of the psychic event or dream image. The next step the differentiation of the *internality* of the psychic event from the externality of the physical event. A still later step is the differentiation of the *immateriality* of the psychic event from the materiality of other physical events. This sequence corresponds to the logical tree in Figure 1.1.

It is apparent that the differentiation of the immaterial from the material presupposes the inside-outside distinction, since all immaterial events are inside the body (but not vice versa). It is also apparent that internality (location of the dream experience inside the body) presupposes unreality (recognition that the dream is not a real object) since a real object could hardly be in the body. The observed sequence, then, is one which corresponds to an inner logic of the concept of reality itself.

It is apparent that dreams are universal features of the child's experience. It is also apparent that a considerable degree of conflict between the dream experience and the waking experience of reality is a universal feature of experience. This experienced conflict or disequilibrium is presumably the "motor" for movement through the sequence in the absence of adult teaching, though the discrepancies and matches in experience in this area have not been clearly specified.

Figure 1.1.

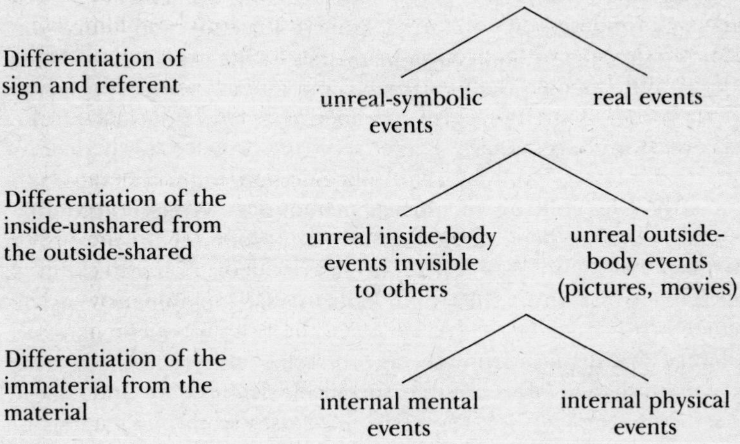

The data on Atayal dream "regression" introduce a useful additional clarification of the nature of the cognitive-developmental approach. The approach is not a theory about the process by which *all* behavior change occurs, as "learning theories" are. It is rather a program of analysis. Some behavior changes are "structural" and "directed" as evidenced by proceeding through sequential stages, while other behavior changes are not. This is the first question for empirical investigation since it determines any further theorizing about processes of development of the phenomena. Behavior changes which are universal, progressive, and irreversible require a different analysis than do reversible situation-specific learnings. While a cognitive-developmental approach may attempt to account for reversible situational learning (as we do in discussing imitative learning), it may also be satisfied with associationistic accounts of situational learning. For example, Turiel's (1969) cognitive-developmental interpretation accounts for Atayal children's "regressive" learning of the adult culture's ideology as a reversible content-learning fitting associationistic notions of social training, modeling, and reinforcement, a learning that is superimposed upon the structural development of subjective-objective differentiation. In Turiel's view, only this latter kind of change requires an interactional equilibration theory of process.

The Atayal example also, however, suggests that a third "regressive" type of behavior change may require elaboration by cognitive-developmental theory. Turiel assumes that the Atayal's dream regression is not a true regression in structure but a content-learning superimposed on a mature cognitive structure and hence does not require special theoretical principles for its explanation. While the Atayal example is an extremely ambiguous case of regression, it is obvious that true regression does occur. As is described elsewhere (Kohlberg 1969), Piaget's cognitive tasks are passed at markedly lower levels by schizophrenic and brain-damaged subjects than by controls of normal mental age. While longitudinal studies have not been carried out, we can assume that where brain damage or the onset of schizophrenia occurred in late childhood, actual regression (rather than failure of development) has occurred. It is obvious that processes accounting for such regressive change are distinct from those producing either progressive sequential change or reversible specific learnings. We may simply decide to exclude such regressive processes from our analysis on the grounds that they are outside the psychological system which assumes an intact nervous system and that we are not required to account for the effects of a blow on the head. Or we may decide that a developmental theory must include a systematic analysis of regression, along the lines outlined by Kramer (1968) and by Langer (1967).

The need to include an account of regression in a cognitive-developmental theory is suggested by some additional data from the Atayal study. The Atayals' learning of the adult dream ideology did not appear to be a smooth and painless superimposition of social content on an underlying cognitive structure. Rather, it appeared to engender complications and conflict in the adolescents' cognitive responses. Atayal children acquired the conservation of mass of a ball of clay at the usual age (7–8). Nevertheless, at age 11–15, the age of dream "regression," they partially "lost" conservation. The loss did not seem to be a genuine regression, but an uncertainty about trusting their own judgment; there was an increase in "don't know" responses. Apparently, adolescent confrontation with adult magical beliefs led them to be uncertain of other naturally developing physical beliefs, even when the latter were not in direct conflict with the adult ideology. The findings on the Atayal, then, seem loosely compatible with experimental findings by Langer (1967) suggesting that some forms of cognitive conflict lead to progressive change while others lead to regressive change. The eventual goal of a cognitive-developmental theory, then, is a specification of the types of discrepancies in experience which lead to forward movement, to backward movement, and to "fixation," or lack of movement.

The Problem of Structure in Socialization—The Failure of Naturalistic Studies

Before elaborating on the application of the cognitive-development approach just outlined to the socialization field, we need to briefly consider the more popular alternatives, the psychosexual-maturational and associationistic-learning approaches to socialization.

For the past generation, socialization research has consisted primarily of naturalistic cross-sectional studies correlating individual and cultural differences in parental practices with differences in children's motivational behavior. The theoretical framework guiding most of this research has represented varying balances of reinforcement learning theory (primarily of a Hullian variety), Freudian psychosexual theory, and anthropological culturology. A clear statement of the theoretical framework, with special focus on the psychosexual-maturational, is provided in D. R. Miller (1969); an earlier statement is provided by Child (1954).

In the last few years, widespread dissatisfaction with the approach has been expressed by many of those most active in its development. This dissatisfaction has arisen because the correlations found in the studies have been low in magnitude and inconsistently replicated from one study to the next. As a result, neither clear practical, nor clear theoretical conclusions can be drawn from the findings. In this section, we shall briefly document the problematic nature of the findings in one sample area, moral development. We shall then go on to consider the reasons for these difficulties, arguing that while some of the difficulties have arisen because of specific defects of theory and of measurement methodology, these defects are incidental to an unfeasible definition of the whole problem of socialization research. In particular we shall argue that studies correlating individual differences in child-rearing practices with individual differences in cross-sectional traits cannot in themselves help answer the problems of the development of universal personality structures to which such theories as psychoanalysis are basically addressed. Our critique, then, is similar to that advanced in the previous section, in which we noted confusions introduced by American misinterpretation of Piaget's theory of the development of cognitive structure as a theory about the quantitative influence of various factors upon individual differences in cognitive influence of various factors upon individual differences in cognitive traits.

My own pessimism about the naturalistic studies of socialization came as the result of engaging in comprehensive reviews of the socialization of moral (Kohlberg, 1963a) and psychosexual (Kohlberg, 1966b) behaviors.

With regard to morality, the hypothetical personality structure focused upon has usually been termed "conscience" or "superego." This "structure" has been studied as behavior through measures of "resistance to temptation" (failure to deviate from cultural standards under conditions of low surveillance) and as affect through measures of guilt (self-critical or self-punitive symbolic response after deviation from such cultural standards). Conscience or superego as studied has been loosely similar, then, to commonsense concepts of moral character (conceived as a set of virtues like honesty, service, and self-control) such as were used by Hartshorne and May (1928–30), and the socialization studies have often employed "moral character" measures as measures of "conscience."

The socialization studies, then, have attempted to relate childhood and adolescent measures of individual differences in "conscience strength" to

1. early experiences of restraint or gratification of oral, anal, and sexual drives;
2. amount and method of moral discipline;
3. parent attitudes and power structures relevant to various theories of identification.

In general, no correlations have been found between parental modes of handling infantile drives and later moral behaviors or attitudes.

With regard to reward, no relations have been found between amount of reward and moral variables in twenty different studies of moral socialization. With regard to physical punishment, two studies find a positive correlation between *high* physical punishment and *high* moral resistance to temptation. Two studies find *no* correlation between physical punishment and resistance to temptation. Two studies find *high* punishment correlated with *high* delinquency, that is with *low* resistance to temptation. Three studies find *high* punishment correlated with *low* projective guilt (low morality). Three studies find *no* correlation between punishment and guilt. One is tempted to interpret these findings as representing a pattern of correlations randomly distributed around a base of zero.

With regard to psychological punishment, findings are more consistent. While only one of six studies found any relation between psychological discipline and moral behavior (resistance to temptation), a majority of studies (eight out of twelve) found a relation between psychological punishment and "guilt," usually defined as making confessional and self-critical responses. In most of these studies, "psychological discipline" has included both parental "love-withdrawal" and parental "induction" in Aronfreed's (1961) sense of verbal elaboration of the bad nature and consequences of the act for other people and for the self. When "induction" is distinguished from "love-withdrawal," it is found to correlate with both verbal "guilt" and internalized moral judgment in preadolescents (Aronfreed, 1961; Hoffman and Saltzstein, 1967), while love-withdrawal is not. Thus it appears that the findings on love-withdrawal are probably an artifact of combining love-withdrawal with induction which is why the relations are found in some studies but not others. Induction, however, is not punishment in the ordinary sense of the term, since it is difficult to view it, as one can love-withdrawal, as the infliction of psychological pain on the child. Rather it appears to be a cognitive stimulation of a moral awareness of the consequences of the child's action for other people. That this is the case is suggested by the fact that induction is also related to internalized moral judgment, which in turn is related to age and intelligence.

In summary, neither early parental handling of basic drives nor amount of various types of discipline have been found to directly correlate with moral attitudes or behavior in the studies surveyed.

With regard to parent attitudes, some consistent findings appear, but their theoretical interpretation is unclear. In particular they give no clear support for the notion that early identifications are central to a moral orientation. Investigators concerned with identification have focused especially upon dimensions of parental power and nurturance. With regard to power, no clear relation to moral variables has been found. For example, three studies report a positive correlation between paternal power and the boy's conscience, three report a negative correlation, and three report no correlation. With regard to affection, the findings are more consistent. Eight studies report a positive correlation of maternal warmth and conscience, one reports a negative correlation (among girls only), and four report no correlation. These findings, while weak, are consistent with a "developmental-identification" theory of conscience. However, a detailed examination of these findings does not support such an interpretation (Kohlberg, 1963a, 1964; Aronfreed, 1969). The common notions that if children like their parents, they will be accepting of their admonitions and that "bad children come from bad homes" are adequate to account for these findings. In other words, both the findings on inductive discipline and the findings on parental warmth suggest that children living in a positive social climate will be more willing to learn, and more accepting of, social norms than children living in a hostile or frightening climate. The finding does not seem to be specific to a moral structure but is a general tendency in the social attitude field (W. Becker, 1964). The same correlations with parental warmth and acceptance are found for the learning of achievement standards, for instance. In general, the clearer and the more consistent the findings in the moral area, the more obviously they fit a common-sense interpretation. For example, perhaps the clearest set of findings in the family and personality literature is that delinquents come from bad homes compared to controls from the same social class. The badness of these homes is nonspecific, and interpretation in terms of single theoretically meaningful variables used to define these homes as bad (e.g., low warmth, use of physical punishment, frequency of divorce) fails to hold up, because the interpretation or variable does not explain much variance in the normal population.

Furthermore, the more clear findings are generally ones relating current parent attitudes to current child attitudes, rather than relating early childhood experience to later personality structure. Correlations such as those mentioned on warmth and inductive discipline are clearest when they are taken as between current parent attitudes and adolescent or preadolescent attitudes. Positive relations between parental warmth and moral attitudes have not been found at the preschool-kindergarten level (Sears, Rau, and Alpert, 1965; Burton, Maccoby, and Allinsmith, 1961), nor does kindergarten parental warmth predict to preadolescent moral attitudes.

Our survey indicates that socialization studies of morality have yielded few empirically powerful predictors of moral behavior. Where powerful predictors have been found (as in the Glueck studies [Glueck and Glueck, 1950] of delinquency), these predictors shed little light on any theory of socialization process. One line of reasoning as to why the studies of socialization have failed is embodied in the writings of social learning revisionists, such as Aronfreed (1969), Bandura (1969), and Gewirtz (1969), who once engaged in correlational child-rearing studies of the kind described. In their view, this failure is partly methodological and partly theoretical. On the methodological side, the assessment of behavior by verbal interview and test methods and the use of a correlational methodology cannot be expected to lead to the firm conclusions found through experimental manipulations of social behavior. On the theoretical side, guidance of naturalistic studies by Freudian (and Hullian) hypothetical constructs concerning internal states (e.g., "identification," "guilt") having vague surplus meaning has led to researchers' inability to agree on appropriate measures of these states or to derive unambiguous predictions from the theories involved.

The cogency of these critiques is indicated by the quite powerful results obtained in their experimental studies of socialization, reported by Aronfreed (1969), Bandura (1969), and Gewirtz (1969), for example, Aronfreed is able to show that all children learn to at least minimally "resist the temptation" to take an attractive toy because of experimental punishment (disapproval and candy withdrawal) but that degree of resistance is regularly related to the timing of punishment. These extremely clear experimental results are not supported by the naturalistic studies, which do not show amount of punishment or timing of punishment (Burton et al., 1961) related to resistance to temptation. From the perspective of the experimenter, one can cogently argue "so much the worse" for the naturalistic studies. Findings based on a clear methodology are not invalidated by lack of support from a muddy methodology. More basically, however, the theory behind the social-learning experiments does not imply any predictions as to the effects of early parental reinforcement upon later social behavior. Reinforcement-learning theories are not theories of structural change; they do not assert that childhood learnings are irreversible or that they should determine later behavior in different situations. It is part of the routine strategy of many social-learning experiments to demonstrate reversibility of the learned performance, that is, to show that the learned behavior extinguishes under nonreinforcement. Social-learning theories do not claim extensive transfer of learning, that is, they do not claim that reinforcement learning creates generalized traits of personality manifested in many situations. The experimental studies of socialization are, in effect, cogent demonstrations of the irrelevance of early home reinforcement parameters for later behavior. Insofar as Aronfreed demonstrates that "resistance to temptation" behavior is largely determined by the experimental manipulation in a given situation and not by individual differences in traits of conscience, he demonstrates the irrelevance of early childhood learnings to the behaviors in question. It can be argued, then, that the failure of social-learning theory to receive support from naturalistic as well as experimental studies is not only due to the measurement problems and the absence of controls in the naturalistic studies but to the fact that they they are misconceived as applications of the theories of learning used in them. An appropriate naturalistic study of social learning would not relate individual differences in parental practices of a global nature to individual differences in later global personality traits. Instead, it would relate trial-by-trial changes in children's situational behavior to the trial-by-trial training inputs of the parents.

Our discussion of the social-learning critique of the naturalistic studies has emphasized that the problems to which the naturalistic studies were addressed are not those to which social-learning theories are addressed. The original assumption of the naturalistic studies were those shared by psychoanalytic and neopsychoanalytic theories of personality development, that is, theories which assumed the existence of relatively irreversible structural changes in generalized personality organization. The problems addressed by the studies were those of the ways in which early experiences formed fixed personality structures, and they have used the term *socialization* to refer to the establishment of such enduring personality structures as were compatible with the demands of the child's culture.

The studies, then, assumed that early childhood represented a "critical period," that is, a period of age-specific irreversible changes in personality. They have also assumed that the social processes and influences (primarily parental) forming personality in this period were different from the general processes of reversible social learning or social influence found in adult behavior. This assumption is most clear in the psychoanalytic theory, which assumes that structural change seldom occurs in adulthood, and that such structural change as does occur in adulthood rests on transference of infantile attitudes. These notions of childhood as a critical period have derived primarily from psychoanalytic conceptions of maturational sequences of basic drives. While psychoanalysis has stressed maturational content rather than cognitive structure, and has conceived of sequences as maturational rather than interactional, it agrees with the cognitive-developmental approach in analyzing behavior change as a process of development, that is, as a directed process of structural change exemplified in culturally universal sequential stages. Because it is maturational, psychoanalytic theory is even more clear than cognitive-developmental theory in distinguishing between the causes of forward movement (which is maturational) and the causes of fixation or of backward movement (which represent environmentally induced strains or frustrations).

It is evident that insofar as the naturalistic studies were based on psychosexual theory, these studies should have started by empirically establishing the natural age-developmental trends postulated by psychosexual theory, since psychosexual theory describes socialization in terms of fixations, regressions, or inhibitions in such developmental trends. Almost none of the myriad studies of socialization have actually attempted to do this. Instead most have "bootstrapped" this essential first phase of the task. Insofar as they have been psychoanalytically oriented, they have (1) theoretically assumed (rather than observed) psychosexual stages, (2) theoretically assumed that some behavior measure was in fact a valid measure of some aspect of psychosexual development, and have then gone on to (3) hypothesize some relation of a child-rearing practice to individual differences in the behavior measure at a given age. The "bootstrapping" strategy has assumed that if the predicted correlation between childrearing practices and the variable was found, this would confirm (1) the postulated psychosexual sequences, (2) the validity of the measures employed, and (3) the postulated relation between the child-rearing practice and fixation of the psychosexual sequences. Obviously this research strategy is unworkable, as the results of the studies have demonstrated.

From one point of view, the strategy might be considered one in which psychosexual stages are considered postulates useful in discovering some reliable and powerful relations between early experience and later personality. From another perspective, the strategy might be conceived as one of testing the validity of psychosexual theory. From either point of view, the strategy has failed. With regard to the first point of view, very few reliable and powerful empirical correlations have been obtained which would aid in predicting the behavior of any individual or group of children. From the second point of view, the boot-strapping approach cannot be said to be testing psychoanalytic theory. If it had worked, it might have provided some support for the theory, but its failure is not evidence against the theory, which cannot be said to be "tested" by such studies.

The objection to the bootstrapping approach is not so much that it was methodologically inappropriate to the difficult problem of socialization as that it was based on a misconception of psychoanalytic theory. We noted that Piaget's (1964) theory of the *development* of cognitive structures found in every human has been frequently misinterpreted by Americans as a theory of the origins of individual differences in intellectual abilities or traits, leading some Americans to view his interactionism as genetic maturationism and others to view his interactionism as a doctrine of the environmental determination of IQ difference. We have noted that theories of reinforcement learning have also sometimes been misinterpreted as theories designed to account for stable individual differences in personality traits, although these theories do not postulate personality traits in the first place. Learning theories are statements of laws or functional relations holding for all human beings, not theories designed to make statements about individual differences. It is an equally American misinterpretation to view psychoanalytic theory as directly relevant to an understanding of individual differences in personality traits. In part, psychoanalytic theory is a theory of laws of mental functioning in all humans; in part, it is a theory of development and maturation; in part, it is a theory of psychopathology. It has never claimed, however, to be a theory designed to predict adult individual differences or traits from specific childhood experiences, a task Freud (1938) claimed was impossible.

While Freud had special reasons for viewing the problem of the prediction of individual differences as unresolvable, a little thought leads to the recognition that there is no general theoretical question as to the origin of individual differences nor any conceivable general answer to such a question. While American researchers will always be obsessed with the problem of the prediction of individual differences, this problem is no more likely to lead to conceptual advance in social science than is meteorological prediction likely to lead to general advance in physical science. This contention may perhaps be clarified by pointing to certain extreme examples of "meteorological" studies of child-rearing antecedents of student activism. Of what theoretical significance could it be to examine the child-rearing antecedents to participation in a transitory social movement in the United States? It certainly can contribute nothing to the understanding of personality development or socialization defined outside of the culture of the American college of the 1960s. It is of equally little sociological or practical significance. One might be practically interested in the current values and personality integration of student activists, but hardly in the childhood correlates of activism. If this criticism is accepted, one must ask whether a study of the child-rearing correlates of variations in American middle class 5-year-old boys' performance on some cheating tasks in the year 1965 is likely to be of conceptual interest, since the correlations are unlikely to hold true in another society, in another moral task, at another year, or in another historical period, as the lack of replicability of the conscience studies suggests.

We have stated that the conceptually interesting problems of socialization are not the problems of accounting for the natural correlates of individual differences in behavior traits. Indeed, some understanding of the inconsistencies of the naturalistic studies arises when it is recognized that socialization seldom gives rise to traits as usually conceived. With regard to "resistance to temptation" or "moral internalization," no findings have been reported suggesting fundamental revisions of Hartshorne and May's (1928–30) conclusions as to the situational specificity and longitudinal instability of moral character, as is discussed in detail elsewhere (Kohlberg, 1964; Sears et al., 1965; Grim, Kohlberg, and White, 1968). Correlations between tests of resistance to temptation are low, and test-retest stability of these measures is low (correlations between cheating tests typically range between 0 and 40, six-month test-retest coefficients range between 30 and 60).

An example of the failure of resistance to temptation tests to represent conscience structure comes from a study by Lehrer (1967). Lehrer made use of Grinder's (1964) ray gun test of resistance to temptation. Grinder reports that a large majority (about 80 percent) of sixth-grade children cheat for a prize badge on this test. Lehrer decided to improve the circuitry and the instructions involved in the test to control for certain minor factors that might discourage cheating. Rather than making cheating more likely, her improvements led to less than 25 percent of the sixth-graders cheating. Probably the increased size and computerlike appearance of the gun led the children to believe it had score-keeping powers. Obviously the behavior of the 55 percent of children who cheat on one machine but not the other is not determined by features of conscience strength.

Long ago MacKinnon (1938) suggested that conscience or superego was only one factor in actual moral behavior such as the decision to cheat. A clearer index of conscience would be provided by assessments of guilt, a more stable or general tendency. While guilt was the moral force in personality, actual moral decisions depended on the interaction between guilt and other factors in the personality and in the situation. This plausible view led socialization analysts to proliferate projective measures of guilt and to relate them to child-rearing practices. There has been little agreement on what constitutes guilt in projective responses to transgression stories, however. The chief disagreement has been between those who view guilt as a conscious cognitive moral judgment (i.e., statements that an actor feels bad and blames him- or herself after transgressions) and those who view it as unconscious anxiety and self-punitive tendencies (projections of harm, punishment, catastrophe, and self-injury after transgression). Needless to say, the two are empirically unrelated. Furthermore, when the latter conception of guilt is employed, varying indices of guilt do not correlate well with one another, and little story-to-story generality or test-retest stability of guilt is found (studies reviewed in Kohlberg, 1963a). Not surprisingly, then, little consistency from study to study has been found as to child-rearing antecedents of guilt (studies reviewed in Kohlberg, 1963a).

Consistencies between studies of child-rearing antecedents of conscience presuppose that the measures of conscience in one situation relate to measures in another, and that measures of conscience at one age correlate with measures at another. While no longitudinal studies of child-rearing correlates of conscience have been carried out, a study of aggression has (Sears, 1961). Sears found that child-rearing correlates of aggression in children at age 5 failed to correlate with aggression in these same children at age 12. This is hardly surprising in light of the fact that measures of aggression at age 5 failed to predict aggression at age 12. Given a similar longitudinal instability in "conscience strength," the lack of consistency in findings on its child-rearing correlates is not surprising.

An Example of Social Development Defined in Cognitive-Structural Terms—Moral Stages

At first, the disappointing results summarized in the previous section suggest that all social behavior is reversible situation-specific behavior to be studied by such methods and concepts as those used by social-learning theorists. However, we shall now try to show that there are stages or directed structural age-changes in the area of social-personality development just as there are in the cognitive area. Later we shall go on to argue that these structural changes are not explainable in terms of the methods and concepts of social learning. In this section, we shall attempt to show that these structural-developmental changes can provide definitions of individual differences free of the problems which have confounded the naturalistic socialization studies, in the sense that they generate situationally general and longitudinally stable measures which relate meaningfully to social-environmental inputs. Our argument will be based on findings in a specific area, morality. However, we shall argue that success in this area is only a special case of the potential success arising from definitions of social development in cognitive-structural terms.

In spite of its obviousness, our focus upon situational generality and longitudinal predictability as a prerequisite for the meaningful study of socialization deserves some elaboration. The bulk of thinking about socialization is thinking about personality and culture, conceived as patterns or structures abstractable from the raw data of the myriad social behaviors in which individuals engage. The legitimate abstraction of a concept of personality from such raw data depends on the ability to predict behavior from one situation or time period to the next for the personality concept in question; that is, it depends upon the demonstration of its situational generality and longitudinal continuity.

In the previous section we pointed out that the ordinary personality "traits" focused upon in naturalistic studies of socialization are not stable in development. The ordering of individuals on motivated traits like dependency, aggression, affiliation, anxiety, need-achievement, and conscience-strength either predicts very little or not at all to later ordering on these same traits, if the two orderings are separated by many years (Kagan and Moss, 1962; MacFarlane, Allen, and Honzik, 1954; Sears, 1961; Emmerich,

1964). The personality traits outside the cognitive domain which have proved most stable are those of little interest to socialization theory, for example, traits of temperament like introversion-extroversion and activity-passivity (Kagan and Moss, 1962; Emmerich, 1964). These traits are uninteresting to socialization theory because their stable components seem to be largely innate (Gottesman, 1963) rather than products of socialization, because they are traits of style rather than content of social action, and because they do not predict the general adjustment of the individual to his or her culture (La Crosse and Kohlberg, 1969).

The study of socialization in terms of personality formation under the assumption of trait stability, then, is unjustified. Most theories of personality formation do not assume trait stability, however. They assume, rather, that personality undergoes radical transformations in development but that there is continuity in the individual's development through these transformations. In other words, they conceptualize personality development as an orderly sequence of change, with the individual's location at a later point in the sequence being related to location at an earlier point in the sequence. In the words of John Dewey (1930), "Psychology is concerned with life-careers, with behavior as it is characterized by changes taking place in an activity that is serial and continuous in reference to changes in an environment which is continuous while changing in detail" (p. 106).

While Dewey assumed that behavior is determined by the current ongoing situation in which the person is engaged, the situation is as that person defines it. This definition, in turn, is a result of sensitivities developing out of earlier situations, for example, "One and the same environmental change becomes a thousand different actual stimuli under different conditions of ongoing or serial behavior" (Dewey, 1930, p. 108).

In this view, early experience determines the choice of one or another path or sequence of development. It does not lead to the stamping in or fixation of traits carried from situation to situation throughout life. As stated by John Anderson (1957), "The young organism is fluid, subsequent development can go in any one of many directions. But once a choice is made and direction is set, cumulative and irreversible changes take place" (p. 39).

While continuity in personality development may be defined in terms of a number of alternative sequences available to different individuals in different social settings, most developmental theories of personality have employed some notion of a single, universal sequence of personality stages (S. Freud, 1938; Gesell, 1954; Erikson, 1950; Piaget, 1929). Such stage theories view the child's social behavior as reflections of age-typical world views and coping mechanisms rather than as reflections of fixed character traits. As a child moves from stage to stage, developmental theorists expect his or her behavior to change radically but to be predictable in terms of knowledge of the child's prior location in the stage sequence and of the intervening experiences stimulating or retarding movement to the next stage.

If continuity in personality development is to be found, then, stage theories hold that personality must be defined in terms of location in regular sequences of age development. The first and grossest implication of this view is that personality description must be phrased in age-developmental terms. In most studies of socialization, concepts of age-development have been theoretically assumed and empirically ignored. We have noted this in psychoanalytically oriented studies which continue to define individual differences with "superego strength" measures theoretically assumed to be related to psychosexual age-development, in spite of the fact that these measures do not relate empirically to age-development. It is also true in more learning-theory-oriented studies of socialization, which define socialization as *learned conformity* to the standards of the group and ignore the relations of such conformity to age-development. Usually these studies assume that social age-development generally coincides with "socialization."

In Child's (1954) definition socialization is "the process by which an individual, born with behavior potentialities of an enormously wide range, is led to develop actual behavior confined within the narrower range of what is customary for him according to the standards of his group." The socialization conception of moral development is implied in its definition in terms of strength of resistance to temptation and strength of guilt. "Resistance to temptation" means amount of conformity to cultural moral rules, "guilt" means degree of conformity to these rules after deviation, in the form of culturally expected forms of reparation for deviance. In the psychosexual field, socialization has been defined as increased conformity of attitudes to cultural norms for masculine or feminine roles, usually as measured by M-F tests.

While it has seemed plausible to equate "moral development" or "psychosexual development" with degree of conformity to the culture, it turns out that conformity does not in fact define trends of age-development. In the area of morality, the dimension of increased "resistance to temptation" as experimentally measured ("honesty" in old-fashioned terms) does not seem to define a trend of age-development at all. Sears et al. (1965) did not find an increase in experimental honesty from age 4 to 6; Grinder (1964) did not find an increase from 7 to 11; and Hartshorne and May (1928-30) did not find an increase from 11 to 14. In the psychosexual area, "internalization" or "identification," that is, sex-typed preference and choice, does not increase regularly or clearly with age after 7 (Kohlberg, 1966b). The lack of longitudinal stability in measures of "conscience strength," then, becomes more intelligible when it is recognized that the child's moral maturity, in an age-developmental sense, does not predict to his or her performance on these measures. In some sense, we know that the average adult is morally different from the average 4-year-old. Measures which fail to capture this difference must completely fail to capture whatever continuities exist in development.

The fact that degree of conformity measures fail to capture age-development is only a special case of the fact that polar traits in the personality area are seldom either age-developmental or longitudinally stable. By polar traits are meant traits defined by a quantitative ordering of individuals on a single dimension (such as aggression, dependency, etc.; e.g., Loevinger, 1966). Most developmental theories of personality assume that such "traits" are differential balancings of conflicting forces and that these balancings differ at different points in the life cycle as new developmental tasks are focused upon. Developmental theories assume that a certain minimal level of certain polar traits must be present for solution of a developmental task, but further increase on the variable is no sign of increased maturity. As an example, achieving a certain level of conformity may become a "milestone" representing the formation of conscience in various theories. Further development, however, may lead to a relaxation of conformity with assurance that impulse control has been achieved, or it may lead to an apparent nonconformity as autonomous and individual principles or values are developed. For example, guilt has typically been measured by number and intensity of self-blaming and reparative reactions to stories about deviation from conventional norms for children (e.g., opening some boxes hidden by one's mother, cheating in a race, etc.). Age-developmental studies indicate that almost no direct or conscious guilt is expressed to such stories of conventional deviation by children under 8, that the majority of children age 11–12 express some guilt, and that there is no age increase in amount or intensity of guilt after this age (Ruma and Mosher, 1967). Ratings of intensity of guilt, then, may group at the low to moderate end both the immature who have not achieved a minimal level of conformity and the mature who have transcended such conformity and have a humorously detached sense that they do not have to show what good children they are in obeying mother in such stories. If one were interested in using projective "guilt" as an index of moral maturity, one would simply note the qualitative presence of conventional guilt reactions to some transgression story as an indication of having passed one of a number of milestones in moral development, rather than construct a polar trait of guilt intensity.

While the study of age-development can go a certain distance using moderate levels of polar traits as milestones, the developmentalist holds that satisfactory definition or measurement of age-development requires definition of changes in the shape, pattern, or organization of responses. The developmentalist holds that a closer look at changes over time indicates regularities representing basic changes in the shape of responses rather than changes in their strength. This is, of course, the implication of an account of development in terms of stages. Stage notions are essentially ideal-typological constructs designed to represent different psychological organizations at varying points in development. The stage doctrine hypothesizes that these qualitatively different types of organization are sequential, and hence that the individual's developmental status is predictable or cumulative in the sense of continuity of position on an ordinal scale.

In what has been said so far, there is little divergence between the views of psychoanalytic, neopsychoanalytic and cognitive-developmental approaches to personality. The cognitive-developmental approach diverges from the others, however, in stressing that directed sequences of changes in behavior organization or shape always have a strong cognitive component. On the logical side, our approach claims that social development is cognitively based because any description of shape or pattern of a structure of social responses necessarily entails some cognitive dimensions. Description of the organization of children's social responses entails a description of the way in which perceive or conceive, the social world and the way in which they conceive themselves. Even "depth" psychologies recognize that there are no affects divorced from cognitive structure. While social psychology for a long time attempted to measure attitudes as pure intensities, the birth of a theoretical social psychology of attitudes (e.g., various cognitive balance theories) has come from the recognition that the affect component of attitudes is largely shaped and changed by the cognitive organization of these attitudes.

On the empirical side the cognitive-developmental approach derives form the fact that most marked and clear changes in the psychological development of the child are cognitive, in the mental-age or IQ sense. The influence of intelligence on children's social attitudes and behavior is such that it has a greater number of social-behavior correlates than any other observed aspect of personality (Cattell, 1957). In terms of prediction, Anderson (1960) summarizes his longitudinal study of adjustment as follows:

> We were surprised at the emergence of the intelligence factor in a variety of our instruments (family attitudes, responsibility and maturity, adjustment) in spite of our attempts to minimize intelligence in selecting our personality measures. Next we were surprised that, for prediction over a long time, the intelligence quotient seems to carry a heavy predictive load in most of our measures of outcomes. It should be noted that, in a number of studies, adjustment at both the child and the adult level, whenever intelligence is included, emerges as a more significant factor than personality measures.

It is apparent that the power of IQ to predict social behavior and adjustment springs from numerous sources, including the social and school success experiences associated with brightness. However, a large part of the predictive power of IQ derives from the fact that more rapid cognitive development is associated with more rapid social development. This interpretation of IQ effects has been thoroughly documented in the area of sex-role attitudes. An example of this fact comes from a semilongitudinal study of the sex-role attitudes of bright and average boys and girls (Kohlberg and Zigler, 1967). In the first place, this study indicated significant IQ effects in performance on seven tests of sex-role attitudes (some experimental-behavior, some verbal, some projective doll-play). In the second place, the study indicated that while there were marked and similar developmental trends for both bright and average children, these trends were largely determined by mental as opposed to chronological age. Parallel curves of age development were obtained for both groups, with the curves being about two years advanced for the bright children (who were about two years advanced in mental age). As an example, bright boys would shift from a preference for adult females to a preference for adult males on experimental and doll-play tests at about age 4, whereas the average boys would make the shift at about age 6. The same findings held in a study of retarded and average lower class black boys, half father-absent, half father-present (unpublished study by C. Smith, summarized in Kohlberg, 1966b). The average boys made the shift to the male at age 5–6, the retarded boys at age 7–8. Clearly, then, sex-role age developmental trends are mediated by cognitive development.

Turning to morality, "resistance to temptation" has a moderate but clearly documented correlation with IQ (Kohlberg, 1963a, 1964). These findings are not too helpful, however, since resistance to temptation does not define any dimension of age-development of morality. We shall now attempt to show that more "cognitive" dimensions of moral judgment do define moral age-development, and that once moral judgment development is understood, the development of moral action and moral affect becomes much more intelligible and predictable. The assertion that moral judgment undergoes regular agedevelopment and that this development is in some sense cognitive has seldom been questioned since the work of Hartshorne and May (1928–30) and Piaget (1948). However, extreme proponents of the cultural relativism of values must logically question both these contentions, as Bronfenbrenner (1962) has done. Bronfenbrenner has claimed that class, sex, and culture are more important determinants of Piaget-type moral judgment than is age-development. Examination of this claim may usefully clarify the sense in which moral judgment is said to have a cognitive-developmental component. One sense of the assertion that moral judgment development is cognitive is that it involves an increase in the child's knowledge of the content of conventional standards and values of his or her group. This is indeed the nature of moral judgment as measured by conventional "moral knowledge" tests like those of Hartshorne and May (1928–30). In this sense, it is plausible to assert that insofar as the content of standards and value labels differs by class, sex, and culture, so will the development of moral judgment. In another sense, however, moral judgments change in cognitive form with development. As an example, it is generally recognized that conceptions and sentiments of justice ("giving each his due") are based on conceptions of reciprocity and of equality. Reciprocity and equality are, however, cognitive as well as moral forms. Piaget (1947) has done a number of studies suggesting that the awareness of logical reciprocity (e.g., recognition that I am my brother's brother) develops with the formation of concrete operations at age 6–7. Our studies (Kohlberg, 1969) indicate that use of reciprocity as a moral reason first appears at the same age.

Another example of cognitive form in moral judgment is the consideration of intentions as oppose to physical consequences in judging the badness of action. According to Piaget (1948), the development of moral intentionality corresponds to the more general cognitive differentiation of objective and subjective, physical and mental, discussed earlier in this chapter. Accordingly, it is not surprising to find that in every culture, in every social class, in every sex group, and in every subculture studied (Swiss, American, Belgian, Chinese-Malaysian-aboriginal, Mexican, Israeli, Hopi, Zuni, Siouxan, Papagoan) age trends toward increased intentionality are found. It is also not surprising to find this trend is always correlated with intelligence or mental development in all groups where intelligence measures have been available. Finally, it is not surprising to find that such cultural or subcultural differences as exist are explainable as due to the amount of social and cognitive stimulation provided by the culture in question.

As an example, in all nations studied, there are social-class differences in the direction of earlier intentionality for the middle class. These are not class differences in values but class differences in the cognitive and social stimulation of development. In each class, the older and more intelligent children are more intentional. If the "retardation" of the lower class child were to be explained as due to a different adult subcultural value system, the older and brighter lower class children would have to be more "retarded" than the younger and duller lower class children, since they should have learned the lower class value system better. Intentionality, then, is an example of a culturally universal developmental trend that is universal and regular in its development because it has a "cognitive form" base in the differentiation of the physical and the mental.

In contrast, however, a number of the dimensions of moral judgment studied by Piaget are really matters of content rather than cognitive form. An example is the dimension of responsiveness to peer, as opposed to adult, expectations. While Piaget (1948) hypothesizes this dimension as part of his autonomous stage, his rationale for deriving this from a consideration of cognitive form is vague and unconvincing. There is nothing more cognitively mature about preferring a peer to an adult. It is not surprising to find, then, that this dimension does not vary regularly with chronological and mental age, that what age trends exist are absent in some national groups (e.g., the Swiss), and that in general this dimension is sensitive to a wide variety of cultural and subcultural influences which cannot be analyzed in rate-of-development terms.

In summary, then, universal and regular age trends of development may be found in moral judgment, and these have a formal-cognitive base. Many aspects of moral judgment do not have such a cognitive base, but these aspects do not define universal and regular trends of moral development.

Using the Piaget (1948) material, we have indicated that there are "natural" culturally universal trends of age-development in moral judgment with a cognitive-formal base. Age trends, however, are not in themselves sufficient to define stages with the properties discussed in our first section. While Piaget attempted to define two stages of moral judgment (the heteronomous and the autonomous), extensive empirical study and logical analysis indicate that his moral stages have not met the criteria of stage he proposes (summarized in our first section), as his cognitive stages do.

Taking cognizance of Piaget's notions as well as those of others, such as Hobhouse (1906), J. M. Baldwin (1906), Peck and Havighurst (1960), and McDougall (1908), I have attempted to define stages of moral judgment which would meet these criteria. A summary characterization of the stages is presented in Table 1.2. The relations of the stages to those of other writers is indicated by Table 1.3.

The stages were defined in terms of free responses to ten hypothetical moral dilemmas, one of which is presented subsequently in Table 1.5. Stage definition is based on a subsumption of a moral judgment under one of twenty-five aspects of moral judgment listed in Table 1.4.

These aspects represent basic moral concepts believed to be present in any society. As an example, "10, punishment," is a culturally universal concept entering into moral judgment as is "19, rights of property," or "23, contract." Each of these concepts is differently defined and used at each of the six stages. Definition or usage of concepts at each stage can logically be claimed to represent a differentiation and integration of the concept as it is used at the pre-

Table 1.2. **Classification of Moral Judgment into Levels and Stages of Development**

Levels	*Basis of Moral Judgment*	*Stages of Development*
I	Moral value resides in external, quasiphysical happenings, in bad acts, or in quasiphysical needs rather than in persons and standards.	State 1: Obedience and punishment orientation. Egocentric deference to superior power or prestige, or a trouble-avoiding set. Objective responsibility.
		Stage 2: Naively egoistic orientation. Right action is that instrumentally satisfying the self's needs and occasionally others'. Awareness of relativism of value to each actor's needs and perspective. Naive egalitarianism and orientation to exchange and reciprocity.
II	Moral value resides in performing good or right roles, in maintaining the conventional order and the expectancies of others.	Stage 3: Good-boy orientation. Orientation to approval and to pleasing and helping others. Conformity to stereotypical images of majority or natural role behavior, and judgment by intentions.
		Stage 4: Authority and social-order maintaining orientation. Orientation to "doing duty" and to showing respect for authority and maintaining the given social order for its own sake. Regard for earned expectations of others.
III	Moral value resides in conformity by the self to shared or sharable standards, rights, or duties.	Stage 5: Contractual legalistic orientation. Recognition of an arbitrary element or starting point in rules or expectations for the sake of agreement. Duty defined in terms of contract, general avoidance of violation of the will or rights of others, and majority will and welfare.
		Stage 6: Conscience or principle orientation. Orientation not only to actually ordained social rules but to principles of choice involving appeal to logical university and consistency. Orientation to conscience as a directing agent and to mutual respect and trust.

SOURCE: Kohlberg, 1967, p. 171.

Table 1.3. Parallel Moral Stages or Types in Various Theories

Author	*Amoral*	*1. Fearful–Dependent*	*2. Opportunistic*	*3. Conforming to Persons*	*4. Conforming to Rule*	*5,6. Principled–Autonomous*
			Moral Stages			
McDougall (1908)	1. instinctive		2. reward and punishment	3. anticipation of praise and blame		4. regulation by an internal ideal
J. M. Baldwin (1906)		1. adualistic	2. intellectual		3. ideal	
L. Hobhouse (1906)	1. instinctive	2. obligation as magical taboo		3. obligation as ideals of personal virtue	4. obligation as rules of society	5. rational ethical principles
Piaget (1948	1. premoral	2. heteronomous obedience to adult authority	3. autonomous–reciprocity and equality oriented			4. autonomous–ideal reciprocity and equality
Peck and Havighurst (1960)	1. amoral		2. expedient	3. conforming	4. irrational–conscientious	5. rational–altruistic
Kohlberg (1958)		1. obedience and punishment oriented	2. instrumental egoism and exchange	3. good-boy, approval oriented	4. authority, rule and social order oriented	5. social contract legalist orientation 6. moral principle orientation

Table 1.3—Continued

	Ego or Character Types					
Fromm (1955) Riesman (1950)		1. receptive, tradition-directed	2. exploitative, anomic	3. marketing, other-directed	4. hoarding, inner-directed	5. productive autonomous
C. Sullivan, Grant, and Grant (1957)		I_2 passive–demanding	I_3 conformist (exploitative)	I_3 conformist (cooperative)	I_4 authoritarian–guilty	I_6 self-consistent I_7 integrative
Harvey, Hunt, and Shroeder (1961)		1. absolutistic–evaluative	2. self-differentating	3. empathic		4. integrated independent
Loevinger (1966)	1. presocial	2. impulse-ridden, fearful	3. expedient	4. conformist	5. conscientious	6. autonomous 7. integrated

Table 1.4. Coded Aspects of Developing Moral Judgment

Code	*Description*	*Aspects*
I. Value	Locus of value—modes of attributing (moral) value to acts, persons, or events. Modes of assessing value consequences in a situation.	1. Considering motives in judging action. 2. Considering consequences in judging action. 3. Subjectivity vs. objectivity of values assessed. 4. Relation of obligation to wish. 5. Identification with actor or victims in judging the action. 6. Status of actor and victim as changing the moral worth of actions.
II. Choice	Mechanisms of resolving or denying awareness of conflicts.	7. Limiting actor's responsibility for consequences by shifting responsibility onto others. 8. Reliance on discussion and compromise, mainly unrealistically. 9. Distorting situation so that conforming behavior is seen as always maximizing the interests of the actor or of others involved.
III. Sanctions and Motives	The dominant motives and sanctions for moral or deviant action.	10. Punishment or negative reactions. 11. Disruption of an interpersonal relationship. 12. A concern by actor for welfare, for positive state of the other. 13. Self-condemnation.
IV. Rules	The ways in which rules are conceptualized, applied, and generalized. The basis of the validity of a rule.	14. Definition of an act as deviant. (Definition of moral rules and norms.) 15. Generality and consistency of rules. 16. Waiving rules for personal relations (particularism).

Table 1.4—Continued

Code	*Description*	*Aspects*
V. Rights and Authority	Basis and limits of control over persons and property.	17. Nonmotivational attributes ascribed to authority (knowledge, etc.). (Motivational attributes considered under III above.)
		18. Extent or scope of authority's rights. Rights of liberty.
		19. Rights of possession or property.
VI. Positive Justice	Reciprocity and equality.	20. Exchange and reciprocity as a motive for role conformity.
		21. Reciprocity as a motive to deviate (e.g., revenge).
		22. Distributive justice. Equality and impartiality.
		23. Concepts of maintaining partner's expectations as a motive for conformity. Contract and trust.
VII. Punitive Justice	Standards and functions of punishment.	24. Punitive tendencies or expectations. E.g., notions of equating punishment and crime.
		25. Functions or purpose of punishment.

SOURCE: Kohlberg, 1967, pp. 172–173.

ceding stage. An example of the six stages of definition of one aspect of moral judgment is presented in Table 1.5. This table indicates how the aspect of intentionality studied by Piaget (1948) has been defined in terms of each of the six qualitative stages. To document the way in which form of moral judgment is distinct from action content, Table 1.5 presents standardized arguments (Rest, 1968) at each stage of intentionality both for and against stealing the drug in the dilemma involved. Table 1.5 also indicates the sense in which each stage of orientation to intentions entails a differentiation not made at the preceding stage.

Table 1.5. **Six Stages of Orientation to Intentions and Consequences (Aspects 1 and 2) in Response to a Moral Dilemma**

In Europe, a woman was near death from cancer. One drug might save her, a form of radium that a druggist in the same town had recently discovered. The druggist was charging $2,000, ten times what the drug cost him to make. The sick woman's husband, Heinz, went to everyone he knew to borrow the money, but he could get together only about half of what it cost. He told the druggist that his wife was dying and asked him to sell it cheaper or let him pay later. But the druggist said no. The husband got desperate and broke into the man's store to steal the drug for his wife. Should the husband have done that? Why?

Stage 1. Motives and need-consequences of act are ignored in judging badness because of focus upon irrelevant physical form of the act (e.g., size of the lie), or of the consequences of the act (e.g., amount of physical damage).

Pro—He should steal the drug. It isn't really bad to take it. It isn't like he didn't ask to pay for it first. The drug he'd take is only worth $200, he's not really taking a $2,000 drug.

Con—He shouldn't steal the drug, it's a big crime. He didn't get permission, he used force and broke and entered. He did a lot of damage, stealing a very expensive drug and breaking up the store, too.

Stage 2. Judgment ignores label or physical consequences of the act because of the instrumental value of the act in serving a need, or because the act doesn't do harm in terms of the need of another. (Differentiates the human need–value of the act from its physical form or consequences.)

Pro—It's all right to steal the drug because she needs it and he wants her to live. It isn't that he wants to steal, but it's the way he has to use to get the drug to save her.

Con—He shouldn't steal it. The druggist isn't wrong or bad, he just wants to make a profit. That's what you're in business for, to make money.

Stage 3. Action evaluated according to the type of motive or person likely to perform the act. An act is not bad if it is an expression of a "nice" or altruistic motive or person and it is not good if it is the expression of a "mean" or selfish motive or person. Circumstances may excuse or justify deviant action. (Differentiates good motives to which an act is instrumental from human but selfish need to which it is instrumental.)

Pro—He should steal the drug. He was only doing something that was natural for a good husband to do. You can't blame him for doing something out of love for his wife, you'd blame him if he didn't love his wife enough to save her.

Con—He shouldn't steal. If his wife dies, he can't be blamed. It isn't because he's heartless or that he doesn't love her enough to do everything that he legally can. The druggist is the selfish or heartless one.

Stage 4. An act is always or categorically wrong, regardless of motives or circumstances, if it violates a rule and does foreseeable harm to others. (Differentiates action out of a sense of obligation to rule from action for generally "nice" or natural motives.)

Pro—You should steal it. If you did nothing you'd be letting your wife die, it's your responsibility if she dies. You have to take it with the idea of paying the druggist.

Con—It is a natural thing for Heinz to want to save his wife but it's still always wrong to steal. He still knows he's stealing and taking a valuable drug from the man who made it.

Stage 5. A formal statement that though circumstances or motive modify disapproval, a a general rule the means do not justify the ends. While circumstances justify deviant acts to some extent they do not make it right or lead to suspension of moral categories. (Differentiates moral blame because of the intent behind breaking the rule from the legal or principled necessity not to make exceptions to rules.)

Pro—The law wasn't set up for these circumstances. Taking the drug in this situation isn't really right, but it's justified to do it.

Con—You can't completely blame someone for stealing, but extreme circumstances don't really justify taking the law in your own hands. You can't have everyone stealing whenever they get desperate. The end may be good, but the ends don't justify the means.

Stage 6. Good motives don't make an act right (or not wrong); but if an act follows from a decision to follow general self-chosen principles, it can't be wrong. It may be actually right to deviate from the rules, but only under circumstances forcing a choice between deviation from the rules and concrete violation of a moral principle. (Differentiates good motives of following a moral principle from natural motives as following a rule. Recognizes that moral principles don't allow exceptions any more than do legal rules.)

Pro—This is a situation which forces him to choose between stealing and letting his wife die. In a situation where the choice must be made, it is morally right to steal. He has to act in terms of the principle of preserving and respecting life.

Con—Heinz is faced with the decision of whether to consider the other people who need the drug just as badly as his wife. Heinz ought to act, not according to his particular feelings toward his wife, but considering the value of all the lives involved.

SOURCE: Rest, 1968.

While it is not surprising to consider concepts of intentionality developing along cognitive-formal dimensions, it may surprise the reader to find that motives for moral action (Aspects 10 and 3 of Table 1.4) also have a cognitive-formal element. Table 1.6 presents the definition of moral motives characteristic of each stage, in a form similar to that of Table 1.5. It should be recalled that we are still dealing with concepts, here concepts of motives manifestly relevant to the concepts of intentions involved in the previous table. As Table 1.6 indicates, each stage involves a differentiation not present at the preceding stage.

The definition of the stages is not dependent on response to a particular set of materials, however, but is based on a system for scoring any moral judgment unit or sentence in any context. As an example, Table 1.7 indicates some statements by Adolf Eichmann which were scored by stage and aspect with good interjudge agreement, using general definitions of each stage at each aspect, such as those provided by Table 1.4 and 1.5 for two aspects.

While the evidence is far from complete, all the evidence to date suggests that the stages do meet the criteria of stages proposed in our first section. This evidence comes from studies conducted in Taiwan, Great Britain, Mexico, Turkey, and the United States. In addition to middle and lower class urban boys, the studies have included preliterate or semiliterate villagers in Turkey, Mexico (a Mayan group), and Taiwan (an Atayal group).

Figures 1.2 and 1.3 suggest the cultural universality of the sequence of stages which we have found. Figure 1.2 presents the age trends for middle class urban boys in the United States, Taiwan,

Table 1.6. **Motives for Engaging in Moral Action (Aspects 10 and 13)**

Stage 1. Action is motivated by avoidance of punishment and "conscience" is irrational fear of punishment.

Pro—If you let your wife die, you will get in trouble. You'll be blamed for not spending the money to save her and there'll be an investigation of you and the druggist for your wife's death.

Con—You shouldn't steal the drug because you'll be caught and sent to jail if you do. If you do get away, your conscience would bother you thinking how the police would catch up with you at any minute.

Stage 2. Action motivated by desire for reward or benefit. Possible guilt reactions are ignored and punishment viewed in a pragmatic manner. (Differentiates own fear, pleasure, or pain from punishment-consequences.)

Pro—If you do happen to get caught you could give the drug back and you wouldn't get much of a sentence. It wouldn't bother you much to serve a little jail term, if you have your wife when you get out.

Con—He may not get much of a jail term if he steals the drug, but his wife will probably die before he gets out, so it won't do him much good. If his wife dies, he shouldn't blame himself; it isn't his fault she has cancer.

Stage 3. Action motivated by anticipation of disapproval of others, actual or imagined-hypothetical (e.g., guilt). (Differentiation of disapproval from punishment, fear, and pain.)

Pro—No one will think you're bad if you steal the drug but your family will think you're an inhuman husband if you don't. If you let your wife die, you'll never be able to look anybody in the face again.

Con—It isn't just the druggist who will think you're a criminal, everyone else will, too. After you steal it, you'll feel bad thinking how you've brought dishonor on your family and yourself; you won't be able to face anyone again.

Stage 4. Action motivated by anticipation of dishonor, i.e., institutionalized blame for failure of duty, and by guilt over concrete harm done to others. (Differentiates formal dishonor from informal disapproval. Differentiates guilt for bad consequences from disapproval.)

Table 1.6—**Continued**

Pro—If you have any sense of honor, you won't let your wife die because you're afraid to do the only thing that will save her. You'll always feel guilty that you caused her death if you don't do your duty to her.

Con—You're desperate and you may not know you're doing wrong when you steal the drug. But you'll know you did wrong after you're punished and sent to jail. You'll always feel guilty for your dishonesty and law-breaking.

Stage 5. Concern about maintaining respect of equals and of the community (assuming their respect is based on reason rather than emotions). Concern about own self-respect, i.e., to avoid judging self as irrational, inconsistent, nonpurposive. (Discriminates between institutionalized blame and community disrespect or self-disrespect.)

Pro—You'd lose other people's respect, not gain it, if you don't steal. If you let your wife die, it would be out of fear, not out of reasoning it out. So you'd just lose self-respect and probably the respect of others, too.

Con—You would lose your standing and respect in the community and violate the law. You'd lose respect for yourself if you're carried away by emotion and forget the long-range point of view.

Stage 6. Concern about self-condemnation for violating one's own principles. (Differentiates between community respect and self-respect. Differentiates between self-respect for general achieving rationality and self-respect for maintaining moral principles.)

Pro—If you don't steal the drug and let your wife die, you'd always condemn yourself for it afterward. You wouldn't be blamed and you would have lived up to the outside rule of the law but you wouldn't have lived up to your own standards of conscience.

Con—If you stole the drug, you wouldn't be blamed by other people but you'd condemn yourself because you wouldn't have lived up to your own conscience and standards of honesty.

SOURCE: Rest, 1968.

Table 1.7. Scoring of Moral Judgments of Eichmann for Developmental Stage

Moral Judgments	*Score**
In actual fact, I was merely a little cog in the machinery that carried out the directives of the German Reich.	1/7
I am neither a murderer nor a mass-murderer. I am a man of average character, with good qualities and many faults.	3/1
Yet what is there to "admit"? It would be as pointless to blame me for the whole final solution of the Jewish problem as to blame the official in charge of the railroads over which the Jewish transports traveled.	1/7
Where would we have been if everyone had thought things out in those days? You can do that today in the "new" German army. But with us an order was an order.	1/15
If I had sabotaged the order of the one-time Führer of the German Reich, Adolf Hitler, I would have been not only a scoundrel but a despicable pig like those who broke their military oath to join the ranks of the anti-Hitler criminals in the conspiracy of July 20, 1944.	1/1
I would like to stress again, however, that my department never gave a single annihilation order. We were responsible only for deportation.	2/7
My interest was only in the number of transport trains I had to provide. Whether they were bank directors or mental cases, the people who were loaded on these trains meant nothing to me.	2/3
It was really none of my business.	2/7
But to sum it all up, I must say that I regret nothing. Adolf Hitler may have been wrong all down the line, but one thing is beyond dispute: the man was able to work his way up from lance corporal in the German army to Führer of a people of almost eighty million.	1/6
I never met him personally, but his success alone proves to me that I should subordinate myself to this man. He was somehow so supremely capable that the people recognized him.	

Table 1.7—**Continued**

And so with that justification I recognized him joyfully, and I still defend him.	1/17
I must say truthfully, that if we had killed all the ten million Jews that Himmler's statisticians originally listed in 1933, I would say, "Good, we have destroyed an enemy."	2/21
But here I do not mean wiping them out entirely. That would not be proper—and we carried on a proper war.	1/1

*The first code number in this column refers to Stages 1–6 (see Table 1.2); the second number refers to the aspect of morality involved (see Table 1.4).
SOURCE: Kohlberg, 1967, p. 177.

and Mexico. At age 10 in each country, the order of use of each stage is the same as the order of its difficulty or maturity. In the United States, by age 16 the order is the reverse, from the highest to the lowest, except that Stage 6 is still little used. At age 13, Stage 3, the good-boy middle stage is most used. The results in Mexico and Taiwan are the same, except that development is a little slower. The most conspicuous feature is that Stage 5 thinking is much more salient in the United States than it is in Mexico or Taiwan at age 16. Nevertheless, it is present in the other countries, so we know that it is not purely an American democratic construct. The second figure (1.3) indicates results from two isolated villages, one in Yucatan, one in Turkey. The similarity of pattern in the two villages is striking. While conventional moral thought (Stages 3 and 4) increases steadily from age 10 to 16, at 16 it still has not achieved a clear ascendency over premoral thought (Stages 1 and 2). Stages 5 and 6 are totally absent in this group. Trends for lower class urban groups are intermediate in rate of development between those for the middle class and the village boys.

While the age trends of Figures 1.2 and 1.3 indicate that some modes of thought are generally more difficult or advanced than other modes of thought, they do not demonstrate that attainment of each mode of thought is prerequisite to the attainment of the next higher in a hypothetical sequence.

The importance of the sequentiality issue may be brought out from two points of view. With regard to the definition of moral development, it is not at all clear that Stages 5 and 6 should be used to define developmental end points in morality. Figure 1.2

Figure 1.2. **Age Trends in Moral Judgment in Middle Class Urban Boys in Three Nations**

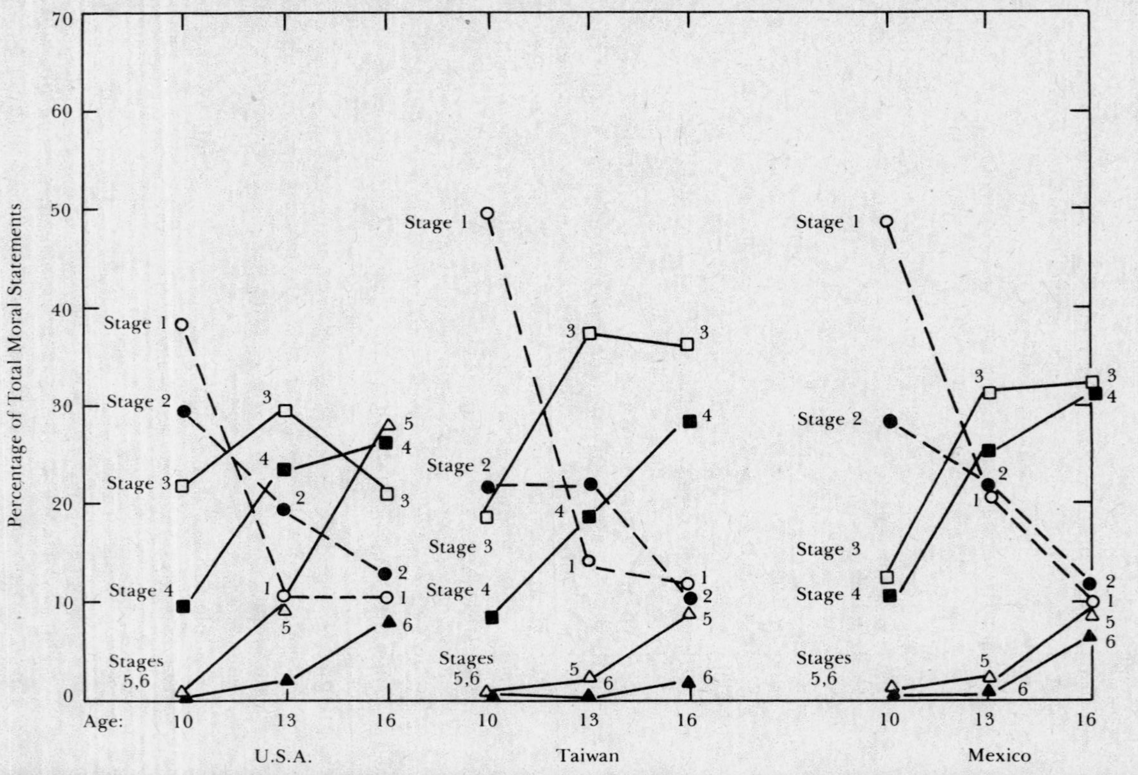

Figure 1.3. **Age Trends in Moral Judgment in Isolated Village Boys in Two Nations**

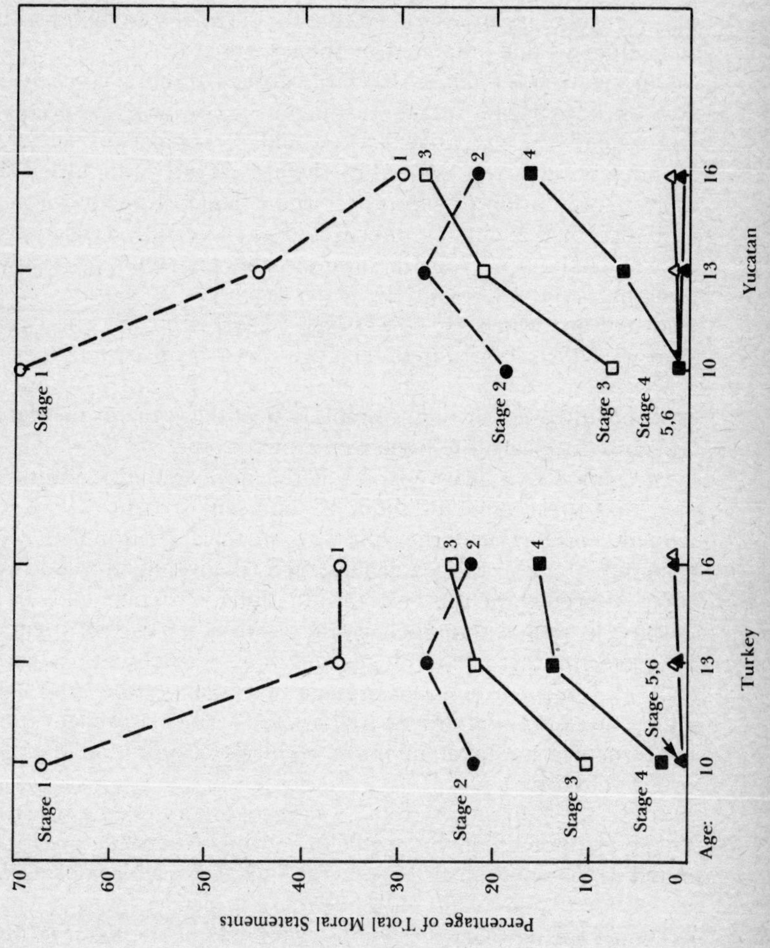

indicates that Stage 4 is the dominant stage of most adults. It is possible to view Stages 4, 5, and 6 as alternative types of mature response rather than as a sequence. Indeed, this is the view of some writers who view conventional-authoritarian (Stage 4) adult character types as opposed to humanistic (Stages 5 and 6) character types as representing alternative channels of personality crystallization. If Stages 5 and 6 persons can be shown to have gone through Stage 4 while Stage 4 persons have not gone through stages 5 and 6, it can be argued that the stage hierarchy constitutes more than a value judgment by the investigator.

Our age trends indicate that large groups of moral concepts and ways of thought only attain meaning at successively advanced ages and require the extensive background of social experience and cognitive growth represented by the age factor. From usual views of the moralization process, these age changes in modes of moral thought would simply be interpreted as successive acquisitions or internalizations of cultural moral concepts. Our six types of thought would represent six patterns of verbal morality in the adult culture which are successively absorbed as the child grows more verbally sophisticated. The age order involved might simply represent the order in which the culture presented the various concepts involved, or might simply reflect that greater mental age is required to learn the higher type of concept.

In contrast, we have advocated the developmental interpretation that these types of thought represent structures emerging from the interaction of the child with the social environment rather than directly reflecting external structures given by the child's culture. Awareness of the basic prohibitions and commands of the culture, as well as some behavioral "internalization" of them, exists from the first of our stages and does not define their succession. Movement from stage to stage represents, rather, the way in which these prohibitions, as well as much wider aspects of the social structure, are taken up into the child's organization of a moral order. This order may be based upon power and external compulsion (Stage 1), upon a system of exchanges and need satisfactions (Stage 2), upon the maintenance of legitimate expectations (Stages 3 and 4), or upon ideals or general logical principles of social organization (Stages 5 and 6). While these successive bases of a moral order do spring from the child's awareness of the external social world, they also represent active processes of organizing or ordering this world.

Because the higher types of moral thought integrate and replace, rather than add to, the lower modes of thought, the Guttman (1954) scaling technique used for the dream concept in our first section is not appropriate for our material, based on the usage of the stages in free responses. It does become appropriate, however, if we measure children's *comprehension* of each stage instead of their *use* of it. Rest (1968) has asked subjects to recapitulate in different words statements at each stage, of the sort presented in

Tables 1.5 and 1.6. In general, subjects can correctly recapitulate statements at all stages below or at their own level, correctly recapitulate some, but not all, statements at one stage above their own, but fail to correctly recapitulate statements two or more stages above their own (Rest, 1968; Rest, Turiel, and Kohlberg, 1969). Even where this is not the case, for example, where subjects can recapitulate a statement two stages above their own, their comprehension still fits a Guttman scale pattern; that is, they will comprehend all the statements below the plus-two statement including the statement one above their own.

While the pattern of actual usage of stages does not fit a cumulative model, it does fit a noncumulative model of sequence. The profile of usage of other stages in relation to the child's modal stage is presented in Figure 1.4. This figure indicates that on the average, 50 percent of a child's moral judgments fit a single stage. The remainder are distributed around this mode in decreasing fashion as one moves successively farther on the ordinal scale from the modal stage. An individual's response profile, then, typically represents a pattern composed of the dominant stage he or she is in, a stage he or she is leaving but still uses somewhat, and a stage he or she is moving into but which has not yet "crystallized."

***Figure 1.4.* Profile of Stage Usage**

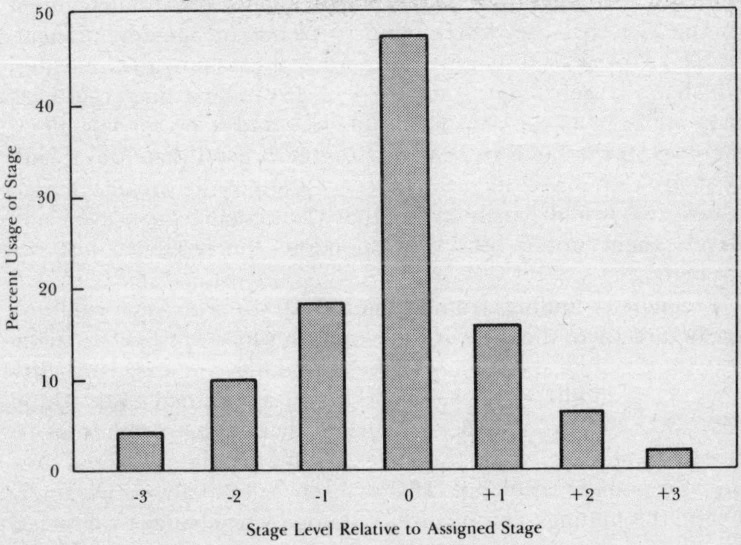

The pattern of usage of different stages becomes intelligible when if is recalled that, in a certain sense, all the lower stages are available or at least comprehensible to the subject. The pattern of usage, then, is dictated by a hierarchical preference for the highest stage a subject can produce. While subjects have difficulty comprehending stages above their own, and do not have difficulty with stages below their own, they prefer higher stages to the lower stages. If they can comprehend a statement two stages above their own, they prefer it to a statement one above. If they comprehend statements one stage, but not two, above their own, they prefer them to statements either two above or one below their own. If hypothetical statements at their own stage are presented to subjects, and they have not yet produced statements of their own, the subjects tend to prefer the one above to their own level statement.

It appears, then, that patterns of actual usage of stages are dictated by two opposed sequential orders, one of preference and one of ease, with an individual modal stage representing the most preferred stage which he or she can readily use. It is apparent, then, that the moral stages empirically meet the criterion of sequence and of hierarchical integration discussed in our first section, and that they logically meet it in the sense that each stage represents a logical differentiation and integration of prior concepts as indicated in Tables 1.5 and 1.6. In some sense, then, one can discuss the stages as representing a hierarchical sequence quite independent of the fact that they correspond to trends of age-development. Table 1.7 presented statements by Adolf Eichmann, a Nazi leader, which are largely Stage 1 and Stage 2. It can be argued that German adolescents grew up into a Stage 1 and 2 Nazi adult moral ideology in the same sense that it can be argued that Atayal children grow up into a Stage 1 or 2 conception of the dream. In such a case, we would hardly argue that the actual sequence of age-development would fully correspond to the sequence just described.

Preliminary findings from a longitudinal study of American boys speak directly to the issue of the extent to which ontogeny actually follows the logical sequence. These findings are based on fifty boys, half middle class, half working class, studied every three years over a twelve-year period. Originally ranging in age from 10 to 16, on terminal study they were 22 to 28. While only the data on development after age 16 has been fully analyzed (Kramer, 1968), the findings fit a picture of ontogenetic change as directed and sequential, or stepwise. The one exception is that at one age period (end of high school to midcollege) 20 percent of the middle-class boys "regress," or drop in total score. They come up again after college, so that none of them are below their high-school level in the late twenties and almost all are above that level. No such temporary "regression" occurs in the noncollege or lower class population. The only cases of "regression" found in the lower class sample were among six delinquents followed longitudinally. For three of these, reform school and jail had an actual "regressive" effect on morality.

The findings on regression are cited to clarify the meaning of sequence in the study of ontogeny suggested in connection with the Atayal dream concept. The claim of the theory is that the "normal" course of social experience leads to progression through the sequence. Special forms of experience, like jail, may have a "regressive" effect. If one finds "regression" because of college experience, one must analyze the college experience in terms different from those appropriate for earlier or later sequential movement, as Kramer (1968) has done using "cognitive conflict" concepts.

In addition to sequence, stages must meet the criterion of consistency implied by the notion of a "structured whole." On the logical side, consistency is found in the fact that twenty-five distinct aspects of moral judgment may be logically defined from the core concepts of the six stages. On the empirical side, both consistency across aspects and consistency across verbal situations are to be found. Such consistency is indicated, first, by the fact that an average of 50 percent of a subject's moral judgments fit a single stage. Second, such consistency is indicated by fairly high correlations in moral levels from one story to another. The highest such correlation is .75, the lowest .31, the median .51. Third, it is indicated by the fact that these correlations between situations are not specific; that is, there is a general moral level factor. A general first moral level factor accounts for most of covariations from situation to situation (Kohlberg, 1958).

While the stage conception implies that stages constitute "structured wholes," the stage notion also suggests that (1) age should lead to increasing consolidation or equilibrium in a given stage and (2) that higher stages eventually represent better or more equilibrated structures than lower stages (Turiel, 1969). As children move into adulthood, then, those who remain primarily at Stages 1 and 2 crystallize into purer types, an extreme being some delinquents with an explicit Stage 2 con-man ideology. Subjects moving into the higher stages (4, 5, and 6) stabilize more slowly then the lower stage subjects but by the middle twenties have become the purest types of all (Turiel, 1969; Kramer, 1968).

We have reported a variety of evidence suggesting that moral stages fit all the criteria of stages in the social domain. Our earlier discussion claimed that if this were the case, we should be able to solve the problem of longitudinal predictability which has frustrated so much of socialization research. Preliminary longitudinal findings indicate that this is the case. The correlation between moral maturity scores at age 16 and in the midtwenties was .78 ($n = 24$).* While only a very small sample ($n = 8$) of middle class 13-year-olds have reached the midtwenties, the correlation between moral maturity at age 13 and in the midtwenties was equally high (r between age 13 and age 24 = .92; r between age 16 and age 24 = .88). It is clear, then that a study of environmental determinants of moral level at 13 can have long-range meaning. The degree of predictability achieved suggests the potential fruitfulness of defining social behavior in terms of development sequence instead of in terms of traits for socialization research.

Relations Between Cognition, Affect, and Conduct in Social Development

We have seen that moral judgment stages provide a definition of continuity through transformations of development necessary before the naturalistic study of socialization can begin. We shall now consider how these "cognitively" defined stages of judgment illuminate "noncognitive" moral development in the spheres of affect and of action. This sentence is, however, a misstatement of both Piaget's position and our own, which is not the position that cognition determines affect and behavior but that the *development* of cognition and the development of affect have a common structural base. Rather than saying, as I did earlier, that "regular age-developmental trends in moral judgment have a formal-cognitive base," I should have said that "age-developmental trends in moral judgment

* Because of shakeup and "regression" in college, the correlations between moral maturity at age 16 and in college were much lower ($r = .24$). As previously noted, the regressors all "straightened out" by the midtwenties (Kramer, 1968).

have a formal-structural base parallel to the structural base of cognitive development." While the notion of cognitive-affective parallelism is not abstruse, it has been difficult for American psychologists to grasp. The doctrine has, however, entered the American research literature as it has been independently elaborated by Werner (1948) and his followers (Witkin, 1969). A structural dimension of development, such as "differentiation," is considered to characterize all aspects of the personality—the social emotional, the perceptual, and the intellective. As measured by age-developmental perceptual tasks, "differentiation" is quite highly correlated with standard psychometric intelligence measures as well as with a variety of social attitudes and traits. Harvey et al. (1961) also elaborated a "structural parallelism" view of personality development in terms of increased structural differentiation and integration of conceptions of self and others, implying both cognitive and attitudinal correlates.

In Piaget's (1952a) view, both types of thought and types of valuing or of feeling are schemata which develop a set of general structural characteristics which represent successive forms of psychological equilibrium. The equilibrium of affective and interpersonal schemata involves many of the same basic structural features as the equilibrium of cognitive schemata. It is generally believed that justice (portrayed as balancing the scales) is a form of equilibrium between conflicting interpersonal claims, so Piaget (1948) holds, "In contrast to a given rule imposed upon the child from outside, the rule of justice is an imminent condition of social relationships or a law governing their equilibrium," p. 291. In Piaget's view, logic also is not a learned cultural rule imposed from the outside but a law governing the equilibrium between ideas rather than between persons. Both violation of logic and violation of justice may arouse strong affects. The strong affective component of the sense of justice is not inconsistent with its structural base. As was already stated, the structure of reciprocity is both a cognitive structure and a structural component of the sense of justice.

What is being asserted, then, is not that moral judgment stages are cognitive but that the existence of moral stages implies that moral development has a basic structural component. While motives and affects are involved in moral development, the development of these motives and affects is largely mediated by changes in thought patterns.

Among the implications of this statement are the following:

1. There should be an empirical correlation between moral judgment maturity and nonmoral aspects of cognitive development.
2. Moral judgment stages or sequences are to be described in cognitive-structural terms even in regard to "affective" aspects of moral judgment, like guilt, empathy, and so forth.
3. There should be an empirical correlation between maturity on "affective" and cognitive aspects of morality, even if affective maturity is assessed by projective test or interview methods not explicitly focused on moral judgment.
4. The way in which moral judgment influences action should also be characterizable in cognitive-structural terms.
5. The socioenvironmental influences favorable to moral judgment development should be influences characterizable in cognitive-structural terms, for example, in terms of role-taking opportunities.

With regard to the first point, correlations between group IQ tests and moral judgment level at age 12 range from .30 to .50 in various studies. These correlations indicate that moral maturity has a cognitive base but is not simply general verbal intelligence applied to moral problems. This fact is indicated by the existence of a general moral level factor found among our situations after correlations due to intelligence are controlled for. The relation of moral judgment to intellective development is suggested by the fact that our stage definitions assume that Piagetian concrete operations are necessary for conventional (Stage 3 and 4) morality and that formal operations are necessary for principled (Stage 5 and 6) morality. Some crude and preliminary evidence that this is the case comes from a finding that moral judgment maturity and a crude test of formal operations correlated .44 with tested verbal intelligence controlled. The Piagetian rationale just advanced, as well as other considerations, suggests that cognitive maturity is a necessary, but not a sufficient, condition for moral judgment maturity. While formal operations may be necessary for principled morality, one may be a theoretical physicist and yet not make moral judgments at the principled level. In fact, a curvilinear relation between IQ and moral maturity is found. In the below-average range, a linear correlation ($r = .53$) is found between IQ and moral maturity, whereas no relationship ($r = .16$) is found between the two measures in the above-average group. In other words, children below average in IQ are almost all below average in moral maturity. Children above average in IQ are equally likely to be low or high in moral maturity. The theories just proposed suggest not only a non-linear relation between IQ and moral maturity but a decline in the correlation between the two with age. Moral judgment continues to develop until age 25 (Kramer, 1968), although only for half the middle class population, whereas general intellectual maturity does not. While bright children attain formal operations earlier than duller children, most of the dull children eventually attain them. The duller children, then, tend to develop more slowly in moral judgment but may develop longer. IQ is then a better indicator of early rate of development than it is of terminal status, which is more determined by social experience.

The second point (that affective aspects of moral development are to be described in cognitive-structural terms) was partially documented by our indicating how our stages defined moral affects in Table 1.6 just as they defined "cognitive" dimensions like intentionality in Table 1.5. Table 1.6 indicates that each "higher" affect involves a cognitive differentiation not made by the next "lower" affect.

Table 1.6 assigns guilt over deviation from conventional rules leading to injury to others to Stage 4 (guilt over violation of internal principles was assigned to Stage 6). Stage 4 guilt implies differentiating concern about one's responsibility according to rules from Stage 3, "shame" or concern about the diffuse disapproval of others. Stage 3 concern about disapproval is, in turn, a differentiation of Stage 1 and 2 concerns about overt reward and punishment characteristic of lower stages.

In a certain sense, the cognitive-structural component of guilt would be obvious if it had not been ignored in psychoanalytic theory. Guilt in its most precise sense is moral selfjudgment, and it presupposes the formation of internal or mature standards of moral judgment. Psychoanalysts have assumed the early formation of internalized guilt, of self-punishment and self-criticism tendencies, and have generally assumed that this formation occurs in the early latency period, ages 5 to 7, as a reaction to the Oedipus complex. In fact, however, researchers who have used story-completion tests of guilt reactions do not find open self-criticism and self-punishment tendencies appearing in response to transgression stories until preadolescence or late childhood. When asked, children under 7 almost never say a deviant child who escaped punishment would feel bad. While young children do not show conscious guilt, they do project unrealistic punishment into incomplete stories of transgression. Psychoanalytically oriented researchers have assumed such punishment concerns reflect the child's unconscious guilt, projected out into the world because it is unconscious. In fact, no satisfactory evidence has been accumulated for thinking this is true, since punishment concerns do not correlate positively with other behaviors which might represent moral internalization. Both the punishment concerns of Stage 1 and the guilt of Stage 4 or Stage 6 represent anxiety about deviating from the rules, structured in different ways. In some sense, the feeling in the pit of one's stomach is the same whether it is dread of external events or dread of one's own self-judgment. The difference between the two is that in one case the bad feeling is interpreted by the child as fear of external sanctioning forces whereas, in the other case, it is interpreted by the child as produced by the self's own moral judgments. When the child reaches adolescence, he or she tends to reject fear as a basis for conformity. If a boy is a member of a delinquent gang, he will deny the anxiety in the pit of his stomach because it is "chicken" to fear the cops. If he has developed more mature modes of moral judgment, he will link the same dread in the pit of his stomach to his own self-judgments and say, "I could never do that, I'd hate myself if I did." The difference between the two is a cognitive-structural difference, not a difference in intensity or type of affect. The difference is a real one, however, since intense fear of punishment does not predict to resistance to temptation, whereas self-critical guilt does.

We have already noted that projective-test studies indicate that self-critical guilt appears at about the same age as conventional moral judgment. The coincidence in the age of appearance of projective guilt and of "mature" or conventional moral judgment suggests that the two should be correlated among individual children of a given age. (As stated, this was the third implication of the structural parallelism interpretation of our stages.) The clearest findings of correlation are those reported by Ruma and Mosher (1967). Ruma and Mosher decided they could avoid the many problems of measuring imaginary guilt by assessing guilt about real behavior through use of a population of thirty-six delinquent boys. Measures of guilt were based on responses to a set of interview questions about how the boy felt during and after his delinquent acts (assault or theft). The primary measure was the sum of weighted scores for responses expressing negative self-judgment and remorse (2) as opposed to responses expressing concern about punishment (1) or lack of concern (0). The correlation between this measure and a moral maturity score based on stage-weighted ratings of response to each of six of our conflict situations was .47 ($p < .01$). This correlation was independent of age, IQ, or social-class effects. They also found a correlation of .31 ($p < .05$) between the life-situation guilt measure and the Mosher guilt scale, a sentence-completion measure of guilt using referents suggested by the psychoanalytic conception of guilt (Ruma and Mosher, 1967). The correlation of moral judgment maturity and the Mosher guilt scale was .55. Maturity of moral judgment ideology, then, related somewhat better to two measures of guilt—one real-life, one projective—than they do to each other.

With regard to moral emotion, then, our point of view is that the "cognitive" definition of the moral situation directly determines the moral emotion which the situation arouses. This point of view has been generally held by the "symbolic interactionist" school of social psychology, which has stressed that socially communicated symbolic definitions determine the actual felt attitudes and emotions experienced by the individual in given situations. The empirical findings supporting this general point of view are cumulative and striking, and constitute much of the core content of many social-psychology textbooks. One striking line of evidence is that on the effects of drugs on behavior. Naturalistic studies by sociologists clearly suggest that pleasurable marijuana experiences and marijuana "addiction" are contingent on learning the "appropriate" symbolic definitions of the experience (H. Becker, 1963). Experimental studies indicate that while autonomic stimulants elicit generalized arousal, whether such arousal is experienced as anger, elation, or some other emotion is contingent on the social definition of the situation attendant on administration of the drugs (Schachter, 1964).

In our view, the basic way in which "affect" is socialized is not so much by punishment and reward as it is by communication of definitions of situations which elicit socially appropriate affect. In addition, our approach points to certain fundamental and "natural" cognitive bases of moral emotion, and views cultural definitions as representing only certain selective emphases and elaborations of these bases. The utilitarians were almost certainly correct in emphasizing that the central basis of moral emotion is the apprehension of the results of human action for the pain and harm (or joy and welfare) to human (or quasihuman) beings. Our studies of moral judgment in a variety of Western and non-Western cultures indicates that the overwhelming focus of moral choice and feeling is such personal welfare consequences. The child's whole social life is based on "empathy," that is, on the awareness of other selves with thoughts and feelings like the self. The analyses of the development of the self by Baldwin (1906) and G. H. Mead (1934) have clearly indicated that the self-concept is largely a concept of a shared self, or a self-like other selves. The child cannot have a self-conscious self without having concepts of other selves. Perceived harm to others is as immediately, if not as intensely, apprehended as is harm to the self. Empathy does not have to be taught to the child or conditioned; it is a primary phenomenon. What development and socialization achieve is the organization of empathic phenomena into consistent sympathetic and moral concerns, not the creation of empathy as such.

Our view of the way in which moral values influence action is generally similar. We noted in our second section that socialization studies of "resistance to temptation" had provided few solid findings because "resistance to temptation" is largely situation-specific, as Hartshorne and May (1923–30) demonstrated. While low correlations between cheating in one situation and cheating in another are to be found, these correlations are not due to internalized moral values or standards in the usual sense. These correlations are largely due to nonmoral "ego strength" factors of IQ and attention, and the correlations between cheating tests disappear when these ego factors are controlled (Grim et al., 1968). Attention, measured as standard deviation of reaction time, has been found to correlate in the 50s and 60s with scores on cheating tests. Moral "values" or attitudes conceived as affective quanta in the usual social attitude sense do not predict directly to behavior in conflict situations. Half a dozen studies show no positive correlation between high school or college students' verbal expression of the value of honesty or the badness of cheating and actual honesty in experimental situations. Undoubtedly part of this failure of correlation is due to "deceptive" self-report tendencies. The same desire leading to a desire to cheat to get a good score leads to an overespousal of conventional moral values. However, the problem is deeper than this, since affect-intensity projective measures of guilt fail to predict resistance to temptation unless they include the cognitive-structural selfcritical components already discussed. The real problem is that general intensity measures of espousal of moral attitudes have little relation to the forces determining behavior in concrete conflict situations.

When cognitive and developmental measures of moral judgments and attitudes are used, better results are obtained. While Hartshorne and May (1928–30) found only low correlations between these tests of conventional moral knowledge ($r = .30$) and experimental measures of honesty, the correlations were at least positive and significant. When my transcultural measure of moral maturity is employed, better results are obtained. In one study, correlations of moral judgment maturity with teachers' ratings of moral conscientiousness were .46, and with teacher ratings of fair-mindedness with peers were .54. In another study the correlation of moral maturity with peer ratings of moral character was .58. These correlations are not too clear in meaning, since moral judgment is a clear age-developmental variable, whereas ratings of moral character are not. Clearer relations of judgment and action come if particular stages of moral judgment are related to theoretically meaningful types of moral decisions.

As an example, in the ordinary experimental cheating situations, the critical issue is whether to follow the norm when the conventional expectations of the adult and the group about not cheating are not upheld. Experimenters explicitly leave the children unsupervised in a situation where supervision is expected. Not only do the experimenters indicate they do not care whether cheating goes on, they almost suggest its possibility (since they need cheaters for their study). While the conventional child thinks "cheating is bad" and cares about supporting the authority's expectations, he or she has no real reason not to cheat if tempted, if the authorities don't care and if others are doing it. In contrast, a principled (Stage 5 or 6) subject defines the issue as one involving maintaining an implicit contract with the adult and reflects that the general inequality or taking advantage implied by cheating is still true regardless of the ambiguity of social expectations in the situation. As a result, it is not surprising to find that principled subjects are considerably less likely to cheat than conventional or premoral subjects. In a college group only 11 percent of the principled students cheated as compared to 42 percent of the conventional subjects. In a sixth-grade group, only 20 percent of the principled children cheated as compared to 67 percent of the conventional children and 83 percent of the premoral children.

In the studies mentioned, the critical break was between the principled and the conventional subjects. Another break occurs where the subject is faced with disobeying the rules formulated by an authority figure who is seen as violating the rights of another individual. An example is the Milgram (1963) obedience situation. In this situation the experimenter orders the subject to give an increasingly severe electric shock to a stooge "learner" who has agreed to participate in a nonsense-syllable learning experiment. In this study, only the Stage 6 subjects would be expected to question the authority's moral right to ask them to inflict pain on another. Stage 5 "social contract" subjects would tend to feel the victim's voluntary participation with foreknowledge released them from responsibility to the experimenter while their agreement to participate committed them to comply. As expected, 75 percent of a small group (six) of Stage 6 subjects quit as compared to only 13 percent of the remaining twenty-four subjects at lower moral stages. Some replication of this result comes from preliminary findings of a study of the Berkeley students who did and did not participate in the original free speech sit-in. As expected, 80 percent of the Stage 6 subjects sat in, as compared to 10 percent of the conventional and 50 percent of the Stage 5 subjects. A similar majority of the Stage 2 subjects also sat in, for different though predictable reasons (Haan, Smith and Block, 1968).

The studies just cited help to clarify the relative role of cognitive definitions and of affect-intensity in determining moral choice. We have seen that cognitive definitions determined cheating behavior whereas attitude-strength measures did not. In the Milgram (1963) situation, Stage 6 cognitive definitions determined choice, but a projective measure of sympathy did not. High-empathy subjects were no more likely to quit than low-empathy subjects. In the Berkeley situation, Stage 6 subjects also chose to disobey authorities in the name of individual rights, but without concern for individual rights involving empathy for a concrete victim, supporting the interpretation that the Stage 6 decision to resist was not based on a quantitative affect base. Some tentative findings suggest that amount of empathy was influential in the conventional level subjects' decisions, though not in the principled subjects' decision. Indeed, the Stage 5 subjects were the most prone to say they wanted to quit but did not; that is, they were restrained by contractual principles in spite of their empathic feelings. This interpretation of the affective and situational influence in the Milgram moral decision is similar to that just advanced for the cheating decision.

When affectively or situationally strongly tempted, conventional subjects will cheat. Similarly, when empathy leads to strong "temptation" to violate the rules and authority of the experimenter, conventional subjects will quit (or when fear of authority leads to strong temptation to violate conventional rules against hurting others, conventional subjects will comply).

The interpretation just advanced suggests that quantitative affective-situational forces are less determining of moral decisions at the principled than at the conventional level. This interpretation coincides with another cognitive-developmental interpretation as to the relation of moral judgment to moral action. It was noted that the "cognitive" traits of IQ and attention correlated with measures of honesty, even though honesty is not directly an age-developmental or a cognitive-developmental trait. Drawing upon Williams James's (1890) doctrine of the will as attention, our interpretation holds that IQ, and especially attention, enter into moral decisions as nonmoral tendencies of "strength of will" or "ego strength" (Grim et al., 1968). In part, the moral neutrality of "ego strength" is indicated by the fact that attentive children simply are not tempted and hence need make no moral decision to resist temptation. Attentive children are not only more likely to resist temptation, but attentive noncheaters are more likely to say that they did not think of cheating after temptation than are inattentive noncheaters (Krebs, 1967). In part, the morality neutrality of "ego strength" or "will" is also indicated by the fact that while "strong-willed" conventional subjects cheat less, "strong-willed" premoral subjects cheat more (Krebs, 1967). Among conventional Stage 4 children, only 33 percent of the "strong-willed" (high IQ, high attention) cheated, as compared to 100 percent of the "weak-willed" (low IQ, low attention). In contrast, among the Stage 2 "instrumental egoists," 87 percent of the "strong-willed" children cheated, whereas only 33 percent of the "weak-willed" children cheated. Presumably the weak-willed Stage 2 children were tempted (distracted and suggested) into violating their amoral "principles." At the principled level, however, resistance to temptation is less contingent on "strength of will" and hence is also less contingent on situational-affective forces of a sort irrelevant to their moral principles. All of the children at the principled stage were low on attention, yet only 20 percent cheated.

In summary, then, while moral judgment maturity is only one of many predictors of action in moral conflict situations, it can be a quite powerful and meaningful predictor of action where it gives rise to distinctive ways of defining concrete situational rights and duties in socially ambiguous situations. The causal role of moral judgment appears to be due to its contribution to a "cognitive" definition of the situation rather than because strong attitudinal or affective expressions of moral values activate behavior. To a certain extent, it is no more surprising to find that cognitive moral principles determine choice of conflicting social actions than it is to find that cognitive scientific principles determine choice of conflicting actions on physical objects. Moral principles are essentially believed by their holders to define social "laws" or realities just as physical principles are felt to define physical laws or realities. This is true less in the abstract than in the concrete definition of the situation. While the "value of trust and contract" sounds like an empty abstraction, the principled subject's awareness that the experimenter in the cheating situation trusts him or her is concrete and real and is an awareness missing at lower stages.

In terms of implication for research strategy, the findings suggest that situational action is not usually a direct mirror of structural-developmental change. Once structural-developmental change has been assessed by more cognitive methods, however, it is possible to define structural-developmental changes in situational behavior, for example, consistent noncheating becomes a "milestone" behavior for Stage 5. Whether the milestones are reached first in action (consistent noncheating) or in judgment (Stage 5) is an open empirical question.

Conceptualizing Social Environment in Terms of Role-Taking Opportunities and Structural Match

We stated early in the chapter that an understanding of hierarchical interactional stages depends upon analyses of (1) universal structural features of the environment, (2) the order of differentiations inherent in given conceptions, and (3) relations between the structure of specific experiences and the child's behavior structures, defined in terms of conflict and match. The universal structural features of the environment relevant to moral stages are partly those of the general physical environment, since moral stages presuppose cognitive stages. At the first moral stage, the regularities of the physical and the social environment are confused and the basis of conformity to social laws is not much different than the basis of conformity to physical laws. More fundamentally, however, there are universal structures of the social environment which are basic to moral development. All societies have many of the same basic institutions, institutions of family, economy, social stratification, law, and government. In spite of greater diversity in the detailed definition of these institutions, they have certain transcultural functional meanings. For example, while the detailed prescriptions of law vary from nation to nation, the form of "law" and the functional value of its importance and regular maintenance are much the same in all nations with formal law.

In addition to common institutions, however, all societies are alike in the sheer fact of having institutions, that is, in having systems of defined complementary role expectations. In cognitive-developmental or "symbolic-interactional" theories of society, the primary meaning of the word *social* is the distinctively human structuring of action and thought by role-taking, by the tendency to react to the other as someone like the self and by the tendency to react to the self's behavior in the role of the other (Mead, 1934; Baldwin, 1906; Piaget, 1948). There are two subsidiary meanings of "social," the first, that of affectional attachment, the second, that of imitation. Both human love and human identification, however, presuppose the more general sociality of symbolic communication and role-taking. Before one can love the other or can model his or her attitudes, one must take the other's role through communicative processes (Mead, 1934; Kohlberg, 1966b). The structure of society and morality is a structure of interaction between the self and other selves who are like the self but who are not the self. The area of the conflicting claims of selves is the area of morality, or of moral conflict, and the modes of role-taking in such conflict situations represent the varying structures of moral judgment and choice defining our various stages. Role-taking itself represents a process extending beyond the sphere of morality or of conflicting claims. Moral role-taking itself may have many affective flavors, as our discussion of attitudes of empathy, guilt, disapproval, and respect suggested. Basically, however, all these forms imply a common structure of equality and reciprocity between selves with expectations about one another. Our moral stages represent successive forms of reciprocity, each more differentiated and universalized than the preceding form.

We have discussed the logical ordering of the stages in terms of the differentiation of twenty-five specific moral categories or aspects. However, we take as primary the categories of reciprocity and equality, that is, the categories of justice, as these are used to define social expressions and rules. The most primitive form of reciprocity is that based on power and punishment, the reciprocity of obedience and freedom from punishment. Next (Stage 2) comes literal exchange. Then comes a recognition (Stage 3) that familial and other positive social relations are systems of reciprocity based upon gratitude and the reciprocal maintenance of expectations by two social partners. At Stage 4, this develops into a notion of social order in which expectations are earned by work and conformity, and in which one must keep one's word and one's bargain. At Stage 5, the notion of social order becomes a notion of flexible social contract or agreement between free and equal individuals, still a form of reciprocity (and equality). At Stage 6, moral principles are formulated as universal principles of reciprocal role-taking, for example, the Golden Rule or the categorical imperative, "So act as you would act after considering how everyone should act if they were in the situation." In other words, at the conventional level, the social order is felt to embody the structures of reciprocity defining "justice," whereas at the principled level the social order is derived from principals of justice which it serves. Principles of justice or moral principles are themselves essentially principles of role-taking, that is, they essentially state, "Act so as to take account of everyone's perspective on the moral conflict situation" (Mead, 1934). At the principled level, then, obligation is to the principles of justice lying behind the social order than than to the order itself, and these principles are principles of universalized reciprocity or role-taking.

If moral development is fundamentally a process of the restructuring of modes of role-taking, then the fundamental social inputs stimulating moral development may be termed "roletaking opportunities." The first prerequisite for role-taking is participation in a group or institution. Participation is partially a matter of sheer amount of interaction and communication in the group, since communication presupposes role-taking. In addition, the centrality of individual in the communication and decision-making structure of the group enhances role-taking opportunities. The more the individual is responsible for the decision of the group, and for his or her own actions in their consequences for the group, the more must the individual take the roles of others in it. It has sometimes been held that the subordinate takes the role of the superior more than vice versa (Brim, 1958). If true, this is true only at the level of the dyad.

The group leader must take all the subordinates' roles and be aware of their relations to one another, while the subordinate is only required to take the role of the leader. It is likely that leadership positions require not only more complex or organized role-taking but more affectively neutral, objective, and "rules-and-justice" forms of role-taking, since the leader must mediate conflicts within the group, as Parsons and Bales (1955) have claimed is the case for the "father" or "instrumental leader" role. While leadership roles might be expected to require more role-taking than follower roles, it is also likely that "democratic leadership" requires more role-taking than "autocractic leadership" on the part of both leader and follower, since the group leader must be more sensitive to the members' attitudes and the members will engage in more communication with the leader and have more responsibility for the group decision, as Lippett and White's (1943) studies suggest.

For the developing child, there is presumably a rough sequence of groups or institutions in which he or she participates. The first, the family, has received the most attention in socialization theories. From our point of view, however, (1) family participation is not unique or critically necessary for moral development and (2) the dimensions on which it stimulates moral development are primarily general dimensions by which other primary groups stimulate moral development, that is, the dimensions of creation of role-taking opportunities. With regard to the first point, there is no evidence that the family is a uniquely necessary setting for normal moral development. An ordinary orphanage is a poor setting in terms of role-taking opportunities, so it is not surprising to find institutionalized retardates more retarded in moral judgment development than control retardates living with their families. On the same Piaget (1948) measures on which institutionalized children are more backward than children in families, however, kibbutz children are equal to city children living in families. In general, kibbutz children are "normal" in moral development in spite of marked reduction in amount of interaction with their parents. Earlier, we pointed out that bad families contribute heavily to delinquency, and it may be noted that delinquency is associated with a low level of moral judgment development. The fact that bad families lead to moral arrest and moral pathology does not imply, however, that a good family is necessary for moral development. While parental rejection and use of physical punishment are both negatively correlated with moral internalization and moral stage-development measures, this again is indicative of the negative rather than the positive influence of the family. Extremely high warmth and complete absence of punishment do not seem to be particularly facilitating of moral development. With regard to the second point, the positive dimensions of family interaction contributing to moral development seem understandable in terms of role taking opportunities. Hostility and punishment obviously do not facilitate the child's taking of his or her parents' role. Peck and Havighurst (1960) report that ratings of maturity of moral character are related to ratings of common participation in the family, to confidence sharing, to sharing in family decisions, and to awarding responsibility to the child, a cluster well summarized under the rubric of "role-taking opportunities." As cited earlier, Hoffman and Saltztein (1967) found "inductive discipline" associated with moral internalization. Inductive discipline, that is, pointing out to children the consequences of their actions to others and their own responsibility for it, would seem to represent a form of creating moral role-taking opportunities.

With regard to my own measure of moral maturity, a study by Holstein (1968) indicates that parental provision of role-taking opportunities in moral discussion is a powerful predictor of moral judgment at age 13. Holstein taped discussions over revealed differences in moral opinions on hypothetical situations between mother, father, and child for fifty-two suburban middle class families. Parents who encouraged their child to participate in the discussion (i.e., who were rated as "taking the child's opinion seriously and discussing it") tended to have relatively mature or conventional-level (Stage 3 or 4) children. Seventy percent of the encouraging parents had conventional children while only 40 percent of the nonencouraging parents had conventional children. Amount of paternal and maternal interaction with the child (play, discussion, affection) was also related to the child's moral level.

The second group in which the child participates is the peer group. While psychoanalysts have taken the family as a critical and unique source of moral role-taking (e.g., identification), Piaget (1948) has viewed the peer group as a unique source of role-taking opportunities for the child. According to Piaget, the children's unilateral respect for their parents, and their egocentric confusion of their own perspective with that of their parents, prevents them from engaging in the role taking based on mutual respect necessary for moral development. While the empirical findings support the notion that peer-group participation is correlated with moral development, it does not suggest that such participation plays a critical or unique role for moral development. Peer-group isolates matched for social class and IQ with children highly chosen by their classmates tend to be quite markedly slower in moral development than the leaders. This slowness, however, is not particularly manifested as an arrest at Stage 1, more or less equivalent to Piaget's heteronomous stage. In particular, peer-group participation is not especially facilitative of development on the moral dimensions focused upon by Piaget, as opposed to other dimensions of moral development. Indeed, no differences have been found on measures of intentionality between sociometric stars and isolates, or between kibbutz (peer-group centered) and city children. In summary, then, while peer-group participation appears to stimulate moral development, its influence seems better conceptualized in terms of providing general role-taking opportunities than as having very specific and unique forms of influence.

A third type of participation presumed important for moral development is that of participation in the secondary institutions of law, government, and perhaps, work. One index of differential opportunities for participation in the social structures of government and of work or economy is that of socioeconomic status. It is abundantly clear that the lower class cannot and does not feel as much sense of power in, and responsibility for, the institutions of government and economy as does the middle class. This, in turn, tends to generate less disposition to view these institutions from a generalized, flexible, and organized perspective based on various roles as vantage points. The law and the government are perceived quite differently by the child who feels a sense of potential participation in the social order than the child who does not. The effect of such a sense of participation upon development of moral judgments related to the law is suggested by the following responses of 16-year-olds to the question, "Should someone obey a law if he doesn't think it is a good law?" A lower class boy replies, "Yes, a law is a law and you can't do nothing about it. You have to obey it, you should. That's what it's there for." (For him the law is simply a constraining thing that is there. The very fact that he has no hand in it, that "you can't do nothing about it," means that it should be obeyed—Stage 1.)

An upper middle class boy of the same IQ replies, "The law's the law, but I think people themselves can tell what's right or wrong. I suppose the laws are made by many different groups of people with different ideas. But if you don't believe in a law, you should try to get it changed, you shouldn't disobey it." (Here the laws are seen as the product of various legitimate ideological and interest groups varying in their beliefs as to the best decision in policy matters. The role of law-obeyer is seen from the perspective of the democratic policymaker—Stage 5.)

Studies of moral judgment development in Taiwan, Mexico, the United States (where class groups were matched on IQ), and Turkey indicate that middle class and lower class urban males go through the same stages and that the lower class is more retarded in development than the middle class. Retardation is more marked when the lower class is more impoverished (Mexico, Turkey) than where it is more stable economically (United States, Taiwan).

To some extent, differences between peasant village and urban groups may also be viewed as representing differential opportunities for role-taking and participation in secondary institutions. The Mexican, Turkish, and Taiwanese villager grows up with a sense of participation in the village, but little in the more remote political, economic, and legal system. To a considerable extent, age progressions of development are similar to those of the lower class urban males except for a total, rather than relative, failure to attain the more generalized stages of moral principle, and except for less tendency toward adult fixation at a morally alienated (Stage 2) level.

These findings contrast with many sociological notions as to how group memberships determine moral development. It is often thought that the child gets some of his or her basic moral values from the family, some from the peer group, and others from the social-class group, and that these basic values tend to conflict with one another. Instead of participation in various groups causing conflicting developmental trends in morality, it appears that participation in various groups converges in stimulating the development of basic moral values, which are not transmitted by one particular group as opposed to another. The child lives in a total social world in which perceptions of the law, of the peer group, and of parental teachings all influence one another. While various people and groups make conflicting *immediate demands* upon the child, they do not seem to present the child with basically conflicting or different stimulations for *general moral* development.

The examples of role-taking opportunities just elaborated are essentially specifications of the general belief that the more the social stimulation, the faster the rate of moral development. These theories do not account for specific transitions from stage to stage or to eventual fixation at a particular stage. Such explanation requires theories of structural conflict and structural match, extensively elaborated in the moral domain by Turiel (1969). The problem posed by stage theory is that the stimulus inputs received by the child are usually either assimilated to his or her own level or are not perceived as stimuli at all. For example, a Stage 2 delinquent is offered "role-taking opportunities" by an understanding psychotherapist, but these opportunities are perceived as opportunities to "con a sucker" and do not stimulate development beyond Stage 2. In the Rest studies (Rest, 1968; Rest et al., 1969), it was found that there was a strong tendency to assimilate higher level moral judgments to the subject's own level or one below it. The problem of moral change would appear to be one of presenting stimuli which are both sufficiently incongruous as to stimulate conflict in the child's existing stage schemata and sufficiently congruous as to be assimilable with some accommodative effort.

With regard to the assimilation of moral judgments made by others, the "match" notions just presented suggest that there would be maximal assimilation of moral judgments one level above the subject's own. The rationale for this was made clear in our earlier discussion of the Rest studies of the hierarchy of comprehension and preference for the six stages. To test this "match" hypothesis, Turiel (1966) divided sixth-grade children (themselves equally divided by pretests among Stages 2, 3, and 4) and randomly to one of three treatment groups. The treatments consisted of exposure to advice by an adult experimenter on two hypothetical moral conflict situations. The first treatment group received advice one stage above their own, the second two stages above their own, and the third one stage below their own. The children were posttested one month later on both the pretest and the treatment situations. Turiel found a significant increase in usage of thinking one stage above in the plus-one treatment group. He found no significant increase in usage of thinking two stages above in the plus-two treatment. He found an increase in usage of thinking one stage below in the minus-one group, but this increase was significantly less than the increase of plus-one thinking in the plus-one treatment group.

Turiel's laboratory study has received naturalistic validation from Blatt's (1969) program of classroom discussions of moral dilemmas held once a week for three months at the sixth-grade level. Blatt's procedure was to elucidate the arguments of the Stage 3 children as against the Stage 2 children on hypothetical moral conflicts, then to pit the Stage 3s against the Stage 4s, and finally to himself present Stage 5 arguments. The effect of this procedure was to raise 45 percent of the children up one stage (as compared to 8 percent in a control group), and 10 percent, up two stages. A majority of the Stage 2 subjects moved to Stage 3, a majority of the Stage 3 subjects, to Stage 4. There was very little movement from Stage 4 to the Stage 5 level presented by the teacher.

One reason the Blatt study induced more change than the Turiel study was that the discussions were carried on over a greater time period. The Blatt procedure also differed in inducing greater conflict through disagreement. Presumably a sense of contradiction and discrepancy at one's own stage is necessary for reorganization at the next stage. A series of studies by Turiel (1969) are systematically exploring the role of such cognitive-conflict parameters in moral judgment change.

Findings on "match" in parent influences on moral development are still ambiguous. No relationship has been found between the moral level of fathers and of their children (Kramer, 1968; Holstein, 1968). A clear relationship between mother's level and the level of her child (of either sex) has been found by Holstein. While 50 percent of forty-one mothers at a conventional level had premoral (Stage 1 or 2) children, none of twelve principled mothers had children at this low level. From a direct transmission or social learning point of view, there is no reason why conventional mothers should be less effective in transmitting (their own) conventional moral ideology to their children than principled mothers. The one-above hypothesis also does not account for the superiority of principled mothers in stimulating movement from the premoral to the conventional level. It may be that it is the match of the principled mothers' action, not their judgment, which is crucial to this effect.

The problem of "match" is not only a problem of the assimilation of moral statements by others but a problem of the assimilation of their actions. With regard to actions, the slum boy may well interpret the behavior of policemen, teachers, and gang buddies as being based on his own Stage 2 individual behavior and exchange conceptions. It may be that if the boy also has a bad family, in the Gluecks' (Glueck and Glueck, 1950) sense, there is no model of altruistic Stage 3 action to generate either conflict in his Stage 2 schema or any Stage 3 moral material to be assimilated. The problem of match is also a problem of assimilation of the child's own behavior to his moral ideology. Freedman (1965) has stressed the accommodation of moral attitudes to actual behavior in the service of reduction of cognitive dissonance, where moral attitudes are defined in the "nonpredictive" sense discussed earlier. Our developmental conception is one in which cognitive balance is not so simple and in which cognitive dissonance can lead to reorganization upward or downward. However, no work has yet been done on moral behavior—moral ideology relations—from this perspective.

In summary, then, a theory of "match" in morality should account for the effect of inputs of moral judgment and moral action at particular stages. In its broadest sense, the match problem is the problem of the fit of the individual's ideology to his or her world. Stage 2 "fits" a slum or jail world, Stage 4 fits the traditional army world, Stage 5 fits the academic and bureaucratic worlds. In this regard, the changes of "world" characterizing adult socialization may require the same types of theoretical analysis as those of childhood.

Experimental Studies of Social Learning and Structural-Development Change

Earlier, I suggested that the major rationale for conducting naturalistic studies of socialization rested on the assumption that personality development involved structural change and that the effects of early experience upon behavior are relatively permanent, irreversible, and different in kind from the effects of experience upon behavior change in adulthood. I noted that theories of socialization based on general learning theories typically do not make such assumptions about structural change. It is not surprising, then, to find that socialization theorists oriented to general principles of learning have turned away from naturalistic studies to studies involving the experimental modification of situational behavior. It is also not surprising to find that these studies have shown social-learning principles to be powerful predictors of behavior, while the naturalistic studies have not. The discrepancy between the degree of support for social-learning theory coming from experimental and from naturalistic findings may be explained on two grounds. The first is that the long-run effects of natural socialization inputs upon structural change require different principles of explanation than are applicable to short-run situational change. The second is that there is no such thing as long-run structural change, and the short-run situational changes explained by social-learning theories cancel each other out so as not to yield long-range predictions at the transsituational and longitudinal level explored by the naturalistic studies of personality. Because the methodological ambiguities of the naturalistic studies are great, most social-learning theorists have not taken a clear position on this issue, but have tended to dismiss the findings of the naturalistic studies as to weak methodologically to require detailed explanation.

With regard to the actual experimental studies, some seem designed with the assumption that there is no such thing as structural change in development. Others seem to be asserting that some behavior changes have more "structural" properties than other behavior changes, but that these changes, too, are explicable by the general principles of learning. As discussed earlier, the empirically minimal properties of structural change are a considerable degree of stability or irreversibility of the change (e.g., resistance to extinction or counterconditioning) and a considerable degree of generalization of the change to situations not manifestly similar to the situations in which change was initially induced.

The simplest type of study based on the first assumption is one showing that conditioning can change or mimic behavior having a label the same as that employed in a structural theory. An example is Azrin and Lindsley's (1956) study of the "learning of cooperation." Cooperation is thought of by Piaget and others as a natural and relatively irreversible developmental trend resulting from the child's differentiation of his or her own "egocentric" perspective from that of others. Parten and Newhall (1943) provide considerable support for this "structural" view of cooperation since they find regular relationships of naturalistically observed cooperation to chronological and mental age, and considerable day-by-day or situational stability to the child's level of cooperation. Azrin and Lindsley conducted a training study inducing "cooperation," apparently to demonstrate that cooperation was a product of operant learning. Their operational definition of cooperation was the matching of one child's placement of a stylus to the other's placement, such matching being a contingency for receiving a candy. Needless to say, the children's rate of stylus matching increased after reinforcement and extinguished after nonreinforcement. The reversibility of the learning of the response, then, indicated that no structural change was induced. No transfer of training was tested, nor was there any definition of what the term "cooperation" might mean in terms of some generalization dimension. ("Sharing" of the reinforcer was not even involved as a learning dimension in the study; from the outset the children shared.) The study, then, leads only to the conclusion that children will adjust the placement of a stylus in such a way as to receive a reinforcer, but this finding does not appear to have any theoretical significance for the problem of structural change in development.*

A second type of social-learning approach to developmental structure is exemplified by Bandura and MacDonald's (1963) experimental induction of changes in Piagetian moral judgment. It is not quite clear whether the intent of the study was to explain structural change in social-learning terms or to demonstrate that Piaget's (1948) behavior definitions did not have any structural component.

The first intent would imply that Piaget had correctly identified a response with some structural properties but had employed a faulty "maturational" theory to explain its development, which could be better explained by social-learning processes. The second intent would imply that Piaget had incorrectly attributed structural properties to his moral stage measures, either because his methods were poor or because moral judgment responses have no structural properties. Piaget (1948) himself believed that his moral judgment stages are structural in the sense that (1) they represent "structural wholes," that is, a constellation of traits indicative of global heteronomous or autonomous attitudes toward rules and (2) that they constitute a relatively irreversible sequence. According to Piaget, one index of the child's stage location is that of his or her judgment in terms of intentions or consequence when the two conflict, for example, judging it is worse to break ten cups while washing the dishes than one cup while stealing candy. Bandura and MacDonald (1963) tested second-grade children on a series of

* The positive side of these studies emerges where the behavior studied is of obvious practical significance. Thus Baer and his co-workers (Baer, Peterson, and Sherman, 1967) demonstrate that specific problem behaviors of preschool children are amenable to replacement with more positive behavior by operant techniques. In light of the tendencies of teachers to inappropriately define annoying behavior as representing pathological personality structures and to respond accordingly, these studies have obvious usefulness. However, except in their impact upon the evaluation of the child by others, the Baer manipulations are presumably as structurally irrelevant to the child's personality development as are the Azrin and Lindslely (1956) induction of changed stylus behaviors in their children.

these items and found some were "at the autonomous stage" (judged in terms of intentions) while some were "at the heteronomous stage." Children at each stage were then exposed to reinforced models emitting the opposite type of judgment. Bandura and MacDonald found substantial learning of the opposite type response. Not only was a "higher stage" readily learned, but it generalized to some new items. Learning was about equal whether it was "progressive" or "regressive." The apparent conclusion to be drawn from the study is that intentionality is learned by ordinary reversible social-learning mechanisms and that the age trends in intentionality found by Piaget correspond to a learning of the adult cultural norms.

The findings from a number of other studies warn us against accepting these conclusions at face value. Some of these findings come from experimental studies of the training of conservation (reviewed in Sigel and Hooper, 1968; Kohlberg, 1968). Almost all of these studies have given great attention to the issue of whether the behavior changes induced by training are "structural" or not. "Structural change" has been assessed by

1. the degree of generality or transfer of conservation (e.g., conservation of liquid to conservation of solids to conservation of number);
2. the degree of irreversibility of conservation in the face of training or trick demonstrations designed to induce nonconservation.

While the findings conflict somewhat, the following conclusions emerge (Kohlberg, 1968):

1. "Naturally" developed concepts of conservation are quite generalized (i.e., there is a general "conservation factor" in conservation tests).
2. Naturally developed concepts of conservation are quite irreversible.
3. Conservation is difficult to teach by ordinary learning methods to children at an appropriate readiness "age" and almost impossible at earlier ages.
4. When taught by some methods, conservation shows some generality and irreversibility. In this it deviates from the specificity and extinguishability of most social-learning study changes. At the same time, however, taught conservation is

far less generalized and irreversible than natural conservation.

In light of these findings, the ready reversibility of moral judgment responses in the Bandura and McDonald (1963) study is suspicious. How are the discrepancies between the ease of learning or unlearning of Piaget's (1948) moral judgment and the difficulty of learning Piaget's (1947) conservation to be accounted for? One answer would be that cognitive tasks (e.g., conservation) do involve structural development but that social or moral tasks do not; they simply involve the learning of cultural values. A second answer would be that morality is an area of structural development but that Piaget's concepts and methods for defining structure are not as adequate in the moral field as are his concepts and methods in the area of logical operations.

A number of facts point to the validity of the second rather than the first conclusion.* Our review of the findings with our own moral stages indicated that they did have structural properties. Our review also indicated that the studies of Turiel (1966) and of Rest et al. (1969) yielded quite different results from those of the Bandura and MacDonald study. "Social learning" of the stage above the child's own was much greater than learning of the stage below the child's own. The discrepancy, however, was one of preference and assimilation, not of cognitive learning, since children recalled the one-below arguments better than the one-above arguments.

The Turiel studies (1966, 1969), then, suggest that moral judgment is an area of structural development but that Piaget's concepts and methods are not good measures of structure in this area. The Kohlberg (1958) assessment method involved classifying open-ended responses into one of six stage categories, whereas Piaget's (1948) assessment involved asking children to choose between two prepackaged alternatives, for example, "Was John who broke one cup or Charles who broke ten cups worse?" This facilitates children's social learning of the content of the "right answer" without necessarily implying development of awareness of the structure underlying the right answer. Furthermore, the Pia-

* The points made here are elaborated and documented in the discussions of replications of the Bandura and MacDonald (1963) study made by Crowley (1968) and Cowen, Langer, Heavenrich, and Nathanson (1968).

get stories do not reveal awareness or unawareness of intentions in moral judgment, but simply how much these are weighted against consequences. Age-developmental studies indicate an awareness of the modifying role of intention among almost all children of the age of the Bandura and MacDonald subjects. Some limitation of the role of intention, as opposed to consequence, is involved even in judgment of adults, who consider it worse to kill someone in a car accident by negligence than to purposefully and malevolently insult someone. Accordingly, the shifts in the Bandura and MacDonald study do not represent an actual learning or "unlearning" of a basic concept of intentions, but a learning to weigh them more or less heavily as opposed to consequence. Piaget asserts that awareness of intention is "structural" in the sense that it represents advance on one of eleven dimensions defining the autonomous stage of moral judgment. However, empirical studies reviewed elsewhere (Kohlberg, 1963a) indicate that children of a given age who are mature on Piaget's tests of intentionality are not more mature on the other Piaget dimensions of the morally autonomous stage; that is, there is no general Piaget moral stage factor (while there is a general moral stage factor in the various Kohlberg situations and dimensions).

In summary, then, Piaget's definitions of moral judgment responses do not meet the naturalistic criteria of structural stages, and hence social-learning manipulations of these responses do not indicate that moral judgment is not structural nor do they indicate that social-learning operations can account for structural development. A hypothetical comparison may clarify the basic point. Bandura and MacDonald's (1963) intent was analogous to operant manipulations of a behavior, such as guilt-strength, that is considered structural in psychoanalytic theory. The theoretical futility of such efforts is self-evident, since the psychoanalyst always says the behavior changed is not structural, and is not what they would term "real guilt," regardless of the outcome of the study. In the moral judgment case, however, the issue of the structural nature of the variable is an empirically definable matter, not an issue of what Piaget's theory might be assumed to say, and this line of experimentation can eventually lead to some conclusions.

Our comparison of the the Turiel and the Bandura and MacDonald studies indicates, then, that prior naturalistic study of structural aspects of development is required before experimental manipulations can lead to conclusions about structural development. The contrast between the intent of the Bandura and MacDonald study and that of the experimental studies of conservation is enlightening. The conservation studies assume the existence of structural development and manipulate inputs in order to accelerate such development. The purpose of such studies is to allow us to conceptualize the conditions for cognitive structural change, not to reduce explanations of structural change to explanations developed for other purposes. It is hard to believe that experimental studies of socialization will not take on the same intent soon.

The Bandura and MacDonald (1963) study suggests an additional positive goal for studies manipulating developmental responses besides the goal of accelerating development common to the conservation studies. While Piaget's measures of intentionality are not direct assessments of "structural" stages, they do reflect some natural or cross-culturally universal trends of development. Age trends toward intentionality have been found in every literate culture studied (Switzerland, Belgium, Britain, Israel, United States, Taiwan), as well as in all but one preliterate or semiliterate culture studies (Atayal, Hopi, Zuni, Papago, Mayan, Sioux). Accordingly, the social learning processes exemplified by the Bandura and MacDonald "backward" manipulations are not only distinguishable from the processes naturally leading to the development of intentionality but in partial conflict with them. The same statement may be made about the Turiel (1966) study which did induce some learning in the one-below condition. This type of learning may not be unusual in actual social life. An extreme natural example offered earlier was the Atayal adolescent's social learning of "regressive" dream beliefs. Perhaps another, more artificial, example is provided by the Milgram (1963) obedience study in which the subjects may "learn" from an authority that it is right to shock people in certain situations.

In the discussion of the Atayal dream concept, I suggested that the "social learning" of such regressive beliefs was not smoothly superimposed upon the child's previous cognitive structure, but engendered conflict and doubt in the child or to his or her other "natural" beliefs. A study by Cowen et al. (1968) suggests that the regressive learning in the Bandura and MacDonald study involved some such conflict and that this learning had somewhat different properties than progressive learning. In one part of their study, Cowen et al. replicated the Bandura and MacDonald findings. Their study also involved a more extensive test of the generality and stability of the learning involved. Such tests indicated that the downward learning was less stable over time than the upward learning, as expressed in the decline of use of the model's downward moral reasons (consequences) in a two-week delayed posttest for the regressive group, in contrast to no such decline in retention of the model's reasons in the upward-learning group. This discrepancy between upward and downward reasoning was especially marked for new, as opposed to retest, items. In addition, the authors note that for both learning groups almost all learning took place in the first two trials, that learning seldom went above the 60 percent criterion, and that the children seemed extremely confused and uncertain as to their reasons after the learning trials. Rather than smooth change following the general laws of learning, the children seemed to have been confronted with the fact that a social authority contradicted their own notions. Their long-range response to this contradiction varied according to whether the authority espoused a view above or below the child's own. In summary, then, the study of the effects of social influence upon responses at various developmental levels may contribute an understanding to that vast border line of socialization in which cultural learning processes and cognitive-structural processes influence each other.

Social-Learning Studies and the Concept of Internalization

The social-learning studies considered so far have been primarily efforts to deny, rather than to explain, structural-developmental change. The work of Aronfreed and others, however, represents a positive effort to explain structural-developmental change within the general principles of associationistic theories of social learning. As Aronfreed suggests, structural-developmental change is usually defined by social-learning theorists as "internalization." According to Aronfreed,

> The young child's behavior is initially highly dependent on its experience of external events which are transmitted through the presence and activity of its socializing agents. But its behavior gradually comes to be governed, to a considerable extent, by internal monitors which appear to carry many of the functions of the external controls originally required to establish the behavior. [Aronfreed, 1969, p. 263]

The concept of internalization is an attractive one since it seems to define basic structural-developmental changes in a way amenable to experimental investigation. As an example, Aronfreed finds that mild experimental punishment will lead children to resist touching attractive toys even in the absence of an adult monitor, and that this punishment is more effective if it is closely timed to follow onset of the touching act. Aronfreed interprets this effect as the result of classical conditioning of anxiety directly to internal proprioceptive cues of incipient action (as opposed to the conditioning of anxiety to external cues of punishment). Such an experimental induction of internalization seems analogous to the basic processes of natural socialization designed to produce reliable conformity in the absence of sanctions. It also seems analogous to the natural developmental trend in children toward increased self-government, self-control, or ego strength. When the analogy to self-control is considered carefully, however, it becomes clear that the child conditioned to feel anxiety over kinesthetic cues of incipient action has no more made a gain in self-control than has the dog conditioned in a similar fashion or the child whose conditioned anxiety represents a phobia. Self-control implies control and inhibition of action by an organized self or ego with cognitive representations of itself and the world, and with an intelligent flexibility as to the cues and conditions of inhibition or release of action. Insofar as inhibition of action is determined rigidly by the paradigms of classical conditioning, it indicates the absence of self-control in the usual sense.

If internalization as experimentally studied has not represented the formation of new structural mechanisms of self-control, neither has it represented structural-developmental change itself. As Aronfreed notes, there is little evidence that experimental inductions of resistance to temptation have the situationally general and irreversible character of structural-developmental change. The sheer fact that a child will follow instructions without someone in the room is itself no evidence that something more than reversible situational learning has been induced. It is clear, then, that experimental inductions of "internalization" cannot be considered to represent the induction of structural-developmental change in the absence of direct evidence of situational generality and irreversibility of such learning.

We have claimed that the experimental studies of internalization have not actually studied either the acquisition of new mechanisms of self-control or the formation of irreversible transsituational learning, and hence do not really shed light on any process of "internalization" distinct from the general processes of reversible situation-specific learning. In this regard, they are no different from the naturalistic studies of internalization discussed earlier. The experimental studies have operationally defined internalization as degree of conformity to the experimenter's instructional or modeling behavior. As indicated earlier, naturalistic studies of moral internalization have also defined it in conformity terms, that is, as behavioral, affective, or cognitive conformity to the moral standards of the child's culture. As another example, sex-role "internalization" has been studied in terms of "masculinity-femininity," or "sex-role identification," that is, in terms of tests of conformity to statistically modal responses of males as opposed to females in the child's culture (studies and measures reviewed in Kohlberg, 1966b).

Earlier, I noted that these naturalistic measures of moral internalization did not seem to represent measures of structural change any more than did the measures used in experimental studies of internalization like Aronfreed's. The naturalistic measures also appeared to be situation specific and longitudinally unstable (i.e., reversible). The same is more or less true of measures of "sex-role internalization" (evidence reviewed in Kohlberg, 1966b). In essence, I argued that conformity definitions of response were inadequate to define structural change in development because they ignored sequential changes in the shape or patterning of responses.

We must ask, then, in what sense the internalization concept is useful in the definition of structural-developmental change. It is evident that natural moral development is grossly defined by a trend toward an increasingly internal orientation to norms. Our moral stages, as defined by the aspect of sanctions in Table 1.6, clearly represent increasing interiorized orientations to moral norms moving from a concern for sanctions to a concern for praise and blame to a concern for internal principles. This stage conception of internalization is similar to that stated by McDougall (1908) in the first textbook of social psychology:

> The fundamental problem of social psychology is the moralization of the individual into the society into which he is born as an amoral and egoistic infant. There are successive stages, each of which must be traversed by every individual before he can attain the next higher: (1) the stage in which the operation of the instinctive impulses is modified by the influence of

rewards and punishments, (2) the stage in which conduct is controlled in the main by anticipation of social praise and blame, (3) the highest stage in which conduct is regulated by an ideal that enables a man to act in the way that seems to him right regardless of the praise or blame of his immediate social environment. [McDougall, 1908, p. 97]

There are certain fundamental differences in this stage concept of moral internalization and the conformity concept, however. In the first place, while "internality" is an essential component of McDougall's idea of mature morality, this internality is not defined relative to degree of conformity to a cultural standard, as in a resistance-to-temptation study. Rather, it is defined in terms of an "ideal enabling a man to act in a way that seems to him right regardless of praise or blame." This ideal hardly needs to be an internalized cultural standard. When Luther said, "Here I stand, I can do no other," he represented McDougall's highest stage, but he was not conforming to an internalized cultural standard of any recognizable sort, since the ideal was self-formulated. In practice, then, the developmentalist is arguing that we can tell whether the norm an individual is following is "moral" or "internal" by looking at the way in which the individual formulates the norm, that is, its form, and without reference to a specific external cultural standard. A cultural norm, common especially in the lower class, is "Stay out of trouble." It is clear that such a norm cannot be held as a moral ideal by an individual regardless of the processes of "norm-internalization" to which the individual is exposed. Our own position is that the only fully internal norm is a moral principle, and that a moral principle (our Stage 6) is definable according to a set of formal attributes which are culturally universal.

The first point brought out by the stage conception, then, is that internality is merely part of the conception of a moral orientation, not a general socialization dimension definable without reference to the concept of a moral orientation. The distinction between moral principles and other cultural standards is just that one is not expected to have as fully an internalized orientation to other cultural standards. Moral principles are categorical imperatives, all other standards are hypothetical imperatives contingent on the individual's aims in the situation. Young children may first require admonition and punishment to brush their teeth and eventually brush their teeth without sanctions. In the adult, such an "internalized" orientation of the norm of toothbrushing is quite different from an internalized orientation to a moral norm. If a man forgets his toothbrush when traveling, he feels no obligation to brush his teeth nor any guilt for failing to do so. He will justify his toothbrushing instrumentally and selfishly (it prevents cavities and keeps his teeth clean) rather than because of respect for the rule or principle of toothbrushing. In sum, then, moral internalization in the sense of development of moral principles cannot be equated with some general dimension of social-norm learning.

The meaning of internalization in the moral domain also makes clear a second point implied by the stage position, which is that internalization must imply cognitive as well as affective correlates. The man in the street knows that a dog or an infant can be trained to refrain from eating meat powder when hungry, even in the absence of surveillance by the socializing agent, but refuses to consider such conformity "moral." Likewise, the dog's deviance is not considered immoral nor does it arouse moral indignation, because the dog is not considered moral. The dog is neither moral nor immoral "because it doesn't know right from wrong." When the dog has "internalized" the rule to refrain from eating meat powder, it is not because it is "acting in terms of an ideal that seem to it right regardless of praise or blame," but because it has not correctly discriminated the occasions where punishment is likely from those where it is not. The animal or infant has no concept of a rule which is guiding its behavior but instead is responding to cues in the physical or social situation to which it has been aversively conditioned. Children acquire conceptions of rules by age 5–6, but it is not until adolescence that children cognitively formulate moral principles in McDougall's sense of ideals guiding the self's behavior regardless of external social or authoritative support.

In summary, then, there is a sense in which socialization agents hold as their goal in the development of internalized moral standards in the young, and there is also a sense in which the development of internalized moral standards is a "natural" trend regardless of the specific expectations and practices of socialization agents. Neither the expectations of socialization agents nor the natural trends of development are well defined by a conformity conception of internalization, however. This is apparent in the case of Western adults who do not define moral internalization as behavioral conformity to the cultural code but rather as the development of a morality of principle which is above actual conformity to cultural expectations. The existence of such parental expectations for socialization "above the culture" must in turn arise from parental recognition of partly natural or autonomous developmental trends in the formation of an internal morality.

Socialization analyses have tended to take an ethnographic description of the content of adult cultural expectations as defining the end point and direction of the socialization process, apart from natural age trends. It is obvious that there is some gross match between trends of age-development and adult expectations in any culture, or the culture would hardly be transmitted. This gross correspondence, however, may as much represent the shaping of adult expectations by developmental realities as the shaping of developmental progressions by adult expectations. There is, we believe, common meaning to the image of maturity guiding socialization in any culture, an image largely reflecting universal and natural trends of social development. In our contemporary culture this core of common meaning is generally called "ego maturity" or "ego strength." There are a large number of competencies expected of adults in our culture which psychologists include in this rubric. The most general of these capacities are those for love, work, and morality. There can be little question that middle class American socialization expectations are more centrally oriented to the development of such basic capacities than they are to the teaching of detailed conformity to the set of specific and culturally arbitrary definitions of behavior in specific roles defined by the ethnographer or the sociologist. It seems likely that there are culturally universal or near-universal values suggested by the words "love," "work," and "morality," and that these values recognize natural developmental trends and progressions. The development of moral capacities (as well as capacities to work and to love) involves an orientation to internal norms, but this development cannot be defined as a direct internalization of external cultural norms.

If students of socialization ignore these maturity components of social development in favor of simpler conformity or internalization concepts, they will not only fail to describe "natural development" correctly but will fail to describe the aims and expectations of socialization agents correctly. As a result they will fail to understand the socialization process insofar as this process is essentially a matching (or mismatching) of the developmental expectations of the parent and the developing capacities of the child.

Imitation as a Fundamental Process in Social Development: Baldwin's Theory*

In the preceding sections, I have argued that the enduring products of socialization must be conceived of in terms of cognitive-structural changes with "natural" courses or sequences of development rather than in terms of the learning of culture patterns. These changes are results of the general processes of cognitive development as these restructure conceptions of the social self, the social world, and the relations between the two. While cognitive, these processes responsible for social development are theoretically different from those responsible for development of physical concepts because they require roletaking. Since persons and institutions are "known" through role-taking, social-structural influences on cognitive-structural aspects of social development may be best conceived in terms of variations in the amount, kind, and structure of role-taking opportunities.

In order to tie my conceptions of role-taking to notions of socialization "processes" (of motivation and learning), I shall now elaborate a cognitive-developmental account of processes of imitation and identification. As I indicated earlier, roletaking is a broader term than imitation, but in my opinion, all role-taking has imitative components or roots. At the adult level, however, we do not overtly imitate, we "role-take."

In the earlier discussion of the Bandura and MacDonald (1963) study of modeling of moral judgment, I indicated some of the ways in which imitation did not help explain structural development. Is there a sense in which it does? J. M. Baldwin (1906) and Piaget (1951) have postulated that imitation is a natural and active tendency in the human infant, and that this tendency is necessary to account for the infant's cognitive and social development.

One sense in which Baldwin and Piaget have claimed that imitation was an explanatory principle of development is the sense in which they equate imitation with a basic functional tendency they call "accommodation." As stated by Baldwin, "Reaction of the imitative type is the original form of mental accommodation to the environment" (1906, p. 528). I will not elaborate this difficult con-

---

*This condensed summary of the theories of development of the social and moral self of Baldwin and Mead is elaborated in Kohlberg (1982) and Hart and Kohlberg (1985).

ception here beyond suggesting some of its intuitive rationale. It is clear that imitation involves a cognitive copying process. There is a sense in which any cognition is a copy of a part of the environment, since an image or symbol has a relation of "likeness to" an environmental object or structure. In Baldwin's and Piaget's view, representation or imagery then implies a distinctive active copying tendency, since they believe all images and representations are forms of action, not passive reintegration of sensations (as introspective associationism and psychoanalysis claimed).

Whatever one's views as to the role of imitation in the development of cognitive representation, there can be little question that imitation is an extremely basic mechanism in the formation of social knowledge. Struck by such phenomena as sociodramatic play, there is hardly a writer concerned with the problem of how the child comes to know his or her society who has not been struck by the place of the child's imitative or role-taking tendencies in the growth of such knowledge.

Baldwin's view that the child's knowledge of society develops at first through imitation seems to be saying little more than the social-learning truism that the child's knowledge of society grows through the observational learning of the behavior of others (learning which, translated into performance, is termed imitation). The more distinctive feature of Baldwin's view is that such imitation provides the structure of the child's social relationships, that is, of his or herself as it relates to other selves. In the social-learning view of imitation, it is a matter of little moment whether a response is learned by imitation or by reinforced trial and error, since it functions in the same way once learned. In contrast, Baldwin argues that imitation is important because it determines the structure of the child's self-concept, and of his or her concepts of others, a structure, in turn, determining the use of the behavior pattern learned through imitation.

According to Baldwin,

> the growth of the individual's self-thought, upon which his social development depends, is secured all the way through by a twofold exercise of the imitative function. He reaches his subjective understanding of the social copy by imitation, and then he confirms his interpretations by another imitative act by which he ejectively leads his self-thought into the persons of others. [1906, p. 527]

Baldwin's central claim (made also by Mead, 1934) is that the child's self-concept and his or her concept of other selves necessarily grow in one-to-one correspondence. The child cannot observationally learn the behavior pattern of another without putting it in the manifold of possible ways of acting open to the self. Once it becomes something the self might do, when others do it, they, too, are ascribed the subjective attitudes connected with the self's performance of the act.

As stated by Baldwin,

> What the person thinks as himself is a pole or terminus and the other pole is the thought he has of the other person, the "alter." What he calls himself now is in large measure an incorporation of elements that at another period he called another. Last year I thought of my friend, W., as someone with skill on a bicycle. This year I have learned to ride and have imitatively taken the elements formerly recognized in W's personality over to myself. All the things I hope to learn to become are, now, before I acquire them, possible elements of my thought of others.
>
> But we should note that when I think of the other, I must construe him as a person in terms of what I think of myself, the only person whom I know in the intimate way called "subjective." My thought of my friend is not exhausted by the movements of bicycling, nor by any collection of such acts. Back of it all there is the attribution of the very fact of subjectivity which I have myself. I constantly enrich the actions which were at first his alone, and then became mine by imitation of him, with the meaning, the subjective value, my appropriation of them has enabled me to make. [1906, pp. 13–18]

According to Baldwin, then, there are two intertwined mechanisms of society, of sharing. The first is imitation of the other, the second is "ejection," that is, empathy or "projection" of one's own subjective feelings into the other. Imitation of the other not only leads to a changed self-concept (e.g., a self who rides the bicycle) but it leads to a changed concept of the other because the activity (bicycle riding) has a new meaning after it is done by the self, and this meaning is read back as part of the other.

The basic starting point of any analysis of the growth of social knowledge, then, must be the fact that all social knowledge implies an act of sharing, of taking the viewpoint of another self or group of selves. This fact is paralleled on the active side by the fact that all social bonds, ties, or relationships involve components of sharing. The word *social* essentially means "shared." The motivational problem usually proposed to socialization theory is the question of why the "selfish" or impulsive infant develops into a social being, that is, one who wants to share activities with others, to share goods with others, to be a member of a common group, to maintain shared norms, and to pursue shared goals. The answer of developmental theory is that the self is itself born out of the social or sharing process, and therefore, motives for self-realization or self-enhancement are not basically "selfish" in the perjorative sense, but require sharing. Developmental theory, then, presents a radically different picture of the birth of social motives from that of all other theories. Other theories have assumed that social motives are either instinctive or result from the association of socializing agents and their behavior with gratification and anxiety to the child. In contrast, developmental theories assume a primary motivation for competence and self-actualization which is organized through an ego or self whose structure is social or shared.

Two basic psychological mechanisms of sharing have been proposed by developmental theory, "role-taking" and imitation. Baldwin (1906) and Mead (1934) engaged in extensive written debate as to the relative priority of the two mechanisms in social development. Baldwin viewed similarity of self and other as directly striven for through imitation, whereas Mead viewed it as the indirect result of role-taking involved in communicative acts. The child's attitude, he thought, became like that of the other because both respond alike to a common symbol or gesture. Because a boy has responded in the past to the other's gesture, when he makes the gesture himself, he calls out in himself implicitly the response he calls out in the other. Mead further points out that much sociality, much mutual role-taking, occurs through cooperative interaction in which each individual's role is different, in which roles are complementary rather than similar. Nevertheless, the study of infancy indicates that similarity to others is directly striven for, and that such striving or imitation precedes, rather than follows, the development of linguistic communication. Accordingly, it seems to me that Mead's conceptions must be embedded in a broader developmental account of the self which includes early imitative behavior and the matrix of infant cognitive development out of which the self emerges.

Like Mead, Baldwin was struck by the fact that the younger child's social interaction is structured in terms of dyadic complementary roles, and that young children tend to play out both sides of these complementary roles as a mechanism of self-development. As stated by Mead,

> The child plays that he is offering himself something, and he buys it; he gives himself a letter and takes it away; he addresses himself as a parent, as a teacher; he arrests himself as a policeman. He has a set of stimuli which call

out in himself the sort of response they call out in others. A certain organized structure arises in him and in his other which replies to it, and these carry on the conversation of gestures between themselves. [1934, pp. 150–151]

According to Baldwin also, the basic unit of the self is a bipolar self-other relationship, with a resulting tendency to play out the role of the other, that is, children either have an "imitative" or an "ejective" attitude toward another person. When children are imitating or learning from the other, their attitude is one of "accommodation," that is, their behavior is being structured by the structure of the behavior of the other. It is a matter of little import whether a child's action is structured by the other in the form of spontaneous imitation or in the form of instruction or command. A modeling is taken as an implicit command, and an explicit command can always be modeled (i.e., "Do it this way," accompanied by a demonstration). In either case, the structure of the activity belongs to both parties, but it is being passed on from the active to the passive one. The central focus is upon a novel structure the active agent has that the passive agent does not.

In contrast, the active or assimilative self is one which knows what it is doing, and which ejects its own past attitudes into the other. Whether the child is active or passive, there is a focus upon an activity of one person with an attitude of accommodation to it in the other. The attitude of the child practicing something already learned through imitation or compliance, then, is always different from the attitude held in the process of learning it. In learning an activity associated with the superior power or competence of the adult, the child's attitude is accommodatory and, in that sense, inconsistent with the prestigeful activity being learned. Accordingly, the child tends to turn around and practice the activity on, or before the eyes of, some other person whom he or she can impress, into whom the child can "eject" the admiration or submissiveness felt when learning the act.

The actual "ejective" phase of self-development appears to first develop in the second year of life. At that age, the child seems to attribute feelings to others and to show things to, and communicate with, others. At the end of the second year, a "negativistic crisis" (Ausubel, 1957) typically occurs. This is a phase in which self and other are sharply differentiated and the difference between copying the self and copying (or obeying) the other are sharply distinguished. An example of the counterimitation of this era is a 2½-year-old's consistent response of "Not goodbye," when someone said "Goodbye" to him.*

Interestingly, however, it is just at this age of "independence" that the child acquires a need for an audience, a need reflected in "look at me" or attention-seeking behavior. Indeed, it is striking to notice that look-at-me behavior often is a phase of imitative acts at this developmental level. The father takes a big jump, the same 2½-year-old imitates, and then demands that the father look at him just as he looked at the father in imitating. Imitation immediately placed the child in the model's role, and led him to eject into the adult his own capacity for admiration.

Thus Baldwin would account for the "show-and-tell" behavior of the 3–4-year-old as the reverse form of the sharing involved in the initial imitative act. Imitation, then, generates social sharing at both the learning and the practicing phase. Seeking to act competently almost always requires another person for the imitative young child. First, the child needs another self as a model of what to do. Second, because the child has learned from a model, he or she needs to practice what has been learned on another self, for example, to be a model to another.

Much of the show-and-tell behavior of the preschool child shades over into "private" of "egocentric" speech (Kohlberg, Yaeger, and Hjertholm, 1968), which accounts for about a third of the preschool child's verbal output. Mead would explain such speech by the need to tell another person what one is doing in order to establish its meaning for the self, a meaning which requires "taking the role of the other" toward the self's activity. According to Mead, the self needs an audience to be a self, to establish the meaning and value of its own action. Eventually, this audience becomes an internal and abstract "generalized other," but first it is the concrete other of the egocentric dialogue.

In spite of these differences in emphasis, Baldwin and Mead would agree that preschool children's need to show and tell others about their activities reflects the egocentric "ejection" of the subjective component of the bipolar self upon another to establish the meaning of the self's activity, an interpretation far different from

---

*This negativism about imitation and obedience is paralleled by a negativism about receiving help, the insistence on "doing it oneself." A typical expression was the same child's insistence that a coat be put back on him so he could take it off himself after it had been removed by a helpful adult.

the usual "dependency motive" interpretations of attention seeking.

An experiment by Emmerich and Kohlberg (1953) provides some crude support for Baldwin's analysis in that it suggests the bipolarity of the imitative and the audience-seeking and egocentric-speech tendencies in the child. The study is discussed further later in the chapter in that it indicated both of two experimental conditions, prior negative criticism by an adult experimenter and prior helpfulness equally led to high imitation by kindergarten children in contrast to a no-interaction condition. These conditions which led to high imitation were, however, the exact opposite of those which led to high audience-seeking and egocentric speech. The "no prior interaction" condition elicited the most such speech in contrast to both of the conditions eliciting imitation. This negative association between the situations eliciting imitation and those eliciting social speech was reflected in negative correlations between situational change scores in the two types of social behavior. Children who went down in social speech (compared to a pretest baseline) were high in imitation; those who went up in such speech were low in imitation ($r = -.34$). This negative association between the situational conditions eliciting imitation and the conditions eliciting audience-seeking speech does not mean that children who imitate do not engage in social speech. In fact the two go together as developmental or personality dispositions, as Baldwin's analysis (as well as others) suggests. The correlation between pretest audiencing speech and subsequent imitation was .45. The negative association was rather between the occasions for audiencing and imitative behavior as bipolar tendencies, not between the two of them as general social dispositions.

Age-developmental studies suggest that look-at-me attention-seeking precedes the seeking of approval from others. It is clear that the child who shows off to the adult the act he or she has just learned from the adult will not seek the adult's approval. As children mature, they recognize that imitation of the act does not make them as competent as the model, and that performance of one competent act still leaves the adult a generally superior performer. As children acquire a stable sense of the superiority of the older model, "Look at me" after imitation becomes the request for approval, "Did I do it right?" Baldwin's (1906) account, then, suggests that much of the need for approval is born from the fact that most of the child's accomplishments are imitative. Almost everything young children strive to do or accomplish is something they see another person do first and which they learn, in part, imitatively. Young children's accomplishments, their talking, walking, dressing themselves, toileting, and so on, are all activities that they see others do and know others can do. Because they are models for activity, their approval of performance counts.*

Following Baldwin, then, we may propose that the motivational basis of social reinforcement is to be found in children's imitative tendencies, their tendencies to engage in shared activities. The child's "look-at-me" behavior is not so much a search for adult response as it is a search for confirmation of social or imitative learning. Insofar as the desire for approval arises developmentally out of "look-at-me" behavior, it, too, is not a sign of some more concrete reward which the child seeks. As I elaborate in a subsequent section, children's dependence on social reinforcement is heaviest at the developmental stage where they are concerned with "doing things right" but have no clear internal cognitive standards of what is right and so must rely on the approval of authorities to define "right" behavior. The child's initial desires to perform competently, to succeed, rest on intrinsic competence motivation. Infants struggle to master a task without the least concern for adult reward for performing the task, and without the least concern for the adult's judgment as to whether or not they are doing it right. Social development up until age 6–7 is not a matter of internalizing "extrinsic" social reinforcement into intrinsic competence motivation; rather, it is a process of growing sensitivity to external social definers of standards of competence, and in that sense an increased sensitivity to "extrinsic" social reinforcement. This increased sensitivity, in turn, is the result of a growing sense of dependence upon having a social model of performance. The tendency to imitate, to seek a model of performance, itself rests primarily upon intrinsic competence motivation, upon the "need" to act or function. Children's fundamental motive in imitation is expressed in the familiar cry, "What can I do?" Relying on models to do something interesting and effective, they come to feel increasingly that they must rely also on models to

* The interpretation just advanced reverses social-learning accounts of the relations between imitation and social approval. Gewirtz (1969) notes, like Baldwin, that almost every behavior which socialization requires is a behavior children see others do first. Accordingly, says Gewirtz, when a child is rewarded for a step in socialization, he or she is also being rewarded for imitating, and so a generalized habit of imitating is born. In a subsequent section, I consider this argument in more detail.

tell them "how they are doing." In this view, competence motivation engenders imitation which engenders social dependency through an increased sense of discrepancy between children's own activities and the norms embodied in the activities of their models.

In Baldwin's account, the development of the imitative process into social dependency, the need for approval, is also part of the development of imitation into "identification," into the combination of attachment, admiration, and desire for normative guidance which forms a focus of children's attitude toward their parents. Identification as discussed by Baldwin is a constellation of attitudes similar to that termed "satellization" by Ausubel (1957). Ausubel distinguishes between an imitative "incorporatory" attitude and a "satellizing" attitude. An incorporative child is a general imitator, always ready and eager to imitate any interesting or prestigeful model because such imitation is a primitive form of self-aggrandizement, of getting something the model has or sharing the model's prestige. In contrast, the satellizing child is loyal to past modelings of his or her parents and to their expectations, and will pass up the opportunity to copy the new prestigeful response of the model. In fact, Ausubel et al. (1954) predicted and found that "imitative" or "suggestible" copying of the preferences of a prestigeful model was negatively correlated with satellizing attitudes toward parents.

The distinctions between an "incorporatory" and a "satellizing" attitude are suggested by the following examples:

Incorporatory—Boy, aged 4, to male adult interviewer: "You're twice as big so you have twice as much brains. I'm going to knock your brains out, and they they'll go in my brains and I'll be twice as smart."

Satellizing—Boy, aged 12, asked about his father: "I'd like to be like my father because I think of him as nice and I was brought up by him and learned the things he taught me so I could be a good boy because he always taught me to be good."

Boy, aged 15: "I try to do things for my parents, they've always done things for you. I try to do everything my mother says, I try to please her. Like she wants me to be a doctor and I want to, too, and she's helping me to get up there."

It is clear that the examples cited illustrate different cognitive and moral levels of thought. Since the 4-year-old's thinking is concrete and physicalistic, becoming like another involves a transfer of body contents.* In contrast, the older boy's conceptions are based on psychological likenesses through processes of teaching and conformity to expectations. Furthermore, the admired quality of the model has shifted from power and smartness to moral goodness.

These identification statements are "moral" in a double sense. First, the content of what is to be shared with, or learned from, the parent is a moral content. The parent both models and expects the good. The boy wants to be like the model in the ways expected by the model. Second, the reasons for identifying with the parent are moral. The boy wants to be like the parent because the parent is good, and the boy wants to be good. More specifically, however, to become good is to give something to the parent to whom one owes something, because what the parent wants is for the child to be good.

As we discuss later, the development of such "moral identifications" presupposes the development of moral thought already discussed. At the same time, however, Baldwin (1906) points out that these identifications rest on a sense of a shared self built up because the child feels he or she shares with the adult everything learned from the adult. This sense of a normative shared self Baldwin terms "the ideal self" and equates it with moral conscience. As we have seen, Baldwin says that the bipolar self involves an active, assertive, controlling self and a passive, submissive, imitative self. The child may be either as occasion arises. With a younger child or a parent in a permissive mood, the child defines what is to be done and the other is merely an object to be manipulated, an agent in terms of whom the action may be carried out. With an older person or in a novel situation, the child expects to be the object in terms of which action determined by the other is carried out.

Whether the self determining the child's action is the other (the adult) or it is the child's own self that is "selfish," it is a bipolar self, not a shared or sharing self. The act of adjusting to or obeying the adult need not imply an experience of selfcontrol and unselfishness by the child since the self-controlling the child and demanding sacrifice of the child's wishes is not his or her own self. Though the child's action may be determined by the dominating self of the other, still that other self is conceived by the child in its own image

* In my opinion, it is the concrete bodily nature of the young child's thought and the resulting magical and destructive notion of becoming like another by physical possession which makes early identification "incorporative," rather than such identification being the result of the child's domination by oral libido.

as a basically impulsive or need-gratifying self (insofar as motives are assigned to it at all). The experience of unselfish obligation requires that the two selves be identified or unified with each other, an integration which is not achieved by motives to imitate or obey in themselves.

How does such a concept of a shared self which wants to be good and to conform to rule arise? The experience required, says Baldwin, is one in which the child perceives the parent as putting pressure on the child to conform to something outside the parent. Such an experience is not bipolar, since the parent wants the child to be like the parent vis-à-vis the parent's attitude toward the rule. The parent's self is seen as simultaneously commanding (the child) and obeying (the rule). Thus, initiating action and conforming are seen as both parts of the same self, a self-controlling self.

Such conformity to a third force might simply be perceived by the child as indicating that a third person dominates the parent as the parent dominates the child. However, the fact that such pressure to conform goes on in the absence of the third person or authority tends to give rise to the concept of a generally conforming self. In addition, the fact that the conformity is shared in the family or group gives rise to a sense of a common self which the child is to become.

Originally such a general or ideal self is largely in the image of the parents. It is ideal to the child, it is what he or she is to become, but it is largely realized in the parents. This does not mean that there is no differentiation of parents from the rule; the parents are seen as obeying the rule. It does mean that the image of a good, conforming self which obeys the rules tends to be in the parent's image.*

In summary, Baldwin holds that in the years 3 to 8, the child develops from seeing interaction as governed by bipolar self-other relations to seeing it as governed by rules. These rules are shared by both members of the self-other dyad. As "ejected" into others in the course of action, they are what Mead (1934) termed "the generalized other," the common rules and attitudes shared by the group. As these rules are felt as governing the self, but being im-

---

*By experience of conflict between models and by perception of their failure to incarnate the rule, the self which is the child's model becomes recognized as abstract and impersonal and is embodied as conscience, according to Baldwin (1906). In this sense, however, a morality of principle is still based on identification, but an identification with a set of principles (or a principled self) rather than another person.

perfectly known and followed by the self, they are the "ideal self." The sense of the rule-following self, "the ideal self," is more personal and more closely equated with the parent than is the system of rules themselves, "the generalized other."

Baldwin's concepts imply that as a young boy develops a sense of himself as a "good boy" governed by shared rules, his relations to others are increasingly dominated by a sense of himself as a "good boy" whose relations of sharing with others (especially those close to him) are based on this common "goodness," this common "ideal self." His nonmoral forms of self-aspiration (his desire to be a powerful, strong, clever self) are neither ideal nor a basis for sharing, and in that sense are not an "ideal self." Given the formation of an ideal self, then, it determines forms of social relationship as well as regulating moral behavior.

As an example of the role of the ideal self in social relations, one might cite the state of "being in love" as conventionally (or romantically) defined. All psychological analyses of love, including the psychoanalytic, agree that it involves a relationship of identification (or sharing between selves) involving idealization of the other and a sense of being governed by an unselfish or sacrificial concern for the love object. In other words, it involves a sense of sharing based on the ideal self, not the concrete self.

In spite of the obvious scope and suggestiveness of Baldwin's and Mead's theories of the role of imitation and role-taking in the function of the social self, these theories have been almost completely neglected by research child psychologists. The remainder of this chapter will attempt to elaborate these concepts, to compare them with more familiar psychoanalytic or social-learning concepts, and to document them in terms of research findings.

General Comparison of Cognitive-Developmental, Psychoanalytic, and Social-Learning Concepts of Identification

It is apparent that Baldwin's cognitive-developmental view of moral development and identification has similarities to the psychoanalytic view in which moral "internalization" is the result of a process of parental "identification," that is, a motivated transfer of norms outside the self-system into the boundaries of the self-system, a process located in the years 4 to 8 by both Baldwin (1906) and Freud (1938).

In the cognitive-developmental account, however, the notion of "moral internalization" does not imply a simple and literal transfer, incorporation, or internalization of something outside the ego to something inside. Assimilation of the "outside" to "inside" depends upon the structural reorganization of the external norm and upon structural reorganization of the self assimilating the norm. At the earlier stages of valuing (Stage 1), cultural standards and values are oriented to as labels of good and bad external physical events and actions (e.g., punishment and other bad happenings) and the self's pursuit of values lies in the avoidance of "bad" physical events and objects. By Stage 3, cultural standards are conceived of as "internal" in the sense that they are defined as internal psychological dispositions or virtues in the self and moral expectations (and virtues) in others, and the self is defined as "someone trying to be a good person." At this conventional level, however, values are still seen as depending upon some actual social relations of sharing, upon a concrete social order with actual shared experiences. The standard is contingent upon its being held and maintained by others, and upon approval and disapproval by others. Only at the stage of principle, rather than at the stage of identification with authority, are norms oriented to as fully internal, in the sense of resting upon a basis of self-selection (and ideal universality or the capacity to be shared) rather than upon actual sharedness.

The cognitive-developmental view holds that the development of morally relevant identifications is a relatively advanced phase of development of the imitative process and, accordingly, that a theory of identification with parents must be part of a much broader account of the development of imitative processes in general. Psychoanalytic theories of parent identification are obviously unsuitable to deal with the bread-and-butter phenomena of imitation which constitute the basis of much of the child's ordinary situational and reversible social learning. As Bandura points out (1969, p. 233):

According to the (neo-psychoanalytic) theories of identification reviewed, in order to get a boy to emulate a baseball player such as Mickey Mantle, it would be necessary for the youngster to develop an intense attachment to the brawny model who would then withhold affectional responsivity. Or the youngster would have to develop strong incestuous desires towards Mrs. Mantle and hostile rivalrous feelings toward the slugger.

Of course, psychoanalytic theories of identification were not designed to account for such phenomena of imitation and presuppose a sharp distinction between identification as a process of structural change in the personality and ordinary imitation. Occasionally psychoanalytic writers use examples of the child's daily imitations as exemplifying principles of identification (e.g., Anna Freud's [1946] child who plays dentist out of "identification with the aggressor") but in so doing run the risk of the absurdities Bandura mentions. Essentially, psychoanalytic identification theory has no detailed way of dealing with daily imitation and presupposes a theoretical discontinuity between processes of imitation and processes of identification.

In the research literature (Kohlberg, 1963a), it has been customary to distinguish between identification (as structural change) and imitation according to the following empirical criteria of structure:

1. Identification, modeling is generalized and transsituational. A variety of behaviors and roles are reproduced in a variety of situations. In imitation, modeling is of specific behaviors in specific situations.
2. In identification, modeling is persistent and occurs in the absence of the model.
3. In identification, performance of the modeled behavior appears to be motivated intrinsically. It persists in the absence of an obvious reinforcement to which it is instrumental.
4. In identification, performance of the modeled behavior is relatively irreversible or nonextinguishable even when it is nonreinforced or punished.

In research practice, these distinctions between identification and imitation have been assumed rather than observed, in the sense that a paper and pencil measure of similarity between the child's self-concept and the child's concept of his or her parent is assumed to have the structural properties mentioned, while an experimental measure of imitation of a strange experimenter is assumed not to have these properties. Given the fact that distinctions between identification and imitation have been assumed rather than studied, it is fair to say, as Bandura does (1969), that a review of the research literature gives no support for the notion of two distinct realms or processes of modeling, one of "deep" identification and the other of superficial imitation. Bandura, as well as Aronfreed (1969) and Gewirtz (1969), argue that the distinctions between imitation and identification are not distinctions between processes but, rather, represent a continuum of stimulus, response, and reinforcement generalization of processes of imitative learning that have the same basic social-learning antecedents whether they are situation-specific or whether they appear to be generalized and functionally autonomous.

The cognitive-developmental approach would agree with these writers in seeking theoretical continuity between the two and in rejecting general theories of identification which cannot directly handle the phenomena of imitation. The developmentalist diverges from the social-learning analyst in holding that, though many of the *functions* and causal antecedents of imitation and identification are continuous, the cognitive-*structure* characteristics of phenomena of imitation and identification are different and discontinuous.* In considerable part, the differences customarily implied by the terms "imitation" and "identification" are differences in the developmental level of structure implied by the two terms. In distinguishing between continuity of function and discontinuity of structure, the developmentalist is employing a familiar strategy. Stages of morality, stages of intelligence, and so on, all imply a continuity of function (e.g., moral value-judgment) together with a discontinuity of the structures (moral stages) fulfilling those functions. Piaget (1951) has attempted to employ this strategy to define the early stages of imitation. In Piaget's view imitation is defined functionally (primacy of accommodation over assimilation) in a continuous fashion, but each new stage of intelligence or cognition leads to new stages of imitation.

The cognitive-developmental view of identification differs from the psychoanalytic in the following regards:

1. Identification is viewed as a cognitive-structural stage of more general imitative or social-sharing processes.
2. Accordingly, it is not uniquely dependent upon particular mo-

---

*It is evident that either the psychoanalytic or the cognitive-developmental conceptions of identification-internalization presuppose a self-concept or ego with boundaries. Since associationistic social learning postulates no self-system, the concept of identification cannot be meaningful within it. In Aronfreed's (1969) treatment, "internalization" refers to the operation of a variety of learning mechanisms (some cognitive, some simple conditioning) that can lead to relatively permanent response-patterns, but does not presuppose an ego or identification processes. The cognitive-developmental theory assumes, like psychoanalysis, that the ego's judgment of perceived similarity between self and other are basic structural components of attitudes of identification but, unlike psychoanalysis, assumes these are conscious cognitive judgments.

tives and ties only present in the early parent-child relationship.

3. Identifications are not totally fixed, irreversible, or "internalized." Identifications are "solutions" to developmental tasks which may change in object or nature with new developmental tasks.

It was said that the cognitive-developmental account distinguishes identification (generalized, enduring modeling and perception of a portion of the self as shared with parents) from imitation, but makes the distinction relative and one of developmental structure, rather than dichotomous processes. In the cognitive-developmental account, however, enduring tendencies to model are only one component of a larger constellation of attitudes termed "identification" or "satellization." The constellation includes the following components:

a. tendencies to imitate the parent or other model,
b. emotional dependency and attachment to the parent,
c. tendency to conform to the parent's normative expectations,
d. perceived similarity to the parent,
e. idealization of the parent or of his or her competence and virtue,
f. vicarious self-esteem derived from the parent's competence or status,
g. ability to derive self-esteem from the parent's approval and so to forgo other sources of prestige or competence, with associated security of self-esteem, moderate level of aspiration, and so on.

This constellation is believed to develop more or less gradually in the "latency" years (4–10) in most (but not all) "normal" children and to wane or decline with the growth of independence in adolescence. Accordingly, the constellation is a major component in the definition of a later childhood stage of ego development in the theories of Baldwin, Ausubel, Loevinger, and myself.*

---

*The major alternative focus for defining this era of social development has been Piaget's (1948) and H. S. Sullivan's (1953) focus upon development of "Stage 2" peer attitudes of egalitarian competition, cooperation, and exchange as opposed to the development of "Stage 3" attitudes of identification, approvalseeking, loyalty, and gratitude toward parents. I have argued that both develop in this era, but that there is typically a hierarchical and unified (rather than conflicting) relation between these two focuses of development.

The existence of such a constellation of attitudes has received considerable support from the research literature. Correlations between affectional attachment responses (wanting to be with the parent), imitation responses, perceived similarity responses, and awarding of authority and competence are consistently reported in the literature and are all related to parental nurturance (evidence reviewed in Kohlberg, 1966b). These attitudes toward parents (though not specifically to the same-sex parent) are also correlated with acceptance of the conventional moral code or of parental moral expectations and to self-report measures of adjustment (evidence reviewed in Kohlberg, 1963a, 1966b). Furthermore, it seems fairly clear that whatever major "positive" or "socialized" contribution to development is made by identification dispositions is based on this constellation. While perceived similarity and affectional reactions to parents are jointly tied to acceptance of the moral code and to self-rated adjustment, measures of dispositions to play adult or same-sex role are not (evidence reviewed in Kohlberg, 1963a, 1966b). In other words, it is not so much that moral content is internalized by identification as it is that the identifying attitude is a "moral" attitude of conformity to share expectations.

I have referred to satellizing or developmental identification as a constellation of attitudes of attachment, imitation, and conformity to the expectations of the model. This is because definite causal priorities are not definitely implied by a cognitive-developmental identification theory. Insofar as these three attitudes are linked in other theories, such causal sequences are assumed. Anaclitic identification theory (Sears, 1957) assumes a sequence in which (1) parental nurturance (and nurturance withdrawal) causes (2) identification (modeling) which causes (3) the internalization of parental moral expectations. While single causal sequences are oversimplified, the developmental view stresses that the desire to model the adult leads to attachment and social dependency, rather than the reverse, a theme taken up at length later in the chapter.

The cognitive-developmental concept that imitative attitudes support and stimulate a dependency relationship is quite different in its implication from psychoanalytic theories of identification, which suppose that is primarily a form of substituting for the relationship to the other person by acting upon the self in the role of the other. As a relationship of sharing with another person, developmental identification is not as fixed, "internalized," or self-directed as is implied by psychoanalytic concepts. In its moral implications, satellizing identification leads to a "semi-internalized" conformity to expectations and concern about disapproval based on a sense of sharing these expectations, not to an "internalized" self-critical and self-punitive "superego." (As noted previously, it is linked to a conventional rather than a fully internalized moral orientation.) Furthermore, satellizing identifications are not the unilateral cause of the formation of conventional "good-boy, good-girl" morality. In actuality, the structure of these identifications partially presupposes conventional moral concepts and attitudes. Such identifications, however, support conventional morality, give it specific content, and deepen its affective significance. A somewhat superficial analogy may be drawn between relations to parents and relations to a personal god in moral development. Children of varying religions (Catholic, Protestant, Jewish, Muslim, Buddhist, atheist) go through the same sequence of moral stages. As they pass through these stages, religious relations are redefined. (For example, a Stage 2 Protestant boy says, "The best rule is to be a good Christian. You be good to God and He'll be good to you." Of being a "good son," he also says, "If you do things for your father, he'll do things for you.") Attitudes toward God, in turn, support moral attitudes, particularly at the conventional levels of morality. This is because they give children the feeling that someone besides themselves really cares that they are good, that is, that they have someone with whom to share their moral expectations of themselves. Similarly, once relations to parents have been defined in moralidentificatory terms, they tend to support moral attitudes because they provide a matrix of generalized support and care about the child's being good. While "society" or other authorities expect children to "be good," children are only one of many for everyone but their parents.*

From the cognitive-developmental viewpoint, then, it is impossible to conceive of such basic and near-universal features of personality development as morality as being directly caused by parent

---

* It may be the loss of this support of the parent's special concern about the child's being good which leads to "regression" to instrumental hedonism on leaving home in some of the college-age population (Kramer, 1968). Decline in attitudes of identification with parents, as well as decline in religious attitudes, appears to characterize both regression to preconventional morality and progression to principled morality in a college population (Haan, Smith, and Block, 1968). If no one else one cares about whether the self is good, one tends to fall back upon self-chosen goals and standards, whether these are amoral or morally principled. In the latter case, one cares about the principle, however, rather than about "being a good self."

identification. There are too many developmental and cultural forces tending to produce "normal" morality to see these attitudes as contingent on special unique relationships to parents. As we elaborate later, the role-taking opportunities required for moral development need not be specifically familial, nor need they imply identification in any specific sense. Accordingly, our view is that identifications do not cause moral (or sex-role) internalization but develop in parallel with them and help to support moral or sex-role attitudes. Cognitive-developmental changes in conceptions of moral rules and social-sex roles are causative forces in the formation of parent identifications as much or more than the reverse. The research evidence supporting the cognitive-developmental (as opposed to the psychoanalytic) conception of the role of identification in psychosexual and moral development will be briefly considered at the end of this chapter, after a consideration of the imitative process and its development.

Cognitive-Structural Stages of Imitation-Identification

A discussion of stages in the cognitive organization of imitation must start by noting that all imitations, including its early forms, are cognitive, as Aronfreed (1969) and Bandura (1969) very convincingly argue. Bandura's studies demonstrate no-trial observational learning and storage by preschoolers of complex new behavior patterns of models. Developmental studies such as Piaget's (1951) document the same characteristics as are true of later infant imitation. It is evident that such acquisition and the resulting generalized and autonomous enactment of an absent model's behavior presupposes what Aronfreed (1969) terms a "cognitive template" and Bandura (1969) "an image" guiding imitation. Such a "cognitive template" is involved in much or most of the ordinary phenomena of infant imitation, such as that involved in language learning.*

The cognitive prerequisites of imitative behavior are further suggested by the fact that it is difficult or impossible to teach highly

*In the Piaget (1951) framework, an image of action is a rather late-developing (age 1) representational schema, one that itself presupposes imitation for its genesis. Before imitation involves copying novel responses, Piaget terms it "pseudo-imitation." A discussion of whether or not imitation is "cognitive" presupposes some distinction between "genuine" and pseudo-imitation (Gilmore, 1967). One condition for defining genuine imitation is that the subject has attended to cues of similarity and difference

generalized imitation by instrumental-learning procedures to most lower animals like rats (Solomon and Coles, 1954). In contrast, cognitively higher animals, for example, primates, readily display generalized imitative behavior and imitative learning (Warden and Jackson, 1935).

While some associationistic (or social-learning) theories of imitation, like those of Aronfreed (1969) and Bandura (1969), recognize the cognitive skill components in imitation acquisition, they fail to recognize stages of imitation, that is, radical reorganizations of the imitative act due to changes in its cognitive structure. With regard to infancy, Piaget's (1951) observations have led him to define the following stages of imitation:

1. *Pseudo-imitation because of lack of differentiation between stimuli produced by self and other (Intelligence Stage 2)* (1–3 months). Stimuli made by other which are similar to those the child makes and which provide feedback to prolong the child's own circular reactions will prolong or elicit the child's response; for example, crying by another child will prolong or trigger the child's own crying.
2. *Pseudo-imitation to make an interesting spectacle last (Intelligence Stage 3)* (3–7 months). The child will employ a schema already in his or her repertoire to maintain a like schema of action modeled by the adult. If the adult imitates what the child is doing (putting out its tongue), the child will repeat the act to "make" the adult continue in this interesting activity.
3. *Imitation of new models (Intelligence Stage 4)* (7–10 months). The child will imitate a visually perceived movement by the adult for which the child has only kinesthetic or auditory, but not visual, feedback, for example, matching a visually perceived mouth movement of the adult. The child will also imitate new schemas by trying out various known schemata which gradually become closer to the model. No effort is made to reproduce models too remote from the child's own schema, but some novelty in the modeled activity is required.
4. *Imitation of unfamiliar models (Intelligence Stage 5)* (10–18

between his behavior and the model's. A second is that the behavior pattern is actually acquired from observation of the model rather than being learned in other ways. Much of what has been studied experimentally as "imitative learning" is not imitation in this sense, but is simply the gradual increase of performance of similar responses under reinforcement, without real specification of the conditions of original acquisition of the responses.

months). The child will imitate visually perceived new movements of parts of the body not visible to it. Imitation of the new is systematic experimental groping toward the new model as in active imitation of new speech sounds not in the child's repertoire.

5. *Deferred imitation (and playful "making believe" one is another) (Intelligence Stage 6)* (after 18 months). Imitates a new action when the model is no longer present. As an example, the child imitates a temper tantrum of another child, not at the time, but the next day (the imitator never having had a temper tantrum previously).

Piaget's observations of these five stages of imitation are sufficiently accurate to generate a test of infant development which is stage-sequential in the sense of defining a cumulative Guttman Scale (Hunt and Uzgiris, 1967). Among other dimensions characterizing this developmental scale are the dimensions of increased situational generality, independence of the presence of the model, and independence of an overt eliciting stimulus customarily used in distinguishing between imitation and identification. At the first stages of imitation the infant simply repeats specific responses made by another which are already in its repertoire and which are modeled before its eyes. At Piaget's final stages of sensorimotor imitation (by age 2) the child will play at being an absent person in the sense of deliberately enacting a set of behaviors characterizing another person. This is the first developmental approximation of identification-like behavior.

From the Piaget point of view, sensorimotor cognitive organization is more or less completely developed by age 2, but the processes of cognitive organization characterizing maturity at the sensorimotor level must be repeated again at the symbolic-conceptual level, a process completed (at the level of concrete concepts) at about age 7–8 with attainment of the logic of classes, relations, and number. With regard to identification, the final stage of sensorimotor imitation launches the child into the beginnings of identification, that is, the symbolic equations of the self with another (rather than the equations of an act of the self with an act of the other). From the Piaget point of view, the psychoanalytic descriptions of identification fantasies involving "magical" or logically impossible transformations of identity belong to this symbolic but prelogical era of thought (2–5). Early in this period children first "fantasy," enact roles other than their own, and then gradually learn (or develop) a firm sense of the limits of their own identity, that is, that they can't change sex or age-status, that they can't take their parent's place, and so on. Associated with (1) clear establishment of the limits of physical identity is the growth of (2) selectively modeling persons similar in identity, (3) selectively modeling in terms of attributes of admired models which can be shared because they are teachable psychological skills and virtues rather than physical attributes and symbols, and (4) awareness that possible sharing is through exhibiting the model's norms of goodness with regard to the child's own role activities rather than directly imitating the grown-up role activities.

These trends were illustrated by the quotations explaining Baldwin's theory and Ausubel's concept of "satellization." They all imply a trend to structure imitative processes in terms of conceptions of structured roles, that is, of categories of persons in defined relations to one another with normatively defined functions. These role conceptions themselves depend upon "concrete operations," that is, the logic of classes and relations.

The developmental trends in cognitive structuring of modeling and identity concepts in the years 4–8 just enumerated have formed the basis of a general theory of psychosexual development in these years that I have propounded (Kohlberg, 1966b; Kohlberg, Slaby, and Uhlian, 1985). The theory explains a large number of age-developmental trends and sequences which seem to occur regardless of any vicissitudes of particular parent-relations. The theory may be summarized as follows:

1. The concrete, physicalistic, and symbolic nature of children's thought and interests lead them to conceive of interpersonal relationships in terms of body actions and to define social roles in terms of physical characteristics and differences. The elaboration of the physical bases of sex-role concepts in the concrete thought of the child leads to a core of common meaning of these concepts, regardless of cultural and family variations in sex-role definition.

2. Accordingly, there are "natural" developmental trends or sequences in sex-role attitudes, trends not directly structured by cultural teaching, which are the products of cognitive development. Because of the universal physical dimensions of sex-role concepts and because of culturally universal developmental transformations in modes of conceptualizing, it is plausible to expect some relatively invariant developmental trends in sex-role concepts and attitudes.

3. The fact that sex-role concepts have physical dimensions suggests that the formation of a sex-role identity is in large part the comprehension and acceptance of a physical reality rather than a process primarily determined by sexual fantasies, social reinforcement, or identification with models. The child's basic sex-role identity is largely the result of self-categorization as a male or a female made early in development. While dependent on social labeling, this categorization is basically a cognitive reality judgment rather than a product of social rewards, parental identifications, or sexual fantasies. The reality judgments "I really am and will always be a boy" or "I really am and will always be a girl" are judgments with a regular course of age-development relatively independent of the vicissitudes of social labeling and reinforcement. This course of age-development is dependent upon complex modes of cognitive organization and development. The stabilization of sex-role identity implied in the judgment "I really am and will always be a boy" is dependent upon the types of cognitive reorganization discussed by Piaget (1947) as "conservation of the identity of physical objects" and is not completed until age 6–7, at the time that other forms of physical conservation are fully stabilized.

4. The motivational forces implied in such reality judgments are general "drive-neutral" motives of effectance, or competence, which orient the child both toward cognitive adaptation to a structured reality and toward the maintenance of selfesteem. Accordingly, sex-typed preferences in activities and social relationships (masculinity-femininity) are largely the product of such reality judgments of sex identity. The boy, having labeled himself as male, goes on to value masculine modes because of the general tendency to value positively objects and acts consistent with one's conceived identity.

5. To a large extent, the value of social reinforcers to the child is determined by his or her sex identity rather than the reverse. As opposed to a social-learning sequence, "The boy wants rewards, the boy is rewarded by boy things, therefore, he wants to be a boy," a cognitive theory assume a sequence, "The boy asserts he is a boy. He then wants to do boy things; therefore, the opportunity to do boy things and the presence of masculine models is rewarding."

6. The tendency to value positively and imitate self-like objects tends to radiate out in the child's development in the form of imitation and liking for the same-sex parent. The boy's preferen-

tial attachment to the father as against the mother proceeds from, rather than causes, basic sex-role identity and basic tendencies to imitate the father preferentially. It depends, not only upon a prior stable gender identity (point 3 above) and masculine values (point 4 above), but upon the formation of abstract cognitive categories of likeness involved in the boy's inclusion of his father in a category of "we males."

7. The effect of father-identification (in the case of boys) is, then, not to cause the child to desire and ascribe to generalized sex-role stereotypes and a basic gender identity, but to aid in defining the masculine role in more individualistic terms related to the father's particular role definitions. This does not make the boy more "masculine," but it may serve to make the boy more conforming to parental expectations. In particular it may lead the boy to define his masculine role aspirations in more "moral" and more achievement-oriented terms as opposed to the more physicalistic power terms found in the young child's sex-role imagery. Same-sex parent identification is less cause than consequence of natural trends of self-categorization and sex-role stereotyping. Its developmental function is primarily to channel relatively crude sex-role aspirations and stereotypes into culturally conforming and "moral" role aspirations.

The fact that the developmental changes in imitation and identification just discussed are cognitive-structural has been well documented. Piaget (1951) and Hunt and Uzgiris (1967) document point-to-point relationships between stages of imitation and general stages of sensorimotor intelligence. The cognitive nature of stabilization of gender identity, of same-sex modeling and same-sex attachment behavior, has been documented by showing its relatively invariant relationships to mental age as opposed to other factors (Kohlberg and Zigler, 1967). The formation of normative "good-boy" identifications with parents is correlated with maturity of moral judgment (in turn, correlated with mental age), so it, too, is in considerable part a cognitive-structural development.

I have just sketched some of the age-developmental cognitive-structural changes through which the imitative process proceeds. These changes are paralleled by clear developmental changes in sheer amount of imitation in experimental situations. During age 2–3 there is a well-documented "negativistic" period (Ausubel, 1957). In the period from 3 to 5 there is a regular increase in conformity to suggestion or instruction, which is accompanied by an increase in imitativeness (Kohlberg and Zigler, 1967). In a study discussed further later in the chapter, Kuhn and Langer (1968) found only 20 percent of 3-year-olds imitated an adult experimenter in a "neutral" experimental condition (children told they could do what they wanted) in which 80 percent of 4-year-olds imitated. Indeed, the 3-year-olds imitated as much (20 percent) under a condition where they were told *not* to imitate as they did in a neutral condition.

From the period 5–8 there is a regular decline in imitativeness of an adult model under "neutral" experimental conditions, (Kohlberg and Zigler, 1967), so that 8-year-olds superficially appear much like the 3-year-olds in disposition to imitate. The trends mentioned are again largely a function of cognitive maturity, of mental rather than chronological age. In the 3–4 period where imitation is developmentally increasing, bright children imitate more than average children, whereas bright children imitate less in the 6–8 period when imitation is declining (Kohlberg and Zigler, 1967). Similar findings are reported by others comparing retarded and average school-age children.

As I document later in the chapter, this curvilinear trend partly reflects changes in definitions of what is good or right or conforming behavior in ill-defined situations. The 4–5-year-old takes the adult's example as his or her cue to what the adult wants the child to do, the 6–7-year-old child is aware that "copying someone else's work isn't good," "you should do your own work," and so on. When a group of twelve 4-year-olds were asked about copying, none said it was bad; whereas a majority of a group of twenty-four 6-year-olds did (Kohlberg, unpublished interview data). This in turn reflects a growing orientation to stable normative patterns of an "ideal self." According to our viewpoint, this developmental decline in imitativeness does not reflect the disappearance of the modeling process, but rather its transformation into more structured identifications with normative models as reflected in "good-boy" concepts. The findings of Ausubel (1954) that *low* imitation in school-age children was correlated with *high* identification with parents or high satellizing attitudes supports this interpretation.

In summary, then, the developmental trends in modeling processes in the years 3–8 broadly summarized by Baldwin (1906) as "the formation of an ideal self" and by Ausubel as "satellization" have a detailed cognitive-structural base in the general development of concepts of roles and rules in this period discussed by Piaget

(1947). While much of the particular content and intensity of these identifications is given by individual family experience, much is also universally derived from the common basic meanings of age and sex-roles at a given cognitive stage.

The Motivation for Imitation Is Intrinsic—Effectance and Interest as Determining Imitation

While few would question that early imitation entails cognitive patterning and skill components, cognitive-developmental theories also hold a "cognitive" theory of the motivation of imitation, a theory of the same sort as that involved in explaining curiosity, and exploratory and mastery behavior. The conditions leading to such behaviors are best conceived along the lines of Piaget's (1952b) notions of assimilation, White's (1959) notion of competence or effectance motivation, and Hunt's (1963) notions of information-processing motivation.

Effectance theories of motivation have always been difficult to grasp because they do not assume any "pushes," "drive states," or other definite sources of activity. They assume that one does not need to ask for specific deficit states to explain why the organism is active, any more or (perhaps) less than one needs to ask for specific states to explain why the organism is at rest. Like operant analyses, it assumes that a motivational analysis is one of (*a*) the conditions under which this, as opposed to that, activity occurs and (*b*) the directed quality of the action. This directed quality, it believes, cannot be defined in terms of goals or end states which are distinct from the activities or the behavior structures seeking them (or from the situation in which the organism finds itself), but must be defined in terms of forms of relation between the action and its results (or between the act and the object), forms suggested by words like *mastery.* It is this refusal to separate the act and the "reinforcer" which discriminates theories of effectance motivation not only from drive theory but from driveless accounts of motivation in terms of external reinforcement. The general rationale for effectance concepts of motivation is most lucidly presented by White (1959). In terming an effectance concept of the motive for imitation "cognitive," we do so because effectance concepts are most clearly required for cognitive activities, which are very hard to account for in terms of "drives" or "reinforcers." It is almost impossible to discuss the "energetic" and the patterning or "structural" characteristics of cognitive activities independently of one another. The "motivational" characteristics of an object arousing curiosity and the activities upon the object terminating curiosity are defined by the relation of the cognitive-structural characteristics of the object to the cognitive-structural characteristics of the child's behavior patterns, relations definable in terms of structural match or balance. If an object fits a schema or behavior structure, but does not fit it too well, it arouses exploratory or mastery behavior, as has been documented repeatedly since the days Baldwin (1895) first formulated the notion of assimilation" and "schema." The assumption that the motivation of imitative behavior is best explained by effectance theory, then, is the assertion that the primary conditions which arouse imitation are a moderate degree of mismatch between the child's behavior structure and the behavior of the model (or later between the behavior structure of the child and the structure of the situation as this mismatch may be reduced by imitating the model), and the conditions which terminate it are a better state of match, balance, or "mastery" between the child's behavior and the model's (or between the child's behavior and the situation).

We shall attempt to elaborate the foregoing view of the motivation for imitation by working from some facts. The first fact is that much imitation appears to be intrinsically motivated, in the sense of having no obvious external reinforcer for which the imitative act is instrumental or contingent. Much apparently nonreinforced imitation is discussed by Bandura (1969) under the heading of "vicarious reinforcement," since none of his studies involve directly reinforcing the child for imitating. One cannot, however, explain his findings of imitation of nurturant or powerful models in terms of vicarious reinforcement, since power leads to imitation but consumption of resources does not (Bandura, Ross, and Ross, 1963c). Furthermore, Bandura gets a high level of imitation in his control groups exposed to his nonnurturant or powerless models.

For example, in one study Bandura and Huston (1961) had an adult make nurturant responses to one group of preschool children while the children played with toys, while ignoring a second group. The adult then made various irrelevant nonaggressive (e.g., marching) and aggressive gestures (knocking down a rubber doll) while performing a simple task which the child then performed. In the nurturant condition, almost all the children imitated the adult (100 percent on aggression, 65 percent on marching). What is also striking, however, is that in the control condition, a great deal of imitation occurred also (80 percent on aggression, 25 percent on marching). The imitation in the control group is not to be attributed to socially learned generalized imitativeness of young children. The discrepancy between the 100–80 percent aggression and the 65–25 percent marching makes that clear enough. Even the 65–25 percent of children marching is high, however, compared to the findings from other studies. Anyone who (like myself, Kohlberg and Zigler, 1967) has attempted to get preschool children to imitate an experimental model will realize it is not that easy. Bandura's success in eliciting imitation is due to the interesting and zany things he has his adult models do. An adult goose-stepping around the room shouting "March, march, march!" or pummeling a Bobo doll is clearly a fascinating spectacle to the child. If the adult is not crazy and seems at all encouraging ("nurturant"), the child is likely to follow suit.

If preschool children often like to imitate interesting behaviors with no extrinsic reinforcement consequences, infants are even clearer in this desire. This is demonstrated by the standard results achievable with infant tests of imitation, such as those developed by Valentine (1942), and by Hunt and Uzgiris (1967) following Piaget (1951). A stranger elicits these imitative behaviors one by one without following them with any clear reinforcement. Yet, the tests work regardless of the prior social reinforcement history of the infant but cannot be made to work with nonimitative species. Any observer of these imitation tests with infants will note two qualitative characteristics of early imitation which further bespeak its basic independence of extrinsic reinforcers. First, it customarily occurs in a play context, rather than in the context of being a means to some external goal. Second, early imitation clearly displays a joy in the reproduction of irrelevant details of the model's action. There seems to be a desire to exactly replicate for its own sake, rather than simply to match to some degree of similarity associated with reinforcement. In other words, the similarity sought is not as a discriminative cue associated with reinforcement, as in a "matching to sample" response, but is sought without regard to a criterion of similarity.

Because early imitation often appears to be intrinsically motivated, because it is species-specific or characteristic of some gregarious species (e.g., primates), and because it is so universal within the species, it has often been taken to be instinctive. There are certain telling characteristics of imitation, however, which do not fit our usual concepts of instinct. The first characteristic is the flexibility of the behavior patterning or structuring of imitative acts. The behavior patterns referred to by the word *imitation* are far from fixed; there is no specific patterned action which is imitative, nor is there any fixed, specific releaser stimulus for imitative behavior. The characteristic of imitation is the absorption of new behavior patterns from the environment. Our characterization of early imitation as cognitive is itself a statement that its patterning is not instinctive or innate. Not only is imitation flexible and cognitive rather than being instinctively fixed and blind, but its forms change with cognitive-structural growth. The second "noninstinctual" characteristic of imitation is the flexibility of the motivational conditions for the performance of imitative acts. Instinctive behaviors are repeatedly performed, with durations of exhaustion followed by periods of readier elicitation. In contrast, imitative behavior is exploratory and playful rather than being repetitive and compulsive. While there is an emphasis on exact reproduction of the model, this reproduction is not repeated in the same way over long periods of time. Typically, the child imitates a behavior only as long as it is novel and interesting and then goes on to imitate something else. This characteristic "seeking of novelty" in the conditions eliciting imitative behavior is as inconsistent with an instinct notion as it is with the operant notion that an imitative act will be repeated as long as it is followed by some extrinsic reinforcer.

The reasons I have just advanced for rejecting the idea that imitation is instinctive are also reasons why I am led to reject Aronfreed's (1969) affect-conditioning theory of the motivational conditions for imitative behavior. As opposed to social reinforcement theories, the cognitive-developmental approach agrees with Aronfreed that the (motivational) "foundations of imitative learning appear to lie in the conditions of the child's observations [of the model] rather than in the modification of the child's overtly emitted behavior by positive or aversive external outcomes" (p. 280). However, it does not appear plausible to define the "conditions of observation" leading to imitation as a contiguity between the behavior of the model and a strong affective state in the child. In the first place, the infant frequently imitates the behaviors of adults who are not emotionally important to him, as the construction of a baby test of imitation by a strange examiner indicates. Second, when the infant does imitate, the behaviors imitated are often not those immediately associated with affectively significant events, as baby tests of imitation of gestures with little affective charge document. Third, the affect-conditioning model suggests a repetitive or compulsive character to imitative behavior which is quite different from that usually found. As noted, behaviors tend to be imitated or reproduced only as long as they are novel.

Having rejected instinct, reinforcement, and classical conditioning accounts of the motivation for early imitation, what positive account of the conditions for imitation may be given? We may start with the simple generalization that the one common condition of stimuli that are imitated is that they are interesting. One simple cue to interest value is attention, so that anything which leads an action to be attended to may be sufficient to lead to its being imitated. Many of the dimensions of interest or attention have been catalogued by Berlyne (1961) under such headings as complexity, novelty, and so forth. The statement that the motivational conditions for imitation are cognitive, then, implies that they are not found in fixed intraorganismic needs but in "objective" dimensions of the stimulus which make it interesting. These dimensions or conditions are not located purely in the stimulus, however, since they also include its match to the child's behavior structure, as is implied by dimensions like "novelty," or by the dimension of similarity of the model to the self (e.g., that it is a person being imitated). In general, if a person does something interesting, the infant tries to assimilate it to his own behavior capabilities; the infant tries to see if he can do it too. If the behavior is not interesting, or if the child, through repetition, is sure he can do it, he is unlikely to imitate the behavior.

One way of looking at Piaget's (1951) stages of imitation is as a series of progressions in the kinds of events which elicit imitation. Following Baldwin's (1895) fundamental insights, Piaget defined imitation and its development in terms of the growing complexity of "circular reactions."

The fundamental unit of directed behavior in infancy is a circular reaction, that is, a patterned action which produces feedback stimuli which are the natural elicitors of the act in question. The first and simplest circular reactions are those innately wired to produce such a reaction (sucking which itself produces the tactile pressure on the mouth which naturally elicits sucking, or clenching the fist which produces the pressure on the child's palm naturally eliciting further clenching). These behaviors, then, naturally lead to cycles of repetition, and soon generate integrations in which activities in one modality (waving the hand) lead to sensory feedback in another modality (the spectacle of a moving hand) which leads to repetition of the activity in the first modality, repetitions with functional value (developing eye-hand coordination). This is termed "primary circular reaction," and is in turn followed by a stage of "secondary circular reaction" (the feedback from the act is from its effect in moving an external object), "tertiary circular reaction," and so on. These progressive complications of the circular reaction define Piaget's (1952b) stages of sensorimotor intelligence. As stages of circular reaction, they define an active tendency to repeat any behavior pattern with a "circular" feedback stimulation output.* Postulating an active tendency toward repetition, it was Baldwin's (1895) further genius to see that the basis for children's imitating another was no different from the basis for imitating themselves. If children by accident performed a behavior leading to an interesting result, they would desire to repeat it. To do so, they must copy their own behavior. The situation is no different if another performs the interesting behavior. Insofar as repetition rests upon accommodation to, or copying of, a model or stimulus pattern, then, it is imitation. Expressed in slightly different terms, almost anything which might lead children to repeat a novel behavior pattern they emitted could lead them to repeat the behavior pattern of another. A specification of the motivational conditions for imitation, then, does not imply a special imitative motive, but derives from the conditions leading to the reproduction of any interesting behavior pattern.

We have so far discussed the interest value of the act to be imitated in terms of dimensions of the structure of the act itself, such as its complexity and novelty. A large part of the interest value of many imitated actions, however, rests upon the effects of the act upon other objects. When infants repeat one of their own acts which has interesting consequences, an operant analysis will claim that the consequences serve as a "reinforcer" for the act. As already mentioned, however, exploratory or playful acts do not appear to be under the stable control of definite reinforcers. An interesting light, sound, or movement resulting from a playful act soon ceases to be interesting and ceases to function to maintain the behavior. Furthermore, while the effect of the child's actions maintains the child's behavior, the relation between behavior and effect does not look Skinnerian under close scrutiny. Close obser-

---

*This active tendency toward repetition is in a sense like the Freudian (1938) "repetition compulsion" without the instinctual underpinnings.

vation of infant learning suggests that the goal state is not defined directly by either external or internal stimuli ("reinforcers") but is defined by a *relation* of mastery between the act and its effects. In other words, the effects of the child's behavior are only reinforcing if they are caused by the self's action, while the self's action is only satisfying if it leads to effects, to mastery. For example (Piaget, 1952b), the infant's kicks start a toy bird swinging and the child delightedly kicks "to make the bird swing." One cannot call the external event itself (swinging of the bird) a reinforcer of kicking, since it is not the external event which is the "reinforcer" but its relation to the act of kicking, a relation of causality or mastery. If the adult makes the bird swing, this leads to renewal of the kicking to reestablish the connection. It is quite difficult for reinforcement theory to explain why the infant kicks when he or she is already being reinforced for lying still. Furthermore, as mentioned, the swinging of the bird is not a stable reinforcer; the infant soon loses interest when he or she has assimilated it (established its relation to his or her own behavior).

This example (Piaget's infant kicking to make the bird swing) is used by Piaget as an example of a "secondary circular reaction." It may also be described as an assimilation of an interesting event. Basically, early imitation of another is also assimilation of an interesting event. This interest may be generated either by the form of the model's act, or by its striking consequences. This simple formulation in terms of assimilation of the interesting is most clearly applicable to infant imitation. However, it is also applicable to much preschool imitation, as was mentioned earlier in connection with Bandura's studies.

Social Reinforcement and Imitation as a Form of Normative Conformity

Gewirtz (1969) suggests that imitation is a generalized response based on reinforcement for making responses similar to those of others. He notes that while adults may not systematically intend to reward an support imitative behavior, almost all the socialization demands of the adult involve expecting the child to make responses or develop skills like those already displayed by other people, by older members of the group. Accordingly, Gewirtz says, any reward for socialization achievement is also a reward for imitating. In our discussion of Baldwin, we observed that he, too, notes the omnipresent connection between the child's social achievements and his or her imitative tendencies, but uses this connection between achievement and imitation to explain approval-seeking (i.e., social reinforcement effects), rather than deriving imitation from it. Baldwin's approach rests on the theory that both early imitation and early mastery of basic skills are motivated by intrinsic competence or effectance tendencies. Children in orphanages try to walk, talk, and so on, as well as try to imitate, with a minimum of social reinforcement. According to the cognitive-developmental interpretation, the fact that the child's achievements are imitative engenders a concern for social approval, as the child comes first to need another self (or an audience) as confirmation of achievement and then to systematically ascribe superior competence to the adult model or audience. In other words, "intrinsically" motivated imitation should come under the control of social reinforcers increasingly with age-development (up to about age 5–6), rather than originating from such reinforcement.

There are three points to the interpretation I have just advanced. The first is that the ordinary social reinforcement effects upon imitation (or any other task) behavior in the child are based upon the child's "primary competence motivation," upon the child's generalized desire for task success. This intrinsic desire for success is mediated by external social definitions through social reinforcement. But the desire for success is not the desire for the concrete reinforcers administered. By this we mean that it is more correct to say that the child wants to secure rewards or approval as a sign that the task has been performed competently than it is to say that the child wants to perform competently in order to obtain situational rewards or approval. The role of reinforcers is primarily that of cognitively redefining success in terms of social standards rather than through directly strengthening an associated response.

The second point of our interpretation is that there is an age increase in the child's concern about external social definitions of correct performance, in the child's "need" for approval, up until about age 6–7. The third (and most questionable) point is that this development is mediated by the imitative process itself, in addition to being mediated by the child's growing awareness of the limits of his or her own competence. While the second point receives some documentation from social learning studies (Stevenson, 19656), this documentation is sketchy, because of the indifference of most research students of social reinforcement to developmental variables. The third point has not been considered at all in research studies.

Accordingly, the remainder of this section will attempt to document the first point. It carries the following implications:

a. Social reinforcement affects children's imitation primarily because it has informational value, that is, because the reward is perceived as indicating that the child's response is correct or in accordance with a standard in the mind of a person more competent than the self. A schedule of social reinforcement functions primarily as a long-winded instruction or definition of the right answer; it does not function like a food pellet to a rat. If the situation is one in which a social reinforcer does not symbolize a judgment of normative conformity, the social reinforcer ceases to function.

b. One-or no-trial extinction of imitation "learned" under social reinforcement will occur under conditions where the child is given relevant information that the situation or rules are "new" or changed.

c. In some cases, social reinforcement functions as the equivalent of a direct instruction to imitate. Where more subtle mediation of imitation by the desire for task success appears, it is primarily in situations in which the definition of the rules of the game are ambiguous.

d. The preschool child's general cognitive ambiguity about the rules of the game encourages both imitation and susceptibility to reinforcement which does not appear to be "normative" or instructional to the adult. Because young children have few clear cognitively defined standards or information concerning correct performance, they do not clearly discriminate between correct performance and being rewarded, and hence are more likely to appear to be governed by extrinsic and arbitrary social reinforcement contingencies.

The first implication is that the effectiveness of social reinforcers is contingent on the child's interpretation of them as a symbol of a competent judgment, of correct performance. To illustrate, a social-learning analyst actually installed in a preschool a machine which emitted a tape-recorded vocalization, "That's good," after a bar was pressed, under various schedules of reinforcement. After an initial amused run on the machine, clearly motivated by the desire for novelty, the machine lay dormant, its reinforcing power spent. Obviously, "That's good" did not stand for a social judgment. Another illustration is suggested by Bandura's studies of "vicarious reinforcement." Models receiving social reinforcement were imitated in Bandura and MacDonald's (1963) study of the modeling of moral judgment. However, in another study adult models who were given concrete social "rewards" (candy, ice cream, etc.) were not imitated more than those who were not rewarded. The most likely interpretation is that the nominated models did not receive their rewards in a way in which they could be viewed as indicating correct performance.

The fact that the effectiveness of social reinforcement depends upon a normative context has been obscured by the preschool child's readiness to assume a normative context, a "rule" on which the reward is based, where none exists. For example, in an unpublished study I told children a story in which a boy faithfully watched his baby brother and was punished by his mother on her return (or abandoned the baby but was rewarded by the mother on her return). Most 4-year-olds (though knowing obedient baby-sitting was "good") said the punished boy was bad for obediently baby-sitting. Most 5-year-olds said the boy's baby-sitting was good but he was a bad boy because "he must have done something bad to get punished" and went through a variety of cognitive contortions to balance the act and the sanction. By age 7, about half of the children were able to completely disentangle "goodness," or the rule, from reinforcement and to say the child was good and there must be something foolish or bad about the mother to punish him (still maintaining cognitive balance but of a more differentiated justice-balance sort). This demonstration of the extent to which "arbitrary" social reinforcement carries a normative meaning for the preschool and kindergarten child suggests that a very arbitrary social reinforcement schedule will still owe much of its power to its ability to define the child's act as good or bad (or as successful or unsuccessful). When concrete reward and punishment are still equated with being good or bad, the value of physical or social rewards administered by an authority is as much due to their assumed connection with competent and correct performance as is the value of correct performance due to its association with physical reinforcers. Furthermore, it is the informational value of reinforcement as defining correct performance which probably leads to any durable generalized effects it might have. Accordingly, the effects of arbitrary and concrete reinforcement would be expected to have more enduring effects at an age where they are confused with the normative, and in a situation where the normative is ambiguous.*

An experimental example of this point is provided by a study of Bandura, Ross, and Ross (1963b), who found children were much more likely to imitate the aggressive behavior of Rocky, the bully, if Rocky was successful in beating up his victim and taking his toys than if he was defeated. In the successful condition, 60 percent of the children said that they would like to be like Rocky "because he was a fighter, he got good toys." While not attributing virtue to Rocky, they said his victim was "a crybaby, didn't share, was mean, dumb," and so on. This is hardly surprising when it is found that most children of this age (4–6) not only say that the "good guys win" but explain that you can tell who are the "good guys" in TV shows because they win (Kohlberg, 1965). Bandura (1969) accounts for this cognitive balancing as *ex post facto* verbal cognitive dissonance reduction, that is, rationalization for imitation the children want to do anyhow for vicarious rewards. In contrast, our interpretation makes it causative and postulates that Bandura would not get this "vicarious reinforcement effect" with children over 7 who are more able to differentiate goodness from arbitrary success.

We have claimed that more enduring effects of social reinforcement are contingent on their normative-informational components. One cannot doubt that a concrete reward or prize engenders more immediate incentive to perform than a mere verbal acknowledgment that the child's response is correct. The effect of a concrete reward as an added incentive may lead to more or faster learning as well as performance. However, there is little reason to think that a concrete reward engenders a longer-range disposition than does a sign of social approval, given that either reinforcer leads to any learning or behavior change. While the children may perform more eagerly to get a physical prize than to be told they are right, long-range maintenance of the behavior depends on the cognitive stability of the children's definition of the behavior as "good" or "right." The effects of reward depend for their stability on either the expec-

---

*To illustrate, children aged 9 to 16 were asked if they would "change their mind" about a moral judgment question for fifty cents in the Kohlberg (1958) study. Moral Stage 1 subjects tended to say, "Yes, because you know the answer, you have the answers in the back of the book [from which the questions were read]." Stage 2 subjects tended to say, "I'd take the fifty cents and tell you I'd changed my mind." Children above Stage 2 tended to say they would not change their minds.

tation of future reward or on the redefinition of successful or good behavior. As already mentioned, the two tend to be equated by young children, who only form generalized expectations of reward if they think the behavior is generally considered good by adults. Children understand that whether or not they get candy for a performance is highly specific to the situation and the adult; the more generalized component of their learning is that of whether the act is good or bad.

An example of the cognitive flexibility or reversibility of imitative learning under concrete reward is provided by a study by Turiel and Guinsburg (1968). The situation used by Turiel was the "conventional" Miller and Dollard (1941) instrumental imitation situation in which the child watches a model find candy under one of two boxes. When told that the experimenter had put two candies under one box, experimenter engaged in "no-trial imitation." When told that the experimenter had put one piece of candy under each box, the child engaged in "no-trial" counterimitation (went to the other box). If the child imitated for many rewarded trials under the imitation-reward condition, the child would nevertheless immediately stop imitating upon being told the second candy had been placed under the alternative box. The point is, of course, that prior rewards for imitation, direct or vicarious, are irrelevant where the situation can be directly defined cognitively. Past rewarded imitation will only be maintained where it is appropriate to the situational "rules of the game" or where "the rules of the game" are cognitively ambiguous.

In summary, I have claimed that the more durable effects of social reinforcement in young children (aged 3–8) are the result of the informational value of such reinforcement in normatively defining the "successful" or "right" response. Only from such a perspective do studies of "vicarious reinforcement" effects, such as those of Bandura (1969) and his colleagues on imitation, make sense. The concept of vicarious reinforcement presupposes cognitive processes of observational learning and is objected to on these and other grounds by Gewirtz (1969). While presupposing cognitive processes, vicarious reinforcement concepts assume these processes are irrational. Such an irrational cognitive component is implicit, not only in theories of vicarious reinforcement, but in Whiting's (1960) "status envy" theory that identification is based on the desire to consume the resources possessed or consumed by the model.

In general, it is not "rational" to believe that doing what the model does will lead to getting the rewards the model gets. Turiel's study (Turiel and Guinsburg, 1968) clearly indicates that if you provide children with information that allows them to infer that they will not get the reward the model received, they will not imitate. The only conditions under which "vicarious reinforcement" will lead to modeling with some persistence are the conditions in which vicarious reinforcement is taken by the child as indicating that the model made the "right" or successful response. This, in turn, is contingent upon the normative context of the situation, and upon the prior beliefs about the good held by the child. Where the child's normative standards are confused and externalized, a rather arbitrary reinforcement pattern will still be interpreted normatively.

The fact that vicarious social reinforcement has a "normative" rather than a "pellet" effect on modeling is indicated by the studies on the imitation of the self-administration of rewards (Bandura and Kupers, 1964; Bandura and Whalen, 1966; Bandura, Grusic, and Menlove, 1967). These studies indicate that children will imitate a model's self-denial in giving themselves physical rewards for performance in a game that a model has imposed upon him- or herself, but that this imitation is partly contingent on perceiving the model rewarded for this self-denial. Bandura's interpretation, in terms of vicarious reinforcement, supposes that children through no-trial observational learning forgo the unlimited and concrete reinforcers they could give themselves for the sake of the "pie in the sky" of the limited and "vicarious" reinforcement of the model. In fact, the reinforcement effect only makes sense as defining the normatively correct pattern of reward for the game, that is, as indicating that the model is following the rules.

We have discussed the fact that much imitation is motivated by the desire to succeed by following "the rules of the game," and that much of the effect of social reinforcement upon imitation depends upon this desire, rather than upon a past reinforcement history or upon fixed needs. The major "motivational" conditions determining experimental imitation, then, are the rules of the game of the task situation as this is determined by the conditions of instruction, on the one hand, and the cognitive-developmental status of the child, on the other. This conclusion is very convincingly documented in a study by Kuhn and Langer (1968). In this study, preschool children were exposed to an adult model who performed three acts (putting marbles in a bowl, putting them in a circle, and building with blocks). The children were then given one of seven instructions ranging from 1, explicit instruction to imitate a stressed act of the model ("While I'm gone you put the marbles in the bowl just like I did. I'll have a prize for you when I come back"), to 4, "neutral" condition ("You can do anything you want while I'm gone. I'll have a prize for you when I come back"), to 7, instructions not to imitate the stressed act ("When I'm gone, be sure not to do what I did. When I come back, I'll have a prize for you").

The results for the stressed act indicated that the "neutral" condition was treated like an instruction to imitate. Under the "explicit" instructions (Conditions 1–3), 100 percent of a group of 4-year-olds imitated the stressed act. In the "neutral" condition, 80 percent of the children imitated the stressed act. Essentially, none of the children imitated the stressed act under the negative instruction condition. With regard to "incidental imitation" (i.e., imitation of the two acts of the experimenter not mentioned in the instructions), the results were equally clear. In the neutral condition, 80 percent of the children engaged in incidental imitation. In the next most neutral condition ("You don't have to put the marbles in the bowl like I did"), there was 50 percent imitation. In all other conditions of instruction, there was no substantial incidental imitation (less than 20 percent imitated) even where the children were instructed to imitate the stressed act. These results clearly indicate that the children only engaged in incidental imitation when they were puzzled as to what they were supposed to do. If they knew what to do, whether told positively (imitate the stressed act) or negatively (don't imitate the stressed act), they did not engage in incidental imitation.

It is unlikely that this tendency of 80 percent of 4-year-olds to incidentally imitate in the neutral condition was due to any generalized disposition to imitate based on prior social reinforcement for imitating. If such were the case, one would expect the children to incidentally imitate when they were told to directly imitate, since this indicated that the situation was one of reinforcement for imitation. Furthermore, one would expect more individual variation than occurred. The individual differences found were purely cognitive-developmental. Most 3-year-olds failed to imitate directly (20 percent) in the neutral condition (as noted earlier), and they also failed to imitate indirectly in this or any other condition. In other words, they had not yet developed a conception that "when in doubt, do what the model does."*

In the Kuhn and Langer (1968) study, almost all of the variance in imitative behavior was accounted for, a rare feat in experimental social psychology. Almost all the variation can be accounted for in terms of variation in the cognitive ambiguity of the instructions and the cognitive maturity of the child, variation which cannot be explained by drive or reinforcement concepts of motivation and habit.

The Kuhn and Langer study indicates how one kind of cognitive ambiguity, that of the definition of the task, determines amount of imitation. The study suggests a continuity between the determinants of childhood imitation (e.g., ambiguity in task definition) and those studied by social psychologists of adulthood interested in the conditions of conformity to group norms as mediated by the behaviors or judgments of others. In other contexts, children's cognitive uncertainty as to their capacity to succeed in the task, independently, is an equally powerful determinant of imitation. This is demonstrated by a study of Turnure and Zigler (1964). Normal children, aged 8, were given two measures of imitation, the Miller and Dollard (1941) measure of looking for a toy under the same box as a child stooge, and Emmerich and Kohlberg's (1953) measures of making sticker designs like those of an adult experimenter. Before the imitation tasks, the children were given some prior tasks. Half were told by the experimenter that they were doing well on the tasks (success), half that they did poorly (failure). After the success condition, none of the children imitated at all in either task, after the failure condition a slight majority imitated on both tasks. Obviously individual differences irrelevant in the success condition (since no one imitated) determined the split between imitators and nonimitators in the failure condition. These individual differences, however, themselves seem largely individual differences in expectations of task success. Turnure and Zigler (1964) ran a retarded group of the same mental age†

*That the age effect in question is primarily a function of cognitive maturity is suggested by the Kohlberg and Zigler (1967) study in which all age differences in imitation were largely mental rather than chronological age effects.

†By using a mental-age control, the study presumably eliminates a further source of the greater imitativeness of retardates relative to controls of the same chronological age, the earlier discussed tendency of less cognitively mature children to imitate more.

through their experimental procedures. About half of the retarded children imitated under the success condition, while 90 percent imitated under the failure condition. Turnure and Zigler present evidence suggesting that this greater proneness to imitate is due to a history of experiences of failure and uncertainty about independent task performance. Accepting this interpretation, it would appear that Turnure and Zigler have predicted and accounted for all the variance in their dependent variable, imitation, by one independent variable (success-failure expectation) since they were able to predict variability from 0 percent imitation in one group to 90 percent imitation in another.

Like the Kuhn and Langer (1968) study, the Turnure and Zigler study indicates that most of the variance in many experimental imitation studies is determined by the child's desire to successfully perform the task, as this is mediated by varying definitions of task success. The fact that failure experiences in a prior task generate imitation in a subsequent task is not derivable from an operant analysis but requires an explanation in terms of the cognitive redefinition of the self's capacities in the task situation.

Like the other studies discussed in this section, the Turnure and Zigler (1964) study indicates that most of the variations in amount of imitative behavior in experimental situations with rules (tasks or games) is to be explained in terms of variations in the normative value of the model, that is, in the extent to which the experimental situation defines the model behavior as indicating the "right answer" for the child to give to the task, and in the extent to which it defines the child's independent or imitative behavior as likely to yield the right answer to the situation. This interpretation encompasses the experimental findings on the effects of prior task reinforcement (Turnure and Zigler, 1964) as well as the effects of direct and vicarious reinforcement upon imitative behavior. Taken together with the findings on the interest value of the model's act discussed previously, this interpretation accounts for the bulk of the reported experimental findings on imitation in young children.* The remaining findings, those on the status characteristics

* The studies which suggest more mechanistic Skinnerian interpretations of imitation learning have been conducted with grossly retarded (Bair et al., 1967), or autistic children (Lovaas, 1967) who have not reached preschool cognitive maturity and do not seem to display the "natural" imitativeness discussed in the previous section, which was said to increase with such cognitive maturity.

of the model in relation to those of the child, are taken up in the next section.

Status of the Model and the Child: Competence and Similarity as Determinants of Imitation

I have considered so far the motivational conditions for imitation as they reside in the interest-value of the act and in the appropriateness of imitative behavior to the situation (its social reinforcement parameters). I shall now consider the conditions of imitation as they reside in the personality or status of the model, i.e., in the quality of his relationships to the child, to other persons, or to the larger social structure. A consideration of the status conditions of imitation takes us closer to the concerns of traditional psychoanalytic and neopsychoanalytic theories of identification, e.g., theories which invoke the model's love withdrawal, his aggressiveness, his possession of envied resources, etc., as major determinants of the child's modeling.

Almost all of the theories of identification just listed have assumed a strong deficit-state motivation for identification, for example, either the model's infliction of pain/anxiety (identification with the aggressor, A. Freud, 1946; Sarnoff, 1951), the model's withdrawal of love (anaclitic identification, A. Freud, 1946; Sears, 1957), or the model's control or withholding of someone or something else desperately wanted by the child (status envy identification, Whiting, 1960). The reason for this focus on strong deficit states becomes clearer if it is recognized, as Whiting (1967) has pointed out, that these theories are really designed to account for illogical fantasy identifications, such as identification with the opposite-sex role. The theories more or less assume some magical thought processes involved in identification, that is, a magical equation of self and other. One may term such equations magical since they are "incorporative," that is, they involve the notion of "being the other" or "absorbing him," not becoming like another person distinct from the self through approximating his behavior. In other words, they assume that the reason for identification is either to do away with another causing the self pain (defensive identification), or to "be the other" so that the self can love or hate itself as it has the other from whom one is separated. The processes involved in identification have been assumed to be illogical in another sense, the sense of being equations of the self with others whom one cannot "really" become, or like whom it is maladaptive to become. Finally, the processes involved have been assumed to be illogical in the sense of leading to self-other equations of a painful or self-punishing sort, for example, in the creation of a "superego."

The two notions of strong deficit state and magical thought process are interlocked, since presumably some strong deficit state must be a motivator for magical cognitive processes. In other words, psychoanalytic and neopsychoanalytic theory has assumed that identification is illogical, that is, a defense, and hence must be a reaction to an intense pain experience or a negative drive state. The defensive character of identification is assumed, not only by its illogical character, but by its presumed fixity, rigidity, or persistence in the face of situational inappropriateness.

As I discuss in more detail subsequently, while psychoanalytic and neopsychoanalytic identification theories were designed to account for the pathological and the structurally fixed, actual research applications of the theories have been to the phenomena of ordinary imitation or to self-conscious perception of similarity to one's parents or one's parents' sex-role. Neither of these sets of phenomena reveal anything rigidly fixed, since perceived similarity measures of identification are not fixed or longitudinally stable (the boy who is heavily father-identified one year is not the next, Kohlberg, 1965). Also, neither of these sets of phenomena involve anything directly illogical or pathological, since there is nothing, per se, more illogical or pathological about thinking one has values or personal traits like the father than the mother.* With regard to sex role, the process by which a child acquires an identification with his own role is not the process by which the child acquires an "illogical" or "pathological" identification with the opposite-sex role, as our cognitive-developmental theory stressed. Since studies of sex-typing in preschool and school children include few children with definite opposite-sex identification, but only children more and less "mature" in development of a logical or conforming identity, these studies also are irrelevant to distress-defense theories of identification.

In light of what has been said, it is not surprising to find that

* There is no positive correlation between measures of perceived similarity with the opposite-sex parent and measures of "maladjustment" or "neuroticism" in women and only a slight one in men.

reviews of the findings of research studies of imitation and perceived similarity provide little support for the neopsychoanalytic theories mentioned (Kohlberg, 1963a; Bandura, 1969). More specifically they suggest the following qualifications about these theories:

1. *Anaclitic theory.* While prior nurturance (and perhaps nurturance-withdrawal) are correlates of imitation-identification in a number of studies, they are not stronger determinants than a number of others. As elaborated earlier, "positive atmosphere" effects seem to best fit these findings, for example, that the instructions and examples of liked persons are more readily assimilated than those of disliked persons.
2. *Identification with the aggressor.* Few studies have found any "identification with the aggressor" effects. The few studies finding such effects can be best interpreted in terms of the concept that "the aggressor" is perceived as powerful, competent, and sex-appropriate (masculine). In any case, the theory does not account for general-power competence effects.
3. *Status envy theory.* Bandura et al. (1963c) found that the experimental owner of resources was imitated, not the consumer of the resources. Admiration of the power of the "owner" rather than envy of the consumer was presumably, therefore, the determinant of imitation.

As theorists concerned with identification have focused more specifically on the phenomena of childhood imitation, sex-typing, and perceived similarity to parents, they have increasingly converged on a notion of power as the central status attribute in modeling. This central focus is to be found in the theories of Brim (1958), Kagan (1958), Maccoby (1959), Parsons and Bales (1955), and Mussen and Rutherford (1963). In contrast to neopsychoanalytic theories, these theories do not assume identification to be an incorporation of the other but view it as a process of role-playing, that is, of enacting the role of the other. The theories assume that roles are packages of behavior performed by classes of persons, so that playing the other's role does not imply magically equating the body or identity of the self with the other, nor does it imply that one plays the other's role in order to "magically" give oneself what the other gives or to magically do away with the other. The most elaborated of these theories (Brim, 1958; Maccoby, 1959) start from G. H. Mead's (1934) analysis of the bipolar or complementary role-taking process. In interacting with another, the child must implicitly take the other's role. Under certain circumstances, covert role-taking will lead to overt role-playing. In some cases, the absence of the other will make playing the other's role realistic or appropriate. For example, it is sometimes found that on the death of a father, the widow or son will not only take over the father's functions but will play out stylistically and interpersonally the particular role of the father, a role they had long taken implicitly in interacting with him. In other cases, the role of the other will be played out as fantasy, a playing out which may promote competence in the child's playing of his or her own role with the other (Maccoby, 1959). From this perspective, it is logical to assume that the basic conditions for taking and playing the role of the other are that the consequences of interaction with the other are important to the child. If the other person controls resources on which the child depends, and access to these resources is contingent on playing a certain role to the other or correcting anticipating the other's role, then the child should "identify with" or play out the other's role under appropriate "free" conditions. It is evident this type of analysis of identification as role-playing or role-practice is fitted to deal with the child's selective enactment of familiar roles (other than his or her own) in an unstructured situation, such as family doll-play. It is not, however, a theory of general conditions under which a child will learn a behavior or attitude of a model or wish to be like another person, including conditions in which the child had not had a history of complementary role interaction with that person.

When one considers the general characteristics of models which elicit imitation, it becomes apparent that power is too narrow a term for the attributes of favored models. As Bandura's (1969) Mickey Mantle example suggests, any form of competence by a model in any (or no) direct relationship to the child may elicit imitation. While power is one index of competence, it is only one of many. As long as this is true, boys will continue to prefer to be like big league ball players or inventive scientists to being like generals or senators or bankers. The cognitive-developmental theory, then, would propose that there are as many qualities of an emulated model as there are perceived forms of competence. In addition to sheer perceived competence, the perception of similarity to, or relevance of, the model to the self is the other major status determinant of imitation-identification.

The statement just made is, in effect, a direct derivative of the notions of the primary competence motivation for imitation discussed in previous sections. The motive for imitating is not a peculiar or special one, as identification theories have assumed. The reason for imitating is to do the competent, "smart," right, or effective thing. Insofar as the model's is an index of competence, it tends also to be an index of the competence or "rightness" of the model's action. Insofar as this is the case, one need not assume that the enactment of the model's behavior is instrumental to some further equation of the self and the model, and hence need not assume that this equation involves magical thinking. The assumption is rather that the power and competence of the model leads the child to see the specific act modeled as competent (or "big-boy") and so makes it gratifying to perform, because the child likes to perform competent acts, which make the child feel more competent. It does not assume that the child's modeling indicates the desire to introject the model, to magically share the model's powers, or to act toward the self as the model has.

We have discussed so far the status determinants of imitation in a way which would account for an adult's tendency to copy the tennis style of a tennis star, or the writing style of a Freud. The account, however, raises a number of issues about the development of concepts of competence and their relations to modeling. Piaget and Baldwin discuss early infant motivation in terms of assimilation of the interesting and circular reaction. As the infant's cognitive structuring of the self and the world progresses, the assimilation of the interesting becomes a definite motive to master, to be competent, to demonstrate power or control over events. Such a development presupposes a differentiation between the self (as a locus of agency) and the other (as a locus of agency), a sense of causal relation, and a differentiation of what the self causes from what others cause. These differentiations in concepts of objectivity and causality develop in sequential order and are completed by the end of the second year of life (Piaget, 1954). At this point, the desire for mastery is reflected in the need to do things oneself. A typical incident is a 2-year-old boy's frustration at putting on his coat, followed by a temper tantrum if his mother tries to help him. The temper tantrum indicates that the child clearly differentiates what he can cause from what others can do, and as a result, only what he can do leads to a sense of "mastery."

We have pointed to he cognitive development of a self-other

differentiation in causality as transforming effectance motivation, the assimilation of the interesting, into a definite desire for power and control over things and people. At first it would seem that such competence strivings would lead only to independent and negativistic rather than imitative behavior. It is clear, however, that such a striving for power and control is a precondition to perceiving superior power and control in a model, and imitating as a result. At an early stage of lack of differentiation of self and world, infants may not imitate the adult's act which generates interesting consequences (swinging the birds) because they will "believe" that they generated those consequences themselves. At a later stage, however, they will imitate the adult to gain the assurance that they, too, can generate those consequences. At the stage of negativism, children make an even sharper differentiation between what they can do and what the other can do. Before this period it is typical that they feel satisfied if the act is completed with the aid of the mother or someone else like the self.* At the negativistic stage insistence on independence in the performance of an act is independence in performing an act "imitatively" learned from others. In our example, "putting on the coat myself" is still an imitation of the mother's care-taking act. So "independence," "doing things oneself," is still an expression of competence motivation which generates further imitation.

The negativistic crisis, then, heralds the clear awareness that there is something more competent and powerful in being the model than in imitating. This first leads to the "look-at-me behavior," the need to turn around the imitator-imitated roles described in connection with Baldwin's (1906) theory. It also leads to an increasing selectivity of models on the grounds of relative power and competence. With growing awareness of relative competence and power, the child will award some generalized capacity or power to adults or others regardless of the particular consequences of the adult's specific act. At this point children take "on faith" the fact that the adult's act is a demonstration of power and competence and imitate it in order to make sure that they, too, can do the "grown up" or "big-boy" thing being modeled.

---

* It is this undifferentiated feeling of mastery which psychoanalysis termed "primary identification with the mother" and "feelings of omnipotence" and which Ausubel (1957) terms "executive dependency associated with volitional independency." The lack of differentiation of causal agency, however, is actually not limited to the mother, as these terms suggest.

The cognitive-structural developments in the differentiation of the competence of self and other just discussed are largely responsible for the growing generalized imitativeness of adult models found in the years 3 to 6. In the period from 5 to 8, there is further cognitive development in concept of competence which leads to selective imitation of good and skillful, as opposed to older and more powerful, models and to a selective modeling of good and skillful behavior by the model (as opposed to other aspects of his or her behavior). These trends were discussed earlier in the chapter, and related to the development of concrete-operational conceptualization of role relations and attributes. In terms of concepts of competence, we shall merely stress here that the change is from physicalistic to psychological-normative notions of the relative competence of individuals. During the earlier (3–5) period, the child assimilates the superior skill and virtue of individuals to their age-status, which is defined in terms of physical size and strength. An earlier quoted example was the boy who discussed the adult's task skill as a product of "bigger body, bigger brain." Children under 5 do not tend to be able to distinguish age from size, and assume that physically growing up automatically leads to possessing adult competence, just as their own growing up has led them to no longer be that worst of all categories, "babies." By the early school years, the child has discriminated physical attributes of competence (being big and strong, and owning things) from "psychological" attributes of competence ("being smart," "knowing things," "doing things right," "being good") which represent the fitness of behavior to a normatively defined role with a status in a social order (Kohlberg, 1965). Associated with this differentiation is a more refined and disciplined imitation of the "good" and "smart" way of doing things of the model rather than a simple sharing of the activity.

Associated with this differentiation of competence from age-size is a growing differentiation of the competences appropriate to males and females. At the preschool level, sex differences are more or less equated with age differences. Insofar as the sexes are different, it is because males are physically bigger and stronger than females, just as grown-ups are bigger and stronger than children (Kohlberg, 1966b). As an example, 4-year-old Philip told his mother, "When you grow up to be a Daddy, you can have a bicycle too [like Daddy's]." As "virtues" or forms of competence are discriminated from age-size, these virtues become increasingly sex-typed. In the years from 4 to 7, girls develop a clear perception that feminine competence and status are based on being "attractive" and "nice," rather than on being powerful, aggressive, and fearless. (Boys come to make grossly similar distinctions, in learning to differentiate the qualities of the "good guys" and the "bad guys," both of whom are alike in physical attributes.)

There are, then, major developmental shifts in statusdimensions of the model leading to imitation. These shifts are not due to the formation of new motives for imitation, but are due to cognitive-structural transformations in conceptions of role-competence. These cognitive changes lead to a rechanneling of primary competence motivation into varying channels of selective imitation. A single example may clarify the point. Psychological discussions of "ownership of resources" have a simple cash meaning in the world of the American child. When asked, "Who is the best one in the family," a majority of twenty-four middle and lower class 6-year-old boys and girls replied, "the father," and give as the single most frequent reason, "because he makes the money" (Kohlberg, 1965). In contrast, a minority of 4-year-old children choose father as "best," and none give "making money" as a reason for choice of "best one in the family." The response that father is the best one in the family forms the highest step in an age-developmental cumulative Guttman scale of appreciation of the father's cash function which includes the following items or the following order of increased maturity.*

1. Father chosen as the one most needed to buy things in the store.
2. Father chosen as most needed in the family in general.
3. Father chosen as best one in the family.

This development in awareness of economic functions of the father closely parallels the following logical development of a general understanding of economic roles, which is stage sequential (Guttman scaleable) and closely linked to Piaget's (1947) stages of logical development (Strauss, 1954; Danziger, 1958):

1. *Preconceptual* (Age 3–4). Money is not recognized as a symbol of value different from other objects, and it is not understood that money is exchanged in purchase and sale transactions.

---

*Obviously, the scale is derived from children in intact families with nonworking mothers.

Money is not recognized as necessary for gaining all objects from stores, that is, as necessary for having food.

2. *Intermediate* (Age 4–5). Children recognize that money transfer is required in stores, but do not recognize that the transfer is an exchange of equal economic value. The exchange of work or job for salary is not understood, nor is the scarcity of money understood. Money is thought to come from a store or the bank without any exchange or input required. The mother is as much or more the supplier of money and goods than the father, because she goes to the bank and gets the money and goes to the store and buys the good.
3. *Concrete operational* (Age 6–8). Children recognize money transactions as involving a logical relation of reversible, reciprocal, and equal exchange of values. They understand that the storekeeper must pay money to others for goods; they understand the work-salary exchange and the scarcity or "conservation" of money. Accordingly, the child recognizes the need and importance of the father's work-role ("otherwise the family will die or starve").

The logical and sequential nature of the development of the valuing of the father's economic function indicates that it is not a cultural learning of the male-dominant and materialistic values of the American culture, but is a natural cognitive development (in families with a sexual division of labor in economic roles). This cognitive development in definitions of family power and prestige, in turn, is a determinant of modeling. At age 4–5, physicalistic sex stereotypes are critical in differentiating mother and father roles (Kohlberg, 1965, 1966b). While fathers are perceived as bigger, stronger, and more aggressive than mothers by age 4–5, social power and prestige are not clearly typed in favor of the father until 6–7 (Emmerich, 1961; Kohlberg, 1965). This, in turn, is linked to the father's economic and work functions, as already discussed.

The developmental tendency to award greater authority to the father-role leads in turn to a developmental increase in modeling the father in the ages (4–7) mentioned. This tendency is true for girls as well as boys.*

---

* In the case of the girls this modeling is not part of a global desire to be like the father, but is due to the notion that he knows the right way to do things better than the mother, is smarter, etc.

To close the cognitive-developmental circle, bright children are advanced on all the trends mentioned, including the trend for boys and girls to increasingly orient to the father as a model.

The fundamental assertion of the present section has been that the general characteristic of the model's status leading to imitation is the model's role-appropriate competence as this is perceived by the child, and that this perception undergoes cognitive-developmental transformations. While this generalization is so prosaic as to scarcely require documentation, it does cast light on the findings of studies of social-power effects on imitation which are otherwise puzzling. In particular, these studies indicate the following points:

a. Interpersonal power over the child is only an aspect of general competence, which is the determining status attribute for modeling.
b. The import of power for the child's modeling is contingent upon whether power is a role-appropriate form of competence, an issue determined by the child's sex-role stereotypes.

With regard to the first point, Van Manen (1967) found that adolescent boys' value-similarity to the father was not correlated with the father's dominance over the boy or the father's dominance over the mother. The boys' identification, however, was correlated with the father's external occupational competence (job success and satisfaction as perceived by father, mother, and in part, "objectively"). Sixty-six percent of the children of the 80 fathers dissatisfied with their jobs were low in value agreement with their fathers, as compared to only 7 percent of the children of the remaining 225 fathers.

With regard to the second point, paternal dominance over the spouse (Hetherington, 1965; Hetherington and Frankie, 1967) has been found to correlate markedly and clearly with boys' same-sex parent imitation-identification as measured in a quasi-experimental setting. These same studies indicated that there was no relationship between maternal dominance and girls' same-sex parent identification. Dominance is a form of competence in fathers because it is role-appropriate (as perceived by children), but it is not a form of competence in mothers.

These findings clarify various puzzles in social-learning experiments on imitation. As an example, among sixteen experimental groupings in the Bandura et al. (1963c) study of control of resources, the single highest modeling effect was that found for boys to imitate a male adult who was ignored by a female adult who dispensed rewards to the boy subject. The rewards were candies, cookies, and so on, typically dispensed by "mother figures." The boys in this condition tended to criticize the lady dispenser and sympathize with the ignored male (e.g., "She doesn't share much, she's greedy. John played bravely even though she didn't share"). Even in preschool, when feminine power violates sex stereotypes of feminine givingness and when masculine impotence coincides with masculine "virtue" and "bravery," it seems to be sex-typed virtue and not bare power which leads to imitation.

In addition to the role appropriateness of the model's competence, a cognitive-developmental theory would stress that the relevance of the model's role to the child's own is a major determinant of imitation. A major determinant of relevance is the degree of similarity between the child and the model. At an adult level, this has been documented by Stotland and his colleagues (Stotland, Zander, and Natsoulas, 1961). At the childhood level, and at the level of gross sameness of role, it is so basic as to have been ignored. We noted that at the earliest stage of imitation, children only "imitate" the behavior of others which is already in their repertoire, that is, infants' repetition of other's actions and their repetition of their own actions are indistinguishable. At large stages, novel behavior of others is repeated, but with an increasing sensitivity to the like-self quality necessary for another to serve as model. While the infant may imitate physical things and animals, this is presumably because the boundaries of self as animate and human are not clearly distinguished from the not-self as inanimate or nonhuman. In any case, by age 5, prolonged imitation of the nonhuman is considered pathological. By age 5, the sameness of sex of child and model has also become a most basic determinant of modeling, as discussed previously. After age 5, there is also a fairly steady increase of imitation of peers, as compared to an adult, in spite of recognition of the superior competence of adults*

* This tendency is, of course, task-relative. In an instructional setting with a right answer, adults are preferentially imitated; in a value-preference situation, peers are preferentially imitated

(Kohlberg and Zigler, 1967). The importance of similarity as a determinant of modeling is not only highly important by age 6, but it is a focus of generalized awareness. In one study (Kohlberg, 1965, 1966b) children aged 4 to 8 were shown animal pictures in sets composed of four animals of the same species, two of which were of the same color. The child was then asked, "Which animals do the same [specified] activity?" and "Which animals like each other?" Over 70 percent of the responses of children 5 and over named the same-colored animals for both these sets of questions, although 4-year-olds did not choose the same-colored animals beyond the level of chance (33 percent). This growing self-consciousness about similarity is suggested by the response of a 7-year-old boy after his 4-year-old brother had just expressed a preference for a male baby-sitter. When the younger boy was asked why he wanted a boy, his older brother intervened to say, "because he's a boy, himself, of course."

While similarity is a major determinant of imitation, it is only one of many determinants of the model's relevance to the child's imitation. The concept of similarity is itself a cognitive-classificatory development of the concrete-operational period. Before the period of categorical-classificatory thought, feelings of "likeness" may be based as much on proximity, familiarity, and dependency as upon similarity in role, status, or attribute. As an example, it is not until about age 6 that the boy preferentially imitates his father even though he preferentially orients to boys as opposed to girls at an earlier age (Kohlberg, 1966b). Before this, the young boy tends to feel his mother is most like him because feelings of social closeness at young ages are based more on association than upon judgments of similarity. As conceptual relations between persons become based on attributes of similarity and class membership, so do definitions of social ties.

As an example, when children were asked to put family dolls together with the ordinary concept-formation instruction ("Put the ones together that go together"), it was not until age 5 that a majority of children grouped the dolls on the basis of similarity (boys together, mothers together, etc.). Before this, dolls were primarily grouped associatively ("the boy and girl go together because they play together"). At age 5–6, then, categorization (object-sorting) and generalized preference in imitation (same-color animals choose each other) develop together. With age and IQ controlled, significant correlations were found between object-sorting classification, same-color choice on the animal test, and doll-play imitation of the same-sex parent, indicating the cognitive roots of a growing same-sex orientation of imitation.

Of the determinants of relevance other than similarity, prior interaction with the model is perhaps most important. Many of the effects of prior experimenter nurturance or reward upon the child's imitation may be understood in these terms. As an example, a study by Emmerich and Kohlberg (1953) involved three groups of kindergarten children. In the first, or nurturance, group, children were given help and praise by the experimenter in a puzzle task; in the second, or conflict, group, children were given help but blamed and criticized in the task; and in a third group the children were ignored by the experimenter during their work on the puzzle. The experimenter then joined the child in a sticker-kit design-making session in which the child's tendency to copy the experimenter's designs could be measured. The results were a significantly lower amount of imitation for the children who had been ignored (0.4 imitative designs) than for either of the other two conditions (3.0 and 3.2 imitative acts respectively). There were no differences between the children who were nurtured and those who were criticized and blamed.

What seemed to count was the mere fact of interaction, whether that interaction was negative or positive. Thus, an interpretation of the nurturance condition as causing responses like the experimenter's to acquire secondary reinforcement value seemed ruled out. In both conditions of high interaction, it seemed that experimenter's helping and evaluating activity defined them as people who were revelant norm-setters for shared activities in the situation. Whether help and evaluation of the child were positive or negative, experimenters defined themselves as evaluators, guides, and participants in the child's activities. If experimenters fairly explicitly define themselves as norm-setters in shared activities with the child, it seems obvious that they are more likely to be imitated than if they do not.

In summary, then, the findings on selective imitation of models may be best explained in terms of the child's perception of the models' competence and of their relevance to the child's own role. The age-development of selective preference for models may be explained in terms of the cognitive development of the child's concepts of role competence, and in the child's conceptions of dimensions of relevance such as similarity.

The Development of Social Dependency and Attachment

Earlier, I sketched a conception of identification in which imitation was one component of a cluster of attitudes of perceived similarity, dependency, attachment, approval-seeking, and moral conformity toward the parent. I said that all the correlational studies supported the existence of such a cluster of attitudes toward parents. I questioned the neopsychoanalytic sequence designed to account for these correlations and pointed out that Baldwin's (1906) theory suggested that under at least some conditions, this sequence might be turned on its head. The alternative sequences proposed are as shown in Figure 1.5.

Examples of the cognitive-developmental sequence appear in the formation of adolescent or adult relations of dependency-identification, where these have no basis in extensive prior interaction and care, and where there is no sexual basis for the relation. A familiar case to the reader is the identification of a student with a same-sex teacher. Such relations are based on the competence and interest value of the teacher's behavior generating (or joining with a prior) desire to be like, or to be in a role like, the teacher, which

Figure 1.5

Neopsychoanalytic	*Cognitive-Development*
1. Child's dependency based on care taking and affection.	1. Child's imitation of competent and interesting behavior of adult.
↓	↓
2. Imitation as a substitute for parental nurturance.	2. Desire for normative conformity, i.e., a sense of shared standards for behavior, desires to imitate.
↓	↓
3. Internal normative conformity in order to maintain self-approval based on 2.	3. Dependency, i.e., persistent sense of need for guidance and approval by the model.

in turn generates a need to share the teacher's normative attitudes and obtain his or her guidance, approval, and so forth. This sequence, familiar enough in young adulthood, is also apparent in childhood relations to older same-sex figures. The 7-year-old boy quoted earlier, who explained that his younger brother wanted a male baby-sitter "because he was a boy himself" went on to say that he (the 7-year-old) wanted a male babysitter because "a girl can't teach me anything."

The sequence just described also best fits the available evidence on the development of the boy's orientation to the father in the years from 4 to 8 (Kohlberg, 1966b). The development of the boy's attachment and identification with the father is of particular interest because it is the first strong attachment which cannot be explained in terms of the physical caretaking or social instinct theories so frequently introduced in discussions of the mother-child tie. The existence of the shift has been documented in studies with various social classes and ethnic groups, using various measures which all show preschool boys as somewhat female-oriented in doll-play and experimental tests of social dependency toward adults and parent figures, and show a shift to male-oriented preference at about age 6 (Kohlberg, 1966b). While all identification theories postulate such a mother-father shift for the boy, none provide a very adequate mechanism for it. It does not seem that the shift could be a result of the fact that the father actually becomes the primary nurturer and rewarder in these years while the mother ceases to be, while the psychoanalytic account in terms of castration anxiety raises many difficulties in accounting for a positive shift in dependency.

The cognitive-developmental explanation of a developmental shift in the boy's orientation to his parents is straightforward. The theory would claim that a boy learns to sex-type himself and his activities during the second and third year. By the age of 3 to 4 the boy knows quite well he is a boy and prefers "boy things" to "girl things" simply because he likes himself and that which is familiar or similar to himself. Up to this point in his development, he has remained mother-oriented, however. Tending now to prefer masculine activities, he seeks a model for these activities. Thus he is led to select his father rather than his mother as a model. Imitation in turn leads to emotional dependency upon the father. The sequence can be diagramed as shown in Figure 1.6.

The existence of such a sequence was confirmed in a semilongi-

Figure 1.6

Neopsychoanalytic Identification Theory	*Cognitive-Developmental Theory*
1. Orientation to father as major rewarder or punisher with associated dependency.	1. Sex-typed identity.
↓	↓
2. Identification or imitation of father.	2. Imitation or identification with father.
↓	↓
3. Sex-typed identity.	3. Orientation to father as major rewarder with associated dependency-companionship.

tudinal study of boys aged 4 to 8 (Kohlberg, 1966b; Kohlberg & Zigler, 1967). Like other studies, this study indicated that there was a clear preference* for appropriately sex-typed objects and activities by age 3 (on Brown's [1956] IT Scale and the Sears et al. [1965] Pictures Test), a clear preference for imitating the male figure by age 5 (on Hartup's [1962] measure of imitating the doll father as against the doll mother and on the measure of imitating a male experimenter more than a female experimenter, and a clear preference for orienting social dependency to the male at age 6 (on the Ammons and Ammons [1949] measure of relative choice of father and mother doll as agent of nurturance and on a measure of amount and "dependency" of talk to a male, as opposed to a female, experimenter).

The age at which an individual child advanced through this sequence varied considerably. One of the major determinants of speed of movement was cognitive maturity. As a group, bright boys, aged 4 (mental age 6), displayed male preference in dependency and imitation as well as in sex-typing, whereas average boys

* "Clear" male preference on these tests denotes over 60 percent of the choices or responses of the age group went to the male object or figure.

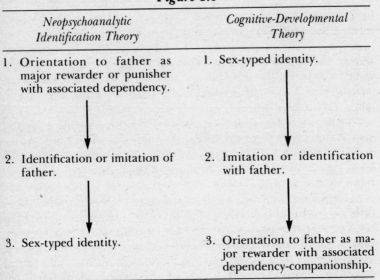

did not display male dependency preference until age 6* (Kohlberg and Zigler, 1967). Regardless of the boy's speed in moving through the sequence, however, he moved through it in the same order, that is, the tests mentioned defined a cumulative Guttman scale. All but three of forty-eight boys fell into one of the four scale-type groups (passes all preference tests, passes sex-typing and imitation but not dependency tests, passes sex-typing tests only, fails all tests).

The existence of such a sequence and its relation to cognitive maturity is extremely difficult to explain in terms of any other theory of identification. All the usual theories that might account for the measured shifts from mother to father between the ages of 4 and 6 seem to be ruled out by a study by C. Smith (unpublished, summarized in Kohlberg, 1966b). Half of the subjects of the study, all black boys, came from father-absent homes, half from father-present homes. These groups in turn were equally divided by age (5 and 7) and by IQ (average and mildly retarded). The boys were administered the same tests as in the Kohlberg and Zigler (1967) study. The age trends for both father-absent and father-present black boys of average IQ were quite similar to those found in an average IQ middle class white population. By age 7 almost all boys had 100 percent masculine choice on the IT Scale, and a clear majority were father, as opposed to mother, oriented on the identification measures. At age 5 identification choice was mixed (about 50 percent) and masculine sex-typing was incomplete. Clear IQ effects were found in both father-absent and father-present groups, similar to those found in middle class children (Kohlberg and Zigler, 1967). Mildly retarded boys aged 7 were more like their mental age counterparts (the average IQ boys aged 5) than they were like their chronological age counterparts (the average IQ boys aged 7). In sum, general cognitive and social development is leading the father-absent boys to develop attitudes of "identification" toward nonexistent fathers that are grossly similar to those father-present boys develop toward their own fathers.

These findings indicate that the age-developmental trend

---

*Bright boys go through the sequence faster than average boys because (*a*) they cognitively stabilize a gender identity faster (as in the "conservation of sex-role" test), (*b*) they become aware of general relations of similarity faster, i.e., become aware that they and their fathers are both male sooner (as in the concept-formation test), and (*c*) become aware of the competence of male adults sooner (as in awareness of the father's economic role).

toward father identification cannot be explained by any of the usual theories, such as anaclitic theory (an actual increase in nurturance and reward by the father), defensive identification theory (fear of retaliation by the father for sexualized attachment to the mother), social reinforcement theory (mother shifts to rewarding the boys for imitating the father). All these theories assume a present and active father.*

In the case of the boy's identification with the father (or with a teacher), we have stressed a definite sequence in which a similar identity precedes imitation, which precedes dependency-attachment. We have done so to stress the fact that the element of the identification-cluster which appears to be the developmentally simplest and earliest in the child, social dependency (the need for proximity, help, and response), is not, in general, the first and prior element in the formation of human bonds.† The case of the development of the boy's identification with the father in the years 4 to 8 is artificial, however, since the cognitive-development requirements of this particular development slow its component down into a definite sequential order. Where developing cognitive abstractions are not involved in slowing down the steps in identification, its different components tend to develop more or less simultaneously.‡

We have stressed the boy-father identification to establish the fact that (1) the formation of human social bonds or attachments requires components of past shared-identity (similarity) and of the disposition to share and learn new behavior patterns (imitation), and (2) therefore, the motivational determinants of attachment are in large part those discussed already as determinants of imitation. These considerations allow us to sketch out briefly a general cognitive-developmental theory of attachment which contrasts markedly

---

*The fact that these theories do not explain sex-typed preference or the child's sense of gender identity goes without saying, since such a sex-typed identity is established before, or in the absence of, a preferential identification with the father and even in the absence of a father at all.

†To recur to the earlier example, the student who displays early help-seeking or instrumental dependency to a teacher is most unlikely to form any social or stable attachment, unlike the student who follows the identification sequence.

‡As an example, girls, too, seem to increase, though less markedly, in father identification in the 4 to 7 period, partly because of increased awareness of the prestige or competence of the father's role. In this development, there seems to be no particular sequence in the relative increase of imitation and dependency components of identification.

with social learning, psychoanalytic, and ethological theories of attachment. (A comprehensive survey of these theories and the relevant research data is provided by Maccoby, 1969.)

Our theory holds that the motivation of social attachment, like the motivation of imitation, must be primarily defined in terms of effectance or competence motivation. The interest value of the activities of the other, the other's competence and social value, the relevance of this competence to the self's own action, and the general degree of similarity or like-mindedness of the self and other are all major determinants of dependency or attachment, as we have shown they are for imitation-identification. All these conditions have repeatedly been found to be important by social psychologists concerned with studying adult affiliation, friendship formation, marriage, and leader-follower relations.

As studied by social psychology, a social attachment or bond is conceived of as a relationship of sharing, communication, and cooperation (or reciprocity) between selves recognizing each other as other selves. In contrast, all popular child psychological theories have denied that experience of, and desire for, sharing and communication between selves and the primary components of a human social bond. Their model of the child's attachment to others has been based on a model of an attachment to a physical object, or to a physical source of physical pleasure or pain. The "physical object" concept of social attachment is equally basic to Freudian (1938) theory (cathexis of the physical body of the other), to secondary drive and reinforcement theory (presence and response of the other is associated with care-taking reinforcement and so becomes a secondary reinforcer, i.e., the presence of the bottle or the breast is desired because it is associated with hunger reduction), and to ethological "social instinct" theory, which implies that clinging responses are imprinted on the body of the mother as the baby chick is imprinted on the body of the mother as the baby chick is imprinted on a physical decoy (Bowlby, 1958; Harlow, 1959).

If, in contrast to physical theories, one takes the desire for a social bond with another *social self* as the primary "motive" for attachment, then this desire derives from the same motivational sources as that involved in the child's own strivings for stimulation, for activity, mastery, and for self-esteem. Social motivation is motivation for shared stimulation, for shared activity, and shared competence and self-esteem. Social dependency implies dependency upon another person as a source for such activity, and for the self's competence or esteem. The basic nature of competence motivation, however, is the same whether self or the other is perceived as the primary agent producing the desired stimulation, activity, or competence, that is, whether the goal is "independent mastery," social mastery (dominance), or social dependence. The differences between the two are differences in the cognitive structures of the self-other relationships involved.*

In my earlier discussion of Baldwin's theory of the bipolar social self, I indicated the exact sense in which the same desire to master an activity or situation would at one time lead the child to imitative following, at another, to dominating "showing off," at a third, to independent "doing it myself." I cited research showing that imitation and "verbal dependence" were tendencies correlated with one another and with brightness and active mastery in preschool children. The research showed that while these tendencies were positively correlated in children, they were negatively correlated in some situations, some situations being appropriate for imitation, others for verbal dependency, others for independent mastery. These situational definitions were in turn related to the cognitive-developmental status and self-concept of the child. The polarity between active mastery and passive dependence is, then, not a polarity between two motives but a polarity of social-situational and self-definition. (Generally passive-dependent children are not ones with a stronger motive for a social bond; if they were, they would engage in more of the independent behavior which would win them social approval.)

The more physicalistic models have found favor in considering early attachment because of the physical dependency of infants and their apparent similarity to infants in lower species with more defi-

---

* An account of social ties in terms of competence motivation and resulting desires for sharing does not deny the importance of sex, aggression, and anxiety in human relations. It does deny that drives provide the basic source of human social attachment. Were human attachments dependent upon instinctual drives, they would have the unstable periodicity, the promiscuity of arousing objects, the narcissistic quality which drives typically have, not only in mammals but in humans. Even the most attached male is capable of fantasy sexual arousal by someone to whom he is not attached, and is capable of sexual drive reduction in nonsocial onanistic ways. Sexual lust is anchored by a social attachment of sharing which makes it love; without such sharing, it is not a cause of attachment. As dryly stated by Kinsey et al. (1953), "In a socio-sexual relationship, the sexual partners may respond to each other and to the responses made by each other. For this reason, most persons find socio-sexual relationships more satisfactory than solitary sexual activities."

nite or rigid instincts. It is clear, however, that there is no such definite attachment to the mother in the infant before the age of six months, that is, there are no separation reactions before this period (Yarrow, 1964; Schaffer and Emerson, 1964). This casts suspicion on mechanistic imprinting or conditioning accounts which are plausible for the early forming attachments of lower species.

Human (and perhaps primate) attachments, even in the first two years of life, reflect the fact that they are attachments to another self or center of consciousness and activity like the self, that is, that they are "identifications."

This fact of human attachment implies the following characteristics:

1. *Attachment involves similarity to the other.* Attachment is only to another person, not toward physical objects. The distinctive sign of instinctual imprinting in lower species is that a decoy object may be imprinted. In baby monkeys, there may be an attachment to a blanket or cloth figure, but it is not a social attachment, as the Harlows (Harlow and Harlow, 1962) discovered. Whether "contact-comfort" blankets or oral drive–reducing bottles are involved, neither creates a social attachment.

2. *Attachment involves love or altruism toward the other,* an attitude not felt toward bottles or cloth mothers. Altruism, of course, presupposes the "ejective" consciousness of the feelings and wishes of the other, that is, empathy or sympathy.

3. *Attachment and altruism presuppose self-love.* The striving to satisfy another self presupposes the capacity or disposition to satisfy one's own self. Common sense assumes that the self (as body and center of activity) is loved intrinsically, not instrumentally (i.e., not because the body or the body's activities are followed by reinforcement or drive reduction). It is this nucleus of self-love which is involved, also, in organizing attachment to others.

4. *Attachment involves a defined possessive bond or relation linking the self and the other.* This is most clear when the bond is least "selfishly" possessive, as in the parent's attachment to the child. The difference between the attachment of the parent and that of the nurse or foster mother to the child illustrates this component.

5. *Attachment presupposes the desire for esteem in the eyes of the other or for reciprocal attachment.* In other words, it presupposes self-esteem motivation and the need for social approval, again presupposing ejective consciousness.

To summarize, a human social bond presupposes a relation to

another self, a relation which involves various types of sharing and of identification between the self and the other.

We have stressed the cognitive structures and self-esteem motivations found prerequisite for postinfant human attachment by social psychology. The rudiments of these prerequisites are also evident in primate and infant attachments. With regard to mammalian attachments, it is striking that the social species are also *(a)* the more cognitive species, *(b)* the more imitative species, and *(c)* the more playful (primary competence motivated) species. The fact that these attributes are primary to monkey sociality is suggested by the Harlows' (Harlow and Harlow, 1962) studies of monkey socialization. First, the studies indicate that monkey attachment is neither the result of drive reduction nor of imprinting in any mechanistic sense. Associations of a wire "mother" with hunger satisfaction do not lead to attachment to the wire "mother" or to anything else. Cloth "mothers" will be clung to by baby monkeys for "contact comfort" in quasi-instinctual fashion, but this does not generate later social attachment either to the cloth "mother" or to other monkeys any more than does experience with wire mothers. The fact that satisfaction of contact-comfort needs and early "imprinting" of these needs on a cloth mother does not generate any forms of social behavior in the monkey is indicated by the absence of social behavior or attachment in adult monkeys to either their cloth "mothers" or to other monkeys. If contact comfort does not generate social attachment by "imprinting" mechanisms, neither does sheer visual exposure to other monkeys (in other cages) generate attachment or lead to social "imprinting," though it does lead to prepatterned responses.

What Harlow has found to be sufficient for the formation of monkey attachments and for "normal" adult social and sexual behavior is social interaction with peers in play. What elements of play interaction are important has not been specified, though it is clear the elements are more than body contact, visual exposure, and drive reduction. It is very likely that it is the social quality of the interaction that is important, where "social" is taken as reciprocity or sharing of behavior. In general, even simple social play and games have the character of either complementarity-reciprocity (I do this, then you do that, then I do this) or of imitation (I do this, and you do this, too). In either case there is a shared pattern of behavior, since reciprocal play is a sort of reciprocal imitation ("you follow me, then I follow you"). One cannot claim that such sharing creates "the ejective consciousness" in the monkey, but the contrast between films of mother monkeys without childhood social experience and those who have had such experience suggests something like "ejective consciousness" in the normal monkey mothers. The socially deprived monkey mothers simply treat their infants as disturbing physical things, in marked contrast to the normal monkey mothers.

Turning to the human data, the widespread notion that a specifically maternal early care-taking relationship is essential for basic social development has borne up poorly under careful research scrutiny (Yarrow, 1964). Where early maternal deprivation has a deleterious effect on social development, it is part of a more general "package" of insufficient stimulation, cognitive as well as social, leading to retardation rather than irreversible "damage," and leading to cognitive, as well as emotional, retardation (Casler, 1961; Dennis and Najarian, 1957). While adolescents and adults with long histories of social deprivation, of mistreatment, and of transfer from institution or foster home to another seem deficient in a capacity for social attachment, there is no clear evidence that these effects are due to infant deprivation rather than to later negative influences in their life. In particular, insofar as deprivation or institutionalization have deep social effects, it seems to be due to the absence of stable and pleasurable social interaction, rather than to a lack of maternal care-taking which produces weakened social ties. A. Freud and Dann's (1951) report of the deep identifications and attachments between young children which developed in a Nazi concentration camp without maternal caretaking suggest, at a deeper human level, the normal social attachments which peer interaction and sharing cause at the monkey level in Harlow's (1959) studies.*

We have pointed out that the evidence suggests that positive social attachments develop out of intrinsic motivation to engage in social interaction and the intrinsic pleasure of social interaction, regardless of specific body instincts and drives. We have also said that the evidence suggests that this aspect of ego development has

---

* Insofar as early social environments cause schizoid and autistic withdrawals from social interaction which are not genetic, the effect appears not to be a sheer deprivation effect so much as an effect of nonresponsive and nonreciprocal mothering. As White (1963) suggests, it is the feeling of noncontrol, incompetence, of not having a predictable and reciprocal effect on the human environment which is probably the experiential agent in the autistic child's focus upon things, not people, as objects for interaction.

a natural developmental course and robustness in early life, so that, like other aspects of ego development, it is responsive to a much wider variety of functionally equivalent types of social stimulation than is suggested by doctrines of "mother love." We shall now trace a few of the steps in the development of social attachment implied by this account.

As was the case for stages of imitation, age-developmental progressions of attachment are generated by cognitive-structural changes. In the infant period this is indicated by the work of Decarie (1965). Decarie found *(a)* close age parallels between Piaget progressions in physical object concepts and social object-relations or psychoanalytic ego-stages, and *(b)* correlations between the two such that infants advanced on one scale were advanced on the other. For various reasons, it is more plausible to assume that cognitive advance is the more basic or causal factor in this parallelism, though there is some reason to think that the cognitive advance is reflected earlier in the social-object world than in the physical-object world. In the preschool period, this is suggested by my own work on father-attachment just summarized. Our sketch of the age-development of attachment stresses the following strands in cognitive-developmental theories of ego-development:

1. The Piagetian development of the concept of the mother as a permanent, causally independent, but familiar, object (completed by age 2).
2. The development of the child's conception of the parent (or older sibling) as having a mind, intelligence, or will different from, and superior to, the child's own mentality or will, but one which the child can share through processes of learning, conformity, and winning affection (completed by age 6–7). This development is termed "satellization" by Ausubel (1957), formation of "ideal self by Baldwin (1906). The cognitive developments involve *(a)* the ability to make comparative judgments of competence, *(b)* the differentiation of the child's own mind and perspective from that of others, *(c)* development of conceptions of shared ascribed social identities of sex, age, and kinship, and *(d)* the development of conceptions of shared rules.
3. The development of conceptions of reciprocity, of choice, of shared but relative self-chosen and individual values and identities (completed in adolescence); and the development of inti-

macy, friendship and love as discussed by Erikson (1950) and Sullivan (1953).

It is obvious that our account assumes that intense and stable attachment (love) is a mature end point of ego-development, not a primitive tendency. A careful analysis of the research on age differences in response to separation and object-loss (Branstetter, 1969) supports this assumption.

As was the case for imitation, I must commence my account by noting that social objects are first responded to more than physical objects because they are much more interesting. It is evident that other people are especially interesting to infants and that this interest is due primarily to the fact that people look familiar and yet they are complex stimulus objects constantly engaging in interesting activities having some relationship to the infant's own activities. While some of the most interesting things done by social objects are to care for the needs of the infant, these activities fall into a much larger class of interesting activities.* The fact that the motivational conditions for early social responses are general information-processing conditions is suggested by recent findings on the determinants of attention and smiling to human-face schemata; for example, "stimuli that resemble the infant's schema will maintain his attention with the greatest intensity. Stimuli that very closely match or have no relation to his schema will hold his attention for a much shorter time" (Kagan, 1968, p. 27). In addition, however, the sudden recognition of the familiar (whether faces or other configurations) elicits smiling, because it leads to a rapid assimilation of an uncertain experience (Piaget, 1952b).† In his sense, children's early social smile is functionally continuous with much of their later smiling and laughter at funny stimuli, that is, stimuli which are first incongruous but suddenly "fall into place"

* Wolff (1965) notes that attentiveness to external stimuli in very young infants was lowest when the infant was hungry or otherwise viscerally excited. The account which follows assumes that the infant's "social responses" are part of this broad attentiveness to the outside world, rather than that the child attends to the outside world only when something external meshes with a visceral drive-state.

† The notion that smiling to human faces is due to an association with feeding satisfaction has been disproved. Association of face-schema with bottle feeding reduced, rather than increased, smiling to a schema of the face in orphanage infants (because it made it overfamiliar) (Wilson, 1962) The notion that the human face constitutes a specific "innate releasing mechanism" for an instinctive smiling response also seems untenable, since a large variety of complex stimuli will elicit smiling (Wilson, 1962).

in a somewhat unexpected way, as all theories of humor emphasize.

We have stressed the role of assimilation of the familiar and interesting in one positive social response, the smile. Failure to assimilate the unfamiliar and incongruous seems to be responsible for another early "attachment" response, the 8–12-month reaction of "stranger anxiety" (Morgan and Ricciutti, 1968). Before the appearance of stranger anxiety, all human faces tend to be assimilated to the familiar "mother" schema. The clear failure to fit the schema seems to induce stranger anxiety. After "normal" stranger anxiety has subsided in development (for example, after 1 year) the donning of a mask by the mother will elicit a similar reaction of anxious response to the incongruity in the apparently familiar (though the sheer presentation of a mask will not).* We do not yet know enough either about the infant's schema development or about the general conditions of schema-stimulus match to specify what is the optimal amount of incongruity to produce pleasurable attention and what is an overload of incongruity-producing distress. However, the burgeoning work on infancy clearly suggests that early "social" responses will be understood in terms of the broad picture of assimilative reactions to patterned stimuli rather than in terms of specific prepatterned, maturationally unfolding responses to innate releasing stimuli for "attachment" or "flight," or by histories of conditioning (Riccuitti, 1968).

The implication of what has been said so far is that infants' "social attachment" responses in the first eight months are simply part of their responsiveness to patterned external stimulation, rather than being genuinely "social" or forming the necessary groundwork for later human ties. We have claimed that preference for parent over stranger, so-called "stranger anxiety," is a negative response to the unfamiliar. In this regard it seems no more "social" than anxiety about being placed in a strange room as opposed to a familiar room. Ainsworth (1963, 1964) suggests that it forms part of a sequential pattern of attachment behaviors, but neither her work nor that of Decarie (1965) has succeeded in arriving at a sequential or cumulative scale of social or mother

---

*Just as smiling to a face has been reviewed as involving an innate releasing mechanism, stranger anxiety has been viewed as an innate "flight" response terminating the period of "imprinting" or attachment (Schaffer, 1966). Not only does the onset of stranger anxiety not terminate the potential for attachment, but it disappears in a way instinctive flight responses do not.

"object relations" which clearly indicates any patterning not due to the sequential patterning of infants' responses to physical objects based on general Piagetian principles of cognitive development. The stages of the infant's construction of permanent independent physical objects have close parallels in the child's growth of awareness of the permanence and independence of social objects like the mother, as Decarie (1965) has documented. The age at which the child first shows stranger-anxiety and separation responses is the age (6–9 months) at which the child first shows awareness of the permanence of physical objects (Decarie, 1965; Schaffer and Emerson, 1964). It is obvious that the permanent existence of the mother is a precondition to missing her. The open question is whether there are steps in the formation of a mother attachment which indicate something more than the child's general cognitive growth in response to external objects whether physical or social. If not, there is no reason to assume that early experience should have a basic effect on capacities for later social attachment unless early deprivation or trauma were so extreme as to retard responsiveness to external stimuli and cognitive development in general.

We have claimed that the 9-month response to the socially unfamiliar is in itself not "social" since it is no different from the child's response to the unfamiliar in general. The child's early separation responses may represent something more specifically social than this, however. The fact of object constancy indicates the beginning of a growth of selfness, a discrimination between the self and outer objects. While the mother must be recognized in some sense as an outer object to be missed when she is not present, she is also more self-like than other outer objects, as psychoanalytic theories of infancy have always stressed.

In a certain sense, the mother may be part of the child to be missed as a part of the child's body might be missed. Separation and stranger anxiety, then, may be a reaction not only to an unfamiliar situation but to the change or loss of a more or less permanent self. While a mother-infant identification may not be responsible for separation reactions in the first year of life, it seems clearly involved in reactions in the second year of life. By the second year of life, there is a self-other differentiation at the level of bodies but not of minds and wills. While "ejective consciousness" is established in the second year of life, the child's confusion between his or her own perspective on objects or mental reactions and those of others (termed egocentrism by Piaget [1947]0 continues in quite gross form until age 5–7. Before the 2-year-old's "negativistic crisis" signals awareness of a differentiation of wills and agencies, the child feels no sense of incompetence or weakness in either imitating others, obeying others (i.e., in being the agent of another's will), or in being helped by others (i.e., in the other being an agent of the child's will). In the second year of life, then, there is a sense in which the psychoanalytic notion of a primary identification or undifferentiated symbiotic bond with the mother is an accurate characterization of social relationships.*

Insofar as this is the case, this tie is not social; it involves neither acts of sharing nor love for the other nor the desire for love. This is brought out in Ausubel's (1952, 1957) account of the development of identification-attachment. According to Ausubel, in this undifferentiated phase, the infant conceives of the caretaker as a mere extension of the infant's own wishes and actions, as an executive arm. Accordingly the infant's dependency upon the parent is essentially an instrumental or executive dependency rather than a volitional dependency; that is, it is not a willingness to subordinate actions to the wishes or responses of the parent. It does not imply any orientation to the psychic state of the mother, that is, no desire to share psychic states, no altruism about her state, and no concern about being loved (as a psychic state in the other, important for self-esteem). Ausubel believes that growing cognitive differentiation of self and other and growing awareness of the superior power of the parents precipitates a third-year negativistic crisis typically resolved by accepting a satellite role in the family. Satellizing children give up a sense of self-esteem based on their own power and achievement (and a controlling executive dependency over the mother which extends their sense of power to what they can get the mother to do) for a sense of vicarious self-esteem as the result of vicarious sharing of parental superiorities and as the result of being loved and being positively evaluated by parents and others. Both identification and volitional dependency are motivated by

---

* Bowlby (1958) and others have exaggerated the specificity and depth of the symbiotic clinging attachment to the mother in the second year of life, however. A recent carefully controlled study of the reactions of infants (aged 1½ to 3) to hospitalization involved comparisons of mother-absent, "substitute-mother" volunteers, and rooming-in groups. While many of the mother-absent infants showed intense distress, there were no differences between the real and substitute-mother groups in distress reactions (Branstetter, 1969).

needs for self-esteem in a satellite role. The need to be loved does not precede identification but is contemporaneous with it in a total process of cognitively realistic ego devaluation where love, acceptance, and attractive adult role models are available.

Ausubel's crisis-oriented typological account is useful as a dramatic sketch of the development of identification, compressing into a single conflict and a single relationship a process of social development going on in the first eight years of life. The account is limited, not only by condensing too much development into the resolution of a single crisis, but by its neglect of the positive experiences of, and motives for, sharing. Shared goals, shared norms, and shared esteem are derived by Ausubel from a clash which leads the child to give up a unilateral primary "egoistic" will and sense of competence or self-esteem for a unilateral "derived" sense of goals and sense of self-esteem, rather than from more positive, unconflicted, and egalitarian experiences of sharing.

In particular, both Ausubel and the psychoanalytic accounts of second-year sociality stress a negative mother-child symbiosis expressed in a physical clinging and a demandingness which results from the child's seeing the mother as a physical extension of the child's own self. In addition, however, the child in the second year of life clearly takes a delight in sharing through imitation, reciprocal play, and communication (e.g., pointing things out to the other). It is this kind of experience, rather than clinging, which clearly indicates that other people are people to the infant, not security blankets or "cloth mothers" to be clung to in unfamiliar situations. The bridge between the physical and the social is suggested by infants' response to their own mirror-image (Dixon, 1957). Eight-month-old children's interest in their mirror "twin" is based largely on the fact that their mirror twin "imitates" them. Infants act repetitively to get the mirror twin to "imitate" their movements. According to Dixon, however, infants are far more interested in their real twin than in their "mirror twin," and this interest is largely connected with simple imitative games in which each takes turns imitating and eliciting imitation from the other.

Social objects early become a special focus of attention and recognition because they do more interesting things. They become differentiated from physical things because a major vehicle for interacting with them is to imitate them rather than to manipulate them. Social objects not only do interesting things, but these interesting activities may be shared and made one's own by imitation or by reciprocal interaction. By the second year of life, most children are tagalongs behind their older siblings, following siblings more than they follow their mothers. They tag along because what their older siblings do is interesting, more interesting than the parents sedate activities. They follow along, not to watch, but to imitate and participate in these activities. The motivation for this "tagging-along" is effectance motivation, the motivation behind the perennial question "What is there to do?" and the satisfaction of the motive is through imitation of the interesting. In large part, then, children are dependent upon the other as a model for their own activities, and the motivation for this dependence is the motivation for imitation I have discussed before. It is also clear that 2-year-olds are not attached to the older brother they slavishly imitate in the sense that they are to their mother; when in a state of insecurity or need, 2-year-olds quickly turn to their mother, not their brother. I argued earlier, however, that sheer physical need for the presence and services of the other does not in itself generate social bonds, because it does not involve a motive to share between self and other or to be guided by the response of the other. It is an open question whether children's symbiotic relation to their mother constitutes a more basic or favorable base than do their relations to peers and other adults for the cultivation of a desire to share, and a "satellizing" renunciation of nonshared wishes and sources of self-esteem for shared ones which is basic to the formation of later stable social bonds.*

The ego-development theories of Baldwin (1906), Piaget (1948), Ausubel (1957), and Loevinger (1966) suggest that the child's further development of social ties and development of moral attitudes become different sides of the same coin. M. Blatt (unpublished research) has found that children's conceptions of love and friendship go through stages parallel to my moral judgment stages. It is not until the onset of Stage 3, "good-boy" morality, at age 6–7 that children express the desire to be liked independently of being given rewards; express the desire to do something for someone they like; feel being a friend of, or being liked by, someone pres-

---

*It must be stressed that psychoanalytic, ethological, or S–R theories basing later dependency or attachments on mother-infant relations in the first two years are not as yet based on any substantial research findings. The facts are more to the contrary. As a single example from many, Kagan and Moss (1962) found a correlation of only .33 between affectional dependency in the first three years of life and at ages 6–9, and a similar correlation of .33 between anxiety at loss of nurturance across the same periods.

tigeful gives them derived self-esteem; or think that they like their parent or friend, even though they are momentarily frustrating them. At this point, the child's social tie to the parent becomes the satellizing moral identification previous discussed. The development of attachment and love past satellization to intimacy must be left for subsequent treatment.

Identification and Psychopathology

I have claimed that specific identifications with specific parent figures may (*a*) speed up (or slow down) development in natural moral or psychosexual sequences and (*b*) may give particular stages of development specific content and affective significance. The child's stage of development in turn colors or gives specific significance to the child's relationship to parents. I have claimed, however, that specific identifications with specific parent figures are neither necessary nor sufficient conditions for normal or psychosexual development.

The need to explain general trends of both moral and sex-role development in terms independent of specific parent-child ties or identification is indicated by research findings reviewed elsewhere (Kohlberg, 1963a, 1964, 1966b).

1. Children and young adults are no more like their parents in level of morality or of masculinity-femininity than they are like a random parental individual of the same social class. All reported studies indicate no correlation between the masculinity-femininity of the child and the masculinity-femininity of their same-sex parents (Terman and Miles, 1936; Mussen and Rutherford, 1963; Angrilli, 1960). There is no significant correlation between the stage or level of moral maturity (as defined by my methods) of male adolescents or young adults and that of their fathers (Holstein, 1968; Kramer, 1968). While "principled" mothers are more likely to have "conventional" children than less-advanced mothers, this is not due to identification mechanisms. If it were, conventional mothers should have more conventional-level children than principled mothers (Holstein, 1968).

2. Measures of identification (perceived similarity) with the same-sex parent do not clearly and consistently relate to moral and sex-role maturity or to moral and sex-role "internalization" (i.e., to acceptance of conventional moral and sex-role attitudes and standards). With regard to sex role, measures of girls' femininity

tend to correlate with measures of identification with the opposite-sex parent rather than the same-sex parent. Measures of boys' masculinity correlate with measures of identification with the same-sex parent at most, but not all, age periods. With regard to morality, low significant correlations are found between parent identification measures and acceptance of the conventional moral code. These are not sex-specific; for example, measured identification with the same-sex parent is not more clearly related to moral attitudes than is identification with the opposite-sex parent. these correlations may be best explained along the lines of the findings on warmth and liking; for example, that if their children like their parents they tend to agree with them and learn more from them as reflected in both moral attitude measures and perceived similarity measures.

3. There is no generalized "identification-internalization factor" in children's personalty. Measures of moral and of sex-role attitudes or development are not correlated with one another. Measures of identification do not correlate well with one another. Measures of identification at one age do not predict to measures of identification at another age.

4. The presence of a same-sex parent is not necessary for normal moral or psychosexual development. Children in the kibbutz and children from father-absent households are little different from children of intact families in all measured or observed aspects of "normality" or development of sex-role, as well as of moral, attitudes and behavior.*

There is a widespread misunderstanding of the research findings as indicating "the importance of the father for the development of the boy's sex-role identity." In fact, no study has shown any marked differences between father-absent and father-present boys with regard to measures of masculine-feminine attitudes (Terman and Miles, 1936; Barclay and Cusumano, 1965; C. Smith summarized in Kohlberg, 1966b). A naturalistic longitudinal study

---

* Differences appear where intactness of the family represents the general "badness" or deviance of the parents and the environment as in the Gluecks' (Glueck and Glueck, 1950) studies of delinquency in which divorce, parent-conflict, criminality, and neglect of children form part of a bad-environment package. Where some control of these correlates of a single-parent household is attained in a research design, the actual presence of a specific parent does not appear salient. One study, however, that of Hoffman and Saltzstein (1967), does report more internalized moral judgment and guilt in father-present boys than in a sample of father-absent boys matched for IQ and social class (Hoffman, 1969).

by McCord, McCord, and Thurber (1962) indicated no difference between father-absent and father-present families in incidence of effeminacy or homosexuality in boys.

While these findings clearly contradict any theory that claims that particular identifications or good parent relations are necessary for normal social development, there are some findings suggesting that bad parent relations are retarding or disrupting of such development. As an example, McCord et al. (1962) found intact families with strong marital conflict produced "effeminate" boys more frequently than either the conflict-free or the father-absent families. Hetherington (1965) and Hetherington and Frankie (1967) also find the sons of extremely submissive fathers to be low on sex-typing and on father imitation compared to the sons of high dominant fathers. The sons of dominant fathers appeared to be no different from a random population, or even from C. Smith's father-absent population, however (Kohlberg, 1966b). In other words, while markedly bad, deviant, or conflictful mother-father relations produce disturbances in sex-role attitudes, exposure to a "good" or conforming mother-father interaction is neither necessary for normal sex-role development (since it does not favor father-present over father-absent boys) nor does it even favor normal sex-role development (since highly masculine and dominant fathers are no more likely to have masculine sons than are fathers in the middle range).

In the moral area, the findings of the Gluecks (Glueck and Glueck, 1950) clearly indicate that delinquent boys are much more likely to come from markedly "bad" families, according to any criterion of "badness.' But again, a specific relation to a specific good parent is neither necessary nor sufficient for normal or advanced moral development, since absence of the father, father's moral level, and use of "good" child-rearing techniques, however defined, do not predict to such maturity (Speicher-Dubin, 1982).

The contrast between the relatively clear findings on effects of deviantly bad parents and the lack of findings on the effects of parent absence (or of normal variations in child-rearing practices) upon socialization is theoretically important for several reasons.* Limiting myself to identification theory, I pointed out that psycho-

---

* The practical implications of this conclusion imply a revolution in current social work and mental health services for children now addressed to helping the child under the presupposition of preserving his relation to a "bad" but intact family.

analytic identification theory (especially identification with the aggressor notions) was designed to account for illogical, pathological, or deviant identifications. I pointed out that a theory as to why boys want to be boys is not a theory as to why a boy wants to be a girl in some generalized sense; nor is an explanation of why boys want to be good in general an explanation of why a particular boy seems to want to be bad or sees himself as bad in some generalized sense. While we cannot conclude that boys low in masculinity or delinquent boys have formed a definite deviant "opposite-sex" or "bad" identification modeled on a parent, it is at least possible that some of the effects of bad families are due to this mechanism.

There is, at present, little definite reason to view "opposite-sex identification" as a valuable explanation of sexual psychopathology, since homosexuals are not clearly more "opposite-sex identified" than heterosexuals (Kohlberg, 1966b). With regard to some forms of moral psychopathology, however, deviant parental identifications seem more directly relevant. Freud's (1938) reasoning that pathological feelings of being blamed by others (paranoia) and of self-blame (depression) require a notion of fixed self-blaming structure, somewhat ego-alien but at the same time internalized within the psyche and based on identification, still seems convincing. Self-criticism and self-punishment by definition require identification in the broad sense of taking the role of the other, and severe forms of self-punishment and self-blame must be modeled in some sense on parental reactions in young childhood, since the parent is ordinarily the only agent who engages in intensive punishment and blaming activities. Explanations of pathological guilt (i.e., guilt in the absence of serious transgression of self-accepted standards) suggest a base in idiosyncratic family and childhood experience, explanations of normal guilt (guilt over transgressions of self-accepted moral standards) do not.

Unfortunately, it is premature to attempt explanations of psychopathological identifications because there are almost no data concerning them except clinical case studies. The research literature is irrelevant to such questions except under the dubious assumption that measures of developmental lag in sexual or moral attitudes, or low scores on verbal measures of conformity to conventional moral or sex-role standards reflect pathological identifications (e.g., that a low score on an M-F test is a measure of a cross-sex identification of an illogical or pathological sort). A consideration of theories of psychopathological identification requires the kind of developmental and longitudinal data on psychopathology not now available. The analysis of such data may provide more of an integration of psychoanalytic and cognitive-developmental concepts than this chapter has suggested.

2. Moral Stages and Moralization: The Cognitive-Developmental Approach

In this chapter I shall present an overview of the cognitive-developmental theory of moralization as elaborated in studies of moral stages by myself and my colleagues. I shall first present a theoretical description of the six moral stages, followed by an account of the development of our methods for identifying or scoring stage. Having presented a picture of what moral development is and how to assess it, I shall go on to present the theory of moralization which can best account for this picture of moral development, and then to contrast this theory with approaches which see moral development as a result of socialization or social learning.

In a sense, this chapter represents an updating of earlier presentations of my theory of moral development stages (Kohlberg, 1969). In this chapter, however, there is no attempt to review research comprehensively, as research reviews have appeared earlier (Kohlberg, 1964, 1969) and are forthcoming (Kohlberg and Candee, in prep.). The philosophic assumptions and implications of our stages are also treated only briefly, having been thoroughly discussed elsewhere (Kohlberg, 1971b, 1981a.).

The Place of Moral Judgment in the Total Personality

To understand moral stage, it is helpful to locate it in a sequence of development of personality. We know that individuals pass through the moral stages one step at a time as they progress from the bottom (Stage 1) toward the top (Stage 6). There are also other stages that individuals must go through, perhaps the most basic of which are the stages of logical reasoning or intelligence studied by Piaget (1967). After the child learns to speak, there are three major developmental stages of reasoning: the intuitive, the concrete operational, and the formal operational. At around age 7, children enter the stage of concrete logical thought; they can then make logical inferences, classify things and handle quantitative relations about concrete things. In adolescence, many but not all individuals enter the stage of formal operations, at which level they can reason abstractly. Formal operational thinking can consider all possibilities, consider the relations between elements in a system, form hypotheses, deduce implications from the hypotheses, and test them against reality. Many adolescents and adults only partially attain the stage of formal operations; they consider all the actual relations of one thing to another at the same time, but do not consider all possibilities and do not form abstract hypotheses.

In general, almost no adolescents and adults will still be entirely at the stage of concrete operations, many will be at the stage of partial formal operations, and most will be at the highest stage of formal operations (Kuhn, Langer, Kohlberg, and Haan, 1977). Since moral reasoning clearly is reasoning, advanced moral reasoning depends upon advanced logical reasoning. There is a parallelism between an individual's logical stage and his or her moral stage. A person whose logical stage is only concrete operational is limited to the preconventional moral stages, Stages 1 and 2. A person whose logical stage is only "low" formal operational is limited to the conventional moral stages, Stages 3 and 4. While logical development is a necessary condition for moral development, it is not sufficient. Many individuals are at a higher logical stage than the parallel moral stage, but essentially none are at a higher moral stage than their logical stage (Walker, 1980).

Next after stages of logical development come stages of social perception or social perspective- or role-taking (see Selman, 1976). We partially describe these stages when we define the moral stages. These role-taking stages describe the level at which the person sees other people, interprets their thoughts and feelings, and sees their role or place in society. These stages are very closely related to moral stages, but are more general, since they do not deal just with fairness and with choices of right and wrong. To make a judgment of fairness at a certain level is more difficult than to simply see the world at that level. So, just as for logic, development of a stage's social perception precedes, or is easier than, development of the parallel stage of moral judgment. Just as there is a vertical sequence of steps in movement up from moral Stage 1 to moral Stage 2 to moral Stage 3, so there is a horizontal sequence of steps in movement from logic to social perception to moral judgment. First, individuals attain a logical stage, say, partial formal operations, which allows them to see "systems" in the world, to see a set of related variables as a system. Next they attain a level of social perception or role-taking, where they see other people understanding one another in terms of the place of each in the system. Finally, they attain Stage 4 of moral judgment, where the welfare and order of the total social system or society is the reference point for judging "fair" or "right." We have found that individuals who move upward in our moral education programs already have the logical capacity, and often the social perception capacity, for the higher moral stage to which they move (Walker, 1980).

There is one final step in this horizontal sequence: moral behavior. To act in a morally high way requires a high stage of moral reasoning. One cannot follow moral principles (Stages 5 and 6) if one does not understand or believe in them. One can, however, reason in terms of such principles and not live up to them. A variety of factors determines whether a particular person will live up to his or her stage of moral reasoning in a particular situation, though moral stage is a good predictor of action in various experimental and naturalistic settings (Kohlberg, 1969).

In summary, moral stage is related to cognitive advance and to moral behavior, but our identification of moral stage must be based on moral reasoning alone.

Theoretical Description of the Moral Stages

The six moral stages are grouped into three major levels: preconventional level (Stages 1 and 2), conventional level (Stages 3 and 4), and postconventional level (Stages 5 and 6).

To understand the stages, it is best to start by understanding the three moral levels. The preconventional moral level is the level of most children under 9, some adolescents, and many adolescent and adult criminal offenders. The conventional level is the level of most adolescents and adults in our society and in other societies. The postconventional level is reached by a minority of adults and is usually reached only after the age of 20. The term "conventional" means conforming to and upholding the rules and expectations and conventions of society or authority just because they are society's rules, expectations, or conventions. The individual at the preconventional level has not yet come to really understand and uphold conventional or societal rules and expectations. Someone at the postconventional level understands and basically accepts society's rules, but acceptance of society's rules is based on formulating and accepting the general moral principles that underlie these rules. These principles in some cases come into conflict with society's rules, in which case the postconventional individual judges by principle rather than by convention.

One way of understanding the three levels is to think of them as three different types of relationships between the *self* and *society's rules and expectations.* From this point of view, Level I is a preconventional person, for whom rules and social expectations are something external to the self; Level II is a conventional person, in whom the self is identified with or has internalized the rules and expectations of others, especially those of authorities; and Level III is a postconventional person, who had differentiated his or her self from the rules and expectations of others and defines his or her values in terms of self-chosen principles.

Within each of the three moral levels, there are two stages. The second stage is a more advanced and organized form of the general perspective of each major level. Table 2.1 defines the six moral stages in terms of (1) what is right, (2) the reason for upholding the right, and (3) the social perspective behind each stage, a central concept to which our definition of moral reasoning now turns.

Social Perspectives of the Three Moral Levels

In order to characterize the development of moral reasoning structurally, we seek a single unifying construct that will generate the major structural features of each stage. Selman (1976) offers a point of departure in the search for such a unifying construct; he has defined levels of role-taking which parallel our moral stages and which form a cognitive-structural hierarchy. Selman defines role-taking primarily in terms of the way the individual differentiates his or her perspective from other perspectives and relates these perspectives to one another. From our point of view, however, there is a more general structural construct which underlies *both* role-taking and moral judgment. This is the concept of *sociomoral perspective,* which refers to the point of view the individual takes in defining both social facts and sociomoral values, or "oughts." Corresponding to the three major levels of moral judg-

Table 2.1. The Six Moral Stages

	Content of Stage		
Level and Stage	What Is Right	Reasons for Doing Right	*Social Perspective of Stage*
Level I: Preconventional Stage 1—Heteronomous Morality	To avoid breaking rules backed by punishment, obedience for its own sake, and avoiding physical damage to persons and property.	Avoidance of punishment, and the superior power of authorities.	*Egocentric point of view.* Doesn't consider the interests of others or recognize that they differ from the actor's; doesn't relate two points of view. Actions are considered physically rather than in terms of psychological interests of others. Confusion of authority's perspective with one's own.
Stage 2—Individualism, Instrumental Purpose, and Exchange	Following rules only when it is to someone's immediate interest; acting to meet one's own interests and needs and letting others do the same. Right is also what's fair, what's an equal exchange, a deal, an agreement.	To serve one's own needs or interests in a world where you have to recognize that other people have their interests, too.	*Concrete individualistic perspective.* Aware that everybody has his own interest to pursue and these conflict, so that right is relative (in the concrete individualistic sense).
Level II: Conventional Stage 3—Mutual Interpersonal Expectations, Relationships, and Interpersonal Conformity	Living up to what is expected by people close to you or what people generally expect of people in your role as son, brother, friend, etc. "Being good" is important and means having good motives, showing concern about others. It also means keeping mutual relationships, such as trust, loyalty, respect, and gratitude.	The need to be a good person in your own eyes and those of others. Your caring for others. Belief in the Golden Rule. Desire to maintain rules and authority which support stereotypical good behavior.	*Perspective of the individual in relationships with other individuals.* Aware of shared feelings, agreements, and expectations which take primacy over individual interests. Relates points of view through the concrete Golden Rule, putting yourself in the other person's shoes. Does not yet consider generalized system perspective.

	Content of Stage		
Level and Stage	What Is Right	Reasons for Doing Right	*Social Perspective of Stage*
Stage 4—Social System and Conscience	Fulfilling the actual duties to which you have agreed. Laws are to be upheld except in extreme cases where they conflict with other fixed social duties. Right is also contributing to society, the group, or institution.	To keep the institution going as a whole, to avoid the breakdown in the system "if everyone did it," or the imperative of conscience to meet one's defined obligations. (Easily confused with Stage 3 belief in rules and authority; see text.)	*Differentiates societal point of view from interpersonal agreement or motives.* Takes the point of view of the system that defines roles and rules. Considers individual relations in terms of place in the system.
Level III: Postconventional, or Principled Stage 5—Social Contract or Utility and Individual Rights	Being aware that people hold a variety of values and opinions, that most values and rules are relative to your group. These relative rules should usually be upheld, however, in the interest of impartiality and because they are the social contract. Some nonrelative values and rights like *life* and *liberty*, however, must be upheld in any society and regardless of majority opinion.	A sense of obligation to law because of one's social contract to make and abide by laws for the welfare of all and for the protection of all people's rights. A feeling of contractual commitment, freely entered upon, to family, friendship, trust, and work obligations. Concern that laws and duties be based on rational calculation of overall utility, "the greatest good for the greatest number."	*Prior-to-society perspective.* Perspective of a rational individual aware of values and rights prior to social attachments and contracts. Integrates perspectives by formal mechanisms of agreement, contract, objective impartiality, and due process. Considers moral and legal points of view; recognizes that they sometimes conflict and finds it difficult to integrate them.

Table 2.1—Continued

	Content of Stage		
Level and Stage	What Is Right	Reasons for Doing Right	*Social Perspective of Stage*
Stage 6—Universal Ethical Principles	Following self-chosen ethical principles. Particular laws or social agreements are usually valid because they rest on such principles. When laws violate these principles, one acts in accordance with the principle. Principles are universal principles of justice: the equality of human rights and repect for the dignity of human beings as individual persons.	The belief as a rational person in the validity of universal moral principles, and a sense of personal commitment to them.	*Perspective of a moral point of view* from which social arrangements derive. Perspective is that of any rational individual recognizing the nature of morality or the fact that persons are ends in themselves and must be treated as such.

ment, we postulate the three major levels of social perspective as follows:

Moral Judgment	*Social Perspective*
I. Preconventional	Concrete individual perspective
II. Conventional	Member-of-society perspective
III. Postconventional, or principled	Prior-to-society perspective

Let us illustrate the meaning of social perspective in terms of the unity it provides for the various ideas and concerns of the moral level. The conventional level, for example, is different from the preconventional in that it uses the following reasons: (1) concern about social approval; (2) concern about loyalty to persons, groups, and authority; and (3) concern about the welfare of others and society. We need to ask, What underlies these characteristics of reasoning and holds them together? What fundamentally defines and unifies the characteristics of the conventional level is its *social perspective,* a shared viewpoint of the participants in a relationship or a group. The conventional individual subordinates the needs of the single individual to the viewpoint and needs of the group or the shared relationship. To illustrate the conventional social perspective, here is 17-year-old Joe's response to the following question:

Q.—Why shouldn't you steal from a store?
A.—It's a matter of law. It's one of our rules that we're trying to help protect everyone, protect property, not just to protect a store. It's something that's needed in our society. If we didn't have these laws, people would steal, they wouldn't have to work for a living and our whole society would get out of kilter.

Joe is concerned about *keeping the law,* and his reason for being concerned is *the good of society as a whole.* Clearly, he is speaking as a member of society." It's one of *our* rules that *we're making* to protect everyone in *our* society." This concern for the good of society arises from his taking the point of view of "us members of society," which goes beyond the point of view of Joe as a concrete, individual self.

Let us contrast this *conventional member-of-society perspective* with the *preconventional concrete individual perspective.* The latter point of view is that of the individual actor in the situation thinking about his interests and those of other individuals he may care about. Seven years earlier, at age 10, Joe illustrated the concrete individual perspective in response to the same question:

Q.—Why shouldn't you steal from a store?
A.—It's not good to steal from the store. It's against the law. Someone could see you and call the police.

Being "against the law," then, means something very different at the two levels. At Level II, the law is made by and for "everyone," as Joes indicates at age 17. At Level I, it is just something enforced by the police, and accordingly, the reason for obeying the law is to avoid punishment. This reason derives from the limits of a Level I perspective, the perspective of an individual considering his or her own interests and those of other isolated individuals.

Let us now consider the perspective of the *postconventional level.* It is like the preconventional perspective in that it returns to the standpoint of the individual rather than taking the point of view of "us members of society." The individual point of view taken at the postconventional level, however, can be universal; it is that of *any rational moral individual.* Aware of the member-of-society perspective, the postconventional person questions and redefines it in terms of an individual moral perspective, so that social obligations are defined in ways that can be justified to any moral individual. An individual's commitment to basic morality or moral principles is seen as preceding, or being necessary for, his or her taking society's perspective or accepting society's laws and values. Society's laws and values, in turn, should be ones which any reasonable person could be committed to—whatever his or her place in society and whatever society he or she belongs to. The postconventional perspective, then, is *prior to society;* it is the perspective of an *individual who has made the moral commitments or holds the standards on which a good or just society must be based.* This is a perspective by which (1) a particular society or set of social practices may be judged and (2) a person may rationally commit him- or herself to a society.

An example is Joe, our longitudinal subject, interviewed at age 24:

Q.—*Why shouldn't someone steal from a store?*
A.—It's violating another person's rights, in this case, to property.

Q.—*Does the law enter in?*
A.—Well, the law in most cases is based on what is morally right, so it's not a separate subject, it's a consideration.

Q.—*What does "morality" or "morally right" mean to you?*
A.—Recognizing the rights of other individuals, first to life and then to do as he pleases as long as it doesn't interfere with somebody else's rights.

The wrongness of stealing is that it violates the moral rights of individuals, which are prior to law and society. Property rights follow from more universal human rights (such as freedoms which do not interfere with the like freedom of others). The demands of law and society derive from universal moral rights, rather than vice versa.

It should be noted that reference to the words *rights* or *morally right* or *conscience* does not necessarily distinguish conventional from postconventional morality. Orienting to the morally right thing, or following conscience as against following the law, need not indicate the postconventional perspective of the rational moral individual. The terms *morality* and *conscience* may be used to refer to group rules and values which conflict with civil laws or with the rules of the majority group. To a Jehovah's Witness who has gone to jail for "conscience," conscience may mean God's law as interpreted by his or her religious sect or group rather than the standpoint of any individual oriented to universal moral principles or values. To count as postconventional, such ideas or terms must be used in a way that makes it clear that they have a foundation for a rational or moral individual who has not yet committed him- or herself to any group or society or its morality. "Trust," for example, is a basic value at both the conventional and the postconventional levels. At the conventional level, trustworthiness is something you expect of others in your society. Joe expresses this as follows at age 17:

Q.—*Why should a promise be kept, anyway?*
A.—Friendship is based on trust. If you can't trust a person, there's little grounds to deal with him. You should try to be as reliable as possible because people remember you by this, you're more respected if you can be depended upon.

At this conventional level, Joe views trust as a truster as well as someone who could break a trust. He sees that the individual needs to be trustworthy not only to secure respect and to maintain social relationships with others, but also because as a member of society he expects trust of others in general.

At the postconventional level, individuals take a further step. They do not automatically assume that they are in a society in which they need the friendship and respect of other individuals.

Instead they consider why any society or social relationship presupposes trust, and why the individual, if he or she is to contract into society, must be trustworthy. At age 24, Joe is postconventional in his explanation of why a promise should be kept:

I think human relationships in general are based on trust, on believing in other individuals. If you have no way of believing in someone else, you can't deal with anyone else and it becomes every man for himself. Everything you do in a day's time is related to somebody else and if you can't deal on a fair basis, you have chaos.

We have defined a postconventional moral perspective in terms of the individual's reasons *why* something is right or wrong. We need to illustrate this perspective as it enters into making an actual decision or defining *what is right.* The postconventional person is aware of the moral point of view that each individual in a moral conflict situation ought to adopt. Rather than defining expectations and obligations from the standpoint of societal roles, as someone at the conventional level would, the postconventional individual holds that persons in these roles should orient to a "moral point of view." While the postconventional moral viewpoint does also recognize fixed legal-social obligations, recognition of moral obligations may take priority when the moral and legal viewpoints conflict.

At age 24 Joe reflects the postconventional moral point of view as a decision-making perspective in response to Heinz's dilemma about stealing a drug to save his wife (see "The Nine Hypothetical Dilemmas," Appendix B):

It is the husband's duty to save his wife. The fact that her life is in danger transcends every other standard you might use to judge his action. Life is more important than property.

Q.—*Suppose it were a friend, not his wife?*
A.—I don't think that would be much different from a moral point of view. It's still a human being in danger.

Q.—*Suppose it were a stranger?*
A.—To be consistent, yes, from a moral standpoint.

Q.—*What is this moral standpoint?*
A.—I think every individual has a right to live and if there is a way of saving an individual, he should be saved.

Q.—*Should the judge punish the husband?*
A.—Usually the moral and the legal standpoints coincide. Here they conflict. The judge should weigh the moral standpoint more heavily but preserve the legal law in punishing Heinz lightly.

Social Perspectives of the Six Stages

This section will explain the differences in social perspective at each moral stage within each of the three levels. It will attempt to show how the second stage in each level completes the development of the social perspective entered at the first stage of the level.

We will start with the easiest pair of stages to explain in this way—Stages 3 and 4, comprising the conventional level. In the preceding section we quoted the isolated-individual perspective of Stages 1 and 2 and contrasted it with Joe's full-fledged member-of-society perspective at age 17, a perspective which is Stage 4. Joe's statements about the importance of trust in dealing with others clearly reflect the perspective of someone taking the point of view of the social system. The social perspective at Stage 3 is less aware of society's point of view or of the good of the whole of society. As an example of Stage 3, let us consider Andy's response to a dilemma about whether to tell your father about a brother's disobedience after the brother has confided in you.

He should think of his brother, but it's more important to be a good son. Your father has done so much for you. I'd have a conscience if I didn't tell, more than to my brother, because my father couldn't trust me. My brother would understand; our father has done so much for him, too.

Andy's perspective is not based on a social system. It is rather one in which he has two relationships: one to his brother, one to his father. His father as authority and helper comes first. Andy expects his brother to share this perspective, but as someone else centered on their father. There is no reference to the organization of the family in general. Being a good son is said to be more important not because it is a more important role in the eyes of, or in terms of, society as a whole or even in terms of the family as a system. The Stage 3 member-of-a-group perspective is that of the average good person, not that of society or an institution as a whole. The Stage 3 perspective sees things from the point of view of shared relationships between two or more individuals—relations of caring, trust, respect, and so on—rather than from the viewpoint of institutional wholes. In summary, whereas the Stage 4 member-of-society perspective is a "system" perspective, the Stage 3 perspective is that of a participant in a shared relationship or shared group.

Let us turn to the preconventional level. Whereas Stage 1 involves only the concrete individual's point of view, Stage 2 is aware of a number of other individuals, each having other points of view. At Stage 2, in serving my interests I anticipate the other person's reaction, negative or positive, and he or she anticipates mine. Unless we make a deal, we each will put our own point of view first. If we make a deal, each of us will do something for the other.

The shift from Stage 1 to Stage 2 is shown by the following change in another subject's response between age 10 and age 13 to a question about whether an older brother should tell his father about a younger brother's misdeed, revealed in confidence. At 10, the subject gives a Stage 1 answer:

> In one way it was right to tell because his father might beat him up. In another way it's wrong because his brother will beat him up if he tells.

At age 13, he has moved to Stage 2:

> The brother should not tell or he'll get his brother in trouble. If he wants his brother to keep quiet for him sometime, he'd better not squeal now.

In the second response, there is an extension of concern to the brother's welfare as it affects the subject's own interests through anticipated exchange. There is a much clearer picture of the brother's point of view and its relationship to his own.

Turning to the postconventional level, a typical Stage 5 orientation distinguishes between a moral point of view and a legal point of view but finds it difficult to define a moral perspective independent of contractual-legal rights. Joe, an advanced Stage 5, says with regard to Heinz's dilemma of whether to steal the drug to save his wife:

> Usually the moral and the legal standpoints coincide. Here they conflict. The judge should weigh the moral standpoint more.

For Joe, the moral point of view is not yet something prior to the legal point of view. Both law and morality for Joe derive from individual rights and values, and both are more or less on an equal plane. At Stage 6, obligation is defined in terms of universal ethical principles of justice. Here is a Stage 6 response to Heinz's dilemma:

> It is wrong legally but right morally. Systems of law are valid only insofar as they reflect the sort of moral law all rational people can accept. One must consider the personal justice involved, which is the root of the social contract. The ground of creating a society is individual justice, the right of every person to an equal consideration of his claims in every situation, not

just those which can be codified in law. Personal justice means, "Treat each person as an end, not a means."

This response indicates a very clear awareness of a moral point of view based on a principle ("Treat each person as an end, not a means") which is more basic than, and from which one can derive, the sociolegal point of view.

Four Moral Orientations and the Shift Toward Greater Equilibrium Within Stages

In discussing social perspectives we have not differentiated *perception* of social fact (role-taking) from *prescription* of the right or good (moral judgment). What are the distinctive features of stages of moral judgment as opposed to social perspective in general?

To define the distinctively moral, we now turn to the moral categories analyzed by moral philosophy. These include "modal" categories (such as rights, duties, the morally approvable, responsibility) and "element" categories (such as welfare, liberty, equality, reciprocity, rules and social order). In describing moral philosophic theories by type, it is customary to analyze the primary moral categories of the theory from which the other categories derive. There are four possible groups of primary categories called *moral* orientations. Found at each of our moral stages, they define four kinds of decisional strategies, each focusing on one of four universal elements in any social situation. These orientations and elements are as follows:

1. *Normative order:* Orientation to prescribed rules and roles of the social or moral order. The basic considerations in decision making center on the element of *rules.*
2. *Utility consequences:* Orientation to the good or bad *welfare consequences* of action in the situation for others and/or the self.
3. *Justice or fairness:* Orientation to *relations* of liberty, equality, reciprocity, and contract between persons.
4. *Ideal-self:* Orientation to an image of actor as a *good self,* or as someone with conscience, and to the self's motives or virtue (relatively independent of approval from others).

In defining the distinctively moral, some writers stress the concept of rule and respect for rules (Kant, Durkheim, Piaget). Others identify morality with a consideration of welfare consequences to others (Mill, Dewey). Still others identify morality with an idealized moral self (Bradley, Royce, Baldwin). Finally, some (Rawls, and myself) identify morality with justice. In fact, individual persons may use any one or all of these moral orientations. As an example, we have the following orientations to the property issue at Stage 3:

Why shouldn't you steal from a store, anyway?

1. *Normative order:* It's always wrong to steal. If you start breaking rules of stealing, everything would go to pieces.
2. *Utilitarian:* You're hurting other people. The storeowner has a family to support.
3. *Justice:* The storeowner worked hard for the money and you didn't. Why should you have it?
4. *Ideal-self:* A person who isn't honest isn't worth much. Stealing and cheating are both the same, they are both dishonesty.

While all orientations may be used by an individual, my colleagues and I claim that the most essential structure of morality is a justice structure. Moral situations are ones of conflict of perspectives or interest; justice principles are concepts for resolving these conflicts, for giving each his or her due. In one sense, justice can refer to all four orientations. Sustaining law and order may be seen as justice (normative order), and maximizing the welfare of the group may be seen as justice (utility consequences). In the end, however, the core of justice is the *distribution of rights and duties regulated by concepts of equality and reciprocity.* Justice recognized as a "balance" or equilibrium corresponds to the structural moving equilibrium described by Piaget on logic (1967). Justice is the normative logic, the equilibrium, of social actions and relations.

A person's sense of justice is what is most distinctively and fundamentally moral. One can act morally and question all rules, one may act morally and question the greater good, but one cannot act morally and question the need for justice.

What are the actual developmental findings regarding the four moral orientations? And do they support our theory's assertion of the primacy of justice? A partial answer comes from our longitudinal data. For this purpose, we group the normative order and utilitarian orientations as interpenetrating to form Type A at each stage. Type B focuses on the interpenetration of the justice orientation with an ideal-self orientation. Type A makes judgments more descriptively and predictively, in terms of the given "out there." Type B makes judgments more prescriptively, in terms of what ought to be, of what is internally accepted by the self. A Type B orientation presupposes both awareness of rules and a judgment of their fairness.

Our longitudinal data indeed support the notion that the two types are relatively clear substages. The B substage is more mature than the A substage in the sense that a 3A may move to 3B, but a 3B can never move to 3A (though he or she may move to 4A). Individuals can skip the B substage, that is, move from 3A to 4A; but if they change substage, it is always from A to B. In a sense, then, the B substage is a consolidation or equilibration of the social perspective first elaborated at the A substage. B's are more balanced in perspective. A 3A decides in terms of What does a good husband do? What does a wife expect? A 3B decides in terms of What does a husband who is a partner in a good mutual relationship do? What does each spouse expect of the other? Both sides of the equation are balanced; this is fairness. At 4A, the subject decides in terms of the questions What does the system demand? At 4B the subject asks, What does the individual in the system demand as well as the system, and what is a solution that strikes a balance? Thus, a 4B upholds a system, but it is a "democratic" system with individual rights.

Because of this balance, B's are more prescriptive or internal, centering more on their judgments of what ought to be. They are also more universalistic, that is, more willing to carry the boundaries of value categories, like the value of life, to their logical conclusion. As an example, a Stage 3 subject responded to Heinz's drug-stealing dilemma by giving a standard A response, "A good husband would love his wife enough to do it." Asked whether a friend would steal a drug for a friend, he said, "No, a friend isn't that close that he has to risk stealing." He then added, "But when I think about it, that doesn't seem fair, his friend has just as much right to live as his wife."

Here we see a tendency, based on an orientation to justice, to universalize obligation to life and to distinguish it from role stereotypes. In summary, the full development and consolidation of moral judgment at each stage is defined by the categories and structures of justice, although stage development occurs in all four moral orientations. (See Appendix C for a more recent formulation of Type A and B.)

Methodology in Assessing Moral Judgment Development

The Aspect-Scoring System

In our original formulation (Kohlberg, 1958, 1969), the moral stages were defined in terms of twenty-five "aspects," grouped, in turn, under the following major sets: rules, conscience, welfare of others, self's welfare, sense of duty, role-taking, punitive justice, positive justice, and motives. Each higher stage had a more internalized and autonomous idea of moral rules, a greater concern about the welfare of others, a broader conception of fairness, and so on.

Our first attempt to identify an individual's moral stage from his interview protocol used "aspect scoring." This was done with two methods: sentence scoring and story rating. Sentence scoring used a manual that listed prototypical sentences on each aspect in each moral dilemma. Every statement of a subject was scored by aspect and stage; and these statements were then converted into percentages, generating a profile of stage usage for each subject.

The second method of aspect scoring was story rating. Here the subject's total response to a story was assigned a stage on each aspect in terms of that stage's overall definition. Stage mixtures were handled by intuitively weighting a dominant and a minor stage of response. An example of a story-rating manual illustrating Stage 1 reasoning on seven aspects is presented in Table 2.2, which refers to the classic example of Heinz's dilemma:

In Europe, a woman was near death from a rare form of cancer. There was one drug that the doctors thought might save her, a form of radium that a druggist in the same town had recently discovered. The druggist was charging $2,000, ten times what the drug cost him to make. The sick woman's husband, Heinz, went to everyone he knew to borrow the money, but he could only get together about half of what [the drug] cost. He told the druggist that his wife was dying and asked him to sell it cheaper or let him pay later. But the druggist said no. So Heinz got desperate and broke into the man's store to steal the drug for his wife.

Q— Should the husband have done that? Why?

To illustrate the aspect-scoring procedure, we present an interview on the dilemma about Heinz and his dying wife, broken down into three statements and scored as Stage 1 by reference to Table 2.2.

Table 2.2. Aspect Scoring: Story Rating Manual with Prototypical Stage 1 Statements on Drug-Stealing Dilemma

Stage 1

1. *Rules:* Thinks Heinz should not steal the drug, since it is bad to steal, whatever the motive; it's against external law and is a violation of the superior power of the police.
2. *Conscience:* Concern about the wrongness of stealing is in terms of fear of punishment.
3. *Altruism:* Thinks about his own welfare, not that of other people, like his wife.
4. *Duty:* Duty is only what he has to do, a husband doesn't have to steal for his wife.
5. *Self-interest:* Yields to power and punishment where rational self-interest would say to stick up for himself or to try to get away with it.
6. *Role Taking:* Since Stage 1 doesn't see things from other people's point of view, and doesn't expect them to see things from his, he expects punishment for stealing, no matter why he did what he did.
7. *Justice:* Justice in punishment is simply retribution for committing a crime, for breaking the law.

Statement 1

Q.—Should Heinz have done that?
A— He shouldn't do it.

Q— Why?
A.—Because then he'd be a thief if they caught him and put him in jail.

In terms of Table 2.2, this statement reveals the following Stage 1 moral conceptions:

1. *Rules:* It's bad to steal or break rules whatever the reason, "he'd be a thief," it's a violation of law and police.
2. *Conscience:* It's wrong because it leads to punishment.

Statement 2

Q.—Is it a husband's duty to steal?
A.—I don't think so.

This statement indicates the following Stage 1 thinking:

3. *Altruism:* Doesn't focus on the welfare of the others, such as one's wife.
4. *Duty:* Obligation is limited to what one has to do because of superior power, not obligation to other people as such.

Statement 3

Q.—If you were dying of cancer but were strong enough, would you steal the drug to save your own life?
A.—No, because even if you did have time to take the drug, the police would put you in jail and you would die there anyway.

This statement indicates the following:

5. *Self-interest:* In thinking about his own welfare, he is not rational and does not stand up for himself or try to get away with a violation where it would be sensible to, because he believes he cannot escape the power and punishment system.

The limits of aspect scoring.

In a sense, aspect scoring by story is still the easiest introduction to the stages, and yields sufficient interjudge agreement (.89). This method turned out, however, to contain too much extraneous content to yield a measure or classification meeting the invariant sequence postulate of stage theory. This failure appeared in our original analysis of twelve-year longitudinal data gathered every three years on fifty males aged 10 to 26 (Kohlberg and Kramer, 1969; Kramer, 1968). The most outstanding inversion of sequence was an apparent shift from a Stage 4 society orientation to a Stage 2 relativistic hedonism in some subjects who became "liberated" and "relativized" in their college years. Based on the fact that these subjects eventually moved on to Stage 5 principled thinking, we eventually concluded that this relativistic egoism was a transitional phase, a "Stage 4½"—a no-man's-land between rejection of conventional morality and the formulation of nonconventional or universal moral principles. The social perspective of Stage 4½ was clearly different from that of naive Stage 2. The Stage 4½ questioned society and viewed himself and the rules from an "outside-of-society" perspective, whereas the Stage 2 saw things as a concrete individual relating to other individuals through concrete reciprocity, exchange, and utilities (see Chapter 6; Turiel, 1977).

A second inversion of sequence was found in a small proportion of individuals who "regressed" from Stage 4 to Stage 3, or skipped from Stage 3 to Stage 5. These inversions, in turn, could be seen as due to an inadequate definition of Stage 4, a definition which equated "law-and-order" ideas (content) with taking a social system perspective (stage structure). As a result, we redefined as Stage 3 (rather than Stage 4) any law-and-order thinking which did not display a social system perspective (for example, an Archie Bunker concept of law and order).

These changes in conceptions of the stages reflected a growing clarity in the distinction between structure and content which led us to abandon aspect scoring. Our aspect scoring was based not on "structure," but on certain statistical or probabilistic associations between structure and content. For example, a social system perspective tends to yield moral judgments whose content is law and order. One can, however, have much of this content at Stage 3 without the social system perspective, or one can have the social system perspective without this content. Accordingly, we decided to generate a new, more structural scoring method, which we call issue scoring.

Intuitive Issue Scoring

In order to develop a more structural scoring system, the first step was to standardize or analyze types of content used at every stage. These types of content, called issues or values, represent *what* the individual is valuing, judging, or appealing to rather than his *mode of reasoning* about that issue. To analyze stage differences, we must first make sure each stage is reasoning about or from the same values. We had attempted to do this with the aspects, but they were a mixture of formal or structural characteristics of judgment (for example, motives versus consequences and sense of duty) and direct issues or value content (for example, law and rules). Accordingly, we developed the following list of issues, values, or moral institutions found in every society and culture:

1. Laws and rules
2. Conscience
3. Personal roles of affection
4. Authority
5. Civil rights

6. Contract, trust, and justice in exchange
7. Punishment and justice
8. The value of life
9. Property rights and values
10. Truth
11. Sex and sexual love

The new content issues each embody several different moral aspects. For example, thinking about the issue of contract and trust involves formal aspects of altruism, duty, rules, role-taking, fairness, and so on.

Our classification of content in terms of issues also gave rise to a new unit to be rated. This unit is all the ideas a person uses concerning an issue in a story. The old system had rated each separate idea separately (sentence scoring) or else rated the story as a whole (story rating). But the sentence unit had proven too small for structural classification, and the story unit had proven too large for analytic, as opposed to ideal, typological scoring.

Having decided on issues, we then defined stage thinking on each issue. An example is the conception of life issue as worked out for Heinz's dilemma about stealing the drug (Table 2.3). To illustrate the use of this issue in scoring, here are excerpts from an interview with Tommy, a 10-year-old boy who spontaneously focuses on the life issue.

His wife was sick and if she didn't get the drug quickly, she might die. Maybe his wife is an important person and runs a store and the man buys stuff for her and can't get it any other place. The police would blame the owner that he didn't save the wife.

Q.—Does it matter whether the wife is important or not?
A.—If someone important is in a plane and is allergic to heights and the stewardess won't give him medicine because she's only got enough for

Table 2.3. Issue Scoring Stages in Heinz's Dilemma

Stage	*What is life's value in the situation?*	*Why is life valuable?*
Stage 1	Wife's life has no clear value here to husband or others when it conflicts with law and property. Does not see that husband would value his wife's life over stealing.	Does not give a reason and does not indicate understanding that life is worth more than property.

Table 2.3—Continued

Stage	*What is life's value in the situation?*	*Why is life valuable?*
Stage 2	It is its immediate value to the husband and to the wife, herself. Assumes the husband would think his wife's life is worth stealing for, but he isn't obligated to if he doesn't like her enough. Life's value to a person other than its possessor depends on relationship; you wouldn't steal to save the life of a mere friend or acquaintance.	Each person wants to live more than anything else. You can replace property, not life.
Stage 3	Life's value is its value to any good, caring, person like the husband. The husband should care enough to risk stealing (even if he does not steal), and a friend should care enough to save the life of a friend or another person.	People should care for other people and their lives. You're not good or human if you don't. People have much more feeling for life than for anything material.
Stage 4	Even though he may think it wrong to steal, he understands the general value or *sacredness* of human life or the rule to preserve life. Sacredness means all other values can't be compared with the value of life. The value of life is general; human life is valuable no matter what your relationship to the person is, though this doesn't obligate you to steal.	Life is valuable because God created it and made it sacred. Or life is valuable because it is basic to society; it is a basic right of people.
Stage 5	One recognizes that in this situation the wife's *right to life* comes before the druggist's right to property. There is some obligation to steal for anyone dying; everyone has a right to live and to be saved.	Everyone or society logically and morally must place each person's individual right to life before other rights such as the right to property.

one and she's got a sick friend in the back, they should put the stewardess in a lady's jail because she didn't help the important one.

Q.—Is it better to save the life of one important person or a lot of unimportant people?

A.—All the people that aren't important, because one man just has one house, maybe a lot of furniture, but a whole bunch of people have an awful lot of furniture and some of these poor people might have a lot of money and it doesn't look it.

Is Tommy's response Stage 1, Stage 2, or Stage 3 in terms of Why is life valuable? Tommy does not seem to fit Stage 1 in Table 2.3, since his response indicates that the wife's life does have a value justifying stealing. His response *is* Stage 1, however, because Tommy does not clearly recognize that life is more valuable to an individual than property. He says the lives of a lot of people who aren't important are worth more than the life of one important person because all the ordinary people together have more furniture or property. This is Stage 1 thinking, not Stage 2, because the value of life depends on a vague status of being important, not on the husband's or wife's interests or needs.

Standardized Issue Scoring

The procedure just discussed is called *intuitive issue scoring* and is theoretically the most valid method of scoring, since it is instrument free, that is, applicable to any moral dilemma. It is adequately reliable (90 percent interrater agreement) in the hands of thoroughly trained or experienced scorers. Reliable intuitive scoring, however, cannot be learned without personal teaching and supervised experience. It also is too intuitive to provide satisfactory test-construction characteristics of item difficulty, item independence, written versus oral interviews, and so on. We are therefore now developing a manual for standardized issue scoring (Colby and Kohlberg, 1984, in press). This manual is based on a standardized interview which probes only two issues on each of three stories. The standard form, Form A, contains three stories covering six issues as follows:

Story III: Heinz steals the drug
Issues: life, property
Story III: the judge must decide whether to punish Heinz
Issues: conscience, punishment
Story I: the father breaks a promise to his son
Issues: contract, authority

There is a second form for retest purposes, Form B, with different stories covering the same issues.

The manual for standardized issue scoring presents criterion judgments defining each stage on each issue for each story. A *criterion judgment* is the reasoning pattern that is most distinctive of a given stage. Theoretically, such reasoning follows from the structural definition of the stage. Empirically, the criterion judgment is actually used by a substantial number of subjects at that stage (as defined by their global score) and not at other stages.

In the old sentence-scoring interview, sentences were matched to "prototypical" sentences of each stage in a manual. In some sense the new system returns to this procedure, but with controls. The first control is for the presence of the response in terms of the content or issue of response. The new system eliminates the problem of whether a criterion judgment at a given stage is not expressed because the subject does not have a stage structure for that concept, or whether it is not expressed because the content (or issue) of response has not been elicited by the interview. The second control distinguishes between matching to a verbal sentence and matching to a criterion judgment. On the unit-of-response side, this implies that the unit of interpretation is bigger than the sentence. It also implies that the stage structure of the criterion judgment is clarified or distinguished from particular examples or exemplars.

The methodology of establishing standardized scoring is like Loevinger's methodology (Loevinger and Wessler, 1970) for scoring ego stage, in that criterion items are defined by reference to their use by individuals who have been intuitively staged. The difference, however, is that the criterion judgments are not the result of sheer empirical item analysis; rather, they must logically fit the theoretical stage description.

In my opinion, this standardized scoring system goes as far toward standardization as is possible while maintaining theoretical validity. We define "validity" as true measurement of development, that is, of longitudinal invariant sequence. A more common notion of test validation is prediction from a test to some criterion external to the test of which the test is presumed to be an indicator. Using the latter notion, some people assume that a moral judgment test should be validated by predicting "moral behavior." In this sense, Hartshorne and May's tests (1928–30) of "moral knowledge" fail to be valid, since they do not predict well to morally conforming behavior in ratings or experiments. We have argued that moral stage development predicts maturity of moral behavior better than Hartshorne and May's measures; but we have also argued that moral behavior is not a proper external criterion for "validating" a moral judgment test. From the point of view of cognitive-developmental theory, the relationship of the development of judgment to action is something to be studied and theoretically conceptualized; the issue is not one of "validating" a judgment test by a quantitative correlation with behavior.

Using the concept of external criterion validation, others have thought that a test of moral development should be validated by its relationship to *age*, a key meaning of the term *development.* While our measure of moral judgment maturity does correlate with chronological age in adolescents aged 10 to 18 ($r = +.71$), such a correlation is not "validating." Many adults are morally immature, so that a test which maximized correlation with age would ecologically relate to age but have little relation to *moral development.* The validity criterion of moral judgment development is construct validity, not prediction to an external criterion. *Construct validity* here means the fit of data obtained by means of the test to primary components of its theoretical definition. The primary theoretical definition of structural moral development is that of an organization passing through invariant sequential stages. The structural stage method meets this criterion in that longitudinal data so rated display invariant steplike change. The criterion for validity for our new standard moral-reasoning test is congruence with, or prediction to, structural scoring.

The construct validity of a moral development measure has a philosophical or ethical dimension as well as a psychological dimension, that is, the requirement that a higher moral stage be a philosophically more adequate way of reasoning about moral dilemmas than a lower stage. This is a judgment about ways of thinking, not a grading of the moral worth of the individual. I claim (Kohlberg, 1971b) that each higher stage of reasoning is a more adequate way of resolving moral problems judged by moral-philosophic criteria. This claim is, again, made for structural scoring stages; a "standardized" test may be said to be valid insofar as it correlates with, or predicts to, structural stage.

An alternative approach to a standardizing measurement of moral development is set forth in Rest's presentation of his Defining-Issues Test (1976). Rest relies primarily on the more usual approach to empirical test construction and validation. Test construction is by empirical item analysis. The test is conceived as assessing a continuous variable of moral maturity rather than discrete qualitative stages. Test validation is primarily defined by correlations with various criteria, such as age, having studied moral philosophy, and so on. Rest, like my colleagues and myself, is interested in construct validity, not simply prediction to an external criterion. His conception of construct validity, however, is the notion of moderate-to-high correlations with other tests or variables expected to be associated with the test or variable in question. Instead, our conception of construct validity implies assignment of individuals to stages in such a way that the criterion of sequential movement is met. In our opinion, Rest's approach does provide a rough estimate of an individual's moral maturity level, as suggested by his reported correlation of .68 between his measure and an issue scoring of moral dilemma interviews.

We believe Rest's method is useful for exploratory examination of the correlates of moral maturity, but not for testing theoretical propositions derived from the cognitive-developmental theory of moral stages. Choice of various methods, then, must weigh facility of data gathering and analysis against relatively error-free tests of structural theory.

In What Sense Are the Stages "True"?

In claiming that our stages are "true," we mean, first, that stage definitions are rigidly constrained by the empirical criterion of the stage concept: Many possible stages may be conceptualized, but only one set of stages can be manifested as a longitudinal invariant sequence. The claim we make is that anyone who interviewed children about moral dilemmas and who followed them longitudinally in time would come to our six stages and no others. A second empirical criterion is that of the "structured whole," that is, individuals should be consistently at a stage unless they are in transition to the next stage (when they are considered in mixed stages). The fact that almost all individuals manifest more than 50 percent of responses at a single stage with the rest at adjacent stages supports this criterion.

Second, in claiming that the stages are "true," we mean that the conceptual structure of the stage is not contingent on a specific psychological theory. They are, rather, matters of adequate logical analysis. By this we mean the following:

1. The ideas used to define the stages are the subjects', not ours. The logical connections among ideas define a given stage. The logical analysis of the connections in a child's thinking is itself theoretically neutral. It is not contingent on a psychological theory any more than is a philosopher's analysis of the logical connections in Aristotle's thinking.
2. The fact that a later stage includes and presupposes the prior stage is, again, a matter of logical analysis, not psychological theory.
3. The claim that a given child's ideas *cohere* in a stagelike way is a matter of logical analysis of internal connections between the various ideas held by the stage.

In short, the correctness of the stages as a description of moral development is a matter of empirical observation and of the analysis of the logical connections in children's ideas, not a matter of social science theory.

Although *the stages themselves are not a theory,* as descriptions of moral development they do have definite and radical implications for a social science *theory of moralization.* Accordingly, we shall now (1) elaborate a cognitive-developmental theory of moralization which can explain the facts of sequential moral development and (2) contrast it with socialization theories of moralization.

Types of Moralization Theory: Cognitive-Developmental, Socialization, and Psychoanalytic Theories

A discussion of a cognitive-developmental moral theory immediately suggests the work of Piaget (1932). Piaget's concepts, however, may best be considered as only one example of the cognitive-developmental approach to morality represented in various ways by J. M. Baldwin (1906), Bull (1969), J. Dewey and J. H. Tufts (1932), Harvey, Hunt, and Schroeder (1961), Hobhouse (1906), Kohlberg (1964), McDougall (1908), and G. H. Mead (1934). The most obvious characteristic of cognitive-developmental theories is their use of some kind of stage concept, of some notion of age-linked sequential reorganizations in the development of moral attitudes. Other common assumptions of cognitive-developmental theories are as follows:

1. Moral development has a basic cognitive-structural or moral-judgmental component.

2. The basic motivation for morality is a generalized motivation for acceptance, competence, self-esteem, or self-realization, rather than for the meeting of biological needs and the reduction of anxiety or fear.
3. Major aspects of moral development are culturally universal, because all cultures have common sources of social interaction, role-taking, and social conflict which require moral integration.
4. Basic moral norms and principles are structures arising through experiences of social interaction rather than through internalization of rules that exist as external structures; moral stages are not defined by internalized rules but by structures of interaction between the self and others.
5. Environmental influences in moral development are defined by the general quality and extent of cognitive and social stimulation throughout the child's development, rather than by specific experiences with parents or experiences of discipline, punishment, and reward.

These assumptions contrast sharply with those of "socialization," or "social-learning," theories of morality. The work of Aronfreed (1968), Bandura and Walters (1959), Berkowitz (1964), Hoffman (1970), Miller and Swanson (1960), Sears, Rau, and Alpert (1965), and Whiting and Child (1953) may be included under this general rubric. The social-learning theories make the following assumptions:

1. Moral development is growth of behavioral and affective conformity to moral rules rather than cognitive-structural change.
2. The basic motivation for morality at every point of moral development is rooted in biological needs or the pursuit of social reward and avoidance of social punishment.
3. Moral development or morality is culturally relative.
4. Basic moral norms are the internalization of external cultural rules.
5. Environmental influences on normal moral development are defined by quantitative variations in strength of reward, punishment, prohibitions, and modeling of conforming behavior by parents and other socializing agents.

Research based on classical Freudian theory can also be included under the socialization rubric. While the classical Freudian psychoanalytic theory of moral development (Flugel, 1955) cannot be equated with social-learning theories of moralization, it shares with these theories the assumption that moralization is a process of internalization of cultural or parental norms. Further, while Freudian theory (like cognitive-developmental theory) postulates stages, these classical Freudian stages are libidinal-instinctual rather than moral, and morality (as expressed by the superego) is conceived as formed and fixed early in development through internalization of parental norms. As a result, systematic research based on Freudian moral theory has ignored stage components of moral development and has focused on "internalization" aspects of the theory (Kohlberg, 1963b).

A forthcoming book (Kohlberg and Candee, eds., in prep.) reports on forty studies which represent an accumulation of replicated findings firmly consistent with a cognitive-developmental theory of moralization and quite inexplicable from the view of socialization theories. The next section elaborates the cognitive-developmental view of how the social environment stimulates moral stage development.

How Does Cognitive-Developmental Theory Characterize Environmental Stimulation of Moral Development?

Moral development depends upon stimulation defined in cognitive-structural terms, but this stimulation must also be social, the kind that comes from social interaction and from moral decision making, moral dialogue, and moral interaction. "Pure cognitive" stimulation is a necessary background for moral development but does not directly engender moral development. As noted earlier, we have found that attainment of a moral stage requires cognitive development, but cognitive development will not directly lead to moral development. However, an absence of cognitive stimulation necessary for developing formal logical reasoning may be important in explaining ceilings on moral level. In a Turkish village, for example, full formal operational reasoning appeared to be extremely rare (if the Piagetian techniques for intellectual assessment can be considered usable in that setting). Accordingly, one would not expect that principled (Stage 5 or 6) moral reasoning, which requires formal thinking as a base, could develop in that cultural context.

Of more importance than factors related to stimulation of cognitive stage are factors of general social experience and stimulation, which we call *role-taking opportunities.* What differentiates social experience from interaction with things is the fact that social experience involves role-taking: taking the attitude of others, becoming aware of their thoughts and feelings, putting oneself in their place. When the emotional side of role-taking is stressed, it is typically termed *empathy* (or *sympathy*). The term *role-taking,* coined by G. H. Mead (1934), is preferable, however, because (1) it emphasizes the cognitive as well as the affective side, (2) it involves an organized structural relationship between self and others, (3) it emphasizes that the process involves understanding and relating to all the roles in the society of which one is a part, and (4) it emphasizes that role-taking goes on in *all* social interactions and communication situations, not merely in ones that arouse emotions of sympathy or empathy.

Although moral judgments entail role-taking—putting oneself in the place of the various people involved in a moral conflict—attainment of a given role-taking stage, as indicated earlier, is a necessary but not a sufficient condition for moral development. As an example, the role-taking advance necessary for Stage 2 moral reasoning is awareness that each person in a situation can or does consider the intention or point of view of every other individual in the situation. A child may attain this role-taking level and still hold the Stage 1 notion that right or justice is adherence to fixed rules which must be automatically followed. But if the child is to see rightness or justice as a balance or exchange between the interests of individual actors (Stage 2), he or she must have reached the requisite level of role-taking. Role-taking level, then, is a bridge between logical or cognitive level and moral level; it is one's level of social cognition.

In understanding the effects of social environment on moral development, then, we must consider that environment's provision of role-taking opportunities to the child. Variations in role-taking opportunities exist in terms of children's relation to their family, their peer group, their school, and their social status vis-à-vis the larger economic and political structure of the society.

With regard to the family, the disposition of parents to allow or encourage dialogue on value issues is one of the clearest determinants of moral stage advance in children (Holstein, 1968). Such an exchange of viewpoints and attitudes is part of what we term "role-taking opportunities." With regard to peer groups, children high in peer participation are more advanced in moral stage than are those who are low. With regard to status in the larger society, socioeconomic status is correlated with moral development in various cultures (Kohlberg and Candee, eds., in prep.). This, we believe, is due to the fact that middle class children have more opportunity to take the point of view of the more distant, impersonal, and influential roles in society's basic institutions (law, economy, government, economics) than do lower class children. In general, the higher an individual child's participation in a social group or institution, the more opportunities that child has to take the social perspectives of others. From this point of view, extensive participation in any particular group is not essential to moral development but participation in some group is. Not only is participation necessary, but mutuality of role-taking is also necessary. If, for instance, adults do not consider the child's point of view, the child may not communicate or take the adult's point of view.

To illustrate environments at opposite extremes in role-taking opportunities, we may cite an America orphanage and an Israeli kibbutz. Of all environments we have studied, the American orphanage had children at the lowest level, Stages 1 and 2, even though adolescence (Thrower, in Kohlberg and Candee, eds., in prep.). Of all environments studied, an Israeli kibbutz had children at the highest level, with adolescents mainly at Stage 4 and with a considerable percentage at Stage 5 (Reimer, 1977). Both orphanage and kibbutz environments involved low interaction with parents, but they were dramatically different in other ways. The American orphanages not only lacked parental interaction but involved very little communication and role-taking between staff adults and children. Relations among the children themselves were fragmentary, with very little communication and no stimulation or supervision of peer interaction by the staff. That the deprivation of role-taking opportunities caused a retardation in role-taking as well as in moral judgment was suggested by the fact that the orphanage adolescents failed a role-taking task passed by almost all children of their chronological and mental age. In contrast, children in the kibbutz engaged in intense peer interaction supervised by a group leader who was concerned about bringing the young people into the kibbutz community as active dedicated participants. Discussing, reasoning, communicating feelings, and making group decisions were central everyday activities.

Obviously, the kibbutz differed as a moral environment from the orphanage in other ways as well. Beyond provision of role-taking opportunities by groups and institutions, how do we define the *moral atmosphere* of a group or institution? We have said that the core of specifically moral component of moral judgment is a sense of justice. While role-taking defines the conflicting points of view taken in a moral situation, the "principles" for resolving conflicting points of view at each moral stage are principles of justice, of giving each his or her due. The core of the moral atmosphere of an institution or environment, then, is its justice structure, "the way in which social institutions distribute fundamental rights and duties and determine the division of advantages from social cooperation" (Rawls, 1971, p. 7).

It appears from our research that a group or institution tends to be perceived as being at a certain moral stage by its participants. Our empirical work on this has been primarily based on the perception by inmates of the atmospheres of various prisons in which they were incarcerated (Kohlberg, Hickey, and Scharf, 1972). Although for reasons of comprehension inmates cannot perceive an institution as being at a higher level than a stage above their own, they *can* perceive it as being at lower stages. Thus, Stage 3 inmates perceived one reformatory as Stage 1, another as Stage 2, and a third as Stage 3. An example of a Stage 3 prisoner's perception of staff in the Stage 3 institution is, "They are pretty nice and they show interest. I get the feeling that they care a little more than most people do." An example of a Stage 3 inmate's perception of staff as being Stage 2 in the Stage 2 institution is, "If a guy messes up in a certain way or doesn't brown-nose as much as he should, the counselor won't do a job for him. It's all favoritism. If you go out of your way for a guy, he will go out of his way for you."

Even more extreme perceptions of the subjects' world or institution as being low stage were shown in the orphanage study. With regard to parents, here is a 15-year-old boy's response:

Q.—Why should a promise be kept?

A.—They aren't. My mother called up and says, "I will be up in two weeks," then I don't see her for eight months. That really kills you, something like that.

On the moral judgment test this boy was beginning to show some Stage 3 concern about affection, promises, and so on; but his world was one in which such things meant nothing. This boy's mother is Stage 2, but the orphanage environment presents no higher-stage moral world. While the nuns who direct this particular orphanage are personally conventionally moral, their moral ideology translates into a justice structure perceived as Stage 1 by this boy. He says:

> It really breaks your heart to tell the truth because sometimes you get in trouble for it. I was playing and I swung a rock and hit a car. It was an accident, but I told the sister. I got punished for it.

Obviously, prisons and orphanages are exceptional in representing monolithic or homogeneous lower-stage environments. It is plausible in general, however, that the moral atmosphere of environments is more than the sum of the individual moral judgments and actions of its members. It is also plausible that participation in institutions that have the potential of being seen as at a higher stage than the child's own is a basic determinant of moral development.

A notion that a higher-stage environment stimulates moral development is an obvious extension of experimental findings by Turiel (1966) and Rest (1973) that adolescents tend to assimilate moral reasoning from the next stage above their own, while they reject reasoning below their own. The concept of exposure to a higher stage need not be limited to a stage of reasoning, however; it may also include exposures to moral action and to institutional arrangements. What the moral atmosphere studies we have quoted show is that individuals respond to a composite of moral reasoning, moral action, and institutionalized rules as a relatively unified whole in relation to their own moral stage.

Using the notion that creation of a higher-stage institutional atmosphere will lead to moral change, Hickey and Scharf (1980) and I developed a "just community" in a women's prison involving democratic self-government through community decisions as well as small-group moral discussion. This program led to an upward change in moral reasoning as well as to later changes in life-style and behavior.

In addition to the role-taking opportunities and the perceived moral level provided by an institution, a third factor stressed by cognitive-developmental theory is cognitive-moral conflict. Structural theory stresses that movement to the next stage occurs through reflective reorganization arising from sensed contradictions in one's current stage structure. Experiences of cognitive conflict can occur either through exposure to decision situations that arouse internal contradictions in one's moral reasoning structure or through exposure to the moral reasoning of significant others which is discrepant in content or structure from one's own reasoning. This principle is central to the moral discussion program that we have implemented in schools (Blatt and Kohlberg, 1975; Colby 1972). While peer-group moral discussion of dilemmas leads to moral stage change through exposure to the next stage of reasoning, discussion without such exposure also leads to moral change. Colby (1972) found, for example, that a program of moral discussion led to some development of Stage 5 thinking on a posttest in a group of conventional level students who had shown no Stage 5 reasoning on the pretest.

Real-life situations and choices vary dramatically in their potential for moral-cognitive conflict of a personal nature. This conclusion comes from our longitudinal data on the movement of individuals from conventional to principled morality (see chapter 6). One factor that appears to have precipitated the beginning of this shift was the college moratorium experience of responsibility and independence from authority together with exposure to openly conflicting and relativistic values and standards. The conflict involved here was between the subject's own conventional morality and a world with potentials for action that did not fit conventional morality. Some of our other subjects changed in more dramatic moral situations which aroused conflict about the adequacy of conventional morality. One subject, for example, moved from conventional to principled thinking while serving as an officer in Vietnam, apparently because of awareness of the conflict between law-and-order "Army morality" and the more universal rights of the Vietnamese.

Moral Development and Ego Development

As we move from general characteristics of environments to the more individual life experiences that seem to promote moral change, a cognitive-developmental theory begins to seem limited and abstract. At this point, one begins to draw upon theories like Erikson's (1964), which present age-typical emotional experiences as they relate to a developing personality or self. It then becomes useful to look at the individual's ego level as well as his or her moral stage. In this sense, ego-development theories represent possible extensions of cognitive-developmental theory as it moves into the study of individual lives and life histories. There is a broad unity to the development of social perception and social values which deserves the name of "ego development." This unity is perhaps better conceived as a matter of levels than of structural stages, since the unity of ego levels is not that of logical or moral stage structures. The requirements for consistency in logic and morals are much tighter than those for consistency in personality, which is a psychological, not a logical, unity. Furthermore, there are relatively clear criteria of increased adequacy in logical and moral hierarchies, but not in ego levels.

Because moral stages have a tighter unitary structure, it would be a mistake to view them as simply reflections of broader ego levels. Writers such as Peck and Havighurst (1960) and Loevinger and Wessler (1970) have nevertheless treated moral development as part of general stages of ego or character development—indeed, as a bench mark for such development. If ego development is seen as the successive restructuring of the relationship between the self and standards, it is natural for ego-development theorists to use changes in the moral domain as bench marks. Similar restructurings are assumed to hold in the relations of the self to values in other areas, such as work achievement, sociability, art, politics, religion, and so on.

We hold, however, that there is a unity and consistency to moral structures, that the unique characteristics of moral structures are defined by formalistic moral philosophy, and that to treat moral development as simply a facet of ego (or of cognitive) development is to miss many of its special problems and features. We believe that

1. Cognitive development or structures are more general than, and are embodied in, both self or ego structures and in moral judgment.
2. Generalized ego structures (modes of perceiving self and social relations) are more general than, and are embodied in, moral structures.
3. Cognitive development is a necessary but not sufficient condition for ego development.
4. Certain features of ego development are a necessary but not sufficient condition for development of moral structures.
5. The higher the moral stage, the more distinct it is from the parallel ego stage.

While these propositions suggest a high correlation between measures of ego development and measures of moral development, such a correlation does not imply that moral development can be defined simply as a division or area of ego development. Moral structure distinct from ego structures can be found, however, only if moral stages are first defined in ways more specific than the ways used to characterize ego development. If this specification is not made in the initial definition of moral development, one is bound to find moral development to be simply an aspect of ego development, as Peck and Havighurst (1960) and Loevinger and Wessler (1970) have. Loevinger's inability to differentiate moral items from nonmoral items in her measure of ego development simply demonstrates that her criteria of moral development were not more specific than her general criteria of ego development.

In summary, a broad psychological cognitive-developmental theory of moralization is an ego-developmental theory. Furthermore, in understanding moral functioning, one must place the individual's moral stage within the broader context of his or her ego level. To see moral stages as simply reflections of ego level, however, is to lose the ability to theoretically define and empirically find order in the specifically moral domain of the human personality.

PART TWO

Moral Stages: A Current Statement and Response to Critics

FOR APPROXIMATELY twenty years the Kohlberg stage theory of moral reasoning has been recognized as the major cognitive-structural perspective on moral development. Detailed statements of this theory (in the order written) and the various claims made about it can be found in Chapter 1 of this volume, "Stage and Sequence" (1969); Chapter 4 of Volume I, "From *Is* to *Ought*" (1971); Chapter 2 of this volume, "Moral Stages and Moralization" (1976); and Chapter 5 of Volume I, "Justice as Reversibility" (1978). In addition to discussions of various psychological and philosophical issues, these statements present (*a*) descriptions of the stage hierarchy, (b) discussions of the changes that have occurred in the methods I and my colleagues employ to score moral reasoning, and (*c*) research data which support our claim that moral development proceeds through our stage hierarchy in a stepwise, invariant stage sequence, regardless of cross-cultural variation in moral norms and beliefs.

This work has stimulated a great deal of debate over the last ten years. Some scholars have challenged the normative-ethical and cross-cultural claims; other have argued that theory and method are sex biased and fail to adequately describe and document a theoretically complete conception of the moral domain. Chapters 3 and 4 present our perspective on these and other issues; Chapter 4 responds specifically to the major criticisms which have been been aimed at our work.

Part Two addresses itself to two related tasks. In Chapter 3 we present a systematic and detailed discussion of the current formulation of the Kohlberg theory. This chapter (*a*) describes the theory as a rational reconstruction of the ontogenesis of stages of justice reasoning; (*b*) provides a discussion of the metaethical assumptions underlying the theory; (*c*) differentiates the normative-ethical from the metaethical assumptions we hold; and (*d*) details our conception of the moral domain. In addition to the above, we draw attention to the distinctions we make between "hard" and "soft" stages, form and content, and A and B substages. Finally, we discuss the nature of our current claims about Stages 6 and 7 and bring the reader up to date on recent research pertaining to (*a*) the relationship between moral reasoning and moral behavior and (*b*) the effects of sociomoral atmosphere on moral development.

Chapter 4 presents synopses of the work of various critics and our response to their claims. We reply to such critics as Gilligan (1982), Schweder (1982), Simpson (1974), Sullivan (1977), and Habermas (1979). In this chapter we acknowledge the constructive criticisms of the theory that many scholars have made, but we defend the Kohlberg theory against, for example, those who claim that it is an incomplete theory and is cross-culturally and sex biased. Our review of the current formulation of the theory in Chapter 3 provides the conceptual basis for much of our response to the critics. There has been considerable empirical validation for the theory and measuring instrument, evidence of which we briefly present now for the reader's information.

In a monograph for the Society for Research in Child Development, Colby et al. (1983) report twenty-year longitudinal data on a sample of fifty-three American males, data which depicts those Piagetian properties of stage progression one would expect in order to consider the Kohlberg theory a valid theory of moral stage development. In only 4 percent of the cases of repeated testing was there downward stage movement observed, and this was mainly movement of half a stage and less than the 15 percent downward movement found in test-retest data. There was no stage skipping observed in the longitudinal data in the three-year intervals of testing. The "structured whole" assumption of the stage notion was supported by the finding of a single general factor in correlations across moral issues and dilemmas and by the fact that, on the average 67 percent of an individual's thinking was at a single dominant stage, with the remainder accounted for by reasoning at an adjacent stage.

Cross-cultural validation of the stage sequence and of stage consistency was found in a Turkish longitudinal sample by Nisan and

Kohlberg (Chapter 8), and in a Israeli kibbutz sample of males and females by Snarey, Reimer, and Kohlberg (Chapter 9).

It should be noted that the above findings answer those strictly methodological and empirical criticisms of the Kohlberg theory and measure that were advanced by Kurtines and Grief in 1974.

Before replying to the critics (in Chapter 4), we wish to make a few general comments about the nature of their criticisms and about the more general issues they address. The critiques of the theory that we shall be discussing are less focused on specific difficulties and questions about our empirical findings or scoring methodology and more concerned with the intersection of psychological and philosophic issues, such as the basic assumptions about the meaning and nature of morality and moral development. Thus, while the critiques to which we respond are written by research psychologists, our focus of discussion will be partly upon metaethical or philosophic issues.

There are some general points of agreement between ourselves and our critics which we should note. First, none of the critics rejects the idea of stages of moral reasoning or the fruitfulness of using a cognitive-developmental approach to understand them. Also, none of the critiques we will respond to are written from a strictly behavioristic or "narrowly positivistic" point of view. In contrast to a narrow behavioristic attitude, all the critics whom we shall discuss accept the legitimacy of a psychology using a hermeneutic approach to interpreting an interview text. We start our chapter on the current status of the theory with an explication of the hermeneutic enterprise and its epistemic relations with our cognitive-structural approach. The latter framework we assume is shared with us by critics of the Kohlberg theory.

In contrast to the above areas of agreement, there are general points of disagreement between ourselves and our critics which we now summarize: (1) There is disagreement about the usefulness or completeness of a purely formal or structural account of moral reasoning; for example, Levine (1979), Simpson (1974), and Sullivan (1977) argue in this vein. (2) There is criticism of the theory in reference to its psychological claim of cultural universality. Critics starting from the empirical assumptions of cultural and historical relativism question the validity of descriptions of development made ahistorically and outside a particular cultural or situational context. Such criticism is offered by Simpson (1974) and Sullivan (1977). (3) Related to (2) is another criticism, the criticism of normative-philosophical or ethical relativity. The normative or ethical relativist questions the criteria we use to claim that moral judgments can be made ethically universalizable; this is, that it is possible to define a universalizable notion of moral maturity or moral adequacy. The ethical relativist claims, instead, that mature moral judgments are contextually relative. This critique is made by Gilligan and Murphy (1979) as well as by others. (4) There are objections to a theory which defines moral stages in terms of moral reasoning or cognition while neglecting the factors of moral emotion or volition. This criticism is made particularly by Gilligan and Murphy (1979), Murphy and Gilligan (1980), and Sullivan (1977). (5) There is criticism of what is seen as our methodological attachment to analyzing individual reasoning extracted from the network of *actual, particular* social relations or social situations in which the moral dilemma has real life. Sullivan (1977), Simpson (1974), Habermas (1979), and Gilligan and Murphy (1979) argue this point. (6) Related to this methodological criticism is the normative-ethical criticism of the direction or end point of moral development described by the Kohlberg theory. Critics point out that our notion of moral maturity, emphasizing the ideas of justice and regard for individual rights, ignores the concept of ideal community (i.e., of human caring and responsibility for others) and is therefore lacking. Gilligan (1982), and to some extent Habermas (1979), raise this point. (7) Many of these criticisms are informed by what is called a dialectical perspective. We believe that this is an overworked phrase in need of clarification. We take it that critics of the Kohlberg theory use the term "dialectic" in one of two ways: (*a*) from a neo-Marxian perspective, interpreting moral theories as expressions of Western capitalist false consciousness and arguing that the authors of such theories are unaware of the fact that their views simply reflect the conditions of socioeconomic, historical evolution (Sullivan [1977] argues in this vein, concluding that the Kohlberg theory is therefore a biased theory of moral development); (*b*) from a perspective that asserts that mature thought or adequate theories about the social world deal with continual transformations of states of this world. From this second point of view, Piagetian equilibrated stages are considered "overstructured" and it is held that there is a "more open" dialectical way of thinking that emerges after Piagetian formal operations and our principled stages of reasoning. This critique overlaps with critiques of the moral stages as neglecting contextual relativist considerations.

Generally speaking, then, critics have argued that the Kohlberg theory and instrument is applying a normative system to individuals whose own normative values may be different from those central to our perspective, and hence whose own perspective is consequently poorly represented by the theory. In addition to this charge of bias is a charge of incompleteness, that is, the claim that the theory leaves out psychologically critical components of the moral judgment process, such as imagination, affect, and a sense of responsibility in specific relationships.

In Chapter 3 on the current status of the theory, we make clear that the theory is a pure theory of *justice reasoning.* However, we are also using the theory to explore the ways in which it can be enlarged into the study of, for example, moral action or a more general theory of moral development which does take into account the affectual, imaginative, and responsibility components of personality.

Although we have organized Chapter 4 around specific authors and their challenges, we will try to be particularly responsive to the above-mentioned concerns of bias and incompleteness.

3. The Current Formulation of the Theory

with CHARLES LEVINE
and ALEXANDRA HEWER

Overview

Before answering critics of the Kohlberg theory in detail, in Chapter 3 we must present an updated picture of the theory of justice reasoning and the domain of research we are investigating, in part because critics have had to rely on what are, by now, rather early statements of the theory, such as those presented in "Stage and Sequence" (Chapter 1), "From *Is* to *Ought*" (Volume I, Chapter 4), and "Moral Stages and Moralization" (Chapter 2). It is also important to indicate which parts of the theory are currently claimed to be validated empirically (e.g., invariant sequence), which parts are claimed to be in principle verifiable but await further research (e.g., the documentation of Stage 6), and which are philosophical assumptions justified on logical rather than empirical grounds (e.g., the assumption of formalism). Part III of the book and the appendices fill in empirically the theoretical positions outlined in this chapter.

To orient the reader to our presentation of the current status of the theory there follows a brief outline of the ten issues our discussion will address.

1. The current conceptualization of the theory as *a rational reconstruction of the ontogenesis of justice reasoning.* Our presentation will draw heavily on Habermas's discussion of the hermeneutic enterprise in social science.

2. *The enlargement of the psychological study of the moral domain* from a concern with justice reasoning into a broader concern with reasoning oriented to issues of care and response in real-life moral dilemmas as well as with the issue of how these dilemmas are resolved in responsible action.

3. A *differentiation between "soft" developmental levels of social and moral reflection and "hard" Piagetian operative stages of reasoning:* Both

critics like Gibbs (1979) and we ourselves agree that there are forms of development occurring in adulthood after the attainment of Stage 4 or 5 moral reasoning. We understand these developments as being based on "soft stages" or levels of existential and reflective awareness and do not believe they can be derived from a Piagetian structural stage model. Our theory, then, has led us to accept different formulations of adult developmental change in addition to the one described by a Piagetian model of change in justice structuring. Examples of these "soft," "post-Piagetian" levels can be found in the work of Perry (1970), Fowler (1981), and Gilligan (1982). Thus, while the Kohlberg theory claims that stages of justice reasoning are hard stages of moral development extending through adulthood, we do acknowledge that our stages do not provide a complete description of adult development after, say, age 30.

4. *The postulation of a hypothetical "soft" Stage 7:* In my writings I have described a "soft" seventh stage of ethical awareness. This psychological description of a "seventh" stage, to be found in "The Aging Person as a Moral Philosopher" (Chapter 4, Kohlberg, 1985, in press) and in "Moral Development, Religious Thinking, and the Question of a Seventh Stage" (Volume I, Chapter 19), delineates an orientation based on ethical and religious thinking involving a cosmic or religious perspective on life. This soft stage is not a strictly moral one, nor do we intend that it be understood as a hard stage of justice reasoning constructed beyond Stage 6.

5. *A growing clarity of the form-content distinction.* Our longitudinal analysis has allowed us to better distinguish the formal characteristics of stage organization and change from the normative content of moral judgments. Some of the normative content which was formerly used in defining stages is now categorized as describing individual and cultural differences in norms, and it is defined independently of the formal properties of stages. Some of the normative content that was formerly used to define stages, especially higher stages, is now used to define a B substage associated with each of the stages.

6. *A revision in the definition of A and B substages.* Current criteria for A and B substages provide further characterization of longitudinal justice reasoning development. With this A–B substage distinction we have annexed the normative content of judgments formerly confused with structural definition. In addition, our new classification and understanding of substages seems to be an important determinant of the passage from moral judgment to moral action. At

each stage, the B substage corresponds to Piaget's notion of an orientation of autonomy, mutual respect, and reversibility, in contrast to the heteronomy of the A substage.

In addition to these Piagetian criteria, B substages are recognized by their intuition of a hierarchy of values, for example, of life over property in the Heinz dilemma, and of promise or contract over authority in the Joe and his father dilemma. In other words, intrinsically more moral norms are intuited by B substage reasoning. This intuition of a hierarchy is only given a logical justice rationale at principled stages of justice reasoning. However, these hierarchically arranged norms are interpreted in a prescriptive and universalizable fashion in the B substage of lower stages; for example, Heinz is seen as having a duty to save a life, even the life of a stranger, at a B substage, whereas at an A substage there is no systematic duty recognized that requires one to save a stranger's life. (Appendix C presents the current substage–moral type theory; also see "Colby and Kohlberg, 1984, in press, for a full elaboration of this theory and the scoring manual.)

7. *The elaboration of the stages as the basis of a theory of moral action as well as of justice reasoning.* In the current state of theory and research we are trying to enlarge the theory of development in justice reasoning to more effectively account for moral action (Kohlberg and Candee, 1981; Chapter 7). In so doing, part of the aim is to construct a more complete theory of moral development than is provided by a theory of justice reasoning per se.

A first elaboration of the theory comes through relating justice stage to the content of deontic choices (i.e., choices seen as intrinsically right without appeal to other consequences) in real and hypothetical situations. The fact that on some dilemmas Stage 5 subjects consensually agree on one choice of action allows us to relate structure to content as one way of accounting for observed relations between justice stage and action.

A second elaboration of the theory recognizes the relevance of judgments of responsibility made in addition to deontic justice judgments. Independent of which content choice is made, there is observed a monotonic increase in consistency between actions and subjects' deontic choices, and we see this increased consistency of judgment with action at higher stages as due to differences in the way in which judgments of responsibility are made at each stage.

8. *The study of socio-moral atmosphere.* A third elaboration of the theory to account for moral action is its sociological extension into

an analysis of moral atmosphere, that is, into an analysis of the collective norms of a group or community. Certain norms not only are held as individual norms of judgment, transformed through socialization by the development of the Kohlberg stages but are also explicitly shared by members of a group. These norms can be defined as having a certain level of collective agreement behind them, their own phase of group institutionalization, and finally, as being based upon their own modal stage of justification and interpretation. This moral atmosphere analysis allows us to explain action patterns more or less common to a group.

9. *The attenuation of claims about Stage 6 justice reasoning.* We no longer claim that our empirical work has succeeded in defining the nature of a sixth and highest stage of moral judgment. The existence and nature of such a stage is, at this moment, a matter of theoretical and philosophical speculation and further empirical data collection.

10. *A differentiation between assumptions made prior to research and implications drawn from research.* In my article "From *Is* to *Ought*" (Volume I, Chapter 4), I made claims from two types of philosophic assumptions tied to my psychological work. The first claims are a set of metaethical assumptions, the second, a set of normative-ethical assumptions. The metaethical assumptions are retained today and are briefly outlined as follows:

a. The assumption of value relevance implies that moral concepts are not to be understood as value neutral but are to be treated as normative, positive, or value relevant.

b. The assumption of phenomenalism implies reference to conscious processes.

c. The assumption of universalism implies that moral development has some features to be found in any culture or subculture and is not be defined in a totally value-relative way.

d. Prescriptivism is the idea that one ought or should do something, not simply the idea that one would do it. Prescriptivism implies that the domain of "ought" statements is not fully reducible to the domain of factual judgments. This concept runs together with the ideal of moral universalizability.

e. Cognitivism or rationalism is the idea that moral judgments are not reducible to, nor directly expressive of, emotive statements but, rather, describe reasoning or reasons for action where reasons are different from motives.

f. Formalism is the notion that there are formal qualities of moral judgments that can be defined or argued upon regardless of whether or not agreement exists on substantive matters.

g. The assumption of principledness implies that moral judgments rest on the application of general rules and principles. They are not simply evaluations of particular actions.

h. The assumption of constructivism implies that moral judgments or principles are human constructions generated in social interaction. They are neither innate propositions known *a priori* nor empirical generalizations of facts in the world.

i. These assumptions lead to a corollary assumption of the primacy of justice. We say that *moral* judgments or principles have the central function of resolving interpersonal or social conflicts, that is, conflicts of claims or rights. Such judgments must also define duties relative to these rights. Thus, moral judgments and principles imply a notion of equilibrium, balancing, or reversibility of claims. In this sense they ultimately involve some references to justice, at least insofar as they define "hard" structural stages.

These metaethical assumptions are made prior to research, and they have helped us to orient ourselves to the empirical study of moral development as justice reasoning. It should be noted that at a philosophical level these assumptions remain controversial, but their use has led to the discovery of empirical findings which seem to justify their continued use.

In addition to the above metaethical assumptions, there is another set of assumptions that we have employed in our work, assumptions that are *normative-ethical* in nature. For example, our claim that a sixth and highest stage of reasoning defines morally adequate principles and that each higher stage is a movement toward fulfilling Stage 6 criteria for just resolutions of moral conflict constitutes one such normative-ethical assumption.

I argue in "From *Is* to *Ought*" that my psychological research can be seen as having an impact on resolving philosophical controversies over normative-ethical claims. However, this claim of mine is itself highly controversial, and it should be emphasized that agreement with it is not required for fruitful psychological theorizing about the nature and process of moral development in general. The normative-ethical claims I make certainly need not be accepted by other psychologists interested in doing research within the cognitive-structural paradigm. However, such psychologists do need to understand the Kohlberg stage theory as a rational reconstruction of the ontogenesis of justice reasoning, and thus, they should be aware of the normative-ethical assumptions it employs.

We will now treat in greater detail the current status of the theory. Our discussion of the various issues will follow the order listed above.

The Theory as a Rational Reconstruction of the Ontogenesis of Justice Reasoning

We begin with the following synopsis of Habermas's article "Interpretative Social Science versus Hermeneuticism" (see Haan, et al., 1983), elaborating and clarifying what he says about the Kohlberg theory. In general we agree with his statements regarding the nature of both the theory and the methodology. We present Habermas's thought rather fully here because its philosophy of social science, the rational reconstruction of ontogenesis, is perhaps unfamiliar to North American thinking, thinking which is often grounded in logical positivism. We believe that Habermas's views are useful, and perhaps crucial, in understanding my perspective and the current status of the theory.

Habermas starts by contrasting "extreme hermeneuticism" with positivism as approaches to social science methodology.

> Extreme hermeneuticism is represented by Gadamar (1975), who argued that social scientific study is basically a matter of interpretation of particular works or "texts" no different than the interpretation practiced in the humanities in fields of study like literary criticism or history. In complementary contrast, positivists hold that there are no general problems of interpretation in social science, there are only issues of "operationalizing theoretical terms, tests of the validity and reliability of particular tests or instruments, and the prevention of experimenter or observer bias in these tests. Recently much social science has taken an interpretative turn, embracing such phenomenological and particularistic modes of interpretation as ethnomethodology. [Habermas, 1983, p. 251.]

Habermas correctly states that our theory and observations lie in this more interpretative vein. We claim, however, that though the study of moral judgments rests on particular acts of interpretation, one can still make a meaningful general social science theory of moral judgment, a view with which Habermas agrees.

In his article, Habermas contrasts the act of interpreting a sentence, such as one in a moral judgment interview, with the act of observing and predicting the sentence as an acoustical pattern or as a behavior.* Habermas says that when doing interpretative social science one must enter with an attitude of communication between the observer and the observed; that is, one must "join a conversation." Interpretation, the hermeneutic art, rests on trying to come to agreement *with* another member of a speech-community who is *expressing his or her belief about something* in the world.

In "How to Interview" (see Part I of Colby and Kohlberg, 1984, in press) the relevance of the hermeneutic posture to the Kohlberg theory and methodology is brought out in several ways. First, "Stages are not boxes for classifying and evaluating persons. The attitude of boxing is reflected in thinking of persons who display Stage 2 thinking as 'manipulators,' 'instrumental egoists,' etc. When we call thinking Stage 2 we do not mean that persons displaying Stage 2 thinking are egoistic or manipulative, for they have as genuine a concern about rightness or fairness as do individuals thinking at Stage 5. Knowing that someone's thinking is Stage 2 is not to say that the person does not behave fairly or morally, it is to recognize his sense of rightness and fairness, to *help* understand his point of view. A good moral judgment interviewer or scorer, like a good counsellor, begins his study by seeing the world through the interviewee's eyes." In other words, as Habermas (Haan et al., 1983) says, "Only to the extent that the interpreter grasps the reasons that allow the author's utterance to appear as rational does he understand what the author could have meant. Thus the interpreter understands the meaning of his text only to the extent that he sees why the author felt himself entitled to put forward as true certain assertions, to recognize as right certain values and norms, to express as sincere certain experiences" (Habermas, 1983, p. 257).

Let us now dovetail Habermas's hermeneutic conception with our cognitive-structural approach. The first meaning of cognitive for us is that observations of others are made phenomenologically, that is, by attempting to take the role of the other, to see things from his or

---

*The positivistic refusal to treat sentences as moral judgments to be interpreted as communications is indicated by an interchange in the early 1960s when I was teaching at Yale, then still a bulwark of behaviorism. I gave a colloquium on my research on moral judgment development and played a tape of children's responses to the Heinz dilemma representing different stages. At the conclusion of the tape, one listener asked, "Why did you present us with these examples of verbal behavior?" At issue was not only a certain cynicism about the relation of moral reasoning to moral action but a refusal to accept that the study of either moral reasoning or moral action could yield reliable knowledge if it was based on an interpretative attitude.

her conscious viewpoint. Second, we mean by cognitive that interviewing and scoring are acts of "interpreting a text" around some shared philosophic categories of meaning. Insofar as each of us has been through the moral stages and has held the viewpoint of each stage, we should be able to put ourselves in the internal framework of a given stage. To understand others, to put oneself in the framework of others, is to be able to generate from their statements other statements that they can or do make from this framework, not because we are imposing upon them a framework to predict future speech acts, but because we can organize the world as they do; that is, for the moment we can share their meanings. Both of these tenets are implied in the example of analyzing the structure of Aristotle's philosophy. We may classify Aristotle's philosophy into a general type (e.g., naturalistic, teleological, or perfectionistic) representing a class of philosophies, but such a type classification makes sense only after we have traced out the pattern of Aristotle's thought and seen nature and human culture through his eyes. As William James once remarked, "Building up an author's meaning out of separate texts means nothing, unless you have first grasped the centre of his vision by an act of imagination." We cannot, of course, legitimately request of moral judgment scorers a lasting potential for "acts of imagination" in the full sense, yet we should keep James's statement in mind.

"Cognitive," then, means not only (1) phenomenological or imaginative role-taking activity and (2) the search for logical or inferential relations and transformations, but also (3) the definition of the subject's structure in terms of the *meanings he or she finds in the world.* We describe the subject in terms of his or her perceptions of the *world* and its *meanings* for him or her, *not* in terms of words which refer to hypothetical entities "inside" the subject's head, such as "the superego." For us, moral judgments refer to *moral meanings in the world* (i.e., to rules, laws, and states of justice), and to grasp this fact our discussion of interviewing has stressed the point that the interview is a dialogue, a communication between two people.

The above hermeneutic view of the acts of interviewing and scoring led me to reject as inappropriate the use of a standardized or psychometric approach to interviewing and scoring. As is well known, my early methodological approach employed "clinical interviewing" and clinical issue-rating. In 1975, however, I and several of my colleagues began to develop a standardized issue scoring manual and a standardized interview for assessing moral reasoning. The result of this work is the measurement instrument currently used and described in Colby et al. (1983). It is an instrument that we believe allows us to have our psychometric cake and hermeneutically interpret it too.

This change from an intuitive scoring method to a standardized scoring technique reflects, for us, a change from a view of interpretation as an art to a view of interpretation as a "science," that is, as a research activity employing a reasonably reliable method of observation. This "method," however, still rests on the communicative and empathic stance of an interpreter, not on a positivistic stance of someone trying to classify and predict "behavior" as distinct from meaning.

Habermas points to a difficulty in accepting social science as interpretative but still a science. This difficulty stems from the fact that interpretation is not value-neutral but is, rather, normative.

There are three consequences of the fact that understanding what is said requires participation, not only observation. One difficulty is that what is understood as a performative attitude, necessary for interpretation, has to become subordinated under the objectivating attitude. Another major hurdle is the impact of values on the fact-stating discourse. These difficulties are due to the fact that the theoretical frame for an analysis of everyday behavior (e.g., moral judgments) must be connected with the frame of the participant's own everyday interpretations (of moral judgments). These interpretations are linked with both cognitive and non-cognitive claims to validity while theoretical properties are just related to truth. These consequences of the participatory role of an interpreter threaten the very context-independence and value-neutrality which seem to be necessary conditions for the objectivity of theoretical knowledge. However, Charles Taylor (1971) and Alvin Gouldner (1972) have convincingly argued against the possibility of value neutral language in our field. [Habermas, 1983, p. 257]

Thus, for Habermas, the position of the interpreter is as follows:

Only to the extent that the interpreter grasps the reasons that allow the author's utterance (e.g., a moral judgment) to appear as rational does he understand what the author could have meant. An interpreter can elucidate the meaning of an opaque expression only by explaining how this opacity arises, that is, by explaining why the reasons which the author might have been able to give in his context are no longer acceptable to us. In some sense all interpretations are rational interpretations, an interpreter cannot but appeal to standards of rationality which he himself has adopted as binding for all parties including the author and his contemporaries. Such an appeal to presumably universal standards of rationality is, of course, no proof of the soundness of that presupposition. But it should be sufficient reason to at least look at theories or metahermeneutical analyses which focus on the conditions for validity of normative (or moral) expressions. [Habermas, 1983, p. 259]

Consistent with the above view is our own. Not only are the moral judgments we score normative judgments, but our theory, upon which our scoring system is based, is itself normative in nature. While we have argued against classifying persons into evaluative "boxes," our scoring procedure does not specify a value-neutral attitude toward the moral judgments of subjects. On the contrary, our method and our theory presuppose a stance toward the greater or lesser moral rationality of the moral judgments being interpreted. Thus, our stage interpretations are not value-neutral; they do imply some normative reference. In this sense our stage theory is basically what Habermas calls a "rational reconstruction" of developmental progress. Our theory is a rational reconstruction because it (*a*) describes the developmental logic inherent in the development of justice reasoning with the aid of (*b*) the normative criterion of Stage 6 which is held to be the most adequate (i.e., most reversible) stage of justice reasoning.

It is for the above reasons that our theory requires moral philosophic as well as social scientific analysis, though it need not claim to have established philosophic "proof" for itself. Given the need for normative reconstruction, however, is it possible to have a social scientific theory resting on interpretation which can be empirically tested?

Habermas says:

Must we conclude that Gadamer's (1965) position should be accepted in the social sciences as well as in the humanities? Should we agree with Rorty's recommendation to put the social sciences side by side with the humanities, with literary criticism, poetry and religion? I observe among social scientists three major reactions to these questions.

1. *Hermeneutic reconstructionism.* Some of us play down the more dramatic consequences of the problem by returning to some version of an empathy theory of Verstehen. This position implies that we can somehow all agree on a correct understanding of, or empathy with, a text.

2. *Radical hermeneuticism.* Extending radical hermeneuticism to the field mistakenly claimed as the proper domain of social science, giving up the claim to objectivity and explanatory power. One of the consequences is a kind of moral relativism, which means that different approaches will just express different moral attitudes and convictions.

> 3. *Hermeneutic objectivism.* Some of us facing the problem of interpretation are prepared to drop the conventional postulate of value-neutrality and abstain from assimilating the social sciences to the model of a natural science of laws. Yet we wish to advocate the desirability and possibility of approaches which promise to generate some sort of objective and theoretical knowledge. Such objective and theoretical knowledge created within the hermeneutic mode depends upon theories as rational reconstructions of the tacit meanings of experiences by human subjects. [Habermas, 1983, p. 258]

Habermas is correct that "hermeneutic objectivism" is the scientific position I take in designing my theory. But Habermas rightly points to a certain confusion I created in the past about the nature of my theory as a normative-ethical, rational reconstruction of higher level judgments. He points out that a theory made in the normative or moral philosophic mode is distinct from a theory as a psychological theory of ontogenesis expounded purely from an "objective" mode of reasoning, related solely to claims of propositional truth. Habermas points out that in my interpretation of my own theory, which Habermas calls the "identity thesis," the above distinction is blurred. As an example of such blurring he cites the following statement made in Kohlberg (1971, p. 233 [also Volume I, Chapter 4]): "The scientific theory as to why people factually do move up from stage to stage is broadly the same as a moral theory as to why people should prefer a higher stage to a lower." We would now agree that this statement blurs claims of empirical truth with claims of normative rightness, and we now restrict ourselves, with Habermas, to what he calls a "complementarity thesis" in relating normative and propositional truth claims. In the complementarity thesis, statements as to the normative adequacy of an ethical thesis like mine cannot be tested by, or be shown to imply, empirical truth claims. Habermas states, "Both the psychologist's subject and the moral philosopher take the same performative attitude of a participant in practical discourse. In both cases, the outcome of moral reasoning, whether it is an impression of the lay-members' moral intuitions or the expert's reconstruction of them, is evaluated in the light of claims to normative rightness." However, Habermas goes on to say that what can happen is that "the success of an empirical theory which can only be true or false can function as a check for the normative validity of a hypothetical reconstruction of moral intuitions." Habermas quotes Kohlberg (1971, p. 223) in this vein: "Science, then, can test whether a philosopher's conception of morality phenomenologically fits the psychological facts. . . . [However] science cannot go on to justify that conception of morality as what morality ought to be."

Habermas interprets this complementarity thesis in a way we accept as meaning that rational reconstructions can be partly tested or checked in the sense that they can fail to work in the empirical domain but they cannot be shown to be valid by standards of empirical truth. As an example, a rational reconstruction of moral judgment through stages increasingly approximating a rational conception of justice can be shown not to work if this sequence is found not to be true empirically. However, the empirical truth of ontogenetic sequence does not guarantee validity for the normative conceptions of justice used in rational reconstruction. In Habermas's (1983, p. 266) words, "the empirical theory presupposes the normative validity of the reconstruction by which it is informed, and yet this validity becomes doubtful as soon as the reconstruction does not 'work empirically.'"

In agreeing with Habermas, we have accepted his distinction between the isomorphism (i.e., identity) and the complementarity theses. This leads us to question the truth of the isomorphism claim we made in "From *Is* to *Ought*" (Volume I, Chapter 4), but to retain the complementarity claim. The isomorphism claim we now renounce states that the normative theory as to the greater adequacy of each stage *is the same thing* as an explanatory theory of why one stage leads to another. This blurs the distinction between what is empirically testable in a psychological theory with the nonempirical or philosophical claims of a normative theory of justice.

The complementarity thesis to which we still subscribe makes the much weaker claim that an adequate psychological theory of stages and stage movement presupposes a normative theory of justice; first, to define the domain of justice reasoning and, second, to function as one part of an explanation of stage development. For instance, the normative theoretical claim that a higher stage is philosophically a better stage is one necessary part of a psychological explanation of sequential stage movement. However, the psychological theory adds explanatory concepts in its explanation of ontogenesis, such as mechanisms of cognitive conflict, which are not reducible to the concepts of the normative philosophic theory.

Thus, the empirical verification of the psychological stage theory does not directly confirm the normative validity of theories of justice as reversibility, theories such as those of Rawls (1971) or Kohlberg (Volume I). However, falsification of the empirical hypotheses of our psychological theory would, we believe, cast doubt on the validity of our normative theory of justice. In this sense, psychological findings can provide indirect support or evidence justification for the normative theory, although that theory also still requires philosophic or normative grounding such as that given by Rawls (1971) or Habermas (see McCarthy, 1978).

This distinction between the objectivating, scientific, psychological theory and the normative theory, upon which the psychological theory partly rests, leads us in later sections of this chapter to make basic changes in the philosophic claims we make. The first such change we will discuss is the attenuation of our claim of having found a single most adequate sixth stage of moral development. It is true that the idea of a rational reconstruction *requires* that we hypothesize a sixth or highest stage, but we cannot say we have yet empirically evidenced it. Second, we discuss two related distinctions: (1) assumptions made in studying moral development which research could falsify but cannot "prove" versus philosophic conclusions drawn from research, and (2) a normative-ethical theory of more adequate stages of justice reasoning versus our cognitivist, metaethical theory of moral judgment which is assumed prior to research and can be evidenced in a noncircular manner by the results of our research.

The Enlargement of the Psychological Study of the Moral Domain

We have classified the Kohlberg theory as a rational reconstruction of the ontogenesis of justice reasoning; we now need to emphasize the nomenclature "justice reasoning," since the Kohlberg stages have more typically been called stages of moral development.

I have always tried to be clear that my stages are stages of justice reasoning, not of emotions, aspirations, or action. Our data base has been a set of hypothetical dilemmas posing conflicts between the rights or claims of different persons in dilemma situations. The standard questions we have asked in order to probe our subjects' reasoning have focused on issues of rightness and justice.

The focus of our dilemmas and probe questions as questions of justice goes back to the assumption that guided my (1958) original interview and study. My definitions of morality and moral development were derived from R. M. Hare's (1963) neo-Kantian definition of morality, phrased in formal terms. According to Hare, essential to the moral quality of a judgment was that it was (*a*) prescriptive, a categorical obligation to act, and (*b*) universalizable, a point of view which any human being could or should adopt in reaction to the dilemma. In this formal sense, I said in 1958 that moral development consisted of the growing differentiation of prescriptive and universalizable moral judgments from aesthetic and prudential judgments.

Preconventional moral judgment, I said, did not differentiate between "rights and shoulds" as prudential hypothetical imperatives and "moral rights and shoulds" as categorical imperatives or prescriptions. In other words, I assumed that the core of morality and moral development was deontological; that is, it was a matter of rights and duties or prescriptions. My assumption about the deontological form of mature moral judgment was associated with the assumption that the core of deontological morality was justice or principles of justice. My assumption concerning the centrality of justice derived directly from Piaget's (1932) own study of the development of moral judgment and reasoning.

In *The Moral Judgment of the Child* Piaget assumed morality to be a matter of justice, and he defined morality as respect for rules and as the fair application of rules to those persons constructing them as well as to those persons to whom the rules applied. In defining morality as an attitude of respect for persons and respect for rules, Piaget aligns himself with Kant (1949). At the heart of the Kantian notion of morality was the notion of respect for persons, that is, the categorical imperative to treat each person as an end, not as a means. However, Piaget, unlike Kant, thought there were two moralities of justice, not one. Children first developed a heteronomous morality of absolute obedience to rules and adult authority, and then a second morality of autonomous mutual respect between equals and of respect for rules as the result of social contract, agreement, and cooperation among equals. Kohlberg's (1958) original study did not confirm Piaget's "two moralities" theory. However, in our more recent work we have distinguished between two substages at each of Kohlberg's stages: a substage A and a substage B. The A substage is more heteronomous, the B substage more egalitarian and flexible in regard to rules and persons. (We will discuss this distinction between A and B substages later at greater length.)

Recently, I wrote a chapter reinvoking the Socratic claim that virtue is not many but is one and its name is justice (Volume I,

Chapter 2). In volume I, chapter 5, I reiterated the claim for the primacy of justice in discussing Rawls's (1971) *Theory of Justice,* a theory in which justice is seen as the first virtue of a society. In the Platonic tradition, the first virtue of a society must also be the first virtue of an individual, so that justice is a name for both. In reality our current position about justice is perhaps as close to that of Aristotle as it is to that of Plato.

Aristotle identifies morality with a number of virtues, not just with one. He enumerates as the several virtues courage, temperance, liberality, magnificence, high-mindedness, gentleness, truthfulness, wittiness, and justice. However, in a sense justice is the primary and general moral virtue for Aristotle, insofar as moral virtue governs relations between a person and other persons in a society. Justice is the only "other regarding" virtue enumerated by Aristotle, the remaining virtues being not "other regarding" but, rather, norms of an ideal of the good life for a single rational individual. Here we quote a summary of Book V of Aristotle's *Nicomachean Ethics,* the book concerned with the virtue of justice:

> A person is said to be unjust (*a*) if he breaks the law of the land, (*b*) if he takes more than his share of anything. Where injustice is equivalent to unfairness it means taking more than one's share of the goods of fortune. The lawbreaker being unjust and the law-abiding person just, it follows that whatever is lawful is in some sense just. The object of the laws is the interest of the community as a whole. All that tends then to create and to conserve happiness in the body politic is in one sense just. Justice as so defined is complete virtue in relation to one's neighbor. Hence justice alone of the virtues seems to be the good of others. This justice is not a part of virtue, but the whole of virtue. The corresponding injustice is not a part of vice, but the whole of vice. Justice and injustice as wholes are generally determinable by law. They are coextensive with the field of lawmaking. Particularly, justice may take two forms: one, distributive justice, which is the distribution of honor and wealth among members of the community, a distribution which is either equal or proportionate to merit. The second form is commutative justice, which is proportionality or equality in private transactions. The latter includes corrective justice aimed at redressing an unfairness or inequality by restitution to the victim which Aristotle distinguishes from retaliation and retribution.*

Aristotle's idea of justice, then, includes what later came to be called utilitarianism or benevolence, a concern for maximizing the

---

*This quotation is taken from *The Ethics of Aristotle* (New York: Carlton House, undated), pp. 271–276. The author's name is not given.

public good or general happiness in the political community. In addition, it includes notions of fairness and equity in the distribution of goods and notions of reciprocity and equality in private transactions.

The above discussion is a brief and limited review of the philosophical and psychological orientations which I drew upon to define my perspective on moral development as the development of justice reasoning. We admit, however, that this emphasis on the virtue of justice in my work does not fully reflect all that is recognized as being part of the moral domain. We may note that, in addition to justice, the moral domain also includes reference to a virtue emphasized by Christian ethical teachings. This virtue, *agape* in the Greek, is the virtue we call charity, love, caring, brotherhood, or community. In modern American research this virtue has been called prosocial behavior (see, for example, Rushton [1982] and Mussen and Eisenberg-Berg [1977] or an "ethic of care and responsibility" Gilligan [1982]).

In the classic studies of moral behavior by Hartshorne and May (1928–30), morality was defined by a narrow conception of justice as honesty and altruism, and care as "service." Modern formalist philosophers such as Frankena (1973) and Peters (1971), however, recognize at least two virtues or two principles: the principle of justice and the principle of benevolence. When benevolence is treated as a principle, it is the principle of utilitarianism and is to be considered part of justice. Both utilitarianism and fairness (Rawls 1971) are virtues or principles regulating the relation of members of society to one another and to the society as a whole. While both of these principles are focused upon in our theory and scoring system, we admit that the "principle" of altruism, care, or responsible love has not been adequately represented in our work. This point has been made forcefully by Gilligan (1977, 1982).

Since 1976, Gilligan and her colleagues have been analyzing the way in which persons construe "real-life" moral dilemmas, such as the dilemma of whether or not to have an abortion. Gilligan has documented both the way in which people resolve these dilemmas and the evaluations they offer for their own resolutions. Very frequently, these dilemmas focus on a conflict between care for the self and care for the other. As a result of using such dilemmas, Gilligan and her colleagues have defined an orientation of care and responsibility which they believe to be distinct from a justice orientation as they have defined it.

Gilligan and her colleagues found that more females than males prefer the care orientation and more males than females the justice orientation, though both orientations are used by most subjects. (We will discuss this issue of sex differences in Chapter 4 in our synopsis and reply to the critiques of Gilligan and her colleagues.)

We have come to understand Gilligan's (1982) claim as the claim that our moral dilemmas and scoring system were limited in the sense that they did not deal with dilemmas (or orientations to those dilemmas) of *special relationships and obligations.* Special relationships include relations to family, friends, and to groups of which the self is a member. We do believe that dilemma situations involving such special relationships can be handled by a universalistic justice ethic of respect for persons or rules and with the concepts of reciprocity and contract. However, we also believe that such situations can also be handled by a morality of *particularistic* relations which differentiates such special relationships from universalistic relationships handled by justice reasoning. Central to the ethic of particularistic relationships are affectively tinged ideas and attitudes of *caring, love, loyalty, and responsibility.* Shakespeare's *King Lear* is about the love and loyalty of Cordelia for her father, and the loyalty of Kent, Gloucester, and the fool for their liege Lord. It is about the betrayal of Lear by his other two daughters, Regan and Goneril. The "injustice" that makes Lear go mad is not Regan and Goneril's injustice in its strict sense, that is, the inequity in the number of retainers they allow Lear to keep after he has given his kingdom to them; rather, it is the disloyalty of two daughters to a "generous" father. In Lear's words: "How sharper than a serpent's tooth it is to have a thankless child!"

Carol Gilligan had the acuity to hear a moral orientation framed to situations or relations of particularistic care "intruding" into the responses to her dilemma of abortion, and both she and we have found this orientation sometimes "intruding" into our standard justice dilemmas. In an interview of a male 30 years old who gives an ideal-type Stage 5 response to the Heinz dilemma in terms of the priority of the right to life over the right to property, we also find a related sense of care between connected selves appearing in his discussion of the husband's duty to his wife: "There is a commitment to another person; marriages being a kind of thing like something in two bodies, and in that sense there is a responsibility; she can't do it for herself. It's like an extension of yourself." Being high in justice stage, this respondent is also able to universalize the special relations of caring to a stranger. He states: "Jesus tells of the guy at the side of the road and the stranger that helped him. He felt human and that was enough of a bond."

This and other material does *not* indicate to us that there are two separate general moralities, one morality of justice and generalized fairness and another completely separate or opposed morality of care. In our view, special obligations of care presuppose, but go beyond, the general duties of justice, which are necessary but not sufficient for them. Thus, special relationship dilemmas may elicit care responses which supplement and deepen the sense of generalized obligations of justice. In our standard dilemmas considerations of special relationship are in some sense supplementary, since they go beyond the duties owed to another on the basis of a person's rights. These considerations, however, need not be seen as being in conflict with a justice ethic; in our example, Heinz's care for his wife deepened his sense of obligation to respect her right to life. Thus, those responses to our justice dilemmas which articulate these special considerations use them as supplements to, rather than alternatives for, justice solutions to the problems posed. We believe that what Gilligan calls an ethic of care is, in and of itself, not well adapted to resolve justice problems, problems which require principles to resolve conflicting claims among persons, all of whom in some sense should be cared about.

From our point of view there are two senses of the word *moral*, and two types of dilemmas, each corresponding to these differing meanings of the word. The first sense of the word *moral* corresponds to what formalistic moral philosophers have called the moral point of view, a perspective which we elaborate upon later when we quote Frankena's *Ethics* (1973). The "moral point of view" stresses attributes of impartiality, universalizability, and the effort and willingness to come to agreement or consensus with other human beings in general about what is right. It is this notion of a "moral point of view" which is most clearly embodied psychologically in the Kohlberg stage model of justice reasoning.

There is a second sense of the word *moral*, which is captured by Gilligan's (1982) focus upon the elements of caring and responsibility, most vividly evident in relations of special obligation to family and friends. As Gilligan herself points out, this sense of the word does not include the notions of impartiality, universalizability, and an effort to come to consensus with all other human beings about the "right" decision, criteria we use to define the moral point of view. However, there are three ways in which the phenomena that Gilligan talks about are moral. The first is that they imply some concern for the welfare of another person. The second is that they involve a feeling of responsibility or obligation. The third is that they involve some effort to engage in communication or dialogue with other parties involved.

The difference between the Frankena and the Gilligan sense of the word *moral* is captured by the distinctions that many Americans make between the sphere of personal moral dilemmas and choices and the sphere of moral choice that is not considered personal, that is, the sphere captured by our justice dilemmas. The spheres of kinship, love, friendship, and sex, all eliciting considerations of care, are usually understood to be the spheres of personal decision-making, as are, for instance, the problems of marriage and divorce.

A 31-year-old American woman is asked to talk about "a decision in which she didn't know what was the right thing to do." She states: "I've had a personal decision, my decision to divorce . . . but I didn't view it as a moral problem. It wasn't. There weren't any moral issues involved really [no children were involved in her situation]. The issues involved were—was it the right thing for us? I don't really see that as a moral problem. But it was a very hard thing to decide. I knew that I'd be giving up my entire life and I'd have to begin again because it involved a geographical change and a change in work." The interviewer asked whether this experience affected the way this woman thought about responsibility. She said: "Yes, it made me more conscious of responsibility in that responsibility is something that has to be taken if you decide to take it, but you better be careful. When you get into a situation where you may have to take responsibility, think it over very carefully and know what you're doing because it's a very heavy load. It involves others, not just yourself. That always puts an entirely different dimension on things for me. If somebody is a part of somebody's life, its [a matter of] mutual responsibility. That's a very serious matter."

In sum, this woman saw her divorce decision as a personal one involving responsibility and concern for her husband, but she did not consider it to be a moral dilemma or decision. In answer to a question about what would make something a moral problem for her, she describes an imagined family dilemma. "Usually where two principles that I consider valuable look as though they may be clashing, then it's very hard to make a decision about things. When I think about things like child abuse, for example, there is the principle of family unity and the principle of the welfare of the child. That to me can be a problem, although I think in that case, I would always look out for the welfare of the child. I think that is the higher principle."

This woman defines moral as opposed to personal dilemmas as those requiring a just solution to a conflict between principles or norms; something which is neither possible nor required in her "personal" divorce decision.

At the beginning of the interview she was asked to describe herself. Her response resulted in a discussion of her moral philosophy. She said: "I'm too much of a perfectionist, I think; but on the other hand, I think I've grown in compassion and understanding. I would like to think those are a part of my character, too. Tolerant, I think, except in my basic principles; they have become stronger." The interviewer then asked what her most important principles were. She replied: "The only one I can really think of that matters more than anything else is human rights. I act very impatient with taking a situational approach to things in many cases when there is a principle involved."

The woman whom we have quoted makes a distinction between personal and moral dilemmas along the same lines of definition of the moral that we used in developing the standard moral dilemmas. She thinks that personal dilemmas and decisions are not moral in the same sense that justice decisions are moral. She has, however, given an example of each of the two senses of the word *moral,* paralleling our distinction, though she herself does not call the kind of decision focused upon by Gilligan a moral decision.

We are willing to agree that the orientation which this woman brings to bear on her divorce is a moral orientation in the second sense of the word *moral* as we defined it earlier. What is noteworthy, however, is that she makes a distinction, which we ourselves would make, between fundamentally different kinds of dilemmas or situations corresponding to fundamental differences in the type of decisionmaking appropriate to each of the two kinds of dilemmas.

Thus, we argue that it is the different kinds of dilemmas noted above that invoke different types of moral considerations. The woman's examples of the two dilemmas or decisions, her own divorce and the imagined case of child abuse, demonstrate the two senses of the word *moral.* Her resolution of the dilemma of child abuse versus family unity can claim to be universalizable, impartial, and agreed upon as right by all human beings. The decision of her own divorce does not claim to be universalizable or impartial and need not be agreed to by any other human being, even her husband. In other words, the decision to divorce, although it involves issues of moral responsibility, can not be resolved from the "moral point of view," whereas the dilemma of child abuse can be, in the way articulated by this woman.

We have presented two cases of Stage 5 or postconventional subjects who use both types of moral considerations in their reasoning. In our first case, the respondent answering the standard justice Heinz dilemma supplementing considerations of care to the justice principles and rights he used to resolve the dilemma. In our second case, the woman placed the moral considerations about divorce in the sphere of personal decisionmaking, which cannot be resolved by rational reasoning and principles aspiring to a universal and right choice. Personal decisions are understood to be culturally, historically, and individually relative, though some degree of empathy, sensitivity, and communication are required to resolve such problems. Considered in this manner, we believe that Gilligan's distinction between a morality of care and a morality of justice is a distinction held in the minds of all human beings, be they male or female, a belief also held by Gilligan (1982). In our view, however, these two senses of the word *moral* do not represent two different moral orientations existing at the same level of generality and validity. We see justice as both rational *and* implying an attitude of empathy. It is for this reason that we make the following proposal: that is, that there is a dimension along which various moral dilemmas and orientations can be placed. Personal moral dilemmas and orientations of special obligation (as we have just discussed them) represent one end of this dimension, and the standard hypothetical justice dilemmas and justice orientations represent the other end.

At the postconventional level of justice reasoning the distinction between these two kinds of dilemmas is understood. Reasoning at this postconventional level leads to a tolerance about the resolution of personal dilemmas of special obligation while at the same time upholding a general framework of nonrelative justice that provides the context within which individually varying personal moral decisionmaking takes place. We may note in this context that Higgins, Kohlberg, and their colleagues have begun pilot research, as yet unpublished, on adult decision making about the care of aging parents. The data indicate a recognition on the part of respondents that justice requires that the aging parent receive care that will insure his or her well-being. The data also indicate, however, that it is considered to be a matter of personal decision based on the intergroup context of the individual. This fact, at least, is one of the findings of a study conducted by Higgins, Power, and Kohlberg (1984).

For reasons somewhat different from Gilligan's, Higgins, Power, and Kohlberg became interested in considerations of responsibility and adapted Gilligan's perspective as an orientation to assess the moral judgments of students who were members of high school "just communities." The educational efforts made in just community schools were not oriented simply to developing a fair democratic society, or *gesellschaft,* enhancing students' rights; they were also oriented to forming a cohesive school community, of *gemeinschaft,* in which participation would lead to a sense of caring and responsibility for other students and the school community.

As a result of asking high school students "real-life" dilemmas related to their high school life, Higgins, Power, and Kohlberg found students sometimes construing and resolving dilemmas in terms of responsibility as well as in terms of justice. Somewhat consistent with the work of Gilligan and Lyons, the high school subjects were assigned for each dilemma a justice stage score, a responsibility stage score, or stage scores on both types of moral judgments. The criteria for defining judgments of responsibility used by Higgins, Power, and Kohlberg appear in Table 3.1.

The design of this high school study involved a comparison of four schools: two just community alternative schools and their two companion high schools. Samples of students from the four schools were given three dilemmas that related to daily high school life; one focused on helping an unpopular student, one on upholding the school agreement against drug use, and one on stealing and taking responsibility for restitution to the victim. In the two just community schools, 55 percent and 46 percent of the sampled students resolved these dilemmas with a focus on care and responsibility. In the regular public high schools only 3 percent and 12 percent of the sampled students focused on care and responsibility concerns.

The expectation of these researchers had been that the just community schools, like families, would develop special ties of responsibility or care among their members. As a result, they expected the decisions on the high school dilemmas, which we generally see as dilemmas of special obligations, to be based primarily on

Table 3.1. Criteria for Defining Judgments of Personal Responsibility

Judgments of responsibility go beyond deontic judgments in one of four ways:

1. Judgments which consider the needs and welfare of the other as an individual, where the other's welfare seems to be a matter of a right or claim the other has or where it is a matter of not harming the other's welfare, are justice judgments. Judgments which consider fulfilling the other's need when it is not based on a right or claim or where it is not a matter of preventing harm, are responsibility judgments.
2. Judgments of responsibility consciously consider the involvement and implication of the self in the action or in the welfare consequences to the other.
3. Judgments of personal moral worth (aretaic) or of the kind of self the actor wants to be (perfecting character), or would be, if he or she failed to perform the action (judgments of blame, guilt, loss of integrity) are judgments of responsibility when explicitly used as a basis for action. They are not judgments of responsibility when used to define rights and/or obligations.
4. Judgments that use an intrinsic valuing of social relationships, such as friendship or relationships of community, as justification for performing a moral action are judgments of responsibility.

concerns of special relationships of group membership and care. As just noted, the data support this expectation and are consistent with the overall perspective we have been discussing here.

We have discussed at length in this section the ideas of Carol Gilligan and her colleagues on the enlargement of the moral domain as a subject for psychological study. We have distinguished two concepts of morality: a formal conception of morality as involving an impartial moral point of view represented by our justice dilemmas and stages, and a morality of special obligations based on interpersonal ties and communication. This more particularistic morality we said was central to many "personal" moral dilemmas and to specific social group contexts. We quoted the response of a 31-year-old woman who thought of this morality as being outside her own notion of the term *moral,* and who defined it as being a "personal" matter rather than a moral concern. In contrast to this respondent, we think that such "personal" morality *is* part of the moral domain, a position similar to Gilligan's, and we also feel that our justice stages can be applied to this "personal" domain, or to considerations of special relationships, though this is not always done by subjects as reflected in the woman quoted.

Another theorist, Elliot Turiel (1980), distinguishes from the moral domain a domain he calls conventional; a domain which some persons seem to consider part of the moral domain while others do not. For Turiel, the core of the domain of the "conventional" is a core of rules and social regulations which are arbitrary in their nature but which provide the uniformity required for group life. An example of the arbitrary nature of the conventional domain can be seen when considering the rule about driving on the right side of the road in the United States. This rule is completely arbitrary in a universalistic sense but does function to regulate driving behavior. Other examples of conventions studied by Turiel are forms of address (i.e., whether a boy should call teachers in school by their first names), modes of dress (i.e., whether dressing casually in a business office is appropriate), sex-associated occupations (i.e., whether a boy should want to become a nurse caring for infants when he grows up), and patterns of family living arrangements in different cultures (i.e., whether it is acceptable for fathers to live apart from the rest of the family) (Turiel, 1980, p. 81).

Turiel believes that even young children 6 years old are able to discriminate between conventional rules and rules of morality and justice. He quotes interviews with American children to support his claim. (However, whether this distinction is made in all cultures is subject to dispute. Unpublished data by Nisan indicate that Arab children believed that calling a teacher by his first name was morally wrong, harmful, or unjust.) Turiel (1980) goes on to propose a set of stages in the development of children's and adolescents' reasoning about conventions, stages which are quite different from our justice stages. He interprets his stages, like Selman's (1980) stages of conceptions of friendship, peer group, and parent-child relations, as stages of social rather than moral cognition.

Given the above, it appears that Turiel's viewpoint is the opposite of Gilligan's in the sense that Gilligan wants to include reasoning about personal dilemmas in the moral domain while Turiel wants to exclude reasoning about conventional dilemmas from the moral domain. We may note that differing claims about the scope of the moral domain are not made just by research psychologists. For example, one of the high school dilemmas used in the Higgins, Power, and Kohlberg study was a dilemma about smoking marijuana, a dilemma which some American adults would call conventional and others moral.

To reach agreement in this context, we believe that claims regarding the scope of the moral domain should be grounded in philosophical analysis and corroborated by psychological evidence. As we argue throughout Part Two our claims about justice reasoning as the core of the moral domain are metaethical claims as well as psychological claims, with the latter being confirmed by empirical evidence. We conclude this section by noting that (*a*) the philosophical analysis of which we speak is not apparent in the works of Turiel and Gilligan and that (*b*) neither author reports psychological evidence for their stages that meets the criteria required to confirm a structural stage model of development. Whether such evidence of structural stage growth can be mustered by these authors, given their domains of psychological study, remains an open question for now. Some distinctions pertinent to this question are discussed in the next section on soft and hard stages.

A Distinction Between Soft and Hard Stages

Perhaps the most important issue in research on psychosocial change in adulthood concerns the question of adulthood stages. The fruitfulness of approaching personality change through adolescence using the concept of structural stages has become an agreed-upon directing premise of a large body of research. Yet, when it comes to studying adulthood personality change, there is neither clear research data nor consensus of theoretical opinion as to the plausibility of a structural stage model. It is our claim that part of what has hindered such consensus has been a confusion about what is actually being studied or measured. This section attempts to elaborate a systematic and general set of distinctions between three types of stage models purported to be appropriate for the study of adult development.

The first and most notable model of adult development is the Eriksonian model of *functional* stages (Erikson, 1963), which traces the maturing person through his or her experiences of new sociocultural spheres and roles. The second type of model is referred to

---

This section is adapted from a chapter by Kohlberg and Armon entitled "Three Types of Stage Models in the Study of Adult Development," in Commons, M. L.; Richards, F. A.: and Armon, C.; eds., *Beyond Formal Operations: Late Adolescent and Adult Development* (New York: Praeger, 1984).

here as a model of *soft* structural stages. Such soft stages on the *form* of development, as do Piagetian stages, but they also include elements of affective or reflective characteristics of persons, characteristics not easily assimilated to the Piagetian paradigm. Of these soft stage structural theories, Jane Loevinger's (1976) theory of ego development is the most completely developed and will serve as our primary example. The third stage type to be distinguished in this section is that of *hard* structural stages, stages that have all the formal properties Piaget attributed to a state. The Kohlberg justice reasoning stages (see Chapter 1) will be used to illustrate this approach to stage definition. (Other examples would include Piaget's [1967] stages of logical reasoning and possibly Selman's [1980] stages of perspective taking. The preliminary work of Armon [1984b] is also an attempt to define hard stages in value reasoning.)

The distinctions to be made here between "hard" and "soft" structural stages have been made by other writers to whom we are indebted. However, the distinctions presented here are a little different and perhaps more fully elaborated. Gibbs (1979a), for example, discusses distinctions between "standard Piagetian stages" and "existential stages." For Gibbs, standard stages involve problem solving through the use of Piagetian reasoning operations while existential stages involve self-reflection upon such questions as What is the meaning of my life or of my self? or What is human life all about? Leaving aside minor differences, Gibbs's "existential" or "self-reflective" structural stages and what are referred to here as "soft" structural stages involve an ego, or self, consciously making meaning for itself. In each case, the focus is on the self or ego, viewed as some form of totality, a system of meaning that confronts the world or the "other." This is the assumption, not only of Loevinger's (1976) *Ego Development,* but also of Kegan's (1982) *The Evolving Self,* Gilligan's (1982) *In a Different Voice* (contrasting a separate and a connected self), Perry's (1970) *Forms of Intellectual and Ethical Development,* and Fowler's (1981) *Stages of Faith.* For each of these authors, self-reflection and totalistic "meaning making" are central to their conceptions of development. Furthermore, Gibbs, Loevinger, Kegan, Gilligan, Perry, and Fowler all acknowledge a moral dimension to self-reflective meaning making. This moral dimension is referred to in Volume I, Chapter 9 as an "ethical and religious philosophy." An ethical philosophy is more than a structure of moral reasoning defined by justice operations and moral conflict resolution. It also includes a conception of human nature, of society, and of the nature of ultimate reality. Classics such as Aristole's *Ethics* or Spinoza's *Ethics* represent such total world views within which moral reasoning is embedded. Viewed in this light, the "strength" of hard stages is limited by the need to subdivide into discrete domains those world views that are, in an ethical and religious sense, unified. What hard structural stages gain by this is precision in their articulation of a structural logic of stages that will survive the ever changing growth of psychological knowledge about the self, its functions, and its development.

The distinctions to be made among the above three types of stage models will rely on the specific criteria of a hard structural stage model. In the traditional cognitive-developmental literature, the following four general criteria have been used to identify Piagetian (1960) cognitive stages:

1. Stages imply a distinction or qualitative difference in structures (modes of thinking) that still serve the same basic function (for example, intelligence) at various points in development.
2. These different structures form an invariant sequence, order, or succession in individual development. While cultural factors may speed up, slow down, or stop development, they do not change its sequence.
3. Each of these different and sequential modes of thought forms a "structural whole." A given stage response on a task does not just represent a specific response determined by knowledge and familiarity with that task or tasks similar to it; rather, it represents an underlying thought organization. The implication is that various aspects of stage structures should appear as a consistent cluster of responses in development.
4. Stages are hierarchical integrations. As noted, stages form an order of increasingly differentiated and integrated *structures* to fulfill a common function. Accordingly, higher stages displace (or, rather, integrate) the structures found at lower stages.

These four Piagetian criteria will be used to distinguish the three types of stage models. We will argue that a close examination of these criteria will allow us to distinguish hard Piagetian structural stage models from both functional and soft structural stage models. If we are successful, it is hoped that our discussion will provide the clarity necessary to reduce some of the ambiguity present in the application of the stage construct to the investigation of adult development.

The distinction between Eriksonian functional stages and hard structural stages will now be briefly discussed.* The central distinctions between the Eriksonian functional stage model and the hard structural stage model can be described in terms of three of the four Piagetian stage criteria just listed. First, the structured whole criterion means that there is a constant form in the activity described, one that remains relatively constant across differing experienced, situations, and functions of the ego. The requirements implied by this criterion are inappropriate for a functional stage model. Functional stages are representative of differing ego functions in response to different "crises" involving particular and differing tasks. Hard structural stages, by comparison, are described in terms of different structures, or ways of thinking, in response to a single function, such as logical reasoning or moral judgment.

Second, functional stage models rely on psychological accounts, rather than logical or moral philosophical ones, of the ways in which each stage brings new "strength" or "wisdom" to the individual. As a result, a functional account may be more culturally relative (though not relativistic) than a hard structural account. Hard structural stage models distinguish the operative *form* of reasoning from psychological accounts of the self's concerns. In so doing, the adoption of hard structural stage models has resulted in the cross-cultural verification of the universality of stage sequences (Chapter 5 Chapter 8 and Chapter 9).

Third, functional stages are not hierarchically integrated. Functional stages are "choices" or uses of new functions by an ego. Earlier functions remain in the background of a new stage. Hard structural stages, on the other hand, *replace* earlier stages in the sense that each succeeding stage transforms the previous one into a more adequate reorganization.

In summary, the differences between Eriksonian functional stages and hard structural stages are relatively straightforward. These differences concern not only the nature of the stages but also the focus of the theories they are based upon. The focus of functional stage

---

*See Kohlberg (1973a) and chapter 6 of this volume for a more complete treatment of the similarities and differences between Eriksonian stages and stages of justice reasoning.

models on the self coincides with the notion of developing stages of an ego, viewed as an executor or chooser that *uses* cognitive and other structures. In contrast, the focus of hard structural stages is upon forms of manifest reasoning rather than upon the ego's processes of affirming or defining itself.

We may note that structural characteristics can be abstracted from Eriksonian functional stages (Snarey, Kohlberg, and Noam, 1983). Erikson (1977, pp. 204–206; 1964, pp. 136–141, 171–172) himself has stated his general acceptance of the Piagetian and Kohlbergian models as "strands" of development that describe the structural basis of the individual's functional unity at each stage. Similarly, Piaget and Kohlberg have alluded to, or argued for, logical parallels between their theories and the Eriksonian model (Chapter 6; Kohlberg, 1973a, 1984, in press; Piaget, 1973). However, Erikson's model does not have as its purpose a structural description of child and adult development.

In recent years, however, a number of theoretical and empirical definitions of "stages" have been published that are usually considered to be essentially structural rather than functional. Many of these stage models do attempt to meet the four general Piagetian criteria of structural stage models. Although these models attempt to meet these criteria, the degree to which they actually do meet them however, is not clear. While these models do have a general fit to the Piagetian criteria, we argue here that it is not a very close fit. To make this argument, we will first carefully examine at a theoretical and empirical level the characteristics of some Piagetian hard stage criteria. Our claim here is that if these criteria are interpreted rigorously they will distinguish hard structural stages from soft structural stages. What follows first is a close examination of two Piagetian criteria: the notions of structured wholeness and of hierarchical integration. Next, we use these two criteria to distinguish Loevinger's (1976) theory of ego development from Kohlberg's theory of moral development. The former theory we see as articulating a soft stage model; the latter, we understand as a theory of hard stage development.

For Loevinger, ego development is characterized by qualitative changes in complexity as the developing ego passes through an invariant hierarchical sequence of stages. The stages integrate "strands" of personality development across the dimensions of character, interpersonal style, conscious preoccupation, and cognitive style. Ego development represents the development of "structures" in the cognitive-developmental sense of "an inner logic to the stages and their sequence" (1976, p. 11). The essence of ego development, states Loevinger, "is the search for coherent meaning in experience" (Loevinger and Wessler, 1970, p. 8).

In order to compare Loevinger's perspective on ego stages with what is claimed here to be a hard structural perspective, we will first note the shared assumptions of both perspectives. The first and the most basic shared assumption is the concept of ego. Both perspectives agree that there is a relative unity to personality, that is, the ego, that reasons, judges, evaluates, and, generally speaking, functions to make sense of the world. Second, both perspectives agree on the general requirements of Piaget's hierarchical stage model: that is, that stage models represent (*a*) a structured wholeness that (*b*) develops in an invariant sequence that (*c*) forms hierarchical integrations. Third, both perspectives accept the idea that moral judgment and character are major aspects or dimensions of ego development which contribute to the formation of general ego stages. A fourth area of agreement between the Loevinger and the hard structural perspective concerns test construction and test scoring. Both Loevinger, who comes from a psychometric background, and hard structuralists, who have been governed by Piagetian assumptions, move away from traditional psychometric procedures and construct tests that attempt to tap underlying structures. Loevinger's approach is consistent with structuralism. She agrees that the test constructor finds developmental structures, not by an inductive method, but by an "abductive" method, a sort of "mutual bootstrapping" that involves a working back and forth between theoretical reflections and the responses subjects actually give. Finally, although Loevinger has not claimed that her model has universal or cross-cultural validity, it appears that it probably does have it, in light of the support received from research in Curacao, Israel, Germany, French-speaking Quebec, and Japan (Kusatsu, 1973; Lasker, 1974a, 1974b, 1977; Limoges, 1978; Snarey and Blasi, 1980; Snarey, 1982; Vetter, 1978).

The above assumptions are those that are generally shared by soft and hard structural models. We will now discuss several theoretical and empirical differences between these two perspectives through an examination of those two Piagetian structural stage criteria mentioned.

The first Piagetian criterion to be closely examined is that of "structured wholeness." This criterion was considered by Piaget

(1960, 1972) to be the central criterion of structural stages. At the outset we shall note that there does appear to be general agreement between hard and soft structural perspectives as to the nature and conception of "structured wholeness." This general notion can be described as a conception of underlying thought organization that determines responses to tasks that are not manifestly similar. The general empirical implication of this conception is that individuals' thinking will be manifested at a single, dominant stage when observed across instances of varying content, though the presence or usage of the stage adjacent to the dominant stage may also be expected (Colby et al., 1983).

However, a closer examination of the Piagetian construction of structured wholeness uncovers a number of marked differences between soft and hard structural stage models. These differences partly revolve around the differing conceptions of structure employed by the two models.

For Piaget (1970), a structure is a system of transformational laws that organize and govern reasoning operations. This formalized governing system is reflected or manifested in individuals' actual *responses* to conflicts or problems (Chapter 5). Since it is only the formal organization of reasoning operations that defines a structure, however, one is led necessarily to additional distinctions between content and structure and between competence and performance in order to maintain a methodology that can identify the structures.

In contrast, Loevinger's scheme considers structure less as a form of thinking and more in terms of fairly stable personality functions and contents. This usage of structure is similar to that notion of structure implied by the psychoanalytic concept of character. Structure in Loevinger's terms is a hypothetical, underlying entity of personality, like that entity defined by the psychoanalytic concept of the ego. Because structure is an underlying hypothetical construct, it can never be directly observed. For Loevinger, the existence of a structure can only be inferred from probabilistic signs of it; it cannot be logically abstracted from observations of a phenomenon. Loevinger's actual assessment measure is based on categories of content, or mixtures of content and structure, as probabilistic signs of an underlying structure.

Since the structures themselves can never be observed, the stages that represent them are constructions of ideal types or illustrative exemplars rather than abstracted forms or expressions of the structures themselves. In this context, an ideal type is the theoretical representation of the stage, which itself contains differing mixtures of content and structure. The glossing over of the distinction between content and structure reduces the plausibility of defining the operations that structures were intended to represent.

Similar to the distinction between content and structure, the distinction between competence and performance is also implied by the structured whole criterion, since the structures themselves are manifestations of competence. The lack of a clear distinction between content and structure in soft structural stage models, however, leads to an ambiguous distinction between competence and performance.

Loevinger has attempted to address this distinction methodologically by counting higher stage responses more heavily and by applying an ogive transformation to individual scores. In so doing, however, she defies the structured whole criterion on two counts. First, her assessment procedure implies that individuals respond at all stages. Second, and more important, the scoring procedure she employs cannot directly test even the most general conception of structured wholeness, since individuals are not assigned to their modal stage.

Theoretically, then, there are differences between soft and hard structural stage models concerning how to articulate the inner logic of the stages. Loevinger defines her stages partly in terms of structures, but also partly in terms of functions and motives pertaining to the whole self and its enhancement and defense (Chapter 5). Loevinger's theory, by definition, addresses the unity of the self (Loevinger, 1982) and is dependent on the individual's reflections upon the self's psychology. Such reflections are composites of second-order or metamodes of thinking. These reflections on the self's psychology represent one example of reflective thought, and there are other examples we may note. For instance, Fowler's (1981) stages of faith represent reflections on the self's ethics and epistemology. Broughton's (1978a) stages of metaphysics represent reflections upon the meaning and nature of reality. It is important here to note the distinction between the forms of reflection described here and Piaget's conception of "reflective abstraction." While Piaget observes that reflective abstraction accompanies movement from one stage to the next, this "reflection" is not to be interpreted as meaning that each later stage involves a self-conscious awareness of itself or of the previous stage. On the contrary, reflective abstraction is considered to be an unconscious structural process, not the conscious formation of a theoretical perspective on one's own development.

Thus, systems of second-order or metamodes of thinking appear to represent theories that individuals construct, rather than structural forms of reasoning. Piagetian structures embody organized systems of operative reasoning where operations are interiorized forms of *action.* In an empirical sense, this implies that hard stages relate to action in direct ways. Soft stages do appear, however, to have qualitatively different organizations. While one may be able to differentiate between soft stages, such stages of reflective and self-reflective forms of development do not appear to be interiorized forms of action, at least theoretically. Loevinger and other soft structural stage researchers have not attempted to construct a methodology based on the assessment of problem solving, nor have they presented a theory relating reasoning in a given domain to actual behavior as is done in Chapter 7.

In contrast, hard structural stage models define structures in a way consistent with the Piagetian construction of structure, that is, as an organization of manifest thought operations. Such structures are those consistent, rational forms of thought organization logically related to the use of sets of logical operations identified in diverse content. This formulation of structure, then, defines the inner logic of the hard stage and it is a formulation based on the identification of the use of specific operations.

In addition to the above, we should note that hard structural stage theories rely on an abstraction from the concrete, unitary, self or ego to the perspective of an epistemic self (in Piaget's logical stages) or a rational moral subject (in Kohlberg's justice stages). This distinction allows a hard structural stage model to define stages solely in terms of cognitive or sociomoral operations rather than in terms of reflections upon the self, morality, or nature.

Within the Kohlberg model, the interiorized forms of action that the operations represent are prescriptive forms of role-taking in concrete moral situations.* The Kohlberg stage model, then, represents the different hierarchically integrated forms of the operations of reciprocity, equality, and equity. For Piaget and for ourselves,

---

* The moral stages have also been found to be empirically related to moral action (Chapter 7; Blasi, 1980).

justice is the structure of conflict resolution for a dilemma of competing claims between or among persons. It is the parallel in the social world to the structure of logical thought in the physical world. The justice operations of reciprocity and equality in social interaction parallel the logical and mathematical operations of reciprocity and equality in science and mathematics. In both the logical and justice domains, the use of operations imply equilibrated or reversible systems which we call hard structures. Both Piagetian cognitive tasks and Kohlbergian moral judgment interviews are set up to elicit these specific, predefined operations. The tasks themselves are focused on transformational reasoning. Reciprocity, for example, is elicited by tasks that present conflicts requiring reciprocity for their resolution. In other words, for the methodology of the hard structural model to be consonant with its conception of structure, it must attempt to elicit the use of operations in order to allow one to distinguish form from content.

An illustration of the evolution of this methodological procedure can be seen by comparing my early and later work. My original definition of the moral stages and the research based on my 1958 method of assessment is summarized in Chapter 1, "Stage and Sequence." There I describe how my stages were assessed in terms of favored content, that is, by holding together all normative content by stage and inferring structure as an ideal type from this content. These earlier stage assessment procedures and stage definitions partially confounded content and structure. However, the current method for assessing moral judgment reasoning (Colby and Kohlberg, 1984, in press) differentiates the form of moral judgment from the norm favored by individuals. To briefly explain, an interview transcript is first classified by the content of the choice; second, it is classified by the content of the justification of the choice; and third, it is classified by the value content appealed to in the justification. Only after classifying content according to these three content categories is an interview then assessed by stage or structure. At this point, formal justice structures are identified that characterize a stage in terms of its justice perspective and its use of the operations of equality, reciprocity, and equity. (This assessment of structure is explained more fully later in the chapter.) Thus, current scoring methods yield an explicit differentiation of content and structure.

In addition to the above, we should note that our current assessment instrument and interview method taps a subject's competence rather than his or her performance, by providing probing questions that attempt to elicit the upper limits of the subject's thinking (Colby and Kohlberg, 1984, in press).

The second criterion to be discussed is that of hierarchical integration. Hard and soft stage models are based upon different interpretations of this criterion. The central feature of the hierarchical integration criterion concerns the inner logic of a stage sequence. What is required for this criterion is both theoretical and empirical support for the notion that later stages not only *replace* but also *transform* earlier stages. Theoretically, hard structural stage models follow Piaget (1970) in asserting that to construct a model of hierarchically integrated stages is to construct a normative model of development. A normative model establishes a standard as a developmental end point. It must include a philosophical as well as a psychological account of this end point or most equilibrated stage. Thus, each stage in the hierarchy represents an increase in correspondence with the end point or highest stage. The normative model assumed by both Piaget (1970) and Kohlberg (1973b) relies on a conception of human rationality in that it presumes an end point upon which all rational agents could agree (see also Habermas, 1983). Piaget's normative model has as its standard the criterion of reversibility. He formulates an end point of logical thought as propositional logic in terms of the "INRC group."

The ambiguity of the inner logic of Loevinger's and others' soft structural stage sequences reduces the plausibility of formulating a normative model of development. However, we claim here that it is not possible to construct a stage sequence that conforms to the criterion of hierarchical integration without specifying the inner logic of the sequence in terms of its end point. Loevinger (1982) herself explicitly denies a normative model and makes no claim that a higher ego stage is a more adequate stage.*

> Who is so wise as to say which is the highest stage? Each investigator in the field has a different idea of how the highest stage should be defined.

From a more empirical perspective, Loevinger's stages are nontransformational. Rather than each new stage representing an *integration* or *transformation* of the previous stage, her new stages stem from the addition of new developmental aspects to those used to

---

* Loevinger has been criticized for this omission. See Habermas, 1979; Broughton and Zahaykevich, 1977.

Table 3.2

Stage: Autonomous
Code: I-5
Impulse Control/Character Development: *Add* Coping with conflicting inner needs, toleration
Interpersonal Style: *Add* Respect for autonomy, interdependence
Conscious Preoccupations: Vividly conveyed feelings, integration of physiological and psychological, psychological causation of behavior, role conception, self-fulfillment, self in social context
Cognitive Style: Increased conceptual complexity, complex patterns, toleration for ambiguity, broad scope, objectivity

Stage: Integrated
Code: I-6
Impulse Control/Character Development: *Add* Reconciling inner conflicts, renunciation of unattainable
Interpersonal Style: *Add* Cherishing of individuality
Conscious Preoccupation: *Add* Identity
Cognitive Style: Same

NOTE: *Add* means in addition to the description applying to the previous level.

define the previous stage. Thus, her stage hierarchy appears to be an increasingly inclusive, cumulative system and not a system based upon successive integrations. The representation of Loevinger's I-5 and I-6 stages in Table 3.2 illustrates this point.*

In contrast to Loevinger's stage hierarchy, Kohlberg's justice stage hierarchy is understood as a hierarchy based upon successive structural integrations. This property of ontogenesis has been described, stage by stage, at a theoretical level (Chapter 2; Volume I, Chapter 4) and has been documented at an empirical level. For example, Rest (1973), using the technique of Guttman scale analysis, reports that individuals maintain a cumulative hierarchy of justice stage comprehension. Rest's subjects comprehended all the stages below their own modal stage but could not comprehend reasoning more than one stage above their modal stage. Rest also reports that individuals tend to prefer the highest stage they can comprehend. These findings are consistent with my explanation of the integrative and hierarchical nature of my stage model.

* This representation of stages I-5 and I-6 is taken from Table 1, "Some Milestones of Ego Development," in Loevinger (1976).

As stated earlier, hard structural stage models attempt to define stages in terms of discrete operations of reasoning in contrast to reflective or self-reflective metathinking. By defining the stages in terms of operations of reasoning, hard structural stage models can plausibly explicate not only the inner logic of the stages but also the inner logic of the sequence from one stage to the next. Building upon the identification of operations in reasoning, hard structural stages are amenable to formulation within a normative model.

Logic is a case of a normative model. Athough different logicians and philosophers prescribe different formulations of logic, most search for one or more formalizations upon which all rational agents could agree. The same could be said of normative models of justice structures. Rawls's (1971) theory of justice is an attempt to construct a normative model of justice, as are the works of Kant (1949), Sidgwick (1887), and Hare (1982). The main activity of normative moral philosophy is the attempt to define and justify a normative end point.

The focus of Piaget and myself on morality as deontological justice springs, in part, from a concern with moral and ethical universality in moral judgment. The search for moral universality implies the search for some minimal value conception(s) on which all persons could agree, regardless of personal differences in detailed aims or goals.

Soft stages, on the other hand, cannot be formalized in a normative model. Development to the higher soft stages is optional, not prescribed. Although such development involves increased reflectivity or complexity, it is unclear whether or not some of these soft stages are of co-equal validity. The terminus of many soft stage sequences is a mystical, transcendental, or postrational level. Most soft stage models stem either from James Mark Baldwin's (1911) hyperlogic to some notion of totality or unity, or from Klaus Riegel's (1973) hypotheses about dialectical adult thought that transcends the subjective-objective distinction. These levels move beyond the criteria of rationality, autonomy, and agreement assumed by a normative model.

In sum, we have attempted to elaborate a set of distinctions between *functional, soft structural,* and *hard structural* stage models. We have argued that a rigorous application of the Piagetian criteria for a hard structural stage can distinguish these three stage models, and that only a hard structural stage model can actually meet these criteria. Nevertheless, the reasons for the success of the Piagetian hard structural stage scheme in charting logic and justice development may be precisely the reasons that it will not be successful in charting the experience and wisdom of adulthood. For example, a rational logic of justice cannot give answers to questions such as Why be moral? or What is the meaning of life? A model of rational justice cannot help the psychologist explain the unique characteristics of adult development, with its existential, reflective theories of the human condition. The *strict* Piagetian stage construction may need to be abandoned in the study of adult development, but the idea of soft stages of development in adulthood should not be. There are hierarchical levels of positive development in adulthood and this development is something other than life phases (Levinson, 1978). In addition, we should note that the soft stages of the sort described here differ from Erikson's functional stages. Soft stage development depends neither on the emergence of new functions nor on the performance of new tasks. Instead, soft stage development depends on formal reflection. Models of soft stage development describe the adult's attempt to interpret the task of metaphysics and religion, the task of integrating the ideals of justice, love, and truth with one's understanding of the ultimate nature of reality. Soft stage models present a new way of doing research in the subject area of adult development, a way that has *emerged from* the Piagetian paradigm.

The Postulation of a Soft Hypothetical Seventh Stage

We conceptualize Stage 7 as a high soft stage in the development of ethical and religious orientations, orientations which are larger in scope than the justice orientation which our hard stages address. Generally speaking, a Stage 7 response to ethical and religious problems is based on constructing a sense of identity or unity with being, with life, or with God. With reference to the work of James Fowler (1981), Kohlberg and Power (Volume I, Chapter 9) present a theoretical analysis and case material concerning this seventh stage of ethical and religious orientation which appears after the attainment of postconventional justice reasoning.

To answer the questions Why be moral? Why be just in a universe filled with injustice, suffering, and death? requires one to move beyond the domain of justice and derive replies from the meaning found in metaethical, metaphysical, and religious epistemologies. Power and I (Volume I, Chapter 9) basing our theoretical conclusions on empirical findings, suggest that meaningful solutions to these metaethical questions are often articulated within theistic, pantheistic, or agnostic cosmic perspectives.

In addressing this issue of a high seventh stage, Shulik, Higgins, and I (see Kohlberg, 1984, in press) present case material based on the use of Fowler's (1981) faith interview with a sample of aging persons. These interview responses suggest that soft stages of what Fowler calls faith and what we call ethical and religious thinking continue to chart adult development which occurs after the development and stabilization of postconventional justice reasoning. Unlike the analytic and dualistic development of justice reasoning (i.e., reasoning based on the differentiation of self and other, subject and object), ethical and religious soft stage development culminates in a synthetic, nondualistic sense of participation in, and identity with, a cosmic order. The self is understood as a component of this order, and its meaning is understood as being contingent upon participation in this order.

From a cosmic perspective, such as the one just described, postconventional principles of justice and care are perceived within what might be broadly termed a natural law framework. From such a framework, moral principles are not seen as arbitrary human inventions; rather, they are seen as principles of justice that are in harmony with broader laws regulating the evolution of human nature and the cosmic order.

Thus, in our opinion, a soft Stage 7 of ethical and religious thinking presupposes but goes beyond postconventional justice reasoning. More generally, we believe that the development of soft stages toward the cosmic perspective just described informs us of trends in human development which can not be captured within a conceptual framework restricted to the study of justice reasoning per se.

The Form and Content Distinction

Our original definition of moral stages (Kohlberg, 1958) and the research based on the 1958 method of scoring moral reasoning (summarized in Chapter 1) assessed stages in terms of chosen content. From this, structure was inferred as an ideal type which connected the normative content favored by the stage. Thus, our earlier stage definitions and assessment procedures partially confounded content and form. However, we believe that the present method for scoring (Colby and Kohlberg, 1984, in press) succeeds in differentiating entirely the form of moral judgment from the content norm favored by individuals.

Today the formal properties of the stages are divided into two components. The first component is social perspective level: for example, Stage 1 has an undifferentiated or egocentric perspective; Stage 2 has a perspective of two actors aware of the individual needs of the other, coordinated through acts of concrete reciprocity; Stage 3 understands the other in the context of shared role expectations in personalized relationships; Stage 4 understands the other in the context of a less personalized social system of norms and roles; and Stage 5 has a prior-to-society perspective. The second formal component of the stages is more specifically moral or prescriptive. Here we refer to the fact that stages structure duties and rights through the use of three justice operations: equality, equity, and reciprocity. (We will discuss these justice operations at greater length later in the chapter.) For example, the core justice structure of Stage 3 is the Golden Rule, Do unto others as you would be done by, or the prescription to choose with an awareness of the other's perspective as if you were in his or her place. The Golden Rule integrates the operations of equality, reciprocity, and equity. This move toward a clearer formalization of the moral stage definition was required to detect longitudinal developmental sequence in the protocols of individuals who used very different normative content in their responses to our standard interview dilemmas. Thus, when we speak of the form of a stage we refer *only* to the justice structure, which consists of justice operations and the social perspective taking level at which moral or prescriptive judgments are made.

Our differentiation of the content from the formal aspects of the stages leaves us with the task of defining those aspects of content which were previously dealt with as part of stage structure. Thus, we define as content the issue or choice, the norms, and the elements used in individual responses. (For an explanation of these terms, the reader should consult Colby and Kohlberg, 1984, in press) It is from this identification that we then move on to analyze moral judgments for their stage structure. As was noted previously, however, we also identify as A and B substages other aspects of moral reasoning that we see as lying between content and form. In contrast to the formal structural characteristics of a stage, these aspects that are intermediate between form and content can be considered as functional characteristics of a stage. Their appearance allows us to observe the equilibrated *use* of a justice structure. (Tables 3.3 and 3.4 list these characteristics of stage function.) When structures are equilibrated, we speak of them as B substages. One criterion suggesting the use of an equilibrated B substage can be seen in the universalization of a justice structure; that is, when its moral choice and justification are extended to *all* persons included in the perspective-taking level being used. Thus, for example, a judgment which asserts a universalizable prescription to save life on the Heinz dilemma is analyzed as substage B, regardless of the stage at which this judgment is made. We now turn to a detailed discussion of this A and B substage distinction (elaborated at more depth and detail in Appendix C).

A and B Substages

In his original work Piaget (1932) distinguished two stages of justice; a first stage of heteronomous orientation to rules and authority, and a second stage of autonomous orientation to fairness, equality, and reciprocity. Piaget also included a rules element in his second form of justice, where rules were made by contract and were considered the basis of cooperation. We view as somewhat misleading Piaget's observation that heteronomous reasoning is a childish orientation disappearing with development since we can trace this orientation through our stages. In our most recent work we have been led to define what we call A and B substages. This distinction corresponds to Piaget's distinction between the heteronomous and autonomous orientations, respectively.

In contrast to earlier scoring techniques (Kohlberg, 1958), our present method is more able to define our stages in formal structural terms. However, in describing stages in pure structural terms we noted that there were features of moral reasoning that seemed to lie midway between form and content, that were developmental, but were not identified by our scoring system. It was our desire to integrate these features into our scoring system that led us to develop the A–B substage distinction. We thought that this distinction would be helpful to us in our attempts to relate moral judgment to moral action; that is, that subjects using B substage reasoning would be more likely to engage in the moral action they believed to be just, than would users of A substage reasoning.

Our classification by substage is based on the content aspect of moral choice as well as on more formal features of moral judgment. When my dilemmas were developed in 1958, they were thought of as posing a conflict between heteronomous concerns for obedience to authority, on the one hand, and autonomous concerns for rights and welfare, on the other. Recently, a relationship between stage of reasoning and choice was found by Colby et al. (1983). This relationship is as follows: that those subjects reasoning at the highest stage, Stage 5, choose the autonomous choice for resolving the dilemma more than 75 percent of the time. In addition to Colby's observation, we may note that American, Israeli, and Turkish subjects tested on Form A dilemmas who used Stage 5 reasoning judged that it was the right choice to steal the drug (Dilemma III), to show leniency to Heinz (Dilemma III'), and for the son to refuse his father the money (Dilemma I).

Thus, there seems to be a linkage between stage structure and content choice. At stages lower than Stage 5 the selection of the autonomous content choice also occurs, although with less frequency than at Stage 5. However, we have also observed that some persons at lower stages making an autonomous content choice display in their reasoning certain formal features (e.g., prescriptivity, universality) which are not displayed by persons who use the same stage reasoning but make the heteronomous choice. We view the association of these formal features with the autonomous choice as an indication that a B substage is being used, a substage which is more structurally equilibrated and more formally moral. Thus, we score a response as substage B when it demonstrates the autonomous choice as well as the presence of certain formal features of reasoning. We have called some of these formal criteria Kantian, because they reflect a neo-Kantian notion of autonomous judgment. These criteria, presented in Table 3.3, include prescriptivity, universalizability, intrinsicality, and a hierarchical ranking of values:

***Table 3.3.* "Kantian" Criteria for Substage B**

1. *Choice:* The subject must choose the more "just" course of action or solution to the dilemma (i.e., the choice which is empirically agreed upon by subjects at Stage 5). In the Heinz dilemma (III), the choice is to steal the drug; in Dilemma III′, the choice is for

the judge to set Heinz free or to put him on probation; and in the Joe dilemma (I), the choice is to refuse to give the father the money.

2. *Hierarchy:* Reflects the second formulation of the categorical imperative: Treat persons never simply as means, but always at the same time as ends. As such, the right to life, the value of acting on one's conscience, and the importance of promise keeping or of respecting earned property (understood to be the only considerations that ensure that persons are treated as ends) are all placed above any other considerations in the resolution of the respective dilemmas in Form A (III, III′, and I).
3. *Intrinsicalness:* The intrinsic moral worth of persons, or an intrinsic respect for persons and personality (including personal autonomy), is recognized and upheld in the course of resolving the dilemma. This may be reflected in responses that refer to the intrinsic value of life, the intrinsic rights that all human beings possess, the intrinsic value of persons and personality in general, or the intrinsic value of promises as a means to ensure respect for persons and personality.
4. *Prescriptivity:* The categorical imperative also implies a categorical moral "ought" that prescribes a certain set of moral actions (e.g., saving a life or keeping a promise) regardless of the inclinations of the actor or various pragmatic considerations. As such, the categorical imperative is distinguished from a hypothetical imperative, which is not prescriptive, and thus takes a simple "if-then" form.

5a. *Universality:* Reflects the third formulation of the categorical imperative: Act so that your will can regard itself at the same time as making universal law through its maxim. Universality implies that the particular set of actions that have been prescribed in the course of resolving the dilemma must apply universally to any and all human beings. As such, human beings are understood to be universal moral objects, and the corresponding universal moral judgment takes the following form: You should act this way (do *x*) toward any and all human beings.

5b. *Universalizability:* Reflects the most crucial of the tests implied by the first formulation of the categorical imperative: Act as if the maxim of your action were to become through your will a universal law of nature. Universalizability implies that the particular set of actions that have been prescribed for the actor in the dilemma must be such that they apply to any and all other *actors in similar situations or circumstances.* As such, a universalizable moral judgment implies a universal moral subject, and the judgment takes

Table 3.3—**Continued**

the following form: All agents in *A*'s position should act this way (do *X*).

While Piaget was influenced by Kant in his notion of moral autonomy, he also differentiated heteronomous respect for rules from a respect for justice based on relations of mutual respect, cooperation, and contract. The latter attitudes give rise to reversible moral judgments, whereas the former do not. This latter distinction gives rise to several additional criteria which we use to define a B substage. These criteria are presented in Table 3.4.

Thus, in addition to content choice, evidence of what we call neo-Kantian and Piagetian formal criteria are also required to classify a response as B substage.

Our longitudinal data scored for substage seem to indicate that where there is change from one substage to another it is from A to B. However, subjects attaining substage B often retain their substage status even when they advance to the next stage, and some subjects remain substage A throughout structural progression through the stages of justice reasoning.

In addition to these developmental findings, the studies relating substage to moral action; Kohlberg and Candee, 1984, Chapter 7 indicate that substage B subjects are more likely to engage in the action expressed by their "just" choice than are substage A subjects.

In conclusion, the above discussion illustrates some of the senses in which we hold justice to be primary (see, in addition, our later discussion of "justice as primary"). It can be seen that our dilemmas are designed to elicit justice reasoning, and our scoring criteria are designed to code justice reasoning. Our stage theory, in conjunction with empirical research, indicates that the development of justice reasoning can occur in two modes: either implicitly, in the A substage, or explicitly, in the B substage. (This implicit-explicit distinction refers to the manner in which justice operations are used and is discussed later in the chapter.)

In other words, all our subjects are understood by us to be reasoning about justice. However, when subjects employ the criteria for substage B, they explicitly use justice operations and articulate them within a fairness deontic orientation. We may note that this self-reflective use of justice criteria, or what we call B substage reasoning, appears to have developmental implications consistent with our view of ontogenesis as a phenomenon that can be ration-

Table 3.4. **"Piagetian" Criteria for Substage B**

6. *Autonomy:* The response to the dilemma must reflect an understanding that the actor in question is an autonomous moral agent and hence must make moral judgments and decide on a moral course of action without determination by external sources of power or authority, using a rational and logical method of decision making.
7. *Mutual Respect:* This criterion reflects the understanding that the actors in the dilemma must have mutual respect for each other as rational and autonomous moral agents. As such, in Dilemma III, Heinz must be understood to view and treat all of the other actors in the dilemma (the wife, the friend, the stranger, and the druggist) with mutual respect; the judge must treat Heinz with mutual respect in Dilemma III′; and in Dilemma I, Joe and his father must have respect for each other.
8. *Reversibility:* The most important criterion from the Piagetian perspective (but also the most difficult one to identify in an interview) is reversibility. It is understood to be present when the judgments made in response to the dilemma consider the interests and points of view of *all* the actors involved, such that it is clear that the subject can, and has, viewed the problem from the perspective of all the actors involved in the situation. Only in this way can the subject make a decision that he or she could logically and rationally support if he or she were to trade places with each and every other actor in the dilemma, that is, a fair and just decision. For Piaget, *logical* operations are equilibrated when they are reversible; hence a formal criterion for equilibrated *moral* judgments (i.e., judgments at the B substage) must be a correlative form of reversibility.
9. *Constructivism:* This criterion reflects the subject's awareness that the rules, laws, and principles used to guide and frame moral decision making are *actively constructed* by the human mind, in the context of a social system, and are made under considerations of autonomy, mutual respect, and reversibility. In other words, all of society (however "society" is interpreted by the subjects), including its institutions, rules, and laws, is understood to be derived from communication and cooperation between and among persons. (Note: This notion of constructivism is understood to refer only to the subject's *normative-ethical judgments,* and not to his or her *metaethical judgments.*)

ally reconstructed. Finally, and as was noted above, the A–B substage distinction is helpful to us in our attempt to understand the relationship between moral reasoning and action.

Judgment-Action Research

In the late 1960s and early 1970s my theoretical articles called attention to a number of studies which reported correlations between higher stages of moral judgment and "moral" action. My interpretation of the results of these studies stressed that moral stages formed a lens or screen (*a*) through which a moral situation and the emotions it aroused were perceived and (b) through which the alternative courses of action available to the subject were formulated. In 1980, Blasi wrote an exhaustive review of the literature and concluded that the majority of studies using the Kohlberg stage measure reported correlations between relatively high stage moral judgment and what is commonly called moral behavior, including such dimensions as honesty, resistance to temptation, and altruistic or prosocial behavior. Despite these correlations however, Blasi concluded that the studies cast almost no theoretical light on the problem of relating judgment to action. Blasi went on to suggest that one theoretical bridge between moral judgment and moral action might be found by focusing on judgments of responsibility, that is, judgments of the self's responsibility to act in a "morally right" manner.

Blasi's (1980) review and the study by Kohlberg and Candee (chapter 7) indicate that the relationship of moral stage to action is a monotonic one. In other words, the higher the stage reasoning, the more likely action will be consistent with the moral choice made on a dilemma. This monotonic relationship has been observed even in situations where the content factor of moral choice is consistent across stage. For example, McNamee (1978) found that a large majority of Stage 3 and Stage 4 subjects in her sample thought it was right to help an apparently drugged stooge who was appealing for help. Even with this agreement on deontic choice, however, Stage 4 subjects were still more likely to actually help the stooge than were Stage 3 subjects. Results similar to McNamee's are reported in (*a*) the Candee and Kohlberg reanalysis of the Berkeley Free Speech Movement data of Haan, Smith, and Block (1968), and in (*b*) the Candee and Kohlberg reanalysis of the Milgram (1963) data, which I reported in 1969 (chapter 7).

Based upon Blasi's (1980) review as well as work by Rest (1983a, 1983b), Candee and I explain the monotonic relationship between moral stage and action reported in the literature by hypothesizing that moral action results from a three-step process. The first step is the making of a deontic judgment of rightness or justice in the situation. The second step is the making of a judgment that the self is responsible or accountable for carrying out this deontic judgment in the moral situation. The third step is carrying it out. In other words, the monotonic increase in consistency by stage, between moral stage and action, is explained by the hypothesis that there is a monotonic increase in consistency by stage between the deontic judgment made and a judgment of the self's responsibility to carry out this judgment in action.

This hypothesized monotonic increase in consistency by stage between deontic judgments and judgments of responsibility has been observed by Helkama (1979) on responses to hypothetical dilemmas. Helkama found, for instance, that at Stages 3 and 4 about 50 percent of subjects said that Heinz should steal the drug, but that of that 50 percent only 28 percent said that Heinz would be responsible if his wife died because he did not steal for her. At Stage 5 (and 4/5) however, over 50 percent of the subjects felt Heinz would be responsible if his wife died. Thus, there was almost twice the consistency between a deontic judgment of rightness and a judgment of responsibility at Stage 5 as was observed at the conventional stages.

Thus, judgments of responsibility to act become increasingly consistent with both hypothetical and real-life deontic judgments as one moves up the Kohlberg stage hierarchy. This increased consistency is what one would expect on the basis of my claim (volume I, chapter 4) that each higher stage is more prescriptive in the sense that it more successfully differentiates moral obligation and responsibility from nonmoral considerations. For example, at the conventional stages subjects may think it is right or just to help a victim (McNamee, 1978) or to refuse to shock a victim (Chapter 7) and yet at the same time feel that they do not have the responsibility to carry out these actions because for them it is the experimenter who has the authority or responsibility to make final decisions in the situation. However, for Stage 5 reasoners (and very often lower B substage reasoners), taking the responsibility to act in a manner consistent with their autonomous deontic choice is considered necessary. Excuses for not taking the responsibility to act, such as an appeal to the experimenter's authority or a concern for his or her approval, are considered as illegitimate by such reasoners.

Thus, we suggest that moral stage influences moral action in two ways: (*a*) through differences in deontic choice and (*b*) through judgments of responsibility. Where situations are controversial, we may expect to find differences in deontic choice with subjects at each higher stage more likely to agree on the choice as determined by moral principles. In situations where there is general agreement on the deontic choice (e.g., in the McNamee [1978] study), we still expect to find a monotonic relationship between stage and action due to increases in consistency, by stage, between deontic choice and a judgment of responsibility.

The notion that judgments of responsibility are consistent with deontic judgments at the postconventional level allows us to avoid certain philosophic issues about what is really morally right or what "moral" action is. This notion also helps us avoid the problem of finding some "objective" standard for making an aretaic judgment of the moral worthiness of an action or actor. Instead, it allows us to rely on the subject's own response to define what is right and helps us to understand increased consistency between moral judgment and moral action as a phenomenon related to moral stage growth. However, in addition to defining moral action as relative to the subject's own judgment and as a function of consistency between action and judgment, we also explore a more universal approach to defining moral action. In doing this we examine whether principled subjects (i.e., subjects using Stage 5 or 6 reasoning) reach consensus in their judgment of a particular dilemma situation. In cultures where we have studied the relation between structure and deontic choice (e.g., in the United States, Finland, and Israel) we find that Stage 5 subjects reach consensus that Heinz is right to steal. Both the philosophers and the lay subjects we have studied at Stage 5 use Kantian or deontological principles of respect for the life or personhood of another to make their deontic choice. The druggist claims the right to property in the story, and this claim shows no recognition of the wife's right to life which, in the deontological view, takes precedence over property rights. We also note that the use of the utilitarian principle of obtaining the greatest welfare for all involved in the dilemma also leads to the same choice to steal.

Our philosophic considerations leave us with the view that a *moral* action is an action (*a*) that is "objectively right" in the sense that the use of philosophic principles by Stage 5 reasoners leads to agreement on what constitutes "right" action, and (*b*) that is "subjectively right" if it is both guided by a moral judgment or reason that is "right" in form and consistent with the objectively right choice.

This controversial philosophic view leads us to say that, in at least some situations, principled or Stage 5 subjects perform actions which are right in both form and content. However, this claim does not only apply to the highest or principled stages. Lower stage subjects sometimes choose the "right," "just," or "principled" content to respond to our hypothetical dilemmas. Furthermore, they choose it in a way which is formally close to what both Kant and Piaget would call autonomous. In terms of content, they choose the alternative of preserving justice or human rights as against obeying laws or authorities in situations where these are arbitrary or in conflict with rights and justice.

In the substage discussion within this chapter on the current status of the theory we have described two different orientations to the standard hypothetical dilemmas and we have used them to define a B substage oriented to fairness rather than to rules or pragmatics. We characterized the B substage as more prescriptive, more reversible, and more universalistic than the A substage. In this way, and in contrast to the judgments of an A substage, judgments of rights and responsibility made at substage B are more like those judgments of rights and responsibility made at the principled states. Holding stage constant, judgments of responsibility made at substage B contain fewer excusing complications than do judgments of responsibility at substage A. Substage B responses reflect the Stage 5 "right answers" to our dilemmas as well as an intuitive understanding of the principled reasons for these choices. While a Stage 5 reasoner is explicit and rational in his or her response, a substage B person is someone who intuitively perceives the central values and obligations in the dilemma and uses these intuitions to generate a judgment of responsibility or necessity in the dilemma. In the Heinz dilemma, this intuition is that of the intrinsic value or worth of all human life and its priority over property. Such an intuition yields a judgment of universal obligation to preserve such life. In Dilemma III′, it is the intuition that an act of moral conscience or rightness, such as that committed by Heinz's theft of the drug, should not be legally punished, regardless of legality, deterrence, or social order considerations. In the "Joe and his father dilemma," Dilemma I, it is the intuition of the sacredness or intrinsic worth of keeping promises (most especially to children) and an intuition of a universal and prescriptive responsibility for keeping promises, that leads the B substage reasoner to judge that Joe should refuse to give his father the money. These substage B judgments on the three Form A dilemmas only receive their full, rational, and principled justification at Stage 5. But at lower stages they can still govern, or predict to, responsible choices and action. We predict, then, that the minority of subjects below Stage 5 who act morally in experimental situations are substage B. In this way we give credibility to the notion that moral action stems from responsible choice guided by an intuition of moral values and is not necessarily dependent on stage sophistication. Implied, then, is the Platonic as well as the Intuitionist view that conscience can intuit principles of justice and act accordingly. (It will be recalled that Kant also hypothesized that the categorical imperative was intuited by ordinary unreflective moral judgment.) Accordingly, if we are going to look for a relationship between moral thought and moral action, we should look to those persons who judge that it is right to perform the more moral behavior, either by virtue of their Stage 5 reasoning or by virtue of their B substage intuitions.

In summary, subjects who are principled or B substage are (*a*) more likely to make judgments of responsibility and to perform actions that are consistent with their deontic judgments of rightness and (*b*) more likely to perform the "right" action, right action being defined by that agreement reached between philosophic principles and postconventional judgments.

So far we have discussed moral action as though it were always preceded by deontic or responsibility judgments. In fact, this may not be the case. One study which assesses the relationship between moral reasoning and moral action in the context of a real-life decision is the Gilligan and Belenky (1980) study of decision making about abortion. This study used our standard hypothetical dilemmas, a standard abortion dilemma, and scored reasoning about the real-life dilemma faced by the subject. This study raises the important question of which comes first, a new stage of moral action, or a new stage of reflective moral judgment revealed in reasoning about hypothetical situations. Piaget (1932) believes that a new moral structure or stage arises first in action or in practical decision making and that it is only later made self-conscious or reflective. This process he calls *pris de conscience.* However, Gilligan and Belenky followed their subjects longitudinally over a year and found some subjects who were higher in real-life reasoning moving to the next stage in their hypothetical reasoning a year later. Other subjects were higher in their reflective or hypothetical reasoning than in their reasoning about their real-life dilemma, a phenomenon that remained stable over time. Thus, the coordination of structures of reflective moral reasoning with structures of practical moral decision making seems to be a process of coordination between action and reflection, rather than a one-way determination of action by reflective action or vice versa.

As a concluding comment to this section, we should emphasize the fact that in exploring the relationship between moral judgment and action we are dealing with issues of philosophic theory for making aretaic judgments. Earlier, we distinguished deontic judgments of rightness and obligation from aretaic judgments of the moral worthiness of persons or actions. We have argued that what counts as morally worthy action is action related to rationally principled or intuitively principled moral reasoning. This claim, we should point out, is itself a matter of philosophic assumption and debate. Kleinberger (1982), a philosopher, identifies three types of ethical theory in relation to this debate. The first type is the rationalist type, an ethic of pure intention, of which he takes Kant and Kohlberg as representatives. This type of ethical theory holds moral reasoning to be necessary and sufficient for moral action. The second type of ethical theory, a naturalistic type which emphasizes an ethic of responsibility, of which he takes Aristotle and Dewey as representatives, holds moral reasoning to be necessary but not sufficient for action. The third "type" of ethical theory is social behavioristic. Of this type, Kleinberger (1982, p. 149) says, "Since philosophers have an occupational bias in favor of reflective morality, there are hardly any philosophic theories of ethics which hold overt behavior in accordance with accepted moral norms to be a sufficient condition for the morality of an act or agent. But common sense tends to focus moral judgment on outward conduct appraised as habitual behavior conforming to the moral norms currently recognized in society. Not only does 'the man in the street seem to adopt this position but so do many social and behavioral scientists including Aronfreed, Bandura, Eysenck, and Havighurst and Taba.' In this view morality can be determined without reference to the actor's thought." (Kleinberger's typology is reviewed in more detail in chapter 7.) In our opinion, the inability of Hartshorne and May's monumental studies (Hartshore and May et al., 1928–30) to establish the proposition that such virtues as honesty and service are empirically demonstrable habits was a function of their social behavioristic approach to defining moral action. Although Hartshorne and May believed in the common sense assumption that there are internal determinants of moral behavior, their definition of moral acts ignored judgments that might have been made by the participants in their experiments. Moral conduct was defined only by the frequency and amount of such behavior as cheating, not by the subject's own judgment of whether that particular act was wrong in a given situation. There was a low correlation between having high standards of honesty, as reported verbally, and honest behavior in the experimental tasks. In our opinion, the results of the Hartshorne and May studies indicate that one cannot define and study moral action successfully with a purely behavioral perspective. Moral actions cannot be understood as such without reference to an internal moral cognition or moral judgment component which must be directly assessed as part of the definition of an action as moral. Studies of moral action seldom do this.

Research on Sociomoral Atmosphere

So far we have discussed moral action as if it were something determined solely by internal psychological factors in the subject. This is not the case, for moral action usually takes place in a social or group context, and that context usually has a profound influence on the moral decision making of individuals. Individual moral decisions in real life are almost always made in the context of group norms or group decision-making processes. Moreover, individual moral action is often a function of these norms or processes. For example, in the massacre at My Lai, individual American soldiers murdered noncombatant women and children. They did so, not because their moral judgment that such action was morally right was immature nor because, as individuals, they were "sick" in some sense, but because they participated in what was essentially a group action taken on the basis of group norms. The moral choice made by each individual soldier who pulled the trigger was embedded in the larger institutional context of the army and its decision-making procedures. The soldiers' decisions were dependent in large part upon a collective definition of the situation and of what should be done about it. In short, the My Lai massacre was more a function of the group "moral atmosphere" that prevailed in that place at that time than of the stage of moral development of the individuals present.

An early study exploring the moral atmosphere of a group or institution in relationship to its effect on action was that of Kohlberg, Hickey, and Scharf (1972). The starting point of the study was our analysis of responses given in group moral discussions of real and hypothetical dilemmas at the Cheshire reformatory. Inmates' judgments and reasoning appeared to be higher about hypothetical dilemmas, both the standard test dilemmas and the hypothetical group discussion dilemmas, than were their judgments about real Cheshire dilemmas. The study found that none of the thirty-four inmates scored higher on the real prison dilemmas than on the standard nonprison dilemmas, and of the sixteen inmates characterized as Stage 3 on nonprison dilemmas, for example, eleven were rated at Stage 2 on the prison dilemmas. Inmates tended to see relationships with other inmates in Stage 2 instrumental terms. Inmates were seen as "ripping each other off," "ratting" on their friends, and "pounding" weaker inmates. While relationships with other inmates were necessary for mutual protection, they were, nevertheless, usually seen as marred by "fronting." Fronting was necessary to defend one's interests and to "con" the guards and other inmates.

In this 1972 study an attempt was made to articulate the notion of a stage of moral atmosphere that might be different from an individual respondent's own moral stage. Subsequent refinement of the concept of moral atmosphere has been achieved in the context of studying three alternative democratic schools and their regular high school counterpart. Our elaboration of the notion of moral atmosphere has been published in preliminary form by Power and Reimer (1978), and by Higgins, Power, and Kohlberg (1984). The Power and Reimer study analyzes moral judgments made in group or community meetings, while the Higgins et al. study analyzes individual moral interview responses, taking the high school student as an "anthropological informant" of the norms and culture of the school. Central to these analyses of moral atmosphere is the observation and definition of collective norms. Norms shared by the group can be discriminated from individual moral judgment in both group discussions and in moral atmosphere interviews. The distinctions these studies make rely heavily on Durkheim's (1961) notion of norms as prescriptions arising from shared expectations in a group. In addition to collective norms, both Durkheim and ourselves have studied the sense of community or the sense of group solidarity and cohesion attained in a group. It is this sense of community, solidarity, and cohesion that we call moral atmosphere.

With regard to collective norms, we have taken the position that there is a collective stage interpretation and justification of norms somewhat distinct from the individual's moral stage. In the Kohlberg, Hickey, and Scharf study (1972), prisoners who were Stage 3 in their thinking perceived the norms of the prison in Stage 2 terms. In addition to the degree of collectiveness of the norm and its stage, our analysis of moral atmosphere also defines group phases of the institutionalization and internalization of collective norms. Power (1979) was able to show that in the course of four years there was longitudinal growth, not only in the stage of collective norms, but in their phase as well in the Cluster alternative school in Cambridge. However, not all norms advanced to a higher phase and stage. While norms of trust and property developed in this way, norms forbidding the use of drugs did not show much increase in phase and stage.

Tables 3.5 and 3.6 present examples of phases in the growth of collective norms and community valuing, respectively. Table 3.7 presents an example of stages in the growth of collective norms and community valuing which developed in the alternative school and which were manifested in group meetings and individual interviews about practical or "real-life" dilemmas.

The studies by Higgins, et al. (1984), report group development over time in aspects of moral atmosphere described in the Tables 3.5–3.7. This development in these dimensions of moral atmosphere was greater in the democratic alternative school than it was in the regular high school sampled.

We should add that moral atmosphere differences in normative perception appear to be related to actual differences in behavior. For instance, in the first year of the Cambridge Cluster School, stealing was endemic. In the second year, collective norms of trust and norms of collective responsibility had developed to the point that each member of the community pledged to contribute twenty-five cents to make restitution for ten dollars stolen from one student's purse. There were no further episodes of stealing in the school for the next three years, and students generally agreed that neither they nor their peers engaged in any stealing during this

Table 3.5. Phases of the Collective Norm

Phase 0: No collective norm exists or is proposed.

Collective Norm Proposal

Phase 1: Individuals propose collective norms for group acceptance.

Collective Norm Acceptance

Phase 2: Collective norms are accepted as a group ideal but not agreed to. They are not acknowledged as expectations for behavior.
- a. Some group members accept ideal.
- b. Most group members accept ideal.

Phase 3: Collective norms are accepted and agreed to but are not yet acknowledged as expectations for behavior.
- a. Some group members agree to collective norm.
- b. Most group members agree to collective norm.

Collective Norm Expectation

Phase 4: Collective norms are accepted and expected (naive expectation).
- a. Some group members expect the collective norm to be followed.
- b. Most group members expect the collective norm to be followed.

Phase 5: Collective norms are expected but not followed (disappointed expectation).
- a. Some group members are disappointed.
- b. Most group members are disappointed.

Collective Norm Enforcement

Phase 6: Collective norms are expected and upheld through expected persuading of deviant to follow norm.
- a. Some group members persuade.
- b. Most group members persuade.

Phase 7: Collective norms are expected and upheld through expected reporting of deviant to the group.
- a. Some group members report.
- b. Most group members report.

period. In contrast, a norm against coming to school high on drugs never developed in stage or phase and student behavior was accordingly lax. The working norm was "be cool"; that is, don't come to school high in a way that could be detected by the teachers. In another school, the Scarsdale Alternative School, there was also marked growth in stage and phase of community valuing and

***Table 3.6.* Phases of the Degree of Community Valuing**

I. Instrumental Extrinsic:	The school is valued as an institution that helps the individual to meet his own academic needs.
II. "Esprit de Corps" Extrinsic:	The school is valued as an institution that helps the individual and the individual feels some loyalty toward the school *as manifested* in team spirit and support of teams or groups in school.
III. Spontaneous Community Intrinsic:	The school is valued as the kind of place in which members feel an inner motivation to help others in the group community and the community generates special feelings of closeness among members.
IV. Communal Intrinsic:	The school as a community is valued for its own sake. Community can obligate its members in special ways and members can expect special privileges or responsibilities from the group and other members.

collective norms. At this school, however, the drug norm did develop to a high phase, leading first to confession of the use of drugs, then to peer pressure to confess, and finally, to the absence of abuse of drugs either at school or on school retreats.

The Cambridge Cluster School's norm of respect for property and the Scarsdale School's norms about using drugs were norms which students tended to feel should regulate behavior during school hours. Students did not feel that the school community had the right to legislate moral norms governing their moral action outside of the school setting. Students felt this way with regard to rules of prohibition. However, with regard to norms about caring for one another and being responsible for the welfare of others in the community, students did not express this time-limited attitude. Such individual judgments of caring and responsibility (studied with the use of an adapted version of Gilligan and Lyons's (1981) method for assessing a caring orientation) were much higher in both frequency and stage in the alternative schools than they were in the regular high school comparison groups.

In summary, moral atmosphere in the form of collective norms and a sense of community can be a very strong force in determining moral behavior, holding individual moral judgment stage con-

Table 3.7. Stages of Collective Normative Values and the Sense of Community Valuing

Collective Normative Values	*Sense of Community Valuing*
Stage 2	
There is not yet an explicit awareness of collective normative values. However, there are *generalized expectations* that individuals should recognize concrete individual rights and resolve conflicts through exchange.	There is no clear sense of community apart from exchanges among group members. Community denotes a collection of individuals who do favors for each other and rely on each other for protection. Community is valued insofar as it meets the concrete needs of its members.
Examples: 1. Do not "rat" on another group member. Ratting or reporting another group member to authorities is disapproved of because it exposes the rule breaker to likely punishment. 2. Do not bother others. Live and let live. 3. Help others out when you want to.	Examples: The community is like a bank. Members meet to exchange favors but you cannot take more than you give.
Stage 3	
Collective normative values refer to relationships among group members. Membership in a group implies living up to *shared expectations.* Conflicts should be resolved by appeal to mutually accepted collective normative values.	The sense of community refers to a set of relationships and things shared among group members. The group is valued for the friendliness of its members. The value of the group is equated with the value of its collective normative expectations.
Examples: 1. Members of a group should be able to trust each other with their possessions. 2. Members of a group should care about other members of the group.	Examples: 1. The community is a family in which members care for each other. 2. The community is honorable because it helps others.

Table 3.7—**Continued**

Stage 4	
Collective normative values stress the community as an entity distinct from its individual members. Members are *obligated* to act out of concern for the welfare and harmony of the group.	The school is explicitly valued as an entity distinct from the relationships among its members. Group commitments and ideals are valued. The community is perceived as an organic whole composed of interrelated systems that carry on the functioning of the group.
Examples: 1. Individuals not only are responsible for themselves but share responsibility for the whole group. 2. Individuals should participate in the political organization of the group by making their opinions known and by being informed voters.	Examples: Stealing affects "the community more than the individual because that is what we are. We are not just a group of individuals."

stant. However, it appears that the influence of moral atmosphere may be limited to the situational and institutional context of the group. Longitudinal studies will be required to determine the long-range effects of forming strong collective norms and a strong sense of community on post–high school moral action.

In conclusion, we believe that moral atmosphere influences not only the content but also the form of moral reasoning and action. Early writings on moral atmosphere (e.g., chapter 2) have hypothesized that moral atmosphere is a factor influencing the growth of individual moral judgment through the stages. Data obtained from the use of ethnographic interviews has revealed that democratic alternative schools as well as a developmentally oriented program for juvenile delinquents (Jennings and Kohlberg, 1983) have produced conditions conducive to moral growth more successfully than have their traditional counterparts. The conditions to which we refer are (*a*) a sense of the degree to which moral discussion and taking into account others' viewpoints occurred within the school; (*b*) the extent to which subjects felt a sense of power and participation in making rules; and (*c*) the extent to which existing rules were perceived as fair. We use the above results to explain why individual moral stage growth is greater for persons in democratic settings than it is for those in traditional, stratified, and bureaucratic settings.

The Attenuation of Stage 6

Stage 6 has disappeared as a commonly identifiable form of moral reasoning as our stage-scoring concepts and criteria have developed from the continuing analysis of our longitudinal data. None of our longitudinal subjects in the United States, Israel, or Turkey have attained it. A fuller treatment of an interview as a case of a possible psychological sixth stage of adult development is presented in Chapter 6 and a broader perspective on adult ethical development is offered in Kohlberg (1984, in press). The case materials from which we constructed our theoretical definition of a sixth stage in Volume I came from the writings of a small elite sample, elite in the sense of its formal philosophic training and in the sense of its ability for and commitment to moral leadership. An example can be seen in the case of Martin Luther King, who was not only a moral leader but also someone with graduate training in the moral theory of Tillich.

While both philosophical and psychological considerations lead us to continue to hypothesize and look for a sixth moral stage, our longitudinal data has not provided us with material necessary to (*a*) verify our hypothesis or (*b*) construct a detailed scoring manual description which would allow reliable identification of a sixth stage.

Until 1972, our conceptualization and test manual definition of Stage 6 was based on our 1958 cross-sectional and ideal-typical method for stage scoring (Kohlberg, 1958). This method classified as Stage 6 high school and college responses which are now scored as Stage 5, Stage 4, and occasionally even Stage 3 in the standardized issue scoring manual (Colby and Kohlberg 1984, in press). The material that was formally scored as Stage 6 is now scored as substage B at one of these lower stages. An example of substage B reasoning is its intuition of the primacy of life over property and the use of this value hierarchy to justify in a universalistic manner the moral duty to save a life (e.g., to save life regardless of relationships of affection). Such reasoning would constitute either a 3B or 4B resolution of the Heinz dilemma, depending upon other response characteristics. Another example can be seen in the Joe and his father story (Dilemma I). Substage B responses to this dilemma reflect an intuitive moral hierarchy in which promise keeping takes priority over the claims of authority in paternal-child relationship. Such reasoning defines a universal moral obligation to keep promises. Thus, substage B reasoning reflects two properties: (*a*) an intuition of the moral content hierarchy explicitly argued for and chosen by our Stage 5 reasoners and (*b*) the fully universalized and morally prescriptive form of judgments of rightness and obligation ascribed to our theoretical notion of Stage 6. However, these substage B orientations lack that which is critical for our theoretical notion of Stage 6, namely, the organization of moral judgment around a clearly formulated moral principle of justice and respect for persons that provides a rationale for the primacy of this principle. Substage B represents an intuition of parts of both the form and content of solutions reached with Stage 5 or 6 reasoning but cannot yet articulate the central principle of justice which rationally justifies this content and form.

Substage B not only handles the moral judgment data we earlier classed as Stage 6, but it also partially handles the judgment-action implication of Stage 6. Substage B subjects not only tend to have as the content of their choice in real dilemmas the action chosen by Stage 5 subjects (or, theoretically, Stage 6 reasoners) but they also tend to act consistently with this choice (Kohlberg and Candee, 1984; Chapter 7).

If Stage 6 is a theoretical construct not needed to order the extensive empirical data we and our colleagues have gathered, then one may ask why we bother to cling to the theoretical postulation of it. Clearly, we do not maintain this postulation of Stage 6 for the usual purposes of the description of personality development and personality differences typically addressed by a psychological theory. Rather, we continue with the postulation because we conceive our theory as an attempt to rationally reconstruct the ontogenesis of justice reasoning, an enterprise which requires a terminal stage to define the nature and endpoint of the kind of development we are studying. In other words, a terminal stage, with the principle of justice as its organizing principle, helps us to define the area of human activity under study.

A final stage of moral judgment should be one for which the theorist can give a rational description and a rational justification. Piaget, for instance, has defined an end point of logicomathematical and physical reasoning in terms of the "INRC group" of formal operations (Piaget, 1983, p. 124). Without claiming to have a *final* "rational model" of an endpoint for the development of moral judgment, we see John Rawls's (1971) model of justice as a rational description of parts of our sixth stage. Our use of Rawls in this manner does not mean that we believe his normative theory of justice is *the* theory of justice which should or will be accepted by moral philosophers as most morally adequate. Rather, we use John Rawls's theory as a rational model of parts of our sixth stage because we see it as an instance of the notions of reflective equilibrium and reversibility which a Piagetian or "hard" structural theory of stages assumes to characterize the domain of justice in social interactions, just as notions of equilibration and reversibility characterize the domain of logicomathematical and physical reasoning (Volume I, Chapter 5).

Even if our general formulation of a hypothetical sixth stage and its partial exemplification via Rawls's model turns out to be incorrect, we consider it important to continue to search for a terminal stage beyond Stage 5. This is so for philosophic interests as much as for psychological concerns.

Our interest in Stage 6 also shares with other theories of principled judgment (like utilitarianism) a striving for, or a claim to having achieved, rational consensus on the content of the right in disagreements about justice. Philosophically speaking, the claim of agreement at a highest moral stage represents a norm of moral rationality analogous to norms of scientific rationality in the discussion of the philosophy of science. Philosophers of science attempt to formulate a conception of the scientific method whose proper use would lead to agreement on various issues among scientific thinkers. Although philosophers of science do not fully agree in their attempts to define proper scientific method and although scientists do not actually agree on many scientific conclusions, the ideal of agreement is still central to science and scientific development. Similarly, a rational ideal of moral development implies the need for *moral* agreement in conclusions about moral problems. In our conception of morality, moral principles at the highest stages are designed to reach agreement in situations of potential moral conflict or disagreement among individuals. At lower stages, such agreement is less likely, a fact which can be associated with inhumane events. For instance, when Stage 4 moral reasoning is associated with clashes in which Americans and Vietnamese kill one another in the name of justice, then morality at this stage has *prima facie* failed to achieve consensus. The philosophic ideal of consensus led us to the empirical or psychological hypothesis that Stage 6 reasoners will agree in choice on all moral dilemmas with which they are confronted, taking the facts of the case as given. Data reported in Chapter 7 on judgment and action indicate that Stage 5 reasoners do agree in action choice on most but not all of the hypothetical dilemmas.

Pilot data by Erdynast (1973), partly reviewed in the Volume I, Chapter 5, "Justice as Reversibility," indicated that graduate students of philosophy, tentatively labeled as using Stage 6 reasoning, agreed on their choices in several dilemmas on which Stage 5 reasoners disagreed. Thus, while there is some tentative empirical support for a psychological claim of agreement in action choice at Stage 6, we are in no position to claim the empirical psychological truth that there is actual substantive moral agreement reached at the terminus of moral development. The metaethical ideal of moral agreement implied by our rationalist assumption has still uncertain meaning in terms of finding empirical agreement in highly developed and experienced moral judgers in various cultures.

In the absence of clearer empirical confirmation of a sixth stage of moral judgment, we are led to suspend our claim that our research provides support for a number of psychological and philosophic claims which I made in Volume I, Chapter 4, "From *Is* To *Ought*." At this point, our stage findings do not allow us to claim evidence for certain normative ethical conclusions which nevertheless remain my own philosophic preference for defining an ontogenetic end point of a rationally reconstructed theory of justice reasoning.

In particular, we cannot claim either that there is a single principle which we have found used at the current empirically highest stage, nor that that principle is the principle of justice or respect for persons. There may be other principles. For example, Carter (1980) and Shawver (1979) have argued that other principles, such as *agape* (i.e., responsible love) or the utilitarian principle, could be included in a highest or sixth stage of moral judgment. Formalist philosophers such as Frankena (1973) believe that two principles, the principle of benevolence/utility and the principle of justice, are both required for making an adequate moral decision.

In distinguishing between normative-ethical and metaethical claims, we would be in general agreement with the position advanced by Carter (1980), a philosophic critic.

Lawrence Kohlberg's work in moral education appears to be significant enough philosophically that one is tempted to use much of it to resolve basic problems of long standing. In this essay, it is argued that it would prove more fruitful for Kohlberg or anyone else to avoid applying his developmentalist position to the settling of such problems as utilitarian/formalist supremacy or the search for a "best" morality. Instead, emphasis could be placed on explicating the fundamental requirements of a non-relativistic, non-egoistic morality of whatever sort.

Such basic moral requirements serve to highlight of what principled morality (i.e., Stages 5 and 6) consists, and why it need not be tied to a Rawlsian formalism, or to any other normative ethical position. In fact, there is considerable cause for supposing that what Kohlberg really achieves with clarity is nothing more than a sequential typology of development in moral thinking from egoism to universalism, and from situation-specific rules to universalizable and reversible judgments of principle. This in itself constitutes, of course, an enormous undertaking and, if successfully defended, would be a very significant breakthrough in Psychology, Education and Philosophy. It is what Kohlberg ought to be about, rather than something unnecessarily contentious.

In summarizing our current thinking about the philosophic issues raised by the idea of Stage 6 in terms of the critics responded to in Chapter 4, we would say that having suspended some claims for Stage 6 we are not thereby impelled to abandon the theory of Stage 6 as an ideal end point for the rational reconstruction of ontogenetic stages of justice. Rather, in pruning the claims made in regard to Stage 6, we have attempted to distinguish as speculative, some primarily normative-ethical parts of the theory from other primarily metaethical parts of the theory, which we believe are more demonstrable. The demonstrable portion of the theory we call the claims of Stage 5. However, we see in the form of Stage 5 the basis or potential for development to a postconventional stage structure which recognizes rational principles and universal rights. In the body of our reply to criticisms in Chapter 4, we will be defending our account of development through Stage 5 but not attempting to "demonstrate" our earlier claims for Stage 6.

Distinguishing Assumptions Made Prior to Research from Implications of Research

In terms of the interests of the readers of this volume on the psychology of moral development, there is an even more important consideration than the dropping of the claim of a sixth moral stage, with its attendant claim that such a stage answers most moral philosophic problems. We refer to the distinction between the philosophic assumptions preliminary to the study of moral development and the moral philosophic conclusions to be drawn from the stage theory for the resolution of problems in moral philosophy and moral education. In "From *Is* to *Ought,*" I put the distinction this way:

> The general questions discussed in this essay are (*a*) What does the psychological study of the development of moral concepts require in the way of moral-philosophic and epistemological assumptions about moral reasoning? and (*b*) What can the psychological conclusions of the study of moral concepts and their development tell us about their epistemological or moral philosophic status? [p. 101]

In distinguishing between these two kinds of philosophic questions, I recognized that anything I said on the second question was much more controversial than anything I said on the first question. My reasons for entering the fray on the second set of questions were, I said, due to my desire to put my psychological theory into practice in the field of moral education.

> A developmental psychologist must be a fool to enter the den of philosophic wolves (even if they were all as tolerant and gentlemanly as Alston and Peters) with a set of "*Is* to *Ought*" claims, unless he has to. It is my belief that developmental psychologists must eventually do so for two reasons. First, it is necessary for any ethically or philosophically justified educational or other practical application of research findings. Second, following Peters and other philosophers, I believe that a psychological theory of ethics is incomplete, even as a psychological theory, if its philosophic implications are not spelled out. [p. 103]

Basically, the second set of questions, the implications of psychological stage findings for moral philosophy, revolve around the "*Is* to *Ought*" issue. In other words, they center on defining and justifying the sense in which a higher stage is a better stage. Educationally, such "*is* to *ought*" claims must be made if stage development is to be taken as an aim of education. They are not necessary, in any strong sense, for the psychological study of moral stages per se. It may be, as some critics have claimed, that the "*ought*" claims we have derived from our research findings are not demonstrable enough to justify a practice of moral education. It might be advisable to give them more hypothetical status, as part of a psychological-normative theory which is a "rational reconstruction of development," as Habermas suggests. However, our normative conceptualization of why a higher stage is a better stage is part of a theory which is also a psychological theory as to why movement proceeds from stage to stage. But it is not necessary to endorse the philosophical adequacy of our normative claims in order to begin the psychological study of moral development as we have done. Personal endorsement of the philosophical adequacy claims of higher stages is a matter of choice, and one's personal stand may simply be that using the moral stage framework is a fruitful tool for scientific research. This was suggested by our discussion of the attenuation of Stage 6 claims. Accordingly, we will not attempt to present detailed arguments for these normative-ethical claims in this volume.

There are, however, certain metaethical assumptions necessary to begin the study of morality, which psychologists using the stage concept and measure must at least partially endorse. In the remainder of this section we discuss these assumptions and provide arguments for endorsing them. It will be clear to the reader that our way of talking here presupposes that normative-ethical, metaethical, and empirical social science beliefs are distinct, and this presupposition, in turn, needs clarification. These three different types of theoretical discourse are defined as follows in Frankena's *Ethics:*

We may distinguish three kinds of thinking that relate to morality in one way or another.

1. There is descriptive empirical inquiry, historical or scientific, such as is done by anthropologists, historians, psychologists, and sociologists. Here the goal is to describe or explain the phenomena of morality or to work out a theory of human nature which bears on ethical questions.

2. There is normative ethical thinking of the sort Socrates was doing in the *Crito* or that anyone does who asks what is right, good, or obligatory. This may take the form of asserting a normative judgment, like the utilitarian principle "It is always wrong to harm someone or cause unhappiness (other things being equal)" and giving reasons for this judgment or for this principle.

3. There is also "analytical," "critical," or "metaethical" thinking. It does not try to answer either particular or general questions about what is good or right. It asks and tries to answer logical, epistemological, or semantical questions like the following: "What is the meaning or use of the expressions 'morally right' or 'good'? How can ethical and value judgments be established or justified? [Frankena, 1973, p. 4–5]

The philosophic assumptions made prior to psychological inquiry are metaethical assumptions; the philosophic conclusions one may draw from the inquiry are primarily normative-ethical in nature. Questions like What is morality? Is it relative to the individual or is it universal? are metaethical questions. These questions were raised in Kohlberg (1958). My answers to these questions come from my reading of analytic moral philosophy as well as from my own reasoning about what words like *moral* and *moral development* might mean. My work has made use of the following metaethical assumption; we will discuss them in this order:

1. Value relevance of definitions of the moral (as opposed to value-neutral definitions).
2. Phenomenological definitions of morality implying moral judgments (as opposed to moral behaviorism).
3. Moral universality (as opposed to cultural and ethical relativism).
4. Prescriptivism as the use of moral judgments (as opposed to descriptivism or naturalism as interpretations of moral judgments).
5. Cognitivism as the reasoning element of moral judgment (as opposed to emotivism).
6. Formalism as defining the nature and competence of moral judgments (as opposed to definitions in terms of content).
7. Principledness as the rule (or principled) governance of moral judgment (as opposed to act theory).
8. Constructivism (as opposed to either empiricism or apriorism).
9. To these metaethical starting assumptions, we must add a more normative or substantive assumption: the assumption that justice is primary, that moral problems as dilemmas are fundamentally problems of justice.

The Assumption of the Value Relevance of Definitions of the Moral

We have said that we have used our psychological studies, together with formalist normative-ethical theory, to generate a moral philosophy or a normative position, and that our concluclusions are philosophically controversial. Less controversial, we said, are the metaethical assumptions I made in studying moral development. These assumptions may be taken as statements of the philosophy of social science.

Our starting assumptions may also be stated in terms of that branch of philosophy called "metaethics." Many social scientists studying morality have been unaware of metaethics and the need to make and justify metaethical or philosophical assumptions. Instead, they have sought to avoid all philosophizing or metaethical reflection in the name of being value-free or -neutral scientists, rather than philosophers.

In this section, we shall state Kohlberg's metaethical assumptions and argue for their value as guides to inquiry. We do this, in part, by pointing out the deficiencies in alternative assumptions.

My line of argument in favor of my assumptions represents a form of "analytical moral philosophy," the enterprise which attempts to logically analyze or explicate the meanings of ordinary language, in this case ordinary language about morality. In originally formulating my approach to moral development in my dissertation, I was heavily influenced by R. M. Hare's (1952) *Language of Morals.*

In contrast to my efforts to state theoretically a concept of moral development consistent with the careful use of ordinary moral language, most modern psychologists discussing morality have assumed that reliance upon the meanings of morality and ordinary moral language is "unscientific" and that instead it is necessary to construct a new "scientific" language to talk about morality. Their conception of the meaning of scientific language has been that of logical positivism, a philosophy of science explicitly or implicitly held by most American psychologists for the last generation. As stated, for instance, in Ayer's (1936) *Language Truth and Logic,* logical positivism assumes that there are two, and only two, kinds of meaning with scientific or truth status. The first kind of meaning is logico-mathematical: that is, analytic or logically necessary truth. The truthfulness of analytic propositions is based on their tautological, self-referential nature. An analytic truth is simply one of self-consistency in the deductive implications of terms. The second kind of meaning that logical positivism identifies is synthetic or empirical meaning. The meaning and truth of synthetic statements typically depends upon their ability to describe and successfully predict observable events. Empirical truth is open to corroboration by sense observation, or to observation in terms of a dispositional language of physical things and of organisms as observable or physical things.

Related to the truth claims of logical positivism is the assumption of scientific value-neutrality: that is, that the language used to describe events in value-neutral.

In contrast to the above, my first assumption is that conceptions of morality cannot themselves be morally neutral. This is best explained by considering a typical definition of morality in social science. Berkowitz (1964) claims that "moral values are evaluations of action believed by members of a given society to be right." This definition implies moral relativism and is being presented as value-neutral by Berkowitz; that is, he does not see it as implying a normative stand but as merely describing scientifically an observable phenomenon. In fact, however, this definition *assumes* moral relativism, it does not find it. (Moreover, based on this definition, research can never uncover anything but relative moral values, values which are not distinguished as more and less valid or even more or less moral in quality.) Such a definition takes a stand on morality without justifying it, without even admitting it. By contrast, we take a stand in our conception of morality which we feel can be justified philosophically. We believe that systems of truly moral thought are more and less valid and that movement from some of these systems to others can represent a developmental sequence in distinctively moral thought. We claim that more valid systems better fulfill criteria of validity laid down by moral philosophers, especially those of the formalist, Kantian tradition.

In our cognitive-developmental theory, our value-relevant stand appears as a formal internal standard of adequacy. Following *Webster's Dictionary* we define development as "to make active, to move from the original position to one providing more opportunity for effective use; to cause to grow and differentiate along lines natural to its kind; to go through a process of natural growth, differentiation, or evolution by successive changes." This definition suggests an internal standard of adequacy governing development; it implies that development is not just any behavioral change but rather, a change toward greater differentiation, integration, and adaptation. In other words, the theorist has to take up a position as to what "more integrated" and "more adapted" means. One can not study the *development* of moral reasoning without some assumptions as to what it means to be moral, without the definite assumption that morality is a desirable thing, not a value-neutral thing. In similar fashion, the theorist of scientific history or development takes a stand on what scientific adequacy and truth means.

With our claim that the value-neutral stance is mistaken, we are not saying that the social scientist can or should derive value judgments directly from his or her actual scientific conclusions. By analogy, the fact that a social scientist studying Darwin's theory of evolution must have, at some level of inquiry, an evaluative stance toward the truth of evolutionary theory is not the claim that the results of his or her study of Darwin's theory can directly generate conclusions as to the truth of the investigator's evaluative stance. We simply mean that the social scientist must take some evaluate stance on the truth of evolution in conducting an inquiry of Darwin's theory.

Max Weber (1949) justly argued that social scientists should be value-neutral in the sense that their conclusions should not represent particular moral or political pronouncements as being the result of social science. He did point out, however, that the selection of a concrete event or person for historical or development study should and did depend upon the value-importance or value-relevance of the event or person. We would go further than this and claim that some value-norms are needed, not only to select a person or event for study, but to guide inquiry into the event's or the person's development. This is why we have said that Kohlberg's theory of developmental stages is a rational reconstruction of ontogenesis informed by the philosophic norms embodied in principled moral reasoning.

The Assumption of Phenomenalism

The assumption of phenomenalism is the assumption that moral reasoning is the conscious process of using ordinary moral language. This assumption distinguishes Kohlberg from behaviorists and psychoanalytic theorists. Psychoanalytic theorists assume that the essence of moral activity is unconscious guilt avoidance, and behaviorists assume that a valid account of moral activity can only be given by reference to overt action and the overt consequences of such action to the self and others. In contrast to these views, we chose to study the use of ordinary moral language (i.e, our phenomenological assumption) because we believe that if one leaves ordinary language behind one robs oneself of valuable empirical data. Behaviorists and psychoanalytic theorists who believe that there is no logical or empirical validity to moral utterances, that they are simply emotive expressions, are throwing out the scientific baby with the emotional bath water. This consequence can be seen in the following behaviorist and psychoanalytic statements by B. F. Skinner, a behaviorist, and James Gilligan, a psychiatrist.

> Good things are positive reinforcers. Physics and biology study things without reference to their values, but the reinforcing effects of things are the province of behavioral science, which, to the extent that it concerns itself with operant reinforcement, is a science of values. Things are good (positively reinforcing) presumably because of the contingencies of survival under which the species evolved. It is part of the genetic endowment called "human nature" to be reinforced in particular ways by particular things. . . . The effective reinforcers are matters of observation and no one can dispute them [Skinner 1971, p.104]

> Morality is dead. It killed itself; the self-criticism to which moral philosophy subjected itself over the past two centuries left it no honest choice but to recognize that the only knowledge possible is of scientific facts, not of moral values. [J. Gilligan, 1976, p.144]

From the point of view of metaethics and ordinary language, behaviorism is mistaken because our actual judgments as the moral nature of an action depend upon imparting motives and moral judgments to the actor. Accidental manslaughter is not immoral, because there is no hostile motivation behind the act. Murder by a child is not immoral, because the child is assumed not to be morally responsible, that is, not to be capable of generating the moral judgments and decisions which proscribe murder. Behavior such as physically assaulting another is a simple case in which we are required to know something of the actor's moral judgment before judging the behavior as moral or not. To assess the "moral" quality of behaviors such as cheating or obeying an experimenter who orders one to shock another requires one to confront complex issues of interpretation, for both motivation and judgment are to be considered in such assessments before behavior can be said to be moral conduct or moral action. Insofar as a behavior may be directly defined and explained as conditioned, it loses its positive moral quality. I was once asked on a television program to comment on the acts of various "heroes" who had saved others' lives. One "hero" was the strong man of a small Maine village, who had held up a portion of a burning house to aid the escape of a trapped victim. Asked why he did it, he said he had a reputation as a hero for doing such feats and he was always congratulated afterwards. Insofar as this man's behavior was definable or explainable simply as seeking, or originating from, social reinforcement, we hold that it loses its moral quality of heroism. Moral conduct is conduct governed by moral judgments; while moral judgment is not always translated into moral action, the assessment of an action as moral depends upon the imputation of judgment to the action. Our point here is not to develop a theory of moral conduct but to point to the fact that the study of moral conduct and moral development per se must consider the motives and the constructions of moral meaning that are expressed in behaviors.

The Assumption of Universalism

Ethical or cultural relativism is explicit in Skinner's writings.

> What a given group of people calls good is a fact, it is what members of the group find reinforcing as a result of their genetic endowment and the natural and social contingencies to which they have been exposed. Each culture has its own set of goods, and what is good in one culture may not be good in another. [1971, p.128]

It is important to see that Skinner's statement is itself not value-neutral. It is an assertion about "true" values, that is, that they are defined by the standard of each culture. Now it is true that in some sense one can observe moral values from culture to culture in an objective manner without attaching any moral significance to these observations. But as soon as these observations are used to make general interpretive and theoretical statements about morality, then such statements cease to be value-neutral and become statements of the validity of a moral stance, in this particular case the stance of moral relativism. In other words, it is conceivably scientifically true that each culture has its own values; however, to translate this fact into a statement of moral theory such as "What is good in one culture may not be good in another" is to make a morally controversial statement. Such a statement is as controversial as a statement which claims that cannibalism is morally right in a cannibalistic society. Neither ordinary moral speakers nor philosophers from a variety of cultures need make moral judgments based on the assumption of moral relativity.

Not only Hare (1952) but other moral language analysts and philosophers such as Habermas (1982) assume that making moral judgments has a universalizable intent: that is, if one makes a moral judgment at all one at least thinks one is making a universalizable statement. One can judge Nazi genocide to be wrong not only in terms of some non-Nazi cultural norms but also in terms of standards having more universal application or meaning. The ordinary moral language user could say, "I judge Nazi genocide to be morally wrong not simply because it's not good in my culture but because it's not good in any culture, even Nazi culture." A cultural relativist may reply that the ordinary moral language user can say this but would be mistaken because he or she would be simply generalizing his or her own culture's values to other cultures. Our empirical studies indicate that it is the cultural relativist who is likely mistaken in this matter, because every culture we have studied has used the same moral norms and elements in the same structural developmental sequence, a sequence that has the property of increasing universalizability (see Table 3.8 for a list of moral norms and elements). In other words, Skinner seems to accept some particular cultural set of norms as a referent for the meaning of morality. In contrast, we start from a hypothesized universal meaning of morality and see if this universal meaning is found in various cultures or whether there is, in fact, variation from what we expect to be potentially universal moral norms and elements.

Our research shows that individual development in moral reasoning is a continual differentiation of moral universalizability from more subjective or culturally specific habits and beliefs. While moral behaviors or customs seem to vary from culture to culture, underneath these variations in custom there seem to be universal kinds of judging or valuing. Sexual mores obviously vary widely by culture and historical epoch, even if norms about life and property less clearly vary. This variation in sexual customs does not necessarily imply, however, differences in basic moral values or ways of judging. The culturally variable customs of monogamy and polygamy are both compatible with the culturally universal underlying moral norms of personal dignity, commitment, and trust in sexual relationships.

Perhaps no one but a cultural relativist would claim there is no difference between cultural conventions and morality, and no one but a cultural relativist would claim that while they are reasoning morally their judgments apply only to members of their own group. As we noted earlier, Elliot Turiel (1980) has researched this difference between custom and morality. He notes that moral speakers and their statements may be products of various cultures but still, in speaking morally, in the sense of *prescriptively* (rather than as cultural documenters), they can speak with a universalizable intent.

All these considerations, cautions, and critiques are an important part of growing theory and research which employs universalistic assumptions. We must ask critics of our universalistic theory, however, whether they are advising us on how to develop a better universalistic theory, or denying the possibility of such a universalistic approach on relativistic grounds. Critics who assert that our theory and findings are culturally biased (e.g., Simpson, 1974; and Sullivan 1977) implicitly assume that the sheer effort to formulate a universalistic theory is, in and of itself, culturally biased. A theory that offers universalizable principles, they assert, is a theory that represents the perspective of Western liberal ideology. This criticism may well be true in the same sense that postmedieval scientific theories and concepts of scientific method are, historically, Western creations. The same is true for rational moral philosophy, which is largely a Western liberal enterprise. The cultural origins of a theory, however, tell us little about its validity. Furthermore, relativistic critiques of our theory confuse our assertion that certain moral principles and stages develop universally with the assertion that our theory about them is adequate, regardless of its relationship to the Western liberal tradition. We do not make the latter claim, nor should it be confused with the former. Our theoretical statement of moral principles and their development may stem from Western Kantian thought. This fact does not mean, however, that the principles stated to be universal are themselves relative in the sense in which the theory is relative. It is true that philosophical theories of morality are constantly changing. This does not mean, however, that the phenomena such theories address are necessarily historically changing and culturally variable—anymore than those phenomena theorized about in the natural sciences.

While our discussion has focused upon relativism as a doctrine about *"is,"* about the fact that individual and cultural morals are variable, we need also to come to grips with relativism as a doctrine of *"ought,"* that is, of the possibility of rational ethics, of the possibility of agreement about issues of right or wrong through guidance by rational standards. Brandt (1961, p. 433) has pointed out that ethical relativism, as understood by contemporary social scientists, usually consists of the following three beliefs: (1) that moral principles are culturally variable in a fundamental way; (2) that such divergence is logically unavoidable, that is, that there are no rational principles and methods which could reconcile observed divergences of moral beliefs; and (3) that people ought to live according to the moral principles they themselves hold. In this context, Brandt states:

> It is important to see that the first two principles are distinct. Failure to see this distinction has been one of the confusions which have beset discussions of the subject. . . . We shall call a person who accepts the first principle a *cultural relativist.* In contrast, we shall reserve the term *ethical relativism* for the view that *both* the first and second principles are true. According to our terminology, then, a man is not ethical relativist unless he is also a cultural relativist; but he may well be a cultural relativist without being an ethical relativist. [Brandt, 1961, p. 433]

As held by many social scientists, however, ethical relativism is often a confusion between the idea that "everyone has their own values" and the idea that "everyone ought to have their own values." In other words, the value-relativity position often rests on a logical confusion between matters of fact (there are no standards accepted by all persons) and matters of value (there are no standards which all persons ought to accept). This last point of view, the value-relativity position, represents the "naturalistic fallacy" of deriving statements of value from statements of fact.

The validity of the *cultural* relativist position is ultimately a question to be decided on the basis of empirical facts, and the facts, we believe, support the universalist position. On the other hand, *ethical* relativism as a philosophic doctrine is the assumption that there is no way for thoughtful or rational persons to resolve their differences in moral values and judgments. For this doctrine the whole enterprise of moral philosophy is nothing more than an exercise in trying to articulate moral concepts and principles in such a way as to help generate moral agreement between reasonable people. However, most writers of modern texts on moral philosophy are "methodological nonrelativists" (e.g., Frankena, 1973; Brandt, 1961). They think that there are methods for defining moral concepts and for conducting moral argumentation which can lead to substantial agreement on moral matters. There are, they assert, methods of moral reasoning which are universally acceptable, just as there are scientific methods which are universally acceptable.

The fact that most social scientists are ethical relativists and most moral philosophers are not is due to the failure of most social scientists to make certain distinctions that moral philosophers make. The first distinction, already pointed to, is the distinction between cultural and ethical relativity. The second distinction, already suggested, is the distinction between moral impartiality, or fairness, and value-neutrality. The attitude of a reasonable social scientist, philosopher, or human being is one of impartiality in making and in analyzing moral judgments. However, it is only positivism or scientism which confuses moral impartiality with value-neutrality and hence fails to understand that to adopt the position of value-neutrality is to adopt an untenable position.

The third, related distinction made by moral philosophers and not often made by social scientists is that between a belief in relativism and a belief in the liberal principle of tolerance or respect for the liberty of conscience of other persons. The principle of tolerance and of fairness in judging other persons and cultures is itself a universalizable moral principle. However, rather than recognizing a universal principle of tolerance per se, the relativist confuses tolerance with relativism and concludes that if every person or culture has "its own bag" then it "should have its own bag."

We believe that it is because the relativist fails to make these distinctions that our claim of universalism has been misunderstood. With these distinctions fresh in the reader's mind, we now phrase our claim of universalism as follows. We claim that there is a universalistically valid form of rational moral thought process which all persons could articulate, assuming social and cultural conditions suitable to cognitive-moral stage development. We claim that the ontogenesis toward this form of rational moral thinking occurs in all cultures, in the same stepwise, invariant stage sequence.

The latter of these claims is not to be confused with our comments about moral norms or issues that are universal in the sense in which we define them but are, at a content level, culturally variable. For example, it is and always has been obvious to us and to the relativist that some persons subscribe to a moral norm of private property (i.e., the right to exclude others from use) while others subscribe to a norm of public property (i.e., the right not to be excluded from use). We grant this variability. The claim we make, however, is that the property norm per se, regardless of its culturally variable content-based definitions, is a moral norm found in all cultures. What we investigate is the development of those structures of justice reasoning which can invoke the relevance of the property norm or other norms, regardless of how they are defined substantively in the context of moral dilemmas.*

Thus, our claim about universalism is first a claim that the development of structures of justice reasoning is a universal development. Second, we claim that the moral norms and elements listed in Table 3.8 are norms and elements that have been used by moral reasoners in all the cultures we have studied. We do not claim that this list of moral norms and elements is necessarily a complete list.

The Assumption of Prescriptivism

There is a further distinction made by moral philosophers and ignored by many psychologists: that is, the distinction between valid or rational judgments and discussions about facts, about what "is," and valid or rational judgments and discussions about values, about what "ought to be." The confusion between "is" and "ought" is called the "naturalistic fallacy" by moral philosophers. Standing behind social science relativism is the naturalistic fallacy, and as practiced by psychologists, it is the direct deriving of statements about what human nature, human values, and human desires *ought to be* from psychological statements about what they *are.* We might add that, typically, this reasoning slides over the distinction between what is desired and what is desirable.

The statement from B. F. Skinner's work (1971), quoted earlier, offers a good example of the psychologist's fallacy. In this statement, Skinner equates or derives a value word (*good*) from a fact word (*positive reinforcement*). This equation is questionable, for one can always question whether obtaining positive reinforcement really is good in any particular situation. Thus, the psychologist's fallacy or the naturalistic fallacy is a fallacy because we can always ask the further question Why is that good? or By what standard is that good? Skinner does not adequately deal with such a further question, called the open question by philosophers. While he also defines good as "cultural survival," the postulation of cultural survival as an ultimate value raises the open question too. We may ask, Why should the Nazi culture (or the American culture) survive? The reason Skinner is not concerned with answering the open question about survival is because he is a cultural relativist and an ethical

---

* We should note that postconventional reasoners tend to define norms in a much more similar fashion than do preconventional or conventional reasoners.

naturalist who believes that any nonfactual reasoning about what is good or about the validity of moral principles is meaningless. As indicated by the statements quoted earlier, the ignoring of the possibility of rational moral discourse distinct from scientific discourse about facts leads to the assumption that whatever is not scientific is relative and arbitrary.

The sophisticated metaethical position lurking behind the naturalistic fallacy is that of naturalism. This position called naturalism is defined by Harman (1977, p. 14) as follows:

> Naturalism is the view that moral judgments and experiences are reducible to underlying natural states as the experience and judgment of color is reducible to statements about light frequencies reaching the retina. This is certainly a plausible suggestion for certain non-moral evaluative facts. Consider, for example, what is involved in something being a good thing of its kind, a good knife, a good watch or a good heart. Associated with these kinds of things are certain functions. Something is a good thing of its kind to the extent that it adequately fits its function, a good knife cuts well, a good watch keeps accurate time, a good heart pumps blood at the right pressure. But a problem arises when this sort of analysis is applied to ethics. It is difficult to state one's obligation to preserve a life in these terms. Is this a factual judgment? If we suppose it a fact that you ought to preserve a human life, how is that fact related to facts of observation. It is not at all obvious that we can extend our analysis to cover this case.

We hold with Hare (1952, 1963) that, as opposed to naturalism, moral language and judgments are fundamentally *pre*scriptive, not *de*scriptive. Hare (1963) argues that some of the meaning of moral judgment is descriptive, since it can refer to facts; but this does not exhaust the meaning of moral judgment. Moral judgments have an additional *prescriptive* element in their meaning. This prescriptive element implies that moral judgments direct, command, or oblige us to take some action. Moral prescriptions are not merely commands to *perform* particular actions, however. They are imperative deriving from some rule or principles of action which the speaker takes as binding upon his or her own actions. These rules or principles may be very instruction-specific and idiosyncratic to the person speaking, but they are still rules or principles with specific features built into them. For example, saying a promise-keeping act is right or obligatory may for a given action have to be phrased as "Let any person who has promised to do something, where the promise was not obtained by force or fraud, do what he has promised to do unless it conflicts with helping a person in overwhelming need" (Hare, 1963, p. 107). According to Hare, then, a moral judgment is an implicit commitment to action by the speaker and by others who share the speaker's principle, a commitment specifiable as a rule or principle.

The notion of a rule or principle in turn requires logically that moral judgments are *universalizable prescriptions.* Kant argued that mature moral principles are morally universalizable in the sense of the categorical imperative, "Let the maxim of thy conduct be the universal will." In this sense principles are universalizable if they are framed to be *justifiable* to, and applied by, *all* moral agents. Hare, however, does not demand universalizability in this strong normative sense. Rather, Hare holds universalizability as a logical or metaethical statement about the meaning of words, as the necessary requirement of moral words. This is a condition which can be met even by cultural or ethical relativists' moral judgments. Hare states:

> By a "logical" thesis, I mean a thesis about the meanings of words, or depending solely upon them. I have been maintaining that the meaning of the word "ought" and other moral words is such that a person who uses them commits himself thereby to a universal rule. This is the thesis of universalizability. It is to be distinguished from *moral* views such as that everybody ought always to adhere to universal rules and govern all their conduct in accordance with them, or that one ought not to make exceptions in one's own favour. . . . Offences against the thesis of universalizability are logical, not moral. If a person says "I ought to act in a certain way, but nobody else ought to act in that way, in relevantly similar circumstances," then, on my thesis he is abusing the word "ought"; he is implicitly contradicting himself. [1963, p. 31–32]

The Assumption of Cognitivism

We have said that the meanings of moral judgments are prescriptive, not descriptive as ethical naturalists claim. This is not to say, however, that moral judgments have no cognitive characteristics, that they are not based on reasoning, even though such reasoning is not the same as scientific reasoning. A common reaction to finding that moral judgments do not have descriptive or natural-science truth is to decide that moral judgments have no cognitive status at all, that they are simply the expression of emotions. This is James Gilligan's (1976) reaction when he says, "Morality is dead. . . . The only knowledge possible is of scientific facts, not of moral values. Moral beliefs and judgments are simply the cognitive counterparts of the painful affects that underlie all morality, shame and guilt."

The ideas expressed by James Gilligan have been systematically elaborated upon by some modern moral philosophers, such as C. L. Stevenson (1963). We shall summarize these views, following Harman (1977, p. 27):

> Nihilism is the doctrine that there are no moral facts, no moral truth, no moral knowledge. Moderate nihilism says that even if this is so, morality should not be abandoned since morality does not describe facts but does something else. One often-made suggestion is that moral judgments express the attitudes and feelings of people making these judgments. To value something is to be in an emotional state of being in favor of something, not a cognitive state.

An emotivist like James Gilligan may recognize that there is a practical reasoning somewhat distinct from scientific reasoning about facts. Such reasoning, however, is limited to means-ends relations. The process of selecting the means to realize one's value may be a rational one to achieve the end, but a claim to ultimate values or ends themselves can not be defended from the standpoint of emotivism.

Emotivism finds it very difficult to account for the fact that we sometimes call moral judgments right or wrong. Feelings and passions cannot be right or wrong for the emotivist, and if moral judgments merely express feelings, it is not easy to see how these judgments are right or wrong. The rightness or wrongness of a judgment depends on reasons offered, and the emotivist position ignores rationality as an aspect of judgment.

It is not clear that the emotivist can account for the relevance of reasoning and appeal to principle in moral judgment. Above, we called the dependence of moral judgment upon principles "prescriptivism." We can now see how moral judgment is cognitive in that it involves reasoning from and to principles. Many psychologists would not want to accept the emotivism of James Gilligan or Stevenson; instead, they would agree that moral judgments imply prescriptive principles and that these principles are justified by, and are applied through, reasoning. Nevertheless, they find our analysis of moral judgment too "bloodless," too much tied to cold reason, not offering a sufficiently formative role in moral judgment to feelings of empathy, compassion, indignation, and so on.

While emotivism excludes the rational component of moral judgment, our assumption of cognitivism, unlike Kantian rationalism, does not deny affect as an integral component of moral judgment or justice reasoning. For example, our theory recognizes affect in appeals to respect for the dignity of persons, as well as in appeals to caring and responsibility between persons. Our theory recognizes affect but always as mediated by, or as structured by, cognitive processes such as role-taking, or putting oneself in the place of the other. This structured affect could be manifested as sympathy for the moral victim, indignation at the moral exploiter, and/or concern for care and taking responsibility.

The ways in which role-taking and other cognitive processes organize moral sentiments are perhaps still best elaborated by Adam Smith (1948) in his *Theory of Moral Sentiments.* Hume (1930) had based the emotive side of moral judgment on empathy for the person affected by the consequences of a moral action. To this observation Smith added the elements of sympathy with the agent and motive of the act as well as sympathy with the person affected by the consequences of the act. For Smith, this self-projection into the actor's role arouses the sentiment of "propriety," that is, our feeling of the fitness of action. Its emotional basis is a sense of pleasure in finding ourselves being similar to or in agreement with the other. For Smith, the strongest moral emotion was the sense of injustice derived both from antipathy toward, or dissatisfaction with, the culprit and sympathy with the resentment of the victim.

According to Smith, our sympathetic or antipathetic judgments of others make us concerned about whether others can sympathize with ourselves. This concern develops into an inner "impartial spectator," a "man within the breast." The most acute moral emotion is guilt, arising when we cannot sympathize with ourselves as actors and share the resentment of the victim as this is experienced by "the impartial spectator" in our breast.

Hume and Smith tried to derive moral judgments from sentiments of empathy or sympathy and in that sense were emotivists. However, they had to include in their theories the idea of an "ideal observer" who would react in a disinterested way with judgments of approval or disapproval stemming from impartial sympathies. We suggest that the introduction of the concept of a disinterested "ideal observer" shows a need to ground emotivist theory in cognitive operations such as reversibility and equity, operations which can lead to the making of principled judgments. One thing not sufficiently noted by Hume and Smith was that role-taking is first of all a cognitive act, a taking of the perspective of the other. There are various cognitive-structural levels of role-taking. In the perspective I presented in Chapter 2, a given level of role-taking is necessary but not sufficient for a parallel stage of moral judgment. The role-taking involved in moral judgment may lead to strong moral sentiments along the lines suggested by Smith. Indeed, in responding to our hypothetical dilemmas, such sentiments are sometimes voiced by respondents.

Hypothetical dilemmas, however, do not typically arouse the strong sentiments generated by role-taking in real situations, or even in those depicted in literature or film. Moral judgments of real-life dilemmas do, however, require the same cognitive perspective-taking structures for their resolution as do hypothetical dilemmas. When we research real-life dilemmas or moral action decisions we find that the cognitive structures associated with our stages are correlated with moral action (Chapter 7; Blasi, 1980).

We find the theory of role-taking and moral sentiments of Hume and Smith compelling, but we reject their emotivist interpretation of moral judgment, since it ignores the central role of principles and reasoning about principles in moral judgment. Their views give us an "aesthetic" view of judgment, an account of the sentiments of a spectator to a moral theater piece. They do not give us an adequate account of a moral actor committed to, and reasoning about, principles. An astronomer's calculation that a comet will hit the earth will be accompanied by strong emotion, but this does not make the calculation less cognitive than the calculation of a comet's orbit that had no consequences for the earth. Just as the strength of the emotional component is irrelevant to the theoretical importance of cognitive structure for understanding the development of scientific judgment, so also is the quantitative role of affect relatively irrelevant for understanding the structure and development of justice reasoning. Our astronomer example is misleading, however, in that affective aspects of mental functioning enter into moral judgment in a different way than they do in scientific judgments. Moral judgments are largely about sentiments and intuitions of persons, and to a large extent they express, and are justified by, reference to the judger's sentiments. The development of sentiment as it enters into moral judgment is, however, a development of structures with a heavy cognitive component, as our discussion of role-taking and moral sentiments illustrates. Thus, while morally relevant emotions and sentiments are part of moral development, it is important to distinguish between the description or expression of a feeling about a moral situation and the making of a moral judgment about it. Expressions of the speaker's emotions about Heinz and the druggist or about the feelings of Heinz or the druggist do not directly constitute moral judgments. Such expressions tell us something about the affective and ego development of the subject, but they do not tell us anything directly about the specifically moral development of the subject. We have said moral judgment is prescriptive, it is not simply the expression of attitudes and emotions. We have said that it is cognitive and reason-giving. A more complete definition of a moral judgment, however, rests on analyzing its formal properties. We now turn our attention to such an analysis.

The Assumption of Formalism

In addition to cognitivism, our starting assumptions in defining the nature and domain of moral judgment and moral development include the assumption of formalism. Our psychological focus upon form comes from the form-content distinction central to structural stage psychology. Our psychological formalism requires, however, a philosophic or metaethical conception of moral form if it is to constitute an appropriate perspective for defining moral judgment as opposed to any other type of judgment. We should note that in some sense formalism is both a normative ethic *and* a way of doing a metaethical analysis, and we and our critics have sometimes confused the two. As a normative ethic, formalism means a deontological ethic like Kant's, which says that rightness is only a matter of the universal form of the principle followed. In contrast, modern moral philosophers like Baier (1965), Hare (1963), Peters (1971), Frankena (1973), and Rawls (1971) have attempted to characterize the formal qualities of a moral judgment or a moral point of view with a metaethical conception. For them, a moral point of view is something that can be agreed upon in defining morality without achieving necessary agreement on the contents or substantive principles of morality. As Frankena (1973) states:

> To develop a theory of the meaning and justification of moral judgments, we must distinguish moral judgments proper from non-moral normative judgments and say something separately about the justification of each. Moral judgments may be characterized in terms of a moral point of view.

Frankena goes on to elaborate criteria for justifying judgments of moral value. Since his writing in this regard aptly expresses our conception of the moral point of view, we quote him at length.

First, we must take the moral point of view, as Hume indicated, not that of self-love or aesthetic judgment, nor the more general point of view involved in judgments of intrinsic value. We must also be free, impartial, willing to universalize, conceptually clear, and informed about all possibly relevant facts. There we are justified in judging that a certain act or kind of action is right, wrong, or obligatory, and in claiming that our judgment is objectively valid, at least as long as no one who is doing likewise disagrees. Our judgment or principle is really justified if it holds up under sustained scrutiny of this sort from the moral point of view on the part of everyone. Suppose we encounter someone who claims to be doing this but comes to a different conclusion. Then we must do our best, through reconsideration and discussion, to see if one of us is failing to meet the conditions in some way. If we can detect no failing on either side and still disagree, we may, and I think still must, each claim to be correct, for the conditions never are perfectly fulfilled by both of us and one of us may turn out to be mistaken after all. If what was said about relativism is true, we cannot both be correct. But both of us must be open-minded and tolerant if we are to go on living within the moral institution of life and not resort to force or other immoral or nonmoral devices.

If this line of thought is acceptable, then we may say that a basic moral judgment, principle, or code is justified or "true" if it is or will be agreed to by everyone who takes the moral point of view and is clearheaded and logical and knows all that is relevant about himself, mankind, and the universe. Are our own principles of beneficence and justice justified or "true" in this sense? The argument in Chapters 2 and 3 was essentially an attempt to take the moral point of view and from it to review various normative theories and arrive at one of our own. Our principles have not been proved, but perhaps it may be claimed that they will be concurred in by those who try to do likewise. This claim was implicitly made in presenting them. Whether the claim is true or not must wait upon the scrutiny of others.

The fact that moral judgments claim a consensus on the part of others does not mean that the individual thinker must bow to the judgment of the majority in his society. He is not claiming an actual consensus, he is claiming that in the end—which never comes or comes only on the Day of Judgment—his position will be concurred in by those who freely and clearheadedly review the relevant facts from the moral point of view. In other words, he is claiming an ideal consensus that transcends majorities and actual societies. One's society and its code and institutions may be wrong. Here enters the autonomy of the moral agent—he must take the moral point of view and must claim an eventual consensus with others who do so, but he must judge for himself. He may be mistaken, but, like Luther, he cannot do otherwise. Similar remarks hold for one who makes nonmoral judgments.

What is the moral point of view? This is a crucial question for the view we have suggested. It is also one on which there has been much controversy lately. According to one theory, one is taking the moral point of view if and only if one is willing to universalize one's maxims. Kant would probably accept this if he were alive. But I pointed out that one may be willing to universalize from a prudential point of view; and also that what one is willing to universalize is not necessarily a moral rule. Other such formal characterizations of the moral point of view have been proposed. A more plausible characterization to my mind, however, is that of Kurt Baier. He holds that one is taking the moral point of view if one is not being egoistic, one is doing things on principle, one is willing to universalize one's principles, and in doing so one considers the good of everyone alike.

My own position, then, is that one is taking the moral point of view if and only if *(a)* one is making normative judgments about actions, desires, dispositions, intentions, motives, persons, or traits of character; *(b)* one is willing to universalize one's judgments; *(c)* one's reasons for one's judgments consist of facts about what the things judged do to the lives of sentient beings in terms of promoting or distributing nonmoral good and evil; and *(d)* when the judgment is about oneself or one's own, one's reasons include such facts about what one's own actions and dispositions do to the lives of other sentient beings as such, if others are affected. One has a morality or moral action-guide only if and insofar as one makes normative judgments from this point of view and is guided by them. [Frankena, 1973, pp. 112–114]

As was noted earlier, one premise of the formalist metaethical position is that it can define the moral point of view in a manner which can be rationally agreed upon without necessarily reaching agreement upon the content or substantive principles of morality. This formalist position parallels, in a way, the distinction between form and content as it relates to our theory of moral stage growth. For us, a given stage has certain formal characteristics which may generate various pro or con moral contents, all of which can be consistent with its form. (We did note earlier in the chapter, however, that persons reasoning at the postconventional level are more likely to generate similar content decisions than are persons who reason at the pre- or conventional levels.) Thus, the development of moral reasoning is, we claim, a movement toward constructing the formal characteristics of a moral point of view.

In reference to our other metaethical assumptions, we have argued largely by pointing out the difficulties inherent in adopting the opposed position. In this case of metaethical formalism, we know of no systematic statement of an opposed position.

The Assumption of Principledness

We have assumed that moral judgments are prescriptive and articulate moral rules or principles, and in the previous subsection, we identified "the moral point of view" as one based on, or referring to, principles. The point of view opposed to our assumption of principledness is a view we shall call "contextual relativism."

An example of a contextual relativist is Munsey (1980), editor of the volume of criticisms and commentaries on the Kohlberg theory entitled *Moral Development, Moral Education and Kohlberg.* In her own chapter in the volume, "Cognitive-Developmental Theory and Moral Development: Metaethical Issues," Munsey takes the position, primarily a metaethical position, of what she calls John Dewey's "act theory" and contrasts this position with Kant's or Rawls's "rule theory." According to Munsey, a rule theory bases moral judgment and choice upon constructive rules (or what we term principles) such as Rawls's two principles of justice.

> In contrast, act theorists hold that moral rules are not a required part of the evidence justifying singular moral judgments. Rather, justified singular moral judgments can be made merely on the relevant particular facts in a given moral dilemma. General considerations (i.e., moral rules or principles) are not required. The identification of the morally relevant particular facts, while facilitated by moral rules, is logically independent of moral rules. . . . Although, according to act theory, moral rules are not a necessary condition for justifying moral judgments, they are an extremely important part of moral deliberations. They are moral generalizations derived from summarizing our knowledge of the morally relevant particular factors which warranted our past moral judgments. . . . The issue concerning the nature of moral rules can be understood as the issue of whether valid moral rules (whatever they are thought to be, rules of utility or rules of justice) are constitutive rules or summary rules. . . . If rules are best seen as summary rules, they function as starting points in subsequent deliberations and are implicit in our spontaneous identification of certain factors as relevant to a justified resolution of a present moral dilemma. However, they do not define our reflective identification of *all* morally relevant factors. It is always possible to recognize *novel situational* factors as relevant to a justified resolution factor which may not be adequately covered by a present structure of summary rules no matter how generally adequate it might be. [Munsey, 1980, pp. 163–164]

The "act theory" position taken by Munsey might be termed "contextual relativism" instead of "act theory." It is a "Deweyite" position taken by a number of our critics, including Gilligan and Murphy (1979) and Aron (1980).

Munsey frames her critique in terms of John Dewey's articulation of contextual relativism. Dewey (see Dewey and Tufts, 1932, pp. 347–353) critiques views of moral theory or moral principles as absolutes.

> Study from this point of view discloses in a concrete fashion the limitation of moral theory and its positive office. It shows that it is not the business of moral theory or moral principles to provide a ready-made solution to large moral perplexities and dilemmas. But it also makes it clear that while the solution to a dilemma has to be reached by *action* based on personal choice, theory can enlighten and guide choice by revealing alternatives, and by bringing to light what is entailed when we choose one alternative rather than another. It shows, in short, that the function of moral theory is not to furnish a substitute for personal reflective choice, but to be an instrument for deliberation more effective and hence choice more intelligent.

Dewey goes on to say:

> Conventional morality conceals from view the uncertainty which attends decision as to what is good in a concrete case and covers up the problematic nature of what is right and obligatory. It puts before us situations where the moral struggle is not just to be kept from departing from what we know already to be right but where we need to *discover* what is right and where reflection and experimentation are the sole means of discovery. There are still those who think they are in possession of codes and principles which settle arbitrarily the right or wrong of divorce, the respective rights of capital and labor. But there are also many other persons who see that such questions as these cannot be deducted from fixed premises, and the attempt to decide them in that fashion is the road to intolerant fanaticism, dogmatism and the closed mind.

Dewey's notion of moral reasoning and choice is primarily directed to "social morality," that is, choices about social or public policy issues.

> One of the chief values of considering the moral bearing of social problems is that we are then confronted with live issues in which vital choices still have to be made and where principles are still in the process of forming.

Dewey's questioning of fixed principles, and his equation of them with conventional as opposed to postconventional moral reasoning, is very appropriate in thinking about moral problems as issues of social or public policy. Judgments about, for instance, divorce and abortion as social issues, inextricably mingle issues of fact about the consequence of public acceptance or rejection with issues of "principle." This inextricable integration of factual and "principled" reasoning is obviously historically and contextually relative, since the very meanings of abortion or divorce change historically.

Dewey's view, however, carries over to situations of personal moral choice as well. He writes that reflective moral choice

> is not between desire and reason, but between a desire which wants a nearby object and a desire which wants an object which is seen by thought to occur in consequence of an intervening series of conditions as in the long run. The moral good is some natural good which is sustained and developed through consideration of it in its relations.

Dewey's metaethical theory, then, is one of naturalism. It is also one of an "experimentalism."

> It implies that reflective morality demands observations of particular situations rather than fixed adherence to *a priori* principles. The business of reflection in determining the true good cannot be done once for all by making out a table of values arranged in a hierarchical order. The business of reflection is to be done again and again in terms of the condition of concrete interactions as they arise.

As we shall try to show in our next section, on constructivism, Dewey's view of the nature of postconventional moral reasoning is not as far from our own perspective as it first seems. We agree that in principled morality choice is not dictated by "absolutes" or by rigid or exceptionless rules. Our conception of a principle, like Dewey's, is not one of principle as a fixed rule; rather, we too understand a principle as a way of construing a concrete moral situation. It is true that principled reasoning leads to an understanding of the value of respecting human personality, phrased by Kant as "Treat each person as an end in himself and not merely as a means." However, it is principled reasoning that does *not* employ this value as a fixed rule, because it understands this value as needing interpretation in concrete situations.

Thus, it is principled reasoning that understands the value of human personality as a way of constructing a resolution of a moral dilemma, but it does not understand this value as a substantive rule dictating *a priori* what that resolution should be.

Kohlberg's Heinz dilemma of stealing to save a life can be resolved by Stage 5 justice reasoning, which uses what Dewey calls a "fixed hierarchy of values," by placing the value or norm of life over the value of property. Such a hierarchy, or an absolutistic view of the value of life, does not resolve dilemmas of euthanasia, however. Another dilemma we use, the doctor's dilemma, asks whether a physician should follow the request of a terminally ill person in great pain. The patient reflectively decides to request that the doctor give her large doses of morphine which will reduce the pain but greatly shorten her life. Should the doctor accede to her request? Not if he holds an absolutist view of the value of physical life over the value of avoiding pain. The dilemma involves, however, a reflective consideration of the quality of life, not its sheer preservation—so a Deweyite might eventually weigh and resolve the dilemma. We can also see the doctor's dilemma as clarifying the ethical principle underlying the valuing of life as the hierarchy of life over property. This principle, respect for personality, dictates stealing the drug to save a life in the Heinz dilemma but determines that the doctor accede to the terminally ill woman's request for euthanasia out of respect for human personality and dignity. Thus, the principle of respect for personality is a general way of seeing concrete situations; it is not a fixed rule.

We have articulated our conceptions of principled morality as a way of seeing human perspectives in concrete situations in our discussion of a sixth stage of principled moral judgment. In our theoretical conception, a sixth stage is based on a process of ideal role-taking or "moral musical chairs" in which each person imaginatively changes place with every other in the dilemma before stating his or her claims as rightful. This conception of ideal role-taking attempts to synthesize Dewey's views, G. H. Mead's (1934) reconstruction of Kant's categorical imperative as universalizable role-taking, Rawls's social contract theory, and Habermas's (1979) conception of discursive will formation.

In Rawls's theory, ideal role-taking is a statement of a moral point of view for choosing the justice principles of liberty and equality. Ideal role-taking is specified as choosing from an "original position," under a veil of ignorance about who in the society one is. This perspective leads to endorsing those principles of justice which should be *socially agreed upon.* From our point of view, one could say that some general commitment to principles of justice enjoins the moral reasoner to engage in ideal role-taking in order to resolve moral dilemmas. In this sense, our view of moral principles acknowledges the situational context of each moral problem.

Even utilitarianism is a form of principled morality that is contextual. It prescribes considering and maximizing the welfare consequences of an action for each person affected by the action. It reduces ideal role-taking, however, to an objectivating and calculating view of interest-weighing, rather than a view springing from an attitude of respect for the personality and the viewpoint of each person. It is these principles, however, that are central to the more justice-oriented version of principled morality that we favor.

Having stated our claim that adequate moral principles consider context, as Dewey himself holds, we should also note and agree with Dewey's emphasis that the most problematic, changing, historically relative aspect of moral choice is attending to the factual aspects of a moral dilemma. For example, the factual meaning of issues of life quality, seen in real-life abortion and euthanasia dilemmas, changes with each new biological or technological advance in knowledge. We agree that such changes cannot be overlooked by principled reasoning.

In summary, our assumption and conception of principled morality is sensitive to specifics of real-life situations which are the concern of contextual relativists. However, our viewpoint assumes that universal principles which are contextually applied are not thereby rendered arbitrary in the face of changing historical circumstance. This notion of principled stability is unavailable within a relativist position.

The Assumption of Constructivism

We pointed out that "contextually relative" critiques of our notions of mature or competent moral judgment often failed to distinguish rules from principles, defined as guides to "seeing" situations. Consistent with contextually relativist criticisms of a rules-morality are criticisms that assume that a morality of general rules or principles cannot avoid being absolutistic and *a priori.* Our own view of principles has been assumed, incorrectly, to be similar to Kant's, whose view was that principles were "constitutive" in Munsey's terms. As Munsey (1980, p. 164) states: "If moral rules are taken as constitutive rules, they would be a set of *a priori* rules which could not admit of exception. If, on the other hand, moral rules were summary rules, empirical generalizations, they could admit of exception."

Given the distinction we (and Dewey) make between rules and principles, we do not see principles as being "summary rules," that is, as inductions from past moral facts. Neither do we see them as "constitutive rules," or *a priori* axioms from which moral judgments are deduced as geometric propositions were deduced from prior Euclidean axioms. As Rawls (1980) has pointed out, not only his principles but also those specified by Kant may be best viewed as constructions, a view compatible with Piaget's constructivistic theory of the development of cognition.

With regard to moral principles, we follow Rawls's account of the formulation of principles as a "bootstrapping" or spiral process of "attaining reflective equilibrium." According to this account, principles or methods for judging are tentatively applied to cases or dilemmas. Where there is a discrepancy between the principle and our intuitions about the right action in the dilemma, we can either reformulate the principle or decide our moral intuition was in error. Whichever we decide, we move on to consider other cases, being open to change until we reach a "reflective equilibrium" between our principles and our moral intuitions about concrete cases.

In the context of the issues raised by Munsey (1980), my view of moral principles is that they are developmental constructions and not *a priori* axioms or inductions from past experience. This view derives from Piaget's central constructivist assumption, that is, the assumption that mental structures are neither *a priori* biological innates nor inductive habits passively learned from sense experience but are, rather, active constructions assimilating experiences while accommodating to them.

In the Munsey (1980) volume, Boyd (pp. 203–288) elucidates this constructivistic aspect of Rawls's and Kohlberg's conceptions of justice.

[In both Kohlberg's theory and Rawls's theory] principled judgments of justice are seen as the constructive emergents of a dynamic process of interaction among persons conceived as self-determining and rule-following agents. In this view, "justice" refers to, as Edward Cahn has argued, "not a state but a process, not a condition but an action. Justice means the active process of remedying or preventing what would arouse a sense of injustice." In the context of justice in this sense, judgments of principle do not derive their validity from an epistemological status of certainty attributed to the principles referred to, but rather from their being viewed as what all persons could agree to when conceived of as persons seeking to regulate their interactions fairly. Rawls's original position and Kohlberg's "ideal role-taking" must be seen primarily as ways of entering moral argument; they are procedural interpretations of how persons seek a provisional, dynamic state of reflective equilibrium with each other about questions concerning their interactions in a world of a certain sort.

In his paper "The Original Position," Dworkin (1976) has interpreted Rawls's theory in a way which illustrates the above point. Dworkin elaborates two philosophic positions which give differing accounts for the way in which ethical theories can be thought of as relating to our basic moral intuitions. He calls one "the natural model" and the other "a constructive model."

According to the natural model, theories of justice, like Rawls's two principles, describe an objective moral reality; they are not, that is, created by men in societies but are rather discovered by them, as they discover the laws of physics. The main instrument of this discovery is a moral faculty of conscience which produces concrete intuitions or political morality like the intuition that slavery is wrong. The second model treats intuitions of justice not as clues to the existence of independent principles but rather as stimulated features of a theory to be constructed, as if a sculptor set himself to carve an animal that best fit a pile of bones he happened to find together. The "constructive model" does not assume, as the natural model does, that principles of justice have some fixed objective existence, so that descriptions of these principles must be true or false in some standard way—It makes the different assumption that men and women have a responsibility to fit the particular judgment on which they act into a coherent program of action. . . . The natural model, we might say, looks at intuitions from the personal standpoint of the individual who holds them, and who takes them to be observations of moral reality. The constructive model looks at the intuitions from a more public standpoint; it is a model someone might propose for the governance of a community each of whose members have strong convictions that differ, though not too greatly, from the constructions of others. [Dworkin, 1976, pp. 27–28]

Boyd points out, in addition, that the constructivist model conceives persons as having attitudes of mutual respect.

Persons are not thought of as independent, isolated "rule-followers," with greater or less direct access to the moral truth, but rather as rule-followers-in-relation who must construct and continually reconstruct through public dialogue the perspective from which rules governing their action have validity. [Boyd, 1980, p. 204]

To a certain extent, a constructivist and interactive metaethical conception of morality has been implied by the following characterization of Stage 5.

> Right action tends to be defined in terms of general individual rights and standards which have been critically examined and agreed upon by the whole society. There is a clear awareness of relativism of personal values and opinions and a corresponding emphasis upon procedural rules for reaching consensus. [Vol. I, chapter 4, p. 154]

The socially constructive nature of Stage 6 has not been as clear in some of my discussions. Thus, some have interpreted my writing in this context as suggesting that fully competent moral judgment comes from an individual's conscientious commitment to, or discovery of, moral principles, through some infallible faculty of conscience. My discussions of Stage 6 in terms of moral musical chairs or ideal role-taking, however, makes it fairly clear that Stage 6 principles are necessarily social constructions preparing the person for a process of moral dialogue. Such principles structure an imaginative process in the individual's mind which attempts to produce an ideal moral dialogue for resolving conflicts. The adequacy of the conflict resolution proposed is determined by the achievement of social consensus under dialogic conditions. We see Rawls's concept of the original position under a "veil of ignorance" about one's own role in society as an instance of this preparation for moral dialogue.

> We call the process by which a reversible moral decision is reached "ideal role-taking." Stage 6 moral judgment is based on role-taking the claim of each actor under the assumption that all other actors are also governed by the Golden Rule and accommodated accordingly. Ideal role-taking is the decision procedure ultimately required by the attitude of respect for persons and of justice as equity. A decision reached in that way is in "equilibrium" in the sense that it is "right" from the point of view of all involved insofar as they are governed by a moral attitude or a conception of justice, insofar as they are willing to take the role of others. [Volume I, chapter 5, p. 197]

Because our constructivistic conception was not clearly built into the idea of a highest stage, Habermas (1979, p. 89) was led to postulate a seventh stage which would have such characteristics. We will discuss Habermas's claim about a seventh stage in some detail in Chapter 4. For now we will simply state that we see Habermas's conception of his Stage 7 as consistent with our view of my Stage 6:

If needs are understood as culturally interpreted but ascribed to individuals as natural properties, the admissable universalist norms of action have the character of general moral norms. Each individual is supposed to test monologically the generalizability of the norms in question. This corresponds to Kohlberg's Stage 6 (conscience orientation). Only at the level of a universal ethics of speech can need interpretations themselves, that is what each individual thinks he should understand and represent as his true interests, also become the object of practical discourse. Kohlberg does not differentiate this stage from Stage 6, although there is a qualitative difference. The principle of justification of norms is no longer the monologically applicable principle of generalizability but the communally followed procedure of redeeming normative validity claims discursively. An unexpected result of our attempt to derive the stages of moral consciousness from the stages of interactive competence is the demonstration that Kohlberg's scheme of stages is incomplete. [1979, pp. 89–90]

The Assumption of Justice as Primary in Defining the Moral Domain

We discussed in previous sections a definition of moral judgment in terms of the formal criteria of the moral point of view. We stressed particularly two formal characteristics of moral judgment, prescriptivity and universalizability.

Our starting assumptions led to the design of a research instrument measuring reasoning about dilemmas of conflicting rights or of the distribution of scarce resources, that is, justice concerns. We did not use dilemmas about prosocial concerns for others that were not framable as rights conflicts. Besides this limitation to justice dilemmas, we focused our probing questions and scoring procedures on eliciting judgments that were prescriptive and universalizable, while ignoring statements of personal feeling and those that attempted to rewrite the dilemma situation in order to resolve it. To some extent this latter type of material, most often elicited by dilemmas about prosocial concerns, is central to Eisenberg-Berg's (Mussen and Eisenberg-Berg, 1977) and Gilligan's (Gilligan and Belenky, 1980) conceptions of caring and responsibility.

Following Piaget's lead, I thought that justice reasoning would be the cognitive factor most amenable to structural developmental stage analysis insofar as it would clearly provide reasoning material where structuring and equilibrating operations (e.g., reversibility) could be seen. With the moral domain defined in terms of justice, we have been successful in *(a)* elaborating stages which are structural systems in the Piagetian tradition and *(b)* honoring the metaethical assumptions we have made prior to research. To imply that justice is the *first* virtue of a person or of a society, as did Kant and Plato, is a more controversial normative claim that is not required for establishing the validity of our measure and theory of justice development. It seems to us, however, that morally valid forms of caring and community presuppose prior conditions and judgments of justice.

Thus, our assumptions prior to research, as well as the results of our research, have led us to hold that the prescriptivity of moral judgments is a fundamental component of justice reasoning which bases prescriptions and duties on a recognition of others' rights.

The universalizability or impartiality criteria of moral judgment also implies that moral reasoning, as we have studied it, constructs judgments of justice. A universalizable judgment that appeals to norms implies a fair or impartial application of the norms. The way in which a concern for universalizability in upholding a moral norm leads to justice as impartiality may be illustrated by the following example. An 11-year-old boy was asked whether a man should steal a drug to save a friend or even a stranger if there was no other way to save that person's life (Dilemma III). He had previously said that a husband should steal the drug for his wife. He answered: "Well he loved his wife very much; it doesn't really seem that you should steal for someone you don't care about or love that much; you really don't care that much about the stranger." After a pause he went on: "But somehow it doesn't seem fair to say that. The stranger has his life and wants to live just as much as your wife; it isn't fair to say you should steal it for your wife but not for the stranger." This boy's second or revised judgment appeals to the value element of equality (i.e., impartiality) to universalize the norm or value of life in judging the dilemma.

The kind of probing question which we have asked in our dilemmas is a deontic question focusing on the right and on rights and duties. The questions we have seldom asked are aretaic questions, that is, questions that focus on the moral value of lives or persons or questions that ask about ideals of the good life or the good person.

To summarize, the focus of Piaget and ourselves on morality as deontological justice springs from a number of metaethical considerations. First, it derives from our prescriptivist conception of moral judgment; in other words, we focus less upon interpretations of situational facts and more upon those interpretations which express universalizable or "ought" orientations. Second, it springs from our concern for cultural and ethical universality in moral judgment. The search for moral universality implies the search for some minimal value conceptions on which all persons could agree, regardless of differences between them in terms of their detailed aims or goals. As stated by Boyd:

> Conceptions of the good and ideals of human perfection are by no means unimportant for Rawls or Kohlberg. But they do not constitute the essence of morality nor adequately circumscribe the proper entry point into moral questions. For both, pursuit of the good and human perfection is subordinated as a concern to adjudicating differences among individuals on how the good and human perfection are to be defined, furthered and distributed. One cannot understand this entry point unless one understands that they assume that individuals do and will differ in this fundamental way. This presumption of human conflict rests on a more fundamental belief that the good, even for one individual, is not one but pluralistic. . . . Choice of the good is seen as fundamentally subjective and pluralistic, and the moral point of view is seen as objectivity seeking, interpersonal and adjudicatory. [Boyd, 1980, p. 187–188]

Morality as justice best renders our view of morality as universal. It restricts morality to a central minimal core, striving for universal agreement in the face of more relativist conceptions of the good.

Another reason for focusing upon justice is our concern for a cognitive or "rational" approach to morality. This is true partly in the sense that justice asks for "objective" or rational reasons and justifications for choice rather than being satisfied with subjective, "decisionistic," personal commitments to aims and to other persons. However, once personal commitments have been made they may become objectively defended by justice conceptions like contract and trust.

Possibly the most important reason for focusing upon justice is that it is the most structural feature of moral judgment. For Piaget and ourselves justice is the structure of interpersonal interaction. Justice "operations" of reciprocity and equality in interaction parallel logical operations or relations of equality and reciprocity in the nonmoral cognitive domain.

It seems likely that our framing the moral domain in terms of justice has maximized the possibility of finding hard stages of this domain of development. It seems likely that part of the success of the instrument in defining a cross-culturally invariant stage sequence in the cultures studied (e.g., in the United States, Turkey, and Israel) has resulted from this definition of the domain.

The fact that our dilemmas and stage definitions assume a centrality of justice in moral judgment is reflected empirically in the consistency of moral stage from one moral dilemma or conflict of rights to another. This consistency is empirically reflected in the fact that over two-thirds of a person's thinking is at a single stage and that there is a general factor of moral stage observed across dilemmas and across issues, as detected by methods of factor analysis. It could have been the case that the development of moral judgments was specific to certain other moral norms or virtues other than justice, such as norms of honesty or norms of loyalty and affiliation in interpersonal relations. If this had been the case, no general justice factor would have emerged but only factors of the development of specific norms. While we presupposed a general factor of justice in defining our moral dilemmas and stage structures, this predefinition did not guarantee empirical success in actually defining a unifying moral domain.*

In focusing on justice, we are not denying the possibility of extending the idea of stages of moral judgment to other and possibly broader conceptions of the moral domain. Particularly absent from our studies has been a concern with moral reasoning about choices which go beyond duty and justice, that is, dilemmas which elicit supererogatory choice. As we have discussed in our prior section on the enlargement of the moral domain, in going beyond justice we believe that Eisenberg-Berg, as well as Carol Gilligan and her colleagues, may end with definitions of what we would call soft stages of development. At least, this is the way in which I have treated supererogatory ethics in a chapter with Shulik and Higgins entitled "The Aging Person as a Philosopher," (Kohlberg, 1984,

* We may note that there have been other attempts to discover unitary cognitive factors, which have failed. In the decade of the 1920s, for example, psychometricians attempted to define a discrete domain of "social intelligence" by employing tests of intelligence about social situations. They found, however, that there was no such general domain of social intelligence separable from general intelligence as previously defined by Spearman. Thus, the concept of social intelligence received no empirical support from studies directed to assessing it.

in press) where I see responsible love as related to Fowler's (1981) levels of ethical and religious orientation in defining a good and meaningful life.

While the assumption of the primacy of justice has not been "proved" by our research, the fact that data collected under this assumption meet the requirements of sequentiality, structured wholeness, and relationship to action indicates the empirical fruitfulness of the assumption.

In constructing our scoring manual we followed Frankena (1973) in discriminating between orientations to, or "theories" of, rightness. We classify these orientations to justice as the normative order or rule-following orientation; the (egoistic and) utilitarian consequence orientation; the perfectionist or harmony-seeking orientation; and the fairness orientation. Our own theory, like that of Rawls (1971), stresses justice as fairness, and we shall try to indicate how fairness has primacy among the orientations. However, as we will see, each orientation can claim to define criteria of justice. After classifying the four orientations toward justice situations, our manual goes on to classify elements or operations used in reasoning within each orientation (see Table 3.8).

We view these elements as functioning to equilibrate relations in the interpersonal or social sphere, and we see them as paralleling formally similar operations defined by Piaget in the logicomathematical domain.

The major justice operations, which we call "value elements" in the fairness orientation, are equality and reciprocity. We call them operations because they are interiorized actions of distribution and exchange which parallel logical operations of equality and reciprocity. In addition, we call them operations because they equilibrate or balance conflicting value claims. This equilibration implies that moral actions are reversible (i.e., valid regardless of initial standpoint).

While the use of the major justice operations is explicit when elements of the fairness orientation are used, we shall explain at some length how the major operations of equality and reciprocity are also used, implicitly, in the other three justice orientations. Because of this implicit use, the other justice orientations can also be seen as forms of operational reasoning. As a result, we elaborate in Appendix A definitions of each stage in terms of justice operations.

Our philosophic theory (Volume I, Chapter 5) stresses the crite-

Table 3.8

The Elements

Upholding Normative Order:

1. Obeying (consulting) person or deity. Should obey, get consent (should consult, persuade).
2. Blaming (approving). Should be blamed for, disapproved (should be approved).
3. Retributing (exonerating). Should retribute against (should exonerate).
4. Having a right (having no right).
5. Having a duty (having no duty).

Egoistic Consequences:

6. Good reputation (bad reputation).
7. Seeking reward (avoiding punishment).

Utilitarian Consequences:

8. Good individual consequences (bad individual consequences).
9. Good group consequences (bad group consequences).

Ideal or Harmony-Serving Consequences:

10. Upholding character.
11. Upholding self-respect.
12. Serving social ideal or harmony.
13. Serving human dignity and autonomy.

Fairness:

14. Balancing perspectives or role-taking.
15. Reciprocity or positive desert.
16. Maintaining equity and procedural fairness.
17. Maintaining social contract or freely agreeing.

The Norms

1. Life
   a. Preservation
   b. Quality/quantity
2. Property
3. Truth
4. Affiliation
5. (Erotic love and sex)
6. Authority
7. Law
8. Contract
9. (Civil rights)
10. (Religion)
11. Conscience
12. Punishment

rion of reversibility as the ultimate criterion of justice. Reversibility is that property of a justice structure of moral operations which enables the structure to construct solutions to dilemmas in such a way that these solutions can be considered acceptable or just from the points of view of all relevant parties. At the highest level of moral reasoning, reversibility implies a conception of justice as "moral musical chairs," a conception which requires each person to systematically take the position of everyone else in the situation until a solution emerges that is balanced fairly. Using this criterion of reversibility, we argue along with Rawls (1971) that orienting to justice as fairness is the most adequate representation of and orientation to justice problems. In this section, however, we want to point out how each of the other three orientations also implies systems of justice operations involving a degree of reversibility.

Let us now turn to the utilitarian orientation, which defines the just solution as that which maximizes good welfare consequences or minimizes bad consequences. In an operation of maximizing there is an implicit equality operation; that is, each individual is more or less to count as one in the calculation. For example, in this orientation saving more lives is considered better than saving fewer lives. In maximizing operations one must count units; that is, each life counts as one.

In addition to the utilitarian orientation's implicit use of the operation of equality in calculating good individual or group consequences, this orientation can also employ an implicit operation of reciprocity. To illustrate this, we offer the following example from our scoring manual (Colby and Kohlberg, 1984, in press), Form A Life Issue, Criterion Judgment #23, which uses the norm of life and the element of good group consequences: Heinz should steal the drug "because his wife can contribute to society." In this response is an implicit notion of fairness as reciprocity; that is, if a person is a contributor to society then he or she deserves the drug. She is a contributor. Therefore, she should get the drug. Another example of an implicit reciprocity operation is found in Form A Law Issue, Criterion Judgment #24, which uses the property norm and an element of good group consequences: Heinz should not steal the drug "because if property rights are not upheld or if many people in such situations were to steal then there would be no encouragement or incentive for the invention of new drugs." This criterion judgment implies the operation of reciprocity in the relationship between working or inventing drugs and a deserved incentive or reward for such work. The harmful consequences of stealing would destroy this reciprocal aspect of justice and societal relations.

A utilitarian concern for group consequences which reflects a concern for consistency and equality is given in Form A Law Issue, Criterion Judgment #25, which uses the norm of law and the element of good group consequences: It is important to obey the law in general "because laws serve to protect the productive and orderly functioning of society; or, because orderliness will be undermined if a precedent for disregarding the law is set; or, orderliness will be undermined if citizens decide individually when to obey and when to disobey the law." The utilitarian concern here involves a focus on justice as consistency. One subject elaborates this idea by saying, "I think we claim to live in a society based on laws not men. It would be nice to believe that man could live without those kinds of rules and regulations, that he is a creature that works always rationally and does those things which each of us say need to be done. But we always have a few in society that don't operate that way." This subject's concern for the impartiality of government by law instead of by men implies not only the idea of consistency but also the idea of equality, that is, treating like cases alike and maintaining equality between normal people with different beliefs, attitudes, persuasions, and so forth.

We have seen the way in which operations of reciprocity and equality, which are explicit in governing reasoning in the fairness orientation, are implicit in the utilitarian orientation. The same may be said about judgments within the normative order orientation. Judgments here appeal to a norm or rule and make a modal moral judgment supporting this norm. Modal elements are morally prescriptive words such as "having a right" or "having a duty" which do not make explicit a terminal value such as maximizing good consequences or treating people equally. While moral judgments in the normative order orientation do not make explicit use of justice operations like reciprocity or equality, these operations are nevertheless more or less implicit in the norm itself. For example, we note Form A Contract Issue, Criterion Judgment #4, which uses the property norm and the element of having a right: Joe should refuse to give his father the money "because it's Joe's, he saved it and has a right to do what he wants with it." This statement applies the norm of property ownership to the dilemma and uses the norm of property ownership as defining a right. In this case, implicit in the norm of property rights is a justice element of reciprocity. This reciprocity element becomes explicitly used in the fairness orientation. This can be seen in Form A Contract Issue, Criterion Judgment #12: Joe should refuse to give his father the money "because he worked hard; or, in good faith; or, he earned the money to do something his father had promised he could do." In this case the idea of reciprocity as deservingness is made explicit; that is, if you work you deserve to keep what you thereby earn. In the earlier property rights judgment, scored under the normative order orientation, the application of the norm to the situation is definitional. "Saved money" is definitional to having a property right to do what you want with it. In contrast, in the fairness orientation the emphasis is rather on the balancing or deservingness of working hard and thereby earning a return.

Implicit in other normative order judgments is the operation of equality, an operation which is explicitly used in the fairness orientation. As an example of the implicit use of the equality operation within the normative order orientation, we note Form A Punishment Issue, Criterion Judgment #28. People who break the law out of conscience should be punished "because people's consciences differ, and you have to have a common standard or rule for judging acts of conscience." Implicit in this judgment, whose explicit element is obedience, is the element or operation of equality, that is, the need for a consistent standard or system which judges people equally regardless of subjective conscience. In the fairness orientation, the use of the equality operation occurs explicitly. An example of this can be seen in Form A Punishment Issue, Criterion Judgment #39. This is a Stage 5 response in which the norm of law is upheld with the element of maintaining equity: The doctor should be reported or receive a token punishment "because if we can assume a just legal system is operating, then citizens ought to abide by due process as provided by that system. Although turning the doctor in may not be perfectly just, leaving such decisions up to each individual's judgment would result in the long run in greater injustice" (e.g., inequities in punishment for the same crime). In this case we can see that equality before the law should explicitly govern the judge's decision, whereas in the previous example following the law was the explicit focus of judgment per se, with the notion of equality being only implicit.

In the last example we found that what was left implicit in a Stage 4 judgment within the normative order orientation became explicit in the fairness orientation in a judgment made at Stage 5. This brings us to a general point about increasing differentiation by stage. In some cases at a given lower stage, no differentiation is made between upholding the norm and upholding the fairness element which we said was implicit in the norm. However, at a higher stage there is a differentiation made between upholding the norm and upholding the fairness element in a way not true at a lower stage.

The perfectionistic orientation is primarily oriented toward upholding moral ideals, the ideals of moral personality, and the ideal of moral community. The central ideal is, arguably, that of personhood and human respect for human personality, including conscience, which is the moral element of human personality. Associated with this central value is that of human community and relationships as the expression of this ideal or the medium through which this ideal is expressed.

We suggest that common to the perfectionist elements is an attitude of respecting and realizing moral ideals. As was the case in the normative and utilitarian orientations, this perfectionist orientation can also be seen to make implicit use of fairness elements. An example of this can be seen in Form A Life Issue, Criterion Judgment #26, where the property norm is used with the element of serving social ideal or harmony. Here there is implicit in the notion of responsibility an operation of, or a fairness element of, equality: [Heinz should steal the drug] because "the druggist in his exploitation has failed to show any responsibility to his fellow man; or, because he should have used this discovery to benefit humanity or society." An example in which the equality element becomes explicit can be seen in Form A Life Issue, Criterion Judgment #30: The druggist doesn't have a right to charge that much "because, first of all, a drug is a potential benefit to mankind and to withhold it from mankind for economic reasons, for his own personal gain, is besides being selfish, unfair. I think people have a certain responsibility to each other, and just because one person has the skill or luck to come into possession of a thing which gives him power over others doesn't mean he should take advantage of this power to the point of exploitation."

In summary, we assume the primacy of justice in our methodology by using it (*a*) to define the domain of investigation, (*b*) to operationalize moral reasoning stages, and (*c*) to differentiate moral perspective-taking from social cognitive perspective-taking capacity.

The domain of justice is partly defined by the problems or dilemmas we set our subjects in the standardized interview. A dilemma such as Joe and the father (Form A, Dilemma I) sets a problem of balancing issues of contract valuing against authority valuing. This is a problem of commutative justice. The judge's dilemma (Form A, Dilemma III′) poses a problem of restorative and procedural justice, of balancing issues of conscience valuing against punishment valuing. The Heinz dilemma (Form A, Dilemma III) poses a problem of distributive justice, of balancing issues of life valuing against law valuing. (The various types of justice problems are elaborated in Appendix A.)

At each stage the justice operations and their elemental expressions are articulated within different justice perspectives. These justice perspectives and the contrasts between them are fundamental in our assessment of stage developmental transition. For example, the critical move from Stage 2 to Stage 3 justice reasoning is expressed by the construction and use of a third party perspective. This new sociocognitive competence recognizes and is further used to prescribe and endorse shared norms defining expected motives in actions. This prescription and endorsement constitutes the specifically *moral* perspective-taking competence that constitutes Stage 3 justice reasoning and differentiates it from Stage 2 justice reasoning. In using this new justice perspective, the Stage 2 operation of concrete reciprocity as fairness is reconstructed to form Stage 3 imaginative or ideal reciprocity as expressed in the Golden Rule. This may mean, for instance, that even though Heinz and his wife have never done anything concretely for the druggist, he still owes the drug to Heinz and his wife, and others like them, including himself, as people ideally (not concretely) related, doing to each other as they *all would wish to be done by,* independent of any actual concrete exchanges that have taken place or will take place among them.

Similarly, at Stage 4, reciprocity is viewed from a single social system perspective which extends and limits reciprocity to that which can be consistently and impartially maintained within the single established system. This may mean, for instance, that even though the druggist was unfair (selfish) in withholding the drug, some form of restitution is nevertheless due him, for he is someone with systematic property rights, regardless of his character or his motives.

In moving to Stage 5, reciprocity practices are extended by or defined through a transforming notion of free agreements which rational persons could accept in any society. The Stage 5 notion of peoples' rationality is not underpinned or defined by idiosyncratic norms of one social system but has a cross-systemic applicability. This may mean, for instance, that even though the cultural and legal system of which the druggist is a member gives him a (Stage 4) right or institutionalized clearance to charge what the particular supply-and-demand regulated market will bear, nevertheless, that form of distribution itself and the actor who uses it is unfair (in Stage 5 terms) because Heinz's wife has rights beyond that of a legal consumer. Her life deserves recognition beyond its function in particular institutions and systems. Her life takes place and value within a more abstract and complex forum, the forum or perspective of human species relevance which is significant and gives significance across systems. Philosophers and political scientists need not agree on the exact content-concerns of a rational actor coming to agreements about justice and reciprocity. However, the *practice* of attempting such discourse by moral philosophers or political scientists presupposes some perspective such as Stage 5 justice reasoning.

We speculate that, at Stage 6, justice or reciprocity is defined by a "second-order" Golden Rule. This idea is expressed by the principle of reversibility stated in Volume I, Chapter 5 as the principle of ideal role–taking or moral musical chairs; by Rawls (1971) as the notion of an original position under the veil of ignorance; and finally, by Habermas (1979) in his notion of dialogic interaction governed by a universally recognized speech ethic.

In the preceding examples we have traced the reciprocity operation through the stages of justice reasoning in order to distinguish justice operations from justice perspectives. We have given examples of how the reciprocity operation is extended and limited in its applicability to persons as those persons and their rights are created and viewed by particular sociomoral perspectives.

Finally, a further word is in order about reversibility, insofar as it may be viewed as a property of a stage of justice reasoning. Earlier we introduced the criterion of reversibility as best fitting the orientation of fairness, as opposed to the other three justice orientations. In doing this, we implied the greater adequacy of the fairness orientation as a description of justice. We then outlined the way in which the operation of reciprocity is redefined at each higher stage as it is sequentially articulated in conjunction with newly developed justice perspectives. Now we wish to show how each new stage perspective can be understood as being more reversible than its predecessor.

At Stage 2 reciprocity is seen as concrete exchange of favors or blows. Piaget (1932) expresses the nonreversibility of such concrete exchange in terms of its leading to an endless cycle of retaliation with no equilibrium or end point. When asked what the Golden Rule would say to do if someone came up and hit you, Stage 1 and 2 reasoning says it means you should hit back. However, at Stage 3 a subject understands that such an endless cycle of retaliation is not reversible or equilibrated. This understanding is apparent when children tell us that the trading of blows could go on forever, thus implying that such behavior does not lead to a solution to conflict. The Stage 3 idea of fairness as ideal reciprocity, "Do unto others as you would be done by," leads to a more equilibrated or reversible conception of reciprocity implying some peaceful end state agreeable to both actors in the dispute. This ideal is what is implied by the third party perspective of Stage 3 when it reasons with fairness operations such as reciprocity.

At Stage 4 the perspective taken is that which Mead (1934) calls the perspective of the generalized other, that is, the perspective of someone who could be in any of society's roles. At Stage 3, reversibility is attained by upholding shared norms of good motives, whereas at Stage 4 reversibility is attained by a notion of impartiality and consistency across social roles in terms of procedures and rights. Stage 3 reasoning has no way of dealing fairly with roles, and normative expectations for those roles, that legitimize nonaltruistic motives like the druggist's property concerns, for example. In contrast, Stage 4 reasoning recognizes these motives as institutionalized rights and recognizes procedural methods in the legal system for attaining reversibility. Stage 4 can judge, for instance, that Heinz should steal the drug but subject himself to the legal process which may legislate punishment for him or restitution for the druggist. Here a recognition of Heinz's motivations to steal, stemming from his being a good husband and a concerned person, must be balanced with his obligations to the druggist as a property owner and law-upholding citizen. The solution obtained at Stage 4 is more reversible in that it could be agreed upon or prescribed by the position of the druggist or the husband in the Heinz dilemma.

At Stage 5 it is assumed that each actor ought to be able to take a prior-to-society perspective in which the priority of valuing life over property could be shared from the point of view of Heinz or the druggist equally. This hierarchy is reversible and equilibrated in the sense that it could be taken by persons in any of the social roles given in the Heinz dilemma. At Stage 6 reversibility would become *the self-conscious operation* of moral musical chairs in making just choices.

In conclusion, we have tried to show how each new justice perspective and its stage reinterprets fairness element operations like equality and reciprocity. Each new stage reinterprets operations in a way that meets two criteria of adequacy in justice reasoning. The first is the greater generalizability and inclusiveness of each higher perspective over its predecessor: for example, a Stage 3 third party perspective is more general and inclusive than a Stage 2 individualistic perspective. The second criterion is the increasing degree of reversibility of the justice structure of each higher stage, as seen from the vantage point of the highest stage of justice reasoning, Stage 6.

In summary, in this section we have clarified the exact meaning of our stages as rational reconstructions of ontogenesis in judgments of justice from the perspective of a theory of justice as universalizability and reversibility. In terms of these criteria each stage is more morally adequate than its predecessor and Stage 6 completely fills these formal criteria. Philosophers may not agree with our working assumption of the primacy of justice in defining moral reasoning or with the criteria of universalizability and reversibility as the criteria by which one form of justice reasoning may be said to be more adequate or rational than another. But at least our theory of adequacy is clearly stated without the problems of postulations of "is to ought" relations of identity which Habermas and other philosophers have found dubious and ambiguous.

Summary and Conclusion

My last general statement of my theory of moral judgment development was published in 1976 (see Chapter 2). The present chapter represents a considerable amount of revision and expansion of the theory. While the 1976 statement in Chapter 2 has been fully supported by the longitudinal studies in America (Chapter 5, Colby et al., 1983), in Turkey (Chapter 8), and in Israel (Chapter 9), both the work and the criticisms of other scholars such as Gilligan (1982), Fowler (1981), Habermas (1979), and Gibbs (1979a), have led us *(a)* to enlarge the domain of moral or ethical development so as to include areas of "soft stage" development as distinct from the development of our "hard stages" of justice reasoning and *(b)* to develop some theoretical constructs basic for relating judgment to action, including our distinction between judgments of responsibility and judgments of justice, as well as our A–B substage distinction.

In a more philosophical view, we have softened our claims for having empirically defined and philosophically justified a final or sixth stage of moral reasoning. Along with this more tentative Stage 6 claim, we have distinguished the identity or isomorphism thesis between psychological theory and normative moral philosophic theory, which I postulated in Volume I, Chapter 4, from the complementarity thesis to which we now subscribe. We now argue that certain elements of our normative theory are assumed by our psychological theory and that empirical support for the latter gives some support to our normative claims. We hold that empirical evidence could nullify or undermine the plausibility of our normative claims but that it cannot positively "prove" them. However, this weakening of our philosophic claims has not lead us to abandon our theoretical construction of a sixth or highest stage, though the exact nature of this stage is in doubt both empirically and philosophically. We hold that the philosophic formulations of such writers as Rawls (1971), Habermas (1979), and myself (Volume I, Chapter 5) offer definitions of an end point of development which are necessary for defining stages as rational reconstructions of ontogenesis. We have pointed out, however, that even if psychologists do not choose to endorse our conception of a highest stage and our claims about the greater moral adequacy of each successive stage, they may find it useful, nevertheless, to accept the metaethical assumptions which we make in order to commence their scientific explorations in the field of moral development. Critics like Habermas, Gilligan, and Gibbs seem to accept our metaethical assumptions, although they do question various aspects of our stage definitions, particularly our definitions of stages at the principled or postconventional level.

In this chapter and the next we have tried to distinguish those issues about which we agree with our critics from those issues about which we disagree with them. In the instances of disagreement, we have tried to summarize both the logical considerations and the empirical findings which have lead us to maintain our position. At this point, however, many of the issues we have raised are still open to debate, a debate which requires further empirical research as well as further philosophic reflection. One such issue for further research is the status of our hypothetical sixth stage. In this context we intend to use dilemmas central to our conception of a sixth stage instead of employing the standard dilemmas we have used in our longitudinal research. In addition, we also hold that this research will require the study of persons who have some recognized competence or leadership in making moral decisions in the adult social world, judges, statesmen, and so forth.

In addition to the issue regarding Stage 6, we believe that much theoretical and empirical work remains to be done on the issue of understanding the relationship between moral judgment and action. Such work should yield information which will tell us more about the logical structure of our justice stages and about our claim that they form a hierarchy of increasing adequacy.

In conclusion, what we believe our critics have successfully accomplished with their writing is to highlight certain theoretical and methodological issues to which we must be sensitive. We do not believe that they have discovered that my work has been biased in any "hard" sense of the word but that my work and any other social scientific investigation can and would be biased if investigators do not take cognizance of the normative and metaethical assumptions employed. In addition, we believe, in line with Weber (1949), Habermas (1983) and others, that objectivity is a "moment" of scientific inquiry; that the essence or "truth" value of objectivity does not reside in some reified, permanent, or factual quality inherent in the object of inquiry, but is rather to be found in and understood as a process of understanding which is the changing relationship between the investigator and what he or she observes. We believe that it is this theoretical and methodological orientation, aptly expressed in Habermas's notion of "objective hermeneutics," that characterizes our work.

4. Synopses and Detailed Replies to Critics

with CHARLES LEVINE
and ALEXANDRA HEWER

IN THE COURSE of our synopses and replies to criticism we shall divide critics into two groups: first, those who critique the theory and its accompanying method as fundamentally flawed or biased; second, those who suggest some revisions in the formulation and use of the theory and paradigm. In the first group are Shweder (1982), Simpson (1974), Sullivan (1977), C. Gilligan (1977, 1982), Gilligan and Murphy (1979), and Murphy and Gilligan (1980). In the second group are Levine (1979), Gibbs (1979a), and Habermas (1979).

Shweder, R.: "Review of Lawrence Kohlberg's *Essays on Moral Development, Volume I: The Philosophy of Moral Development,*" in *Contemporary Psychology* (June 1982).

Synopsis: Rick Shweder's critique is expressed in the subtitle of his review, "Liberalism as Destiny." He begins by stating,

> Kohlberg believes that reason is on the side of those who oppose capital punishment, hierarchy, tribalism, and divine authority (pp. 21, 30, 176, 289). Moved by the spirit of developmentalism (pp. 87, 134, 136, 137), he holds out secular humanism, egalitarianism, and the Bill of Rights as rational ideals or objective end points for the evolution of moral ideas (pp. 164, 165, 215). For Kohlberg, the history of the world (p. 227) and the history of childhood (in all societies) (p. 25) is the story of the progressive discovery of the principles of the American Revolution (pp. 8, 38, 154, 237). Hegel's Prussian state has been replaced by Western liberal democracy. Liberalism has become destiny (p. 227, 253).

Shweder, an anthropologist, is fundamentally critical of my claim that what is moral is not historically and culturally relativistic.

> The dominant theme in Kohlberg's essays is that what is moral is not a matter of taste or opinion. Kohlberg abhors relativism. He shudders at the idea that the moral codes of man might be like the languages and foods of

man, different but equal. Kohlberg's project in these essays is to establish that there is an objective morality which reason can reveal; to define that objective morality in terms of justice, equity, equal respect for all persons and the "natural" rights of man; and to defend that formulation against relativists, behaviorists, romantics, emotivists, psychoanalysts and advocates of capital punishment and character education. What Kohlberg seeks is a conceptualization of what is moral derived from premises which no rational person could possibly deny, by means of which no rational person could possibly avoid—preferably deductive logic (p. 226, 293).

Philosophically, Shweder draws primarily upon *After Virtue,* a recently written book by the historically relativistic philosopher Alisdair MacIntyre (1982). This book presents a critique of modern liberal moral philosophy from Locke, Hume, and Kant to what Shweder calls two recent great books: Rawls's (1971) *A Theory of Justice* and Gewirth's (1978) *Reason and Morality.* He considers MacIntyre's critique of these last two books itself a third great book, a book which fundamentally reveals the lack of viability of modern (post-medieval) philosophy, Rawls and Gewirth being recent "liberal" examples.

MacIntyre persuasively argues that every notable attempt since the Enlightenment (including Rawls and Gewirth) to construct a rational foundation for an objective morality has been built out of non-rational premises, premises which any rational person might reasonably deny. . . . Kohlberg quite properly criticizes "emotivist" theories about the meaning of moral terms, and instead defines moral concepts by their impersonality and their implication that as a person with reason you are obligated to behave in such-and-such a way. That is what we mean when we say "that's good" (or "bad"), but, if MacIntyre is right, we have no rational warrant for meaning it. We speak to each other (or at least to those with whom we are still on speaking terms) as though our moral choice had a rational foundation. Upon examination, that rational foundation turns out to be the soft sand of preferred (and often shared) assumptions. At its limit, moral discourse becomes ideology, a deceptive form of "mock rationality."

Shweder claims that we are unsuccessful in both our effort to separate form and content and our effort to hold that at the higher postconventional stages there is a formal similarity of moral judgment and reasoning across both culture and particular moral theories. He holds that I have confused a postconventional or principled form of moral judgment with the content of liberal ideology.

To decide how particular people are to be treated as alike or different is to introduce non-rational assumptions; for example, that to be just is to treat everyone as though they had the same natural and inalienable rights. That quite substantive idea of justice is faithfully endorsed by secular humanists but is not required by fact or reason.

Shweder concludes that I run into both empirical and conceptual difficulties in my "quest for a rationally dictated objective morality."

Besides believing that a rational and nonrelativistic morality is an impossible quest, Shweder finds Volume I to be full of conceptual contradictions and inconsistency. As is argued in the reply to follow, a number of these inconsistencies seem to be *distinctions* made in the Kohlberg theory rather than contradictions.

Shweder also holds that the data base of the theory is weak. He believes that available research data do not support the idea that principled or Stage 5 and 6 reasoning is to be found in non-Western cultures. He also argues that the empirical data do not support the Piagetian assumption of invariant stage sequence and structural wholeness. In Shweder's words:

> Finally, the world of cognitive-developmental psychology has changed over the last ten years. The idea of general stages has taken a beating. It is no longer 1970. In 1981 the waning of the orthodox Piagetian paradigm cannot be ignored. Kohlberg's silence on the issue is deafening.

Reply: As a reply to Shweder's review, we reprint Kohlberg (1982c), which appeared in *Contemporary Psychology* in November 1982, "Moral development Does Not Mean Liberalism as Destiny: A Reply to R. Schweder."

Rick Shweder's (1982) recent review of my book *Essays on Moral Development* consists of two parts, an exposition of the argument of the book and a critical reply to the argument. As an anthropologist Shweder wishes to uphold cultural, historical, and ethical relativism and relies upon Alisdair MacIntyre's historically relativistic critique of modern moral philosophy to do so. My major purpose in writing this reply is not to deal with this complex issue but to point out that (1) Shweder's statement of the theory expounded in the book is an inaccurate caricature of its thesis; (2) his claims that I contradict myself in various parts of the book are usually incorrect; and (3) his assertion that I have no data base for my basic stage claim is inaccurate. Shweder uses the paraphernalia of scholarship, that is, reference to specific pages in his exposition, but the reader who actually refers to the pages cited will usually not find what Shweder claims I say. Shweder's title, "Liberalism as Destiny," as the supposed theme of the book is stated in the opening of his review.

If one turns to page 227 of Volume 1 to find the basis of Shweder's critique, one finds instead a statement that liberalism as an ideology which has dominated the West is in trouble and, to be viable, requires some reconstruction or further development. My book, however, is not about the history of ideologies; rather, it is about the ontogenesis of forms of reasoning about justice in various cultures based on longitudinal studies done in Turkey (Chapter 8), Israel (Chapter 9), and the United States (Colby, Kohlberg, et al., 1983). In these longitudinal studies we find universal stages defined by *forms* of reasoning. As Chapter 7 (Volume I) elaborates, *sometimes* the form of Stage 5 or 6 moral reasoning is associated with the content of a moral or political view, like "liberal" opposition to capital punishment. While moral-political liberal ideological *content* is sometimes found to be associated with a stage or *form* of moral reasoning, the book represents a theory about the ontogenetic growth of forms of moral reasoning, not a theory about the growth of societies toward an ideology of liberalism. In the sections listed by Shweder, I do report a generational advance in the usage of principled or Stage 5 reasoning in our longitudinal sample, now adults, compared to their parents. I note that in constitutional democracies like the United States there is a trend toward a growing extension of rights to disenfranchised persons and groups if one takes a two-hundred-year perspective. Finally, I note that in 1906 Hobhouse's *Morals in Evolution* reported studies using cross-cultural and historical data which found a correlation between technological and sociopolitical complexity and "stages" of juridical practices, laws, and moral customs from society to society. Hobhouse described his "stages" in ways greatly similar to my own. The burden of my point in the section on page 227 is that increased sociopolitical complexity poses new problems for members of a society, which give impetus to the growth of a new stage to cope with these problems. But principled reasoning was also used by Socrates 2,500 years ago; it is not a modern development.

While my book is a presentation and defense of what might be called "liberal thought," a tradition including thinkers from Locke and Kant to Rawls, Dewey, and Piaget, my argument is not based on a claim for liberalism as destiny or as a necessary movement to a present or future ideology.

If Shweder's page citations do not lead to the statements he claims I make, neither do these citations document the basic inconsistencies in my book which he claims to find. It is true that the book is a collection of essays written over a period of ten years; it is not a presentation of tight systematic moral theory like Rawls's *A Theory of Justice.* But most of the "inconsistencies" Shweder reports reflect distinctions made by the theory which Shweder fails to note or understand.

As a single example, Shweder finds it inconsistent to say that "there may be long-range trends toward a sociomoral evolution (p. 227)" and to say that moral principles (or stages) "are not scales for evaluating collective entities (p. 111)." My theoretical claim that a higher stage of justice reasoning is a more adequate stage is a claim about deontic judgments and reasons (judgments of rightness or obligation about an action or practice). As textbooks on ethics (like Frankena's) note, a deontic judgment is one thing and an aretaic judgment of the moral worthiness of persons or cultures is another. I explicitly state that my stage theory is not a theory claiming to aretaically grade individuals or cultures on some scale of moral worthiness.

The same distinction between deontic and aretaic judgment is used by Shweder to make another charge of inconsistency against me. He says, "We are told that Stage 6 ethics cannot tell us what is virtuous or worthy of praise or blame (p. 172). Then Kohlberg states the opposite" (pp. 192, 272). I do not state the opposite on pages 192 and 272. I say there that deontic judgments of rightness are more adequate and more likely to lead to consensus at Stage 5 or 6, but this does not mean that I assume that a morally conscientious and consistent actor using Stage 4 deontic reasoning to guide his actions is to be assigned lesser moral worth on some aretaic scale I explicitly say I do not have.

Besides inconsistency, Shweder charges me with the failure to have a data base. Piagetian stages, he tells us, are out. Our own previously cited longitudinal studies in the United States, Turkey, and Israel, however, indicated 5 percent or less of subjects studied violated the invariant progressive sequence criteria of stage growth, a percentage lower than that observed within acceptable levels of test-retest error. Subjects use, at most, two adjacent stages in their reasoning and tend to have one predominant stage, a finding consistent with Piaget's claim that "stages are structured wholes." Finally, Shweder's claim that principled thinking is "Western" confuses a principled form of thinking with the Western liberal content of reasoning. In India, Turkey, Taiwan, Zambia, and other non-Western societies, Stage 5 reasoning has been found by various researchers.

In critiquing my work Shweder draws on Alisdair MacIntyre's *After Virtue.* MacIntyre defines modern moral philosophy as the "Enlightment project" begun in the seventeenth and eighteenth centuries. This project marked the collapse of the Aristotelian approach to science which held that all things had an aim or telos and that man's virtue and happiness could be defined in terms of a telos for human nature living in a political community. Modern moral philosophy, "the Enlightenment project," replaced this view. It began with Hume and the British school of utilitarianism and with the continental deontological school headed by Kant. It held that morality consisted of those laws and principles which an autonomous and rational moral agent would consent to as ordering his or her own society or any other. From MacIntyre's point of view this project or theoretical program has failed despite the vigorous recent involvement and contributions of Rawls, Gewirth, Peters, Hare, and others. MacIntyre says that these scholars have failed because, as a social scientist, he finds educated Western thinkers to be relativists and emotivists, unconvinced of the validity of the rational principles outlined by "the Enlightenment project." He also says the project has failed because there is a lack of consensus among these liberal theorists in both their normative-ethical theories and their resolution of substantive dilemmas of moral life, such as abortion and the distribution of wealth.

I would like to point out that all these modern theorists can be characterized as postconventional in their form of reasoning despite their divergence on the substance or content of the theories that come out of this form of reasoning. In this sense there are formal similarities among these thinkers, despite divergence of content. However, there is also considerable agreement on substantive moral questions among both philosophers and lay adults in several cultures that we have studied. For example, the right thing for Heinz to do in our story is to steal the drug to save his wife's life, rather than to follow that law that upholds the druggist's property rights and let his wife die. Whether someone is a Kantian deontologist or a utilitarian, they agree that it is right for Heinz to steal the drug—if they use postconventional reasoning. While there is vigorous disagreement among philosophers about theory formulation, these disagreements exist within what could be called a common paradigm.

In this paradigm of modern moral philosophy, basic assumptions are shared as to rigorous methods of argument. Similarly there is a common paradigm shared by modern psychology which harbors large areas of agreement about assumptions and method of argument despite diversity of theoretical viewpoint. This at least would be my answer to Shweder's opinion that "what we mean when we say 'that's good' is something we have no rational warrant for meaning. We speak to each other as though our moral choices had a rational foundation. Upon examination that rational foundation turns out to be the soft sand of preferred assumption."

Whether my argument is correct or not, Shweder does not present my fundamental standpoint as a moral psychologist, which is to create a theory that is a rational reconstruction of ontogenesis, drawing jointly on philosophy and psychological data. As Habermas (1981) has pointed out, empirical theorizing about moral development *presupposes* some standard of adequacy defining the direction of development; such theorizing cannot be value-neutral. Even value-neutrality, implying relativism, has its own underlying moral assumptions. My own effort to rationally reconstruct the ontogenesis of moral reasoning makes use of what MacIntyre has called the "Enlightenment project," the project of constructing arguments and theories which would lead rational people to agree on principles of justice to define an end point of ontogenetic development. The validity of my assumption of such a standard of adequacy in describing the moral development of individuals can only be assessed by the extent to which it provides order to empirical data and by the intelligibility of the order it defines. Like the "Enlightenment project" itself, a psychology of moral development based on it should be an open and growing enterprise. It thrives on disagreement, including some of Shweder's disagreements, but it does require a fair exposition of what it tries to say.

Simpson, E. L.: "Moral Development Research: A Case Study of Scientific Cultural Bias," *Human Development 17* (1974), pp. 81–106.

Synopsis: At the core of Simpson's critique is the argument that the Kohlberg stages need not be and actually are not culturally universal. She argues that our claims of universality have no validity because I have not studied a sufficient number of cultures to substantiate such claims. In addition, Simpson asserts that the fact that we have not found postconventional reasoning (Stages 5 and 6) in all the cultures we have studied also undermines our universality claim. She goes on to claim that if postconventional reasoning is found more prevalently in urban cultures that are Western influenced, then it follows that the Kohlberg stage scheme or definition of higher stages is ethnocentric or culturally biased.

Simpson objects to the idea of a culturally universal sequence of stages on two grounds, empirical and philosophical. On empirical grounds she claims: (a) that the validity of the stage sequence is contradicted by findings reported in some cross- cultural studies (i.e., in some cultures reasoning beyond Stages 3 and 4 is not found); (b) that in some cultures reversal in developmental sequence has been found (p. 99); and (c) that lagging in, or absence of, postconventional reasoning in some cultures may not reflect differences in moral judgment *competence* but simply differences that arise due to researchers' insensitivity to conditions of *performance* from one culture to another. To make this last point, Simpson uses three illustrations: (1) that rating a subject as postconventional may not reflect the presence of underlying structure but simply linguistic sophistication (p. 94); (2) that the situation or context in which competence is tested may not be a familiar one for certain subjects; and (3) that insensitivity to cultural meaning on the part of the researcher may lead to the down-scoring of responses from unfamiliar cultures.

On philosophical grounds Simpson claims: (a) that a research-based scale of development cannot be applied universally or objectively, because it is the product of a researcher or theorist who has a particular cultural identity and background (thus, my search for universal principles must therefore be recognized as necessarily biased and limited by its genesis in modern Western society and ideology [p. 85–86]); and (b) that our claims to universality are objectionable because they imply a scale for grading some cultures as "morally superior" to others (p. 91).

Reply: We will first address the empirical criticism raised by Simpson. First, we claim that the sequence hypothesis of the Kohlberg stage model is not invalidated by the current empirical finding that all human beings in all cultures do not arrive at the postconventional stages of reasoning. We have observed in our own studies the low frequency of Stage 5 reasoning in Western as well as in non-Western cultures. Nevertheless, while low in frequency in non-Western cultures, Stage 5 reasoning has been found in a fairly large number of such cultures (Parikh, 1980; Lei and Cheng, 1982; Chapter 9, Grimley, 1973; and Edwards, 1975a). The researchers in these studies have expressed their open-mindedness to the possibility of finding alternative forms of Stage 5 reasoning in response to those typified dilemmas used by us.

The following example from Israel illustrates the existence of Stage 5 reasoning even in a largely Western culture, that uses norms not included in our standard manual norm list (See Table 3.8). This example is from Snarey's (1982) work and is a kibbutznik's response to the Heinz dilemma.

> It [stealing] will be illegal not against the formal law but against the moral law. If we were in a Utopian society my hierarchy of values and those of others would be actualized through consensus. [What are those values?] Socialism, but don't ask me to explain it. In the Utopia there will be all the things I believe in, everyone will be equal. In this society the value of life is perfectly held. I believe everyone has the right to self-growth and happiness. People are not born equally genetically, and it is not fair that one physically or mentally stronger should reach happiness at the expense of someone weaker, because the right to happiness is a basic right of everyone and equal to all.

This respondent's concern with norms of equality and socialism is different from the typical value of equal opportunity expressed by Stage 5 American respondents. However, this response nevertheless demonstrates Stage 5 prior-to-society perspective taking combined with Stage 5 equity operations.

Thus, while our manual was constructed on the basis of responses of American subjects it can still be used to identify Stage 5 reasoning used in conjunction with different cultural norms and values not identified in our manual. Other examples of cross-culturally observed Stage 5 reasoning are given by Lei and Cheng (1982) and Parkih (1980).

For us, the fact that postconventional reasoning occurs with low frequency has no logical bearing on the claim that Stage 5 exists as a structure. In this context, the pertinent question for us becomes one of identifying those socioenvironmental conditions that impede or facilitate the emergence of principled reasoning.

Simpson's concern with how my theory can handle "regression" will not be dealt with, since longitudinal and cross-cultural data, scored with a scoring system developed since Simpson's article, do not show reversal and regression. However, to some extent we take up this issue later, in the context of a competence-performance distinction discussed with reference to Levine's (1979) criticism.

With regard to the fact that Stage 4 and Stage 5 reasoning are comparatively rare, Simpson argues that our moral judgment interview techniques and our scoring system may be incapable of asking the kind of questions, and coding those responses, that would elicit and document higher stage reasoning in other cultures. In response, we agree.

We agree that it is important to be sensitive to this kind of criticism, and indeed, we have attempted to frame our dilemmas in ways that are meaningful, that do produce conflict, in the populations we have studied (e.g., in the Turkish and Indian studies). Insofar as the dilemmas used did produce conflict and did elicit responses that were scorable, they seem to have been meaningful in these other cultures as well as in our own. Since longitudinal and cross-cultural study has validated the stage sequence we hypothesized and has provided examples of postconventional reasoning, we retain confidence in our measuring instrument. Also, we have no reason to think that the dilemma interviews we use are particularly suited only to American populations, since we have found postconventional reasoning in only a minority of our American longitudinal subjects. However, it is true that in some cross-cultural research, minor features of the interview dilemmas were altered to make them more meaningful (e.g., Heinz needs food, not a drug, for Taiwanese, Mexican, and Turkish respondents). Thus, we accept Simpson's general point that one has to be sensitive to such methodological issues in cross-cultural research, and we believe we have been.

Part of Simpson's general argument that our method may not tap competence in cultures other than our own is that it is a method which is linguistically dependent. Studies conducted in the United States, however, indicate that there is a low to moderate correlation ($r=.30$ to .40) between verbal fluency or complexity and moral stage (Colby and Kohlberg, 1984, in press). This finding suggests that assessment of high stage reasoning is not dependent on verbal sophistication. There are, of course, multiple problems in the interpretation of moral concepts defined in different cultures. Thus, being sensitive to problems of translation has been important and usually has been stressed by those researchers conducting cross-cultural studies. Furthermore, we are in agreement with Simpson's general point that we must be very careful about assuming that our methodology allows us to translate differences in performance on our instrument into cultural differences in competence. Kohlberg's longitudinal study within the United States, showing validation of the moral stage sequence, does not lead us to assume that our test is methodologically adequate as a test of competence in all cultures. The fact that Stages 3 and 4 appear more slowly in a Turkish village than in an American city may reflect a difference in competence, but it also may reflect different performance factors in Turkish and American subjects. The fact that the developmental *sequence* of stages is the same in both cultures, however, indicates that our methodology is adequate to capture competence as defined by the logic of developmental theory.

Since Simpson's paper was published, some longitudinal cross-cultural studies have been completed in Turkey (Chapter 8) and in an Israeli kibbutz (Chapter 9). These studies indicate that the *sequence* of movement through Stage 4 into Stage 5 is invariant in the urban settings of these cultures, among their college-educated subjects. In the small-scale village samples of the above studies, Stage 5 reasoning and sometimes Stage 4 reasoning was not found, nor has it been found in other studies of small-scale societies (Edwards, 1981, 1982). Given the urban findings, however, it seems fair to conclude that the fact that Stage 4 or 5 reasoning is not found in small-scale villages is not simply because these stages express Western values. Rather, it seems more likely that such stages have not been observed in these villages because their social structure is relatively simple and their populations have little or no formal education. In all societies, including the United States, we have found that Stage 5 is a relatively infrequent form a reasoning, and again, this finding suggests that the occurrence of Stage 5 is not a reflection of Western ideological content biasing our definitions of moral stages.

We now turn to the nonempirical criticisms made by Simpson. At the heart of her claim that our theory and method is culturally biased is her objection to rating one culture as having more moral worth than another. We share Simpson's concern here. We do not believe that the comparison of one culture to another in terms of moral development is a theoretically useful strategy for the growth of scientific knowledge. However, it is useful to compare the conditions leading to development in one culture with the conditions leading to development in another culture and to establish relations between environmental conditions and moral stage growth that are universal across cultures. An example of such work is the study by Parikh (1980) which replicated in India the relations between parental values and adolescent moral reasoning found in America by Holstein (1972). However, such studies do not employ direct comparisons of mean moral stage scores between cultures; such comparisons have no scientific justification or value, since they would imply that it makes sense to speak of one culture having more moral worth than another. It is difficult to understand what a valid concept of "comparative moral worth of culture" might be, but in any case, such a concept could not be established on the basis of comparison of means on our moral judgment assessment scale. There is no direct way in which group averages can be translated into statements of the relative moral worth of groups.

Like most anthropologists, we would agree that cultures should be treated evaluatively as unique configurations of norms and institutions which help social organizations to adapt to local conditions as well as to universal normative problems. In this sense anthropological cultural relativism is compatible with our philosophic assumption of the universal validity of moral principles. However, our agreement with relativism in this sense does not require us as moral agents to adopt an ethically relativistic position and so claim, for example, that Aztec human sacrifice is right. While it is true that the principles compatible with postconventional reasoning would lead one not to endorse the Aztec practice of human sacrifice, such a judgment constitutes a moral evaluation of a specific cultural practice, not of a culture per se. In a similar view, the argument against the morality of capital punishment in Volume I, Chapter 7, is not a moral evaluation of the American culture as a whole, for the complexity of cultural institutions and norms precludes overall cultural assessment. We do not understand how a "moral ranking" of cultures could either be done or be scientifically useful.

Just as there is nothing in the Kohlberg theory that justifies using the moral judgment scale to compare the moral worth of cultures, so to there is nothing in it which justifies the use of the justice reasoning scale to rank or evaluate the relative moral worth of individuals. In our opinion, what is to be morally evaluated about individual persons are their specific moral actions. It is true that the stage of reasoning associated with a specific action may help determine the moral quality or value of the action. However, the claim that Stage 5 reasoning is more adequate to resolve more moral problems than is Stage 3 reasoning is not a claim that an individual scored as a Stage 5 reasoner has more moral worth than a person scored at Stage 3. There is a difference between the moral adequacy of a process of thought and the moral worth of those who use it. Principled moral reasoning awards equal moral worth to all persons even though it recognizes that specific moral *actions* may be more, or less, moral.

In other words, the fact that our theory and related instrument are not morally neutral, that they are designed to provide a rational reconstruction of moral ontogenesis, does not mean that the instrument is a measure of the moral worth of individuals. It does not tell us how to judge the moral worth of people. It does not imply that it is morally fair to treat preferentially someone scored Stage 5. Assuming the desirability of Stage 5 reasoning is quite a different matter from judging and treating differently Stage 5 and Stage 2 reasoners.

The final philosophical issue we wish to respond to is Simpson's claim that our theory and instrument are biased because of their (and our) historical and cultural location:

> Like each of us, Kohlberg himself, his interest in cognitive development and moral reasoning, his choice of a Kantian or Deweyian infrastructure for this theory and his predilection for abstractions of such principles as justice, equality, and reciprocity are all, in a sense, accidents of time and place and the interaction of his personality with a specifiable social environment and the norms of the subgroups within that environment. [1974, p. 85–86]

Simpson's statement expresses a truism that we accept, that is, that the environment a theoretician is socialized in is likely to have an influence on his or her theory. However, to go on to infer from this that the validity of the theory is *ipso facto* suspect is to commit an instance of the genetic fallacy. This is a fallacy, like the naturalistic fallacy, of drawing conclusions about the validity or truth of a theory from reference to its genetic origins.

Simpson's implicit assumption is that the only way to avoid the bias inherent in a theory because of historical and biographical circumstance is to be self-consciously a relativist about one's own views. In response, we believe that the way to avoid bias in the development of a theory is to subject its development and validation to the scientific method and critical appraisal. The intent of my theory is that it be used, verified, or revised by people other than myself; by people of different social origins, cultures, and classes. The scientific method as we understand it is a product of modern Western history. However, we claim that it represents the most adequate cross-culturally understood method available for avoiding the kind of bias that Simpson in concerned about and that it constitutes the best available method for assessing the truth value of claims to objective knowledge. Like my theory, the scientific method is primarily a product of modern Western thought, but it, like my theory, cannot be dismissed as therefore biased because of its genetic origins.

Sullivan, E. V.: "A Study of Kohlberg's Structural Theory of Moral Development: A Critique of Liberal Social Science Ideology," *Human Development 20* (1977), pp. 352–376.

Synopsis: Edmund Sullivan evaluates my theory as a "style of thinking" and suggests that as a style of thought it is rooted in certain sociohistorical circumstances and therefore reflects the interests of those who live(d) within those circumstances. In other words, Sullivan's article is an exercise in the "sociology of psychological knowledge," and his purpose is to argue that theories in social science, including mine, are "tied to the infrastructure of a society or socially defined groups."

With this conceptual posture, Sullivan correctly identifies my theory as an example of liberal ideology. It is a "style of thought" developing from the period of the French Revolution and thus reflects many of those ideas articulated by the Philosophes; that is, notions of social contracts; an emphasis on the rights of individuals; and a view of persons as ideally rational. The Kohlberg theory, Sullivan claims, has both the content and methodology of the style of thinking he calls "natural-law thought."

With the above introduction, Sullivan directs himself to a critique of my conception of Stage 6 justice reasoning. Given its Enlightenment roots, he argues that my notion of Stage 6 reasoning constructs a parochial rather than a universally accurate model of "moral man" (p. 360); that "Kohlberg sees his Stage 6 structure as synonymous with the Rawlsian conception of justice" (p. 358); and that this Stage 6 model is both impersonal and ahistorical, recognizing only an "atomistic" social agent in the individual and thus ignoring the moral significance of the individual's ties with the community. For Sullivan, my conception of "Stage 6 man" is based on an intellectual posture of abstract formalism, a posture which results in a "falsely conscious" understanding of moral development. Sullivan draws from the writings of Marx, Engels, and Lukacs to critique my position of "abstract formalism." He writes that "abstract formalism was the organizing principle structuring social relations of production within Western capitalism" and that "abstract formalism implies" a "universality that," in actuality, only "masks middle-class ideology" (p. 360). Sullivan argues that Rawls's "original position," because it is a hypothetical perspective for seeing how one might contract into society based on principles of justice, serves, in fact, the vested interests of powerful social groups. Presumably, this is the case because the hypothetical nature of the original position requires the assumption of a just society *a priori* and thus fails to address itself to real injustices in our present society. In diverting our attention away from actual injustice in the here and now, the method of reasoning implied by adopting the original position therefore functions as conservative ideology in support of the status quo. Thus, for Sullivan, the abstractly formal, impersonal, and ahistorical nature of Rawl's views and my own constitutes an unconscious "defense of exploitation" while standing in theory for human freedom (p. 362).

In addition to the above "problems" with my perspective, Sullivan perceives others which he attributes to my structuralist bias. Sullivan reasons that I, like other structuralists, dichotomize thought and action, form and content, and in so doing, incorrectly equate the more abstract with the more moral. Not only does my theory fail to grasp what is, in reality, the dialectical tension between reflection and action, it also ignores those factors that one must attend to if one's goal is to develop an adequate theory of moral commitment. In this context, Sullivan points to my failure to integrate into my theory an account of "moral sensitivity," emotion, and moral imagination.

In sum, Sullivan is arguing that the ideological and structuralist basis of my perspective has produced a "morally blind" understanding. It is a theory which expresses an alienated view of the moral being, because it uses what are essentially false dichotomies in its description. For Sullivan, a theory of moral development must be more than a structuralist account of the ontogenesis of justice reasoning.

Reply: In our view, Sullivan's article raises the following three points of criticism: (*a*) that the Kohlberg theory is biased because of its liberal intellectual roots; (*b*) that it is biased because of its structuralist orientation; and finally, (*c*) that it is insufficient as a theory of moral development because it ignores such factors as emotion and moral imagination. Our reply to Sullivan is relatively brief and selective since our replies to Simpson (1974) and Gilligan (1982), as well as our review of Habermas's work, contain material which would make a lengthy reply to Sullivan redundant.

Kohlberg's Liberal Bias

In our opinion, Sullivan's description of my intellectual roots is an accurate one. It is accurate in a sociohistorical sense, and it is accurate in the sense that it depicts my concern with developing a formalist account of morally adequate procedures for adjudicating moral conflicts. What we disagree with is Sullivan's contention that these intellectual roots and interests have produced (*a*) theory that articulates a parochial rather than a universally valid view of Stage 6 and of the development of structures of justice reasoning and (*b*) a theory that can only function as a false-conscious justification of the exploitive practices endemic to Western capitalist societies.*

In response to the above, we believe, in the first place, that whether my theory articulates a parochial or universal valid *description* of justice reasoning and its development is a question to be answered on the basis of empirical test. In our opinion, this is not a question that can be answered *a priori,* through an analysis of the ideological and intellectual foundations of the theory.

In the context of the discussion of revisions to the theory, we have stated in general terms our reply to Sullivan's charge of parochialism regarding Stage 6 per se (see Chapter 3). In that discussion I no longer claim to have empirically verified the existence of Stage 6 reasoning. However, given our posture of a rationally reconstructive perspective, we maintain and, in a normative-ethical sense, defend the conception of Stage 6 as the end point of the ontogenesis of justice reasoning. We noted earlier that the conception of Stage 6 is open to philosophical debate and that researchers need not accept our normative-ethical views as their own in order to carry out research in the area of justice reasoning. From our perspective, we defend our notion of Stage 6 because it represents for us a structure of justice reasoning that is fully reversible. While Habermas (1979) has questioned this claim, we believe that we successfully defend our perspective against his critique. (Our discussion of Habermas com-

* With these assertions, Sullivan appears to have committed the genetic fallacy in two ways. The reader will recall that the genetic fallacy is the tendency to evaluate a theory, not on its own merits, but on the basis of either (*a*) the interests or biographical characteristics of its author or (*b*) its sociohistorical underpinnings.

pletes this chapter.) However, Sullivan does not critique our conception of Stage 6 in this way. Instead, he raises questions regarding both Stage 6 and my general theory, arguing that they constitute a false-conscious defense of the status quo and misrepresent the domain of the moral due to our reliance on the perspective of structuralism.

We disagree with Sullivan's contention that my theory can only function as a false-conscious justification of the status quo. Sullivan may be correct in believing that the spirit of the Enlightenment is dead, that throughout the last three hundred years liberal ideals have been espoused dishonestly and used to disguise the vested interests of some powerful groups. However, just because the Kohlberg theory of justice reasoning grows out of the liberal tradition does not mean that it will or can only be used in similar fashion. Hammers can be used to drive nails or to bludgeon people, and to which of these uses hammers are put cannot be predicted on the basis of an understanding of the technological, cultural, or sociohistorical factors that led to their creation.

We are not claiming that because it can be used for various purposes the theory is therefore "value-free," for we have acknowledged that it is not independent of various normative-ethical assumptions that we hold. In this context, we are simply claiming that how the Kohlberg theory is used cannot be predicted on the basis of a consideration of its intellectual roots. It could and perhaps has been used to preoccupy minds with "moral" rationalizations for immoral acts. However, it can be more easily used, and we hope will be more frequently used, to occupy minds with moral reasons for moral acts. If the principles articulated by Stage 6 reasoning can be used by a Machiavellian as "moral slogans" to disguise exploitive realities, it is also true that they can be used as moral justifications for denouncing such realities.

Kohlberg's Structuralist Bias

It will be recalled that Sullivan perceives a formalistic and structuralist bias in my work that prevents me from coming to grips with concrete moral reality. Instead of developing a theory that acknowledges the "dialectical tension" between "thought and action" and "form and content," Sullivan argues that I am preoccupied with "thought" and "form" and ignore their dialectical complements. Sullivan assumes that "Kohlberg sees his Stage 6 structure as synonymous with the Rawlsian conception of justice"

(p. 358). This assumption allows Sullivan to rely upon his perception of the hypothetical nature of Rawls's "original position" to bolster his critique of my work as being too abstract.

While our task is not to defend Rawls, we should point out that the procedure of "assuming the original position under a veil of ignorance" need not be interpreted as a strategy which avoids dealing with the real world. Rather, we understand it as a procedure that has the potential to allow one to reflect upon the world in a just manner because it requires one to control, not forget, the bias of vested interest when adjudicating moral conflicts. However, even if one questions the legislative potential of Rawls's work, even if one sees it simply as a hypothetical moral exercise for constructing hypothetical moral communities, we still see it as an excellent example of justice reasoning at a postconventional level.

More to the point, however, is the fact that we do not interpret Rawls's notions as synonymous with our conception of Stage 6 reasoning. We understand Stage 6 prescriptive role-taking as a procedure which requires one to avoid the biasing impact of vested interests by evaluating their worth as legitimate moral claims, not by ignoring them. In fact, prescriptive role-taking is a procedure for resolving moral conflicts that *requires* one to focus on the stated claims and interests of real people in real situations. This fact should not be confused with another, that is, that we derived, in part, the procedure of prescriptive role-taking through the use of fictitious actors involved in hypothetical dilemmas.

We believe, more generally, that the nature of theorizing often requires one to buy abstraction and generality at the expense of concreteness. Like many theorists, I have paid this price. However, I have not *ignored* action and content. Instead, I have *emphasized* thought instead of action and form instead of content with the intent of defining what thought and form are. My work should not be construed as denying the "dialectical tension" between thought and action, for I have involved myself more recently in the study of this relationship with Daniel Candee (Chapter 7). Thus, we believe that this work should be understood as a necessary contribution to what we hope will become a greater appreciation of the complexities of the dialectical tensions to which Sullivan has referred.

Kohlberg's Failure to Deal with the Issue of Moral Commitment

In calling for a more complete theory of moral development, Sullivan correctly understands that we have not sufficiently addressed the role played by such factors as moral sensitivity and moral imagination. Of course, we understand Sullivan's comments in this context as constructive rather than critical.

The Kohlberg theory of moral development is one that focuses on moral decision-making processes and the cognitive-moral structures assumed to give rise to these processes. We have acknowledged earlier that we understand the theory of justice reasoning to be necessary but not sufficient for defining the full domain of what is meant by moral development. Thus, we welcome any constructive attempt to enlarge our appreciation of this domain.

However, in conclusion, we wish to emphasize one point which for us is obvious, that is, that a cognitive approach to the study of justice reasoning is, by definition, a perspective which studies the development and use of cognitive-moral processes. As we define and study them, moral judgments are "reasoned" judgments. We agree that their construction most probably is influenced by their relationships with emotion, imagination, and moral sensitivity, and we encourage anyone who is interested in doing so to investigate these relationships. However, we believe that the study of moral reasoning is valuable in its own right.

To embellish his argument about the importance of moral imagery and imagination in fostering a sense of moral commitment, Sullivan quotes at length from one of Martin Luther King's most memorable speeches. It is true that the moral imagery and imagination used by Martin Luther King to foster commitment to action in the service of civil rights is ample evidence justifying Sullivan's concerns. We also believe that it is probable, however, that if one could ask Dr. King *why* it was important to "Let Freedom ring from the hilltops of New Hampshire and from the mighty mountains of New York," that he would have articulated for us a Stage 6 moral reason.

Gilligan, C.: *In A Different Voice: Psychological Theory and Women's Development.* Cambridge, Mass.: Harvard University Press, 1982.

Synopsis: In 1982 Carol Gilligan published a book collecting and integrating her essays on the subject of women's development and morality, *In a Different Voice.* In our synopsis of this book we will try to define positions that she adopts that we agree with and positions she takes that we disagree with, and we will ignore a number of interesting statements in the book which are not directly relevant to moral development.

The general thesis of this book, with which we are in partial agreement, is that the influential theories of personality development for the most part have been created by males and reflect greater insight or understanding into male personality development than into female personality development.

With regard to morality, Gilligan points to the fact that the two greatest theorists of personality development, Freud and Piaget, both identified morality with justice. In addition, both theorists noted that their observations of females suggested to them that either females were less developed in their sense of justice than males or that the nature and development of women's morality could not be fully explained by their theories. Freud saw morality and justice as a function of the superego, that heir of the Oedipus complex which stemmed from identification with paternal authority. In addition he saw superego formation as a more clearly defined phenomenon in male than in female development. In a similar vein, Piaget related early morality to heteronomous respect for the parents, especially the father. This heteronomous respect was a *sui generis* mixture of fear and affection which defined the young child's moral attitude toward other people as well as rules. Observing the games of children, Piaget noted a much greater interest in the codification of rules on the part of boys than girls. This interest developed in a context of peer interaction, a factor which was instrumental in leading to Piaget's second stage of morality based on peer cooperation.

Gilligan suggests that morality really includes two moral orientations: first, the morality of justice as stressed by Freud and Piaget and, second, an ethic of care and response which is more central to understanding female moral judgment and action than it is to the understanding of judgment and action in males. Gilligan correctly notes that my original work (1958) began with an acceptance of Piaget's conception of morality as justice and of moral development as a movement toward autonomy. In addition to Piaget's work, I also focused on the work of Freud and of George Herbert Mead. To investigate Piaget's theory of peer interaction as the source of moral autonomy, I compared the moral orientations of peer group sociometric "stars" with peer group sociometric "isolates." To test the effects of George Herbert Mead's notion of "generalized-other" role-taking, I compared the moral orientations of working class and middle class males. To investigate several psychodynamic hypotheses, I constructed a measure of father identification for boys. After controlling for IQ and other variables in making these comparisons, I decided not to add the complicating issue of sex differences to my study and so did not include girls in my doctoral thesis sample. The major part of my work on the development of moral judgment has been based upon longitudinal analysis of the follow-up data from my original cross-sectional male sample. I did not collect longitudinal data on females until I began a longitudinal study of kibbutz males and females in 1969. Thus, Carol Gilligan points to the possibility of sex bias in my theory and measures, a bias presumably shared by my predecessors, Freud and Piaget. Unlike Freud and Piaget, however, I have never directly stated that males have a more developed sense of justice than do females. In several publications (volume I, Chapter 2; Kohlberg and Kramer, 1969) I did suggest that youthful and adult females might be less developed in justice stage sequence than males for the same reasons that working class males were less developed than middle class males. I suggested that if women were not provided with the experience of participation in society's complex secondary institutions through education and complex work responsibility, then they were not likely to acquire those societal role-taking abilities necessary for the development of Stage 4 and 5 justice reasoning.

However, what Gilligan postulates is a second moral orientation different from a justice orientation, an orientation which is neither adequately elicited by our justice dilemmas nor adequately identified by our 1984 standard issue scoring manual for assessing moral stage on the dilemmas. In our chapter on the current status of the Kohlberg moral theory (Chapter 3), we have largely agreed with Gilligan that the acknowledgment of an orientation of care and response usefully enlarges the moral domain. Philosophers such as Frankena (1973) have agreed with Gilligan in stating that there are two distinct principles or moral orientations, one of beneficence and care, the other of justice, and that both must be accounted for by a moral theory. Gilligan asserts, and Lyons (1982) documents, that it is these two different moral orientations that are reflected in sex differences in spontaneous ways of framing personal moral dilemmas. While Lyons notes that most males and most females form moral dilemmas by using both orientations, she reports that females are likely to use the orientation of care and response as their predominant mode and males are more likely to use justice as theirs.

Gilligan's book does not cite quantitative findings. However, in collaboration with Nona Lyons, she is in the process of reporting quantitative findings on sex differences in the use of the ethic of care and the ethic of justice. These differences are reported in Gilligan, Langdale, Lyons, and Murphy (1982).

In these pilot findings Gilligan and her colleagues found that in the personal constructions of real-life dilemmas in a sample of sixteen women and fourteen men, both orientations were used by both sexes. They also calculated whether each subject had a preponderant use of one orientation over the other, with preponderance defined as more than 50 percent of responses scored in one orientation to the dilemmas. They found that 75 percent of the females used predominantly the response orientation, and only 25 percent used predominantly a rights orientation. The balance was reversed among males; 79 percent used predominantly the rights orientation and 14 percent the response orientation. Seven percent of male responses were equally distributed in both orientations.

In an appendix to Gilligan et al., the authors report on responses from a larger sample of subjects. This larger sample responded, not only to the personal moral dilemmas studied by Lyons, but also to Kohlberg's justice dilemmas. This cross-sectional sample consisted of 144 males and females. Their responses were scored by graduate students I had trained.

The adult males and females of this sample were matched for the most part, all being highly educated and involved in professional work. Among children and adolescents, the authors report no difference in average stage between women and men in justice reasoning. In the adult sample of sixty-four (thirty-two females and thirty-two males), however, they report a difference in mean moral maturity score with the mean for males being 413 and that for females being 400. Parametric tests of this difference failed to attain significance. Given this, they used a nonparametric test to assess this sex difference. Their dependent measure was the frequency of postconventional "points" used by respondents with a "point" defined as one interview judgment. The chi-square test calculated indicated that the difference between male and female response means was significant at the .02 level.

In reference to the statistical significance of the point system, we note that for us the creation and use of a dichotomous variable (i.e., the use of some postconventional "points" versus the use of none) raises two problems. First, it is difficult for us to evaluate the importance of the Gilligan et al. study's findings because there is no interjudge or test-retest reliability data available on a "point" matching scoring technique. Second, the act of classifying subjects on the basis of whether they did or did not utter a single postconventional "point" is of unknown significance to us since the validity and reliability of the Kohlberg scale has been established by assigning individuals to a global or mixed stage score with the intent being to uncover longitudinal progression in such scores. In other words, for us a "point" scoring technique cannot capture the conceptual integrity of a person's moral development.

In terms of psychological significance, we should note that the field does not regard a difference of fifteen points in moral maturity scores between groups (and Gilligan et al. report a difference of only thirteen points) to be a psychologically meaningful difference. A fifteen-point difference is well within the limits of test-retest error variance found in various studies (Colby et al, 1983).

Gilligan et al. (p. 36) draw the following conclusion from the preceding analysis:

> Thus, in replicating under well-controlled conditions the previously reported sex difference favoring men in Kohlberg's standard of moral maturity, the current research suports critics of Kohlberg's theory who claim that, particularly at the postconventional level, that theory reflects a limited Western male perspective and may therefore be biased against women and other groups whose moral perspectives are somewhat different.

We totally disagree with this conclusion and think it is unwarranted, given their own findings. In our reply we will discuss in depth the evidence for our disagreement with their conclusion, based on a review of the field of research in general. Gilligan hypothesizes that, to solve problems of interpersonal conflict and relationship, males are more likely to use Piagetian balancing operations of reciprocity and equality. In contrast, she hypothesizes that females are more likely to construe a moral problem as lying within the boundaries of unquestioned relatedness and to use altruism or self-sacrifice as the solution to interpersonal problems.

In her book and in the above cited research with her colleagues, Gilligan makes a leap to a conclusion of test bias with which we do not agree. We do agree that our justice dilemmas do not pull for the care and response orientation, and we do agree that our scoring manual does not lead to a full assessment of this aspect of moral thinking. We do not agree, however, that the justice reasoning dilemmas and stages lead to an unfair, biased downscoring of girls' and women's reasoning, as Holstein suggests, because it measures them using a stage sequence and scoring manual developed on a sample of males.

This charge of sex bias in the test may have been partially true of the original (Kohlberg, 1958) method for stage scoring. At that time a respondent's concern with norms of caring and affiliation tended to be scored Stage 3, and a concern with norms of law tended to be scored Stage 4. We now see such concerns as content characteristics of reasoning. The 1984 standard issue scoring system now holds such normative content constant and assesses formal differences in the use of sociomoral perspective and justice operations to define justice stage. The justice stage methodology is intended to be an assessment of competence rather than of preference and spontaneous performance. Therefore, even though some females may spontaneously prefer thinking within the care and response orientation, our standard methodology, which pulls for optimal competence in justice reasoning, is, we believe, still a fair measure of that very basic aspect of moral judgment development. In our reply to follow we will cite a variety of sex-difference studies whose findings are pertinent to the issues we have been discussing.

Of more theoretical interest than the charge of test bias is another claim made by Gilligan's colleague, Nona Lyons, with which we disagree.

Lyons says: "This thesis offers the empirical confirmation of two explicit hypotheses generated by Gilligan's observations and speculations: (1) that there are two modes of thinking about moral conflict—justice and care—and (2) that these two modes of moral judgment—although not confined to an individual by virtue of gender—are gender-related" (1982, p. 14).

The implication of this statement seems to be that justice and care define two separate or distinct tracks of moral development. We shall indicate in our reply that considerations of care and considerations of justice are interwoven in working out resolutions to moral dilemmas. We do not think that the experiences that lead to development on the justice side of moral judgment are distinctly different from those experiences that lead to the development of the caring side of morality. The educational approach of our colleagues to stimulating moral judgment development is called the "just community" approach. Their work indicates that experiences of democratically resolving issues of conflicting rights are interwoven with considerations of community and considerations of caring and responsibility for the group and for each of its members. In our philosophic end point of moral reasoning, the hypothetical sixth stage, there occurs, we believe, an integration of justice and care that forms a single moral principle. We shall attempt to describe this idea in our reply.

We should note that implicit in Gilligan's (1982) book is a second set of issues pertaining to the appropriateness of justice principles when placed in conjunction with an awareness of contextual relativity. These issues we shall discuss separately in our synopsis and response to two articles not included in Gilligan's book, articles by Murphy and Gilligan (1980) and Gilligan and Murphy (1979).

Before we move to a detailed reply, however, let us summarize what appears to be the essence of Gilligan's perspective. Gilligan believes that there is a different moral orientation characteristic of females as compared with males. Females employ a care and response orientation, whereas males are primarily concerned with justice. This difference in orientation, Gilligan implies, leads to a sex-biased assessment of the moral judgment development of females, since the Kohlberg instrument, she argues, misrepresents the caring orientation as Stage 3 justice reasoning. Thus, it is asserted that women have been inappropriately downscored. While Gilligan has not defined structural stages in the caring orientation, she does distinguish among three levels in this orientation: a preconventional level which is primarily egocentric; a conventional level which is primarily concerned with caring for others; and finally, a postconventional level which balances care for self and care for others.

Reply: In Chapter 3, in our discussion of the enlargement of the moral domain, we discussed at length Gilligan's view that there is a caring orientation distinct from a justice orientation and assumed that this is Gilligan's most important thesis. However, the claim by Gilligan that has received the most popular attention, and that is most critical of my theory and method, is the claim that the standard moral dilemmas and scoring system have a built-in sex bias and downgrade female responses.

To deal with this issue we shall briefly summarize the studies on sex differences in justice reasoning on our standard dilemmas. Two issues are involved here. The first issue with which we will deal is whether there are mean sex differences between males and females on our justice reasoning dilemmas. The second issue is whether women's responses to the dilemmas can be scored in terms of the justice stages and yield the same results of invariant sequence and structured wholeness which the longitudinal studies of Colby et al. (1983) have found for males.

Sex Differences in Mean Scores

With regard to the issue of mean sex differences in moral judgment stages, we shall quote from an extensive literature review by Walker (1982) of fifty four studies using the Kohlberg moral judgment interview and twenty four studies using Rest's (1979) DIT measure of moral judgment.

Walker starts by noting:

> A theory could warrant the charge of sex bias for either of the following reasons. First, a theory could advocate or popularize a poorly founded claim that the sexes are fundamentally different in rate and endpoint of moral development. For example, Freud (1927) asserted that women lack moral maturity because of deficiencies in same-sex parental identification. Second, a theory might offer no such opinion, but entail various measurement or scoring procedures which inadvertently favor one sex or the other, and thus create a false impression that real differences in moral maturity do exist. The allegations of sex bias against Kohlberg's theory have been primarily based on the latter reason.
>
> If there is sex bias in Kohlberg's approach, how could it have arisen? A trite response is that because Kohlberg is a man, he has taken a masculine point of view in theorizing about moral development. An equally trite rejoinder would be to point out that Kohlberg has had a number of female colleagues and that the senior author of the recent editions of the scoring manual is a woman, Anne Colby. A second and much more important possible source of bias is that the stage sequence has been constructed from the longitudinal data provided by an exclusively male sample (Colby and Kohlberg et al., 1983). While this lack of representativeness is a real threat to the generalizability of the model and could easily be a source of sex bias, the stage sequence has now been corroborated by both longitudinal (e.g., Holstein, 1976) and experimental intervention studies (Walker, in press) using

both males and females. Nonetheless, it is impossible to determine whether the same stages and sequence would have been derived if females had originally been studied. A third potential source of bias is the predominance of male protagonists in the moral dilemmas used as stimulus materials in eliciting reasoning. Females may have difficulty relating to these male protagonists and thus exhibit artifactually lower levels of moral reasoning. Three studies have examined the theory about effect of protagonist's sex; one found more advanced reasoning with same-sex protagonists, another found more advanced reasoning with opposite-sex protagonists, and the third found no evidence of differential responding when protagonist sex was varied. Thus, the data are equivocal regarding this potential source of bias.

To summarize, it is possible that sex bias exists in Kohlberg's theory, in particular due to his reliance on an exclusively male sample, but this remains to be determined.

In order to summarize the research concisely, the studies are presented in three tables which divide the life span into the somewhat arbitrary period of (*a*) childhood and early adolescence, (*b*) late adolescence and youth, and (*c*) adulthood.

Studies which examined sex differences in moral reasoning in childhood and early adolescence are first summarized. There are 27 such studies, involving a total of 2,430 subjects who range in age from about 5 years to 17 years. The overall pattern revealed by these studies is that sex differences in moral reasoning in childhood and early adolescence are infrequent; for the 34 samples, only 4 significant differences were reported.

Next, thirty-four studies of sex differences in adolescence and youth are summarized. Of those studies not employing methodological variation or artifacts, only nine report sex differences.

Five findings indicate significant sex differences remain after removing methodological artifacts. Two of these were reported by Bar-Yam et al. (1980) in a study of Israeli high school students. In both the Moslem-Arab and Youth-Aliyah samples, boys were found to have higher levels of moral reasoning than girls (296 vs. 249, and 376 vs. 350, respectively). Both samples were drawn from ethnic groups where the status of women has traditionally been low, with few opportunities for decision making within the family and society and with typically low levels of education. (Youth Aliyah were recent immigrants who were typically from North Africa or the Middle East.) It is interesting to note that no differences were found in the kibbutz and Christian samples in which attitudes would be more egalitarian.

Eleven studies examined sex differences in moral reasoning in adulthood.

These studies involve a total of 1,131 subjects who range in age from 21 years to over 65 years. Sex differences in moral reasoning in adulthood are slightly more frequent than earlier in the life span; or alternately, sex differences are more frequent in this generation than in later generations. (It is impossible to separate developmental and cohort differences with these data.) Of the 19 samples considered, 4 significant differences were reported, all favoring men.

Unlike the studies discussed in previous sections which involved rather homogeneous samples of school and university students, it is apparent in these studies revealing differences in moral reasoning that sex was grossly confounded with education and/or occupational differences. Haan et al. (1976) found that men scored higher in both the 21- to 30-year-old sample and the 47- to 50-year-old sample (parents of the younger group). The older women in this study were mostly housewives (according to Haan, 1977).

In the two remaining studies that revealed differences, sex was similarly confounded with occupational differences. Holstein (1976) found differences on her first test favoring men (409 vs. 366), but none on the retest. In her upper middle class sample, nearly all the men had careers in business, management, or the professions, whereas only 6 percent of the women were employed. Similarly, Parikh (1980) found that the men in her Indian sample scored higher than women (326 vs. 280). The men were all self-employed professionals, whereas most of the women were housewives.

To summarize, it is apparent that sex differences in moral reasoning in adulthood are revealed only in a minority of studies, and then when sex differences are confounded with differences in level of education and occupation. There is no evidence of sex differences in dominant stage of moral reasoning in adulthood.

In Rest's (1979) review of sex difference in DIT research, he found that only 2 of 21 samples yielded sex differences. In both samples, females evidenced higher scores. Since that review, a few additional studies have yielded sex differences, all with females evidencing higher moral development (Cistone, 1980; Garwood et al., 1980; Leahy, 1981). An additional, and particularly relevant, finding reported by Garwood et al. (1980), was that males exhibited greater preference for Stage 3 statements than did females.

To elaborate on Walker's review, the only studies showing fairly frequent sex differences are those of adults, usually of spouse housewives. Many of the studies comparing adult males and females without controlling for education and job status, as defined by the Hollingshead index or some similar measure, do report sex differences in favor of males. These include Holstein (1976); Kuhn et al. (1977); Haan, Langer, and Kohlberg (1976); and Parikh (1980). Two studies comparing middle class husbands and wives have been conducted using the new Colby et al. (1983) standard issue scoring instrument. These studies are by Speicher-Dubin (1982) and Powers (1982). Both studies report sex differences in favor of males. However, both studies report that these sex differences disappear when the variables of higher education and job status are statistically controlled for by step-down multiple regression techniques.

The need to control for higher education and job status in examining sex differences is documented by the Colby and Kohlberg (1984, in press) longitudinal study of males. In this study, movement to Stages 4 and 5 after high school was found to be systematically related to higher education and to job satisfaction and responsibility. Given these results, as well as our general contention that moral Stages 4 and 5 depend upon experiences of participation, responsibility, and role-taking in the secondary institutions of society such as work and government, it appears necessary to control for such factors as education and employment when assessing sex differences in the use of advanced stages of justice reasoning.

Studies which match males and females on education, job status, and responsibility are better suited to testing for sex differences within an interactionist cognitive-developmental paradigm than are studies which employ techniques of control through step-down regression analysis. The single most clear-cut study of this sort is the longitudinal study by Snarey (1982). In this longitudinal study of kibbutz males and females aged 12 to 24, no significant mean sex-differences were found. On the kibbutz, both males and females were found scoring Stage 4, 4/5, and 5, even though not exposed to higher education. We explain this by the fact that in the egalitarian framework of the kibbutz, females' job responsibility and participation in the democratic governance of the kibbutz is formally equal to that of males. In line with the Kohlberg cognitive-developmental theory, then, no mean differences in justice reasoning stage would be expected, and indeed, none were found.

Another study controlling for education and occupational status was Weisbroth's (1970). This study compared male and female graduate students, thus equalizing the sexes in higher education and in occupational aspiration. As cognitive-developmental theory would predict, no sex differences were found. In summary, studies comparing the sexes in justice reasoning stage either report no sex differences or report sex differences attributable to higher education and role-taking opportunity differences related to work.

Female Data and the Invariant Sequence Hypothesis

A second hypothesis raised by Gilligan's theory is that our standard justice reasoning dilemmas and issue scoring system will not reproduce the findings of invariant sequence and structured wholeness for females that they have for males as reported in the Colby and Kohlberg longitudinal study (1984, in press). This hypothesis would be anticipated if, as Gilligan claims, our justice scoring system is not applicable to females given that their preference is for a caring and response orientation. Again the Snarey (1982) study provides the best data on this hypothesis. The same findings of invariant sequence and structured wholeness found in American males were found in this longitudinal study of both females and males. A second study showing upward movement and no stage skipping in females, within the limits of test-retest reliability, was the study by V. Lois Erickson (1980). In addition, clinical analysis of the Snarey data suggests that many females, as well as some males, made some use of Gilligan's caring and response orientation in response to our standard justice dilemmas. This fact, however, did not lead to downscoring on the standard issue scoring instrument, which pulls for the justice orientation. In other words, while there may be sex differences in preferential orientation to framing moral dilemmas, as Gilligan suggests, this does not lead to the conclusion of bias or invalidity of the justice reasoning test as an assessment of competence in justice reasoning.

Sex Differences in Orientation

A third implication of Gilligan's theory is the notion that women are more likely to spontaneously use the care and response orientation in their reasoning than are men. While Lyons (1982) found that both sexes use both rights and care considerations in construing personal dilemmas, she also noted that there was some preference by females for the caring and response orientation. These results stem from a scoring system which dichotomously classifies response as either rights-oriented or care-oriented. In our discussion about enlarging the moral domain, we suggested that these orientations were not bipolar or dichotomous, but rather that the care and response orientation was directed primarily to relations of special obligations to family, friends, and group members, relations which often included or presupposed general obligations of respect, fairness, and contract.

Our standard moral dilemmas tend to be framed and probed in terms of justice. We believe that Lyons's study indicates, not that women prefer care over justice in responding to such general justice dilemmas, but rather that they more often choose as examples of personal dilemmas, dilemmas of special relationships to family or friends. As noted in Chapter 3, however, many women do not define or select special relationship dilemmas as moral. We quoted a 31-year-old woman who said:

> Take my decision to divorce. I didn't view that as a moral problem. It wasn't. . . . Because there weren't any moral issues involved really. The issue involved was whether it was the right thing for us. I don't really see that as a moral problem. . . . Usually where two principles that I consider valuable look as though they may be clashing, then it's very hard to make a decision about things. . . . That would be a moral problem for me.

This woman defined moral dilemmas, as we have done, as conflicts between two general legitimate norms or "principles." She does not see dilemmas of responsibility in special relationships as moral in the same sense.

The study by Higgins, Power, and Kohlberg (1984), summarized in Chapter 3, reported that both sexes used justice and responsibility considerations in school dilemmas. The major differences in the use of the two orientations were attributable to (*a*) the type of dilemma asked and (*b*) the sociomoral atmosphere of the school situation. The dilemma about helping another student elicited caring considerations, while a dilemma about theft elicited justice concerns. The most striking differences, however, were not dilemma differences (and there were no sex-differences) but, rather, differences in the nature of school environments. In the alternative democratic community schools a responsibility orientation was much more frequently used than in the high school counterpart. In summary, this study suggests that both considerations are used by both sexes and that preferential orientation is largely a function of the type of moral problem defined and of the sociomoral atmosphere of the environment in which the dilemma is located. Dilemmas located within a "community" or "family" context are likely to invoke caring and response considerations, so too do dilemmas of responsibility and caring that go beyond duty (i.e., supererogatory dilemmas and dilemmas of special obligation to friends and kin). In brief, choice of orientation seems to be primarily a function of setting and dilemma, not sex.

In our work we have also attempted to isolate a care and response orientation in our standard justice dilemmas, based on the description of this orientation given in Chapter 3. To maximize the possibility of finding such an orientation we focused on the females in the Israeli kibbutz sample, assuming that we were most likely to find the orientation being used by females and in a setting which, like our just community schools, would have strong ties of interpersonal caring and of caring for a special group or community.

Our tentative findings are (1) that the use of such a global orientation was rare, even in the female sample; (2) that, when found, it was dilemma-specific rather than occurring in all dilemmas (Form A was used in this study); and (3) that, when found, it was stage specific (i.e., it was most likely to be found at the age at which the subject was "early conventional," or Stage 3, and would be replaced by a justice orientation at a later stage).

A female kibbutz case example illustrating these points is Case 252. At age 14, when she is scored Stage 3, she answers the Heinz dilemma (Dilemma III, Form A) as follows:

> He's debating whether he should steal. He loves his wife, he doesn't want her to die, so he's doing the right thing. He didn't have any other way. [Is it a husband's duty?] It's a moral obligation. It depends on the person whether he loves his wife and is willing to steal for her. There might be another person who won't. She's so dear to him that he's willing to steal for her.

Although scorable using our standard manual, this response perhaps could be classified in the caring orientation. In Dilemma III′ (Should Heinz be sentenced or shown leniency?) she more clearly uses the deontic and justice orientation at Stage 3:

> It's a hard question. Yes he should send him to prison because a law is a law. He breaks the law and it doesn't matter for what reason. What would happen in the country if everyone would steal? It would be terrible.

On Dilemma I (Joe and his father) she focuses on the special relationship between the two people. Again this response perhaps could be classified in the caring orientation:

> If Joe thinks the reason his father is asking for the money is really important, then yes, but if not he shouldn't give him the money. I think if it was my father I'd give him the money. I really want to go to camp but I understand, it's worth helping him.

At age 21, when case 252 is scored Stage 4 (3), her responses were classified as being primarily in the deontic orientation, though considerations of caring were integrated into this orientation. On the Heinz dilemma (Form A, Dilemma III) she says:

Absolutely, because when human life is at stake and the only way to save it is getting money, life is more important than money. The ends justify the means in this case. Especially when his wife's life is at stake and it is not a stranger. That enhances the obligation. I think that human life is such an important thing and has great value. [What if Heinz doesn't love his wife?] Yes, because as a moral and humane person he should do everything he can to save another human life. If he didn't have enough courage to do it, he is not guilty, because it was his inner obligation to do it and no one has the right to force him to do it.

Her response to Dilemma III′ (i.e., whether Heinz should be sentenced to jail) was again scored primarily in the justice orientation. However, elements of care were integrated in her response.

The judge should suspend the sentence because Heinz is not a criminal. Heinz is not stealing for his own benefit, and the judge should recognize that fact. He has to take into account the special circumstances that led Heinz to the crime. From the moral perspective, he is acting from his own morality. He is breaking the law for morality. From the moral point of view, it was not a crime. Yet a suspended sentence is also a sentence, since I don't think he is innocent in that he did commit a crime and that should be recognized. The law is to protect society, otherwise the condition of society would break down. If a person would behave only according to his conscience, there would be chaos, but if Heinz's conscience is identical with society's conscience or morality then he should not get a severe punishment: both society and Heinz feel life is important.

In response to Dilemma I (Joe and his father) she says:

Joe shouldn't give his father the money because he had promised and is working very hard. It's unfair to break a promise, it's a kind of exploitation by the father of the son. [Is the promise the most important consideration?] Yes, it is a principle that has its own value, a promise is creating a trust, and breaking a promise is like a betrayal. [How about to someone you don't know?] Yes, if you disappoint your son or a stranger, it makes no difference. In both cases the other side expects you to keep your promise and has placed confidence in you.

Related to our questioning of the dichotomy between the justice and care orientations, and linked to the dichotomy of gender, is our general view that many moral situations or dilemmas do not pose a choice between one or the other orientation but, rather, call out a response which integrates both orientations.

As an example of that observation, consider the fact that for most individuals the Heinz dilemma is not a dilemma of caring and response for Heinz's wife as opposed to a concern for justice considered vis-à-vis the druggist's property rights. Rather, the wife's right to life is often linked to a caring concern for her welfare and the druggist's right to property is often related to concerns about the welfare to persons in general and to society as a whole (i.e., to a concern about the impact of theft on the social fabric). In other words, it would appear that the concerns for justice and care are often hard to distinguish.

A case example illustrates the two points we have made: first, that males also have the capacity for caring and response considerations and, second, that caring and response considerations need not pose a tension or conflict between care and justice but may be integrated into a response consistent with justice, especially at the postconventional level. The Stage 5 response of Kohlberg's longitudinal subject 42 to the Heinz dilemma follows, with our analysis of its justice and caring components.

Q.—Should Heinz have done that?

A.—Well, I don't think there is enough here to indicate that he had tried every alternative before he did it, so it is not necessarily the case whether or not he should have done it but whether he had an alternative and it isn't in the facts here. But he might have approached other people or local authorities or doctors or something like that before getting desperate. On the other hand, the fact that he was desperate might have meant that he had already done that, so . . .

Presumably, if he was desperate, he had tried everything he knew of. Now it may not have been adequate. Getting right down to that choice of theft versus that chance of saving his wife's life, I think, yes, he should steal it.

Q.—In what sense would it be worth it?

A.—In the sense of the value of human life, because it is all well and good to talk about the sanctity of private property and property rights and so on, but I don't think they mean much in a society that doesn't value human life higher. I guess that is the sense in which I am thinking. In the sense that it is his wife and he has made some kind of commitment to her and so on, but basically because of the value of human life.

Q.—Was it actually wrong or right for Heinz to have done that?

A.—Well, with all my conditions . . . I guess it was right. I get entangled in the sense that sometimes I am not even sure if terms like right and wrong apply, but yes.

Q.—Is it a husband's duty to steal the drug for his wife? If he can get it no other way?
A.—Yah, I think so.

Q.—Why?
A.—Well, because of the commitment to the marriage, what it means to me. I guess that is why I respond that way. It is, I just am trying to think of what, it is—I think I know what I mean but I don't know how to say it. The commitment to another person is a total commitment and in a sense he is taking this action because she can't take it herself, in the sense of marriage being something in two bodies. And in that sense there is not much difference in terms of responsibility of her trying to do something for him. This is an ideal proposition.

Q.—You are sort of arguing from the position of marriage being the union of two persons . . .
A.— . . . that involves a commitment to each other and to some kind of form of life or something like that. And it's a commitment that means essentially that. I think I have said it already, that whatever that he would do for her, as much as he would do for himself. It is like an extension of yourself, yah, I guess that is what I am saying.

Q.—Would you say that that comes in under the idea of duty?
A.—Yes, it's a part of the commitment that he made at the time they were married.

Q.—Suppose the person dying is a stranger?
A.—Then he should.

Q.—Why?
A.—Again, because I think the value of human life is higher than the material values that the druggist is after. I was working towards something about not feeling an obligation for someone you don't know, but that doesn't make any sense at all. I am balking. I am groping. What I am thinking of is the parable that Jesus tells of the guy at the side of the road and the stranger that helped him. That was kind of preaching the value of human life whether it is someone you know or not. *He felt human and that was enough of a bond.*

To understand this case it is helpful to turn to Table 3.1 in Chapter 3, in which we elaborated characteristics of the caring and response orientation as described by Gilligan (1982) and by Lyons (1982). The central feature of this adult male's caring orientation is his assumption of a connectedness or union between husband and wife. This sense of the connected self lead to a feeling of psychological responsibility, necessity, or "desperateness" about the obligation to take care of his wife. The bond is seen as intrinsically valuable. As noted in Chapter 3, this subject is able at the same time to universalize this bond of caring in order to declare that Heinz would have a responsibility for stealing even to help a stranger. He does not come to this conclusion directly from the stranger's right to life (as would happen in the justice orientation) but from the Christian notion of the Good Samaritan, from caring, from a sense of *agape* for all human beings who are in relationship to one another. "He felt human and that was enough of a bond."

In other words, the decision to help the stranger comes from a caring orientation to universal bonds, to the connectedness of all selves in the human community. We also note in Case 42's response a quality of cautious contextual relativism, uncertainty about deontic rightness, and a search for alternative means of dialogue and communication which both Gilligan and Lyons suggest are part of the considerations of their caring and response orientation. However, while showing these signs of care and response, this subject also equally relies on justice considerations which support and define his response to the dilemma in terms of a hierarchy of rights, that is, of the right to life over property.

This subject's justice orientation is indicated by the basic way in which he justifies the rightness of the husband stealing. He does this by establishing that societies in general must recognize the hierarchical value of the right to human life before property rights. "It would be worth stealing in the sense of the value of human life, because it is all well and good to talk about the sanctity of property rights but I don't think they mean much in a society that doesn't value human life higher." This statement expresses a Stage 5 justice criterion judgment in the standard scoring manual (i.e., the Life *issue,* the Life *norm,* the *element* of serving human dignity or autonomy), which specifies a prior-to-society sense of a hierarchy of rights that forms the foundation of the social contract. In addition, we note that this respondent supports his caring responses regarding the husband-wife relationship with a contractual judgment of justice when he is asked the deontic question "Is it a husband's duty to steal the drug for his wife?" He replies: "Yes, it's part of the commitment he made at the time of marriage." Thus, this subject's sense of the responsibilities of caring is supported by and integrated with his deontic judgments of justice and duty.

We are more clearly able to score his responses in the justice orientation in terms of our justice stages than we are able to stage score his responses in the caring orientation. We leave to Gilligan and her colleagues the task of defining more fully and formally levels and stages within the caring orientation. For the purposes of this theoretical reply, however, we see the responses we have cited as *nonsupportive* of Lyons's hypothesis that justice and caring are two different tracks of moral development that are either independent or in polar opposition to one another.

We may note that at the postconventional stages there is typically an effort to integrate concerns of benevolence and care, on the one hand, with justice concerns, on the other. At this level of moral reasoning, justice concerns lose their retributive and rule-bound nature for the sake of treating persons as persons, that is, at ends in themselves. This principle of persons as ends is common to both the ethic of care and the ethic of justice. The former ethic sees the other person in relationship to self and others; the latter sees persons as autonomous ends in themselves, relating to one another through agreement and mutual respect.

As an example of the above convergence of the justice and care orientations, we have just suggested two responses to the Heinz dilemma that focus on issues of rights and justice and yet center on issues of care as well. Another example of this convergence can be seen in responses to caring dilemmas used by Higgins et al. (1984) which asked whether Billy, a classmate, should volunteer to drive an unpopular student, Harry, to a college interview.

In order to demonstrate how both the caring and justice orientations come together at our postconventional level, we will answer the Higgins et al. dilemma with the logic of Stage 6 reasoning as described in Volume I, Chapter 5, "Justice as Reversibility." Let the dilemma be called "Billy's dilemma." The question to the respondent is as follows: "Should Billy drive Harry to Harry's interview or should he sleep in?" Some adolescent high school students answer this question in terms of a potential relationship between Harry and Billy as classmates and friends. In this sense they are responding within Gilligan's caring orientation. Many students at the conventional moral stages respond in terms of notions of fairness as captured by the Golden Rule; that is, if they were in Harry's situation, they say, they would want someone to help them get to the interview. This idea of the Golden Rule would be formulated with the Kohlberg conception of Stage 6 as the following question: "If Billy did not know whether he was the needy student Harry, or himself with the car who could not sleep in if he drove

Harry, he would choose the option to offer to drive Harry. He would make this choice reasoning that, not knowing his own identity, the loss of not attending the interview was far greater than not being able to sleep in for one morning. This is an example of Stage 6 justice reasoning which resolves a dilemma which might normally be expected to elicit an ethic of care; and it should be noted, it resolves the dilemma in the same direction as a mature ethic of care would.

In the New Testament there are two alternative statements of the Golden Rule. The first can be seen in the fairness orientation as "Do unto others as you would have them do unto you." The second version is phrased in terms of the orientation of care as "Love thy neighbor as thyself." Like other statements of postconventional morality, the teachings of the New Testament often integrate considerations of care and justice presenting, as modern moral philosophy does, a view of justice which is beyond either strict contract, strict retribution, or strict obedience to rules. Rather, it is a view of justice which focuses on ideal role–taking, a principle which can be called, alternatively, respect for persons (i.e., justice) or caring for persons as ideal ends in themselves (i.e., the ethic of care).

In the parable of the vineyard, the vineyard owner gives the same wage to those who come late as he does to those whom he hires first and who, therefore, work longer. The vineyard owner, in making the last who come equal to the first, is acting out of a generosity which is not unfair to those who came first, since he has kept his contract with them. In terms of justice as equity or distribution according to need, the last to come are as needy as the first. As discussed in Volume I, postconventional justice reasoning, particularly that reasoning called Stage 6, is blind to many of the considerations of merit and retribution which are the connotations of justice to many who reason at lower stages. Earlier stage reasoning often separates justice from an ethic of care. For the sake of a regard for respecting persons as ends in themselves, however, the Stage 6 vineyard owner's action represents not only justice but also the ethic of care.

Not only at the postconventional stages but at the conventional stages as well, we see persons responding to both real-life and hypothetical dilemmas in ways which include and attempt to integrate concerns for both justice and care. Justice and care, we believe, do not represent different tracks of moral development. Piaget spoke of childhood morality as representing two moralities, not one, that is, a morality of heteronomous respect and a morality of mutual respect. Our own work suggests that these differences represent different substages within the sequential growth through my stages of justice reasoning. Similar to our recognition of "Piagetian" substages within a larger context of sequential stage growth, we partially accept Gilligan's differentiation of two orientations in moral judgment which may vary in emphasis from person to person and from situation to situation. We do not believe, however, that the growth of justice and the ethic of care represent two distinct tracks of moral stage (i.e., structural) development.

We may summarize the above discussion by stating that Gilligan's emphasis on the care and response orientation has broadened the moral domain beyond our focus on justice reasoning. However, we do not believe that there exist two distinct or polar orientations or two tracks in the ontogenesis of moral stage structures. In the last chapter on revisions to my theory, we indicated why our focus on justice was more amenable to a formulation in terms of "hard" Piagetian structural stages than would be some other focus on other elements of the moral, such as a focus on considerations of care. It remains for Gilligan and her colleagues to determine whether there are, in fact, "hard" stages in the care orientation. If she wishes to claim that there are stages of caring in a Piagetian sense of the word *stage,* she will have to demonstrate the progressive movement, invariant sequence, structured wholeness, and the relationships of thought to action for her orientation in a manner similar to the way we have demonstrated such ontogenetic characteristics for the justice orientation (see, for example, the presentation of the longitudinal data on justice reasoning in Colby and Kohlberg, 1984, in press).

The questioning of the notion of two distinct moralities made in this reply is paralleled in a paper by Gertrude Nunner-Winkler (1984) entitled "Two Moralities? A Critical Discussion of an Ethic of Care and Responsibility Versus an Ethic of Rights and Justice."

Nunner-Winkler says that insofar as there are differences between the caring and justice approaches they are not differences in basic ethical position but differences in emphasis on two types of moral duty. Following Kant, Nunner-Winkler takes perfect duties to be negative duties of noninterference with the rights of others. Perfect or negative duties can be followed by everybody at any time and location and with regard to everybody. Imperfect duties, in contrast, are positive duties which do not prescribe specific acts but only formulate a maxim which is to guide action, for example, the practice of care.

> Such a maxim delineates a broad set of recommendable courses of action, some of which the actor realizes by at the same time applying pragmatic rules and taking into account concrete conditions such as individual preferences or locations in space and history. Imperfect duties can never be observed completely; it is impossible to practice caring all the time and with regard to everybody. Positive maxims or principles do not specify which and how many good deeds have to be performed and whom they are to benefit so that the maxim can be said to have been followed. This orientation to imperfect duty, which Gilligan characterizes as an ethic of care, finds its most precise expression in the following quotation Gilligan (1977) cites: "Is it right to spend money on a pair of shoes when I have a pair of shoes and other people are shoeless?"
>
> The form this reflection takes, the questioning, is proof of its being derived from an imperfect duty, namely, the principle of charity which does not define its own form of application, its own limits, and the degree to which it is binding. . . . No one would deny that both kinds of duties are considered part of one's morality, the unity of which is constituted by adhering to some universalizing procedure which Kant would hold applies to both types of duties.

From this point of view Nunner-Winkler interprets Gilligan's claim as meaning that females (1) feel more obliged to fulfill imperfect duties than do males and (2), in case of conflict, are more likely to opt for the fulfillment of imperfect duties, whereas males opt for the fulfillment of perfect duties.

Gilligan sees a consideration of contextual particularity as lacking in the ethic of rights and justice. Gilligan's equation of an orientation to imperfect duties with contextual particularity, Nunner-Winkler says, holds true only for a very specific aspect of Kant's moral position which is hardly shared by anyone, namely, that perfect duties allow for no exceptions. Such a position is not held by Kohlberg, she says,

> even though he presents his construction of rights in such a misleading way that it does provoke the kind of criticism that Gilligan voices. . . . Therefore one cannot very well hold context orientations to be a feature to constitute contrasting approaches to morality. Context orientation is a prerequisite for all actual moral judgments.

Given the above, Nunner-Winker then rephrases Gilligan's theory as implying that females feel more obliged to fulfill imperfect duties and males to fulfill perfect duties, though both apply to the field of morality. She presents both logical arguments for her case as well as empirical data from her study with adolescents in which she did not find sex-differences in orientation to imperfect as opposed to perfect duties. As an example, females are not more likely than males to endorse the "caring" or "imperfect" duty of relieving a terminally ill person of her pain, where this is in contrast with the perfect duty of preserving the woman's life (Kohlberg's Form B, Dilemma IV). Since Nunner-Winkler did not find these sex-differences in moral judgment, in the strict sense of justice reasoning, she suggests that what Gilligan is really talking about are sex-differences in ideals of the good life. These ideals of the self and of the good life may be related to the image of the self as connected, but operate, not through moral judgment, but through specific ego interests. As an example, Nunner-Winkler quotes Gilligan's example of one male and one female 6-year-old responding to the dilemma created when in playing with a friend they discover they want to play a different game. "Gilligan cites as characteristic of the little girl 'We don't have a real fight and we agree about what we will do,' while the little boy says 'I wanted to go outside, he wanted to stay in. I would do what I want, he would do what he wants.'" Nunner-Winkler then states:

> As long as it is so described, however, this dilemma is not a moral dilemma but the inner conflict of an individual choosing among his own inner needs. Each child has two desires, the desire to play a specific game, and the desire to play with a specific friend. The little girl prefers foregoing the chance to play the preferred game for the chance to play with her friend. The little boy proves to be more interested in playing the preferred game, and be it alone, than to play with his friend. Thus far each child may have chosen among different needs which proved not to be simultaneously satisfiable. On the face of it there is nothing moral about this choice; it is well known that females are more interested in relationships and males more in things (objects). Neither one nor the other of these preferences is morally more recommendable.

Nunner-Winkler's relating of an ethic of care to an ego interest or an ideal of the good life, rather than to morality in its strictly more other-regarding and universalizable sense, coincides with our statement that many of the judgments in this orientation are personal rather than moral in the sense of a formal point of view.

Further research should attend to differences in what may be considered either "moral content" or "moral style," but we believe it unlikely that such research will find divergent moral "hard" stage sequences for justice and care.

Murphy, J. M., and Gilligan, C., "Moral Development in Late Adolescence and Adulthood. A Critique and Reconstruction of Kohlberg's Theory." *Human Development 23* (1980), pp.77–104.

and

Gilligan, C., and Murphy, J. M., "Development from Adolescence to Adulthood: The Philosopher and the Dilemma of the Fact." In D. Kuhn, ed., *Intellectual Development Beyond Childhood.* San Francisco: Jossey-Bass, 1979.

Synopsis: In these two articles Murphy and Gilligan claim, first, that there is regression in prescriptive reasoning about justice on our "classical" dilemmas in early adulthood. Second, and leaving aside the reported regression on classical dilemmas, they report continued progression on real-life dilemmas as measured with the Perry (1968) scale of epistemological and metaethical development. They interpret this finding in light of their own theorizing about a "responsibility orientation" to moral judgment which they seem to consider as more context-relevant than Kohlberg's justice orientation.

In other words, these essays by Murphy and Gilligan (1980) and Gilligan and Murphy (1979) deal with Gilligan's contrast between the justice and responsibility orientations in terms of a different issue: that is, Gilligan believes that postconventional reasoning in the responsibility orientation does not rest on "abstract principles" but, rather, on contextually relative perceptions of the factual moral situation and its psychological implications. In some sense Gilligan and Murphy believe that the principled morality of justice which we have defined as Stage 5 and 6 represents an adolescent form of overly theoretical and overly abstract moral perception which in more mature adulthood is modified or develops into a more mature adulthood is modified or develops into a more contextually relative form of moral perception. This relativism results from actual experiences of what adults take to be contradictions in conflicts between generalized principles and the factual complexities and ambiguities of real-life situations, situations to which late adolescents attempt to apply their justice principles.

In developing their notion of a postadolescent movement to a moral methodology of contextual relativism, Gilligan and Murphy rely upon William Perry's (1968) statement of intellectual and ethical development in the college years. Gilligan and Murphy make two quantitative empirical claims in this context. The first claim is that there is developmental advance on the Perry scale, moving toward responsibility in the context of relativism, detected in longitudinal data in the college and postcollege years. The second claim they make is that there is some regression on the Kohlberg scale from principled (Stage 5) moral reasoning to transitional (4/5) moral reasoning. They assume that this regression is a *consequence* of the advance observed on the Perry scale. With the use of case material, they interpret quantitative findings as indicating the development of a mature awareness that questions the validity of general or universal principles and their application in the context of confronting concrete moral "dilemmas of the fact."

Gilligan and Murphy (1979) paraphrase Perry's important developmental work as follows, and we quote them at length:

> Empirical evidence for such a divergence in ethical orientations comes, instead, from the work of Perry who, like Kohlberg, followed intellectual and ethical development in the college years. However, where Kohlberg speaks of the order of reason and the conception of the moral ideal, Perry talks of the disorder of experience, the realization that life itself is unfair. How thought comes to account for experiences that demonstrate the limits of both knowledge and choice is the problem that Perry sets out to address. In doing so, he describes a revolution in thinking that leads to the perception of all knowledge as contextually relative, a radical "180-degree shift in orientation" that follows from the discovery that, "in even its farthest reaches, reason alone will leave the thinker with several legitimate contexts and no way of choosing among them—no way, at least that he can justify through reason alone. If he then throws away reason entirely, he retreats to the irresponsible in Multiplicity ('Anyone has a right to his opinion'). If he is still to honor reason, he must now also transcend it." Because "the ultimate welding of epistemological and moral issues" makes the act of knowing an act of commitment for which one bears personal responsibility, Perry centers the drama of late adolescent development on the theme of responsibility which enters first as a new figure on the familiar ground of logical justification. However, because the understanding of responsibility demands a contextual mode of thought, the concern with responsibility signifies a fundamental shift in ethical orientation that ushers in what Perry calls "the period of responsibility." Following this shift, judgment "is always qualified by the nature of the context in which one stands back to observe," so that the interpretation of the moral problem determines the way in which it is judged and resolved. Thus principles once seen as absolute are

reconsidered within a contextual interpretation. As a result, moral problems formerly seen in philosophical terms as problems of justification come to be considered in psychological terms as problems of commitment and choice.

Reply: The Murphy and Gilligan findings are of particular interest because they stem from interviews with a *longitudinal* sample of Harvard students in the upper range of intellectual and moral sophistication. While Murphy and Gilligan claim to find regression in moral stage on our classical dilemmas, we hold that their findings do not support this conclusion. This is because a conclusion of regression in longitudinal data must make some allowance for measurement error, an allowance they did not appear to make. The test-retest reliability reported in Colby and Kohlberg et al. (1983) also indicated some "regression" among subjects tested and retested over an interval of one month. We argue that Murphy and Gilligan cannot establish that the "regression" they found is not just due to test factors, unreliability in scoring, and so forth. When Colby and Kohlberg et al. (1983) tried to determine if regression actually did occur in Kohlberg's longitudinal data, they used a one-month test-retest "regression" score as an error margin. With this margin they found that on average only 4 percent of the longitudinal subjects dropped a half stage or more in a three-year test interval as compared to 17 percent of the one-month retest sample. On this basis Colby and Kohlberg et al. (1983) concluded that there was no determinable regression data in my longitudinal sample. If one applies this line of thinking that corrects for measurement error, to the Gilligan and Murphy sample, one has to conclude that they too have no determinable regression data. If one counts only those cases which contain more than one dilemma (our standard issue scoring instrument requires a full protocol of three dilemmas), and if one assesses change, as Colby and Kohlberg et al. (1983) do, on the basis of a nine-point scale (e.g., 3, 3/4, 4, 4/5, etc.) then one finds only four cases of "regression" in the Murphy and Gilligan data, three of which are a drop of half a stage and only one of which is a full stage drop. Out of all possible occasions for regression, there were only 15 percent observed (four out of twenty-six). This is within the limit of 17 percent "regression" due to test factors found in test-retest data by Colby and Kohlberg et al. (1983). Thus, we can not know whether Murphy and Gilligan's four cases are truly regressors.

Though we have argued that the Murphy and Gilligan findings of regression are within the limits of measurement error, there is another aspect of their data which needs to be noted. The students in their study all participated in a course on ethical and political choice taught by Gilligan, Kohlberg, and others. The course focused on discussion of hypothetical and real-life moral dilemmas as well as on the study of classical moral philosophers. An explicit goal of the course was the moral development of students and the formation of a principled moral orientation. Two assessments of moral reasoning were made in this class. There was about a quarter stage upward movement observed from Time 1 to Time 2, though the data are not reported by Murphy and Gilligan. This upward stage movement is the same in magnitude as that found in other experimental and intervention projects. Some of these studies (e.g., Blatt and Kohlberg, 1975) have also reported occasional regressions on follow-up testing, where higher stage reasoning had been only superficially assimilated and was more than one stage above the subject's pretest level. Thus, some of the questioning or partial rejection of principled reasoning, noted anecdotally in a few cases by Murphy and Gilligan, may reflect a later questioning of didactic content rather than a later rejection of an acquired natural stage of reasoning.

Another point made by Gilligan and Murphy is that despite apparent regression in their sample on the Kohlberg scale, their sample of subjects demonstrate continued development as measured by Perry's scale of ethical reasoning in adulthood. We agree with their view that there is a development in moral epistemology or metaethical reflection upon the validity of "absolute" interpretations of morality in late adolescence and adulthood. We also believe that this development may occur after the attainment of principled stages of justice reasoning. However, we do not agree with their interpretation that this development leads to retrogression in justice reasoning or in the questioning of or abandonment of principles of justice when applied to real-life moral dilemmas.

In our discussion of revisions to the theory (Chapter 3), we discussed the distinction between "hard" Piagetian structural stages and "soft" levels or stages of reflection upon the self, the social world, and the larger cosmos. We said that these "soft" stages might characterize adult development that is based on personal reflection, a development which "hard" stages would fail to define. Perry's levels or stages, in our opinion, also represent forms of metaethical reflection on the validity of standards of truth and rightness, on the source of their authority, and on their limits in the face of disagreements between persons and authorities who hold them. Like the

Fowler levels of faith (1981), Perry's stages reflect adult metaethical or reflective development not captured by our "hard" structural stages. In our discussion in Chapter 3, we dealt with the nature of moral judgments as rule-governed versus principled, and we clarified that our interpretation of principles sees them as human constructions rather than as the application of absolute *a prioris* to moral conflicts. Unlike fixed and absolute moral rules, moral principles were characterized as methods or ways of seeing, and of constructing responses to, complex moral situations. Our own "constructivistic" view of the nature, source, and validity of moral principles is itself a metaethical position based upon psychological research and moral-epistemological reflection. In this sense our position is not a normative statement of principles which would be captured by the justice stage descriptions but is, rather, characterizable by schemes of epistemological and metaethical development such as those of Perry and John Broughton (1982a, 1982b). In this sense, our own constructivistic position is consistent with Perry's notion of development in adulthood that goes beyond, or implies more than, the attainment of principled (Stage 5) justice reasoning.

Let us now turn to the example supplied by Gilligan and Murphy which they claim demonstrates simultaneous development on the Perry scale and abandonment of principled (Stage 5) moral reasoning on the Kohlberg scale. We will argue, instead, that their case material does not indicate that continuing development in "contextual relativism" leads to the abandonment of Stage 5 principles, but rather that such development leads to a more contextual framing of these principles. We will be claiming that there is *not* a contradiction between a principled and contextually relativistic framing of moral conflict as Gilligan and Murphy imply. We will use as an example of the issue a case which Gilligan and Murphy report as Philosopher 2's "dilemma of the fact." They interpret Philosopher 2's integration of his experience with this dilemma as representing a relativistic erosion of his formerly held Stage 5 principles of justice. In contrast, we see his growth over time as a more contextualized search for the correct application of his principles, to which he remains committed.

The dilemma facing Philosopher 2 (a respondent scored at Stage 5 on "classic" hypothetical dilemmas) was that the husband of the woman with whom he was having an affair was uninformed of this fact. This lack of information raised for Philosopher 2 a question of moral obligation to see that the husband knew of the affair. He said:

"If I see some kind of ongoing unjust situation, I have some kind of obligation to correct it in whatever way I see. . . . The husband should be told, since otherwise he would not be getting the information he needed to judge what his best interests should be in the situation. . . . I would have wanted to know the full truth. I think that truth is an ultimate thing."

We would agree with Gilligan and Murphy's interpretation that Philosopher 2 orients to the dilemma in terms of justice or rights and in terms of some role-taking of the positions of the others in the situation. They interpret as a Stage 5 or 6 principle his idea that "truth is an ultimate thing." Reflecting later on his thinking about the dilemma he says, "I was always aware of the kind of situation in which truth was not absolute. If a person comes up to me with a gun in his hand . . . in that sense I never thought truth was ultimate." Thus, he was aware, though not in a clear way, that truth telling, while a basic *prima facie* rule, was not a final decisional moral principle. Either a Stage 5 principle of justice or a Stage 5 principle of choosing the greatest welfare would dictate not telling the truth in situations in which other basic values, say the value of life, were at stake.

Philosopher 2's idea that justice to the husband dictated informing him was complicated by his taking the point of view of his lover and her needs and claims. Overwhelmed by other pressures, she was unable to face the additional stress of informing her husband of the affair at that time, and said that she would tell him at a more peaceful time. In the interim, the husband discovered the affair. "So my dilemma was whether I should call the guy up and tell him what the situation was. I didn't, and the fact that I didn't has had a tremendous impact on my moral system. It did. It shook my belief and my justification of the belief that I couldn't resolve the dilemma of the fact that I felt that someone should tell him. I did feel there was some kind of truth issue involved here, higher than the issue of where the truth comes from. The kind of thing that no matter what happens the other person should have full knowledge of what is going on, is fair. And I didn't tell him."

From our point of view, Philosopher 2's confrontation with the dilemma of the fact led him to a greater awareness of the inherent ambiguity of factual definitions of dilemmas like his; that is, an interpretation of the facts of a dilemma may be difficult to achieve or to get consensus on. He says, "It led me to question whether somehow there is a sense in which truth is relative. Or is truth ever relative? That is an issue I have yet to resolve." This growing relativism about factual interpretation is not in itself a questioning of the universality or validity of moral principles, like the principles of justice or human welfare, but it is a growing awareness of the difficulties encountered in getting clarity or consensus on their application to concrete situations. This experience has also led Philosopher 2 to question further the absolute value of truth telling in favor of some more contextual application of the principle of justice, a principle he does not yet feel he can define for himself. As Philosopher 2 states, "With interpersonal situations that dealt with psychological realities and with psychological feelings, with emotions, I felt that the truth should win out in most situations. Then, after that situation, I became more relativistic about it. As you can tell, right now I have not worked out a principle that is satisfactory to me that would resolve that issue if it happened again tomorrow. If I were the husband I would certainly want to know the truth, but if I were the wife would I see what I [Philosopher 2] wanted to do as being the right thing? And was her right to sanity, which I think was being jeopardized, less important than his right to know? That is a good moral dilemma. Now you figure it out."

In our interpretation, Philosopher 2 is struggling to formulate a principle of justice which would resolve the situation of conflict between the husband's right to truth and the wife's right to sanity. In trying to do this, he attempts to engage in a process of what we call ideal role-taking or "moral musical chairs," a process at the heart of our hypothetical notion of a sixth stage of moral judgment (see "Justice as Reversibility," Volume I, Chapter 5). He says, however, that he cannot find a principle which is morally valid or reversible, seeing the situation from all perspectives. If, following the ideal role-taking process we have referred to and assuming it is correct that disclosure of the truth would risk the wife's sanity, then if Philosopher 2 were to imaginatively continue the process and ask whether the husband's claim to truth would be valid if he placed himself in the wife's position, he would be likely to conclude that justice is better served by withholding the truth, because if the husband puts himself in the wife's position he sees her right to sanity. In other words, in this case Philosopher 2 realizes that choosing sanity over truth telling is a more reversible decision than the converse. In this sense it is not different from his earlier awareness that truth was not an absolute, but that choosing life over truth was a more just solution if "someone came up to me with a gun in his hand . . ." Philosopher 2's increased relativism arising from the conflict represented a growing awareness of the complexity of moral decisions about particularistic relationships. His relativism is partly a relativism about the psychological complexity of defining "facts" about a person's immediate and long-term feelings. However, it is also a growing awareness of the ambiguity of defining principles of justice or respect for the personhood of others in particularistic relationships. In conclusion we would see Philosopher 2 as engaged in a search for the refinement and differentiation of his principles of justice; he is attempting to apply them in more complex situations, rather than abandoning them either in favor of a sceptical or nihilistic relativism or in favor of some orientation to moral decisions other than one of principles or justice.

How do Gilligan and Murphy interpret Philosopher 2's response? In the first place, they assume that our Stage 5 orientation of principled justice implies a rule-based rigor or fixity of application of a principle and a sense that such a principle is an immutable, absolute, defining choice. In fact, we use the term *principle* to mean a human construction which guides perceptions and responses to human claims in conflict situations (see our discussion in Chapter 3 on morality as principledness). Gilligan and Murphy seem to believe that Philosopher 2 has changed from an absolutistic Stage 5 moral orientation to a "morality eroded by relativism." They say, "Thus, the relativism that has begun to erode his former claim to absolute knowledge of the 'right thing to do' arises from his incipient awareness of the possible legitimacy of a different point of view." In contrast, while we grant a growth in contextual relativism has occurred for Philosopher 2, we cannot see any inconsistency between this fact and his use of principled reasoning.

A more central thrust of Gilligan and Murphy's interpretation of the case is that it represents adult development away from a justice orientation to a more contextually relative responsibility and care orientation. We noted earlier that Gilligan defined this orientation partly in terms of sex-differences, as a preferential orientation of women. In the context of Philosopher 2, Gilligan and Murphy say that his response represents development in a male toward a greater awareness of the responsibility and care orientation, one which they see as being in conflict with a justice orientation to the same dilemma. "Thus, the question becomes one of definition as to what is included in the moral domain, since the justice approach does not adequately address the responsibilities and obligations that come from life choices." According to Gilligan and Murphy, for Philosopher 2, "a contextual morality of responsibility for the actual consequences of choice thus enters into a dialogue with the abstraction of rights, resulting in a judgment with contradictory normative statements scored as a mixture of Kohlberg's Stages 4 and 5." They go on to state, "Our interpretation that Philosopher 2's apparent regression is an artifact of a new, more encompassing perspective is supported by his retrospective reflection at age 27 on the dilemma he had reported five years earlier. Now the moral discussion 'about who tells the truth and who doesn't' appears to him in a 'very different perspective,' as legitimate to 'the justice approach' but ancillary to 'the more fundamental issue' of the causes and consequences of infidelity. Focusing his discussion at age 27 on his understanding of why the situation arose in the first place and the problem of life choice its occurrence presented, he attributes his previous unawareness of these issues to 'an incredible amount of immaturity on my part' which he sees reflected in his 'justice approach.'"

We would agree with Gilligan and Murphy that life experience in relationships has given Philosopher 2 a more complex perception of the factual realities of interpersonal relationships and of the personal values that enter into interpersonal choice. What we question is that this is a qualitative shift in moral orientation, from the justice to the responsibility orientation. I have speculated that there are indeed dilemmas and conflicts of interpersonal responsibility and choice which are not fully resolved by principles of justice, but it is not clear to us that Philosopher 2's dilemma constitutes one of these instances. In reference to his later interview at age 27, Gilligan and Murphy state: "His revolution combines the absolute logic of a system of moral justification with a probabilistic contextual assessment of the likely consequences of choice." Without the word "absolute," we would agree that this statement by Gilligan and Murphy describes Philosopher 2's development. But we also believe that this statement, without the word "absolute," describes the task of moral principles of justice, whether they be utilitarian principles of justice as the greatest welfare maximization or Kantian principles of justice as respect for human personality or ideal role–taking.

For Gilligan and Murphy, Philosopher 2's judgment at age 27 occurs in "two contexts that frame different aspects of the moral problem: the context of justice in which he articulates the universal logic of fairness and reciprocity and the context of compassion in which he focuses instead on the particularity of consequences for the actual participants." For us, both these concerns enter into the hypothetical dilemmas of justice which define our moral stages throughout the stage hierarchy. Whether the dilemma is one of whether to convict an escaped but reformed convict of his previous crime, or whether the dilemma is one of an air-raid captain leaving his assigned post out of concern for the immediate welfare of his family, our stages of justice attempt to define choices in which both fairness or reciprocity and compassionate concern for consequences are enmeshed. We believe moral stage development is the development of one morality, not of two, because moral situations and choices always involve both issues of justice and care.

The work of Gilligan and her colleagues has added depth to the description of moral judgment focused on responsibility and caring, but we do not believe that it defines an alternative morality confronted in adulthood by Philosopher 2. More than justice is required for resolving many complex moral dilemmas, but justice is a necessary element of any morally adequate resolution of these conflicts. Future work by Gilligan and her colleagues may modify our general conclusions, but we believe that this continuing work will primarily clarify the reflective and metaethical "soft" stage levels through which adolescents and adults develop, rather than give us a different picture of the development of "hard" structures of moral reasoning.

Levine, C. G.: "Stage Acquisition and Stage Use. An Appraisal of Stage Displacement Explanation of Variation in Moral Reasoning." *Human Development 22* (1979), pp. 145–164.

Synopsis: Three models of the structuralist assumption that moral stages constitute a hierarchy are presented and critically discussed by Levine. The most radically structuralist model identified by Levine is Turiel's (1974, 1977) "displacement" model. The displacement model claims that when a new stage is acquired the previous stage is totally reorganized and no longer exists as a structure; that is, any empirical example of the use of the previous stage is conceptualized by Turiel not as the use of structure but as the content of the subject's current modal stage undergoing reconstruction. Turiel holds this view because he argues that one must see instances of apparent lower stage use in this way in order to be loyal to the requirements of transformation and nonregression implied by a strictly structural stage model. Levine argues that Turiel's interpretation of stage transformation, based on a literal interpretation of displacement, is a view which can not explain fluctuations in stage use predicted on the basis of the hypothesized effects of situational stimuli.

The next model discussed by Levine emerges from Rest's (1979) work and has been called by Turiel the "layer cake" model, in contrast with his own. This model asserts that stages are acquired in an invariant sequence but postulates the continued availability of lower stages. Nevertheless, it is argued that there is a hierarchical preference to use the highest stage available. Levine calls this model a much less radical displacement model than Turiel's. It is only the assumption of hierarchical preference (not the assumption of sequential stage acquisition) that Levine finds problematic, because he feels that this assumption has biased inquiry against a systematic study of social conditions that can elicit the use of stages below the most advanced stage acquired.

The third model presented is Levine's "non-displacement, additive-inclusive" model of stage development. He believes that this model remains consistent with the premises of structural developmental theory but more adequately justifies adopting a method which measures fluctuations in rates of moral stage use based on a concern for the effects of variation in dilemma and situational stimuli. The basis of Levine's concern is his adherence to interactionist assumptions in order to understand performance rather than competence. Though Levine believes that patterns of performance probably have a bearing on development, his major point seems to be that if this is so it ought to be investigated more than it has been, and must be investigated by any theory which claims to offer a complete explanation of the ontogenesis of justice reasoning in the real world.

Levine suggests that his concern for investigating performance is not in any way incompatible with the logic of the Kohlberg theory, but that it may not have been pursued too rigorously because of my primary concern with assessing patterns of development from a competence perspective. In developing his interactionist orientation, Levine is interested in demonstrating that a research perspective which defines competence as the highest stage of reasoning calculated over standardized dilemmas may not be a perspective which enables one to predict reasoning in other situations. Given studies by Rest (1973) and Turiel (1969) which demonstrate that hierarchical preference is a characteristic of moral stage use, as well as my theoretical emphasis on stage growth as movement toward principled reasoning, Levine thinks that a lag between competence and performance, if there is one, is likely to be greatest at the lower end of the Kohlberg stage hierarchy. Levine acknowledges that his thoughts stem from an earlier study (Levine, 1976) in which he demonstrated variation in rates of Stage 3 and 4 use as a function of varying the identity of actors in the dilemmas presented to respondents.

Reply: We do not see Levine's article as a criticism of the Kohlberg theory; rather, we understand it as suggesting that the theory be used for assessing research questions from a social interactionist perspective.

We agree that I have focused on attempts to assess optimal competence, not fluctuations in everyday performance, since my interest has been focused on a theory of structures of moral development and not on a theory of the use of stages of moral reasoning. Levine's (1976) findings, however, while showing fluctuating proportions in the use of *adjacent* stages, do not violate the *performance* expectations I have had from the point of view of a competence perspective.

The issues raised by Levine about interaction between the stimulus situation and stage performance seem to lead into the study of performance in terms of moral action, a study which has been explored under the name of moral atmosphere (Kohlberg, 1981b; Higgins, Power, and Kohlberg, 1984). However, it is true that a concern with moral atmosphere does not amount to an extensive research program into performance questions. In sum, we see Levine's argument as an extension of social psychology theory compatible with the premises of my structural developmental theory. A good portion of Levine's (1979) article explores some of the implications of applying an interactionist approach to the Kohlberg theory. We see it as a useful article which specifies some of the research questions one might ask when attempting to explore patterns of stage use in conjunction with social environmental factors.

Gibbs, J. C.: "Kohlberg's Moral Stage Theory: A Piagetian Revision." *Human Development* 22 (1979), pp. 89–112.

Synopsis: Gibbs's interpretation of moral development is based on a two-phase model. Phase 1 is a Piagetian model of development which maps Kohlberg Stages 1 through 4. Within Kohlberg Stages 3 and 4 Gibbs sees the development of second-order thought, which for him constitutes the basis for the construction of his existential phase of adult development, a developmental period which he calls his second phase. Gibbs claims that his second phase is not structural in the Piagetian sense but is, rather, developmental in a "purely phenomenological and functional" sense (p. 106). By this Gibbs means that his second phase cannot be described in hard structural stage terms since it explains the development of a search for meaning, identity, and commitment as described in writing by Erikson (1963) and Fromm (1947).

The reason Gibbs develops this model is to compensate for what he considers to be a lack of evidence supporting my structural treatment of postconventional reasoning. The lack of evidence Gibbs refers to is both theoretical and empirical. Theoretically, Gibbs argues that the Kohlberg stages do not constitute operative structures (i.e., Piaget's notion of a "system in action") and that they do not appear to be "spontaneous" (i.e., they appear to be nonspontaneous utterances based on the education and understanding of intellectual traditions of a particular society). In addition, Gibbs (p. 97) claims that the cross-cultural empirical rarity of postconventional reasoning suggests that the Kohlberg postconventional stages are not Piagetian structural stages. If my moral stages are Piagetian structural stages, they should, for Gibbs, empirically correlate with the use of similar structures in the cognitive domain. Gibbs (p. 108) charges that no relation as been found between Piaget's cognitive-logical stages of development and postconventional moral thinking.

Given the above, Gibbs concludes that the Kohlberg postconventional stages are not structural in Piaget's sense but are, rather, metaethical positions that adults develop in the courses of their existential growth. Thus, Gibbs would say that the postconventional stages are different but are not more structurally advanced than the "B" substages at Stage 3 or 4. Gibbs's model, then, uses Kohlberg Stages 1 through 4 as a structural explanation of moral development and explains existential nonstructural development with Kohlberg Stages 3B, 4B, 5, and 6.

Reply: In our reply we start by accepting the usefulness of Gibbs's distinction between Piagetian structural stage development in adulthood and the development of nonstructural levels of reflection upon existential issues in adulthood. Gibbs says that this latter type of development is more closely related to Erikson's (1963) and Fromm's (1947) notions of ego development than it is to an extension of Piaget's idea of stages.

As noted above, Gibbs has offered several reasons for questioning whether Stages 5 and 6 really define new moral stages. In the comments to follow, we deal primarily with Stage 5 because, as we have noted in our discussion of the current status of the theory, there is not extensive or sufficient empirical data to substantiate any claims as to use of a sixth stage, even though we still maintain its usefulness as a theoretical construct (see Chapter 3). The core of Gibbs's criticism is that Stage 5 moral reasoning is not a new operative structure or system-in-action. Thus, Stage 5 is not a new form of normative-ethical judgment but is only a new set of theoretical reflections upon already given normative judgment structures, that is, only a new position of metaethical reasoning associated with the normative-ethical reasoning of Stages 3 and 4. (We refer the reader to our discussion of the basic distinctions between normative and metaethical reasoning in Chapter 3).

Gibbs wishes to call our postconventional stages "existential" positions rather than new moral or normative-ethical structures. Central to his conception of existential thinking is the notion that it is "second order," for example, "the ability to adopt the detached meta-perspective on not only logical physical problems, social relationships and social systems, [but also on] consciousness, ethics, reason and life itself" (p. 102). It seems, then, that second-order thinking requires formal operational thought, that is, the capacity to reflect on thought. Thus, in this context, what we have distinguished as metaethical reasoning, as opposed to normative-ethical reasoning, is what Gibbs would call "existential thinking." What Gibbs calls "existential thinking" at Stages 3B, 4B, and 5 we identify as the development of the ability to generate statements about what morality is, to identify the grounds for it in conceptions of human nature and metaphysics, and to justify its necessity. An example of such moral theorizing would be a generalized theoretical statement about the nature of a social contract, typical of Stage 5 thinking. Such a statement might identify the laws of a society and then provide a theoretical justification or criticism for them with the use of a prior-to-society perspective. Although Stage 5 thinkers sometimes generate such moral theories (i.e., metaethical ones), it is their normative-ethical reasoning about particular dilemmas which we use in classifying them as Stage 5. This normative reasoning involves new justice operations in the sense in which justice operations were discussed in Chapter 3 on the primacy of justice. The fact that Stage 5 justice reasoning is not a particularistic, "existential" moral theory rooted in culturally specific metaethical thinking (i.e., Stage 5) is indicated by the fact that Stage 5 appears to be used by "educated" persons in Eastern countries as well as in the West (Chapter 8; Chapter 9; Parikh, 1980; Lei and Cheng, 1982).

Another criterion of Piagetian or "hard-stages" is their relationship to action. A variety of studies of judgment and action (Blasi, 1980; Kohlberg and Candee, 1984; Chapter 7) indicate that Stage 5 judgment is more predictive of moral action than is any lower stage. We introduce this evidence from the judgment-action research because it documents to us that the moral structures are, in fact, "hard" structures and systems-in-action in the Piagetian sense.

Thus, while we do not agree with Gibbs's elimination of Stage 5 as a natural Piagetian hard stage, we do agree that moral development in adulthood beyond Stage 5 appears to be characterizable by metaethical and "existential" reflection and theorizing, phenomena that can be studied with "soft" stage models of epistemology (Perry, 1968), faith (Fowler, 1981), responsibility (Gilligan, 1982), and conceptions of "the good life" (Erdynast, Armon, and Nelson, 1978).

As our discussion of the substage B construct indicates (see Chapter 3), thought content linked with the B substage is not a matter of metaethics as moral theory but is firmly defined as a normative-ethical orientation to specific dilemmas. Finally, we note that Gibbs's argument that postconventional reasoning is rare and is therefore suspect as a natural Piagetian system-in-action is a criticism we have already addressed in our reply to Elizabeth Simpson.

Habermas, J., "Moral Development and Ego Identity." In *Communication and the Evolution of Society.* Translated by T. McCarthy. Boston: Beacon Press, 1979.

Synopsis: In closing this section of our reply to critics, we felt that a review of Habermas's (1979) article "Moral Development and Ego Identity" would be appropriate. While Habermas raises one criticism of the Kohlberg theory in this paper (i.e., that it is insufficient because it does not define a seventh stage), we understand his article, nevertheless, as a clarification and constructive extension of certain aspects of my work. Since this review of Habermas's article is selective, the reader is encouraged to read his book, *Communication and the Evolution of Society* (1979), in order to gain a fuller appreciation of his important contribution to the moral development literature.

As was noted in Chapter 3, Habermas is a critical theorist who sees his task to be the theoretical reconstruction of social evolution at various levels of analysis, that is, the interactive-communicative, the cognitive-affective, and the social-structural. For Habermas these levels of analysis reflect at an empirical level the three interacting and interpenetrating realities of communication, self, and society. Habermas investigates each of these levels of analysis by reconstructing what he perceives to be the developmental logic inherent in each. In other words, there are structures of communication, self, and society that can be ordered hierarchically from a developmental point of view. Habermas seems to use the words self and ego interchangeably and it is this unit of analysis with which the present review is primarily concerned. However, the reader should understand that invariably Habermas's perspective is both critical and social-psychological, and that for him any complete social inquiry must address the interaction between structures of communication, self, and society.

"Moral Development and Ego Identity" is an essay which describes and validates the logic of development I employ to understand the ontogenesis of my moral stages. However, to understand how Habermas develops this justification of my perspective we must momentarily digress to a brief discussion of Habermas's theory of communication. (This discussion is based on his article "What is Universal Pragmatics?" to be found in *Communication and the Evolution of Society*.) Habermas's theory of communication is based on the assumption that the ontogenesis of the communicative competence necessary to engage in "speech-acts" has universal and formal developmental characteristics. Specifically, Habermas argues that communicative competence evolves through three levels or structures of communicative action, that is, incomplete interaction, complete interaction, and finally, communicative action and discourse. A fuller description of these structures will follow shortly. For the moment, it is important to understand the basic point, that communicative competence develops through these three stages of communicative action.

What is communicative competence? It is the ability to engage successfully in speech-acts, an ability acquired by an individual through the mastering of those rules of speech necessary to "fulfill the conditions for a happy employment of sentences in utterances."

For a speech-act to be competently performed, the speaker must utter a sentence in such a way that (*a*) its propositional content appears to fulfill the requirement of "truth"; (*b*) its linguistic content expresses his or her intentions "truthfully"; and (*c*), as an utterance, it is "right" in the sense that it conforms to a recognized moral or normative context. In other words, communicative competence is manifested in the speaker's ability to "embed a well-formed sentence in relations to reality" in a manner which is defined as acceptable by the hearer. The hearer must be able to share the speaker's knowledge, trust his or her expressions as sincere, and finally, share the value-orientation implicated by the speech-act. Thus, speech-acts situate the speaker and hearer in an interpenetrating matrix composed of the following three "reality domains": (*a*) "'The' world of external nature," about which we make statements of truth; (*b*) "'My' world of internal nature," about which we make truthful expressions of our needs and intentions; and (*c*) "'Our' world of society," about which we make statements implying rightness or legitimacy (and in so doing, normatively sanction interpersonal relationships). It is important to note that when situations arise that threaten to undermine consensus between speaker and hearer, the former must articulate and successfully redeem assertions about truth, truthfulness, and rightness as explicitly raised validity claims.

In more simple terms, Habermas is stating (*a*) that communicative competence is the ability to articulate, and, if necessary, argumentatively redeem, claims of truth, truthfulness, and rightness through the medium of speech and (*b*) that communicative competence is developmental in the sense that it is structured by three levels or stages of communicative action.

Before reviewing Habermas's perspective on moral reasoning, we must first briefly comment on his conception of ego-identity formation. For Habermas, the ideal end point of ego-identity formation is a state of rational autonomy, that is, a state of self-awareness and communicative competence which allows the individual to maintain and reinterpret his or her identity through "communicative action." Speech-acts at the level of communicative action foster the autonomous realization of self through dependency on interaction with other individuals. The competence to engage in such speech action is based upon a postsociocentric, "postconventional" awareness of actions and motives of self and other and hence constructs and employs "communally followed procedures" for redeeming validity claims of truth, truthfulness, and rightness. Ego-identity as a state of rational autonomy is, in other words, a state in which both cognitive and affective components of self can be articulated and realized through a communicative process allowing for "discursive will formation." Thus, for Habermas, ego-identity is based on a notion of autonomy as dependent on interaction with others.

From this discussion, it should be obvious that, rather than being tangentially related to his theory of ego development, Habermas's theory of communication provides the conceptual basis for it. As we shall now see, this interpenetrating relationship associating communicative competence and ego development is displayed in Habermas's analysis of moral reasoning. For him, a moral judgment is a manifestation of the use of communicative skills to redeem a validity claim of rightness, which, in turn, is an interactive expression of ego-identity formation.

It should now be noted, however, that when focusing on the topics of ego and moral development, Habermas speaks of interactive rather than communicative competence. Interactive competence is a concept which synthesizes the notion of communicative competence, developing within structures of communicative action, with (*a*) those cognitive stages whose existence must be assumed as prerequisites for communicative competence and (*b*) the ways in which social roles are perceived throughout the ontogenesis of communicative competence. This idea of interactive competence is represented in Table 4.1. The rows of Table 4.1 represent the three levels of interactive competence (i.e., a synthesis of the competencies within "General Structures of Communicative Action" with "Qualifications of Role Behavior"). These levels of interactive competence are also depicted in the first two columns of Table 4.2, where they are labeled "Role Competence" by Habermas.*

It appears, from Tables 4.1 and 4.2, that Habermas considers levels of interactive competence as based in part upon transformations of an actor's perceptions of norms, motives, and other actors.

---

*Tables 4.1 and 4.2 are schemas 3 and 4, respectively, to be found in Habermas (1979; pp. 83, 89).

Table 4.1

General Structures of Communicative Action					*Qualifications of Role Behavior*		
					Perception of		
Cognitive Presuppositions	*Levels of Interaction*	*Action Levels*	*Action Motivations*	*Actors*	*Norms*	*Motives*	*Actors*
I Preoperational thought	Incomplete interaction	Concrete actions and consequences of action	Generalized pleasure/pain	Natural identity	Understand and follow behavioral expectations	Express and fulfill action intentions (wishes)	Perceive concrete actions and actors
II Concrete-operational thought	Complete interaction	Roles, systems of norms	Culturally interpreted needs	Role identity	Understand and follow reflexive behavioral expectations (norms)	Distinguish between "ought" and "want" (duty/inclination)	Distinguish between actions and norms, individual subjects and role bearers
III Formal-operational thought	Communicative action and discourse	Principles	Competing interpretations of needs	Ego-identity	Understand and apply reflexive norms (principles)	Distinguish between heteronomy and autonomy	Distinguish between particular and general norms, individuality and ego in general

Table 4.2

	Role Competence			Stages of Moral Consciousness				
Age Level	*Level of Communication*		*Reciprocity Requirement*	*Stages of Moral Consciousness*	*Idea of the Good Life*	*Domain of Validity*	*Philosophical Reconstruction*	*Age Level*
I	Actions and consequences of action	Generalized pleasure/pain	Incomplete reciprocity	1	Maximization of pleasure—avoidance of pain through obedience	Natural and social environment		IIa
			Complete reciprocity	2	Maximization of pleasure—avoidance of pain through exchange of equivalents		Naive hedonism	
	Roles	Culturally interpreted needs		3	Concrete morality of primary groups	Group of primary reference persons		
II	Systems of norms	(Concrete duties)	Incomplete reciprocity	4	Concrete morality of secondary groups	Members of the political community	Concrete thought in terms of a specific order	IIb

Role Competence				*Stages of Moral Consciousness*				
Age Level	*Level of Communication*		*Reciprocity Requirement*	*Stages of Moral Consciousness*	*Idea of the Good Life*	*Domain of Validity*	*Philosophical Reconstruction*	*Age Level*
III	Principles	Universalized pleasure/ pain (utility)	Complete reciprocity	5	Civil liberties, public welfare	All legal associates	Rational natural law	III
		Universalized duties		6	Moral freedom	All humans as private persons	Formalistic ethics	
		Universalized need interpretations		7	Moral and political freedoms	All as members of a fictive world society	Universal ethics of speech	

As we noted above, one of Habermas's major purposes in this paper is to validate the developmental logic underlying the Kohlberg stage hierarchy. Habermas accomplishes this task by deducing my stages of moral reasoning from his stages of interactive competence. For Habermas, moral reasoning can be appropriately seen as "the ability to make use of interactive competence for consciously processing morally relevant conflicts of action" (p. 88). Thus, moral reasoning can be understood as a facit of interactive competence, manifested in asserting a validity claim of rightness. As such, moral reasoning is, for Habermas, a manifestation of ego-identity formation. Habermas (1979, p. 82) expresses his task of validating my stage hierarchy in the following manner:

> I should like to arrive at this goal through connecting moral consciousness with general qualifications for role behavior. The following steps serve this end: First I introduce structures of possible communicative action and, indeed, in the sequence in which the child grows into this sector of the symbolic universe. I then coordinate with these basic structures the cognitive abilities (or competencies) that the child must acquire in order to be able to move at the respective level of the social environment, that is, taking part first in incomplete interaction, then in complete interaction, and finally in communications that require passing from communicative action to discourse. Second I want to look at this sequence of general qualifications for role behavior (at least provisionally) from developmental-logical points of view in order, finally, to derive the stages of moral consciousness from these stages of interactive competence.

Habermas derives my stages from his own stages of interactive competence through his emphasis on reciprocity as a fixed property of the structures of interaction possible at each level of communicative action.* As noted earlier, these structures of interaction are first incomplete interaction, then complete interaction, and finally, communicative action and discourse (see column 2 of Table 4.1). With the assumption that reciprocity is not a norm per

---

*It is important to note that Habermas uses the concept of reciprocity to denote a property of interaction structures, and thus, this use of the concept should not be confused with our use of it to denote a justice operation. For Habermas, reciprocity as a fixed property of structures of interaction can be either complete or incomplete. (As a point of further clarification, this notion of complete or incomplete reciprocity should not be confused with Habermas's reference to complete or incomplete interaction.) For Habermas, "Two persons stand in an incompletely reciprocal relation insofar as one may do or expect *x* only to the extent that the other may do or expect *y* (e.g., teacher/pupil, parent/child). Their relationship is completely reciprocal if both may do or expect the same thing in comparable situations ($x = y$)."

se but, rather, "belongs *eo ipso* to the interactive knowledge of speaking and acting subjects," Habermas reasons that incomplete interaction, because of its egocentric nature, is compatible with either incomplete or complete reciprocity; that complete interaction is compatible only with incomplete reciprocity, and finally, that communicative action is compatible only with complete reciprocity (see column 3 of Table 4.2). Based on this observation, Habermas (1979, pp. 89–90) derives the Kohlberg stages.

> Stages of moral consciousness can be derived by applying the requirement of reciprocity to the action structures that the growing child perceives at each of the different levels [Table 4.2]. At Level 1, only concrete actions and action consequences (understood as gratifications or sanctions) can be morally relevant. If incomplete reciprocity is required here, we obtain Kohlberg's Stage 1 (punishment-obedience orientation); complete reciprocity yields Stage 2 (instrumental hedonism). At Level II the sector relevant to action is expanded; if we require incomplete reciprocity for concrete expectations bound to reference persons, we obtain Kohlberg's Stage 3 (good-boy orientation); the same requirement for systems of norms yields Stage 4 (law and order orientation). At Level III principles become the moral theme; for logical reasons complete reciprocity must be required. At this level the stages of moral consciousness are differentiated according to the degree to which action motives are symbolically structured. If the needs relevant to action are allowed to remain outside the symbolic universe, then the admissible universalistic norms of action have the character of rules for maximizing utility and general legal norms that give scope to the strategic pursuit of private interests, under the condition that the egocentrism of the second stage is literally raised to a principle; this corresponds to Kohlberg's Stage 5 (contractual legalistic orientation). If needs are understood as culturally interpreted but ascribed to individuals as natural properties, the admissible universalistic norms of action have the character of general moral norms. Each individual is supposed to test monologically the generalizability of the norm in question. This corresponds to Kohlberg's Stage 6 (conscience orientation). Only at the level of a universal ethics of speech (*Sprachethik*) can need interpretations themselves—that is, what each individual thinks he should understand and represent as his "true" interests—also become the object of practical discourse. Kohlberg does not differentiate this stage from Stage 6 although there is a qualitative difference: the principle of justification of norms is no longer the monologically applicable principle of generalizability but the communally followed procedure of redeeming normative validity claims discursively. An unexpected result of our attempt to derive the stages of moral consciousness from the stages of interactive competence is the demonstration that Kohlberg's schema of stages is incomplete.

Reply: Our review has emphasized Habermas's concern that we understand structures of moral reasoning as embedded within structures of communicative action. In understanding moral reasoning in this way, Habermas offers us a detailed analysis of what we believe Piaget (1932) meant when he stated that "apart from our relations to other people, there can be no moral necessity." What Habermas seems to be stating is that it is the nature of our relations to other social actors, as defined by structures of interactive competence and the property of reciprocity, that determines our conceptions of moral necessity.

Before we address Habermas's claim that my stage hierarchy is incomplete because it does not define a seventh stage, we wish to emphasize the following point. In our view, Habermas's conceptualization of ego and moral development does not define structures of justice reasoning per se. For us, structures or "hard" stages of justice reasoning include operations of equality, equity, and reciprocity, operations which we understand as interpersonal interaction analogues of logical operations Piaget describes in the cognitive domain. What Habermas's work appears to define are levels of communicative and role competence which, together, seem to us to be analogous to Selman's (1980) social perspective taking levels. If this interpretation is correct (and with it we certainly do not mean to imply that Habermas's article simply reflects Selman's work), then we understand Habermas's levels of interactive competence to have the same logical relationship to the structures of moral reasoning as do Selman's levels of social perspective taking; that is, we understand them as necessary but insufficient to define the structure of the moral stages. While the justice operations of moral structures are transformed at each level of social perspective taking, these structures are not conceptually reducible to social perspective taking levels.

We will now address Habermas's claim to have discovered a seventh hard stage of moral reasoning. In this context, Habermas makes several observations which he sees as justifying his derivation of a seventh stage. As we implied above, he sees this seventh stage as both one of the manifestation of ego-identity and one of the competencies contributing to the maintenance of ego-identity. Ego-identity is, from the perspective of Habermas's ideal speaker, an awareness of self and other as formative, that is, as involved in a creative, ongoing process of articulating and validating needs. This ideal end point of ego-identity as an ongoing process of discursive will formation can only exist in an unfettered manner when its basis, interactive competence at the level of communicative action and discourse, is itself given free rein. In other words, speech, at the level of discourse, must be protected if ego-identity is to emerge and be maintained. Thus, dialogue per se must be raised to the level of a principle.

In arguing for the principle of dialogue, for a "communally followed procedure for redeeming normative validity claims discursively," Habermas is defining and defending a universal speech ethic as the basis of an evolving, unconstrained, and autonomous ego. (One point of interest, which may have some bearing on certain aspects of Gilligan's critique, is to be seen in Habermas's conception of ego autonomy. For him ego autonomy can only exist through dependence on others, since speech and interactive competence cannot exist otherwise. Thus Habermas's emphasis on the principle of dialogue denies the differentiation, which Gilligan makes between separation and attachment and conceives of ego-identity and a seventh stage of justice reasoning as dependent upon both.)

While my theory has not explicitly addressed the topics of ego-identity or the development of communicative competence, we understand Habermas's treatment of these subjects as being consistent with our conception of human development generally, as well as with our conception of moral development specifically. We also appreciate the contribution Habermas's analysis is likely to have on subsequent research in the areas of ego and moral development. However, we believe that Habermas's derivation of a Stage 7 of justice reasoning is unnecessary, since we understand our conception of Stage 6 as being consistent with his writing.

It appears that Habermas argues in favor of a seventh stage because he reasons that my conception of a sixth stage overlooks the principle of dialogue. However, in Justice as Reversibility (Volume I, Chapter 5), I attempted to include a process of dialogue in moral judgment making via the introduction of my concept "moral musical chairs" (i.e., ideal reversible role-taking). Though this process was primarily expressed in reference to a cognitive-moral structure I call Stage 6, it is based upon principles of respect for persons that are perfectly consistent with the notion of actually engaging in dialogue. Thus, we consider this aspect of my writings to be equivalent to Habermas's emphasis on the notion of "discursive will formation."

Further evidence that we consider the principle of dialogue to be consistent with Stage 6 descriptions can be seen in my work on moral education within "just communities" (see Kohlberg, 1982a). In these intervention studies, actual dialogue over moral conflicts continues until a consensus is reached through the reciprocal modification of participants' understanding of their own needs.

It is probably because of the use of hypothetical dilemmas that the participatory and dialogic nature of the Stage 6 justice procedure has not been apparent. However, my position on the Stage 6 justice procedure is that in the "moral musical chairs" activity of prescriptive role-taking one can only proceed so far intellectually. I believe that my Stage 6 reasoning procedure logically requires dialogue in actual, real-life moral conflicts, otherwise its intension to achieve fairness could be easily subverted by an egocentric interpretation of the needs and perspectives of self and other. Thus, we disagree with Habermas's conception of Stage 6 as employing a "monological" procedure. However, in closing this review, we may note that Habermas (1982) has come to agree with me. He now understands monologic "moral musical chairs" and dialogue discursive will formation protected by a universal speech ethic as similar conceptions of a sixth stage of justice reasoning.

PART THREE

Empirical Methods and Results

FROM 1972 until 1979, a group at Harvard including Anne Colby, John Gibbs, Dan Candee, Marc Lieberman, and others worked with me to develop a standard issue scoring manual and used it to blind-score longitudinal data from approximately sixty American males. The detailed technical results have been published as a Society for Research in Child Development monograph by Colby, Kohlberg, et al. (1983). This manual was used to blind-score Turkish male longitudinal data by Mordecai Nisan (Chapter 8 of this volume and to blind-score Israeli male and female longitudinal data by John Snarey and Joe Reimer (Chapter 9 of this volume). The manual, its theoretical rational, its scale properties, its reliability and validity with longitudinal data, and detailed instructions for scoring stage and substage, along with practice cases, is being published as a two-volume compendium by Colby and Kohlberg (1984, in press).

While covering some of the same ground as the 1984 compendium, or of the Colby et al. (1983) monograph, Part Three of this volume ignores the technical detail of empirical method and results to focus upon the central issues of theory as these relate to empirical data and method. Chapter 5, "The Meaning and Measurement of Moral Judgment" consciously uses a title similar to a classic paper by Loevinger (1966) entitled "The Meaning and Measurement of Ego Development." By comparing similarities and differences between Loevinger's theory and test construction method and our own, the chapter tries to highlight the assumptions underlying our method by comparison with the only other classical test of stages of social development using open-ended material, that of Loevinger and Wessler (1970a) and Loevinger, Wessler, and Redmore (1970b).*

---

* A multiple choice test of our stage concept of moral development was devised and validated by Rest (1979) in the early 1970s. More recently, Gibbs and Widaman

Our first chapter in this section, comparing our method with Loevinger's, stresses two themes. The first is that both of us start with theoretically defined stages but engage in an empirical bootstrapping modification of both theoretical concept and empirical data on test items to achieve a valid measure. Within this similarity, Loevinger clings more closely to the classical assumption of personality testing, that a single response is a probabilistic sign of an underlying construct, while we cling to the face validity of a response as structurally matching a theoretical stage definition. Our theoretical structuralism, distinguishing form and content, has, however, also bent to the regularities in our empirical longitudinal data rather than maintaining adherence to a an *a priori* theoretical system. Many stages sequences could be constructed having a tight logical sequence, but only some, or one, exist in the real empirical world of the development of moral judgment. The back-and-forth interaction between theoretical stage definitions of sequences and empirical data is one of the main focuses of our second chapter in this section, Chapter 6, "Continuities and Discontinuities in Moral Development Revisited—Again" (a different essay was published by me in 1973 as "Continuities and Discontinuities in Childhood and Adult Moral Development Revisited").

Centering on youthful relativism and adult life experience, Chapter 6 reports the data which led us to redefine principled reasoning as an adulthood development rather than the adolescent stage discussed in Kohlberg (1958) or in Chapter 1. Parallel to this redefinition was the definition of an autonomous substage at high school conventional stages which looked principled or postconventional. Data and method on substages is contained in appendix C. This change in location of the postconventional moral stages to adulthood was the result of what Kohlberg and Kramer (1969) called "retrogression" in youth (using the Kohlberg [1958] stage definition and scoring method). Chapter 6 also continues a theme that begins in Chapter 5, the theme that moral judgment stages are an autonous subdomain of the larger domain called by Loevinger

---

(1982) have developed a written and partly open-ended test of the first four moral stages and have generated validity data upon it. Obviously the test of choice for these various stage measures is a complex issue largely dependent upon the researcher's purpose. In some cases, the test of choice for confirming, extending, and revising my own theory of moral development is that described in the Colby and Kohlberg (1984) compendium, but there are many purposes or uses for tests of social development and we make no claim that our method, (Kohlberg, 1979; Kohlberg, 1982d) is the optimal one for many of these purposes.

ego development or, more recently, development of the self, a domain which Loevinger believes to be unitary and indivisible and of which moral development is one dimension or aspect. In contrast, Chapter 5 reasserts the thesis elaborated in Part One, Chapter 2, that Piagetian cognitive development is a necessary but not sufficient condition for Selman's (1980) social perspective taking level which is, in turn, necessary but not sufficient for moral stage development. Two recent studies by Walker (1980) and by Walker and Richards (1979) support these necessary-but-not-sufficient assumptions. The parallelisms postulated by Walker are presented in Table 1.

On pretesting 146 fourth- through seventh-grade children, all moral Stage 2, Walker found that all children were either at the same stage in logical and social perspective taking or were one stage higher on logical reasoning than social perspective taking reasoning. He found that all but one child were either at the same stage in social perspective taking and in moral judgment or were one stage more advanced in social perspective taking. After a brief two-sided exposure to Stage 3 moral reasoning, the children were posttested. Of all 146 children, *only* the children who passed the necessary early formal operations task and the necessary Stage 3 social perspective task on pretest moved to moral Stage 3 through the moral stimulation intervention. *Most* of the 15 children passing the prerequisite did move to moral Stage 3.

Remaining within the structural paradigm and testing for competence, not performance, Walker was able to get almost perfect predictions from the necessary-but-not-sufficient hypothesis. No such clarity can be expected for relating moral stage to Loevinger's ego stage, because the two models' assumptions and test methodology are different. Selman (1980) speculates that there is a fairly close relation between his social perspective taking stages and Loevinger's ego stages. Empirical data of Lambert (1972), Noam (1983), Erickson (1980), and Whitely (1982) indicate a considerable correlation between moral stage and Loevinger's ego stage. But there does not appear to be any close logical relation—for example, a necessary-but-not-sufficient relation—between the two. Erickson (1980) and Whitely (1982), studying undergraduates, tended to find that where discrepancies exist the subjects are usually higher on ego stage than moral stage. Snarey (1982) found the reverse relations among kibbutz adults. Clear relations between domains can only be found if the same paradigm is used for the study of the domains.

Table 1. Parallel Stages in Cognitive, Perspective-Taking, and Moral Development

Cognitive Stage[a]	*Perspective-taking Stage*[b]	*Moral Stage*[c]
Preoperations The "symbolic function" appears, but thinking is marked by centration and irreversibility.	*Stage 1 (subjectivity)* There is an understanding of the subjectivity of persons but no realization that persons can consider each other as subjects.	*Stage 1 (heteronomy)* The physical consequences of an action and the dictates of authorities define right and wrong.
Concrete operations The objective characteristics of an object are separated from action relating to it; and classification, seriation, and conservation skills develop.	*Stage 2 (self-reflection)* There is a sequential understanding that the other can view the self as a subject just as the self can view the other as subject.	*Stage 2 (exchange)* Right is defined as serving one's own interests and desires, and cooperative interaction is based on terms of simple exchange.
Beginning formal operations There is a development of the coordination of reciprocity with inversion; and propositional logic can be handled.	*Stage 3 (mutual perspectives)* It is realized that the self and the other can view each other as perspective-taking subjects (a generalized perspective).	*Stage 3 (expectation)* Emphasis is on good-person stereotypes and a concern for approval.

Early basic formal operations The hypothetico-deductive approach emerges, involving abilities to develop possible relations among variables and to organize experimental analyses.	*Stage 4 (social and conventional system)* There is a realization that each self can consider the shared point of view of the generalized other (the social system).	*Stage 4 (social system and conscience)* Focus is on the maintenance of the social order by obeying the law and doing one's duty.
Consolidated basic formal operations Operations are now completely exhaustive and systematic.	*Stage 5 (symbolic interaction)* A social system perspective can be understood from a beyond-society point of view.	*Stage 5 (social contract)* Right is defined by mutual standards that have been agreed upon by the whole society.

a. Adapted from Colby and Kohlberg (Note 1).
b. Adapted from Selman and Byrne (1974) and Selman (1976).
c. Adapted from Kohlberg (1976).

Loevinger's paradigm is a mixed one; it is partly structural-hierarchial like Piaget's, and it is partly functional like Erik Erikson's (Snarey, Kohlberg, and Noam, 1983).

The theme of the relation between moral development and ego development continues from Chapter 5 to Chapter 6. The origins of Chapter 6 lie in Kohlberg and Kramer's (1969) effort to explain "retrogression to Stage 2" as "regression in the service of the ego" to address youth's Eriksonian identity task or crisis. In Chapter 6, we now take the position that we cannot mix the oil of Erikson's functional ego stages with the water of structural moral stages, but that Erikson's life cycle wisdom helps relate personal experience in youth and adulthood to structurally conceived moral development. The extent to which different paradigms and aspects of moral and ego development can be intergrated to provide ideal-type pictures of eras in the life span is the subject of Kohlberg, 1985.

As a whole, Part Three addresses the three central questions psychologists ask about our stages of justice reasoning judgment. The first, whether they really are sequential, holistic, culturally universal stages of judgment, is addressed in Chapters 5, 8, and 9. The second question is whether they have any meaningful relationship to moral conduct or moral action. Chapter 7 not only indicates correlation between judgment and conduct but proposes a model through which moral stage influences action, drawing upon the conceptualization of Blasi (1980, 1983) and of Rest (1983b). Rest proposes four phases of moral decision, from (1) sensitization to the problem, to (2) definition of a right action, to (3) definition that it would be the self's action, to (4) execution of the action. As social perspective taking, moral judgment enters into (1) sensitization, but the model proposes that moral stage enters centrally into (2) defining a deontic right or just action and (3) making a judgment that it is the self's responsibility to engage in the deontically right action. Chapter 7 takes up a number of interrelated issues. For moral stage to predict action, moral stage structure must define moral judgment content, that is, the judgment that a given action is a dilemma is right or wrong. The chapter reports that in both hypothetical (Heinz) dilemmas and real-life dilemmas, like the Milgram or the California Free Speech Movement dilemmas, there is usually a Stage 5 consensus on what action is right as well as use of Stage 5 reasons why it is right. On many dilemmas there is a monotonic increase in judgments that the Stage 5 content choice is right as one goes up the stages. Even more clearly, there is an increase in consistency between a judgment of rightness (deontic judgment) and a judgment of responsibility to engage in the deontically right action as one moves step by step up the stages.

In Volume I, I asserted that each higher stage is more autonomous, universalizable, prescriptive and reversible. In this volume, we use this assumption about stages (and substages) to infer that higher stage subjects will be monotonically or progressively more consistent or responsible in relating the content of their deontic moral choice to their actual action, a consistency mediated by a judgment of responsibility. The nature of this judgment of responsibility will be more fully elaborated in Volume III in connection with data on high school students' responses to moral dilemmas which occur in the high schools.

Using the findings of Hartshorne and May (1928–30) Chapter 7 stresses a theme brought up in Part One, the pitfalls of behavioral definitions of moral conduct. It argues that the judgment of whether an act is morally right or good, morally bad or wrong, or morally neutral can be decided only by studying the moral judgments and motivations which inform it. The second, related theme which Chapter 7 pursues is the critique of social relativism as a way of defining morality. Proponents of behavioristic conceptions of moral conduct typically define conduct as moral if it conforms to a socially or culturally accepted norm. All of us recognize this is intuitively incorrect, since moral exemplars like Socrates, Gandhi, and Martin Luther King consistently acted in opposition to, and in order to change, social norms—in terms of the moral principles of Stage 5 or 6.

The question of what is a morally right or good action must turn to moral philosophy for its answers. Right action is action defined by valid universalizable moral principles. The fact that Stage 5 (or Stage 6) persons agree in content choice in many dilemmas does not mean that moral rightness is judged by an opinion poll of high-stage subjects; rather, it means that Stage 5 and Stage 6 subjects rely on the principles defined by, and justified by philosophers, principles of justice like that of respect for people and their liberty and dignity, or like that of utility or the greatest welfare for the greatest number. These principles converge in defining what is just in certain situations, yielding a philosophically just solution. Not only is it a philosophic question as to what choice is "objectively" right, but it is a philosophers' question as to what motives and judgments held by an action are required to make it "subjectively" right.

As Piaget's work points out, moral action is defined largely by intentions, not consequences. Following Kant and Hare (1963, 1982), we consider a moral action to be one based on autonomous moral judgment, one implying a sense of obligation or duty which is universalizable, not made for, or limited to, the self. We find not only principled subjects but subjects who are at the autonomous or B substage of conventional (Stage 3 and 4) morality engaging in moral action from a base of autonomous moral judgment.

The issue of relativism central to this section is perhaps most definitely handled by Chapters 8 and 9 showing the universality of the stage sequence in longitudinal data in Turkey and Israel. These data indicate the universality of the sequence, though they suggest that individuals in a village culture in Turkey do not develop to postconventional, or Stage 5, reasoning. They also indicate Stage 5 consensus on dilemma choice in Israel as well as in Finland and the United States.

In summary, Part Three puts empirical meat on the theoretical bones addressed in Part Two. Our empirical meat centers on justice reasoning stages, leaving open to a large extent the enlargement of the moral domain to include real-life and hypothetical dilemmas of care and responsibility discussed in Part Two. This task is left for Volume III.

5. The Meaning and Measurement of Moral Judgment

THE TITLE of this chapter consciously evokes the work of Jane Loevinger (1966) on the meaning and measurement of ego development, reported in her Heinz Werner memorial lecture (Loevinger, 1979). In reporting the work that I have done in recent years with Anne Colby, John Gibbs and others (Colby and Kohlberg, 1984, in press) on the measurement of moral development, I will compare assumptions and results with those of Loevinger, indicating the assumptions which we share and the assumptions on which we diverge. The central theme of my comparison with Loevinger is that developmental tests, tests assuming qualitatively different types of response ordered in an invariant sequence, presuppose different theoretical and methodological assumptions about personality and its assessment than do psychometric tests or traditional personality tests.

Before engaging these issues, we need to ask whether we should try to make stage-developmental tests at all. Piaget and many Piagetians rejected the idea of constructing a stage test, relying instead upon a clinical interview, theoretically interpreted and used to examine hypotheses derived from Piagetian stage theory. When I started work in the area, reported in my 1958 dissertation (Kohlberg, 1958), I did not think that my clinically probed interviews about hypothetical dilemmas constituted a test, nor that I should aim in that direction. I thought I was operating in the tradition of Henry Murray, who got numbers for research exploration by asking for clinical ratings of TAT's or other open-ended material. If there was reasonable agreement among raters in assigning numbers, and if the numbers yielded theoretically meaningful results, that was sufficient warrant for the method. I called my 1958 dissertation method a rating system for assessing developmental ideal types. When Kurtines and Grief (1974) criticized this 1958 method for failing to meet psychometric criteria for a test, including test-retest reliability, I was extremely surprised since I had never claimed that the method was a test.

Somewhat before the Kurtines and Grief article appeared, both Jim Rest and I had decided that one or more tests of moral stage development were required. After our exploratory work which yielded clinical definitions of stages, we entered a second phase of research which required a more reliable and valid assessment method, that is, a test. The first and most obvious consideration was that starting with the work of Moshe Blatt (Blatt and Kohlberg, 1975) we had become involved in work in moral education, which requires a test for evaluation or interpretation of experimental change.

A more basic reason was that revision, refinement, or even rejection of our moral stage theory rested on developing a reliable and valid method of assigning individuals to a stage. This become apparent to me in reflecting upon the problem of apparent "regression" in moral stage in the college years (Kohlberg and Kramer, 1969; Kohlberg, 1973a). Using the 1958 dissertation method, Kramer found that almost 25 percent of our longitudinal cases "regressed" or dropped in stage in late adolescence. We could have interpreted these cases as casting doubt on our method, as an indication that our assessment method had low reliability or validity. Instead, Kramer and I concluded that many of the anomalies represented genuine retrogression, which a theory of invariant stage response had to address, rather than being method error. Further reflection led me to reassert our belief in the theoretical postulate of in variant sequence and to interpret the anomalies not as retrogression but as representing weakness in our clinical method's ability to handle subjects who were in transitional states. Rather than retrogressing from Stage 4 social morality to Stage 2 instrumental egoism, many of our anomalous cases should be considered Stage 4½, a highly relativistic transitional level between conventional and principled moral judgment. Their skepticism, conflict, and questioning about the stage they had been in, Stage 4, was the dominant feature of their response, and the reasoning was only superficially like Stage 2. It was in fact a step out of Stage 4, and further longitudinal observation suggested that it was eventually a step into Stage 5. Such alternations, between revision and doubt about the theory and revision and doubt about the method, clearly indicated the need to develop a more precise or reliable stage-scoring system. In work prior to 1969, we had claimed substantial support for moral stage theory based on results with groups, cross-sectional age data in a variety of cultures. The real data required for testing and revising stage theory, however, is not group data but individual longitudinal data. While the group data, as reported in Chapter 1, indicated a hierarchy of difficulty or advance in our moral types, they did not demonstrate an invariant sequence of stages. This is done only by following individuals longitudinally through the sequence. Following individuals longitudinally through the sequence requires a method with a minimum of measurement error and for that reason implies the need for a reliable and valid assignment of a stage score to an individual interview, in other words, a test.

I have explained how my theoretical concerns and clinical assessments led me after over ten years of research to construct a test. Jane Loevinger's movement has been in the reverse direction, from an early concern for developing a test of personality or ego to theoretical statements such as her recent book, *Ego Development* (Loevinger, 1976). In comparing the views of Loevinger and myself, I shall first consider the topic of theoretical assumptions about personality development and morality. Next, I'll consider assumptions of test construction and classification of responses. Finally, I shall consider the topic of the reliability and validity of the test, once constructed.

With regard to each topic, I shall first review the assumptions I share with Loevinger, then our divergences.

The first shared assumption is the assumption of ego, that there is a relatively unitary, conscious part of the personality, the ego or self, which reasons, judges, or evaluates. The second shared assumption is the assumption of stages. These stages form (1) an invariant sequence of (2) hierarchical transformations, which are (3) structured wholes. Loevinger and I both, then, accept the applicability of Piaget's hierarchical stage model to the characterization of ego development. In addition, we both accept the idea that moral judgment, reasoning, and character is one major part, aspect, or domain of ego development, relating to a more general ego stage. Third, there are striking parallels in the stage descriptions which emerge from Loevinger's writings and mine. This parallelism is empirical as well as conceptual. Lambert (1972) and Sullivan, McCullough, and Stager (1964) find significant correlations between the Loevinger test of ego development and our moral stage assessments after age and IQ are partialled out.

Assumptions Concerning Personality and Development: Divergences

While Loevinger does seem to get her conception of hierarchical stages from Piaget, her dominant orientation is primarily to neopsychoanalytic conceptions of ego development (see Table 5.1). In contradistinction, I orient not to psychodynamic theory but to the cognitive-developmental theories of moralization: to that of Piaget (1932) and of the American forerunners of Piaget—James Mark Baldwin (1895), John Dewey (1930), and George Herbert Mead (1934). The difference in theoretical orientation leads to at least four differences in the nature of the development we seek to assess or measure.

First, there are differences between us on how to define stages and articulate their inner logic. Loevinger defines her stages partly in terms of structures, partly in terms of functions and motives pertaining to self-enhancement and defense. I define stages solely in terms of cognitive structures, or ways of thinking or judging. Our different theoretical orientations, then, lead to differences in the formulation of a "stage," and hence to differences in what we are trying to measure. We both seek to measure thought and judgment structures used by the ego; Loevinger tries to measure ego functions and motives as well.

Second, there are differences between us in dividing the domain of ego development. Loevinger posits a single differentiated but yet indivisible ego simultaneously engaged in cognitive, interpersonal, and moral functioning. From Loevinger's point of view, there is no need to divide the ego domain. In our view, the ego comprises relatively circumscribed and self-contained subdomains, each possessed of a distinct structure, regardless of the functioning of a unitary ego. Whereas Loevinger seeks to capture in her ego stages the interpenetration of ego development, cognitive style, self concerns, and moral or character development, we take these different aspects of functioning as governed by different cognitive structures. Thus cognitive style, for us, points to the domain of structure defined by Piaget's stages of cognitive or logical operations. Interpersonal style and self concerns point, for us, to the domain of structure studied by Selman in his attempt to delineate the stages of role-taking, social perspective, and concepts of interpersonal relations (Selman and Jaquette, 1977). Impulse control and character terms denote, to us, the domain of structure called

Table 5.1. The Loevinger and Kohlberg Stages Compared

Approximate Ego Level	*Sullivan, Grant and Grant Levels of Integration*	*Peck Character Type*	*Kohlberg Basis for Morality*	*Bull Type of Morality*	*Perry Intellectual-Ethical Paradigm*
Presocial	1. Separateness				
Impulsive	2. Non-self differences	Amoral	Punishment and Obedience	Anomy	
Self-Protective	3. Rules ("Cons")	Expedient	Naive Instrumental Hedonism	Heteronomy	Duality
Conformist	3. Rules (Conformists)	Conformist	Good Relations and Approval	Socionomy	Multiplicity Prelegitimate
Conscientious-Conformist	4. Conflict and Response		Law and Order		Multiplicity
Conscientious		Irrational-Conscientious	Democratic Contract	Autonomy	Relativism
Individualistic	5. Continuity	Rational-Altruistic	Individual Principles of Conscience		
Autonomous	6. Self-Consistency				Commitment
Integrated	7. Relativity				

Ego Stage Types of Sullivan, Grant, and Grant; Peck; Kohlberg; Bull; and Perry are from Loevinger, 1976 moral judgment and reasoning. We attempt to assess only this latter domain—the development of moral judgment.

On the basis of Piagetian theory, as modified under the impact of empirical findings (cf. Chapter 2), I have been led to hypothesize parallel and corresponding stages in each ego domain, and also to argue that attainment of a stage in any one domain is dependent on attainment of a certain stage in one of the other domains. Thus, I assume that attainment of Piaget's stage of formal cognitive operations is a necessary but not a sufficient condition for the attainment of Selman's fourth stage of interpersonal conceptions. This stage requires taking a third-person perspective on dyadic relations, requires conceptions of responsibility in relationships, and requires social achievement. In turn, I assume that Selman's fourth stage of social cognition must be attained in order for our fourth stage of moral judgment to be achieved, that is, for the emergence of concepts of duty defined by conscience and by the underlying values and laws of the individual's society. Here again, it is a question of a necessary but not a sufficient condition. The notion of necessary but not sufficient conditions includes our notion of the meaning of moral judgment stage for motivation and behavior. What we conceptualize as moral reasoning is a cognitive competence, necessary but not sufficient for given kinds of motivation and conduct.

In summary, then, Loevinger defines and seeks to assess a unitary ego which uses various structures or competencies but which is a concrete unity of function reflected in motive and action. We claim less: only parallelisms in thought structure which are necessary but not sufficient for given kinds of action.

Third, and in part derived from the first two, there are differences between Loevinger and myself about what we are trying to measure. Loevinger, it would seem, was not oriented toward constructing a test useful for educational and experimental change studies, although her test has been used for this purpose more recently. I wanted to construct a test that not only would assess the current stage of moral functioning and would validly and reliably assess stage change, but also would reflect my concern with educational goals and my belief that a higher stage is a better stage. In other words, I include in my approach a normative component which Loevinger does not.

Fourth, then, this normative concern has led me to rely upon philosophic as well as psychological theory in defining what I study. That is, I assumed the need to define philosophically the entity we study, moral judgment, and to give a philosophic rationale for why a higher stage is a better stage. My philosophic conception of moral judgment has been based on principles of justice and has depended upon the theories of Kant and of Rawls (1971) to justify the principles of the highest stages.

Having discussed the commonalities and differences between Loevinger and myself with regard to theoretical issues, let me turn now to the assumptions, shared and divergent, with respect to test construction and test scoring.

On Test Construction and Test Scoring: Shared Assumptions

A traditional psychometrician, in scoring, let us say, the Binet test, is concerned solely with whether a given response is "right" or "wrong" as defined by the content of the response. The manner in which an individual arrives at the response is irrelevant. The psychometrician's act of scoring is then, in essence, no different from that found in machine scoring. The scorer need have no knowledge of theory and is, indeed, precluded from making a clinical interpretation in the light of theory.

In contrast, one who seeks to locate responses with regard to underlying structure makes a distinction between "achievement" and "process," to use Heinz Werner's formulation: a distinction between the correctness of the response according to some standard of correctness and the ways of arriving at the response. In order to arrive at the underlying structure of a response, one must construct a test, for example, the Pinard-Laurendeau scale, so that the questions and the responses to them allow for an unambiguous inference to be drawn as to underlying structure. The stage of causal reasoning, moral reasoning, and so on, at which an individual is functioning cannot be arrived at here merely by correlating manifest similarities and differences in the content or "correctness" of responses. Instead, this test constructor must postulate structure from the start, as opposed to inductively finding structure in content after the test is made. Thus, the kind of structure to which we refer is not that derived from the factor analysis of psychometric tests, exemplified in the work of Thurstone and Guilford. If a test is to yield *stage* structure, a concept of that structure must be built into the initial act of observation, test construction, and scoring; it will not emerge through pure factor-analytic responses classified by content.

Loevinger, who comes from a psychometric background, and I, whose testing of subjects has been governed by Piagetian assumptions, both move away from the traditional psychometric procedures. A first point of agreement, therefore, is that we both are trying to construct tests which will tap underlying structures. We also agree that the test constructor finds developmental structure not by the inductive method but by an abductive method which involves a working back and forth, or mutual bootstrapping, between theoretical assumptions such as postulated structures, on the one hand, and empirical reflections of those structures in the responses subjects give, on the other.

A further point of agreement is that the test scorer as well as the test constructor must know the underlying theory and also function as a "clinician" who can infer structures from the content in responses. The test scorer must function in a quasiclinical manner, going from a response to postulated underlying structures and then testing the inference to particular structures by looking at additional response material.

On Test Construction and Test Scoring: Divergent Assumptions

Of greater interest and significance are those issues with regard to which Loevinger and I diverge. As I have just done with regard to the shared assumptions, I shall summarize these briefly with minimal comment. I shall then use an item on my test and an item on Loevinger's test in order to show more concretely what each of us takes into account in constructing the items, scoring the items, or both. My hope is that this examination will flesh out our divergent assumptions, and clarify our differences in "arriving at structure."

There are three basic ways in which Loevinger and I are in disagreement with regard to test construction and test scoring: (1) Loevinger does not oppose content and structure—I do. (2) Loevinger constructs and scores her items so as to be able to infer a hypothetical entity, a kind of underlying structure akin to the psychoanalytic ego. The structures we seek to tap in test construction and arrive at in test scoring are abstractable from responses as their form or quality. (3) Loevinger makes use of a "sign approach," one which combines empirical probabilities with theoretical considerations in a bootstrapping process which she calls "saving circularity." My colleagues and I reject the "sign approach," and have required each item in the manual to clearly reflect the structure of the stage to which it is keyed.

Illustrations of Test Construction and Test Scoring (Loevinger vs. Kohlberg)

All of this, of course, is quite abstract and condensed. I therefore turn now to the illustrative material so that we may better see how Loevinger's work and mine relate to each other on matters of testing.

My test, as some of you know, consists of two forms—A and B. Each form includes three hypothetical moral dilemmas: one exhibiting a conflict between helping someone to enhance the quality of life, in violation of the law, versus obedience to the law; a second dealing with conflict between regard for character and conscience versus the meting out of retributive justice or punishment and deterrence; the third involving a conflict between the maintenance of a contract as opposed to the upholding of legitimate authority. Thus, in one of the dilemmas, subjects are asked whether a doctor should give an overdose of morphine to a terminal cancer patient if she requests it. This dilemma is the counterpart on Form B to the better known Heinz dilemma, which deals with whether a husband should steal a drug to save his wife's life. In both instances, the dilemma pertains to the moral conflict between quality of life at the expense of law and obedience to law at the sacrifice of quality of life. Taking the construction of this Form B dilemma and the scoring of responses to it as paradigmatic, I shall try to show how we put structure into the test items and arrive at structure from the responses.

As I discuss the construction of this dilemma and the principles and rules governing the analysis of responses in order to arrive at stage structure, keep before you Tables 5.2, 5.3, and 5.4. Table 5.2 represents a page from our manual for stage-scoring responses to the "mercy-killing" dilemma.

First a word about the alternate forms. For us, constructing a test with alternate forms for the assessment of developmental structure required a prior mapping out of the domain of content as well as a logical delimitation of the domain of structure. This

Table 5.2. Example of Moral Judgment Manual Item

Criterion Judgment #7

Dilemma: IV
Issue: Law
Norm: Law
Element: Seeking reward (avoiding punishment), 11.7
Stage: 2

Criterion Judgment

[The doctor should not give the woman the drug] because he would risk losing his job or going to jail.
[Note: Do not match score this point if it is a response to the general question "Why is it important to obey the law?" unless the response refers to the doctor in this mercy-killing situation.]

Stage Structure

Not killing the woman is justified because it involves a risk (rather than certainty) of punishment. Punishment is seen as something to be instrumentally avoided. The risk of punishment overrides the recognition of the pragmatic reasonableness from the woman's point of view of giving her the drug.

Critical Indicators

One of the following must be used as the central justification for not killing the woman: (*a*) punishment as possible or probable, a risk to be weighed in the decision; *or* (*b*) other disadvantageous consequences to the doctor (he might lose his job, etc.).

Match Examples

1. Should the doctor give her the drug that would make her die? Why? No, the doctor could be charged with killing her. He should give something to calm her. [Why?] He would lose his career and go to prison. He should protect himself first and not kill her.
2. Should the doctor give her the drug that would make her die? Why? No. He would be blamed for killing her. She could take her own overdose. If he did, he could lose his license and be out of a job.

Guess Example

[Note: Guess scored only if no other scored material on the issue and weighted ½ match. Otherwise, material is a nonmatch.]

1. Should the doctor do what she asks and give her the drug? No, I don't think so. I think it's asking too much of a doctor for one thing, that she should ask this even though she is in great pain. A doctor isn't supposed to do this. [Why?] I believe it's in their code

that you shouldn't give a drug to any person to help them die sooner or to put them to death right away. *If he were found out to have given her this drug, he'd probably be kicked out of his profession and he might not be able to get into something else.*

[Note: This refers to the likelihood that the doctor will lose his job as required by critical indicator (b), but the risk of undesirable consequences is not used as the central argument against mercy killing as the critical indicators specify.]

was necessary, if only to hold content themes constant in constructing the alternate forms. The classification of content themes which we try to embody in our items and expect to provide in the responses is derived from moral philosophy and the sociology of morals, in which disciplined attempts have been made to arrive at universal moral norms and issues. These themes, which we refer to as *elements* and *norms,* are listed in Table 5.3. In designing our test, we, the constructors, had to make a thematic analysis of content as well as consider issues of structure. The procedure in our manual requires that the test scorer be able to do the same.

I now turn to the process of scoring responses to the "mercy-killing" dilemma. Here you should refer to Table 5.2.

The aim of the scorer is to arrive at stage structure, to discern the structure underlying responses. Before scorers can do this, they must perform successive classifications with regard to the content of the responses. The first involves a determination as to which of the two value issues in conflict the response falls under. In the example in Table 5.2, the response falls under the category of upholding the law. This response in itself does not determine the stage structure of the response. Valuing law obedience may take place at any stage.

The second act of classification of content, therefore, is directed toward *determining the reasons* for valuing law obedience in this instance. These reasons take us closer to structure. As we have seen, Table 5.3 lists seventeen "elements of value." These are derived from the efforts of moral philosophers to classify types of moral value. As you will note, the response in the example falls under Element 7, "avoiding punishment." Now, one untutored in our system of scoring, or only superficially acquainted with it, might be led to conclude that the response is Stage 1 on the basis of this second act of content classification. But Stage 1 is not unequivocally indicated by a response reflecting the valuing of the element of punishment avoidance. The valuing of punishment avoidance may also emerge from a Stage 2 structure as it does in this case. An instrument is

Table 5.3. The Elements and Norms for Classifying Content

The Elements

I. *Modal Elements*
1. Obeying (consulting) persons or deity. Should obey, get consent (should consult, persuade).
2. Blaming (approving). Should be blamed for, disapproved (should be approved).
3. Retributing (exonerating). Should retribute against (should exonerate).
4. Having a right (having no right).
5. Having a duty (having no duty).

II. *Value Elements*

A. *Egoistic Consequences*
6. Good reputation (bad reputation).
7. Seeking reward (avoiding punishment).

B. *Utilitarian Consequences*
8. Good individual consequences (bad individual consequences).
9. Good group consequences (bad group consequences).

C. *Ideal or Harmony-Serving Consequences*
10. Upholding character.
11. Upholding self-respect.
12. Serving social ideal or harmony.
13. Serving human dignity and autonomy.

D. *Fairness*
14. Balancing perspectives or role taking.
15. Reciprocity or positive desert.
16. Maintaining equity and procedural fairness.
17. Maintaining social contract or freely agreeing.

The Norms

1. Life	6. Authority
a. Preservation	7. Law
b. Quality/quantity	8. Contract
2. Property	(9. Civil Rights)
3. Truth	(10. Religion)
4. Affiliation	11. Conscience
(5. Erotic Love and Sex)	12. Punishment

therefore needed to discriminate a Stage 2 from a Stage 1 structure where a punishment response is given. One such tool is a theoretical statement of Stage 2 structure pertaining to the issue of law and the element of punishment avoidance. This is presented in the paragraph called "Stage Structure" in the sample manual item of Table 5.2.

A second, and complementary, tool for arriving at stage structure is presented in the paragraph designed "Critical Indicators." This category comprises those indicators reflecting whether a certain kind of set (here, a Stage 2 egoistically pragmatic set) is involved in thinking about punishment.

Consider now the examples of responses. The *match examples* pass the critical indicators. The *guess example* fails the critical indicators but seems to give some evidence of matching the stage structure of the manual item. A *fail example* would not only fail to embody the critical indicators but would suggest a different structure involved in valuing punishment avoidance than that characterizing Stage 2. For example, it might suggest valuing punishment avoidance in light of conventional-stage concerns for reputation in a societal context, rather than Stage 2 pragmatism.

Before contrasting this item from our manual with a parallel item from Loevinger's, let me review and elaborate some differences in our approaches. The concept of structure in Loevinger's scheme refers less to a form of thinking than to general stable and consistent personality content and function—the usage implied in psychoanalytic concepts of character structure. That is, structure in Loevinger's scheme is a hypothetical underlying entity of personality like the psychoanalytic ego. In contrast, the structure to which I refer is not potentially tangible rather, it is a construct to subsume a variety of different manifest responses. The responses of subjects to the dilemmas and their subsequent responses to clinical probing are taken to *reflect, exhibit,* or *manifest* the structure. They are the realizations of the "archetypal" structure in actuality, under special conditions. There may be disagreement by investigators concerning the correctness of the attribution of a certain structure, given certain responses (i.e., interrater reliability questions), but there can be no error in the sense of a mistake in inferring from a judgment to some state of affairs concurrent with, precedent to, or subsequent to the judgment. Thus, my procedure is not of the same order as that which one adopts in predicting from clouds to rain or smoke to fire or high white-cell count to appendicitis, or a response from an item on the MMPI to the conclusion of schizophrenia or hypochondriasis. In those cases one is dealing not with reflections, exhibitions, or manifestations but with indices or signs.

The sign approach fundamentally links signs to signs, and does not go beyond the manifest signs, in principle. My own approach does not go from sign to sign, but rather from expressions or "symbols" to what is postulated as a common theme or "structure." There is no way of discovering that structure or uncovering the structure as another sign. It is, in that sense, a construct rather than an inference, and is warranted only on the grounds of "intelligible" ordering of the manifest items. One might say that the hypothetical structure is the principle of organization of the responses. To treat it on the same level as the responses would be, in Ryle's sense, to commit a category mistake.

Because Loevinger sees her test items as signs which are probabilistic indicators of an underlying personality organization, there is no need for her scoring categories to be structurally defined in the same sense that ours are. In fact, she does not make a clear distinction between structure and content in her stage definitions and scoring procedures. A look at one of her items illustrates this.

Table 5.4 presents an item from Loevinger's Sentence Completion Test. A comparison of the manual item from Loevinger with the one presented earlier from our own manual should illustrate both our differing conceptions of structure and the resulting differences in our approaches to test construction. To simplify comparison, I chose items holding content focus and stage structure constant. Both the Kohlberg and Loevinger items are moral in content, both are Stage 2 (Delta in Loevinger's scheme). If we impose on Loevinger's manual the distinctions between content and structure used in our own scoring system, the result is that some of her scoring categories do seem structural in our sense. That is, they are conceptually direct reflections of the organizational principles of the stage. Others are closer to what we would see as content. They may be logically consistent with not only the stage they represent but also other stages; in fact they are empirically most highly associated with the stage to which they are keyed.

Category 2 in the sample item comes fairly close to what we call structure but is still content associated with structure. The issue or content of value is our issue of conscience. Category 2 reflects a nonvaluing of this issue. We would call this an issue content value probabilistically associated with a Stage 2 structure, a devaluing of

Table 5.4. Example of Ego Development Manual Item

Item 35: My Conscience Bothers Me If

Delta

Characteristic Delta reactions displayed on this item are callousness ("I let it") and willful demanding ("always do what I want to do"). "I have to lie to someone who trusts me" displays also denial of responsibility for one's actions. "I can't have my own way" is illogical as an answer but clear as an expression of willfulness. Answers based on not succeeding or on being talked about indicate a lack of conscience almost as clearly as saying one does not have one. The one category here that names transgression of a rule refers to stealing; one may surmise that it is the concrete character of this transgression that impresses it on people earlier in development than lying or cheating.

1. —I steal
   If I take his money
   I take something that is not mine
2. —I don't have a conscience; my conscience never bothers me
   none
   it doesn't
   I don't have any bothers
   always do what I want to
3. —I let it
   I realize it
4. —I am being talked about, suspected
   my mother is suspicious of what I have been doing
   I feel that someone is watching me
5. —I happen, have to lie, cheat, etc. (1-3,1)
   I have to lie to someone who trusts me
   I happen to lie about something
   I am forced into a white lie
6. —I don't succeed in what I want to do (1-3, 13; 1-3/4, 14)
   I can't have my own way
   I'm inconsiderate & don't succeed in making a fool out of Jan
   do something stupid

Unclassified
   I waste precious time taking tests like this

conscience which might probabilistically derive from an instrumental egoistic structure of valuing.

Category 1, "My conscience bothers me if I steal," is even farther than Category 2 from representing what we would call the structure represented by Loevinger's self-protective stage. The Loevinger manual notes that stealing is a more concrete content of moral valuing than lying or cheating. But in our terms, it is clearly content, a statement of what *is* wrong or right, not a direct expression of structure or of form of reasoning about *why* something is wrong or right.

Category 3 comes closer to representing the structure itself, as opposed to being a probable sign of the Delta stage. "My conscience bothers me if I let it" suggests that guilt and shame are affective states subject to ego control in light of an instrumental valuing of a purposive ego, rather than Stage 1-2 impulses and feelings. It also suggests that guilt and shame have no legitimacy or value as representing social morality or social values, the hallmark of conventional thinking past the second stage. This kind of analysis is representative of what would be contained in the stage structure paragraph in our manual. It would not, however, appear in Loevinger's manual. Her manual does not include interpretive statements which explicate the structure of manual items and tie them to the overall structure of the stages they represent.

In terms of test methodology, the differences between Loevinger's epistemology and mine are expressed in differences in attitude to face validity, on the one hand, and to empirical item analysis, on the other.

Our current test rejects both the sign approach and the selection and scoring of items through empirical item analysis. Each item must have face validity in representing the stage as defined by the theory. It cannot be placed at the stage simply because empirical item analysis indicates it has a probabilistic value as a sign of the stage.

Loevinger's assumptions in test construction are intermediate between the radical extremes of our Piagetian approach and the MMPI. She accepts the empirical sign approach of the MMPI, but only if it can be squared with some degree of logical or theoretical analysis, with some degree of face validity. She calls her approach one of saving circularity between theoretical logic and empirical item analysis.

In this context, "saving circularity" means a bootstrapping relation between the ego concept and empirical item analysis. As an example, the response "My conscience bothers me if I steal" has no clear face validity as reflecting a self-protective stage. If it had been initially placed at the conformist stage by clinical inference and theory, Loevinger would move it to her self-protective stage, on the basis of the item analysis which indicated that it is associated with clinical assignment of the total protocol to that stage. Loevinger calls it saving circularity, rather than brute empiricism or empirically patching up the internal consistency or reliability of a test, because it is a spiral process which modifies or improves the conception of each stage and not just the test's internal consistency or concurrent validity in the psychometric sense.

The evolution of my own theory and methods reflects a somewhat different kind of circularity or bootstrapping. I have already referred to the sequence anomalies which resulted from Kramer's original analysis of our longitudinal data (Kohlberg and Kramer, 1969). Several years of reflection led me to decide that the data called into question the construct validity of my measure rather than the truth of the Piagetian sequence hypothesis. More accurately, it led me to doubt some parts of the conceptual definitions of the stages underlying the rating guides which were our measures. Our stage definitions had confused content or surface structure with the deeper structure we meant to describe with our stages.

The reinterpretation led us to try to distinguish more clearly the structure from the content of the response in both stage definition and scoring. This led us first to a clinical rating of stage structure by a set of issue-rating guides, after classifying content by issue, as already described. Level of social perspective on the issue was the basis of rating. Stage 4, for example, was defined, not by valuing the issues of law and order, or the element of concern for the consequences to the group, but by a social system perspective.

The final step was to score a subsample of the cases clinically, with all the bias that implies, to see if we, not a skeptical audience, would have evidence confirming or disconfirming our sequence expectations. We found regular sequence in these ratings. We then constructed a standard interview with the same questions for all and developed a standardized scoring manual out of the responses to our longitudinal subsample in conjunction with our clinical rating guide. We then proceeded to blind score the remaining interviews for each of the fifty eight subjects in the longitudinal sample.

Our subjects were 10, 13, or 16 years old in 1956 and were interviewed every four years from then until 1977. Each interview included the presentation of nine hypothetical moral dilemmas—Interview Forms A, B, and C. The analysis of Form C has not yet been completed, so I'll be reporting the results of Forms A and B.

Before going on to look at the results of the longitudinal study, let's look at the reliability of the scoring system. The test-retest figures are especially important because they give us the estimate of measurement error that is most relevant to our longitudinal analysis. Since we can't expect our measure to be error free, we need some estimate of measurement error against which to evaluate deviations from perfect sequentiality. Therefore, the analysis of longitudinal sequence involves a comparison of the frequency of sequence deviations or downward stage movement in the longitudinal data with the frequency of downward Time 1–Time 2 changes in our test-retest data. If sequence deviations exceed test-retest instability, we can't consider our data to support the invariant-sequence assumption.

Test-retest reliability figures are summarized in Table 5.5. As shown in that table, correlations between Time 1 and Time 2 for Forms A and B are both in the high .90s. Since the correlations

***Table 5.5.* Test-Retest Reliability of Standard-Form Scoring**

Correlation $T_1 - T_2$: Form A: .96 (Rater 1); .99 (Rater 2)
Form B: .97 (Rater 2)

Percent agreement within one-third stage:	Form A	93%
	Form B	94%
	Forms A&B	100%

Percent agreement using pure-stage and mixed-stage scores [9 categories: 1, 1/2, 2, 2/3 3, 3/4, 4, 4/5, 5]

Form A	70% (Rater 1), 77% (Rater 2) (N=43)
Form B	75% (Rater 2) (N=31)
Forms A&B	80% (Rater 2) (N=10)

Percent agreement using major/minor stage differentiations [13 categories: 1, 1(2), 2(1), 2, 2(3), 3(2), 3, 3(4), 4(3), 4, 4(5), 5(4), 5]

Form A	59% (Rater 1), 70% (Rater 2)
Form B	62% (Rater 2)
Forms A&B	70% (Rater 2)

could be very high without much absolute agreement between scores at Time 1 and Time 2, we have also presented percent agreement figures. For almost all subjects, the scores on Times 1 and 2 were within one-third stage of each other. If we look at global scores based on a nine-point scale—the five stages and the four transition points between stages—we find between 70 and 80 percent complete agreement.

Overall, then, it appears that on two interviews conducted about a month apart almost all subjects receive scores within one-third stage of each other. About three quarters receive identical scores on the two interviews when a nine-point scale is used, and between one half and two thirds receive identical scores with the most finely differentiated thirteen-point scale.

Test-retest interviews described above were also used for assessing interrater reliability. The figures for interrater reliability (Table 5.6) look roughly comparable to the test-retest figures: Almost all interviews were scored within a third of a stage of each other by any two raters, and on about one half to two thirds of the interviews the two raters assigned identical scores even when using the thirteen-category system. The correlation between raters 1 and 2 was .98.

Alternate-form data are based on those test-retest subjects who

Table 5.6. **Interrater Reliability of Standard-Form Scoring**

Correlation, Raters 1 and 2, Form A test-retest interviews = .98

		PERCENT AGREEMENT	
Rater Pair	*Within ⅓ Stage*	*Complete Agreement (9 categories)*	*Complete Agreement (13 categories)*
FORM A			
1	100	88	53
2	100	88	63
3	100	75	63
4	88	88	63
5	88	88	63
FORM B			
6	100	78	78

received both Forms A and B and on the 233 longitudinal interviews which included both forms. A single rater scored independently both forms of the test-retest sample interviews. Percent agreement between Forms A and B for this sample was comparable to test-retest and interrater reliability: 100 percent of the interviews were given scores within one-third stage of each other for the two forms, 75 percent received identical scores for A and B using the nine-point scale, and 67 percent received identical scores for the two forms using the thirteen-point scale. The correlation between moral maturity scores for Forms A and B in this sample was .95.

The level of agreement across forms for the longitudinal data is not as high (see Table 5.7). This is to be expected since Form A was scored by rater 1 and Form B by rater 2. That is, the reliability figures confound form and rater differences.

A review of the correlational reliability data for the standard form indicates that the instrument is well within the limits of acceptable reliability. A comparison with related measures may be helpful here. Loevinger and Wessler (1970) report interrater reliability correlations for their Sentence Completion Test of ego development in the mid .80s, as compared to our correlations in the .90s. Jim Rest (1979) reports test-retest reliability in the .80s and internal consistency reliability in the .70s for the Defining Issues Test of moral development.

Considering percent agreement, the standard form again compares favorably with Loevinger's Sentence Completion Test. Interrater agreement on total protocol Sentence Completion score

Table 5.7. Alternate-Form Reliability

Longitudinal Sample (N=193)

Correlation Form A–Form B = .84

(Rater 1 for Form A, Rater 2 for Form B)

85% agreement within ½ stage

(other percent agreement figures not yet available)

Test-Retest Sample

Correlation Form A–Form B = .95

(Rater 2 for both forms)

Percent agreement (9 categories) = 75%

Percent agreement (13 categories) = 67%

Percent within ⅓ stage = 100%

using a ten-point scale is reported to range from 50 to 80 percent (median 61 percent). This is substantially lower than the 75–88 percent that we obtain using our nine-point standard form scale.

Turning to the longitudinal sample, let's look first at the sequence data. Table 5.8 presents global stage scores for Interview Forms A and B separately and for the two forms combined. The

Table 5.8. **Longitudinal Sequence**

Subject and Testing Time	*Global Score Form A*	*Global Score Form B*	*Global Score Forms A&B Combined*
1–1	*1	2	2(1)
1–2	1(2)	2	2(1)
1–3	2(3)	*2	2(3)
1–4	3(2)	3	3
1–6	4(3)	3(4)	4(3)
2–1	2(1)	2(1)	2(1)
2–2	3	3	3
2–3	4(3)	3(4)	4(3)
2–4	3X	2(3)X	3(2)X
2–5	5(4)	4(5)	5(4)
2–6	5(4)	5(4)	5(4)
3–1	2(1)	2	2
3–2	2(3)	2(3)	2(3)
3–3	4(3)	3	3(4)
3–4	4(3)	3(4)	3(4)
3–5	4(3)	4(3)	4(3)
3–6	4(3)	4	4
4–1	2(3)	2	2
4–2	3	2(3)	3(2)
4–3	3(4)	3(2)	3
4–4	3(4)	*3(2)	3(4)
4–5	3(4)	4(3)	3(4)
5–1	2	1(2)	2(1)
5–2	2(3)	2	2(3)
5–3	2(3)	2(1)X	2X
5–4	3X	2	3(2)
5–5	3(2)	2	2(3)X
6–1	—	2(1)	2(1)

Table 5.8—Continued

Subject and Testing Time	*Global Score Form A*	*Global Score Form B*	*Global Score Forms A&B Combined*
6–2	—	*2/3	2/3
6–3	—	3	3
6–4	—	3	3
6–5	—	*2/3	2/3X
8–1	2	2(1)	2(1)
8–2	2	1X	2(1)
8–4	3(4)	3	3
9–1	2(1)	2(1)	2(1)
9–2	2(3)	2(3)	2(3)
9–3	3(2)	3	3
9–4	3	3	3
9–5	3(4)	3(4)	3(4)
9–6	4	*4(3)	4
11–1	1(2)	2	2(1)
11–2	3(2)	*2	2(3)
12–1	2	1(2)	2(1)
12–2	3	2	3(2)
12–3	3(4)	3(4)	3(4)
12–4	3(4)	3	3(4)
13–1	2(1)	2	2
13–2	2	2	2
13–5	3	3	3
14–1	3(2)	2	2(3)
14–2	2(4)(3)X	3(2)	3(2)
14–4	4	4	4
14–5	—	4(5)	4(5)
15–1	2(3)	2(3)	2(3)
15–2	3(2)	3	3(2)
16–1	3(2)	2(3)	2(3)
16–2	3(4)	3	3
16–3	4(3)	4(3)	4(3)
16–4	4	4	4
16–6	4	4	4
17–1	—	2	2
17–2	3(2)	2/3	3(2)

Table 5.8—Continued

Subject and Testing Time	*Global Score Form A*	*Global Score Form B*	*Global Score Forms A&B Combined*
17–3	3(4)	3	3
17–4	3(4)	3	3(4)
17–5	4	4	4
17–6	4(5)	5(4)	4(5)
18–1	3	3	3
18–2	3(2)	3	3
18–4	3/4	3(4)	3(4)
18–5	3/4	*3/4	3/4
18–6	4	4	4
19–1	2	2(1)	2(1)
19–2	2/3	3(4)	3
19–4	3	3(4)	3(4)
19–5	3(4)	4(3)	4(3)
19–6	4(3)	4	4
21–1	2	*2(1)	2
21–2	3(2)	2	2(3)
21–3	3	2/3	3(2)
21–4	3(2)X	3	3
22–1	2	2(1)	2
22–2	2(1)X	2(3)	2(3)
22–3	4(3)	3(4)	4(3)
22–4	4(3)	4	4
22–5	4(3)	—	4(3)X
22–6	4	*4(5)	4
23–1	2	2(1)	2
23–2	2/3	3(4)	3(4)
23–3	3/4	4(3)	4(3)
23–4	4(3)	4(5)	4
23–5	4(5)	5	5(4)
23–6	5(4)	—	5(4)
24–1	3	1(2)	2(1)
24–2	3	3(2)	3(2)
24–3	3(4)	3	3
24–4	3(4)	3(4)	3(4)
25–1	3(2)	2(1)	2(3)
25–2	3(4)	3	3

Table 5.8—Continued

Subject and Testing Time	*Global Score Form A*	*Global Score Form B*	*Global Score Forms A&B Combined*
25–5	4(3)	4(3)	4(3)
25–6	4(3)	4	4
26–1	2	2	2
26–2	3	*3(2)	3
26–4	3	3	3
26–5	3	*3(4)	3
26–6	3(4)	3(4)	3(4)
27–1	2(3)	1(3)	3(2)
27–2	3(4)	3	3
27–4	4(3)	3	3(4)
27–5	3(4)X	3(4)	3(4)
29–1	2(3)	2(3)	2(3)
29–2	3	3	3
29–4	4(3)	3	3(4)
29–5	4	4(3)	4(3)
31–1	1(2)(3)	2	2(1)
31–2	3	2(3)	3(2)
31–5	3(4)	3(4)	3(4)
32–1	2(1)	2	2
32–2	2(3)	2	2
32–5	3	4(3)	3(4)
32–6	4(3)	4(3)	4(3)
36–1	2(3)	2(1)	2
36–2	2(1)(3)X	2	2
36–5	3(4)	3	3(4)
36–6	4(3)	3(4)	4(3)
37–1	3	3(2)	3
37–2	3(4)	3(4)	3(4)
37–3	*4(3)	3(4)	3(4)
37–4	4	*4(5)	4
37–5	4(5)	5(4)	5(4)
37–6	—	5(4)	5(4)
38–1	2(3)	2	2
38–2	3(4)	3(4)	3(4)
38–5	4(3)	4	4(3)

Table 5.8—Continued

Subject and Testing Time	*Global Score Form A*	*Global Score Form B*	*Global Score Forms A&B Combined*
38–6	4(3)	3(4)X	3(4)X
39–1	2(3)	2(3)	2(3)
39–2	3(4)	3	3(4)
39–3	3(4)	3	3X
39–4	4	4(3)	4
41–1	3(2)	2	2
41–2	3(2)	3(2)	3(2)
41–3	3	3	3
41–4	3	3	3
41–5	3	3	3
41–6	4(3)	—	4(3)
42–1	3(2)	3(2)	3(2)
42–2	3	3	3
42–4	4(5)	4	4(5)
42–5	5(4)	4(5)	4(5)
42–6	5(4)	5(4)	5(4)
43–1	*3	3(2)(1)	3
43–2	3(4)	4(3)	3(4)
43–3	4(3)	4(3)	4(3)
43–4	4(3)	4(3)	4(3)
44–2	2(4)	3	3
44–3	4(5)	4(3)	4
44–4	4X	4	4
44–6	4(5)	4(5)	4(5)
45–1	3(2)	2	2(3)
45–2	3	3(2)	3
45–4	4	4(3)	4(3)
45–5	4	4	4
45–6	4	4	4
47–1	2(3)	3(4)	3(2)
47–2	3(2)	4(3)	3(4)
47–3	3	—	3X
47–4	3	3(4)X	3(4)
47–5	3(4)	3(4)	3(4)
47–6	4(3)	2(4)X	4

Table 5.8—Continued

Subject and Testing Time	*Global Score Form A*	*Global Score Form B*	*Global Score Forms A&B Combined*
48–1	2(3)	—	2(3)
48–2	3(4)	3(2)	3
48–4	4(3)	3	3(4)
48–5	4(3)	4(3)	4(3)
48–6	4(3)	4	4
49–1	3(4)	3	3
49–4	4(3)	4(3)	4(3)
49–5	3(4)X	3X	3(4)X
49–6	3(4)	4(3)	3(4)
50–1	3	3(2)	3
50–4	3(4)	3	3
50–5	4(3)	4	4
50–6	4(3)	4	4
51–1	2	2	2
51–4	3(4)	3(4)	3(4)
51–5	3(4)	4	4(3)
51–6	3(4)	3(4)X	3(4)X
53–1	3	*3(1)(2)	3
53–2	3(4)	*3(2)(4)	4(4)
53–4	3X	3(4)	(4)
54–1	2(3)	2(3)	2(3)
54–5	3	4(3)	3(4)
56–1	2	—	2
56–4	3	—	3
56–6	4(3)	—	4(3)
59–1	2(3)	1(2)	21(1)(3)
59–2	3	2/3	3(2)
59–4	3	3	3
59–5	3(4)	3(2)X	3
62–1	2(3)	3	3(2)
62–2	3(4)	4	4(3)
62–4	3X	*3X	3X
62–6	4(3)	4	4
64–1	3	3(2)	3

Table 5.8—Continued

Subject and Testing Time	*Global Score Form A*	*Global Score Form B*	*Global Score Forms A&B Combined*
64–4	3	3(4)	3(4)
64–5	3(4)	4(3)	4(3)
65–1	3(4)	3(4)	3(4)
65–2	4	*2X	4
65–4	4(3)X	4(3)	4(3)X
65–5	4(3)	4(3)	4(3)
65–6	4(3)	4	4
67–1	3	2(3)	3(2)
67–2	3	3	3
67–4	4(3)	3(4)	4(3)
67–5	4(5)	3(4)	4
67–6	5(4)	4(3)	4(5)
68–1	3	3	3
68–2	3(4)	3	3(4)
68–4	4(3)	3(4)	3(4)
68–5	4	*3(4)	4(3)
68–6	4	3X	4(3)
70–1	2(3)	3(2)	3(2)
70–2	3(4)	3(4)	3(4)
70–4	3(4)	4(3)	4(3)
70–5	4	3(4)X	4(3)
70–6	3(4)X	4	4(3)
71–1	3	3	3
71–2	3(4)	3	3
71–4	4(3)	3(4)	3(4)
71–5	4(3)	3X	3(4)
81–1	3	2(1)	3(2)
81–2	3	3(2)	3(2)
81–3	4(3)	3(4)	3(4)
91–3	3	4(3)	3(4)
91–4	3(2)X	3X	3X
91–5	3(4)	3	3
91–6	4	4	4
92–3	3(2)	3	3(2)
92–4	3(4)	3(4)	3(4)

Table 5.8—Continued

Subject and Testing Time	*Global Score Form A*	*Global Score Form B*	*Global Score Forms A&B Combined*
92–5	3X	*3(4)	3(4)
93–3	4(3)	3	3(4)
93–4	3(4)X	3	3(4)
93–5	3(4)	3(4)	3(4)
93–6	4(3)	4	4
95–3	3	3(2)	3
95–4	4(3)	—	4(3)
95–5	3(4)X	3	3X
95–6	—	3	3
96–3	4(3)	3	3(4)
96–4	3X	3	3X
96–5	4(3)	3(4)	3(4)
96–6	3(4)X	3X	3X

X—sequence inversion *scores were all guesses

sequence reversals are noted with an *X*. In Form A these downward changes occurred in 7 percent of the adjacent time points (using our most differentiated thirteen-point scale of global interview scores). The reversals in Form B were 8 percent, and in Forms A and B combined were 7 percent. A comparison with downward stage change in test-retest data is presented in Table 5.9. You can see that in every case the test-retest reversals are well over twice as great as the longitudinal reversals, so it seems reasonable to attribute the violations of longitudinal sequence to measurement error.

The concept of invariant stage sequence also implies that no stage will be omitted as development proceeds. In fact, if you look carefully at Table 5.8 you'll see that in no case on either form did a subject reach a stage in the sequence without having gone through each preceding stage. For the most part, changes across the four-year intervals were less than a full stage. According to the cognitive-developmental theory, the logic of each stage forms "a structured whole." In line with this assumption, one would expect to find a high degree of internal consistency in stage scores assigned. The data support this assumption as clearly as they do that of invariant sequence.

One indication of degree of internal consistency in moral judg-

Table 5.9. Comparison of Downward Stage Change in Longitudinal* and Test-Retest Data

	Pure- and Mixed-Stage Scores		
	Form A (Rater 1)	*Form B (Rater 2)*	*Forms A&B Combined*
Longitudinal T_n to T_n+1	2% (3/177)	4% (6/160)	1% (2/171)
Test-Retest T_1 to T_2	19%	23%	10%
	Major/Minor and Pure-Stage Scores		
	Form A	*Form B*	*Forms A&B*
Longitudinal T_n to T_n+1	7%	8%	7%
Test-Retest T_1 to T_2	19%	33%	20%

* Only the longitudinal interviews which were scored blind are included in this analysis.

ment is provided by profiles for each subject of proportion of reasoning scored at each of the five stages. Our analysis of these profiles showed that most subjects received the great majority of their scores at either a single stage or at two adjacent stages. The mean percentage of reasoning at the individual's modal stage was 68 percent for Form A and 72 percent for Form B. Percentage of reasoning at the subject's most heavily used stages was 98 percent for Form A and 97 percent for Form B. (Remember that there are three dilemmas per form and that each dilemma was scored without knowledge of responses to the other dilemmas, so these figures cannot be an artifact of scorer bias.) The high correlations between alternate forms reported in the section on reliability provide further support for the consistency of a subject's stage of reasoning across differing content.

There remains a problem in interpreting these seemingly clearcut results, however. It results from the circularity in the way the numbers were generated—a circularity that explains the differences between the results of Kramer's analysis (Kohlberg and Kramer, 1969) and the current one. From one extreme point of view, the data represent a desperate effort to save a theoretical hypothesis after it was disconfirmed by the Kramer data. From a second extreme point of view, they simply represent progress in an inductive description of stages.

To me, the most plausible point of view is neither inductive nor hypothetico-deductive theory testing, but the point of view of what Loevinger calls "saving circularity" in the definition and measurement of a construct. Loevinger revised her stage definitions in light of empirical item analyses designed to increase the reliability and validity of her test. I did the circular revision not so much with the criterion of item consistency or reliability but with the criterion of sequence, our basic criterion of construct validity. From this point of view, the results in Table 5.8 define the construct validity of our test. I shall quote a statement about the appropriate criterion of construct validity of our moral stage measure which I made in Chapter 2.

> Construct validity means the fit of the data obtained by means of the test of primary components of its theoretical definition. The primary theoretical definition of structural moral development is that of an organization passing through invariant sequential stages. [Kohlberg, 1976, p. 46]

In other words, data on longitudinal sequence tell us less about truth of theory than about the construct validity of a test based on the theory. It is less a synthetic or explanatory statement about nature than it is an analytic statement about structural stages. It says: Before you try to explain data of change and development with a cognitive-developmental theory, make sure your data can be observed with a measure you have made up to fit the sequence rule.

The same thing is true for assessments of reliability of stage tests. From the point of view of stage theories like Piaget's or mine, test reliability and test construct validity are one and the same thing. In the case of structural stage, construct validity demands high test-retest and alternate-form reliability. A stage is a structural whole; the individual should be consistent over various stimuli and occasions for testing structure. I don't have the time to expand, but our reliability data in Tables 5.5–5.7 fit this demand rather well.

I have already noted that there is a certain circularity involved in assumptions about truth of a theory and validity of a test. Only a bootstrapping spiral can make this a saving circularity. Loevinger's saving circularity is at the heart of scientific method in the epistemologies of pragmatism of Charles Sanders Peirce and John Dewey. It is the heart of the method which is neither induction nor deduction, but what Peirce called abduction. He compared scientific theory to a leaky boat you patch in one place and then stand on in another place while you patch or revise elsewhere. Sometimes the patching doesn't work and the boat sinks. But not, as Kuhn (1970) points out, until another boat comes along which the scientist can move to. I'd be happy to stop patching up Piagetian assumptions if I could see another boat on the horizon which handled my problems and data better than the stage concept. Until the critics point to that boat, I'm stuck with doing research with my test, one of a number of ways of doing useful research in moral development. Until that boat comes along, I might express the wish that psychologists interested in morality might get off stage bandwagons or antistage bandwagons and get on with the hard work of studying the enduring problems of moral development with the tools available. Our test is one.

Let me conclude that saving circularity doesn't always save all cherished assumptions. Sometimes one has to at least temporarily abandon a leaky stage boat without higher stage rescue. Our tables contain no Stage 6 scores. As far as we can ascertain all our Stage 6 persons must have been killed in the 1960s like Martin Luther King. Stage 6 remains as a theoretical postulate but not an operational empirical entity.

Our discussion of the construct validity of the test has been restricted to its internal characteristics, structural wholeness and invariant sequence. There is a recurring demand to know about the validity of the test as a predictor to external criteria, particularly moral action or behavior. I have stated at the beginning of this chapter that our test was a measure of judgmental competence necessary but not sufficient for real-life moral decision making and judgment. The study of real-life moral decision making I take up in Chapter 7.

6. Continuities and Discontinuities in Childhood and Adult Development Revisited—Again

with ANN HIGGINS

IN THE PREVIOUS chapter, I sketched out the process my colleagues and I used to construct a scoring manual for defining purely formal or structural stages of moral development and its validation on our American longitudinal data. I differentiated our moral stages from Loevinger's ego stages, both in terms of method of stage definition and in terms of the theoretical assumptions of her ego development approach to moral development and our cognitive-developmental or structural approach. I mentioned in passing that our efforts to define a stage system clearly differentiating structure from content, and moral judgment from ego development, were motivated by failure of my earlier (Kohlberg, 1958) stage definitions and scoring method to meet the upward invariant sequence hypothesis of stage theory, a defect particularly apparent in charting development after high school, the oldest age group on which the Kohlberg (1958) stage system was developed. In this chapter, using case examples, I shall discuss post-high school development, not only as it led to reconstruction of our stage definitions and measures, but also in terms of some of the more general theoretical issues our data raise for the study of development in youth and adulthood.

Theoretical Issues

In this chapter, we shall present some evidence on the existence of adulthood moral stages and consider the way experience in young adulthood leads to stage change. A number of issues are involved. The first is whether experience occurring after completion of maturation of the body and the nervous system can lead to a qualitatively new structural stage. If so, stages can be defined independently of changing maturational capacities and drives.

The second issue, raised in Chapter 3, is that of whether young adult development may be defined as development of "hard" structural stages of moral reasoning or what we shall call "soft ego stages," either the "soft structural ego stages" of Loevinger or the functional ego stages of Erikson (1963). In Chapter 4, we noted that Gibbs (1979) questioned whether Stage 5, the stage developing in youth or early adulthood, or Stage 6, presumably developing even later, are "hard" or "standard" Piagetian structural stages. Gibbs interprets Stages 5 and 6 as merely conscious theoretical self-reflections rather than new forms of moral reasoning operations for solving moral problems. In the Gibbs formulation Stages 5 and 6 represent more theoretically sophisticated levels of responding to why questions supporting conventional or Stage 4 moral operations of problem solving. This question, however, has to be more directly related to longitudinal cases of development in youth.

The third issue is that of regression. Kohlberg and Kramer (1969) reported evidence suggesting that, entering college, some subjects temporarily (for 2–3 years) "retrogressed" to Stage 2 instrumental egoism and later returned to conventional (Stage 4) or principled (Stage 5) morality. Finding this apparent moral "retrogression" and return to morality, Kramer and I in that paper concluded that Stages 5 and 6 were not new adulthood stages but had developed by the end of high school and were shaken by the identity questioning Erikson (1959) attributed to adolescence and youth. This identity questioning in the adolescent and youth moratorium, Kohlberg and Kramer (1969) reported, led to a questioning of morality, whether Stage 4 or 5, and a consequent retrogression to a relativistic and egoistic orientation similar to that of our Stage 2 instrumental relativistic egoism. This retrogression was "in the service of the ego" in its search for its own identity. The return from "Stage 2 retrogression" to Stage 4 and 5 morality implied that adulthood was a period of stabilization of morality rather than a period of new moral stage growth. In this chapter we will define moral development in youth not as a phenomenon of ego development but in its own terms.

Thus, in the Kohlberg and Kramer (1969) paper I believed that youth was a period of "soft" functional ego stage development in Erikson's terms but not of "hard" structural cognitive and moral stage growth, which merely stabilized in youth and early adulthood. For a variety of reasons which we shall discuss in this chapter, the Kohlberg and Kramer (1969) "solution" to the problem of college relativism as "retrogression" followed by moral stage stabilization was an unsatisfactory one to us. Because it was unsatisfactory to include regression or retrogression in a moral stage scheme, we were led to (*a*) revise definitions of Stage 5 (and 6) and (*b*) to make a distinction between a more morally autonomous B substage and a less autonomous A substage at the conventional level (Stages 3 and 4).

The fourth issue discussed in this chapter involves the kind of experience that stimulates movement to principled thought. Our findings suggested that moral development did not occur only through the processes described in the earlier theoretical chapters (2 and 3). I earlier described moral stage change as a cognitive reorganization of normative conceptions of society and related fundamental norms of justice. Change factors include (*a*) "pure" cognitive growth to a higher logical stage, (*b*) social-cognitive growth through opportunities for enlarged role-taking and (*c*) experiences of cognitive-moral conflict between one's own moral reasoning and those of others (or between one's own structures of reasoning and moral dilemmas one cannot resolve). All of these kinds of factors are factors of relatively vicarious moral experience rather than of personal moral choice.

These "vicarious experience" processes seemed relatively adequate to account for movement through the preconventional and conventional stages, where movement represents an increasingly adequate picture of society as it is. They seem inadequate, however, to account for movement to a level of self-chosen but universalized principles going beyond society and coming into possible conflict with it. The construction of principles would seem to require a much more self-reflective process of construction and choice of principles coming from processing of one's own experiences. In favor of a notion of a different process in movement to principled thought is that the movement to principled thinking is much more difficult than are previous movements. Also supporting the notion is that the transition is often associated with a self-conscious moral crisis of relativity.

The Existence of Adult Moral Stages and Retrogression—The Kohlberg and Kramer (1969) Conclusions

Kohlberg and Kramer (1969) reported that they did not find any new structural moral stage with adulthood (p. 105):

> The first question to be asked, "Are there adult moral stages?" is answered by the fact that there is no Stage 7 on the graph. In other words, there was no way of thinking about our moral situations found in adulthood and not found in adolescence. Principled thought of the Stage 5 variety is pretty completely developed by the end of high school. There is no clear increase in Stage 5 thinking from high school to age 25 and the slight increase in Stage 6 thinking is nonsignificant (p.<.20).
>
> The cross-sectional comparison of our longitudinal subjects at 24 with their fathers aged 40 to 50 also suggests that little development occurs after the early twenties. Our middle class college-educated fathers are slightly (not significantly, p<.20) *lower* on Stage 5 and 6 thought than their sons.

Instead, they reported the following conclusions: (1.) Some subjects at lower stages of moral judgment (Stages 1 to 3) continued to develop toward Stage 4 from age 16 to 24. (2.) Stabilization among the higher stage subjects was found with age. Higher stage subjects (Stages 4, 5, and 6) increasingly dropped out lower stage thinking with age; they became more consistently high-stage. "Adult development is primarily a matter of *stabilization*, a dropping out of childish modes of thought rather than the formation of new or higher modes of thought."

While they reported that the major change past high school was "stabilization" of higher stages rather than the formation of a new stage, they also reported that this "stabilization" was often a dramatic developmental process. Prior to stabilization at a higher or principled stage, they sometimes found "retrogression" or an increased usage of preconventional Stage 2 thinking. Under ordinary conditions, individuals are capable of using all stages below their own but prefer to use the highest stage they understand and are capable of using (Rest, 1973). They found, however, that at around the age of a college sophomore, individuals often did not seem to use the highest moral stage of which they were capable but, instead, made use of preconventional though previously abandoned.

"Between late high school and the second or third year of college, 20 percent of our middle class sample dropped or retrogressed in moral maturity scores. Retrogression was defined as a drop in moral maturity scores greater than any found in a two-month test-retest sample. This drop had a definite pattern. In high school, 20 percent who dropped were among the most advanced in high school, all having a mixture of conventional (Stage 4) and principled (Stage 5) thought. In their college sophomore phase, they kicked both their conventional and their Stage 5 morality and replaced it with good old Stage 2 hedonistic relativism, jazzed up with some philosophic and sociopolitical jargon.

"While these 'retrogressors' chose to use Stage 2 relativistic egoism, they had not lost their earlier capacity to use Stage 4 and Stage 5 thinking. This was evidenced by three facts. First, the retrogressors continued to use a little Stage 4 and 5 thinking. Second, when asked to give what the world would consider a high moral response to our stories, the retrogressors tended to give straight Stage 4 responses. Third, the retrogressors eventually returned to Stage 4 and 5, suggesting that these stages were never lost.

"The mysterious forces of development which led our 20 percent from upstanding conventional morality to Stage 2 hedonism set them all to rights. Every single one of our retrogressors had returned to a mixed Stage 4 and 5 morality by age 25, with a little more Stage 5 or social contract principle, a little less Stage 4 or conventional, than at high school.

"An example we cited was Case 65, or 'Raskolnikov.' As a 'retrogressed Stage 2' he was a 'Nietzschean' who, as a Chicagoan, went to a Southern all-white college and accepted a Social Darwinian racism. Case 65, previously Stage 4, had been the most respected high school student council president in years. In his college sophomore interview, however, he told how, two days before, he had stolen a gold watch from a friend at school. He had done so, he said, because his friend was just too good, too Christ-like, too trusting, and he wanted to teach him what the world was like. He felt no guilt about the stealing, he said, but he did feel frustrated. His act had failed, he said, because his trusting friend insisted he lost or mislaid the watch and simply refused to believe it had been stolen." [Kohlberg and Kramer, 1969, p. 108]

On reinterview in his midtwenties, he was a lawyer in a large city firm, living in the suburbs and espousing Stage 4 moral thinking.

The findings on "retrogression" and return to the social contract, the Kohlberg and Kramer paper interpreted in terms of Erikson's concepts of moratorium, identity crisis, and renewed commitment. After individuals had formed the capacity for morally principled thought, they still had to commit themselves to do so. This commitment often was part of the resolution of an identity crisis or moratorium in which the individual displayed "retrogression" in moral thought.

"This pattern of 'retrogression' and stabilization may be seen as reflecting Eriksonian ego development rather than representing the development of moral stage structures themselves. Ego development in the moral sphere is learning how to use the moral structures one has for furthering one's personal goals. From this point of view, modes of moral thought are structures developed in childhood, but the uses of these modes of thought, their significance for the individual self, are matters for late-adolescent development. Until late adolescence, children live within a world they did not make and in which the choices they must make are circumscribed. Erikson has made us familiar with the fact that Western society provides post–high school students with a psychosocial moratorium which allows them to live out either hedonistic or morally idealistic impulses (reflected in anything from life in pursuit only of pleasure to life in the Peace Corps) with a freedom they have neither earlier nor later in life. This moratorium comes to an end when inner establishment of an identity or outer pressure to take responsibility in a role of work and parenthood lead the individual to a commitment as a 'social contract' to a pattern of moral values now chosen voluntarily." [Kohlberg and Kramer, 1969, p. 110]

The interpretation of retrogression and return in terms of Eriksonian ego development was juxtaposed with the interpretation of the same phenomena as structural "stabilization." The Kohlberg and Kramer paper said that a Piaget-Kohlberg structural stage theory could only interpret the phenomena as "stabilization," not as adulthood structural stage change. What could be seen by structural theory only as stabilization could be seen from another theoretical perspective, the Eriksonian, as adult development. Accordingly, they suggested that if there were adulthood stages and adulthood development, they would have to be defined in terms of Erikson "functional" stages rather than in terms of structural stages or of qualitatively new patterns of thought and judgment, and the clarification of functional stages was a task for the future.

The Work of Perry (1968) as Complementary to the Kohlberg and Kramer (1969) Interpretation

While Kramer and I were unaware of it, the work of Perry (1968) suggested a position rather close to that of the Kohlberg and Kramer (1969) position. Rather than relying on Erikson's stages, Perry charted his own stages, stages of epistemological reflectivity. Using longitudinal data with Harvard undergraduates, Perry (1968) charted nine epistemological positions, designed to describe student attitudes to questions both of knowledge and of values. A summary of the positions is presented in Figures 6.1 and 6.2.

It seems clear that the radical relativism which characterized Case 65 represents Perry's position *4a* the "oppositional" form of multiplicity in which "everyone has a right to his or her own opinions on anything." Coming after position *4a* is 5, "contextual relativism," and successive positions are degrees of personal commitment measured against a background of contextual relativism. Recalling Chapter 3, it is clear that the line of development described by Perry is epistemological and metaethical, whereas our moral stages are stages of normative moral judgment. Furthermore, the movement through positions of commitment is less something definable as "hard" or structural stages and more something like the personal ego stages of Erikson, steps in attainment of an identity. While being a useful map of development in youth, the Perry work did not resolve the problem of retrogressions in our normative ethical "hard" moral stages, any more than did the Kohlberg and Kramer (1969) interpretation using Erikson's theory.

Case analyses did not seem to match up development in the Perry schema in a direct or straightforward way to normative moral development. For instance, analysis done after Kohlberg and Kramer (1969) indicated that Case 65 moved out of the Perry position *4a*, oppositional multiplicity, to personal commitments in marriage and work in a contextually relative position 7 without advancing to Stage 5 in our moral stage scheme.

Note: Figures 6.1 and 6.2 are excerpted from Perry, W. G., "Cognitive and Ethical Growth," Chapter 3 in Chickering, A., ed., *The Modern American College*, San Francisco: Jossey-'Bass, 1981.

Figure 6.1. Scheme of Cognitive and Ethical Development

			Labels
Dualism Modified ↓	Position 1	Authorities know, and if we work hard, read every word, and learn Right Answers, all will be well.	Basic Duality
	Transition	But what about those Others I hear about? And different opinions? And Uncertainties? Some of our own Authorities disagree with each other or don't seem to know, and some give us problems instead of Answers.	
	Position 2	True Authorities must be Right, the others are frauds. We remain Right. Others must be different and Wrong. Good Authorities give us problems so we can learn to find the Right Answer by our own independent thought.	Multiplicity Prelegitimate
	Transition	But even Good Authorities admit they don't know all the answers *yet!*	
	Position 3	Then some uncertainties and different opinions are real and legitimate *temporarily*, even for Authorities. They're working on them to get to the Truth.	Multiplicity Subordinate
	Transition	But there are *so many* things they don't know the Answers to! And they won't for a long time.	
	Position 4a	Where Authorities don't know the Right Answers, everyone has a right to his own opinion; no one is wrong!	Multiplicity (Solipsism) Coordinate
	Transition *(and/or)*	But some of my friends ask me to support my opinions with facts and reasons.	
Relativism Discovered ↓	Transition	Then what right have They to grade us? About what?	
	Position 4b	In certain courses Authorities are not asking for the Right Answer; They want us to *think* about things in a certain way, *supporting* opinion with data. That's what they grade us on.	Relativism Subordinate
	Transition	But this "way" seems to *work* in most courses, and even outside them.	
	Position 5	Then *all* thinking must be like this, even for Them. Everything is relative but not equally valid. You have to understand how each context works. Theories are not Truth but metaphors to interpret data with. You have to think about your thinking.	Relativism (Contextual) Generalized

***Figure 6.1*—Continued**

Commitments in Relativism Developed →

Transition	But if everything is relative, am I relative too? How can I know I'm making the Right Choice?	
Position 6	I see I'm going to have to make my own decisions in an uncertain world with no one to tell me I'm Right.	Commitment Foreseen
Transition	I'm lost if I don't. When I decide on my career (or marriage or values) everything will straighten out.	
Position 7	Well, I've made my first Commitment!	Initial Commitment
Transition	Why didn't that settle everything?	
Position 8	I've made several commitments. I've got to balance them—how many, how deep? How certain, how tentative?	Orientation in Commitments
Transition	Things are getting contradictory. I can't make logical sense out of life's dilemmas.	
Position 9	This is how life will be. I must be wholehearted while tentative, fight for my values yet respect others, believe my deepest values right yet be ready to learn. I see that I shall be retracing this whole journey over and over—but, I hope, more wisely.	Evolving Commitments

Figure 6.2. A Map of Development

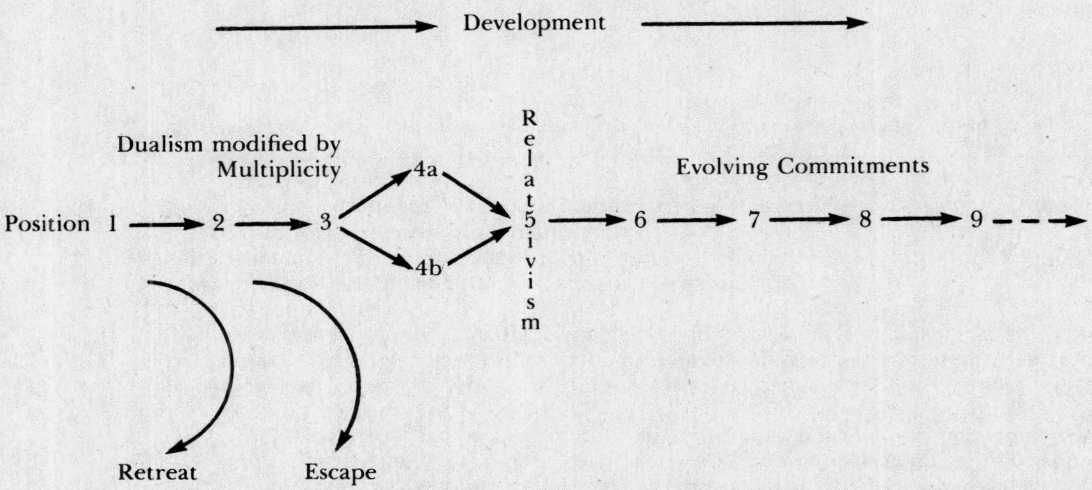

Terms

Dualism. Division of meaning into two realms—Good versus Bad, Right versus Wrong. We versus They. All that is not Success is Failure, and the like. Right Answers exist *somewhere* for every problem, and authorities know them. Right Answers are to be memorized by hard work. Knowledge is *quantitative.* Agency is experienced as "out there" in Authority, test scores, the Right job.

Figure 6.2—Continued

Multiplicity. Diversity of opinion and values is recognized as legitimate in areas where right answers are not-yet known. Opinions remain atomistic without pattern or system. No judgments can be made among them so "everyone has a right to his own opinion; none can be called wrong."

Relativism. Diversity of opinion, values, and judgment derived from *coherent* sources, evidence, logics, systems, and patterns allowing for analysis and comparison. Some opinions may be found worthless, while there will remain matters about which reasonable people will reasonably disagree. Knowledge is *qualitatitive,* dependent on contexts.

Commitment (uppercase *C*). A process of affirmation, choice, or decision (career, values, politics, personal relationship) made in the awareness of Relativism (distinct from lowercase *c* of commitments never questioned). Agency is experienced as within the individual.

Temporizing. Postponement of movement for a year or more.

Escape. Alienation, abandonment of responsibility. Exploitation of Multiplicity and Relativism for avoidance of Commitment.

Retreat. Avoidance of complexity and ambivalence by regression to Dualism colored by hatred of otherness.

NOTE: Figures 6.1 and 6.2 are excerpted from Perry, W. G., "Cognitive and Ethical Growth," Chapter 3 in Chickering, A., ed., *The Modern American College,* San Franciso: Jossey-'Bass, 1981.

Relativism as Moral Stage Transition: The Kohlberg (1973a) and Turiel (1974) Interpretation

By 1973, it was clear to me that neither appeals to Erikson nor appeals to Perry could salvage our post–high school data. While relativism and "retrogression" were the most striking problems, there were a number of other anomalies in the data which required developing or revising our stage scoring system and better differentiating structure from content in moral thought in stage definitions. Once these revisions were made, I suggested, a new conclusion arises, the conclusion that there are adulthood stages (Kohlberg, 1973a). Fully principled or Stage 5 thinking is an adult development, typically not reached until the late twenties or after. Structural development and stabilization are not two different things. That the apparently Stage 5 thinking of high school students was vulnerable to "retrogression" or was not yet stabilized was, in fact, evidence that such thinking was not really principled, or beyond the conventional Stages 3 and 4.

With regard to the first point, the theoretical status of regression, Kohlberg and Kramer had interpreted the apparent resurgence of Stage 2 reasoning in college sophomores as a "structural retrogression," that is, a return to a lower structural stage but a "functional advance." It was, they said, a functional advance in flowing from a questioning of previous commitments and standards necessary before these standards could be stabilized as "one's own identity." This question, in turn, reflected a new awareness of the relativity of value and choice, which was a developmental advance, though the response to it appeared to be a regression to Stage 2 instrumental egoism. They were suggesting, then, that one could regress in the service of development. In the breakup of one stage and the movement to a higher stage, one could recycle to an earlier position. This view, of course, is one held by Gesell, Werner, and other developmental theorists. Turiel (1974, 1977) held, we think basically correctly, that the apparent regression involved in stage development is a disequilibrium of transition very different than the disorganization or dedifferentiation involved in regression. According to Turiel, our relativistic "regressions" to Stage 2 are in a disequilibrated transitional stage in which the breakup of conventional morality is easy to confuse with the resurgence of preconventional morality.

The position taken by Turiel (1974, 1977) implies that movement to the next higher stage typically involves some questioning and some sense of contradiction within the stage in which the subject is currently functioning. In other words, the Piagetian equilibration model suggests that subjects will experience contradiction within their own stage of thinking, a sense of contradiction reflected in an unwillingness to make firm or generalized moral judgments. The outstanding indicator of such a sense of contradiction within a stage should be a sense of relativism, that is, a questioning of the validity of the one's ability to make moral judgments about or for others or for others to make moral judgments applicable to oneself.

Turiel (1977) reports some longitudinal verification of relativism as disequilibrium and as transitions. In his 1974 report, he studied fourteen undergraduates, five of whom he found to be transitional and relativistic. After two years, Turiel (1977) reinterviewed his original subjects. All of the transitional subjects, he reports, had become clearly Stage 5. The other subjects all were conventional on retest as they had been in the first testing.

In contradiction to Turiel's findings, not all cases of marked relativism or subjectivism are those of youthful disequilibration. This is suggested by a recent book by Fishkin (1983). Fishkin interviewed individuals in their thirties and forties, who had graduated from Yale University or Cambridge University in England. A number of these subjects held positions which might be called radically subjectivistic, and seemed to hold these positions because to them they seemed to be the only possible responses to certain metaethical questions or to metaethical difficulties about the foundation of any normative ethic. Fishkin devised a logical Guttman scale type scheme to classify metaethical positions presented in Figure 6.3.

According to Fishkin, his types represent an order of strength of claims about moral judgments.

Claim 1, the *Absolutistic Claim,* is that it is always wrong to violate moral principles and that this judgment of wrongness is rationally unquestionable (the claim of Kant).

Claim 2, the *Inviolability Claim,* is that it would be objectively wrong to violate principles, but not that these are rationally unquestionable.

Figure 6.3.* Fishkin's Ethical Positions

	I *Absolutism*	*II* *Rigorism*	*III* *Minimal Objectivism*	*IV* *Subjective Universalism*	*V* *Relativism*	*VI* *Personalism*	*VII* *Amoralism*
1. The Absolutist Claim	+	−	−	−	−	−	−
2. The Inviolability Claim	+	+	−	−	−	−	−
3. The Objective Validity Claim	+	+	+	−	−	−	−
4. The Universalizability Claim	+	+	+	+	−	−	−
5. The Interpersonal Judgment Claim	+	+	+	+	+	−	−
6. The Judgment of Self Claim	+	+	+	+	+	+	−

* Fishkin (1983), p. 16.

Claim 3, the *Objectivist Claim,* is the claim that principles or judgments should be consistently applied to everyone and are supported by considerations that everybody should accept if they are to take a moral point of view (the claim of Rawls, 1971).

Claim 4, the *Universalizability Claim,* accepts that moral principles or judgments may be subjective and arbitrary, but are bound by the condition that they are to apply consistently to everyone in similar situations (the claim of Hare, 1963).

Claim 5, the *Interpersonal Claim,* implies that the person not only judges for him- or herself, but judges for some others besides the self, though not necessarily in an universalizeable way. He or she might, for instance, judge others in the culture or group but not consider his or her judgments applicable to those outside it.

Claim 6, the *Judgment of Self Claim,* is that judgments can only be made by the person for himself or herself. Persons who reject even this claim are amoralists.

Fishkin claims that the Kohlberg (1973a) and the Turiel (1974) explanations of subjectivism and relativism as a disequilibrated transitional state between Stage 4 (conventional morality) and Stage 5 postconventional morality are inadequate. First, he points to the stability of some subjectivists over time. Second, he points to the fact that subjectivism and relativism may appear at other stages, i.e. one can find "Stage 3½," and "Stage 5½" subjectivists. Colby (1978) has described "Stage 3½" cases and in this chapter we shall describe a "Stage 5½" decisionist personal relativist. Most basically, he claims that subjectivism primarily is a posture or response to metaethical problems, not to normative ethical problems, a distinction elaborated in Chapter 3. In part we agree with Fishkin's distinction. Relativism and moral egoism are metaethical problems, not problems of what is right to be solved by an elaboration of a specific normative ethic. Subjectism and relativism will be metaethical positions found in historical and cultural conditions of low consensus on any basic moral norms or on any metaphysical or religious foundation for moral belief.

For all these reasons, we have given up calling relativism and subjectivism "Stage 4½," a transitional stage. We do, however, retain our conviction that some form of subjectivism or relativism is a necessary but not sufficient condition for movement to Stage 5.

This is because a conception of liberal tolerance and universal individual rights represents a Stage 5 principle that presupposes a questioning of the legitimacy or absoluteness of the culture's rule system (Stage 4). This chapter documents this relationship in depth. We have not yet studied metaethical positions in our longitudinal subjects who never reached Stage 5. We might note that the types of metaethical or moral epistemological positions assumed by youth and the conditions for their development is an ongoing research area occupying a number of researchers, including Fishkin (1983), Perry and his followers, Boyd (1980) Broughton (1982a), and others.

In analyzing our longitudinal cases, we arrived at a typology of forms of relativism that bears some relation to Fishkin's ordering, but comes directly from the qualitative data without implying a logically necessary order among the types. This typology is presented in Table 6.1.

As an example, Case 65 at time A, cited in the Kohlberg and Kramer (1969) article as retrogressing to Stage 2 after reaching Stage 4 in high school, in his college interview responded to the Heinz dilemma question, "Should Heinz steal the drug?" by saying "Do you mean legally or morally? Legally, no. Morally, yes—after all, all our mores are not laws." This appears to be a position V, political or social relativism. He was further asked however. "Is it a husband's duty to steal? Would a good husband do it?" He said, "It isn't a husband's duty; it is a husband's wish only. Terms like 'good' or 'bad' shouldn't be used."

Here Case 65 takes a philosophic position about the use of moral language that is what Fishkin calls amoralism or what others term moral skepticism or radical relativism. Moral prescriptions and moral language have no validity except as representations of the conventions (mores) of a group or the personal inclinations of the individual.

In line with Table 6.1, Case 65 at time A is classified as an example of radical relativism. As we noted earlier, he not only rejected moral terms as a sophomore but acted out his relativistic questioning of morality by stealing to "prove" the invalidity of morality. In Kohlberg (1973a), Case 65 was cited as a "Stage 4½," someone in transition from Stage 4 to Stage 5. In Turiel's (1974, 1977) interpretation, while every stage change would be expected to have some sense of contradiction and uncertainty, Stage 4's self questioning or

Table 6.1.

Radical Relativism *(Fishkin's VII Amoralism)*	*Personal Relativism* *(Fishkin's VI Personalism)*	*Egoistic Relativism*	*Political Relativism* *(Fishkin's V Relativism)*
1. Will not make prescriptive (right, should, duty) judgments either for another (Heinz) or for self. 2. Emotivistic—Believes moral actions and moral judgments to be simply the expression of emotions of liking and disliking, approving and disapproving; they are nothing more. 3. Explicitly states that decisions of self and other are relative to the individual or the individual's culture and therefore have no intrinsic validity. 4. Explicitly rejects moral or prescriptive terms like *duty, rights, good, bad.*	1. Can make prescriptive judgments for self but will not make them for another (Heinz). a. phrases moral responses in terms of what I would do in Heinz's place. 2. Emotion-centered—much of what goes into a moral action or judgment is based on the self (or other's) feelings about other persons. 3. Explicitly states that one's own and other's decisions are relative to the individual's values or culture.	1. Thinks one's primary responsibility is to oneself and that such an egoistic ethic is equally or more valid as a morality of regard for the welfare and rights of other persons. 2. Sees that it is possible for society to operate with individuals with an egoistic morality and thinks that, in fact, much of the world does operate in this way.	1. Believes that since societies vary and one's own society does not meet minimal conditions of justice is unwilling to make general prescriptive judgments for what an individual should do in his or her own society. 2. Takes an outside-of-society perspective which is not clearly grounded on a prior-to-society conception of principles or rights that should be universal across societies.

	Decisionistic Relativism *(Fishkin's IV Subjective Universalism)*	
	1. Hesitates to make a strict duty or responsibility judgment for another (Heniz) because of uncertainty that the self would really perform the right action when it entails sacrifice. 2. Axiom-centered—hesitates to say there is one rational assumption, principle, or axiom from which the good or the right can be deduced, many moral axioms are possible. 3. Explicitly states that ideals of the good life or life philosophies are relative to persons or cultures. Does not differentiate between relativism of good life ideals or life philosophies (teleologies) and relativism about rights and justice (deontologies).	

disequilibrium should be especially focused on relativism and egoism. This is because "Stage 4½" already has the beginning of the core of Stage 5 thinking, a concern for universal individual rights. While unable to articulate as a positive position Stage 5's principle of rights to liberty especially liberty of conscience, Stage 4½ has sufficient awareness of individual rights to doubt that morality should be prescribed for anyone including oneself. Stage 5 sees society's morality (and laws) as a contractual support for individual rights, Stage 4½ sees morality as society's imposition of its consensus or authority upon free individuals and accordingly rejects it. Case 65, however, did not develop some Stage 5 thinking until his forties, "retreating" into Stage 4 thinking after college.

The characteristics of radical relativism are summarized in Table 6.1, where it is compared with other kinds of relativism.

One of our longitudinal subjects who seemed to fit the Turiel formulation was the youngest subject to reach Stage 5, Case 2. Case 2 was Stage 4 (3) at age 17. As a college sophomore, "Stage 4½" relativist, he judges his high school Stage 4 position as conventional, saying, "I was trying to please the norms of society and, in essence, conforming to the prevailing thought about moral right. I was concerned about other people and society in general when I was younger. Now I think more of a moral responsibility to oneself. Self-concern takes precedence over morals."

As a "Stage 4½" sophomore, he is aware of two points of view, the "selfish" point of view and "society's point of view" and thinks each point of view can equally be said to be "moral." From his relativistic perspective, which point of view is more moral "depends on how you mean moral, too. If it is 'moral to me.'" Case 2 is a case of egoistic relativism as listed in Table 6.1.

At age 25, Case 2 seems to have resolved the conflict between "the moral" as Stage 4 regard for society and the "moral" as the individual's self-centered view. He has done so because he now has transformed the individual's self-centered view into a conception of individual natural rights and correspondingly recognizes society's demands as justified because they are based upon society's recognition of these rights.

His general responses about morality are as follows:

As noted in Chapter 5, a score of 4(3) represents a mixture of Stages 3 and 4, with more usage of Stage 4 than Stage 3.

Q.—What does the word *morality* mean to you?
A.—Nobody in the world knows the answer. I think it is recognizing the right of the individual, the rights of other individuals, not interfering with those rights, act as fairly as you would have them treat you. I think it is basically to preserve the human being's right to existence, I think that is the most important. Secondly, the human being's rights to do as he pleases, again without interfering with somebody else's rights.

Q.—How have your views on morality changed since the last interview?
A.—I think I am more aware of an individual's rights now. I used to be looking at it strictly from my point of view, just for me. Now I think I am more aware of what the individual has a right to.

Moving to a perspective prior to that of his own society, he identifies morality with justice (fairness, rights, the Golden Rule), with recognition of the rights of others as these are defined naturally or intrinsically. "The human's right to do as he pleases without interfering with somebody else's rights" is a formula defining rights prior to social legislation and opinion that defines what society may expect rather than *being* defined by society's expectations. Case 2 is able to apply this moral point of view in a consistent principled way to concrete moral decision situations, like the Heinz dilemma.

When Case 2 is 25 years old, he responds using Stage 5 reasoning:

Q.—Should Heinz steal the drug?
A.—I think he was justified in breaking in because there was a human life at stake. I think that transcends any right that the druggist had to the drug.

Q.—Did the druggist have a right to charge that much when there was no law setting the limit?
A.—He has a legal right, but I don't think he had a moral right to do it. The profit was excessive, it was ten times what he bought it for.

Q.—Is it the husband's duty or obligation to steal the drug for his wife if he can get it no other way?
A.—Again, I think the fact that her life was in danger transcends any other standards you might use to judge his action.

Q.—Why?
A.—Well supposedly man is the supreme being and we are the most valuable resource on the planet; it is important to preserve a human life.

Q.—Suppose it was someone dying who wasn't even close. But there was no one else to help him. Would it be right to steal the drug for such a stranger?

A.—It's something he should do. In order to be consistent, yes, I would have to say. Something he should do again from a moral standpoint.

Q.—What is this moral standpoint?

A.—Well, I think every individual has a right to live, and if there is a way of saving an individual I think an individual should be saved if he wants to be.

Case 2 illustrates a clear structural and logical progression from Stage 4 to "4½" to 5. In high school, when his moral thinking was scored Stage 4(3), he had accepted what in previous chapters we called the conventional member-of-society point of view. At Stage "4½" he questioned the right of society to impose its morality on the individual. Relativism was confused with a conception of individual rights. He equated individual rights with taking an ego-centered perspective. Continued reflection beyond his sophomore relativism led him to see that the underlying validity of egoistic relativism was a more general principle of respect for individual rights. Like the authors of the Declaration of Independence, he saw the legitimacy of laws as based on their function in preserving rights to life and liberty. This movement to Stage 5 did not lead him to absolutism but to a more moderated relativism. In response to the question "What does morality mean?" he answers, "Nobody in the world knows the answer."

The Role of the Phenomena of Relativism in Reformulating Conceptions of Postconventional Stages of Morality—The Substage Issues as Exemplified by Cases 2 and 65

The phenomena of relativism have been crucial to our locating principled moral thinking as a moral stage occurring in youth and adulthood.

In the previous section we discussed Case 65 as Raskolnikov while a sophomore at college. His first interview occurred when he was a junior in high school, on the student council and headed for class president. He seemed to be one of the most morally advanced of my subjects who were aged 10 to 17, and in the appendix of my 1958 thesis I reported his case in full as an example of Stage 5 moving to Stage 6.

In high school when I had scored him Stage 5 moving to Stage 6, he had answered the Heinz dilemma saying, "In that particular situation Heinz was right to do it. In the eyes of the law he would not be doing the right thing, but in the eyes of the moral law he would. If he had exhausted every other alternative I think it would be worth it to save a life."

Asked, "If it wasn't Heinz's wife but an acquaintance to whom nobody else was offering help, what should be done?"

He said, "If nobody else was doing anything, and the man was just lying there dying, I would still think it would be right. A human life is still involved."

This emphasis on a higher moral law based on valuing human life I scored Stage 6 in 1958. His response to the next dilemma, should the judge give Heinz a sentence, was, "If I was the judge taking these circumstances into consideration I would compromise and give him a very short penalty and try to help Heinz raise the money to repay the druggist."

Asked why send Heinz to jail at all, he said, "You have to protect the welfare of the citizens, too. Since the majority rules, you have to have the welfare of them—the people should be protected in some way, some small sentence."

This was scored as Stage 5, contractual democratic legalism. As the phenomena of college relativism led us to redefine the scoring system, Case 65's high school responses were scored conventional, Stage 3/4. Their principled-sounding quality we now interpret as representing substage B, the orientation of moral autonomy which recognizes the moral value of life as taking precedence over obedience to laws or authority.

As a college sophomore, as we noted earlier, Case 65 answered the Heinz dilemma by saying, "Legally, no, morally yes. All of our mores are not laws, but most of our laws are mores." In addition to this response, which we called radically relativistic, his whole interview was pervaded with radical and egoistic relativism.

Asked "Would you steal a drug to save your wife's life?" he says, "Who can say, would you?" Asked, "If you were dying of cancer, would you steal to save your own life?" he replies, "You're damned right."

Asked whether it was right to help an escaped slave before the Civil War, he said, "At that time slaves were chattel property, it was part of a logical and legal system."

Asked, "If a person's conscience made him think the slavery law was wrong, should he help the slave?" he responds "No, because you'll be behind bars."

Asked how about in a dictatorship like Russia, he says, "A dictatorship is just another form of government, a good dictatorship is probably the best form of government. A dictator's laws are just as good as anybody else's."

Obviously Case 65's high school ("Stage 6") respect for a higher moral law based on conscience and valuing human life for anyone and his "Stage 5" democratic legalism had disappeared with hardly a trace. In the college interview he was asked "Can you think of any action that you would consider wrong for yourself or others to do, whatever the environment?" He answered, "Well, an action could be illegal and wrong in the eyes of the majority of the society, but I myself wouldn't judge the person. I have a hard time thinking of anything that would be wrong, except maybe hypocrisy. I try not to be a hypocrite, and when I am a hypocrite, I know darn well I'm doing it. I may be achieving my own ends, that's how I feel now; I don't feel any qualms about it. The only reason I follow laws is that I'm afraid of spending ten years behind bars. There are a lot of people who just blindly follow rules, but I don't. I see the need for laws because otherwise there would be anarchy and piracy. Everybody owns something, and they want to protect it, so they make laws to protect themselves against the pirates of the world."

Asked, "Would you condemn the pirates?" he says, "I wouldn't pass judgment on their stealing—I would not condemn them for their act. But I might hire a few more guys to protect my rights."

Asked, "If there were no laws would you become a pirate?" "Yes, but wait a minute, if I became a pirate and I was lucrative enough I'd set up my own government."

Thus we saw Case 65 as a radical and egoistic relativist who still had a Hobbesian awareness of the need for laws to prevent the war of "all against all."

Later in this chapter we will return to Case 65 as an example of movement from Stage 4 to Stage 5 in middle adulthood at the age of 40. In contrast, Case 2, using our current scoring system, was the youngest subject to reach Stage 5, which he did at the age of 25.

Like Case 65, Case 2 spoke of "conscience" and or "moral rights" in high school, which had led me to believe that he had a principled perspective that was prior to social laws and conventions. The fact that this was not the case seemed evident to us in light of later relativistic questioning of his high school morality as merely conventional.

Case 2, you will recall, uses the notion of conventionality in talking about his previous high school opinions. His actual response to dilemmas like the Heinz dilemma had sounded principled to me using the 1958 system.

In high school, at age 17, he had answered the Heinz diemma as follows: "Should Heinz steal the drug?" "What he did was legally wrong but as I see it, what he did overruled anything that might have been legally not proper such as stealing the drug. Legally it wasn't right, but morally it was. Saving a life is much more important than the action that he took. We were put on this earth to live a full life, and we weren't put on to be put off again by what somebody else does."

"Suppose the husband doesn't love his wife?" "Yes, if he likes her or not she is still a living human being, she has as much right to live as anyone else."

In Kohlberg and Kramer (1969) his putting morality before the law and his perception of an intrinsic obligation to save life were interpreted as an example of principled moral thinking defining a moral hierarchy of life over law. In fact these criteria of moral prescriptivity, hierarchy, and intrinsicality are the criteria by which we now define substage B in Stages 2, 3, and 4, as was briefly discussed in Chapter 3. We can see, looking backward, that, while it is substage B, Case 2's high school Heinz response was structurally a Stage 4 orientation to rules of a legal and religious system. For instance, when asked, "What makes saving a life more important than following the law?" he said, "Well, religiously and morally, that's what. The First Commandment, one of the Ten Commandments, is 'Thou shall not kill.' "

Thus, his eventual rationale is in terms of a system of religious rules. This orientation to a system of legal and religious rules is confirmed by the fact that he says that the judge would have to convict Heinz because, "If the judge let everyone off free that committed an act of burglary there would actually be no justice. The judge is not supposed to be a philosopher, he is supposed to stick to the legal question involved. He'd be stepping out of bounds, if he didn't [convict him]."

As noted earlier Case 2's response to the Heinz dilemma at age 17 we now score Stage 4(3) substage B. His response to the dilemma of convicting Heinz was scored Stage 4(3) substage A. His response to the Joe and his father dilemma was also scored Stage 4 substage B. Asked, "Shouldn't Joe refuse to give his father the money?" he responded, "Yes, Joe earned the money, his father didn't, and Joe had a much better reason for using the money than his father did. If he gave him the money, it would open the door for more requests by the father and not keeping his promises." Asked, "Why should a promise be kept, any promise?" he responded, "Friendship is based on trust and if you can't trust an individual there's little ground to converse with him. By trust I mean you can rely on an individual to perform certain acts which you might request and you know that these acts will be done."

Just as in the Heinz dilemma, Case 2 at age 17 orients to moral rights, to a hierarchy of property rights and promises over authority, and to the intrinsic value and prescriptivity of keeping promises.

By the criteria stated above, he was scored substage B on two out of the three dilemmas on Form A, a criterion which defines him as substage B on that form. He was also substage B on Form B at this time and remained substage B in his following interviews, including his college sophomore relativistic interview. He first moved from Substage A to substage B between age 13 and age 17 and remained substage B thereafter.

In Chapter 2, "Moral Stages and Moralization," I briefly explicated the notion of substage B as consisting of the use of either the fairness or the perfectionistic orientations, each of these in turn being defined by a group of value elements defined in Table 5.3 of the previous chapter, elements basic to the construction of the standard issue scoring manual. This approach of defining substages by element did not work in the sense that the postulated greater equilibrium of substage B was not borne out, subjects moved from B to A as well as from A to B. The more global rating system for substage reported in Chapter 3 and in appendix C related more directly to one of our two purposes in defining substages, discriminating earlier stages of justice reasoning which "sounded" to us like principled reasoning from postconventional principled reasoning itself. (Our second purpose, relating moral judgment to action, is discussed in the next chapter.)

In Chapter 2 and in this chapter, we elaborate what we now define as Stage 5 principled reasoning by reference to the sociomoral perspective or justice perspective it employs. This conception of a prior-to-society justice perspective was missing from my 1958 scoring system, which identified principled reasoning with a differentiation of moral values such as life and conscience from legal and customary values and gave priority to such "moral values" in resolving the moral dilemmas. This now represents the core meaning of the autonomous, or B, substage of conventional reasoning. The fact that a conventional morality intuitively giving priority to moral values over legal and customary ones (the B substages) could be almost completely eroded by relativistic and emotivistic questioning and thinking indicates that criteria other than the priority of conscience is required to define principled thinking.

As Cases 2 and 65 illustrate, a number of the relativists we have studied thought that a morality of conscience was just as relative, subjective, and arbitrary as was the morality of conventional norms. Accordingly, the primacy of conscience found in our adolescent substage B cases could not serve as a basis for defining a new and equilibrated stage of thinking, which, for us, the notion of principledness implies.*

Is Postrelativist Moral Thinking Really a New Structural, Hard Stage?

A first question is whether a phase of relativism, emotivism, and egoism is necessary for eventual attainment of principled reasoning. This question we shall address in this section. In the following section, we shall address the data and reasoning which suggest that experiences of adult responsibility are conditions involved in the movement to principled moral thought. In Chapter 3, we noted

---

*We may note that our construction of substage to account for the existence of what appeared to be principled thinking in relatively earlier adolescence represented a very different strategy for stage definition and assessment than that employed by Loevinger and discussed in the previous chapter. Erickson (1980) and others have found occasional cases of gifted adolescents as young as 14 scoring at the I-4/5 and the I-5 levels on the Loevinger measure. The existence of young adolescents scoring at the "autonomous" or "interdependent" level is counterintuitive to the notion that achievement of an autonomous or interdependent I-5 level requires a certain degree of maturity acquired through life experience. Our circular bootstrapping approach between theory, measurement, and intensive case analyses of longitudinal data on a small group of ten construction cases like Case 2 has prevented the appearance of such anomalies in the larger pool of longitudinal data reported in the last chapter. We may note that, at the age of 20, when Case 2 adopted a relativistic and egoistic metaethical posture we tentatively labeled "4½" and "retrogressed" in standard issue scoring from Stage 4(3) to Stage 3 (as noted in Table 5.8 of the last chapter), he was scored Δ/3 on the Loevinger sentence completion test. Presumably the Δ or self-protective component of his Loevinger score reflected the same stance of relativism and egoism reflected in his moral thinking. Thus, if we had been developing an ego test as Loevinger did, we would have been led to make the distinction between an adolescent autonomy which preceded a relativistic-emotivistic or egoistic watershed and that which succeeded this watershed.

that the use of elements of both the form of Stage 5 reasoning and its content at Stage 3B and 4B led John Gibbs (1979) to question whether postconventional or Stage 5 reasoning was really a hard Piagentian stage at all. In Chapter 2, "Moral Stages and Moralization," we called Case 2 "Joe" and used him to illustrate the difference between a conventional and postconventional sociomoral or justice perspective in his responses to "Why respect property?" or "Why keep promises?" In describing his age 17 substage B responses to the father-son dilemma, we found his reason for keeping promises not only intrinsic (substage B) but Stage 4, taking the sociomoral perspective of the societal "generalized other," the perspective of anyone in the (American) society entering into a relationship with anyone else. In Chapter 2, we quoted "Joe" (or Case 2) when he has reached age 25 as illustrating a postconventional "prior-to-society" perspective to the question "Why keep a promise?" when he said, "I think human relations in general are based on trust. Otherwise it become everyone for himself. Everything you do in a day's time is related to somebody else, and if you can't deal on a fair basis you have chaos."

In this chapter we shall argue that the distinction made in Chapter 2 between the conventional and postconventional sociomoral perspectives and illustrated by quotations from "Joe," or Case 2, genuinely represent a new stage of moral reasoning rather than simply being an advance in abstractness and theoretical sophistication in giving answers to why questions, which Gibbs has interpreted the sociomoral perspective levels to be. He interpreted our notion of levels of sociomoral perspective as reducing the distinction between Stage 4 and Stage 5 to merely an increase in abstractness of answers to questions like "Why keep a promise?" That is, as justifying a societal moral practice, rather than as the radical change in justice reasoning operations we call a hard stage. Thus, such a difference in levels of response to why questions might reflect more the sophistication of a course in philosophy than a radical restructuring of justice operations. In dealing with this question, we may note first that in Chapter 2 we identified sociomoral perspectives in terms of "what was thought right" as well as with "reasons why something was right."

At first the distinction between "What is right?" and "Why is it right?" might sound like the distinction between content and structure made in the last chapter, in which we said our scoring method controlled for content as the norms and elements of Table

5.3 and looked at the form of reasoning about those contents. Such an equation would be incorrect, however, since *what* the element means is different at each stage, as we shall illustrate shortly from Case 2. This "what" differentiates Stage 5 reasoning from Stage 4 reasoning and more clearly demonstrates that Stage 5 is a hard stage of operational reasoning. First, however, let us consider the why.

When we compare Case 2's responses to "Why keep a promise?" at Stage 4 at age 17 and at Stage 5 at age 25, we see a generalization from trust as a ground for friendly relations to (1) trust as fairness and (2) trust and fairness as a precondition to society and human relations in general without which there would be chaos and no cooperation at all.

Clearly this is a shift to a prior-to-society perspective and to a social contract rationale for a social practice, the rationale that the practice must be agreed to in order to secure individual rights and the possibility of cooperation.

What assurance, have we, however, that that is a new way of justice reasoning rather than an accrual of cognitive and philosophic sophistication? First, with regard to answering "Why keep a promise?" at age 20 when Case 2 went through his relativistic and egoistic phase, his egoism was present in his response. He answers, "You can't trust a person who breaks a promise to you and friendship is based on trust. Well, losing friends doesn't seem to be as basic as I want to put it. You lose respect. If you want to get anywhere in life you have to be respected."

Clearly Case 2's "4½" relativism and egoism do not lead him to question the idea of respect as a socially shared and accepted way that people judge each other in society, though it may have led him to question the need to take moral responsibility for other persons. His answer to "Why follow the basic moral practices of society?" at age 25 is a very genuine reversal of figure and ground. At age 17 and at age 20 his answers were addressed to another individual making his way in society. At age 25 his answer to "Why?" is that of someone imaginatively constructing a society, that is, someone who can imagine what life without society would be like and who can imagine what society without moral norms and rights would be like. He rejects his age 20 egoism, "being responsible for me" in the given American society, for the notion that once and for all by participating in society he has contracted to respect and uphold the primary and basic values and rights constituting that society.

In ancient Greece, the relativism of the Sophists was the prelude to Socrates' acceptance of the social contract, even at the cost of death, as I discussed in Volume I. In modern society, we see youthful relativistic questioning as still necessary for constructing a postconventional adherence to the underlying justice structure of one's own or any society, a position enabling a person to answer the question "Why adhere to the core justice norms of society?"

Perhaps more convincing in seeing Stage 5 as a hard stage of justice operations occurring in adulthood, different from Stage 3B or Stage 4B adolescent moral reasoning, is its answer to "What is just?" as distinct from "Why be just?" This was most vividly evident in Case 2's response about Dilemma III', whether the judge should send Heinz to jail. It will be recalled that Case 2 at age 17 responded, "If the judge let everyone off free that committed a burglary, there would actually be no justice." In this response justice clearly is defined as regularity or impartiality in enforcing the written law rather than as a principle from which laws are generated and in terms of which the regular maintenance of the social order is evaluated. Justice is impartial social order. In contrast, when Case 2 has moved to Stage 5 at age 25, justice represents a concept of "justice as fairness" which should guide the making and enforcement of laws and normatively define the meaning of social order. On Dilemma III', Case 2 says: "I think he should let him go free. I don't think he should sentence him to jail. There is the legal right and the moral right and usually they coincide. In Heinz's case they conflict. The judge should weigh the moral aspect more heavily because the human life is more important than the drug."

Asked, "How do you feel about the law?" he says "If it's just. Without laws there would be chaos, there wouldn't be any order. I'm talking about just laws now, laws that are as fair to as many people as can be. I think some laws are unduly restrictive where they needn't be. Sometimes it's hard to be objective about it, a law seems just to you but it doesn't seem just to someone else. It's a question I can't answer very easily except to say, as I did, that it is recognizing the rights of the individual, first, to existence and, second, to liberty without interfering with somebody else's rights."

The sheer fact that at age 25, Case 2 says that the morality of life should weigh more heavily in the judge's decision than consistency of law enforcement could in itself be a conventional substage B response to the dilemma. The fact, however, that he continues to clearly articulate the notion that laws should derive from, and be interpreted in terms of, a principle of equity or fairness is postconventional. This is what he means when he talks about "just law" and the justice that a judge's decision should represent.

To us, Case 2's development in responding to this and other dilemmas at age 25 represents a new and qualitatively different way of justice reasoning that what he displayed at age 17 or 20. Justice is now equity and fairness rather than upholding the sociomoral order. It reflects not only a more sophisticated answer to the questions "Why maintain the moral norms or institutions of society like life and promise keeping?" but a new way of justice reasoning about these moral institutions and resolving conflicting situational moral claims.

Personal Experience of Moral Responsibility as a Precondition of Stage 5 Thinking: Case 2

So far we have used Cases 2 and 65 to illustrate two theses. The first is the Turiel thesis that relativism represents a disequilibration of transition from conventional to postconventional morality. The second has been the thesis that postconventional reasoning involves a transformation of reasoning which clearly implies a new "hard" moral stage. We want now to add a third consideration, first introduced in the Kohlberg and Kramer (1969) paper, that movement to principled reasoning relates to life experience of personal moral responsibility. This life experience in turn may be divided into two phases, a first phase of responsibility for self in contexts of moral conflict inducing relativisim and a second phase of social responsibility, often work-related, leading to consolidation of Stage 5 thinking.

In presenting case data on work experience,we will find that the transition from Stage 4 to Stage 5 may take a long time; it may not be the rapid process suggested by the Turiel (1977) data. We will also find that while transitional relativism is necessary for movement to Stage 5, it is not sufficient for movement to Stage 5. A case in point is Case 65, who went from radical and egoistic relativism to a return to Stage 3/4 thinking, then stabilized for a long period at Stage 4 during a time in which he worked successfully as a lawyer and had a family. Only at age 40 does Case 65 attain a scorable (greater than 25 percent) amount of Stage 5 reasoning. This case, and other cases, we shall explore in terms of the influence of work experience upon attainment of Stage 5. A second influential experience for a number of our subjects was the conflicts they felt about military service in Vietnam.

Before going into these cases, we will conclude our discussion of the transition to postconventional morality of Case 2. Case 2 was relatively eloquent about the experiences which precipitated his egoistic form of relativism.

Case 2 attributes his idea of "putting responsibility to myself first" as due to his move to college. Asked, "What accounts for your change to thinking more of yourself first?" Case 2 answers, "College mostly. You see what a dog-eat-dog world it is. Everyone seems to be out for himself. When you are living at home you are always trying to please your parents in some way. You may not notice it at the time but you are. I live at school seven days a week and I hang around with guys that I wouldn't particularly try to please as I would if I lived at home. After I came to college I stopped going to church. So did the other guys. They weren't getting anything out of it and I realized I wasn't either."

Case 2 was asked to elaborate his idea of a "dog-eat-dog" world, and responded as follows:

> Morally right and wrong is mostly platitudes, and adults usually don't believe that way themselves. I was in an accident last fall, someone ran into the rear of my car. The cop who investigated the accident said, "Do you have any injuries?" I said, "No." He said, "That's too bad, if you feel like you have to go to a doctor and see what he can do, it's a dog-eat-dog world." In other words get what you can, take a falsified doctor's report. I thought, "How true it is," but I didn't want to go through all the trouble. All I wanted was to get my car fixed.

Asked, "Do you think the world is a cruel place?" he answers, "Basically yes. That's just the way things are, it's realistic. I'm not going to get upset about it, I'll try to make the most out of it, trying to get as much for the car as I can without becoming totally dishonest or totally bad."

While Case 2 was quite articulate about the experiences leading him to ethical egoism, he was less clear about the experiences leading him out of "4½" to his Stage 5 view of justice and human rights. At the time he moved to Stage 5 he had been working as a chemical engineer, had married and was working part-time on a master's degree in business. He couldn't remember his previous interview, but said, "I seem to remember saying last time it was important for me to be successful. I've modified that, it's not important to be successful, but it's important to enjoy what you are doing, it doesn't have to be anything important if you are enjoying it. Before, I was more materialistic, get out and make that dollar. In my chemical engineering job I'm tired of what I'm doing, I am not really using my talents and education in the job. I have to do to the best of my abilities, that's why I'm getting the master's degree."

Four years later, in his last interview at age 28, where his Stage 5 thinking is even more consolidated, he feels his job as a young executive challenges both his abilities and his sense of responsibility.

We have stressed the fact that the movement to Stage 5 was a personal active construction of new operational moral logic rather than merely the theoretical reformulation of conventional morality at a higher level of abstraction and reflectivity than that used in the high school years. In this sense, development to principled morality we thought to be an even more active construction and commitment than movement through the conventional stages. Movement through the first four stages is, at least in America, a passage through stages of increased reconstruction of the existing sociomoral world, culminating in a Stage 4 understanding of the existing sociomoral order and a justice perspective necessary for maintainence of that order. In contrast, principled morality is not created or supported by sheer cognitive comprehension of the social and moral world, so that personal experience involved in movement to Stage 5 must, we believe, be of a somewhat different sort than the increasing complexity and equilibration of the perception of the world of family, school, and community characterizing development through the stages to Stage 4.

Though nondramatic, Case 2's example of the car accident in the context of college life indicates that his transition from Stage 4 to 5 was not like earlier transitions, a simple increase in ability to take society's point of view. In its first phase of increased relativism, it included an experience of awareness that society was not just in a context in which he had freedom to choose his moral (or amoral) responses without being subject to a disapproval by authorities or peers. In his movement beyond relativism to Stage 5, he reformulated his life goals from "getting ahead" in a "dog-eat-dog world" to "enjoying what you're doing," which included work that was both challenging and of use to others in the context of a social orientation to a world of honesty and the recognition of rights.

Some Generalizations About Cases Who Moved to Stage 5

Before going into further cases, we will note some simple quantitative generalizations emerging from our longitudinal sample. These generalizations are derivable from Table 5.8 of the preceding chapter. The first is the late appearance (age 24 or older) of any substantial (i.e., more than 25 percent) usage of Stage 5 thinking.

This finding is consistent with studies of experimental and control high school students in high school interventions designed to stimulate moral growth. These studies, reviewed by Lockwood (1978) and Higgins (1980), indicate that essentially no student attained major Stage 5 reasoning by the end of high school.

Cases 2, 14, and 23 were the youngest of our sixty longitudinal subjects on whom we have data through their twenties to show Stage 5 reasoning. They first showed Stage 5 thinking at age 24. This means that only 5 percent of our subjects used Stage 5 thinking by age 25. Three of our sixty subjects, Cases 17, 37, and 42, or 5 percent, first used Stage 5 thinking at age 28. Two subjects, or 3 percent of our sample, Cases 44 and 67, used Stage 5 reasoning at age 32. Thus, only 13 percent of our subjects reached Stage 5, and all between the ages of 24 and 32. We reinterviewed a few subjects at 40, and one, Case 65, had moved to Stage 5. Stage 5, then, is an adulthood stage.

The second generalization is that all of the 13 percent of our subjects who reached Stage 5 had some graduate education, for example, a masters degree or a doctorate in business, medicine, theology, law, or one of the social or physical sciences. This fact suggests that either or both advanced education and a prolonged moratorium from immediate work were a condition for the development of Stage 5 thinking in this American sample. Our interpretation of the role of graduate education in attaining Stage 5 in this sample is colored by two findings. First, graduate education may be necessary in our American sample, but it is not sufficient, for attainment of Stage 5. Of the twelve subjects with graduate training, five, or about half, failed to attain Stage 5 reasoning at all during or after graduate training. The other subject besides Case 2 who attained Stage 5 while in graduate school is Case 14, who had been in the Marine Corps, had worked for a department store in the security section, and had married during the four years between finishing college and entering graduate school.

Second, and more important, an additional finding suggests that it is not merely advanced education but actual experience of moral decision making and job responsibility following an advanced or professional education, rather than education itself, which leads to Stage 5 reasoning. Case 2, the case featured in our earlier sections, first displayed Stage 5 thinking while completing his masters in business and working as a chemical engineer. Cases 17 and 44, the two doctors in the sample, were scored Stage 4 while in medical school but attained Stage 5 thinking only after medical school and residency were completed and they were in a period they described as marked by high moral job responsibilities. Case 65 has been recently interviewed (in 1983) for the seventh time, at the age of 40; we will discuss later the moral responsibilities he perceives in practicing law and its relation to his movement into Stage 5 reasoning.

Continued Development to Principled Reasoning After Age 30

We shall briefly report a pilot study by Bakken (1983) of age differences in moral judgment stage in a middle class sample age 30 to age 55. This is the one of the few studies using the current scoring system that covers the middle adult years. Her sample included thirty-two males and sixty-two females. She used three age categories, 28 to 36 years, 37 to 45 years, and 46 to 55 years. Our attention will be focused on the males in order to project from findings in our longitudinal study. But we should report that sex differences were found with a significant correlation between education and moral judgment stage for women but not for men. These results point out the importance of educational experience for women's moral development and are consistent with the discussion of education and moral reasoning in Chapter 5.

For the purposes of this chapter, the major conclusion of the Bakken study was the increase in use of Stage 4/5 moral reasoning by males between age 30 (28–36) years and age 40 (37–45 years) and between age 40 and age 50 (46–55 years). None of her 30-year-old subjects showed any Stage 4/5 or 5 thinking. Ten percent of the 40-year-old group showed Stage 4/5 thinking and 50 percent of the 50-year-old male group were predominately Stage 4/5. While these dramatic cross-sectional changes probably are partly due to accidents of sampling, they suggest that our longitudinal findings of increased use of Stages 4/5 and 5 thinking in the twenties and thirties can be extrapolated to continuing increase through the forties and fifties. Similar findings of an increase in moral judgment Stages 4 and 5 from 20 to 40 are reported by Pratt, Golding, and Hunter, (1983).

In conclusion, the continued increase in the development of principled or Stages 4/5 and 5 reasoning after completion of formal higher education in the twenties suggests the importance of posteducational moral experiences in movement to principled reasoning.

The War in Vietnam

Before considering work responsibility, we should note an experience of significance to a number of our subjects, the decision whether to be drafted to go to Vietnam, and their experiences subsequent to that decision. This experience rendered very concrete both the issues of the justice of their own society and their personal moral responsibility for choice when social standards were questioned.

The disequilibrating role of the Vietnam situation is perhaps most dramatically caught by the story of Case 23. Case 23 attained Stage 4/5 at age 24 while in graduate school. At his graduate school interview, Case 23 said that at the end of high school he was very conservative like his father, but by the end of college

> I had become what you would call a contemporary liberal American. Then I went away to graduate school in London and became radicalized. It was a very turbulent year. The school was closed for twenty-five days and the British authorities blamed it on American students. I was studying political science, but all of a sudden I saw things not in terms of being harmonious, but I saw a lot of conflict going on in society and I started to think about it in that perspective. Then I came back and taught in an inner-city school for a year and I became further radicalized.

Case 23, of all our longitudinal cases, went through the most extensive moral and political questioning centering on the war in Vietnam. He saw his father and his upbringing as extremely conservative, saying, "My father has practically all the evils of American society wrapped up in one person, his military enthusiasm, his business orientation, and reactionary ideology. We spent our summers going to military conventions and riding in tanks, and that was part of existence, the military, the other was the business representing the capitalist part of his character and along with it the whole racial bit. Everything was all right if we didn't question. And then in college we started questioning and we knew what type of reaction we would get.

"Then when I was in London I got more passionately committed to a position, and when I came back I grew my hair and had a beard. My father was away and came home unexpectedly early and he just stood there with a gaping expression and then launched into this speech about my being a no-good hippie and he was a super-patriot. And he physically threw me out of the house and I was completely shocked."

Case 23 had been disregarding induction notices from the U.S. military, and his father had been able to aid him in this delay because of his community and military connections. His father was willing to help delay Case 23's induction on the condition he would go to Officer Training School. Case 23, however, decided to take a job teaching in the inner city "since I wanted some time off and I didn't want to serve in the Army; I could effectively serve both objectives by becoming a teacher."

Eventually, on the date of induction, Case 23 failed the physical. He said, however, "What I would have done had I not failed the physical is I would have refused induction and taken legal action, but I dismissed running away. I figured I would have a year or two to resolve my own conflict of conscience and what I would do about fleeing the country or going to jail or actually serving, though the possibility of serving was remote.

"I would go to jail because of the fact that I don't think I could serve without a conflict of conscience in the Army. In jail I would not be in an environment I could consider comfortable, what I would like, but at the same time I think I could live with myself a lot more than actually going out and serving in the Army, a system that was basically abhorrent to what I felt was morally right."

Case 23 at this time was scored 4(5) and was a political science graduate student at an American university. As might be expected from our quotations thus far, he exhibited, along with his moral concern about the war, much of the relativism and the outside-of-society perspective we have labeled "4½". In response to the Heinz dilemma, he said, "Heinz was justified [in stealing]. The druggist is just a participant in a capitalist type of society and hopefully Heinz could be outside it. Heinz would be outside the basic liberal norm that dominates both Europe and American and he would be in the same position as a black or a Chicano. He has broken one of the rules of liberal society in the sense that property is sanctified."

While Case 23 at this time has a perspective outside of American and Western society, this perspective does not yet clearly define the universal rights and values of Stage 5. Asked whether Heinz was morally right, he answers, "He is acting passionately moral. He is violating property rights in light of something based on the instincts, I guess, human passion."

Asked, "Suppose it was a case of stealing for passion but not to save a life?" Case 23 answers "I don't think there would necessarily be a difference."

Thus, Case 23's response exhibits one quality of personal relativism, emotion-centeredness, as defined in Table 6.1. A second criteria of personal relativism, cultural relativity, when accompanied by a description of the injustice of one's present society, we term political relativism (Table 6.1). Case 23 is willing to make a judgment that the current American society is unjust but is not willing to define some more universal principles of justice to which societies should adhere. Overall, Case 23 is representative of political relativism according to the criteria in Table 6.1.

In response to the dilemma about the captain ordering a man to go on a dangerous mission, he says, "The whole thing is buried in the context of responsibility, promise, and consent, and everything else that America has had as a society. I just conceive of everything outside that. So the situation is just completely outside of my frame of reference, so I couldn't say one or the other. Each person's conscience is different." On the Joe and and his father dilemma (Dilemma I, Form A), he says, "This is too abstract. Not knowing the position of the father, it is very difficult to answer, not knowing where Joe is at or his father is at." On these two dilemmas he refused to take a position, simply considering both sides, the father or the captain's (Dilemma V, Form C) authority and the son or the soldier's rights.

Four years later at age 28 his responses were scored as Stage 4/5. For a time he had combined community organization with working as a commodity broker to support himself. Then he had terminated work as a community organizer because of irregularities and conflicts of interest in the position taken by his superior in the community organization. Thus, he had partially reentered what *he thought* to be "liberal society," that is, a society centered on property rights and norms, to the extent of working as a commodity broker and rejecting the financial irregularities in the community organization operation. He felt morally obligated to both give evidence of the irregularities and to leave the organization.

He still maintained a fairly high degree of relativism but of a more contextual sort. He responded to the Heinz dilemma, saying, "It is difficult to comment on moral questions without taking account of the social and economic environment, which hypothetical situations do not do. There should be a society in which Heinz would not have to rob to obtain the drug, a society like Britain with its health service." He initially recommends nonviolent protest, arguing that robbery would lead to a bad precedent.

He goes on to say, "I think the moral problem one takes is going to be part of the type of society you live it. If you live in the U.S. you abide by the law as interpreted by the Supreme Court; if you lived in the Soviet Union the law or decisions would be part of the Government of the Soviet. On the other hand, if you are a representative of a small body of humanity that has principles that are so universal and just you might interpret it from another perspective. Where morality is dictated by the particular structures, who is to say what is morally right?"

Case 23's relativistic position at Stage 4/5 differs from that of the other longitudinal subjects in that it is highly politicized. But in both interviews he shares with other subjects the two basic characteristics of relativism, the unwillingness to make prescriptive judgments for others on many of the dilemmas and the explicit statements about cultural relativity.

The personal relativist centers on his unwillingness to prescribe for others the decisions of his own personal conscience. Case 23 instead focuses on the fact that a judgment of justice with some universal claims could be valid only if it were embodied in a just political structure. While he is willing to make judgments about the justice of societies and to condemn American society as unjust because of its capitalist nature, he is not able to make consistent or universalizable moral judgments about what a moral individual ought to do given what he perceives as the nonexistence of just society. He is unable to articulate the principles of justice which should guide a moral individual or a just society, that is, to articulate a moral prior-to-society perspective taken by someone with a more consolidated Stage 5 structure of reasoning.

Obviously our positioning of extreme political relativism as coming prior to full attainment of principled or postconventional morality rather than being consistent with it represents our own philosophic and theoretical perspective, one which is rejected by some of our critics discussed in Chapter 4, for example, Sullivan and Simpson. Our own position, however, we think will be supported by further longitudinal follow-up of cases like Case 23.

In our opinion, Case 23 is still in a process of development in his moral reasoning stage, in his thinking about issues of relativism, and in his moral life. His activity as a community organizer may have represented his hope to join "the small body of humanity that has principles that are so universal and just that you might interpret it from another perspective." Rather than providing a sense of helping society to move to more universal and just principles, his work was not even compatible with Stage 4 legal probity. At 28, his work aspiration is "to be in a position financially where I could sit and write critically about what is going on in the U.S." But in the meantime he has made an uneasy peace or a partial social contract with "liberal" American society and its property values. Seeing no possibility of revolution in America, he says there is no real option other than going along with the system.

A particularly interesting case suggesting the impact of the Vietnam War on development in the late twenties is that of Case 67. Case 67 passed through college and graduate school with no "identity crisis" and no real questioning of conventional morality. Interviewed at age 25, he had just received his Ph.D. in chemical engineering and was still Stage 4. An example of his thinking at this time is provided by his reasoning about euthanasia.

Q.—Why get the church's permission?

A.—Well, the church, of course, stands opposed in general to such mercy-killing and the church might look the case over and act as a mediator and okay it. I think, also, to some extent you have to get the authority of the legal government to concur, too. There is a commandment "Thou shalt not kill." Christ set up the church to, not speak for him, but certainly try to bring about his kingdom. As He set up the church, He gave the authority to men on earth to spread His word and act as His representatives.

At age 29, after a stint as a captain in Vietnam, he felt his moral views had changed.

The Army was a shock. I have a lot of personal views on the military. I just basically disagree with most of what the armed forces do in terms of rank, in terms of saying because a man is captain, he's got to be right. If it were up to me, in the best of all possible worlds, we could do away with the military.

Q.—How have you changed in your moral beliefs?
A.—Things are in more shades of gray and are not nearly as black and white as I used to see them in the past. Perhaps I am a lot less rigid in a lot of things, but a lot more rigid in my beliefs in the value of people. In other words, how can I say it, less "laws are laws" and this kind of thing.

While moving to a differentiation of the value of persons over rules, he says his judgments are centered on personal feelings and are not to be universalized. His thinking is well expressed by the following general statement he made about morality:

Morality is a series of value judgments. For me to say something is morally right means that in my own conscience, based on my experience and feelings, I would judge it right. But it is up to the individual, based on his individuality, to determine if something is right; it need not be right all the time. I guess what *I am saying is, I don't think I have a moral right to impose my moral standards on anyone else.*

In his response to other dilemmas he still was scored overall as Stage 4, but there were identifiable Stage 5 ideas in his thinking. Perhaps of greater moment, using the criteria in Table 6.1 to define personal relativism, he had become a personal relativist. He responded as follows to the Heinz dilemma:

I suppose if a person believes in the rules of society, no, he shouldn't have. I suppose if I were in his position with no other recourse I suppose I would do the same. It was the right thing in his mind, although it's against the law. It goes back to what the person himself feels. If you want to maintain society by law, no, you shouldn't. If it was myself, I would say there would be a moral justification for it based on my personal experiences and feelings.

Q.—Do you feel it would be morally right for anyone or is he the only one who can decide whether or not it is morally right?
A.—You can't say it's right for anyone in the situation. I don't think I can make a judgment looking at it through his eyes. I don't think I can generalize to anybody in this situation. I can make judgments about what I feel is morally right. I don't think that if somebody else's experiences are different I can say his judgment is right or wrong.

Q.—Would it be morally right in your view to steal for a friend?
A.—It would depend on the circumstance, and how I felt. I'd probably do it.

Q.—How about for an acquaintance?
A.—No I don't feel I would have any motivation to do it for a stranger. I suppose we have a common bond with all humanity, but the fact is the world is peopled by acquaintances.

Case 67's personal relativism at age 29 ceases when his own view coincides with that of society's rules and laws and he makes a Stage 4 judgment. Of mercy-killing, he says, as he did before going to Vietnam:

A doctor can't legalistically or moralistically do it. He had taken the oath of Hippocrates to preserve life. What I perceive to be the value of life, it would be morally wrong in my own judgment. We don't have the right to ask to be born and we don't have the right to ask to die, though that gets into religion which is another thing.

By age 33, Case 67 has moved to a more universalistic view of morality and was scored as Stage 4/5 on the standard dilemmas. He responded to the Heinz dilemma as follows:

He should steal the drug because life is more important than money or anything else in this world. Man can't create it, though he can destroy it. It's the one single thing that everyone has in common with everybody else. Maybe that's the way we see it in the Western world with the Judeo-Christian ethic. In Vietnam they do not value it so highly. But I think moral standards have to treat life as important. It is the person. Each person is unique and each has his or her own worth. Those tenets pervade our society with or without being raised in a faith.

Q.—Do you feel an Eastern society might be wrong then?
A.—I don't think that we in the West have a handle on all of reality. I think in this case we are correct in believing in the worth of the individual.

Q.—Do you think Heinz should steal for an acquaintance?
A.—I would feel that the personal value of his or her life overrides everything else.

We have tried to make two claims about Case 67. First, after a period of stabilization at Stage 4 through graduate school, the moral conflicts of his Vietnam War service caused disequilibrium in his Stage 4 framework. This disequilibrium was first manifested in a growing questioning and a growing relativism which we called personal relativism. Second, this was followed by movement to a position with substantial Stage 5 thinking and the decline of personal relativism in favor of a more integrated, universalistic perspective.

Less clear-cut than Cases 23 and 67 is Case 14. Case 14 in his college interview was scored Stage 4 and was in great moral conflict about being drafted to go to Vietnam. Asked about the Vietnam War, he says:

I don't want to go and I'm completely confused as to what we ought to do. We got into something we shouldn't have gotten into. I don't see how we can get out. The deeper we get in, the worse it gets. We made a lot of commitments to the people over there and we can't just walk out of it. So I honestly don't know. I'm completely confused. I'm trying to get into England as a graduate student. If they try to haul me back, I don't know what I'm going to do. I'd be inclined to tear up the notice, because I don't want to get myself involved in a war I can't be committed to. I hate to be put in the position of shooting it out with someone for a war I don't believe in and a situation I don't understand. If it had been World War II there would have been no problem there.

However at age 24, Case 14 tells us he had been in the Marine Corps. His experience in the Marines he describes as one of responsibility and of being required to take other people's points of view. He says:

Well, I ended up doing a lot of fairly high-level staff work and that doesn't hurt anybody. It teaches you organization and how to get things done on time. And to work with people, you know, different sorts of authority roles and get along with them. It was sort of interesting. I was in lots of places in Southeast Asia. . . . I came from a conservative family. I took my father's basic libertarian conservatism and moved it about three notches to the right, *which is total disregard for anybody else.* I realize now that if you follow that idea that you are not your brother's keeper, it's an easy moral thing to believe, because it relieves you from any responsibility for anyone else. I think that's basically why people follow it.

In summary, each of the cases we have discussed in this section, Cases 23, 67, and 14, came from a conservative background. The perceived injustice of the war in Vietnam led to various degrees of questioning of their own background, of the society, and of the objectivity of moral judgments. For each, however, the relativity issue was not immediately resolved by taking a stand one way or the other on Vietnam but required some further years of reflection and responsibility to attain some ability to make Stage 5 judgments in a manner which was tolerant but not in one of the modes of relativism described in Table 6.1.

Work Responsibility and Role-Taking as Stimulating Movement to Principled Thinking

In addition to relativism, we think work experience with a certain level of moral complexity requires a person simultaneously to take the perspective of individuals within a system and of the system as a whole and that this experience aids development to principled thinking. When the rules of a system or an institution conflict with the welfare or rights of an individual within that system, the person who is in a position of responsibility for solving that conflict must necessarily formulate ideas or principles which reccognize the just or fair claims of both in order to resolve the conflict and to act fairly and responsibly. A central aspect of work experience is role-taking. To what extent does a job allow, encourage, or necessitate empathic or moral role-taking rather than nonmoral or strategic role-taking? Who are the persons or groups whose role one must take—clients, peers, authorities, subordinates, the organization as a whole, or some combination of these constituents?

A second and related central aspect is the extent of responsibility for a fair or moral outcome. Does the job require that one take responsibility for decisions and consequences that affect others?

In combining these aspects we ask the following question: Does the job encourage one to use strategic role-taking with those in positions of authority over one, those *to whom* one is responsible or accountable, and to use empathic or moral role-taking with one's clients, peers, and subordinates, those *for whom* one feels responsible?

In general, we believe that positions higher in responsibility encourage moral role-taking more than do positions lower in responsibility. Such lower positions more often limit role-taking of superiors to strategic concerns about gaining rewards or approval and avoiding sanctions or disapproval. Needless to say, executives at the top of work organizations also may and often do engage in a great deal of strategic role-taking toward subordinates, but overall they do have greater freedom and opportunity for moral role-taking.

We will first use the only two physicians in our longitudinal sample to illustrate the role of work experience in movement to Stage 5. Both physicians reasoned at Stage 4 at the end of their professional training and after three years of work. Both, however, moved to Stage 4/5 on the standard hypothetical dilemmas while in the first decade of practicing medicine as autonomous physicians. In 1969, Case 17 as a pre-med student and Case 44 as a medical student both said the doctor should not mercy-kill the woman on the euthanasia dilemma. Case 17 argued that only God can make such a decision, and Case 44 argued it violated the Hippocratic oath. Both used much Stage 4 reasoning and showed no signs of personal relativism.

By 1972 Case 17 is 24, a medical school student and purely Stage 4.

> I personally think it is morally wrong to mercy-kill, but other people are strongly in favor of euthanasia. I think it should be left to the discretion of a panel of three physicians.

He has also become a personal relativist, saying:

> I am in a quandary right now. I've been through this and it's a real tough question. I've seen doctors do it to prevent anymore suffering for the patient and emotional strain in the family. I don't think I could do it, I'm against taking a life, *but I hate to put it in the morally wrong or right* [category].

Whereas earlier he recommended life imprisonment for the doctor, this time he recommends probation. The hard work of medical school adds a practical side to his relativism when he tries to decide whether the doctor should lose his license. He said, "You work damn hard for your license and then do something that you feel is right. I just don't know."

Case 44 at age 31 was older than Case 17 when he entered a period of personal relativism and scored transitional Stage 4/5 while a medical resident.

Before, he used the Hippocratic oath to say that mercy-killing is "something that is not done," but as a resident in 1972 he said:

> Okay, as I say, it is a fairly common situation. It's a situation that almost anyone in medicine long enough is going to run across more than once. From my own point of view, when a person is this sick and it becomes obvious to those of us taking care of him or her that survival is impossible, and they know there's no chance of survival, it becomes a kind of gradation of treatment in that it's very easy to say, "Okay, this person is having a lot of pain so therefore we will not withold any medication to make her comfortable." Now, there are times when the situation is exactly this, the amount of medication necessary to make her comfortable may very easily be lethal, and this is the route that we may very well take.

> Q.—And how do you justify it?

A.—You justify it on the basis that my job as a physician is first and foremost to make the patient as comfortable as possible rather than to say just dogmatically that my job is to preserve life at all costs.

So now we hear Case 44 give a contrary idea of the ethical oath he has taken, one that is embedded in a sense of his own personal responsibility for the patient's welfare.

In 1976 at the last interview time, both doctors used primarily Stage 5 reasoning. For the first time, both thought the *woman* should have the right to make the final decision.

Case 17 said:

Q.—But should she have the final decision?
A.—I believe if a patient is competent, knowing all the facts and everything, yes.

Q.—Why?
A.—I believe that a person should have the dignity to go out in the style that he chooses in his last 3 to 6 months and whether he wants to live in almost incapacitating pain. It's a value decision. I definitely feel that a person should have some say in the way he should die.

Case 44 appeals to the idea that being autonomous is uniquely human and has to be the basis for the decision:

I think that people should have the right to determine their own fate. That basically is what makes us human, having some control over our fate. If we can assume the hypothetical, nonexistent situation, and also assume that the woman has all of the facts at her disposal, and that she is rational, then I would say yes, she should have the right to determine her own fate.

Both doctors also felt the law against mercy-killing is wrong and should be changed, although acknowledging the complexity of trying to create a just law in the case of mercy-killing. Also, both doctors point out that in real life no doctor can with assurance predict someone's death, thus making real-life decisions more difficult than that posed by the dilemma. For them, then, the expertise that has come with being a physician has not provided the answers, but the experience of being a doctor has instead posed dilemmas that can only be adequately delineated, though not always solved, at Stage 5.

The concurrent increase in job responsibilities from medical student to intern, resident, and practitioner for the doctors parallels their development from conventional to principled reasoning.

Case 44 was director of anesthesia for a university hospital. His job in 1976 involved practicing anesthesiology, teaching, and doing administration.

He describes that doing his job well is fulfilling two major responsibilities, the responsibility of patient care and the responsibility of teaching residents and medical students. In his description, his relationships with both students and patients are characterized by moral role-taking. He said in response to questions about his responsibilities and his job philosophy:

I am responsible for seeing that anesthesia is administered safely and efficiently to the patients, that the patients get good care, in other words. Also, I am responsible for seeing that the educational part of the program is carried out, and when I administer anesthesia myself, I am responsible for the patient that I am caring for; overall I am responsible for all of the patient care related to anesthesia. I find that there isn't a conflict between the two responsibilities but that at varying times I enjoy them both and am glad to be able to have both types of responsibility, that I find it very satisfying to take care of patients and to administer anesthesia well. It is also very satisfying to see a resident learn how to give anesthesia. I am very satisfied when I do a case myself and it goes smoothly and the patient comes out of it well and the patient expresses the fact that it was a pleasant experience. I am also satisfied when a resident who has been under my supervision has the same experience and also when a resident in one way or another expresses that he is happy with the teaching.

He never spoke of his relations with other people in terms of his superior position as director or alluded to the hierarchy among staff that we know exists in the medical world.

Case 17 was 29 and a fellow in gastroenterology in 1976. While training in this subspecialty he spent his days consulting on patients with extreme gastrointestinal problems, deciding what diagnostic studies should be done, what therapy instituted, and actually doing many of the procedures he recommended.

When he was asked how he felt about his responsibilities, he described how they increased and were coming close to what he saw as the ultimate responsibility of a physician, the well-being of the patient:

I like having responsibilities, I mean being able to make these decisions; I feel very competent in my decisions, usually, and I find it to be a very rewarding and satisfying experience. I like undertaking these responsibilities and hopefully doing a good job. It is interesting, when you are an intern, you have less responsibility and with each passing stage you have more and more of the ultimate responsibility for the overall well-being of the patient, and right now I am getting almost to the top and I enjoy it even more so.

He saw the doctor-patient relationship as a personal one of friendship based on the ideas of trust and honesty, a characterization of both the moral functions of his role and the centrality and pervasiveness of moral role-taking as the means for carrying out his role.

I tend to go in with a very positive attitude and I tend to be very open, I tend to be very warm. I am convinced that the best way to attain a person's trust is to have these attributes and to take time and spend an extra five or ten minutes with the patient at the bedside, actually listening to their complaints, and relating to them, rather than giving them the feeling at times you are shrugging their problems off and saying okay, next, next, next. And once you have won their trust, you have won their respect most of the time, too.

Case 17's clear description of the moral function of a physician combines the aspects of moral role-taking and feeling direct and personal responsibility for the welfare of patients.

Later in the interview, Case 17 extends the realm of this philosophy of respect and trust to include his relations with the rest of the hospital staff.

I think the approach that I take of being open, personable, and trusting and spending a little extra time with patients, people you are dealing with, is very critical to your work. And not only does that mean patients, but it means your paramedical help, too, and everything else. You can only function as well as the other medical personnel, surrounding you, and if they are not happy with you, they can sometimes make life a little more intolerable, and you just—you have to permeate the entire atmosphere.

We have noted that both our doctors went through some degree of personal relativism while still scoring as Stage 4 when both were in graduate or medical school. Eventually both moved to Stage 4/5 after a period of responsible work practice. The experience of work responsibility after graduate or professional school appears to be less conducive to movement to Stage 5 for lawyers than for doctors in our sample. To clarify this point, we will take up again Case 65, the "Raskolnikov" of Kohlberg and Kramer (1969) and the sophomore radical relativist we discussed earlier in this chapter. As we noted, Case 65 was our prototype of radical relativism. We stated earlier that while Turiel (1977) reports a smooth transition from radical relativism to Stage 4/5 or 5 thinking in the college years, Case 65 did not develop in the way Turiel theoretically expected and found, that is, from a disequilibrated relativist Stage 4 ("Stage 4½") to Stage 5 by an internal process of re-equilibration.

From Case 65's "4½" position as a college sophomore he returned to a Stage 4(3) position at age 26 when beginning law practice in a corporate law firm in a large city. Between the ages of 26 and 36, he continued to practice corporate law, he married and had children, and his responses to the dilemmas stabilized at Stage 4 but continued to reflect his earlier relativism, albeit in the milder form we call personal relativism.

Case 65 at age 36 was scored as pure Stage 4. His Stage 4 combined with a moderate degree of personal relativism. When asked, "Should Heinz steal the drug?" he says:

> From his point of view, yes. I couldn't harshly judge him morally for having done it. If he thinks he should, he should. On the other hand, I couldn't judge him if he didn't. I couldn't say he was a terrible person morally because he didn't steal the drug.

Asked about stealing for a stranger, Case 65 says, "I can't answer that. Would I do it for a total stranger? That's a tough one. I wouldn't condemn for stealing for a stranger but whether I would do it, I really don't know. I would just have to be there at the time, I can't visualize that situation enough to be able to answer."

Asked, "If Heinz thinks its wrong to steal, would he be right in not stealing?" he says, "From his standpoint, yes. I couldn't say he was wrong. It's not like physics, so I don't see the problem at all. That it's being inconsistent to say that."

Then he is asked, "As a lawyer you know it's against the law for Heinz to steal, does that make it morally wrong?" he says:

> Of course not. . . . Even a law that's based on morality gets gray in many cases, and therefore, I would say that the law should be upheld because of the fact that we have to have some order in our society and therefore the laws should be upheld and Heinz should be found guilty and given a minimal sentence. So therefore I would not say the law should be flouted. The law should be changed and this would be a "cause celebre" to change the laws by the legislature, but he should still be found guilty.

Case 65 continued his mixture of personal moral relativism and a nonrelativistic legal approach to the family in Dilemma I. Asked, "Should Joe refuse to give his father the money?" he says:

I couldn't condemn Joe for whatever he did, morally I couldn't. Legally I am not sure of the law; I don't know enough family law to know what the law says on this subject. What I would do if I were the boy, I don't know.

Asked, "Why in general a promise should be kept?" he answers both in moral terms of maintaining the family structure and in legal pragmatic terms; he says:

A family situation is built on believing in each other and relying on each other. In general I think it takes on some practical aspects, too. It's bad business to be known as a promise breaker because then your reputation will be hurt and this is particularly true in my profession. To me that is the overriding standpoint, the practical one.

Case 65's responses to the hypothetical dilemmas is not inconsistent with his moral orientation to work, but the practical or strategic element comes out more strongly in his work interview. He is a trial lawyer who handles cases for large corporations with sums of money from $25,000 to $10 million as a member of a large law firm with 120 lawyers.

Of course I have a philosophy, every lawyer does. One, as far as the combatant aspect of litigation, I try to throw my opponent off balance in court. I consider my opponent an enemy, somebody to fight. That does not mean that I can't sit down and talk to him about things of mutual interest and that we can't swap data of mutual help. But when push comes to shove, he is my enemy. I can get along with him and be polite, but he is my enemy, and I think that every litigator has to have that attitude. When he calls up I instantly turn my mind and become circumspect.

Another thing, with my clients I am brutally honest. Quite contrary to how I am with my opponents. And thirdly you have to be somewhat of a psychologist in dealing with clients and witnesses and juries. And so I try to get inside the skin of these people to the extent that I can. And fourthly, I am very reliable. I make appointments, I return phone calls, or give a damn good reason why. I think I am very honest within my partnership. The only people I am at all cagey with are my courtroom opponents and other lawyers. But other than that I try to be reliable and honest and straight with partners and clients.

Case 65 describes his responsibility to his client as doing what his client wants him to do.

The only person I am answerable to is the client, who will say, "I demand that we settle this case, I'm scared to death of a trial, I will not try it, settle it for the best terms that we can," and of course, I do that. If he demands I try it, and he is going to pay me, I will try it.

Case 65 recognizes to some extent that his pragmatic and adversarial philosophy involves some clash with standards of fairness.

The big corporations have the money to not only get good legal talent but fight issues even though they are bad, they are on the wrong side. They have the time and money to fight them and I represent those big corporations and I do those cases. But there are times I feel like I am beating some little guy to death and his lawyer doesn't have the time or the money and my client does. So there is a certain unfairness in that. . . . I take advantage of the big corporation and the money that it has. So that's not fair.

How does he live with himself? Does he see himself as responsible for unfair outcomes in cases? No, he is articulate and convincing to himself that his job does not include being responsible for the resolution and outcome of cases. He lays the responsibility for fair and just outcomes at the feet of the system of law—the procedures of law, juries, and judges. This neat division of responsibility between himself as a lawyer and the justice system allows him to say he can cope and "so far I haven't had any real sleepless nights over the issue."

The issues of unfairness or the moral conflicts he sees himself facing in his work are two types—the extent of honesty with one's opponents and the taking advantage of the money and talent of his clients, the large corporations. He describes the first type thus:

I try to be honest with opponents in court, to the extent that it is my client's best interest. But the law lets me keep secrets and I do keep them. I do keep them, but I have had some dilemmas where maybe I should have disclosed something to an opponent in one way or another and I didn't. So that is always a continuing problem. . . . The law lets you keep secrets and lets you hide things, so I take advantage of that. The law *must* operate that way. Occasionally I have had some things I really didn't like having to do, but the client wanted it, and the law let me do it, so that I did it and it helped win the case. So that is just a thing that comes with the territory and the alternative is to get out and I don't want to do that.

The role of the law as a procedure to guarantee just outcomes is graphically portrayed in Case 65's discussion of what happens when the big corporation meets the little guy in court.

If the other side has a good case, it will win out in the end. He will have his day in court, because the lawyers are not slouches on the other side, and even though their client is poor they are quick enough to spot a good case and the fee agreement is such that they often get rich representing poor people. So I really don't feel that sorry for them. Also, I assume juries are fair. I have total faith in juries, they ultimately are very wise and they ultimately make the right decision, even though at the time I may disagree with it. They have a greater wisdom than you can possibly imagine. I don't think they ever make the wrong decision, given what they saw in court.

Case 65 implicitly also holds judges responsible for the moral resolution of cases, but not to the same extent as he does juries. He also shows less faith in judges. He says, "A good judge is nice. Not too many of them are good, maybe half the judges are good judges and a quarter of them are excellent judges. It is nice to see a good judge working and giving decisions and making rules, who knows the law and is intelligent and is paying attention."

Turning to the place of morality in his work, Case 65 explicitly states that to be a good trial lawyer one should make very few moral judgments. In answer to a question about the appropriate philosophy a trial lawyer like himself should have, he says:

Total flexibility, total mental flexibility. Not to say you are immoral, but—I am speaking strictly professionally, I am not saying it is good for the person—it is good professionally to be able to defend the indefensible, that is an excellent quality to have, I am not saying it is the morally good quality, and I want to tell you the best trial lawyers I know have that quality, they can defend anybody and sound halfway good defending them, which is another way of saying there are very few moral judgments at all and this is a good thing to have to be a trial lawyer; it may be bad as a person, it may destroy you as a person, but it is good to have as a trial lawyer.

There is one area of his work, however, in which Case 65 feels that people should treat each other fairly, that is in the relations among partners in his firm. Politics in his law firm he experiences as problematic, unavoidable, and something he feels he has learned to cope with. In other words, when the aspect of his work in which he expected morality to be a central component turns out to be otherwise, he reconstructs his expectations, moving them from the moral to the pragmatic realm.

I have got some senior people in my law firm, that I have had some bitter, bitter experiences with, that are almost traumatic, and which I am slowly overcoming and it has made me a better and wiser person. I haven't been hurt physically or financially because of the experiences, but the politics in a larger law firm, as in any large company, can be extremely vicious, because there is a lot at stake, there is a lot of money at stake, and prestige. . . . I find it dissatisfying because part and parcel of it is deviousness and dishonesty, which I don't really mind when I am dealing with an arm's length competitor in court—that is part of the game—but I do mind when it is within a group that is supposed to be analogous to a brotherhood, as it were. A partnership is about as close a business relationship as you can have with a person, a professional relationship, and it bothers me that among partners, there is—with certain people anyway—a good deal of not total candor; that bothers me. It still does and probably always will, I am just learning to cope with it and live with it.

In this interview at age 36, we have stressed that Case 65's Stage 4 moral judgment forms part of a work philosophy of strategic legalism, one which he is not entirely comfortable with. During this interview he also showed some signs that morality was moving into a more central position in his thinking about his work and his life. He feels that becoming financially secure has allowed him to think of being less self-interested.

I think unfortunately that most people act in terms of their self-interest to the maximum extent that their own moral code lets them. They stretch the code to the maximum extent possible for their self-interest. In my own case, it used to be that way, and I think it is now changing. I think morality, and I'm talking about a higher level morality, has become more important than it was. I know it's become more important to me than it was even three or four years ago. I'm not sure I'm unique. I think I have reached a point where a lot of self-interest has been satiated. Materially I have achieved all that I have ever wanted, more than I ever wanted, more than I ever needed. I think I'm not alone; unless a person is insatiable I think he reaches a point of thinking in terms of right and wrong more, in both what I do professionally and also privately. But three years ago I would have said that the only thing stopping my self-interest—the only limit—I won't kill somebody. Anything I could justify short of that I would do. Now I think of a moral question sooner in the problem than I have in the past. I guess I can afford to say no more or to do the right thing more than four years ago.

Seven years later in 1983 Case 65 responded to a written interview of the Form B moral judgment and to questions about his work. He was scored as Stage 4/5. When asked, "What does the word *morality* mean to you?" he answered:

I find this extremely difficult to answer, particularly in these times of no consensus as to codes of conduct. So to me it means a basic way of acting toward one's fellow man to preserve mutual respect and dignity and trust among humans.

Thus Case 65, finding no moral guidance in the changing and relative mores of American society, defines morality in terms of a fundamental principle of respect for human dignity.

As a lawyer, Case 65 still enjoys "the challenge, the competition, and the winning" of trial law. He also raises the same moral dilemma arising in his work, about "whether or not to disclose in a lawsuit the complete truth to the court or to the opposing side about a fact required, by law, to be revealed."

Although he posed the same problem, this time he resolves it differently. He says, "Each case is different. The pressure to win, from various sources, is quite strong. I prefer to reveal and then reconcile the adverse fact with my legal theory—make it consistent." His resolution of this work dilemma now gives greater weight to the moral obligation to reveal the truth in presenting his cases than was true at his earlier interview.

As was said before, Case 65 earlier felt the best trial lawyer was one who makes very few moral judgments. He felt this characteristic "may destroy you as a person, but it's good to have as a trial lawyer." He also felt at that time that some of the partners in his firm did not display much real moral integrity. Now in 1983 he has decided to differentiate himself from the going morality of his profession and some of his partners. He says, "I have met and worked with, and against, some incredible liars. It has affected me in that I try *not* to be like them—a reverse teaching device. More than once I was hurt in my feelings by them; I have become more hardened to their arrows yet endeavor *not* to treat others that way. It taught me some compassion and humility."

To summarize the moral history of Case 65, he was the most dramatic example of sophomore radical relativism and egoism, a development from high school conventional morality to college Stage "4½." His movement from Stage "4½" to principled or Stage 4/5 morality was not a process of smooth re-equilibration to a higher stage nor of the positive affects of higher education in law school. In the almost twenty years between being a college sophomore and becoming principled, Case 65 reasoned primarily at Stage 4 but retained a relativistic attitude, although it was the milder version, personal relativism.

Unlike the process of work moral decision making for our doctors, the relation of moral concerns and principles to work role expectations and success was much less positive and direct for this lawyer. This seems to be true for the one other lawyer in our longitudinal sample as well, a corporate lawyer who has reasoned conventionally at Stage 4 throughout his adult life to the last interview in 1983 at age 39. It is also interesting to note that this lawyer never went through a period of relativism of any sort during his youth.

While the role of lawyer involves a high level of job responsibility for these two men, it divorces the responsibility for defense from that for the fairness of the outcome of a trial, responsibility which is placed on the court system, instead. In addition, for them the role of lawyer clearly defines toward whom one should be empathic, honest, and open and toward whom one should act strategically. Thus, it would seem that different professions provide different incentives and opportunities for moral or empathic role-taking even though they are of the same high social status and responsibility. Finally, we want to point out that there does seem to be a fairly direct correspondence between these subjects' responses to the hypothetical standard moral dilemmas and their moral judgment orientation to their work situations.

The Effect of Relativism Without Higher Education

We have discussed our two physicians as reaching Stage 5 after actual experience of extensive job responsibilities, which we believe stimulated their moral role-taking thought about the patients and staff for whom they are responsible. There is, of course, not an automatic relationship between holding a position of power and responsibility and having one's capacity for and use of principled thinking stimulated. We will inevitably recall Bryce's dictum, "Power corrupts and absolute power corrupts absolutely." Marcus Aurelius, a principled Roman emperor, was succeeded by Caligula. American constitutional democracy and the bureaucratic and professional organizations of American society have attempted to develop an elaborate system of checks and balances on such abuses of power, a system last conspicuously seen in operation during Watergate. As our discussion of Watergate in the next chapter indicates, it was possible for the whole Nixon group to develop a "moral atmosphere" of individuals reasoning at the conventional stages to morally justify actions clearly in violation of both the basic Stage 5 principles implicit in the American constitutional system and of Stage 4 considerations of established law. Both moral development and moral action are highly dependent on historical and sociological variations in moral experience, most evident in our account of the role of the Vietnam War in the movement of some of our subjects to Stage 5. The role of both graduate school and subsequent professional responsibility in movement to Stage 5 does not appear to be a cross-culturally universal generalization. In the study of moral development on the kibbutz described in Chapter 9, subjects were found to develop to Stage 4/5 without either formal education past high school or visibly high job responsibilities of the sort we have just described. They did, however, go through a phase of personal relativism similar to our American subjects. On the Heinz dilemma, one kibbutz subject said:

> Yes, according to my values, but I have no right to come and tell you that you are not right. Every human being has his own set of values, his own morality. The more people agree on a value the more objective it is. It will be closer to the truth, though I don't know what truth. I can't say there is an absolute justice or morality. I am speaking from a specific time and place, and that is relative.

This subject and two other kibbutz subjects also reached Stage 5 in the early twenties. We may tentatively hypothesize that they have a sense of moral responsibility and moral role-taking in work, even in jobs which do not involve the life-or-death responsibility of physicians or the definitions of the responsibility in terms of care for particular others characteristic of the medical profession, because of the situation of egalitarian community in the kibbutz in which the work is embedded. Unfortunately we do not have work interviews on kibbutz subjects which might support such a hypothesis.

Speculations—A Relativity Crisis at Stage 5 and a Resolution at Stage 6

We have reported data indicating that Stage 5 is a genuine adulthood stage based on personal life experience, first of relativistic questioning, and subsequently of personal experience of responsibility and its conflicts. Our longitudinal data do not provide any clear evidence of still further disequilibration after consolidation of Stage 5 and its resolution by our philosophically postulated Stage 6. Even without direct longitudinal confirmation of our formulation, it is worth reporting some case data which illustrate our notion of Stage 6, although they do not in any way confirm it.

One, and only one, of our cases who was first scored Stage 5 at both age 28 and 32 expressed his Stage 5 reasoning with a growing sense of its relativity and of an existential gap between the abstract rightness of a Stage 5 orientation to universal human rights and a commitment to action.

At age 28, Case 37 responds to the Heinz dilemma as follows:

If I thought it would be any good, I would steal. My doing of it presupposes I think it is morally right because of the value of human life. That is, from a perspective, we are reaching for an absolute on this one. I don't think there is an absolute on this one. It is absolutely relative to the point of view the guy has.

Q.—Does the husband have an obligation to steal for his wife?
A.—As far as the role of a husband goes, no. I would do it and there is a covenant. Obligations are agreed upon, they are covenantal and reciprocal.

Q.—How about for an acquaintance?
A.—I cannot say honestly I would feel obligated to steal for somebody I did not know. There is an obligation for man to care for his fellow man, but I can't exist if I choose this obligation in every situation. Unless I want to be a Jesus and die on the cross, theoretically I am choosing to do this for everybody. It is difficult for me to talk about that except philosophically, because I am not ready to do that. Still, I get back to the original presupposition of life being more valuable than property. Either you take it seriously or you don't.

Q.—Should everyone acknowledge the value of life over property?
A.—No, I don't think everyone has to construct that. That is imposing my values on them. They may choose to pursue different kinds of life. Obviously I think my perception of it is best.

Q.—Should the judge sentence Heinz, or let him go free?
A.—He would have to let him go free. Because not giving him a sentence would contribute to the overall growth and development of a more humanistic society which valued life over property.

Case 37 is a completely consistent and articulate Stage 5 elaborator of the implications of the value of life over property. but he is also a relativist of a quite sophisticated sort, a "decisionist" relativist. The axiomatic value of life over property, like any decision, can be questioned as arbitrary and relative. His is one construction of a kind of a (good) life, but he cannot "universally impose my values on them; they may choose to pursue a different kind of life."

Philosophers in the deontic justice mode like Kant, Hare (1982), Rawls (1971), Habermas (1982), or ourselves (Volume I) would argue that, though ideals of the good life, or the limits of personal responsibility, must be left relative or open, there should and can be universal agreement or consensus about the basic conditions or principles of justice or fairness which persons with varying conceptions of the good life must share to cooperate with respect for one another. This is taken for granted in a somewhat unreflective way by the other Stage 5 cases we have reviewed, because they make their moral judgments primarily in the deontic justice mode in which a respect for tolerance beyond relativism is guaranteed by conceptions of universal rights and fairness. Case 37, construing moral problems as problems of personal responsibility and seeing moral choice as a selection of an ideal of a good life, is haunted by continued relativistic questioning, a questioning which may have led him to drop out of theology school, where he was at the time we just quoted him, to become a salesperson, and then to go into business with a relative. By age 32, his relativism became an even stronger refusal to make moral judgments except about his own personal responsibilities.

In response to the Heinz dilemma, he says:

> You can look at it from various points of view. I don't know about Heinz but if it was me, yes; because a life is involved that is close to me and important to me. If Heinz wants to, that's up to him. Each person has to make up his mind. If you have to have some kind of "should," I don't really care if he does or not. I would take responsibility for it myself. I can't say what Heinz should do. I don't think people have the right to tell other people what they ought to do or claim some absolute value.

We see Case 37's relativism as the most philosophically sophisticated form of relativism, one accepted by a number of existential philosophers and in social theory articulated by Max Weber. According to Weber (1946, p. 112), "In the area of ethical choice ultimate world views clash and in the end one has to make a choice."

For Weber, there are two maxims of conduct "fundamentally differing and irreconcilably opposed." The first ethic is an ethic of intention represented by the Christian ethic of *agape* or by Kant's ethic of a pure moral will, and the second is an ethic of responsibility or consequences based on the foreseeable results of one's action and not by the principle or intention behind it alone. The choice between these two starting points for ethical action is, in a sense, arbitrary or relative for Weber. Commitment to one or the other is an act of faith rather than a rational choice. As a decisionist, Case 37 seems to be saying that there are a number of possibilities of the good or of the good life, and choice among them is arbitrary. His hesitation to make his assertion of the value of human life universal or nonrelative arises from his awareness that such a universal valuing of human life opens up the possibility of having to lead an utterly sacrificial or exemplary life "like a Jesus and die on the cross."

Interviewed at age 40 in 1983, he had a sense of the rightness or nonrelativity of an action like stealing to save the life of a stranger together with a deepened sense of disquiet about his comfortable life in business, in its contrast with the moral demands and responsibilities of an unjust and suffering world to which his current life seems unresponsive. Pursuing a loosely Christian enlightenment through meditation, he seems on the threshold of a "spiritual journey" of the sort described in one chapter of Kohlberg 1985, in press, "The Aging Person as a Philosopher." In some sense then, Case 37 is, in his own words, "still reaching for an absolute" in his own life. A partial resolution to Case 37's decisionistic relativism is provided not by an absolute but by the constructivistic view of moral principles discussed in Chapter 3 and related to our conception of Stage 6. Constructivism, a basic feature of Piaget's genetic epistemology, is also at the heart of modern elaborations of Kant's basic position, such as those of Rawls (1971, 1980), Hare (1981), Dworkin (1977), and Boyd (1980).

As articulated by Rawls's article "Kantian Constructivism in Moral Theory" (1980), one major aspect of constructivism is "contractarianism," the notion that moral principles are generated and receive their validity through the agreements which autonomous, rational, and moral persons would arrive at. For Rawls, the specifications of these principles may be arrived at by the device of imagining each person to be in an "original position" under "the veil of ignorance" as to what place in society he or she would be in, in coming to agreement about a society's basic principles of social justice. As stated by Rawls (1980, p. 517) "We take our examination of the Kantian conception of justice as addressed to a response in our recent political history. The course of democratic thought over the past two centuries shows there is no agreement on the way basic social institutions should be arranged if they are to conform to the freedom and equality of citizens as moral persons. Now, a Kantian conception of justice tries to dispel the conflict between the different understandings of freedom and equality by asking which traditionally recognized principles of freedom and equality would free and equal moral persons themselves agree upon if they were fairly represented solely as such persons and thought of themselves as citizens living a complete life in an ongoing society?"

Closely linked to the respect for rights of life, liberty, and equality discussed by Rawls is the notion of "justice as reversibility" outlined in Chapter 5 of Volume I, which relates Rawls's decision process to the Golden Rule, the prescriptive role-taking or reversibility of "moral musical chairs." In the construction of Stage 6 in that chapter, I said that, first, the persons whose responses we call Stage 6 do agree on principles of justice, such as the two principles of liberty and equality of Rawls. They agree in their resolutions of moral dilemmas more than do Stage 5 persons. Second, Stage 6 persons spontaneously resolve moral dilemmas by entering something like Rawls's "original position" or impartiality. They engage in role-taking with every person involved in the dilemma. They imagine themselves as the wife and the druggist, as well as the husband, and they ask themselves whether they could live with the alternative choices. In a sense, they "play moral musical chairs" to decide what's fairest.

Using the Golden Rule, they imagine themselves in the druggist's place as well as the wife's. But then they imagine the druggist's claim if the druggist put himself in the wife's place. The druggist might put property before life, but not if he were to step into the wife's shoes. The wife places life before property; she could still hold that position standing in the druggist's shoes. In the original position, imagining they didn't know who they were, morally rational persons would usually agree, given common knowledge of the facts. Thus, Stage 6 thinkers come to agreement on the principles of justice which should guide moral choice (Volume I, Chapter 5).

Why is justice the central principle at Stage 6? Our conception of Stage 6 justice does not, itself, adequately define the moral value of love or *agape.* I return to this issue in Kohlberg (1985, in press). I point out that love involves us in the realm of supererogation, not duties on which all could agree. Of our various values, some define merely desirable actions, but others define obligations or duties. Choices that are moral obligations are choices not just for ourselves but for all people. Kant said that the idea of an obligation implied a categorical imperative: So act as you would want all humankind to act in your place.

Moral values are distinct from other values, such as values of the good life, then, in defining duties as universalizable. In addition, duties imply rights to which in some sense they are correlative. Ideals of the good life thereby develop, but ideals of the good life are not assessed by our justice dilemmas. In Chapter 3, I suggested that life ideals do not seem to be "hard stages" like our justice stages, nor do they need to be agreed upon, to require consensus, or to require they be universalized, as do principles of justice. Christians, Buddhists, Marxists, and liberal secular humanists seem to have quite different ideals of the good life, and can validly maintain these variations. Case 37's relativism represents his notion that he should not impose his ideals of the good life on others. In contrast, effort at agreement on principles of justice or fairness is presupposed for peaceful, caring, and cooperative relations between human beings.

Reversible role-taking, "moral musical chairs," is a component not only of Rawls's contractarian theory of social justice but of Habermas's (1979, 1982) theory of a universal communication ethic. According to Habermas an ideal communication situation is governed by norms or assumptions of freedom and equality of each communicator, a "nondominative" communication situation. In such an ideal communicative situation, reversible role-taking is lived out in actual dialogue among the parties involved in a potential conflict situation, with a resulting "discursive will formation in which each individual is willing to reconstruct his or her needs and preferences in light of the needs and claims of others." Such a universal communication ethic is broader than the Kantian contractarian ethic of Rawls but is obviously constructivistic and "contextually relative" rather than being absolutistic or rigoristic. In Chapter 3, I said both our own lack of empirical data and the current state of philosophic discussion led us to question our claim that a sixth stage principle could not be utilitarian but must be a "Kantian formulation of respect for persons involving a formal process of reversible role-taking different from the utilitarian calculations of maximizing average welfare or preferences in determining rules or principles to follow. The presentations of Hare (1981, 1982) and of J. C. Harsanyi (1982) indicate that formal use of reversibility and universalizable role-taking can be part of a utilitarian solution to justice dilemmas, whether based on an underlying attitude of universal care or *agape* or an underlying attitude to fairness or equality or respect for persons.

Furthermore, the two principles of utility and of respect for persons come close to yielding similar solutions to many moral dilemmas. In Chapter 7, on judgment and action, I show this to be true empirically for most of our standard hypothetical dilemmas.

With this philosophic prologue, we shall now present an interview which seems to represent Stage 6 reasoning. The numerous Stage 5 cases we have quoted resolve dilemmas by use of a hierarchy of rights and values, such as the hierarchy of the wife's life over the druggist's property in the Heinz dilemma. In contrast, a cross-sectional case responds to our standard hypothetical dilemmas in terms of a single, general, universal, and reversible ethical principle. The principle is the principle stressed in Volume I, the principle of equal respect, or treating each person as an end not as a means. She starts with the claims and rights of other individuals, not with their interests or wants, as do utilitarians. But her use of the principle clearly involves a sense of caring and responsibility that is slightly different from the usual stereotypes of Kantian principles of justice. Her principle, that is, integrates the mode of personal care and responsibility and the mode of deontic justice discussed in Chapter 4 in connection with the work of Gilligan. It should be noted that she is a 32-year-old woman with graduate training in philosophy, whom we will call Joan. Joan starts by framing the Heinz dilemma as one of potential communication and dialogue, the reversible role-taking stressed by Habermas.

Q.—Now the first question is, what do you see as the problem in this situation?

A.—The problem for Heinz seems to be that his wife is dying and that he's caught inbetween obeying societal law of not stealing and committing a crime that would result in saving his wife's life. I would like to think that here's a conflict for the druggist as well, in that the druggist has to make a profit, and assuming it's a capitalistic society, doing all those things that are a part of that. But at the same time, I would like to think that there is a conflict for him, too; of the fact that his desire to make money and fulfill his own desires are done at the expense of another person. There might also be a conflict for the woman as well in that she would prefer to live—but at the same time her desire to live is what is putting Heinz in the dilemma.

A.—And why do you think it's important to take into consideration the conflicts facing the other two characters in the situation?

A.—Well, because I think anytime there are conflicts in a situation . . . As soon as more than one person knows about a situation, OK, that there's shared conflicts and the conflicts of each person sort of play off one another. And I think that the conflicts can be resolved to some extent by kind of pooling—so that as soon as more than one person becomes aware of the conflict that there are automatically problems to be resolved by each, things to be considered by each; and each person then has the power to affect what happens in the conflict. If I were

Heinz I, you know, would keep trying to talk with the druggist . . . I have a hard time thinking of any decision as being static, and it seems to me that dialogue is very important and a continuing dialogue in this kind of situation. But if it came to a point where nothing else could be done, I think that in consultation with his wife, if he and his wife decided that that would be an acceptable alternative for Heinz, then yes he should. Because I think that ultimately it comes down to a conflict of duties . . . I hate to put it this way, but I really tend to think of things in a Kantian sense—I don't think that Heinz should do anything that he wouldn't be willing to say that everyone should do. And breaking into a store and stealing is not an action that can be prescribed for humanity, for our societal group as a whole. On the other hand, Heinz, I think, just by virtue of being a member of the human race, has an obligation, a duty to protect other people; I guess that's a way to put it. And when it gets down to a conflict between those two, I think that the protection of human life is more important.

Q.—Is it important for people to do everything they can to save another's life?

A.—No. I have this natural responsibility I'm talking about—to preserve your dignity, integrity, as an autonomous human being. And now when I think "Do I have a responsibility to save your life?" I think that depends a lot. If I'm walking down the street, yes, I would do anything I could to save somebody's else's life. I mean if I saw somebody walking in front of the car, I would jerk that person out of the way of the car. That would be the way I would react automatically. But, in other situations it depends. If you are terminally ill and you have decided that you would prefer rational suicide, or would prefer to not go through any more chemotherapy, any number of those things, I don't feel that I have the right to intrude on that position of yours, to say that you must take this chemotherapy, it's going to extend your life for a week longer, or a month longer, or something. I don't see myself doing that, no.

Q.—Let me ask you this question: In looking at the original situation of Heinz and the drug and deciding whether to steal or not, is there any one consideration that stands out in your mind, above all others, in making a decision of this sort?

A.—I would say that there are two things. The first thing is that no person has the right to make a decision that affects the dignity and integrity of another person without there being cooperative discussion among the people involved. Number one. The second thing is that, you know, in this very strange situation where it would come down to being, you know, the single person's decision, and I have trouble conceiving that as ever happening, then it comes down to preserving the dignity and integrity . . . and for the reason of life usually is involved in that, of another person. So I guess I'm saying that, well . . . I'm not saying that preserving life is *the* essential or ultimate thing. I think that preserving a person's dignity and integrity are the important things.

Q.—If Heinz doesn't love his wife, should he steal the drug for her?

A.—I don't think that he should steal it out of a sense of love. I think that Heinz should steal the drug, if it comes down to that far-reaching point, out of a sense of responsibility to preserve life, not out of love. I think responsibility, as I'm using it here, means a recognition of dignity, on the part of every living being, but I could narrow it down, if you like, to persons. And responsibility is really something that's entailed in that recognition. If I respect you as a creature with dignity and your own unique, special being, in recognizing that I won't intrude on you, I won't purposefully harm you—there's this whole series of negatives that go along with being responsible and there's also some positives. And that's to recognize you as being unique, important, and integral, in some sense, and to do what I can to preserve all that.

Q.—Suppose the person dying is not his wife but a stranger. Should Heinz steal the drug for a stranger?

A.—Assuming going through the whole situation again—you know, of talking and . . . sure, yes.

Q.—Is it a duty or obligation for Heinz?

A.—When I think of my being obliged, to do something, I think of another person as having a special claim, a claim that goes beyond the sort of minimal claims we all have on one another. To me that's obligation. And responsibility is what I naturally feel for every person. It's not imposed on me from the outside, it's part of my nature as a human being.

Q.—Is there really some correct solution to moral problems like Heinz, or when people disagree is everybody's opinion equally right?

A.—Well, of course there is some right answer. And the right answer comes out of the sense of recognition of other people in the ways that I described and out of a recognition of one's responsibility, well, to do a couple of things: to preserve all of the integrity, dignity, and to, in a general sense, act as you would like to see other people acting. I don't know really how to explain that except that when I do things, particularly things that I do not really want to do very much, you know, but what I really feel is the right thing to do, usually what sort of sets me over the edge and makes the motivation enough for me to do it has to do with, well, how would I like to see people in general act in this case. What do I think is right in general, and that's what I do.

We may summarize this interview around several points. First, this woman, Joan, believes in actual dialogues or communication and a correlated reversible role-taking or moral musical chairs in coming to a solution. Second, she follows Kant in thinking that a decision must be universalizable. Third, she has a single general principle for resolving moral dilemmas, responsibility to other human beings as autonomous moral beings possessing dignity and integrity. This single general principle is clearly distinguished from a general rule to preserve life since she spontaneously says that it need not dictate keeping a person alive under conditions such as our euthanasia dilemma (Dilemma IV). Fourth, this principle defines both rights and caring responsibilities, or integrates the two. Fifth, she is a nonrelativist but not an absolutist; for instance, she does not define the preservation of human life as an absolute in all situations, rather she has a sense of the features of a moral point of view which she thinks everybody should take to resolve moral dilemmas.

We will give a brief summary of Joan's review of her life in order to indicate some of the origins of her moral point of view and its relationship to her actions and life career. In childhood she suffered physical abuse at the hands of both her parents and felt a lack of esteem and respect which she translated into the thought "I'm just not doing a good job as a child" and somewhat later developed the strong feeling that no one should treat a child the way she had been treated.

During her later high school years, Joan became involved in both the civil rights and anti–Vietnam War protests and rallies. She spent a lot of time away from home and held various jobs. She felt this both allowed her to separate herself from and become independent of her parents and helped her to put into action an intuitive belief that every person has intrinsic value and should be respected.

Joan got married during college, and after finishing, returned with her husband to his hometown in the Midwest. She took a job with a local judge working with juvenile wards of the court. The judge was very strict in her treatment of the juveniles. One of the girl runaways for whom Joan was responsible ran away yet again and came to Joan's home for refuge. Without knowing the home life of the runaway or her reasons for running, Joan recognized that the girl had serious problems and needed counseling. Violating her work role and the court rules, Joan kept the girl for one week while she found a foster family and a psychologist willing to help. After these arrangements were made she took the girl to the judge and told the judge, "I know I shouldn't have done this, but here is the child, and I made these arrangements so that she can get help, and I believe it will be best for her."

The judge decided differently and sent the runaway to the state juvenile facility. Joan's job included driving the girl to the facility, which she did. However, on the trip she described a halfway house in the next state and gave the girl bus money. At a stoplight the girl jumped out; Joan stopped for a cup of coffee and called the court to report her ward had run away. Joan was fired but later learned the girl was, indeed, in the halfway house she had discussed with her.

Thus, rather early in her life she faced a dilemma formally similar to our hypothetical dilemmas which pit the welfare and rights of another against rules and fixed authority. Her resolution in favor of the runaway girl showed an effort, if limited and unsuccessful, at dialogue with the judge. Her resolution of the dilemma also showed moral courage and some sacrifice of her own interests.

Finishing this brief sketch of Joan's life, we continue by noting that after being fired she went to graduate school in education to get teacher certification. Joan then taught high school for two years, requesting and getting a diverse group of adolescents which included the very bright and the handicapped. She felt that she was successful in creating a classroom atmosphere of mutual respect and pleasure in learning. She considered this a genuine success, not so much for herself but for the moral values in which she believed.

At the same time, Joan's moral values became articulated for her in a graduate class in philosophy by reading Kant. She felt reading Kant's ideas was like recognizing that the beliefs and intuitions that she had long held within her could be objectively and rationally articulated and justified. To date, Joan has continued her career in education and has been intensely involved in volunteer work with troubled and abused adolescents and women.

Our presentation of this 32-year-old woman reasoning at Stage 6 is not strict evidence for a clearly theoretically defined "hard stage" grounded on cross-cultural and longitudinal data. It does suggest some of the themes of our ongoing empirical search for a definition of a sixth stage arising in adulthood, and our dissatisfaction, like the dissatisfaction of Case 37, with Stage 5 as a statement of the end point of development of moral reasoning.

Adult Experiences Involved in Moral Stage Development—Relations to Erikson's Views

If new moral stages do form as a result of adult experience, we need to understand how this happens. In particular, we need to integrate a Piagetian cognitive-structural model of experience leading to development with a model of adulthood personal experience. The bulk of moral stage development occurs in childhood and adolescence and does not require the extensive personal experience of moral choice and responsibility found in adult life.

Many findings support the notion that the experience necessary for moral stage development in childhood and adolescence is largely cognitive and symbolic and does not require particular kinds of personal experience. In using the term "cognitive," as opposed to "personal," we do not mean to oppose cognition to the emotional, the social, or the behavioral. The moral structures of judgment we study as stages can be hotly emotional, are manifestly social, and are related to choice and action. But in calling moral stages cognitive, we do mean that they are centrally *forms of thinking*, they are *generalized* and *symbolic*. However, we have noted that the experiences involving thinking that lead to moral development are not simply logical experiences. Moral stage development is not merely the horizontal decalage of logical thought to social situations. A formal operational adolescent, to attain morally principled reasoning, must undergo social and moral experiences which cannot be conceptualized as experiences that aid in transferring logical principles to social situations. They are experiences, rather, which lead to transforming modes of judgment of the morally right and the fair. Often, the experiences which promote such change have a fairly strong emotional component. As emotion enters into experiences leading to change, it is, however, the emotion which triggers and accompanies rethinking.

Because structural moral stages represent general forms of thinking, both the capacity for higher conventional stages and the preference for higher stages can develop relatively speedily in a cognitively and socially rich environment. A great deal of experience of personal moral decision and choice is not necessary for movement from one stage to the next in childhood and adolescence. Our tentative finding, however, that principled thinking does not appear until adulthood suggests that perhaps a different kind of experience is required for attainment of principled moral judgment than is required for attainment of the prior stages. While our cognitive-developmental theory stresses that children construct each new stage "for themselves," the sense in which the individuals construct the stage of principled moral reasoning for themselves is somewhat different from the sense in which they construct earlier stages. Up through Stage 4, each new stage represents a wider and more adequate process of role-taking, of perception of the social system. Principled thinking, however, is not a more adequate perception of what the social system *is,* rather, it is a postulation of principles to which the society and the self *ought to be committed.* To be principled in moral judgment is not just to cognitively "see" principles. It is to *(a)* see their ideal adequacy in spite of the fact that they are not a social reality to conform to, *(b)* see a basis for commitment to these ideals, and *(c)* at the same time, see a commitment to a real society in which one acts consistently with these ideals. This seems to require more than the vicarious experiences of role-taking sufficient for movement through the stages to Stage 4, which represents a fairly adequate cognition of the social system.

While our evidence is limited, there appear to be two different sorts of "personal" as opposed to vicarious-symbolic experience important in movement to principled thought. Both share common features, and both occur, at least typically, only after high school. The first experience may be the experience of leaving home and entering a college community with conflicting values in the context of moratorium, identity questioning, and the need for commitment. As we have seen earlier in this chapter, this experience itself may not be sufficient, and such moral crises as Vietnam may precipitate a "relativist phase" of the kinds we have described in Table 6.1. This questioning seems part of the process of movement to Stage 5 rather than a process of questioning of and commitment to morality separable from moral stage development itself, as either the interpretation of Kohlberg and Kramer (1969) or of Perry (1968) might suggest.

Until college, the adolescent usually lives within a world he or she did not make and in which the choices made are circumscribed. Insofar as there is movement to principled thought in the college or graduate school period, it is in relation to anticipated commitment. Only later, however, does the person typically have *(a)* the experience of sustained responsibility for the welfare of others, and *(b)* the experience of irreversible moral choice, which are the marks of personal moral experience in adulthood and which Erikson (1959) makes central to the development of the ethical sense in the stage of generativity. In this chapter we have chosen to illustrate these aspects of adult personal moral experience as they are manifest in moral responsibilities in work.

In summary, personal experiences of choice involving questioning and commitment, in some sort of integration with stimulation of cognitive-moral reflection, seem required for movement from conventional to principled (Stage 5) thought. It is probably for this reason that principled thought is not attained in adolescence. The Kohlberg and Kramer conclusions as to the "facts" of moral development in postadolescence were in essential agreement with Erikson's (1964) perception of the "facts." That paper supported Erikson's belief that the adolescent is capable of awareness of universal ethical principles, though only the adult can consistently *be ethical.* According to Erikson:

> Between the development in childhood of a man's *moral* proclivity and that of his *ethical* powers in adulthood, adolescence intervenes when he perceives the universal good in ideological terms. In adolescence, then, an ethical view is approximated. . . . The true ethical sense of the young adult goes beyond moral restraint and ideal vision, while insisting on concrete commitments to those intimate relationships and work associations by which man can hope to share a lifetime of productivity and competence. But this may engender its own dangers, the *territorial* defensiveness of one who has staked out his earthly claim and seeks eternal security in the super-identity of organizations. [1964, pp. 224–225]

According to Erikson, the ethical sense or power of the adult depends, not only upon resolving one's identity, but upon establishing relations of care or generativity toward others. In Erikson's view, when this generativity combines with a more inclusive identity with the human species, there may result a lived ethic which is universal or Stage 6 in our terms.

Our current data suggest that the original Kohlberg and Kramer (1969) conclusions that Stage 5 and 6 principles are available to adolescents as ideologies was incorrect and, accordingly, an Eriksonian distinction between capacity and functional use is not needed to chart adult development.

Erikson's formulation suggests that for all individuals there should be an adulthood movement from an "ideological" to an "ethical" orientation as there is ego progression through the phases of identity crises and commitment. In contrast, our current "single" view of development implies that the experiences of youth and adulthood lead to a "stabilized" or "ethical" use of moral judgment only in the relatively few adults who also move to a principled stage of moral judgment.

We wish now to introduce some broader basis of integration between our structural theory and Erikson's theory of ego stages in adulthood which our line of thought suggests.

Before suggesting lines of integration, however, we need to briefly review the differences between the two approaches, differences summarized in Table 6.2.

The first central distinction between the models is that the structural model starts with relatively rigid distinctions which the functional model slides over. These are the distinctions between

Table 6.2. **Erikson Functional and Piaget-Kohlberg Structural Stages**

Piaget	*Erikson*
Nature of Stages	
Stages are different structures for a single function, e.g., moral judgment, logical reasoning. Accordingly, later stages replace earlier stages. Experience leading to development is cognitive experience, especially experiences of cognitive conflict and match.	Stages are choices or uses of new *functions* by an ego—earlier functions or choices remain on background to the new stage. Experience leading to development is personal experience, especially experiences and choice of personal conflict.
Focus of Stages	
The developmental change is primarily a changed perception in the physical, social, and moral *world.* The outcome of movement is perceptual *change.* The stability of the new stage is not the result of choice.	The developmental change involved is primarily a self-chosen self-perception identification with goals. The outcome of a movement is relatively permanent and results in a *choice* or a commitment.
Later stages are more cognitively adequate than earlier stages: *(a)* including the earlier stage pattern, *(b)* resolving the same problems better, and *(c)* being more universally applicable or justifiable, i.e., in the universality and inclusiveness of their ordering of experience.	Later stages are more adequate than earlier stages, not in cognitive inclusiveness, but in virtue or ego strength, i.e., in their ability to order personal experience in a form which is stable, positive, and purposive. Attainment of a stage and adequacy of stage use are distinct, however.

"structure" and "content," between "competence" and "performance" (behavioral use), and between "quality" and "quantity" in development. Related to the rigidity of these distinctions is the fact that the structural model insists that *(a)* the nature of each new stage is a definitely definable structure, a structure defined by an internal logic, and *(b)* each higher stage is logically, cognitively, or philosophically more adequate than the preceding stage and logically includes it.

The second basic distinction between the stage models is that as we move from pure structuralism in defining stages, we turn to a psychological rather than a logical account of stages and of the sense in which a later stage is more adequate than its predecessor. This distinction between logical and psychological adequacy is, in turn, related to the third basic distinction, the focus of ego stages upon the ego or the self as that which changes and becomes more adequate with development. While both structural and functional stage theories hold that there is a parallelism between development of the self and orientations to the world, cognitive and moral stages stress the world-pole whereas functional stages stress the self-pole.

Piaget cognitive stages and my moral stages represent a series of increasingly adequate cognitions of a relatively constant physical and social world. The objective moral world the child lives in is grossly or basically the same throughout his or her development from the point of view of structural theory. The basic changes in the child's moral world come from the developmental changes in the child's perception of it. In contrast, the focus of the Erikson model is upon changing self. While the sociomoral world is more or less constant, the child's self, the child's competence and position in that world, is constantly changing. Erikson attempts to characterize these changes around an invariant sequence of challenges and accretions of a sense of the self's competence. These define an order of increased adequacy in the sense of an increase of ego strength, ego integration, or solidity of a sense of self-worth.

The self-focus of ego stages, in turn, implies another basic contrast between Piagetian or my stages and Erikson's stages, that of Erikson's focus upon choice. Stages of perception of the world cannot be defined directly as choice. In contrast, stages in the perception of and movement of the self are stages in a self's choice. Moral decisions and moral development may be viewed as either a choice (or change) in the moral self or as a change in perceived moral principles. The former is the central perspective of Erikson's stages, the latter, of our moral stages.

In summary, both the focus upon the self and the focus upon choice coincide with the notion of stages of an ego, of an executor or chooser who uses cognitive and other structures. In contrast, the focus of our moral stages is upon the form and content of "objective" moral principles, rather than upon the process of their choice, use, or application to the self. An "integrated" theory of social and moral stages would attempt to combine the two perspectives.

Erikson's ideal person has passed through the seventh stage of generativity and becomes an ethical person, an ideal corresponding to our Stage 6. There remains for Erikson's person a task which is partly ethical but more basically religious (in the broadest sense of the term *religious*), a task defining an eighth stage whose outcomes are a sense of integrity versus a sense of despair. The problem of integrity is not the problem of moral integrity but the problem of the integration and integrity of meaning of the individual's life; its negative side, despair, hovers around the awareness of death. This problem is also psychological.

Our discussion of Erikson's eighth stage in "The Aging Person as a Philosopher" in Kohlberg (1985, in press) is primarily an effort to make Erikson's concept philosophical, drawing upon Fowler's (1981) stages of faith. A first basic notion is that there is a postconventional religious orientation, as there is a postconventional ethical orientation. A second basic notion is that an adequate postconventional religious orientation is both dependent upon, and demanded by, a Stage 5 or 6 orientation to universal human ethical principles. As I have phrased the problem, after attainment of a clear awareness of universal ethical principles valid against the usual skeptical doubts, there remains the loudest skeptical doubt of all, the doubt of Why be moral? Why be just, in a universe which is largely unjust? That is, of course, one of the problems thought to be unanswerable at the stage of transitional relativism and skepticism. The Stage 5 answer, the social contract, is essentially a compromise answer, the answer that I pursue my own happiness socially or with due regard to the rights and welfare of others. While Stage 6 ethical principles offer a more complete solution to the problem of relativity of values than Stage 5, it has an even less complete solution for the problem Why be moral? There is a sharper contrast between ethical principle and egoistic or hedonistic concerns than there is between the social contract and hedonism. I have argued that the answer to the question Why be moral? at this level entails the question Why live? (and the parallel question, How face death?), so that ultimate moral maturity requires mature solution to the question of the meaning of life.

7. The Relationship of Moral Judgment to Moral Action

with DANIEL CANDEE

THE FIRST question raised by the study of moral judgment is that of the relationship between moral judgment and action. Blasi's (1980) recent work reviewing a large number of studies indicates that most studies do show a correlation between stage of moral judgment and action. The existence of correlations only sets the problems for moral psychology and for moral philosophy, however. It is the goal of this chapter to review empirical studies which help move toward a theory of moral action. A theory of moral action must be both a psychological theory and a philosophic theory. As I discussed in Chapter 3, the empirical study of moral development must start with some normative or philosophic assumptions, it cannot be value-neutral. At the same time, we believe that a normative philosophic theory of moral development may be developed through a "bootstrapping" spiral between refinement of philosophic assumptions and empirical findings. As in the study of moral judgment development, we assume that an action considered moral must meet some standard adequacy. But what is adequate or "virtuous" moral action? This is the question debated by Socrates and his partners in the Platonic dialogues, but it is as far from being answered today as it was in the time of Plato and Aristotle. Before elaborating our own philosophic assumptions, we will try to demonstrate the need for such philosophic clarification by reviewing the confusing and contradictory results found by Hartshorne and May (1928–30) in what remains the classic empirical psychological research on moral conduct and character.

The Hartshorne and May Studies

In starting these studies of moral character, Hartshorne and May were not explicit value-free relativists holding that whatever norms were held by a given group at a given time in a given situation were right. They did, however, start their studies by polling religious, educational, and community leaders about the basic virtues of morality, arriving at a list including honesty, service, and self-control. (The alternative would have been to start with some philosophically defined and justified principles, such as the principle of justice, of which honesty is a derivative or part.) Given this starting point, they did hold that the less frequently a child cheated, the better the child's character was with regard to the virtue of honesty. They also assumed that there was an internal cognitive and attitudinal component of honesty and the other virtues they studied, service and self-control. In a loose sense, they accepted something like Aristotle's assumption that virtues are both learned through habit and also cognitively guided. Plato and Aristotle thought that honest behavior is an expression of a rational principle of justice. Presumably a modern psychologist who oriented to the philosophic issues involved would set up an ideal model of just or honest action and analyze children's or adolescents' behavior in relation to this model. Hartshorne and May instead simply looked inductively at behaviors loosely corresponding to common-sense conceptions of honesty, correlating these behaviors with one another and with tests of moral knowledge and moral attitude. In the late 1920s Hartshorne and May (Hartshorne and May, 1928–1930), through a series of studies involving ten thousand children, hoped to show that some children would be consistently honest and others consistently dishonest. Their experiments allowed the opportunity to cheat on a number of experimental tasks conducted in home, school, and community settings.

Specifically, Hartshorne and May began their work with the following hypotheses: (1) adolescents could be divided into honest and dishonest types; (2) adolescents who cheated in some situations were likely to cheat in others; (3) an individual's moral behavior could be predicted from his or her verbal report of valuing a high standard of honesty and his or her knowledge of conventional norms of honesty.

Despite an elaborate series of studies, Hartshorne and May's hypotheses were, for the most part, not borne out. Their results showed that adolescents could not be divided into honest and dishonest types. Cheating behavior was not distributed in a bimodal fashion but rather was distributed in a normal bell curve around a mean of moderate cheating. Further, they found that cheating on one test situation did not predict well to cheating in other situations. The average correlation between different tests of honesty was low, $r = .25$ in the 1928 studies of Hartshorne and May (p. 383) and $r = .21$ in the 1930 studies (p. 169). Insofar as there was any order among tasks, it was in terms of riskiness. Tasks for which the likelihood of detection was perceived as high elicited less cheating. One qualification to these results is that where tasks were similar (e.g., two tests of eye-hand coordination) and were performed in the same setting (e.g., school or home), the correlations of cheating behavior were higher. The third hypothesis, concerning the connection of honesty with moral knowledge, showed an equally modest relationship. The median correlation between eight tests of moral knowledge and a composite scale of honesty was $r = .22$ (Hartshorne and May, 1930, p. 157). In our opinion, these studies indicate that one cannot define and study moral action with a purely behavioral approach. An alternative explanation, which we favor, is that moral actions involve an internal component. Two possible major components are, first, a moral cognition or moral judgment component and, second, a moral emotion component. We argue that the first component, and often the second, must be directly assessed in order to define an action as moral.

The reader's first reaction is probably to decide that Hartshorne and May overlooked the moral emotion component in their behavioral studies. Perhaps their studies did not sufficiently arouse an emotional conflict within their subjects.

The Moral Emotion Component

To start thinking about this question of why Hartshorne and May failed to find evidence of internal determinants of moral behavior, it would be helpful for the reader to actually take the test presented in Figure 7.1.

This figure presents the test and instructions for it as administered to schoolchildren. The test is an adaptation of Hartshorne and May's improbable achievement test of cheating. On the task, subjects are asked to place numbers in a series of circles while keeping their eyes closed. No one can place more than a few numbers in the circles correctly, so that a high score indicates cheating. In spite of this, you will hardly be convinced that anything basic about your honesty was tested by such an exercise.

Why don't people feel their honesty is fully indicated by such a test? There seem to be two sources of skepticism. One is that the

***Figure 7.1.* MacQuarrie Eye-Hand Coordination Test**

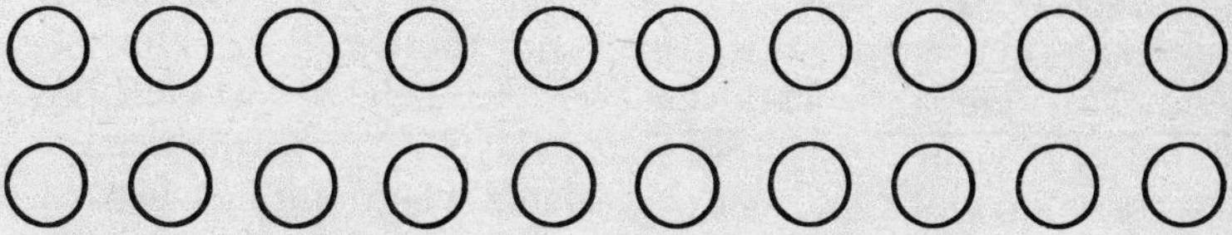

INSTRUCTIONS: This test is to be completed with your eyes closed. Place pen or pencil in the first circle. Then mark the first circle with the number 1, the second with number 2, the third with number 3, etc. With eyes closed move to the second row and insert the numbers 11 through 20.

test does not arouse strong motives either for or against cheating. Honest behavior results from a conflict between a temptation and a moral standard. A test of moral behavior should have a strong emotional component. The lineage of emotion in psychology's notion of conscience and morality comes from the prophets through Saint Paul to Freud's conception of the battle between the id and the superego. As expressed by Saint Paul, "The flesh lusteth against the Spirit and the Spirit against the flesh so that ye cannot do the things ye would." And all this has passed into many psychology textbooks; moral behavior is resistance to temptation resulting from the algebraic outcome of two forces, the lusts of the flesh or of needs, and the anticipation of the guilt of the conscience as mediated by an ego, self, or will. Thus, the first explanation we must consider is that Hartshorne and May's failure to find internal determinants of moral behavior was due to a test method in which subjects were not emotionally invested in following or violating a standard.

In an attempt to overcome this deficiency, Lehrer (1967) tried to create a moral test that would evoke "a battle of conscience." She built a ray gun test following Grinder's (1961) model. Grinder's gun was preprogrammed to yield a marksmanship score just a little below what was needed to get a marksmanship prize, a handsome silver-plated army identification bracelet. The 12-year-olds for whom the test was designed had the opportunity to fudge on their score a little to get the prize. Unlike the reader taking the circles test, these children might be thought to be thrown into a battle between their impulses and their conscience. In any case Grinder (1962) reports 80 percent of the children ended up cheating. As Saint Paul said, "Ye cannot do the things you would." Lehrer, however, was not satisfied with the Grinder design. She wanted to tempt the children even more, by a carefully programmed sequence of scores leading the children to the brink of success in a realistic but random fashion. The resulting electronic gadgetry cost a thousand dollars, but Lehrer and myself thought it would be worth it to get a real moral dilemma for the children. To our surprise, however, when Lehrer took the machine out to two junior high schools and ran one hundred children, only 15 percent of the children cheated, as opposed to the 80 percent who cheated with the Grinder model (Lehrer, 1967). In other words, our gadgetry had strengthened the conscience of 70 percent of the population. The machine apparently struck the children as being a computer that kept its own score, while the Grinder model did not. It is apparent that the 70 percent who cheat on the Grinder ray gun but does not cheat on the Chicago ray gun have hardly made a decision of conscience. Thus, even if we are successful in arousing stronger emotional conflicts based on the methodology discussed so far, we still have to conclude that moral behavior is essentially defined by situational factors, including expediency.

In Kohlberg (1963*a*, p. 292), I systematically reviewed the relation between measures of emotional strength of conscience or superego and Hartshorne and May types of measures of honesty or "resistance to temptation." I concluded, surveying over a dozen studies relating emotive measures of conscience strength to behavioral measures of honesty like Lehrer's that "the evidence fails to support the psychoanalytic hypothesis relating projective test guilt to actual resistance-to-temptation behavior. Neither fantasy punishment reactions nor 'total guilt' measures seem to be positively related to measures of behavioral conformity or internalized standards." Thus, we also feel that emotional arousal does not seem to be an internal determinant necessary to define moral behavior.

Cognitive and Attitudinal Factors

The simplest internal determinant of moral behavior is the individual's statement of what he or she should or should not do. This can be stated in either a general or a specific form. In the specific form it is simply the actor's judgment of which action in a moral conflict is right. However, such judgments are rarely recorded in studies of moral conduct. This is because until recently studies in this area examined behavior, such as cheating on an exam, in which it was assumed that all subjects would choose the same behavior as being "correct." Earlier, studies relating cognition to action began by measuring cognition in terms of a more general construct, moral knowledge. Moral knowledge refers to the actor's awareness of conventional moral rules, though as used by Hartshorne and May, it may include an actor's moral opinions and social attitudes, as well.

Studies in this tradition go back to the early part of the century. A number of researchers during that period devised tests which asked subjects to define moral words, such as *good,* and *right* (Kohs, 1922) or asked them to rank moral terms (Fernald, 1912; Brotemarkle, 1922) or moral behaviors, such as dancing, drunkenness, and flirting (Pressey and Pressey, 1919; McGrath, 1923). The culmination of research during this era was Hartshorne and May's attempt to relate some of these tests of moral knowledge to actual moral behavior. As reported above, Hartshorne and May found the correlation between any single test of children's moral knowledge and any single measure of their behavior to be low. The highest correlations ($r = .35$) occurred between tests in which intelligence played a major part. Partialling out mental age reduced the correlation to zero. Somewhat higher associations ($r = .39$) were achieved only when scales of moral knowledge or moral behavior, containing multiple tests, were constructed.

A particularly graphic study which dramatizes the findings of early researchers in this area was conducted by Weber (1929). Weber attempted to associate differences in moral behavior with differences in moral knowledge by comparing two populations. First, he asked women at the University of Texas (presumably his "righteous" population) to rank twenty-five vices in terms of their viciousness. Vices such as "gossiping" or "idleness" were considered to be bad, though they were rated somewhere in the middle of the list. Others, such as stealing and lying, were rated much closer to the top. However, the vice which was rated as the worst of all is one which few people even know the meaning of today. That vice was "sex irregularity." In order to show the expected relationship between moral knowledge and moral behavior the researchers then gave their survey to the most immoral group of women they could find, those at the Texas Penitentiary. To their surprise, the rankings were exactly the same. Though the women appeared to differ on gross aspects of their life behavior, they did not differ on what they "knew" to be right.

Research in the period following Hartshorne and May (1930 to the mid-1960s) placed moral cognition in the context of larger personality constructs, such as superego, conscience, or character. If the early research focused on knowledge of what an individual should do, that is, moral knowledge, later research focused on indications of the strength with which the individual would do or resist doing certain acts. This set of factors may be referred to as moral attitudes. Moral attitudes, during this period, were measured by the strength of guilt or self-blame or the denial of transgression in response to projective stories involving the violation of common moral prohibitions.

However, the relationship of moral attitudes to behavior was low, as suggested by my 1963 review. The conclusions of that review are similar to those of a review by Pittel and Mendelsohn (1966) which looked at nonprojective attitude tests as well. They conclude:

> A number of studies have shown low correlations, no relationship, or even negative relationships between values and resistance to temptation (e.g., Hartshorne et al., 1929; Mills, 1958), guilt, and resistance to temptation (e.g., Grinder, 1962; Burton, 1959; Allinsmith, 1960; Maccoby, 1959; Sears et al., 1960) and no studies have demonstrated that strength of moral values, resistance to temptation, and proneness to give projective guilt responses all co-vary. [Pittel and Mendelson, 1966, p. 34]

Thus, the picture of the relationship of moral cognitions to moral action painted by most researchers until the mid-1960s was primarily one of inconsistency. Inconsistency in intraindividual behavior (Hartshorne and May) and inconsistency between moral thoughts and behavior. This state of affairs led some researchers, for example, Grinder (1964), to suggest that we were dealing with two essentially different systems, one a system of moral thought and the other a system of moral behavior. We may learn on a verbal level that certain actions are supposed to be right, but we learn on a situational level that other actions can be rewarded as actually being right.

Similar conclusions are drawn by Brown and Herrnstein (1975) in a well-written introductory psychology chapter on moral reasoning and moral action. This chapter plays off Kohlberg kinds of studies of moral reasoning with social psychology kinds of studies by Milgram, Zimbardo, Latane, and others, which suggest that undergraduates and adults act immorally despite their moral judgment action capacities under suitable institutional and situational incentives and pressures.

In their introductory psychology textbook, Brown and Herrnstein call the relation of moral judgment to moral action a paradox and state the paradox as follows:

> This is a chapter about a paradox. Students of the development of moral reasoning in children and young people have found that a great majority attains a conventional "law and order" morality, which involves obeying the laws and trying to treat people decently. In the same research period, students of social psychology have outdone one another in discovering that in certain circumstances respectable young people are capable of deceitful conformity, vandalism, and indifference to life-and-death problems of strangers who ask for help, are capable even of endangering the lives of others. For the most part, the subjects in the developmental studies and in the social psychological studies were drawn from the same population—American young people, especially college students. Therein lies the paradox.
>
> The two kinds of psychologists—developmental and social—seldom read each other's work, and since their studies are described in different courses, the paradox has largely gone unnoticed. But if a young person believes in being lawful and decent, how can he sometimes lie, destroy property, ignore a threatened stranger, and be willing to endanger another's life?
>
> Actually, there is no paradox unless you make a certain assumption. You must assume that the way people think about moral issues determines the way you act. You must believe act and thought are normally in harmony. If you do not, then there is neither paradox nor even surprise in someone talking on the high road and acting on the low road. [Brown and Herrnstein, 1975, p. 289]

Brown and Herrnstein resolve the paradox by assuming a two-track theory of moral learning and development. Moral judgment, they think, develops according to Piagetian principles of cognitive conflict and sequential stage reorganizations. In contrast, moral action develops or is learned through some other process, possibly the laws of situational social learning and reinforcement discussed by a variety of social learning theories.

In contrast, reviewing some of the social psychological studies described by Brown and Herrnstein, we see moral development as a single-track process. In our view moral judgment development both causes moral action and arises out of moral action itself. A new moral judgment may guide new behavior while the performance of a new behavior may lead one to construct a new moral judgment. In either case, however, there is a unitary developmental process involved in the development of both judgment and action.

Before elaborating our own view, however, we should call attention to the philosophic implications for the social behavioristic approach to moral character, or virtue, of positing a lack of relation between judgment and action. Behavioristically, Hartshorne and May did not find a clear or strong character factor or virtue of honesty, though Burton (1963) has reanalyzed their correlations in a way that suggests a small factor or pattern of consistency or honesty in their data. The repeated finding of low correlations between the content of moral cognitions and behavior indicates that these measures of both moral cognition and moral behavior fail to define a moral virtue or a trait of honesty worthy of a judgment of positive moral worth.

It may be noted that infants and dogs are not considered to be morally virtuous, because they are assumed not to have the capacity for moral judgment. If studies of the content of moral cognitions and attitudes have little relation to behavioristic measures, we must doubt whether either set of measures allow us to assume the existence of moral virtues or character. Psychologists are quick to write off moral cognitive assessments if they have no relation to conduct measures, but if they considered philosophic concepts of morality, they would be forced to acknowledge that they would also have to write off the behavior measures as well. This is, indeed, the stance taken by thoughtful and "pure" behaviorists like Skinner (1971) and Gewirtz (1969), who view "morality" as a conventional labeling or language behavior which is simply, like any other behavior, situational behavior under the control of situational social reinforcement.

Putting the matter in slightly different terms, philosophical analysis of ordinary moral language (for example, Hare 1963), indicates that moral virtue terms imply a cognitive component to virtue. Clear and consistent behaviorists like Skinner and Gewirtz treat moral language as useless to a scientific psychologist, as "prescientific (as does James Gilligan [1976] on the psychoanalytic side), and replace it with a morally neutral scientific language which is "Beyond Freedom and Dignity." This seems to us the only legitimate stance for a behaviorist in light of the data from Hartshorne and May onward. Such a stance may indeed lead to prediction and control, the goals of positivistic psychology, but it cannot lead to a theory for judging moral action.

Reasons for the Failure of Hartshorne and May to Define Character

From our point of view, the philosophic mistake of Hartshorne and May was to define both their measures of moral judgment and their measures of moral behavior in terms of a culturally relative definition of a "bag of virtues," a definition I critiqued in Volume I. As we noted, some of these virtues have almost disappeared from the American scene since Hartshorne and May's time, like sexual purity or absence of "sexual irregularity" rated as "worst" by Weber's (1926) subjects. "Honesty" is a more historically universal value, but its definition is individually, historically, and culturally relative. It does not appear in the lists of Plato or Aristotle, who would subsume it under justice. Diogenes searched Greece with a lamp looking for an honest man but could not find one. Diogenes' research was confirmed by Hartshorne and May, who could not find an honest child among their ten thousand. Presumably Diogenes thought he himself passed the test of honesty, but Hartshorne and May failed their own test. Seeking to find scientific truth about morality they lied to ten thousand children, saying they were giving them tests of intelligence and achievement while they were secretly trying to catch them cheating. Their behavior was consistent with their socially altruistic moral values involving establishing a social scientific base for moral education. It was, however, inconsistent with their socially relativistic definitions of honesty in either moral cognition or in behavior.

Just as Heinz stealing a drug to save a dying person considers himself moral though "dishonest," so too did Hartshorne and May. They did not, however, give their subjects the option of defining their own social judgments or principles in either their attitudes or their moral behavior. Second, they ignored what is central to both moral judgment and actions, its form and reasons as distinct from its content.

Thousands of Americans in the 1960s failed to pay federal taxes.

The bulk did it because of instrumental morality which allowed them to be "dishonest." Others did it "honestly" as civil disobedience during a war they considered unjust and undeserving of tax dollars. The difference was not so much in the content of behavior and cognitions but in its form and reasons. This focus on form or reasons allows us to find consistency between judgment and action where Hartshorne and May failed. In summary, in our view the Hartshorne and May or socially relative behaviorist approach failed (*a*) because it ignored the *internal* definition of moral action content as the subject internally perceived or judged it and (*b*) because it ignored the *form* of the subjects' judgments of morality. In addition it failed (*c*) because it defined morality in terms of a list of separate traits or norms "a bag of virtues," ignoring the way in which subjects must organize these norms to make an integrated moral choice.

In Chapter 5, Table 5.3 lists twelve culturally universal moral norms. Adherence to norms of property and truth represents the "virtue" honesty, but what if these norms conflict with norms of human life or of marital love and affection, the "virtue" of loving or caring? Not only in the Heinz dilemma, but in real life, virtues or norms conflict and moral integrity requires consistent organization of these virtues or norms. Like Plato, we have called the integration of these virtues or norms justice, and like Plato, we recognize that while the organization of virtues may have a single name "justice," the actual exercise of just action may entail other virtues, especially (*a*) care, altruism, or responsibility and (*b*) moral courage or will. To find "moral character" or an internally organized and consistent disposition to moral action, one must find an internally organized system of judgment and relate this to action. Starting by breaking character down to a list of traits and measuring them destroys the possibility of finding the organization of personality called character. We share this assumption with theories of the ego or self like that of Loevinger (1976), Blasi (1981), Peck and Havighurst (1960), and J. M. Baldwin (1906). Empirically, however, these researchers assume a unity of internal judgment and motivation and outward action, using personality or projective tests and interviews to assess both. Remaining within the structuralist approach, we assess judgment and conduct separately and then ask questions about the relations between the two. Our test of moral judgment is just that, not a test of moral character or conduct. Empirical studies relating the two begin to build a theory of character, rather than such a theory being a starting point for research.

Philosophic Assumptions

The statement that Hartshorne and May's approach "failed" is not a positivistic conclusion reached because of the very limited power they achieved in predicting behavior. It is, rather, in part a philosophic conclusion.

There are two central philosophic issues in defining moral or morally commendable action. The first is that of the issue of relativity: Whose standard of rightness do we use in defining an action as moral; is it that of the actor him- or herself, that of society, or that of some universal philosophic judgment of right action in light of moral principle? On both philosophic and psychological grounds, we argue that Hartshorne's use of generally accepted or majority-accepted norms, social relativism, is invalid. This is so, first, because it ignores the individual actor's own judgment, a necessary part of considering whether an action is moral or not. As cited, Hartshorne and May's judgment that it was right to deceive children to increase knowledge of character is a necessary part of judging their action as moral. One part of our approach to defining moral conduct rests on the individual actor's own judgment, defining moral action as consistency between judgment and behavior. What, however, if the actor's own judgment of rightness is clearly wrong, for example, Lieutenant Calley's judgment that it was right to massacre civilians at My Lai? We shall argue that analysis of an action from the point of a moral principle like Kant's respect for persons or Mill's maximization of welfare help in this discussion. Here we shall adopt the bootstrapping relationship between normative philosophical views and principles and empirical data that in Chapter 3 we discussed as the complementarity strategy for relating philosophy and psychology. If in general there is agreement about the facts of the case, we shall claim that in many situations consideration of principle, even those posed as conflicting principles by moral philosophers, like the utilitarian principle of welfare and the Kantian principle of justice, are in agreement about particular situations. The empirical support for this claim is that principled Stage 5 thinkers indeed do agree upon which action is right in many conflicting situations. While this does not prove that a Stage 5 concensus defines moral action, it is an empirical support for an otherwise falsifiable philosophic claim that various formulations of moral principles still lead to agreement about what is right in certain situations. Thus, all the philosophers quoted in Volume I, like Stage 5 (or 6) laymen, agreed Heinz was right to steal the drug. From this point of view, when both the individual actor's point of view and that of the consensus of principled persons agree, and the action is actually carried out, we have a clear case of moral action.

Aside from the issue of relativism there is a second fundamental philosophic issue in defining moral action, that of whether the morality of an action is dictated (*a*) by the behavior itself as it conforms to a norm, (*b*) by the intention, judgment or principle guiding the act, or (*c*) by the welfare consequences of the act, which depends upon how the individual processes factual information about the situation and the interests and feelings of others and predicts outcomes to the action. These options are the focus of an article by Kleinberger (1982). Kleinberger notes that Hartshorne and May, as well as more recent social behaviorists, end up by adopting the view that it is the conformity of the behavior itself to a social norm like "Don't cheat" that defines moral action. Kleinberger lists a number of modern American social learning theorists who take this point of view.

The second point of view is that which defines the morality of an action in terms of its social welfare consequences to the self as well as others affected by the action. Of course this cannot be judged by a single action, where good consequences might be a matter of chance, but only as a settled disposition of character to foresee good results and act in terms of them. Kleinberger lists John Dewey as an example of the consequential conception of moral action. Aristotle might be listed as well, as could John Wilson (1973), a modern philosopher of moral education.

Wilson attempts to specify an ideal of "a morally educated person" based on all the components or elements which would lead that person to do actions having good consequences for others and the self. Accordingly, his components include all factors important for a good outcome whether these factors or abilities are distinctly moral or not. His list included (*phil*) a moral principle of respect for persons (which is distinctively moral), (*krat*) a will factor, (*emp*) a psychological knowledge factor, and (*gig*) a factor of factual knowledge and skills of information processing.

Finally, Kleinberger lists philosophers who equate the morality of action with the principle of judgment behind it, including Kant and myself in this camp. Kleinberger argues that these three conflicting views of morality spring from *a priori* philosophical assumptions, and empirical data cannot help to solve them. Clearly Kleinberger is partly right, and no amount of gathering empirical correlations between judgment, behavior, and factual knowledge can reconcile these views. But we do not agree with Kleinberger's own conclusion, which is similar to that cited in the preceding chapter as Max Weber's "decisionistic relativism." As noted there, Max Weber's (1946) decisionistic relativism states an impasse between an "absolute ethic" of acting on pure intentions and a "responsibility ethic" of acting in a less principled way in terms of the effort to realistically foresee good consequences.

Kant (1949) did endorse an "absolute ethic," that is, an ethic which said that principle, or a universalizable and categorical or prescriptive judgment determining action, was both necessary and sufficient to define an action as worthy, regardless of the consequences. Other factors influencing action, he thought, were not strictly moral. An example is what in this chapter we will call self-control or ego strength. Of this factor Kant says, "Moderation in the passions, self-control, and calm deliberation are not only good in many respects, but even seem to constitute part of the intrinsic worth of a person; but they are far from deserving to be called good without qualification, although they have been unconditionally praised by the ancients. For without the principle of a good will, these qualities may become extremely bad. The coolness of a villain not only makes him far more dangerous, but immediately makes him more abominable in our eyes than he would have been without it."

We can clarify this position of Kant's by reference to findings discussed later in the chapter.

Ego strength or will is an example of a factor closing the gap between moral judgment and moral action. In Kant's terms, principled moral judgments meet the requirement of the "categorical imperative," that is, that they are experienced as a moral duty which is universalized. The categorical imperative states, "Act only on that maxim through which you can at the same time will that it should become a universal law" (Kant, 1949). Kant points out, however, ego strength or attention-will is not in itself positively moral, it only "amplifies" moral judgment, making action based on principled moral judgment more moral and action based on unprincipled judgment more immoral. We will point this out in discussing the results of the Krebs and Kohlberg (Kohlberg and Candee, in preparation) study showing that ego strength makes students high in moral judgment more "moral," that is, makes them cheat less, but makes students lower in moral stage cheat more.

For the Kantian reasons just given, Kleinberger attributes to ourselves this Kantian philosophic presupposition about moral action.

> Why does the cognitive-developmental approach to moral education focus so heavily upon moral reasoning? Firstly because moral judgment is claimed to be the single most influential factor in moral behavior. But the main reason is that moral judgment is the only distinctively *moral* factor among all the factors which influence moral behavior. Therefore it is only by virtue of this factor that behavior may be considered genuinely moral. [Kleinberger, 1982, p. 154]

Kleinberger attributes to me the Kantian (and Christian) view that the only thing that counts in evaluating a moral action is the intention or principle that lies behind it, not the consequences, or the ability to foresee the consequences, which determines the good effects of the action upon other people. In fact, I do not adhere to this Kantian position, but rather hold a modified version in which a distinctively moral judgment is a necessary component of an action judged moral, but it need not be sufficient for evaluating the morality of an action or actor. Other factors of knowledge and motiviation which are not distinctively moral may be required for assuring a good outcome. Hence, while necessary, moral judgment principles may not be sufficient for good action or good character, in its broader sense, but it is only by starting theory and research with an examination of the necessary moral judgment component that one can move on to identifying other factors sufficient to complete the terms *moral action* or *moral character.*

In our view, the word *moral* presupposes a normative stance, it is not a "value-neutral" word. The word *moral* has two meanings. One meaning distinguishes the context of moral relevance. The Heinz dilemma is a "moral" dilemma since it involves a conflict between two universal norms, and typically, judgments about the dilemma of which of two houses to buy is not a moral dilemma, it is a practical or economic dilemma. In its second meaning, "moral" is distinguished from "amoral" or "immoral." Not all judgments to moral dilemmas are moral judgments. Sometimes children adopt a practical, economic, or pragmatic set to the Heinz dilemma, as when Taiwanese children argue that Heinz should steal the drug to avoid paying for an expensive funeral. These judgments we called partly "premoral" or "amoral," reflecting a lack of development of moral judgment. To call a judgment "moral" or "morally developed" in this second sense is in some sense to commend it or to claim it is good or adequate. It requires then, both some philosophic argument about the use of the word *moral* and some agreement about the adequacy of the judgment in question.

The same is even more true for moral action. In the *Laches,* Socrates asks, "When is diving in a well an act of moral courage and when of foolhardiness?" If a man jumps into a well in which a person is drowning our judgment of the act as moral depends in part upon the reasons he gives for the action. These may not be moral, they may be that he wanted to test his endurance or he hoped to get a reward from the person he saved. In such a case, most philosophers and most laymen would judge the action as being morally neutral rather than as being a moral action.

As stated earlier, it is our position that moral judgment is a necessary factor, and other factors are not necessary to the definition of an act as moral. Empirical study is required to investigate the sufficient conditions of moral action.

With regard to factual and psychological knowledge, Gilligan (1982) points out, correctly, that in particularistic relations like that of parent to child we inevitably take a responsibility or consequentialistic ethic in Weber's terms. Our morality is assessed not by our principles alone, but also by our ability to foresee and secure good consequences for our children, largely a matter of understanding and predicting psychological and social facts.

This, however, holds true in a world like the family in which we are responsible for consequences. In the larger world of universal humanity, a responsibility ethic of consequences may easily degenerate to Stalin's utilitarian decision to let four million kulaks starve to insure the collectivization of Soviet agriculture. Orienting in this chapter, and in our work in general, to norms of how human beings should treat one another qua human beings, we focus on the principled or intention component of action, since a consequentialistic act-utilitarion ethic cannot in our opinion be universalized. In saying this, we do not wish to deny the validity of a consequentialist or responsibility ethic within its limits, the limits where interpersonal care and concern can effectively operate and knowledge of the other is possible.

In holding that rational moral judgment is necessary but not sufficient for moral conduct, we take a position that is in broad agreement with the naturalistic theories of Dewey and Aristotle. Dewey and Aristotle hold that moral reasoning and judgment is not sufficient for developing moral virtue, which they would say requires the development and teachings of habit in order to acquire the sensitivity to the values achieved by virtuous action. Dewey and Aristotle insist that moral learning or development comes through doing, through habitual exercise, this being the distinction between moral and intellectual virtue for Aristotle (since intellectual virtue can be taught). But virtue also has a reasoning component, according to Aristotle: "It is necessary that the agent at the time of performing a just act should satisfy certain conditions, that is, in the first place, that he know what he is doing, secondly, that he should deliberately choose to do it and do it for its own sake, and thirdly, that he should do it as an instance of a settled and immutable state" (*Ethics* bk. II, chap. 3). "Moral purpose is more than volition. There are things that are voluntary, that are not purposed. Moral purpose implies reason and thought, it indicates previous deliberations" (bk. III, chap. 4).

Aristotle, then, held that moral reasoning judgments, or principles, were a necessary component of moral action. He did not, however, think that they were sufficient for moral action. This was his basic disagreement with the "rationalist" or "idealist" position of Socrates and Plato. He says (*Ethics* bk. VI, chap. 13), "Socrates thought the virtues were rules or rational principles (for he thought they *were* all of them forms of scientific Knowledge) while we think they *involve* a rational principle."

In Volume I, I elaborated a philosophic theory of deontic justice reasoning and judgment which claimed that a principled deontic judgment was more adequate than a lower stage judgment. Our philosophic theory of deontic justice reasoning is not, however, a theory guiding aretaic judgments, that is, judgments about the moral worthiness of an action or person. Persons who make Stage 5 or Stage 6 judgments are not in our theory more worthy persons or morally better persons than those who make Stage 3 or Stage 4 judgments. A more adequate mode of reasoning is neither necessary or sufficient to define the person who makes those judgments as morally worthy or virtuous. A first approximation to a philosophic theory of moral worth, an aretaic theory, would be to say that an individual who consistently acts on Stage 5 or 6 principles is morally worthy. This, however, is a stronger claim to having an aretaic theory than we would wish to make. Other elements or components of moral action besides justice principles may be involved in actions deemed worthy by a theory of aretaic judgments for guiding judgments of moral worthiness.

This chapter, a first step to formulating a philosophic theory of aretaic judgment, that is, a theory guiding judgments of moral worth, is just that, a first step. The strongest claim we could possibly make for it is the claim that is made in Chapter 3 for the philosophic theory of moral judgment. Following Habermas, we distinguished between using empirical psychology data to confirm or "prove" our normative theory to saying that empirical data could only lead to disconfirmation of our normative theory. Insofar as the development of human morality was not in the direction of the principles of Stage 5 and 6, it would be difficult to hold to these normative principles as more morally adequate. Similarly, if there were no conceptually clear relations of judgment to action, our own philosophic definition of moral action would be falsified empirically.

A successful research program must start by identifying some regularities in action which can reasonably be called moral. Our basic criticism of the behavioristic approach to defining moral action was that in its most well worked out implementation, that of Hartshorne and May, it did not allow the identification of a situationally general and intrinsically moral component of conduct. It is the claim of this chapter that the findings reviewed in this chapter do warrant the cognitive-developmental definition of judgment and action as a starting point for research. One focus of such research will obviously be upon "gaps" between judgment stage and action. But the study of gaps between judgment and action presupposes that these are a puzzle in the context of a paradigm that orders a great deal of data already. As quoted earlier, Brown and Herrnstein (1975, p. 289) find no puzzle or problem reaching explanations about discrepancies between judgment and action. They say, "You must believe action and thought are normally in harmony. If you do not then there is neither paradox nor even surprise in someone talking on the high road and acting on the low road." We believe that such discrepancies do represent puzzles requiring research and, in contrast to Brown and Herrnstein, we think there needs to be a unified conceptual solution.

The alternative approach to defining specifically moral judgment in action would be a positivistic approach specifying the amount of variance in a "moral" action attributable to a variety of moral and nonmoral factors. In Chapter 3, we specified that our approach to study of the development of moral reasoning was a "rational reconstruction." This approach both elaborated a normative or rational model of judgment and moved back and forth between such a "rational reconstruction" and regularities (or irregularities, puzzles) in empirical data.

The present chapter is a first step in an effort to do something similar in the way of a rational reconstruction of moral action, to begin a sketch of the "moral actor" which can serve as a guidepost for studies of moral action.

Forms of Reasoning About Moral Conflicts as a Distinct and Better Antecedent of Moral Conduct Than Tests of Moral Knowledge and Attitude

Earlier in the chapter we suggested that the most significant moral situations involve a conflict between a standard or norm that the individual accepts as being right and some other value or norm. If moral conduct itself involves conflict, then it makes sense that if we are looking for consistency of behavior and moral thought we should examine how the individual thinks about conflict situations. In other words we should look for a mental analogue of justice conduct.

Moral judgment is essentially a way of seeing and resolving moral conflicts. To know whether an action is moral or not we must know how the person judges the situation with which he or she is confronted. We would expect this assumption to be true in actual situations as well as in hypothetical verbal ones. Our approach to studying consistency or generality in real behavioral situations is not essentially different from the way we have looked for and found consistency in hypothetical verbal situations. In hypothetical situations this has been done by presenting subjects with dilemmas, complex situations in which two or more norms conflict. We then look at ways of reasoning to resolve these conflicts in order to determine a course of action. It is these ways of reasoning which are general across verbal situations. In other words, while Hartshorne and May found great variability in the behavior of individuals from situation to situation we find the person's stage at response to one hypothetical dilemma corresponds closely to his or her response to others. In chapter 5 and in Colby et al. (1983), we report that 90 percent of a subject's reasoning is scored either at the subject's major stage or at one adjacent stage. It is this generality that we would expect to be revealed in moral actions, not the endorsement of a particular standard or virtue.

All stage structures function situationally, that is, they define what is right as a balancing of conflicting norms and claims. At the highest stage this balancing is done in a form that philosophers call "principles." Common sense or conventional thinking tends to equate the idea of principle with holding a norm such as "telling the truth," or "not stealing" as absolutes which admit of no exceptions. At every stage, however, situational factors are considered in making a judgment. For example, in the Heinz situation, the formulation principle is of justice or respect for human personality. This principle may dictate that one violate the law or violate norms of honesty. However, in other situations the principle dictates conformity to the law or conformity to the norms of honesty.

Deontic and Responsibility Judgments

But what does an individual's "operative moral structure or principle" tell us about his or her moral actions? The prediction from stages or principles to action requires that we take account of intermediary judgments that an individual makes. One does not act directly on principles, one acts on specific content judgments engendered by those principles. We hypothesize that moral principles or "structures of moral reasoning" lead to two more specific judgments, one a judgment of deontic choice, the other a judgment of responsibility. Moral judgments serve two psychological functions which we deem are necessary for moral action. The first is a deontic decision function, a judgment of what is right. The second is a follow-through function, a judgment of responsibility to act on what one has judged to be right.

According to Frankena (1973), a deontic judgment is a judgment that an act is right or obligatory. Deontic judgments typically derive from a rule or a principle. Application of Kant's justice principle, the categorical imperative, or Mill's utilitarian principle of the greatest good would be examples of deontic judgments.

Deontic judgments serve as the decision function of moral reasoning. They answer the question What act is right to do? The second judgment, the judgment of responsibility, includes an element which Frankena calls aretaic, "a judgment of the morally good, bad, responsible, or blameworthy." Following Galon (1980), a deontic judgment may be seen as a first-order judgment of rightness, and responsibility as a second-order affirmation of the will to act in terms of that judgment. Deontic judgments are propositional deductions from a stage structure or principle while responsibility judgments are acts of a choosing will. For Galon, responsibility judgments answer not only the question Why is *X* right? but also Why me? Why must I do *X*?

Following Blasi (1983, p. 35), "Moral judgments, before leading to action, are at times processed through a second set of rules or criteria, the criteria of responsibility. The function of a responsibility judgment is to determine to what extent that which is morally good or right is also strictly necessary for the self." In this way responsibility judgments serve the "follow-through" function. According to Blasi, "The criteria used to arrive at responsibility judgments are related to one's self-definition or the organization of the self. The transition from judgment of responsibility to action is supported by the tendency toward self-consistency. . . . Following an action inconsistent with one's judgment of responsibility, guilt is experienced as an emotional response to the inconsistency within the self."

We have, then, a model in which the relationship of moral stage (and as we shall see, moral substage) to moral action is mediated by two intervening judgments, deontic choice and responsibility judgments. We shall return to this model after completing our discussion of what constitutes a moral action.

Definition of Moral Action

We have concluded at this point that the definition of moral action would have to include the actor's conception of right action and would have to consider his or her judgment of responsibility to perform the action. This leaves open two general approaches to the definition of moral action. The simpler approach defines moral action as that which is consistent with the subject's own judgment about the action. This approach considers an actor to be moral if "he practices what he preaches." The second approach involves more philosophic assumptions and is more controversial. This approach defines an action as being moral in reference to objective and universal standards as well as to the individual's own moral judgment. This position argues that at least in some situations one behavior can clearly be designated as "right."

Personal Consistency or Responsibility Approach

The first approach is consistent with the philosophic position of individual relativism. It says not we the psychologists but the subject him- or herself should decide whether the act is right or wrong. Moral action is action consistent with the content of moral judgment whatever that be. We could call this approach quite simply the idea of personal consistency. However, implied in consistency is the more meaningful idea of "moral responsibility." As a personality attribute, responsibility denotes, first, a concern for, and acceptance of, the consequences of one's actions. Second, it denotes a consistency between what one says one should or would do and what one actually does. It is dependability or follow-through in action of one's verbal moral commitments and judgments. We shall claim that persons at each higher stage of moral reasoning are more likely to act with responsibility, that is, to act in accord with choices about situations that they judged to be right when they were somewhat removed from the situation itself.

Judgments of responsibility are usually preceded by a deontic judgment of rightness. However, Gilligan (1982) who studied women's reasoning and judgments about a real decision of abortion, observed that subjects often made a judgment of responsibility without first making a deontic judgment of rightness. This may be true when acts of moral sacrifice are made for children, family, and friends, that is, in "judgments of special obligation." It may also be true of supererogatory altruism toward strangers and of moral actions which benefit a group, community, or institution, that is, acts of social responsibility which go beyond the requirements of rights, duties, or principles.

The action situations we will consider in this chapter, however, are actions engaging a deontic judgment of rightness or justice. We propose that there is a monotonic increase in making a judgment of responsibility consistent with the deontic judgment of rightness as we move from stage to stage. This in turn means that there is a monotonic increase in the proportion of subjects acting "morally" or in consistency with their deontic judgment made outside the situation. We shall cite studies showing this monotonic trend toward moral consistency. The first, a study by Helkama (1979), shows that there is a monotonic increase in consistency between a deontic judgment of "should" and a verbal judgment of responsibility in the Heinz dilemma. The second study, by McNamee (1978), shows that there is a monotonic increase in consistency between deontic judgment and actual behavior.

Table 7.1 is taken from Helkama. It shows that there is some increase by stage in the first row labeled deontic judgment (i.e., Heinz should steal); there is a much more dramatic increase by stage in the second row, "Heinz is responsible if his wife should die." The third row shows an increase in the proportion of subjects whose judgment that Heinz was responsible was consistent with their judgment that Heinz should steal.

To illustrate a stage-wise increase in the consistency of actual moral behavior, we will review a study by McNamee (1978). McNamee describes the experimental situation as follows:

Undergraduates who agreed to be interviewed on the standard moral dilemmas were led to a testing room. As they were entering the room they were intercepted by a student presenting himself as the next subject for the experiment. The student stated that he had just taken drugs and was having a bad time. He had come to the experiment because he thought that the experimenter, being a psychologist, could help him. The response to the experimenter was that she was a research psychologist, not a therapist. The

Table 7.1. **Responses to Choice and Responsibility Questions of Heinz Dilemma**

Question	*Stage* *3*[a]	*4*	*5*
1. Should Heinz steal the drug? (Yes)[b]	42%	56%	67%
2. If Heinz does steal the drug and his wife dies, is he responsible? (Yes)	17%	28%	53%
3. Percent thinking Heinz should steal who also hold him responsible.	27%	29%	50%
N at stage	(52)	(43)	(15)

NOTE: Entries are percentage of subjects at each stage making the response in parentheses. Method of scoring: 1975 standard issue scoring.

a. Stage 3 includes Stage 3(4). Stage 4 includes Stage 3/4. Stage 5 includes Stage 4/5.

b. Other choices include "should not steal" and "may steal."

SOURCE: Helkama, 1979.

drug-user persisted in soliciting aid, hoping that the experimenter could refer him to help. The experimenter replied that she had no experience with drugs and did not know what facility could help him. She told him to reschedule his testing session. The drug-user slowly left the room. The subject was faced with the choice of whether to remain an uninvolved by-stander or whether to intervene. [McNamee, 1978, p. 27]

Subjects' moral behavior was assessed first by whether they helped or not and second by the degree to which they intervened: offering information about other sources of assistance to the drug-user, or offering personal assistance, such as taking him home or to a source of help. Subjects were 102 college students, ages 18–25, containing an equal number of males and females. The results of this study are displayed in Table 7.2.

The first column indicates the percentage of subjects at each moral stage who verbally decided it was right to help the drugged student. Column 2 presents the percentage of subjects who actually did help by referring the student to some other agency. Column 3 describes those subjects who intervened to counsel or personally escort the victim to a helpful source. The last column contains a measure of consistency, that is, the percentage of subjects at each stage who advocated helping and who actually did so.

***Table 7.2.* Percentage Helping Drugged Student by Stage of Moral Reasoning**

Stage	*Thought They Should Help*	*Helped by Referring Victim*	*Helped by Personal Intervention*	*Consistency*[a]	*Stage N*
2	36%	9%	0%	25%	(11)
3	77%	27%	0%	38%	(29)
4	69%	38%	0%	55%	(17)
5	83%	73%	20%	88%	(29)[b]

NOTE: Columns are percent of subjects at that stage making the response. Mean MMS of subjects who helped by referring = 430, of subjects who did not help = 350 (F = 19.4 d.f. = 1/88 p <.01. Method of scoring: 1972 issue method.

a. Consistency is the percentage of subjects who thought they should help who actually did so by referring victim.

b. Five of these subjects were originally scored at Stage 6. Results for them would have been 100%, 100%, 60%, and 100% across the columns.

SOURCE: Adapted from McNamee, 1978.

The overwhelming effect that is revealed by Table 7.2 is the monotonic nature of the act of helping. In virtually all cases the decision to help and the action of helping are evidenced increasingly more often at each higher moral stage. Furthermore, the consistency betweeen deontic choice and action increases with moral stage.

We should note that the measure of consistency (Column 4) is based only on those subjects who judged it was right to help. Although subjects who did not think it was right to help and who subsequently failed to do so may also be considered consistent, their behavior has a very different meaning. In studying moral behavior we are concerned with studying actions in which the subject gives up something or takes risks where not doing so would appear to be to his or her more immediate advantage. In the McNamee situation the rewards and pressures appeared to be on the side of not helping the drugged student. Thus, it is the overcoming of these situational pressures on either a verbal or a physical level that constitutes the test of moral behavior.

How can we account for the increase in consistency of moral behavior in the Helkama and McNamee studies? Following Hare (1963), we may say that in formal terms each higher stage is more prescriptive and universalizable (see Volume I). Prescriptivity (with universalizability) refers to the consideration that if one judges that an action should be done then one is not only judging that the action is right but also that all persons, including oneself, have a duty or are responsible for performing that action in the given situation.

From a psychological point of view, the increasing consistency may be due to a decrease in what we call excuses or "quasi-obligations," at each higher stage. Each stage generates not only its own moral obligations but its own justifications for failure to act in terms of those obligations. These excuses are considered "quasi" obligations because in other situations they may be legitimate obligations. However, in the context of the situations we are studying they cannot, from the viewpoint of moral principles, be considered binding.

Since quasi-obligations can only stem from reasoning that is not principled in the philosophic sense, they, by definition, are unlikely to exist at Stages 5 and 6. At Stages 3 and 4 Helkama found that the quasi-obligations of obedience to the law or of norms of honesty were most commonly used as reasons for not holding Heinz responsible for his wife's death. In the McNamee experiment the most frequent reason among Stage 4 subjects for not helping the drugged student involved a quasi-obligation to the experimenter in his or her role as an authority. Fifty-five percent of nonintervening Stage 4 subjects gave the following reason for not helping: "My role was that of a subject. I'm not qualified as a psychologist. I had to trust the experimenter's judgment. It's dangerous to be a Peanuts psychiatrist." At Stage 3, it was personal disapproval or the personal relationship with the experimenter which most frequently determined nonintervention. Typical of the reasons for not helping at Stage 3 was the following: "I was concerned about what the experimenter would think of me—her disapproval" (24 percent). At Stage 2 the most frequent reason for not helping was not a quasi-obligation to the experimenter but the absence of any instrumental necessity of the helping act itself. Typical of Stage 2 reasons for not intervening was the following: "It's not necessary. It's none of my business. It's his responsibility. He should have thought of the consequences before taking drugs" (44 percent).

The Helkama and McNamee studies have been used to exemplify the moral responsibility or personal consistency approach to defining moral action. By this definition, subjects at each higher stage were more likely to act morally in that they were more likely to make a judgment of responsibililty consistent with their deontic choice and to act on this judgment. Lower stage subjects often left responsibility in the hands of the experimenter because of a quasi-obligation to the experimenter and accordingly did not help. As we shall see in our discussion of the Milgram situation, a similar phenomenon occurred in that study.

Universal Morality Approach

Let us now turn to a more philosophically disputable approach to the definition of moral action. This is the claim that some actions may be judged right or wrong "universally" or "objectively." For example, in Volume I, I argued that it is universally right or just for Heinz to steal the drug under the circumstances of that classic dilemma. Similarly, in chapter 7, Volume I, it was argued that capital punishment is wrong or unjust under nearly any circumstances. The empirical springboard for this claim is the fact that almost all Stage 5 subjects (and subjects which our theory might label Stage 6, though this stage is not well defined empirically) agree or have consensus in such judgments. The philosophic claim involved is not that moral rightness is solved by an opinion poll of high stage subjects. It is rather that the function of judgments of fairness is to resolve conflicting claims in a way that all could agree with; adequate principles of justice have the function of leading to agreement in the content of deontic judgment, given agreement on the facts. Thus both Kant's principle of justice, or respect for personality, and Mill's principle of utility (whether act- or rule-utility), or the greatest welfare of the greatest number, would agree in judging Heinz right to steal.

Our stages of moral judgment are defined by the form of moral judgment, not its content. Higher stages, we claim, are more moral in their form. Many moral philosophers argue that there is a "moral method" for arriving at moral judgment, which can lead to considerable substantive agreement about what is right and just in moral problem situations. Even if following the moral method does not lead to substantive agreement, it is the critical moral component of value judgment. An example of a critical element of "the moral method" is impartiality, the effort to consider the interest and point of view of all parties involved in moral problems, not to consider the situation only from the point of view of oneself and one's own group. "Methodological nonrelativism" has been particularly stressed by formalist moral philosophers from Kant to contemporaries like Hare (1963), Frankena (1973), Baier (1965), Peters (1968), and Rawls (1971). All stress that a "moral point of view" or a moral method implies certain formal features of moral judgment, features including universalizability, prescriptivity, reversibility, and generality.

From our point of view, then, we can define morality in moral judgments formally without commitment to a particular code. Consider the following Stage 5 responses to the Heinz dilemmas.

Q.—Should Heinz steal the drug?
A.—Yes, he should. His obligation to save his wife's life must take precedence over his obligation to respect the druggist's rights.

Q.—Which is worse, letting someone die or stealing?
A.—Letting someone die. Because the value of human life is logically prior to the value of property. That is, property can have no value unless human life is protected.

This subject makes a judgment which is *prescriptive* (states what Heinz should do), *overriding* (life is overriding of other moral and nonmoral considerations), and *universalizable* to any life and to anyone's point of view, including the druggist's. It is in this formal sense that we call the judgment fully moral. However, a respondent can argue for supporting the law in the Heinz situation and still be classified at Stage 5, as in the following:

Q.—Why do we need laws?
A.—Because it is so hard for people to live together unless there are some laws governing their actions. Not everybody is good certainly, and we have to go by some code to make sure that everybody has their own individual rights.

This response, too, is prescriptive (states what we "have to do"), is overriding (the protection of rights is paramount), and is universalizable (everyone's individual rights should be protected). As we shall see, few subjects at Stage 5 actually conclude that arguments favoring the law outweigh those favoring life in deciding what Heinz should do. What is important here, though, is to point out that the classification of reasoning as being Stage 5 is based on the *form* of the subject's argument (i.e., prescriptivity, universalizability, and preemptiveness) regardless of whether he or she is defending the wife's right to life or the law's role in protecting rights generally.

From Structure to Choice: Stage 5 Consensus

We have clarified the sense in which judgments about the Heinz dilemma or other of our standard dilemmas can be said to be "moral" or "morally principled" in formal terms. This, however, does not yet answer the problem of defining moral action. To define moral action, we need to be able to define the content of an action, the choice made, as being moral. We must show the connection between the form of a judgment and its content.

The Heinz dilemma asks a subject to judge whether it is right to obey the law. The dilemma is preframed so that only one of the two opposed actions can be judged as right, either serving the moral norm of human life or serving the moral norm of law (or property). Such dilemmas tend to call for a solution by reliance upon a moral principle. As previously discussed, philosophers distinguish between a moral *rule,* or a moral norm, and a moral *principle.* Don't steal, Respect property, Be honest, are various statements of a moral rule or moral norm of property. In the Heinz dilemma the norm is opposed by another moral norm or rule, the norm of preserving human life. The deontic question asks, Following which rule is right? When rules or norms conflict, a principle seems required. A moral principle, as distinct from a rule, implies two things. First, it is not a "thou shalt" or "thou shalt not" statement about a kind of action, it is a way of seeing, a way of choosing when two rules are in conflict. It is a method of moral choice. Second, it is something underneath a rule, the spirit underneath the law rather than the rule itself, it is an attitude or idea which generates rules. It is more general and universal than a rule. Among ethical principles put forward by philosophers we have noted Kant's principle of justice and Mill's principle of utility. Kant's principle of justice is the principle of respect for human personality or dignity, Treat each person as an end in him- or herself, not a means. Mill's principle is the principle of maximizing human happiness or welfare and minimizing human suffering. In the Heinz situation both moral principles lead to the same judgment, that is, that it is right to steal. It is in this sense that in Volume I we considered the actions of stealing the drug to be morally right.

Empirically, we have found that subjects who reason at Stage 5 do, in fact, agree that Heinz is right to steal the drug. More than 90 percent of Stage 5 subjects in the United States, Finland, and Israel make this choice, compared to about 60 percent of subjects at lower stages (Chapter 8 and Chapter 9). Thus, we have found that in certain cases there is both philosophic and empirical support for a "universal right" in defining moral action.

Table 7.3 indicates the relationship between stage of moral judgment and choice for our nine standard dilemmas, plus a tenth dilemma on capital punishment.

Table 7.3 indicates that Stage 5 (or 4/5) subjects have near consensus on the Heinz dilemma (III), on not punishing Heinz (III′), on refusing an unjust request by a father (I), on agreement to willed euthanasia of a fatally ill cancer patient (IV), on rejecting capital punishment (C.P.), on refusing to report a reformed convict unjustly punished (VIII), and on judging an act of trust betrayal for money as worse than impersonal stealing for the same amount of money (VII). Stage 5 subjects do not attain consensus on whether to report a lie to a mother confided in confidence to a sister (II) or whether a captain should order a man on a suicide mission or go himself when his ability to lead the retreat weighs against going himself (V).

In reporting the data of Table 7.3, we are pointing to two separate but related issues. The philosophic issue is that of whether

Table 7.3. **Percent of Kohlberg's Longitudinal Subjects Choosing the Principled or Autonomous[a] Alternative at Each Stage on Each Kohlberg Dilemma**

Stage	*N*	III	III′	I	IV	IV′	*C.P.*	II	V	VIII	VII
1/2	(14)	42	33	31	57	23	00	27	33	20	40
2	(10)	64	12	50	60	60	11	36	78	50	16
2/3	(43)	67	52	67	60	57	00	57	47	53	53
3	(48)	62	46	58	35	37	20	79	76	74	74
3/4	(75)	74	40	63	30	78	41	67	82	71	71
4	(24)	63	42	63	29	36	36	37	100	91	100
4/5	(10)	90	100	89	81	50	100	50	50	100	100

a. Autonomous choices were as follows:

FORM A

III Stealing is right

III′ Judge should not send Heinz to jail

I Joe should refuse to give his father the money he earned

FORM B

IV Doctor should give morphine at woman's request

IV′ Judge should not send doctor to jail. C.P. (capital punishment) is wrong

II Sister should not tell mother about sister's confidence

FORM C

V Captain should not order a man to a suicide mission

VIII Acquaintance should not report a reformed and unjustly sentenced convict to the police.

VII Cheating a trusting philanthropist is worse than breaking into a store.

certain actions may be called moral by some universal or universalizable criterion. The fact of consensus by principled subjects, by those who strive to take a universalizable moral point of view, does not of course prove that the action they agree upon is morally right or just. It does, however, suggest that moral or philosophic arguments will converge in some controversial dilemmas (in the case of Table 7.3 dilemmas, I, III, III′, IV, C.P., VII, and VIII). In other words, it extends the range of actions and situations which may be labeled "moral" beyond those on which most participants agree, like the McNamee dilemma, to less consensual dilemmas. Each situation studied empirically, if it is to be useful for developing an aretaic theory of moral worth, must be subject to moral philosophic analysis and argumentation. The empirical fact of consensus, whether by all subjects, as in the McNamee dilemma, or by principled subjects, as in the Heinz dilemma, does, however, offer guidelines to the outcome of such reasoning. In the McNamee situation, where responsibility to aid a stranger in distress does not conflict with an equally strong responsibility to aid the experimenter, our intuition is that it would have been right for the subject to help the stranger in need. The consensus on deontic choice found by McNamee after Stage 3 tends to confirm this intuition but is not itself the grounds for labeling the act moral. The same line of reasoning applies to more controversial situations on which only principled reasoners agree.

Turning to the psychological issues, the findings in Table 7.3 and similar findings are more direct in linking stage structures to content of choice. Presumably, for stage structure to determine action there must be an intervening judgment of the content of deontic choice. We expect to show later in the chapter that on those dilemmas where there is Stage 5 consensus on deontic choice there will be a monotonic increase at each higher stage of performing that action in practice.

Judgments of Responsibility and Monotonic Increase in Moral Action by Stage

In the case of the McNamee study, there was a monotonic increase by stage in moral action with near consensus on deontic choice by most subjects. The remaining studies we will report in this chapter closely fit this general pattern. Accordingly, we need to strengthen and clarify our thesis that in addition to a deontic choice pattern, which need not be monotonic, there is a monotonic pattern of a judgment of responsibility increasingly consistent with a judgment of deontic choice, leading to increasingly "responsible" or consistent action. One verbal study showing a monotonically increased consistency of deontic judgment and judgments of responsibility was the Helkama (1979) study reported in Table 7.1. A second study showing a similar pattern is a study by Candee (1976) of public responses to the My Lai massacre, a moral action situation discussed later in the chapter.

In a survey conducted following the My Lai incident we found that while nearly all Americans agreed in their deontic choice (the massacre was wrong), they disagreed on the degree to which Lieutenant Calley, the commanding officer at the scene, should be held personally responsible for his actions. The results of the survey (taken from Candee, 1976) are reproduced in Table 7.4. The question most pertinent to deontic choice is whether respondents

***Table 7.4.* Percentage of Subjects Choosing the Responsibility Alternative on My Lai Questionnaire**

	Moral Stage					
Question	*2*	*3*	*4*	*5*	x^2	*tau*
1. Do you approve or disapprove of Lt. Calley having been brought to trial? (Approve)	0	45	78	89	36.29[a]	.43[a]
2. Should American officers be convicted for war crimes ordered by their superiors? (Should)	20	22	53	84	38.72	.46
3. Do you consider Calley guilty or innocent of murder? (Guilty)	60	40	66	97	27.86[a]	.38[a]
N at stage	(5)	(85)	(74)	(27)		

NOTE: Entries are percentage of subjects at each stage choosing the response in parenthesis. Method of scoring: 1976 standard issue scoring
a. Significant at p <.005.

SOURCE: Candee, 1976.

considered Calley's action wrong. Ninty-three percent of all respondents considered Lieutenant Calley's actions to be wrong. Thus, it is a consensual dilemma for deontic choice. In the area of judgments of personal responsibility (questions 1, 2, and 3), we find a monotonic pattern. At each higher stage subjects were more likely to hold that Lieutenant Calley should be held accountable for his actions either by direct judgment (question 3) or by calling for a public trial (question 1).

Why is there a stage-by-stage increase in judgment of responsibility while there is no general monotonic pattern in deontic choice? This is because with increasing moral development subjects have an increasing sense of the necessity of being responsible to act as one thinks right regardless of whether there is agreement among subjects on what is right.

This is suggested by two developmental studies of the reasons advanced by subjects about responsibility for carrying out what was defined as internal deontic choices.

The first is a study by Blasi (1982). Blasi presented first-graders, sixth-graders, and eleventh-graders a dilemma, which, like the McNamee situation, pitted an action of helping another with obedience to authority. For sixth-graders the story was as follows:

> A boy at summer camp thinks of taking some food to a punished boy, against the orders of the director. Having decided not to do so, he was blamed by his father for not helping his peer.

For eleventh-graders the story was as follows:

> A nurse thinks of revealing to a patient's family the patient's condition, but this is against the hospital's rules. She is later blamed for her silence by the patient's family.

In both these dilemmas, not only were the needs of other people objectively described, but the subjective moral stand of the hero was explicitly presented. Children were told that the hero of the first story believed that it would be good to take food to the punished camper, that the nurse thought it right to tell the family.

Sixth-graders almost unanimously believed that the child had no responsibility to give food to the punished camper and should not be criticized even though the child thought it good to help. Responsibility was believed to be defined by rules and authority, not by the story's hero's ideas of what was good or right. A typical response was: "He is not running the camp and it's not his [the hero's] camp to do whatever he wants to do . . . just like a teacher can tell a student to do something." Some, but relatively few, sixth-graders recognized that the hero's own moral judgment, even when it conflicts with the authoritys', is a sufficient reason for choosing a specific course of action. A typical expression was: "If he thought it would be nice and everything, if he believes very strongly that people should help each other, then he doesn't really have to do what the director said."

Not only was this type of reasoning rare, but most significantly, it was explicitly rejected as a valid criterion by a large number of children.

Blasi said (p. 47), "No sixth-grader, even among those who had accepted subjective morality as a valid criterion for action, felt that inconsistency between action and one's moral views, as was manifested by the hero, is blameworthy, an understanding that seems rather common among adults and that was found among eleventh-graders. Only two children paid attention to, and seriously considered, the interviewer's insistence that the hero himself, according to the story, had judged helping as the right decision. However, in the last resort, even these children could not agree that blame was fair in this situation."

While most of the eleventh-graders responded in a way similar to that of the sixth-graders, important differences were found. Blasi summarizes these differences as follows: "Eleventh-graders, even more than younger children, form a heterogeneous group and begin to show the variety of attitudes that are found in an average adult sample. Behind all these attitudes, one usually finds a clear consciousness of the distance of the individual moral agent from the norm of obedience and of his freedom from social norms. The tendency to evaluate moral issues in terms of subjective criteria is strong and general among the oldest children, especially in deciding about strict obligation ('has to' or responsibility)."

Examples are: "If it comes to a question and she asks what her morals are and she's going to have to break them to go along with the hospital, she shouldn't;" "I think she should have her own principles that she should live by, because if you don't have your own principles . . . you are not going to really be yourself anymore. You're just going to be one huge mass along with the rest of them." "The orders . . . it's no excuse, because then she's like a robot. You are also a person. I mean, just because you're a nurse doesn't mean you lose your personality." These comments indicate a relationship between consistent responsibility and autonomy, a characteristic of our more advanced stages and substages.

In summary Blasi, found general age developmental trends toward increased verbal consistency between ascribed judgments of deontic choice and of responsibility. Judgments of responsibility considered as either backward-looking accountability to criticism or forward-looking "must do," or strict personal obligation, became increasingly subjective, increasingly related to the actor's internal judgment, with age.

Similar developmental trends in responsibility judgments, explicitly related to our moral stages, were found by Helkama (1979). Blasi identified one class of what we called excuses or quasi-obligation, those involving commands from a legitimate authority. In the Helkama study of the Heinz dilemma a parallel "quasi-obligation" is that of obedience to law. In most situations obedience to law is a moral obligation. From the Stage 5 point of view of a Stage 4 deontic judgment which holds stealing right in the dilemma it is also a "quasi-obligation." It is, however, given as a reason why Heinz is not responsible by Stage 3 and 4 subjects who think Heinz should steal. While a concern for law may become a quasi-obligation in the Heniz dilemma, so too may a very different concern, a concern for conscience. Stage 3 and 4 subjects gave as a reason why Heinz was not responsible for his wife that stealing was morally impossible for Heinz, or that he had to be a respectable citizen. The concept of conscience used was that of a concern for fixed social rules, rather than that of a principled decision of conscience. It illustrates, however, how even a concern with conscience can reflect a quasi-obligation in making judgments of responsibility.

We have clarified the sense in which judgments of responsibility become more prescriptive by stage, and the sense in which higher stages are able to eliminate excuses or quasi-obligations in judging responsibility. It is important to distinguish quasi-obligatory excuses from conscious or preconscious defenses against admission or awareness of wrongdoing, such as denial or projection. Quasi-obligatory excuses are moral reasons generated by moral judgment stage structures, reasons which under certain conditions are genuinely moral or *primafacie* obligations but which are ruled out by considerations of justice in the particular situation. For some subjects love and care for one's wife in the Heinz dilemma is even used as an excusing reason when deontic judgment is based on obedience to law. From a principled point of view, where deontic choice is based on the right to life, obedience to law is in that particular situation only an excuse for failure to act responsibly.

We need now to consider the monotonic growth of responsibility by stage in terms of a developing positive conception of responsibility. This may be best stated as the growth of a positive idea of moral freedom or autonomy with each stage. Responsibility is centrally a metaethical concept and judgment. In the end a judgment of responsibility involves a metaphysical stand, or a stand on the nature of human nature, with regard to the metaphysical issues of free will versus determinism. A judgment of responsibility is always partly a judgment of fact, of causality; it is not a purely prescriptive or normative statement of what should be. It is not, however, a pure judgment of factual causality; it implies that someone ought to be *held* responsible, not just that someone *is* responsible in a purely descriptive causal sense. Responsibility judgments do relate to moral stages, because the judgment of moral responsibility is an answer to the question What ought someone to be responsible for? At the principled level, one ought to be responsible for acting in light of principle.

At every stage, judgments of responsibility imply a judgment of freedom and power by the subject. Only at the postconventional level, however, is the freedom involved, a freedom to choose principles or ultimate values.

At Stage 3 and 3/4 Helkama finds subjects saying things like, "Heinz is not responsible because he is a 'respectable citizen.'" For these subjects Heinz is not free to choose his moral stand about stealing or to choose whether or not to be a "respectable citizen" when his wife is dying. In contrast, postconventional subjects see Heinz as morally free, that is, free to choose his own ultimate values or principles or to choose between the conflicting norms of life and property in the dilemma. One Stage 4/5 subject says, "Heinz is responsible because he has been forced to choose and he has chosen the simpler attitude. He lets his wife die and he is not legally guilty. He has no moral right to shirk his responsibility and let his wife die. The ultimate decision is in his hands." Postconventional subjects have a sense of tolerance and relativity about choice of principle but a sense that an actor is or should be responsible for the choice. Persons may choose differently, but the choice must be made responsibly. "Heinz is responsible. He placed his own ideals of honesty above human life. It's his view, which is different from mine. It would be interesting to discuss it with him."

In summary, the Blasi, Candee, and Helkama studies of judgments of responsibility show:

1. Judgments of responsibility clearly display a monotonic pattern of increased responsibility to verbal dilemmas which is not always shown by deontic judgments.
2. This monotonic trend is one of increased prescriptivity (or consistency) of responsibility judgments.
3. This increased prescriptivity may be interpreted as the discounting of excuses or "quasi-obligations" in making judgments of responsibility at successively higher stages.
4. It may also be interpreted as a growing concept of moral freedom or autonomy with higher stages.

These monotonic patterns in judgments of responsibility found in verbal dilemmas lead us to expect a monotonic increase in moral or just action in situations in which most subjects agreed on deontic choice, as in the McNamee study. It leads to the same expectation where there is Stage 5 consensus or deontic choice and some monotonic increase of such choice by stage.

Our philosophic considerations left us with the view that a moral action is an action that is (*a*) "objectively right" in the sense that philosophic principles as used by Stage 5 reasoners agreed that the action is right, and (*b*) "subjectively right" if it was both guided by a moral judgment or reason that was "right" in form and consistent in content with the objectively right choice. We observed psychologically, that (*a*) there are many situations in which there is a monotonic trend toward the deontic choice which is favored at Stage 5 and (*b*) in all situations there is a monotonic increase in judgments of responsibility with higher moral stage. Thus, even in situations where all subjects agree on the deontic choice, there should be a monotonic increase in behaviorial manifestations of that choice due to increased judgments of responsibility.

Substages

Our controversial philosophic view leads us to say that, in at least some situations, principled or Stage 5 subjects perform actions which are right in both form and content. This claim does not only apply to the highest or principled stages. Lower stage subjects sometimes choose the "right," "just," or "principled" content on our hypothetical dilemmas. Furthermore, they choose it in a way which is formally close to what both Kant and Piaget would call autonomous. In terms of content, they choose the alternative of preserving justice or human rights and welfare as against obeying laws or authorities in situations where these are arbitrary or in conflict with rights and justice. How can we identify and characterize such lower stage subjects?

In Chapter 6 and Appendix C, we have discussed two different orientations to the standard hypothetical dilemmas. Substage B is oriented to autonomy and fairness, substage A, to heteronomous respect for rules and authority. Each substage can occur at any of the major structural stages. We characterized the B stubstage as more prescriptive, more reversible, more universalistic, and more autonomous than the A substage. In this way, judgments of responsibility made at substage B are more like judgments of responsibility made at higher stages than are the judgments of substage A. Judgments of responsibility made at substage B contain fewer excusing complications, fewer "quasi-obligations," than do substage A judgments, just as higher stage judgments of responsibility contain fewer excusing complications than do lower stage judgments of responsibility. Substage B responses reflect the Stage 5 "right answers" to our dilemmas and an intuitive understanding of the core reasons for these choices. A substage B person is someone who intuitively or in his or her "heart or conscience" perceives the central values and obligations in the dilemma articulated rationally by Stage 5 and uses these intuitions to generate a judgment of responsibility or necessity in the dilemma.

In the Heinz dilemma (III), this intuition is that of the intrinsic value of the worth of all human life, its priority over property, and a resulting judgment of universal obligation to preserve such life. On the question of Heinz's punishment (III′) it is the intuition than an act of moral conscience or rightness, such as that of Heinz, should not be legally punished regardless of legality and utilitarian deterrence or social-order considerations. In the Joe and his father dilemma (I), it is the intuition of the sacredness or intrinsic worth of keeping promises (most especially to children) and the universal and prescriptive responsibility for keeping promises. These substage B judgments on the three Form A dilemmas only receive their full rational and principled justification at Stage 5. But at lower stages they can still govern, or predict to responsible choices and action. We predict, then, that subjects below Stage 5 who act morally in experimental moral situations are substage B. In this way we give credibility to the notion that moral action is responsible choice guided by intuitions of moral values not dependent on stage sophistication. Implied, then, is the "Platonic," "Kantian," or "intuitionist" view that conscience can dimly intuit rationally principled justice and act accordingly. Kant hypothesized that the categorical imperative was intuited by ordinary unreflective moral judgment. Accordingly, if we are going to look for a relationship between moral thought and moral action we should look to those persons who judge it is right to perform the moral behavior either by virtue to their Stage 5 reasoning or their substage B intuitions.

Model of Judgment-Action and Theoretical Propositions

We turn now to a model of moral judgment and moral action represented in Figure 7.2. Four psychological functions are identified, as indicated at the top of the figure. Each function is served by a cognition or set of cognitions. The first function, defining the problem or interpretation of the situation, is served by Selman's (1980) cognitive structures of social perspective taking, which are necessary but not sufficient for moral stage. These structures interpret the moral situation, sensitize the actor to relevant claims and to the feelings of each character in the situation. Moral stage and moral substage, in turn, determine two more specific judgments which are tied directly to moral action. These are the judgments of deontic choice (which serve function II, decision making), and judgments of responsibility (which serve function III, follow-through).

Deontic choice is tied to stage and substage in the sense that where all universalizable moral principles lead to a single alternative as being "more moral," that choice will be made almost invariably by persons at Stage 5 and at substage B. The choice will be made less often at lower stages and at substage A. Judgments of responsibility are also tied to both moral stage and substage as well as to moral action, in that subjects at each higher stage and at substage B should more often hold themselves responsible for carrying their deontic choices into practice.

A fourth function involved in the judgment-action relationship is the nonmoral skills needed for follow-through. These include such cognitive skills as intelligence (i.e., figuring out a plan to achieve the moral result), attention (i.e., avoiding distractions), and delay of gratification (i.e., persevering in one's chosen plan).

Figure 7.2. **Model of the Relationship of Moral Judgment to Moral Action**

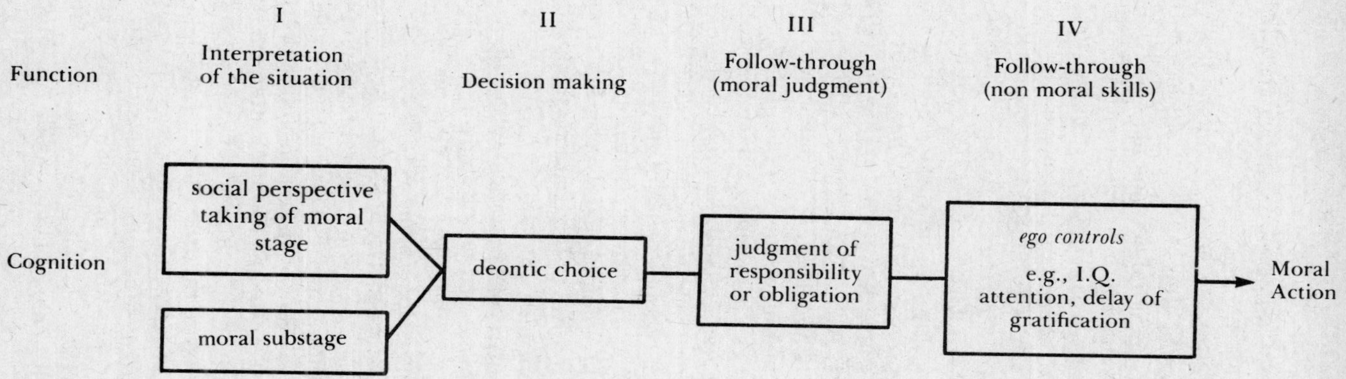

These nonmoral follow-through factors will be discussed more fully later in the chapter.

The model outlined above is intentionally related to one recently proposed by Rest (1983). Rest's model contains four phases or components of moral decision making: (I) interpreting the situation, (II) formulating a moral course of action, (III) evaluating the various courses of action and deciding to undertake the moral action, and (IV) executing and implementing a plan of action. One of the major values of Rest's work is that his components enable him to organize a myriad of studies in social, developmental and personality psychology as they bear upon the moral judgment–action relationship. To illustrate, among the studies involving component I processes, defining the situation, are those by Darley and Latane (1968), Staub (1974), Shantz (1975), Kurdek (1978), Collins (1973), Barrett and Yarrow (1977), and Hoffman (1975, 1976, 1979). Though done in different fields of psychology, all provide information about how morally relevant situations are interpreted. Research varying characteristics of the situation (e.g., Darley and Latane, Staub) has shown that ambiguity in the cues defining a moral emergency is a powerful deterrent to moral action. Milgram's famous series of studies in obedience to authority (Milgram, 1963) has shown a similar effect. Research with children (e.g., Collins) has found that "young subjects have trouble understanding the motives of the characters, misunderstand the patterns of interaction, miss relevant cues, fail to integrate information from various parts of the presentation and consequently draw false inferences, make erroneous evaluations, and advocate inappropriate behavior (Rest, 1983a)." We may hypothesize that adults vary along these dimensions as well.

Among component II processes, Rest cites not only our own work in the development of moral reasoning but also several studies in the tradition of social psychology. Social psychologists studying such areas as social responsibility (Berkowitz and Daniels, 1963), equity (Adams, 1963; Walster, Berscheid, and Walster, 1973), reciprocity (Gouldner, 1960), and generosity (Leeds, 1963) tend to emphasize the role of norms as triggering the recognition of patterns of learned behavior which are appropriate in certain morally relevant situations. Component III, valuing and deciding among different courses of action, involves research ranging from Fishbein's (1967) highly cognitive algebraic model of decision making to Rosenhan, Underwood, and Moore's (1974) study of the effects of mood on acts of altruism. Under component IV, execution, Rest includes many of the same factors which we will later discuss under the heading of ego controls.

While Rest's model identifies nearly the same psychological functions as ours does, its purpose is somewhat different. The major difference is that we do not try to integrate studies from various psychological traditions. Were we to do so it is doubtful our conclusions would differ substantially from his. Rather, our goal is to explore the extent to which one particular set of constructs, moral stage and moral substage, illuminate the judgment-action process.

In some cases we may attribute to moral structures some characteristics that other researchers have explored independently. This is especially true in the area of interpreting the situation. Since moral structures are by their nature integrative they can be considered to sensitize one to morally relevant cues and to define their meaning in terms of moral categories. Such functions undoubtedly overlap with processes studied by other researchers under Rest's component I. The function of interpreting a moral situation would seem to have some aspects that are general to all social information gathering strategies and other aspects that are unique to the moral area. Likewise, there are probably some cognitive skills of defining the situation that are either personality traits or situationally determined, while there are others which we believe are structural-developmental.

In another area, we may consider some of the processes studied independently as the act of commitment (part of component III) to be purposeful moral decisions involving judgments of responsibility. For example, one research cited by Rest, Schwartz (1977), found that "subjects who do *not* score high on [his measure of] denial of responsibility have personal moral norms highly correlated with their behavior; whereas subjects who *do* score high on denial of responsibility have personal moral norms that are not correlated with their behavior" (Rest, 1983a, p. 565). It is likely that Schwartz's measure of denial of responsibility captures some of the features of our judgment of responsibility. As discussed, we expect the judgment of responsibility, and hence the correlation between deontic choice (or what Schwartz calls "personal moral norms") and behavior, to increase with moral stage and with substage B.

Other models have recently been proposed by Blasi (1983) and by Locke (1983). Both are compatible with ours. Blasi's model pays particular attention to the role of ego factors in regulating judgment-action consistency.

Locke's set of models points out the recursive nature of the judgment-action process. Functions are not unidirectional. For example, the experience of one's past moral behavior and the perceived consequences of contemplated behavior influence one's actual interpretation of a morally relevant situation. We are in agreement.

Returning to our own model, we may postulate four theoretical propositions that may be tested empirically.

1. In situations where subjects at Stage 5 tend to perform a given action we will find subjects at lower stages performing that action less often. Stated another way, we expect to find a monotonic relationship between moral stage and action in cases of Stage 5 behavioral agreement. Behavioral agreement may be set at 75 percent or more subjects performing a given action.
2. There will be monotonically increasing consistency between deontic choice and action at increasingly higher moral stages. Following the "personal consistency" or "responsibility" definition of moral behavior, all such consistent behavior can be considered "moral." This hypothesis will be best tested in the McNamee and in the Haan, Smith, and Block (FSM) studies.
3. In cases where subjects at different stages differ on their deontic choice (i.e., nonconsensual situations) but where Stage 5 subjects agree, we expect to find a monotonic increase in subjects acting on the Stage 5 choice. Following the "universal right" definition of moral behavior, the Stage 5 action can be considered "morally right." This hypothesis will be best tested in the FSM study.
4. In all situations we expect the behavior of subjects at the B substage to resemble the behavior of Stage 5 subjects compared to subjects at the corresponding A substage.

Situations in which we would expect to find no relationship between moral stage and moral action are these in which moral principles do not converge on a single, "more moral" alternative. In these cases, either behavior can be considered to be morally right. In practice, such situations can be identified as those in which Stage 5 subjects do not agree on either judgment or behavior. While theoretically important, we will not examine such studies here.

An exhaustive review of studies relating moral judgment to moral action was conducted by Blasi (1980). Although he revealed a number of empirical relationships between moral action and several measures of moral reasoning, Blasi concluded that they shed little light on the theoretical connection between the two variables. We hope to correct that in this section. To do so we shall examine particular studies selected from Blasi's review. The studies were selected either because of the uniqueness of the issues they addressed or because of their methodological clarity. In all cases the results of the studies cited are typical of other studies in their area, which used the standard moral judgment interview and scoring manual (Colby et al., 1983).

Free Speech Movement Study

We turn first to the FSM study. The study was originally reported by Haan, Smith, and Block (1968) but was rescored using the 1983 scoring system by Candee and Kohlberg (in Kohlberg and Candee, in preparation). The FSM study examined the relationship between moral stage and the act of illegally occupying the administration building at the University of California, Berkeley. The sit-in was the culmination of a series of disputes between the Board of Regents of the University and groups of students advocating civil rights and radical causes. The disputes arose over the Regents' recent enforcement of a rule banning the use of university grounds for the distribution of political literature and recruitment to political causes. The researchers gave written forms of the moral judgment interview and a special FSM dilemma to 339 students, 129 of whom had been arrested for sitting in and 210 chosen randomly from a cross-section of the Berkeley campus.

To begin our discussion, we must first determine whether the case is, in fact, a moral situation. From our perspective, it is. A moral situation can be defined as one involving issues of justice, that is, a conflict of rights or claims. In the Free Speech Movement this emerged as a conflict between the right to free speech and one's general duty to respect the social contract "signed" with the university administration. Stated as such, we may not expect this situation to be one in which moral principles necessarily yield a single right answer. However, from all accounts, the Board of Regents seemed to be particularly intransigent and supported its position by appeals to authority. Thus, in this case, the lines between free speech and the authority of the Board of Regents were especially well drawn. Accordingly, 83 percent of the Stage 4/5 subjects thought it was right to have a sit-in, regardless of their own action.

The first hypothesis to be tested is whether a monotonic relationship exists between moral judgment and action in this situation. These results are presented in Table 7.5. As Table 7.5 shows, the pattern is strongly monotonic. At each higher stage of moral reasoning a greater proportion of subjects sat in. Stage scores were assigned on the basis of standard dilemmas, not on responses to the FSM situation itself.

The pattern is consistent with the results of the McNamee study discussed earlier and with most of the studies cited by Blasi in his 1980 review. Indeed, of the 160 hypotheses using the moral judgment interview cited in the Blasi review, 92 were consistent with a monotonic trend. This includes hypotheses which were tested by linear correlation or by *t*-tests. Sixty-one hypotheses showed no relationship between moral reasoning and various measures of moral behavior, while only 7 hypotheses showed a distinctly curvilinear trend. Of these 7, 4 were found in the original Haan, Smith, and Block report.

Thus, while the rescored FSM data is consistent with the vast majority of studies in this area, it is inconsistent with the results originally reported by Haan, Smith, and Block in 1968. In their analysis of the data using the 1958 scoring system they found sitting in to be bimodal. Half of the Stage 2 subjects, about 12 percent of the Stage 3 and 4 subjects, and more than half of the Stage 5 and 6 subjects sat in. In comparison, we scored no individuals at Stages 2, 5, or 6. This absence of Stage 2 subjects represents a real finding and is consistent with other recent studies of college populations. The absence of Stage 6 subjects can be explained by the elimination

Table 7.5. **Relationship of Moral Stage to Sitting In**

	Stage			
	3	*3/4*	*4*	*4/5*
% at Sit-In	10%	31%	44%	73%
(Total N at stage)	(39)	(138)	(125)	(37)

of that stage from the standard scoring system (though it exists as a theoretical stage). Stage 4/5 and Stage 5 subjects could not be distinguished in the written form of the interview. However, among those stages that were represented in the reanalysis, the pattern is clearly monotonic, not bimodal.

The second hypothesis to be tested in the current data is that there is greater consistency between judgment and action at higher stages of moral reasoning. In order to test this proposition, we must control the effect of deontic choice. We measured deontic choice by response to the question "Do you think it was actually right or wrong for the students to sit in?" Responses were grouped into those that clearly stated it was right, those that clearly stated it was wrong, and those that mixed statements of right and wrong. Interestingly, the relationship between deontic choice and moral stage was itself monotonic. Thirty-six percent of the Stage 3 subjects, 50 percent of the Stage 3/4 subjects, 62 percent of Stage 4 subjects, and 83 percent of the Stage 4/5 subjects thought the students were clearly right to sit in. The clear approval given to sitting in at Stage 4/5 (83 percent) indicates that, in fact, principled subjects did agree on a single deontic choice.

In considering these results, we must caution the reader that the data were collected two months after the sit-in took place. Thus, subjects' deontic choice as well as their supporting justifications may have been influenced by the realization that one either did or did not sit in. Nonetheless, we consider these measures to be a useful test of our hypotheses, though not as definitive as a prospective study would have been. There is little reason to expect that the standard moral judgment responses were distorted by the FSM events.

The hypothesis of consistency is tested in Table 7.6.

This table presents the relationship of moral stage to sitting in among subjects grouped by deontic choice. As Table 7.6 shows, the judgment that it was wrong to sit in seems sufficient in this case to explain why no subject who felt it wrong did so. However, as discussed in relation to the McNamee study, a true theoretical test of consistency requires that a "moral" behavior involve relinquishing some other value or reward. In this case it was the students who judged it right to sit in who risked being punished or who relinquished their duty to obey the law. Thus, the data that are most interesting for our hypothesis can be found in the left-hand third of the table. As can be seen, among subjects who thought it

Table 7.6. Relationship of Moral Stage to Sitting In, Controlling for Deontic Choice

	Choice											
	Right				*Mixed*				*Wrong*			
Stage:	3	3/4	4	4/5	3	3/4	4	4/5	3	3/4	4	4/5
% at Sit-In	23%	54%	63%	75%	11%	17%	12%	60%	0%	0%	0%	0%
(Total N at stage)	(13)	(66)	(71)	(29)	(9)	(30)	(24)	(5)	(14)	(37)	(20)	(1)

was right to sit in, a greater proportion at each higher stage of moral reasoning actually had done so. In other words, the consistency between judgment and action increased monotonically with moral stage. We expect such consistency to be mediated by a judgment of responsibility. However, we were unable to measure that variable directly in the FSM study.

We have seen that the vast majority of higher stage subjects judged it was right to sit in and actually did so. How can we account for the act of sitting in when it occurred among lower stage subjects? It is here that we examined the effect of substage. As previously discussed, lower stage subjects who are at the B substage intuitively make moral judgments which have many of the same formal characteristics as do judgments made by Stage 5 subjects. Thus, if Stage 5 subjects (represented here by Stage 4/5 subjects) commonly sat in, we would expect substage B subjects at every stage to also sit in more often than would their substage A counterparts. The test of this hypothesis is shown in Table 7.7.

Table 7.7. displays the relationship of stage and substage to sitting in. It includes substage A, substage B, and an intermediate group which was scored as ambiguously substage B. As Table 7.7 shows, the effect of stage and substage on sitting in is additive. At each higher stage and at each substage closer to B, more subjects sat in. The effect held even when controlling deontic choice, that is, within subjects who judged the sit-in to be right. This indicates

***Table 7.7.* Percentage of Subjects Sitting In by Stage and Substage of Moral Reasoning**

	Stage			
	3	*3/4*	*4*	*4/5*
Substage A				
% Sitting In	0%	21%	21%	60%
(N at Stage)	(30)	(85)	(57)	(5)
Ambiguous B				
% Sitting In	44%	44%	53%	58%
(N at Stage)	(9)	(41)	(40)	(12)
Substage B				
% Sitting In		57%	67%	83%
(N at Stage)	(0)	(7)	(18)	(18)

that our construct of substage is more than simply deontic choice alone.

Milgram Situation

The second study in which we were able to measure substages involved the Milgram situation. Moral judgment interviews were given to twenty-six undergraduates who participated in an early version of Milgram's well-known series of experiments. In those experiments a naive subject is recruited to "shock" an innocent victim under the guise of studying the effects of punishment on memory. While the victim was not actually shocked, the reality of the setting convinced nearly all subjects that their behavior was real. We recently rescored this data according to our current stage and substage scoring systems. The results appear in Table 7.8.

The features of Table 7.8 which we will focus on here are found in the marginals. The relationship of quitting the Milgram experiment by moral stage appears in the lower margin. Most important, we find that nearly all subjects at the highest stage (in this study, Stage 4) quit (87 percent). This compares to only 6 percent at Stage 3/4. Quitting was also high at Stage 3 (50 percent), though there were only four subjects at that stage. Perhaps what is most striking is found in the right-hand marginal, which summarizes the

Table 7.8. **Percentage of Subjects Quitting Milgram Situation by Stage and Substage of Moral Reasoning**

	Stage			
	3	*3/4*	*4*	*Substage Totals*
Substage A				
% Quit	0%	0%	0%	0%
(N at Stage)	(2)	(6)	(1)	(9)
Ambiguous				
% Quit	100%	0%	100%	18%
(N at Stage)	(1)	(9)	(1)	(11)
Substage B				
% Quit	100%	50%	100%	86%
(N at Stage)	(1)	(2)	(4)	(7)
Stage Totals	50%	6%	87%	
	(4)	(17)	(6)	(27)

results for each substage. Here, as in the FSM study, we find a monotonic increase in performing the more moral action at substage B. No substage A subject quit, 18 percent of the ambiguous subjects quit, and a full 86 percent of pure substage B subjects quit. Thus, as expected, principled moral judgment and substage B judgment both lead to quitting the Milgram experiment.

To explain the patterns, we again appeal to the hypothesized mediating judgments of deontic choice and responsibility. Deontic choice was measured by the questions of whether subjects wanted to quit regardless of whether they actually did so. Such judgments were made by all Stage 4 subjects and all substage B subjects. The judgment of responsibility was measured in the standard moral dilemmas by our substage classification. While it was not measured directly in our version of the Milgram study, there is evidence from other versions conducted by Milgram that such judgments strongly influenced behavior. According to Milgram (1974), there is pressure for all subjects in the obedience experiments to enter what he calls the "agentic mode." Once in this mode individuals no longer evaluate the morality of actions for themselves but rather see themselves as agents carrying out the commands of their superiors. However, Milgram reports that persons who quit the experiment seemed to relinquish their sense of responsibility considerably less often than did subjects who were obedient. For example, one subject in Milgram's experiment who quit reasoned as follows:

Q.—It is absolutely essential that you continue.
A.—Well, I won't—not with the man screaming to get out.

Q.—You have no other choice.
A.—I do have a choice [incredulous and indignant]: Why don't I have a choice? I came here of my own free will. . . . I think I've probably gone too far already, probably.

Q.—Who was responsible for shocking the learner against his will?
A.—I put it on myself entirely. [Milgram, 1974, p. 51]

In contrast, subjects who did not quit the experiment typically reasoned as follows:

Q.—Whether he likes it or not we must go on through all the word pairs.
A.—I refuse to take the responsibility. He's in there hollering!

Q.—It's absolutely essential that you continue, teacher.

A.—[Indicating the unused questions]: There's too many left here . . . I mean who's going to take the responsibility if something happens to that gentlemen?

Q.—I'm responsible for anything that happens to him. Continue, please.
A.—All right. [Milgram, 1974, p. 53]

Although we do not have standard moral judgment interviews on the two subjects cited above, it seems clear that the responsibility judgments made in the first case is consistent with substage B and with Stage 4/5 while the lack of personal responsibility in the second quote is consistent with substage A and with Stage 3/4.

Studies of Cheating Behavior

The Milgram situation, just discussed, and the McNamee situation mentioned earlier are both ones where the subject was required to break the normative expectations of an authority in order to aid the welfare of another. However, the more commonly studied moral situation is one like that designed by Hartshorne and May, in which subjects are tempted to break normative expectations for their own interests. These situations are generally called studies of honesty or studies of resistance to temptation.

We will briefly discuss three experimental studies in which subjects were tempted to cheat in ways which apparently could not be detected by the experimenter. These studies are reported directly from the literature. They were not rescored; thus substage is not included. The first study was conducted at the University of Michigan by Schwartz, Feldman, Brown, and Heingartner (1969). In this study a short form of the moral judgment interview was administered to thirty-five undergraduates along with an extremely difficult vocabulary test. The correct answers to the vocabulary test were printed in blurred, reverse form on the back of the page. Thus, with great effort, subjects could discern the correct answer *through* the page. Temptation to cheat was aroused by the experimenter indirectly calling attention to the correct answers (though she asked that such answers not be consulted), by not closely supervising the subjects, and by allowing subjects to grade their own papers. A desire to do well was aroused by providing a small financial reward for correct answers and by (falsely) reporting that some undergraduates had scored 11 out of 14 points by intelligent guessing. Subjects were divided into two moral judgment levels, conventional and principled. The result, as shown on Table 7.9, was that the

***Table 7.9.* Percentage Cheating on Vocabulary Test by Level of Moral Reasoning**

Level	*Level N*	*Percent Cheating*
Conventional	(17)	53%
Postconventional	(18)	17%

NOTE: Percentages are proportion of subjects at that stage who cheated. $X^2 = 3.64$ (df = 1), $p < .05$. Method of scoring: 1958 story rating method
SOURCE: Schwartz, Feldman, Brown, Heingartner, 1969.

principled subjects were much less likely to cheat than were conventional subjects. Only 17 percent of the principled subjects cheated compared to 53 percent of the conventional subjects.

A second study of resistance to temptation was conducted in England by Simpson and Graham (in preparation). This time two behavioral tests of cheating were given, along with the moral judgment interview. The first test was one of verbal intelligence. Copies of each subject's test were made before the subject was asked to correct his or her own paper. The second test consisted of a series of fake Chinese characters with the subjects being asked to choose among the alternative meanings for the symbols. The subjects were told that the test measured creativity. Although subjects were told they would be given their own answer sheet to correct, in fact, they were given a different, specially prepared answer sheet on which the number of correct answers was controlled. Cheating scores were the number of items changed on both the secondary verbal test of intelligence and the creativity test.

Table 7.10 indicates there was a virtually monotonic relationship between cheating and moral stage. At each progressively higher moral stage (with one exception) fewer subjects cheated. At Stage 1, 73 percent of the subjects cheated on either test; at Stage 2, 80 percent cheated; at Stage 3, 64 percent cheated; and at Stage 4, 43 percent cheated.

A third study of cheating behavior was conducted by Krebs and Kohlberg (in preparation; Krebs, 1967). Subjects were 123 students rawn from sixth-grade classes in two schools, one primarily upper middle class and one primarily working class. In this experiment children engaged in four tasks involving psychomotor abilities. This experiment extends the range of cheating tests beyond

***Table 7.10.* Percentage Cheating on Either Secondary Verbal IQ or Foreign Characters Test by Stage of Moral Reasoning**

Stage	*Percent Cheating*
1	73%
2	80%
3	64%
4	43%

NOTE: $X^2 = 11.30$, $p < .02$, $N = 302$. Method of Scoring: 1958 story rating method

SOURCE: Simpson and Graham

the intellectual ones used in the Schwartz et al. and the Simpson and Graham studies. The tasks in the Krebs and Kohlberg experiment included a ray gun game in which scores were, unbeknownst to the subject, predetermined and three tasks in which subjects were asked to perform nearly impossible tasks of coordination (circles task, model house game, and blocks task). For example, the circle task (adapted from Hartshorne and May and presented in Figure 7.1) asked subjects to place consecutive numbers in circles with their eyes closed. Although few persons can get more than one right, subjects were led to believe many more correct marks were possible. In the case of the ray gun and model house games, subjects received a prize for obtaining high scores.

The dependent measure in this experiment was a dichotomous classification of subjects into those who cheated on any test versus those who were honest on all. A dichotomy is theoretically more meaningful than a count of the number of tests cheated on since, as noted earlier, an individual can be "infused with honesty" merely by raising the risk of detection. In fact, because of the elaborate gadgetry of the ray gun and house games, few subjects cheated on them. Most of the subjects classified as having cheated did so on the circles and blocks tasks.

The stage scores reported are based on the 1958 scoring system, since the protocols were unavailable for standard issue scoring (Colby and Kohlberg, 1984, in press). The relationship between moral stage and cheating is presented in Table 7.11. Again, we find the familiar monotonic decline from a high of 81 percent of Stage 1 subjects cheating to only 20 percent cheating at Stage 5.

***Table 7.11.* Percentage Cheating on Any Krebs and Kohlberg Test by Stage of Moral Reasoning**

Stage	*Stage N*	*Percent Cheating*
1	(27)	81%
2	(28)	64%
3	(32)	78%
4	(31)	55%
5	(5)	20%

NOTE: Percentage is the proportion of subjects at that stage who cheated. Scoring method: 1958 story rating ($X^2 = 8.65$, $p < .01$, Stage 5 vs. all others.)
SOURCE: Krebs and Kohlberg.

The previous three studies of cheating can, from the principled point of view, be seen as situations in which subjects were tempted to break an implicit contract with the experimenter to achieve rewards for their own interest. It is the issue of contract and trust as seen by subjects at different stages that is, in our view, the central element in explaining these judgment-action relationships.

We would expect the role of contracts to be best seen in a situation where an individual's commitment to perform an action was freely and explicitly made beforehand. This was the case in a study conducted by Krebs and Rosenwald (1977). In their study, subjects agreed to complete a battery of psychological questionnaires. After completing a written form of the moral judgment interview but before finishing the entire battery, subjects were told that they would no longer be able to use the testing room. When requested by the experimenter all subjects agreed to complete the remaining questionnaires and return them by mail. They were paid in full for their participation and were reminded that in accepting the money they were obligating themselves to complete the remaining questionnaires.

The results, as shown in Table 7.12 again reveal the familiar monotonic pattern. At each higher stage of moral reasoning a greater percentage of subjects did, in fact, mail back the questionnaire.

While most Stage 2 subjects failed to fulfill their contract, virtually all Stage 4 and 5 subjects did fulfill their contracts. The con-

***Table 7.12.* Percentage Returning Questionnaire by Stage of Moral Reasoning**

Stage	*Response*			*Stage*
	On Time	*Late*	*Not at All*	*N*
2	33%	0%	66%	(3)
3	40%	33%	27%	(15)
4	91%	0%	9%	(11)
5	100%	0%	0%	(2)

NOTE: Percentage is proportion of subjects at that stage making the response. $X^2 = 6.90$, $p < .01$. Method of scoring: 1972 issue method.
SOURCE: Krebs and Rosenwald, 1977.

flict, though, seems to have been particularly great at Stage 3. Whereas 73 percent of Stage 3 subjects eventually returned their questionnaires, half of them did so late.

Each of the last experiments involved the issue of contract. In the Krebs and Rosenwald study the moral behavior consisted of fulfilling an explicit contract made with the experimenter. In the three cheating studies (Krebs and Kohlberg; Simpson and Graham; and Schwartz et al.) the "contract" to be honest was less explicit but can, from the principled viewpoint, be considered to exist nonetheless. In the McNamee experiment (helping the drugged student), the Milgram situation, and the FSM study—all cited earlier—breaking an implicit contract with the experimenter or authority was required in order to perform the moral action. Considering all seven of these studies, we find that the moral action was performed by the minority of preconventional subjects, by roughly half of the conventional subjects, but by a large majority of postconventional subjects. A further understanding of these results can be achieved by considering these situations as they might have been seen by persons at each moral stage.

Preconventional subjects view the moral world through a variety of egocentric "operative principles." At this level authoritative expectations must be linked to rewards and punishment. In the cheating situations the minority of subjects who did not cheat may have thought that the authority continued to require honest behavior. However, the much larger number of preconventional subjects who did cheat may have done so because the authority gave no indication that the usual requirements would be enforced. In the cheating situations there were, typically, no penalties for cheating and no rewards for being honest. Since the expectations of the authority were considerably weakened, preconventional subjects may have felt that they were "free" to do what they wanted. They may even have justified cheating to themselves by reasoning that if the authority had not wanted them to cheat he or she would have explicitly prohibited cheating and announced sanctions for doing so. We do not know whether preconventional subjects in these situations actually made the deontic judgment that it was right to cheat. More likely, the behavior of the authority enabled such subjects to judge that they were not responsible for upholding the usual prohibitions on cheating. Thus, our explanation of cheating would appear to lie in the follow-through phase of our model, and perhaps also the decision phase (functions 2 and 3 of Figure 7.2).

In the prosocial (McNamee) situation the authority's expectations were not ambiguous. In that case subjects were clearly expected to refrain from helping the drugged student. Since no reward was given for violating the experimenter's perceived expectations almost no preconventional subjects did so.

Moving to the conventional level of moral reasoning, we find that Stage 3 subjects seem to have experienced considerably more conflict in their thinking about these situations. As evidenced in the Krebs and Rosenwald study, whereas 73 percent of Stage 3 subjects returned the questionnaire, nearly half of those subjects returned it late. We can assume that for all Stage 3 subjects keeping one's promise or fulfilling one's contract was a positive value. The apparent conflict that this group experienced may be explained by the fact that many aspects of the Stage 3 moral structure that would normally support promisekeeping as a value were absent in the experiments. At Stage 3 promisekeeping is valued as part of maintaining good, lasting relationships. Such reasoning confuses fulfilling a contract with another person with being approved of by that person. In the cheating and contract studies, subjects would neither be likely to see the experimenter again nor to receive approval from him or her. Therefore, the usual obligations to the experimenter were weakened.

Another aspect of Stage 3 reasoning which leads to the inconsistent pattern of behavior is the belief that actions are considered responsibilities only as long as they are generally accepted by the group. However, in these situations, subjects typically made the decision to perform or not to perform the moral action alone.

Thus, an individual subject had no way of knowing whether the norm of maintaining one's contract with the experimenter was still in operation. The result of these forces was to produce roughly 40 percent performance of the moral behavior among Stage 3 individuals.

A greater amount of honest behavior was found at Stage 4. This may have been due to the greater likelihood of Stage 4 subjects seeings their obligation to the experimenter in the context of a total social system. In order for such a system to work, people must be expected, in general, to fulfill their contractual obligations. While in this case the experimenter may have appeared to weaken those expectations, many Stage 4 subjects presumably adhered to what would have been the experimenter's normal expectations, in order to be consistent with other situations.

The almost total fulfillment of the contract among Stage 5 subjects in the cheating experiments and the almost total breaking of the contract in the McNamee, Milgram, and FSM situations may be explained by the fact that such subjects see contract and trust as the foundations of all social relations. Contracts which are freely agreed upon are considered valid unless they jeopardize the rights or welfare of others, a condition present in the McNamee, Milgram, and FSM cases. From the Stage 5 point of view, the more trusting a legitimate contractor is, the more obligated and honor-bound the principled individual must be.

So far we have explained why the normal obligation to keep one's promise was weakened, especially at lower stages. However, we have not explained why the alternative force to actually violate the contract existed. The temptation to cheat is not a sheer instinctual force but has a cognitive-developmental structure itself. This was apparent in the McNamee situation where we explained the failure to help as due not to sheer selfish impulse but to a quasi-obligation to conform to the experimenter's expectations. In the cheating studies there was also a quasi-obligation "tempting" the subject—the quasi-obligation to do well, or get a good score on the test. The force of this quasi-obligation seems to explain why, in the Krebs and Kohlberg experiment, more cheating occurred on the circles and blocks test than on the ray gun and house tests, although high scores on the two latter games would have been rewarded with an actual prize.

The monotonic pattern of decreased dishonesty stage by stage strengthens our argument that moral action includes both a judgment of deontic justice and a follow-through judgment of responsibility to perform the just acts. In the Krebs and Rosenwald study a contract was made on the spot, but performing the contract involved a delayed follow-through. Those who did not follow through presumably thought they were not responsible for fulfilling the contract, reasoning that others probably would not follow through so what difference did it make if one less subject did not return the questionaire to the experimenter.

Theoretical Summary

Hypothetical dilemmas pose situational conflicts to people and the resulting classification by stage represents ways in which individuals characteristically define concrete rights and duties in concrete situations. The observed relationship between moral judgment stage and action indicate that there is often a relationship between the way in which subjects define rights and duties in hypothetical verbal situations and the ways in which they define them in actual ones.

Thus, an understanding of an actor's reasoning is a necessary condition for explaining moral action. This does not mean that an action is moral merely because the actor believes it is moral. Rather, our point is that no explanation of moral behavior is possible without an inclusion of the reasoning that led to that behavior.

Moral situations are defined by the actor in terms of specific rights and duties attendant to that situation. One way of measuring individuals' constructions of such rights and duties is through their moral stage structures. These structures are the individual's way of filtering and interpreting the various environmental and interpersonal factors that are involved in moral situations. At the highest stages, these structures take the form of moral principles. Moral principles are not fixed rules but are ways of resolving or balancing competing moral claims in a situation.

Moral action is determined not only by judgments of deontic justice (e.g., rights and contract) but by follow-through judgments of responsibility in a particular situation.

In stressing the idea that moral stages are conceptual filters defining perception of situational rights and responsibilities, we are pointing to the fact that moral action is an interaction between moral stage and particular features of a moral conflict situation. The same Stage 5 orientation which leads to subjects feeling they have a responsibility to return a test to an experimenter leads them to judge that they have the responsibility not to obey an experimenter in the McNamee and Milgram situations. Stage 5 subjects are not in general for or against obeying or conforming to experimenters or authorities. Their actions are determined by their judgment of rights and responsibilities in particular situations.

Finally, it should be noted that we expect that, as distinct from deontic justice judgments, judgments of responsibility are determined by special features of the situation of the sort stressed by social psychologists. In bystander intervention situations patterned after the Kitty Genovese case, Darley and Latane (1968) found that the greater the number of people present, the less often an individual will feel the responsibility to intervene; someone else will do it. With increased stage development, however, judgments of responsibility are made more autonomously. There is less tendency to diffuse responsibility to others. This we shall see when we examine two studies later in the chapter: the My Lai massacre and the Watergate affair.

Ego Controls

Philosopher-psychologists like William James and Piaget have conceived of the existence of an important factor, will, as entering into performing moral action. William James (1890) defined (moral) will as the ability to align action with the weaker but evaluatively preferred stimulus or line of action. The notion of will is introduced by common sense where action does not seem to be in line with minimizing tension (or with expression of the strongest of two conflicting impulses). According to James: "If a brief definition of ideal or moral action were required, none better would fit the appearances than this: it is action in the line of the greatest resistence" (p. 549). James went on to account for moral will in terms of attentional processes:

> We reach the heart of volition when we ask by what processes it is that the thought of any given object comes to prevail stable in the mind. Attention with effort is all that any case of volition implies. The essential achievement of will is to *attend* to a difficult object and hold it fast before the mind.

Building on William James's thinking, Piaget (1968) relates will to an "affective decentering" to regulate or stabilize a hierarchical value preference, a decentering analogous to that of attention in maintaining perceptual constancies. Piaget elaborates on the functioning of will by saying:

> Will is a regulation that has become reversible, and in this sense it is comparable to a [logical] operation. When a duty is momentarily weaker than a specific desire, will re-establishes values according to their pre-established hierarchy and ensures their subsequent conservation. Will gives primacy to the tendency of lesser strength by reinforcing it. Thus is acts exactly like the logical operation when the deduction (equivalent to the superior but weaker tendency) and operational reasoning corrects actual (but misleading) appearances by referring to previous states. [p. 60]

Building on these conceptions, Grim, Kohlberg, and White (1968) collected a variety of measures of attentional stability, including a low standard deviation of reaction time to pushing a button in response to a preparatory signal, randomly varying the time before the actual signal to respond; a number of measures of autonomic stability such as galvanic skin response; and a number of Hartshorne and May kinds of honesty tests and teacher ratings of moral behavior. Using factor analysis, they found a single first unrotated factor cutting across attentional stability, autonomic or "affective" stability, and the various moral ratings by teachers. This factor they thought to be a "will" or ego control factor along the lines of the thinking of James and Piaget. The best or most highly loaded variable on this factor was stability or low standard deviation of reaction for both first-graders and sixth-graders (the two groups sampled). There was an important difference in the single factor found for the two grades. For the first-graders, the Hartshorne and May honesty tests were not significantly loaded on this factor, whereas they were for the first factor using the sixth-graders. Grim, Kohlberg, and White interpreted this discrepancy as suggesting that for the first-graders the factor is a general behavior control factor but not a specifically moral factor, in the sense of inhibiting self-interested behavior (gaining points by cheating on a test) when authorities or sanctions were absent. For the sixth-graders, the Hartshorne and May honesty tests significantly loaded on the first factor, suggesting to the authors that, by that age, moral values and judgments had developed sufficiently to make the ego or behavioral control factor one they felt truly represented moral will.

The measure of low standard deviation of reaction time was then used by Krebs (1967) as reported by Krebs and Kohlberg (in preparation) to distinguish a "will" or "ego control" factor from a stage of moral judgment factor as each might contribute to cheating behavior in a variety of tasks, including the "ray gun" and "circles" tasks described in our earlier discussion on the findings of Hartshorne and May. In addition to the "will" factor or reaction time variable, a second "ego control" factor, psychometric intelligence, was also used. Both these "ego control" variables were found by Hartshorne and May to correlate with honesty on their tests. Tests of persistence and attentional motor control correlated from $r = .03$ to $r = .36$ with individual tests of honesty. Correlations between IQ and resistance to cheating ranged from $r = .18$ to $r = .49$.

Krebs (1968) set up groups who were high and low on IQ and high and low on the reaction time measure of attention. The range of moral judgment stage for the whole sample went from Stage 1 to Stage 5 (1958 scoring system). The sample was adolescent, early high school students. The study then was designed to examine the interaction between moral judgment stage and ego controls in determining honest behavior. The expectation was that ego controls would only enhance moral action when associated with relatively mature moral judgment (Stages 3 and 4). Using the model in Figure 7.2, we can say that ego controls will serve a follow-through function but only when associated with relatively mature moral judgment. This assumption generated some hypotheses about groups showing varying amounts of cheating. The group most likely to cheat would be the preconventional, high ego control subjects. Having no basis for internal valuing of resistance to cheating, those preconventional subjects with high ego strength were in the position to act in accordance with their self-interest, which justifies the cheating response. In comparison we should expect the least amount of cheating to be performed by conventional (Stage 3 and especially Stage 4) children who were also of high ego strength. In their case, high ego strength would allow them to carry out moral beliefs which, relative to the preconventional subjects, mitigated against cheating.

The basic monotonic relationship between stage of moral judgment and the percentage of subjects cheating has already been presented in Table 7.11. The influence of the first ego control factor, IQ, is presented in Table 7.13.

Table 7.13 shows that, on the whole, adolescents of high IQ are somewhat less likely to cheat than adolescents who are below the

***Table 7.13.* Percentage Cheating on Any Krebs and Kohlberg Test by Intelligence and Moral Level**

	High Intelligence		*Low Intelligence*	
	N	*Cheating*	*N*	*Cheating*
Preconventional	(22)	82%	(33)	67%
Conventional	(41)	49%	(27)	85%

NOTE: Percent is proportion of subjects in that cell who cheated. Scoring method: 1958 story method.
SOURCE: Krebs and Kohlberg.

median in IQ. Sixty percent of high IQ adolescents cheated as compared to 75 percent of the low IQ adolescents. What is of more interest is the interaction of IQ and moral stages. Grouping the adolescents into conventional and preconventional, we see that the two groups who are most likely to cheat were the *high* IQ *preconventional* subjects (82 percent of whom cheated) and the *low* IQ *conventional* subjects (85 percent of whom cheated). If we regard IQ as an ego control factor, then we see that high IQ gives the preconventional subjects the ability to live up to their preconventional "principles" and thus cheat. High IQ also allowed conventional subjects to live up to their conventional "principles" and to refrain from cheating. Ego controls appear to operate in different directions depending on the valuing structure of the subjects.

We expected our findings in regard to the second ego control, attention, to parallel those found for IQ. Table 7.14 presents the actual results.

As expected, preconventional subjects who were high in attention were more likely to cheat than those low in attention. Being less distracted from the task, the high attention, preconventional subjects were more able to "stick to their goal" of cheating. However, among conventional subjects the expected differences were not found. Thus, attention does not appear to be as strong or as clearly understood an ego control as is IQ.

When we combine all three variables, MJ, IQ, and attention, we are able to make powerful predictions about the incidence of cheating. As Table 7.14 shows, we can clearly identify the characteristics of those subjects who are almost certain to cheat, that is, preconventional subjects who are high in both ego controls and conventional subjects low in both ego controls. As we have stated,

Table 7.14. Percentage Cheating on Any Krebs and Kohlberg Test by Intelligence and Moral Level

	High Attention		*Low Attention*	
	N	*Cheating*	*N*	*Cheating*
Preconventional	(30)	83%	(25)	60%
Conventional	(33)	64%	(35)	64%

NOTE: Numbers, method, source, as in Table 7.13.

the reasons for cheating are presumed to be very different in the two cases. In the case of preconventional subjects high ego controls probably made them attuned enough to the situation that they felt they could cheat and get away with it. Having little or no moral reason to refrain from cheating, they did so. In the case of conventional subjects, we presume that low ego controls enhanced the temptation to cheat.

Brown and Herrnstein's Interpretation

We have reviewed several studies covering different types of moral behaviors and found that all can be explained by the same set of factors. In our view, there is ample evidence of a linear connection between moral thought and moral action and for our model outlined earlier. However, another position which finds less congruity between thought and action is expressed by Brown and Herrnstein (1975). While sympathetic to the cognitive-developmental approach, these authors argue that the situations cited here are either highly atypical or can be explained by other nonmoral considerations. The highlights of their discussions are as follows:

> The relation between moral reasoning and moral action is not a simple one. Perhaps the best way to summarize the complications is first to describe a study (Krebs and Rosenwald) whose results showed the relations to be as simple as the title of this chapter may have led the reader to expect: the more moral the subjects' reasoning, the more moral their conduct. . . . The result is clear: the higher the moral stage, the greater the probability of moral action. However, this seems not a typical or expected result, but a quite odd effect produced by special features of the experiment's design and certain accidents of subject sampling. Using the Krebs and Rosenwald results as a kind of baseline, what are the factors that our discussion has led us to believe would usually operate?
>
> We have already described experiments other than that of Krebs and

Table 7.15. **Percent Cheating on Any Krebs and Kohlberg Test by Intelligence, Attention, and Moral Level**

	High IQ				*Low IQ*			
	High Attention		*Low Attention*		*High Attention*		*Low Attention*	
	N	*% Cheating*	*N*	*% Cheating*	*N*	*% Cheating*	*N*	*% Cheating*
Preconventional	(12)	92%	(10)	70%	(18)	78%	(15)	54%
Conventional	(18)	55%	(23)	48%	(15)	80%	(12)	92%

NOTE: Numbers, methods, sources as in Table 7.13.

Rosenwald in which one of two actions was believed by everyone or nearly everyone to be the more moral action, and yet the relation between morality of thought and morality of action did not seem to have been the linear one that Krebs and Rosenwald found. In the Asch conformity experiment, everyone seemed to agree that he ought to report the lengths of the lines as he himself saw them.

In Asch's experiment we guess that the conforming subjects were simply somewhat deficient in their concern with acting morally. To speak the truth was to separate oneself from the group and, perhaps, to be cognitively wrong, risks that may have prompted one-third of the subjects to prefer conformity to morality. Obviously, moral reasoning is not the only determinant of behavior; there are many others. One we have introduced is the degree of moral concern. It must be a variable that helps, other things equal, to determine how much correspondence is found between a person's reasoning and his morally relevant actions. This variable probably always operates, but it is perhaps most clearly suggested by the Asch experiment. . . .

The Latane and Darley bystander experiments involve another actor—the assignment of responsibility or, as the authors say, "the diffusion of responsibility." . . . Latane and Darley nicely showed that the more bystanders there are in an emergency, the easier it is to believe that the prime responsibility belongs to someone else. . . .

Milgram's study of obedience involves something quite different from all the others. Those who said that shocking an innocent victim was immoral were outside the relevant situation of hierarchical authority and so presumably were operating in the autonomous mode. People actually in the situation mostly fell into the agentic mode; they seemed to have believed that it was right to obey orders, though it pained them to do so. . . .

We have thus far considered only cases in which one of two proposed actions seemed morally superior to subjects at just about any stage of moral reasoning. In accounting for the fact that in the Asch, Milgram, Latane and Darley, and Zimbardo studies substantial proportions of subjects did not do what they presumably thought they ought to do, we have hypothesized a collection of complicating variables: degree of personal moral concern; assignment of moral responsibility; discrepancies between the perceived morality of acts verbally described and of the same acts experienced in a situation of authority; acts becoming morally neutral when there is evidence that no one cares. We believe that all these factors have a part in explaining the numerous familiar cases in which moral reasoning and moral action do not match.

Brown and Herrnstein's point here is that in cases where moral choice is universally agreed upon, differences in behavior are due to nonmoral considerations. In answer to this point, even where the morally right choice is agreed upon, stage-linked judgments of responsibility lead to differences in moral behavior.

Moreover, in our view the Krebs and Rosenwald study, far from being unusual, is rather typical of laboratory studies of moral behavior. In fact, while the other studies cited here involved implicit contracts between subject and experimenter, in the Krebs and Rosenwald situation the notion of contract was *ex*plicit. It is also typical of most situations in that there is a "right choice" at Stage 5 that is also verbally endorsed by most subjects at lower stages. As is true in the other laboratory studies, there are more reasons to support the more moral choice at each higher stage and more ability to discount countervailing quasi-obligations which pull in the opposite direction.

Brown and Herrnstein cite other studies (Asch, Latane and Darley; Milgram; Zimbardo) in which they doubt that the monotonic relationship between moral stage and moral action would be found. In fact, though, nearly all of these experimental situations have now been studied using the moral judgment interview. Results of these studies indicate that here, too, the relationship between increasing moral stage and greater performance of the moral action exists.

Such studies include Saltzstein, Diamond, and Belenky (1972, Asch situation), McNamee (1978, Darley and Latane situation), Candee and Kohlberg (in Kohlberg and Candee, in preparation, Milgram situation). Brown and Herrnstein predicted that consistent patterns would not be found in their studies, because they believed that, since everyone would verbally agree on the morality of the action, differences in behavior must be attributable to situational concerns unrelated to moral judgment. However, despite an agreement on deontic choice we have seen that there may still be a monotonic increase in moral behavior due to an increase in judgments of responsibility at higher stages. Furthermore, "situational concerns" cited by Brown and Herrnstein are, in our opinion, themselves aspects of moral judgment, though they are interpreted differently by persons at different moral stages. For example, in the Asch experiment, what Brown and Herrnstein refer to as the nonmoral concern of conformity we see as quasi-obligation to maintain a group norm in determining the length of a line. This type of quasi-obligation should be most appealing to Stage 3 subjects. Indeed, in the Saltzstein et al. study this turned out to be true. In the Milgrim experiment persons operating in the agentic mode are, from our viewpoint, trying to fulfill the quasi-obligation of keeping one's promise and conforming to the expectations of the experimenter. As Candee and Kohlberg found, those subjects who were

Stage 4, substage B, did not perceive this quasi-obligation as a legitimate duty and therefore quit the experiment. In this sense these subjects showed greater moral consistency since they reasoned in the situation in the same way as those in Milgram's autonomous mode reasoned outside the situation. In McNamee's version of the Darley and Latane experiments, subjects at each higher stage were more likely to accept their individual responsibility for helping the drugged student and were less likely to assign it to someone else, in this case to the experimenter.

The major difference, then, between our perspective and that of Brown and Herrnstein is that they distinguish too sharply between situational forces, on the one hand, and the stage of moral reasoning, on the other. From our viewpoint one's stage of moral reasoning is a filter through which these situational forces are perceived, interpreted, and acted upon.

Judgment and Action in Nonlaboratory Settings: My Lai

So far we have demonstrated that moral judgment influences moral behavior under experimental conditions by defining the situation in terms of rights and responsibilities appropriate to an individual's moral stage. The predominant trend was that persons at each higher stage of moral reasoning acted more consistently in the direction of supporting rights and acting responsibly and less often in the direction of supporting what we termed quasi-obligations. In addition, we found greater consistency between one's deontic choice and one's action at each higher stage, a consistency we believe is mediated by a judgment of responsibility. In moving outside the laboratory, we should expect the same relationship to be true.

One nonlaboratory situation, the FSM study, has already been discussed. Two others we will discuss here are the mass murder at My Lai, and Watergate. Not only are these nonlaboratory situations but they are also political situations in the sense that they are made by one group of people in relationship to another.

The first situation, which like the Milgram experiment involves questioning the legitimacy of an authority, is the My Lai massacre. This event took place during the Vietnam War and involved the murder, by American troops, of twenty-two civilians in a village which had been suspected of Vietcong activity. The soldiers' main defense was that they were acting on orders which had previously been given by their superiors. This event fits the gloomy social-psychological perspective that situational forces produce immoral behavior in Milgram-type social situations. In fact, for nearly all members of the company this was true. All but one of the soldiers present at My Lai participated in the mass murders.

On November 24, 1969, an interview on CBS television was held with Paul Meadlow, a soldier who admitted his involvement in the massacre of civilians at My Lai. Meadlow (according to his own testimony) had, upon orders from Lieutenant Calley, fired several magazines of M-16 bullets at Vietnamese civilians. Meadlow's thinking, as revealed in the interview and subsequent testimony at the Calley trial, appears to be a mixture of Stage 2 and Stage 3 moral thought. For example, his conception of authority appears to be preconventional. One obeys an officer, not because one respects the society he represents, but rather because one wishes to avoid the punishment which might result from disobedience. Meadlow states:

> During basic training if you disobeyed an order, if you were slow in obeying orders, they'd slap you on the head, drop-kick you in the chest and rinky-dink stuff like that. If an officer tells you to stand on your head in the middle of the highway, you do it. [*CBS Evening News,* November 24, 1969]

Meadlow's conception of retribution was equally preconventional. He believes that it was right to "waste" the Vietnamese in order to get "satisfaction."

> Why did I do it? . . . We was supposed to get satisfaction from this village for the men we lost. They was all VC and VC sympathizers. I felt, at the time, I was doing the right thing, because, like I said, I lost buddies. I lost a damn good buddy, Bobby Wilson. [Hammer, 1975, p. 159]

> It seemed like the natural thing to do at the time. I was getting relieved from what I had seen over there . . . my buddies getting killed or wounded—we weren't getting no satisfaction so what it was—merely revenge. [*New York Times,* November 25, 1969]

In another area of his thinking, Meadlow seems to have little intuition that what he has done offends even conventional moral sensibilities. He exhibited only the barest understanding that killing babies in war is not acceptable conduct:

Q.—You're married.
A.—Right. Two children. The boy is two and one half; the girl is one and one half.

Q.—Obviously the question comes to mind . . . the father of two little kids like that. How can he shoot babies?
A.—I didn't have the little girl. I just had the little boy at the time.

Q.—Uh huh. How do you shoot babies?
A.—It's just one of those things. [*New York Times,* November 25, 1969]

Lieutenant Calley, the officer charged with ordering Meadlow to shoot the civilians, provides something of a contrast in moral judgment with the young private. Calley's conception of right and wrong is largely in terms of conventionalized Stage 3 expectations. He orients to what he anticipates others will regard as a model of being a good officer. He attempts to win praise for fulfilling this role and is chagrined when he violates others' expectations. When asked, in his trial, why he shot a group of civilians he encountered while moving through the village, he responded:

Because that's what I was instructed to do, Sir, and I had delayed long enough. I was trying to get out of there before I got criticized again. [Hammer, 1975, p. 105]

Further, Stage 3 thinking often relies upon a "legitimate" personal authority to define what is right and wrong. The following quote shows a confusion by Lieutenant Calley between relying on his supporters to plan military strategy (a legitimate function of the military from the principled point of view) with relying on them to decide the morality of actions.

I was a run-of-the-mill average guy. I still am. I always said the people in Washington are smarter than me. If intelligent people say communism is bad, it's going to engulf us. I was only a second lieutenant. I had to obey and hope that the people in Washington were smarter than me. [Calley, 1975, p. 105]

The reliance on "legitimate" others extends even to the point of adopting the others' social perceptions. Once the Stage 3 moral reasoner incorporates the social categories of the other, traditional role behavior based on those new categories is facilitated.

We commented earlier that political situations such as My Lai tend to create a uniform group moral perception of the situation. The effect of this phenomenon on Lieutenant Calley appears in the following quotation:

Q.—What was your intention in terms of the operation?
A.—To go in the area and destroy the enemy that were designated there

and this is it. I went into the area to destroy the enemy.

Q.—Were you motivated by any other fact besides that they were the enemy?
Q.—Well, I was ordered to go in there and destroy the enemy. That was my job on that day. That was my mission I was given. I did not sit down and think in terms of men, women, and children. They were all classified the same and that was the classification, we dealt with them, enemy soldiers . . . I felt, and still do, that I acted as I directed . . . and I do not feel wrong in doing so. [Hammer, 1975, p. 256]

The limits of Calley's moral reasoning is vividly evidenced by his failure to understand the testing of superiors' orders, as defined by the Geneva conventions, in even Stage 4 terms.

Q.—Were you instructed by anybody in connection with the Geneva convention?
A.—Yes, Sir, I was.

Q.—What was the extent of that tutoring?
A.—I know there were classes. I can't remember those classes. Nothing stands out in my mind what was covered in those classes.

Q.—Did you learn anything of what the Geneva convention covered as far as the rules of warfare are concerned?
A.—No, Sir. Laws and rules of warfare, Sir?

Q.—What were the principles involved?
A.—That all orders were assumed legal, that a soldier's duty was to carry out the order given him to the best of his ability . . . You could be court-martialed for refusing an order.

Q.—Were you required in any way, shape or form to make a determination of the legality or illegality of an order?
A.—No, Sir, I never was told that I had a choice.

Q.—If you had a doubt about the order, what were you supposed to do?
A.—If I questioned the order, I was supposed to carry out the order and then come back and make my complaint. [Hammer, 1975, p. 241]

A contrast to the mixture of Stage 2 and 3 reasoning found in soldiers Meadlow and Calley is provided by the reasoning of Michael Bernhardt. Bernhardt was the only member of the Calley company who refused to shoot civilians. Seymour Hersh comments:

After a week the company arrived at LZ dotti. Lieutenant Calley ordered Michael Bernhardt to shoot at a running woman. He half-heartedly ran

> after her yelling, "Dong lai," the Vietnamese expression for "Stop," but she got away. [He decided] "I just would fire and miss on purpose after that." [Hersh, 1975, p. 25]

Bernhardt's thinking on the standard hypothetical dilemmas to which he responded after his return to the United States was predominantly Stage 4B with some postconventional Stage 5 thought.

The following are excerpts from his response to the Heinz dilemma.

> Q.—What is the moral dilemma here?
>
> A.—First of all, the moral problem, I guess, is evidently that this druggist assumed that it was his property and his right, his legal and probably his moral right to charge what he wanted to. Maybe the druggist has to develop it, maybe he has to work to acquire a certain amount of knowledge, but the ability to acquire that is given to him for nothing, and just because he has it, he shouldn't be at any more of an advantage than anyone else. All right, so he worked on it and he developed this thing. What should he get for it? Should he get something for it? He did put a lot of effort into it. Whatever it is he is getting for it, he should never value that or what he puts into it more than somebody living. That's the way I would figure it.
>
> Q.—Would you say it is actually the right thing for Heinz to steal that?
>
> A.—I would say it was the right thing to do . . . because he wasn't going to kill the druggist by stealing it but his wife would die more than likely. Let's say it is a question of she will live or die. Sure he was right, he was trying to save her life, anybody's life, as a matter of fact. It would have been right if it was somebody down the street.

From these quotations we see that Bernhardt orients to the druggist's legal and moral rights as well as to the wife's. However, he interprets the druggist's moral rights in terms of equity. In Bernhardt's view the druggist, too, should recognize the hierarchical value of life over property. Furthermore, Bernhardt sees all human life as being of equal value and universalizes the wife's life to all human beings. The value of a person "down the street" is as important as the value of the life of someone close to you. In other words, Bernhardt sets a priority on human life but is also able to see that life is valuable regardless of the social categories into which an individual falls. This reasoning meets the criteria for substage B (hierarchy, prescriptivity, and universality), at least at the Stage 4 level.

It is reasonable to believe that it was the moral attitude expressed above which enabled Bernhardt to respect the human life of all persons at My Lai be they Americans or Vietnamese. In contrast, other members of Bernhardt's company defined human beings as being essentially different when the social characteristics of those human beings changed. The inability of many American soldiers to understand the language and customs of the Vietnamese seems to have led them to redefine the Vietnamese as "less human." This phenomenon is reported by Bernhardt in the following statement:

It has to do with the fact of communication. [That is] one of the aspects of humanity and these people [the Vietnamese] did not appear to be communicating with the men in my company. Like I said, one of the aspects of humanity is the ability to communicate, and since they lose this they sort of slide one level down on the human scale—not quite human—and it makes them a whole lot easier to wipe out. But to me, I can understand now that they were still on the same level of humanity as I was so far as I was concerned. Altogether, from the very first time I saw them and I saw how our men reacted to the Vietnamese, right then and there I decided that this was no good.

A second aspect of higher stage thinking which Bernhardt displayed on the moral dilemma was the view that obedience to the law and authority must be put to the test of conscience.

The law is only the law and many times it's wrong. It's not necessarily just because it's the law . . . my kind of citizen would be guided by his own law. These would be more strict than in a lot of cases the actual laws are. People must be guided by their own standards, by their self-discipline.

His ability to question the legitimacy of authority in light of considerations of conscience led Bernhardt to wage "his own war."

I was telling Captain Franklin about an old woman that was shot. I couldn't understand why she was shot because she didn't halt. First of all, she is in her own country. We never found anything to indicate that she was anything but what she appeared to be, a noncombatant. It wasn't the case that we had been wiped out by an old woman with a fish bag full of grenades. I told them that she was shot at a distance. They said that to shoot her was brigade policy. They couldn't think of a better way of stopping her. I would have said no. I just wouldn't have stopped her at all. Nothing needs an excuse to live. The same thing goes for bombing the village. If there are people in the village, don't bomb it. . . . When I thought of shooting people I figured, "Well, I am going to be doing my own war and let them do their own war," because we just didn't agree on anything.

In Bernhardt's case, his actions at My Lai stem from a conscious moral decision, a decision that did not seem to have been made by many of the men who participated in the massacre:

> When I think about it, there is some kind of moral judgment involved, and so far as they were concerned, there was practically no moral judgment whatsoever. I would just go right down the line, all the way to the bottom. What it might have just been was a confused state of mind. Like you say, getting back at them, getting back at the people who did this to us.

Not only did Bernhardt make a clear moral judgment in the situation, but in his view moral judgment is a determinant of moral action.

> If I recognize something is right or wrong and you get pretty close to it . . . this is the first step to actually doing right. And this is the thing. I can hardly do anything if I know it is wrong. If I think about it long enough, I am just positively compelled.

In summary, then, our analysis of the events and of the thinking of the participants in the My Lai massacre reinforce the conclusions about the relationship of moral judgment to moral action that we drew from previous studies. We may list them as follows:

1. *Higher stage and substage B subjects are more likely to perform the moral action.* In the My Lai situation we may reasonably argue that all ethical principles would define not killing civilians as the more moral action. The only participant to perform that action was scored at Stage 4B or 4/5 on our moral judgment interview. The reasoning of two other participants for whom we have public data was scored at lower stages. Both of these other participants did shoot.
2. *Higher stage and substage B subjects are more likely to judge the moral action as being right (deontic choice).* As stated by our Stage 4B subject Michael Bernhardt, "If I recognize something is right or wrong . . . this is the first step to actually doing right. . . . If I think about it long enough, I am just positively compelled." In this case, Bernhardt judged that shooting was wrong. Both the action of making a deontic choice and the motivating nature of a responsibly moral judgment ("think about it long enough to feel compelled") at higher stages is demonstrated by this quotation.
3. *Higher stage and substage B subjects are more likely to make a judg-*

ment of responsibility. Bernhardt's conscious decision to take responsibility for his own actions is stated in his comment that "I am going to be doing my own war and let them do their own war, because we just don't agree on anything." In comparison, our lower stage subjects (Meadlow and Calley) left the responsibility for determining the morality of their action up to "the people in Washington."

4. *Reasons for not performing the moral action may take the form of quasi-obligations.* In the case of Meadlow, his obligation to shoot was determined partly by the obligation of revenge: "I felt at the time I was doing the right thing because I lost buddies."
5. *There is greater consistency between moral judgment and moral action with increasing stage development.* Again, we refer to the statement from Michael Bernhardt: "The first step to actually doing right" is to see "that something is right. . . . If I think about it long enough. . . . I am just positively compelled."

While we have seen that each individual's perception of a moral situation at My Lai differed due to moral stage, the decisions were not made solely by individuals acting alone. Moral decisions in real life, and especially in political situations such as the ones discussed here, are almost always a group norm or group decision-making process. Moreover, individual moral action is often the function of these norms or processes. For example, in the massacre at My Lai, individual American soldiers murdered noncombatant women and children. They did so partly because as individuals they were subject to a series of obligations and quasi-obligations which allowed them to, at least in part, justify what in other circumstances they themselves might have considered immoral behavior. The reason that these soldiers were able to justify actions that they might normally not have is that My Lai was essentially a group action taken on the basis of group norms and hierarchical authority. The moral choice made by each individual soldier who pulled the trigger was embedded in a larger institutional context of the army and decision-making procedures. Their decisions are dependent in large part upon a collectively shared definition of the situation and of what should be done about it, in short, the group "moral atmosphere."

The Watergate Affair

Under certain circumstances a group primarily composed of conventional individuals may elaborate a group definition of what's right, or justified, that is in violation of the standards of conventional morality of the society at large. This will come about when the potential rewards to the group are great and when the contemplated behavior can be justified within the structure of conventional reasoning as a "quasi-obligation." A good example of such a case is the thinking and behavior of the group associated with former president Richard Nixon during the "Watergate affair," when some members of Nixon's 1972 re-election committee and members of his White House staff attempted to justify their covering up a series of crimes that had been carried out in pursuit of getting the president re-elected. An examination of the moral reasoning of the participants in Watergate, gathered primarily from their testimony before the Senate investigating committee, reveals that such reasoning was exclusively at Stages 3 and 4 (Candee, 1975). It is on this basis that we conclude that the moral atmosphere of the Nixon group was indeed that of conventional morality.

What were the quasi-obligations that comprised the Nixon group's "moral atmosphere?" One common theme was that of interpersonal loyalty to the image of the president himself. An example of such thinking can be seen in the plight of Herbert Porter, an assistant to Jeb Magruder at the Committee to Re-elect the President. Porter explained why he told the grand jury that the money which had gone to the Watergate burglar Gordon Liddy in order to finance the break-in had actually been given for a "more legitimate purpose" (infiltrating a student radical organization):

PORTER: Well, Senator Baker, my loyalty to one man, Richard Nixon, goes back longer than any person that you will see sitting at this table throughout any of these hearings. I first met Mr. Nixon when I was 8 years old in 1946, when he ran for Congress in my home district. . . . I felt I had known this man all my life—not personally, perhaps, but in spirit. I felt a deep sense of loyalty. I was appealed to on this basis.

[And in a preceding exchange]

BAKER: At any time, did you ever think of saying, I do not think this is quite right?

PORTER: Yes, I did.

BAKER: What did you do about it?

PORTER: I did not do anything about it.

BAKER: Why didn't you?

PORTER: In all honesty, probably because of the fear of group pressure that would ensue of not being a team player. [*The Watergate Hearings,* 1973, p. 227]

Porter's reasoning forms a consistent structure of conventional morality. At Stage 3 right is determined by the quasi-obligation of adherence to group norms. It is not surprising, therefore, that Porter is appealed to positively on the basis of favors established by his reference group (the Nixon campaign) and negatively by fear of sanction by that group. Unfortunately for Mr. Porter, besides being less than fully moral, decisions based on loyalty are not always even practical. When Porter's name was mentioned to the former president on one of his White House tapes, Mr. Nixon responded, "Who?"

The progression to Stage 4 is marked by the awareness that individual relationships are part of a larger society. Roles become structured with definite duties and privileges. The overriding concern in Stage 4 is to maintain a system which allows the society to function smoothly and avoid chaos. Such a system need not be conventional society; it may be an "ideal" system, humanistic, religious, or communal. But if the system itself is seen as more basic than the rights of its individual members, it is being viewed from a Stage 4 perspective.

A classic instance of such reasoning seems to have motivated the former chief "plumber," Egil Krogh, to authorize the break-in at the office of Dr. Fielding, Daniel Ellsberg's psychiatrist. Recalling his reasoning at the time, Krogh reflects:

I see now that the key is the effect that the term "national security" had on my judgment. The very words served to block my critical analysis . . . to suggest that national security was being improperly invoked was to invite a confrontation with patriotism and loyalty and so appeared to be beyond the scope and in contravention of the faithful performance of the duties of my office . . . the very definition of national security was for the President to pursue his planned course. [Krogh, 1974, p. 16]

While Stage 4 achieves the awareness of a social system, Stages 5 and 6 proceed to ask, What is the moral validity of that system? At these higher stages the response is in terms of those features which every human being desires to maximize: physical life and liberty and equity in distribution. Liberty, the ability to make one's own decisions and to pursue one's inclinations, necessarily includes the freedoms of speech, assembly, and action. From the moral viewpoint such rights are basic to human beings and exist prior to societies. As a procedural matter these rights must be adjusted when they conflict with the equal valid assertion of such rights by another. However, any action which purports to support a law or maintain a system at the expense of individual rights would be logically and thus morally incorrect, since the very legitimacy of the system is the maximization of such rights.

We were unable to find any Stage 5 reasoning among the Watergate participants. However, as can be seen in the following statement by Special Prosecutor Archibald Cox, it lay at the very crux of their most sophisticated critics.

If man is by nature a social being—if we are destined to live and work together—if our goal is the freedom of each to choose the best he can discern—if we seek to do what we can to move toward the realization of these beliefs, then the rights of speech, privacy, dignity and other fundamental liberties of other men such as the Bill of Rights declares, must be respected by both government and private persons. [Cox, 1974, p. 67]

Why is it that participation in Watergate was justifiable within the reasoning of conventional morality while it was not justifiable within the structure of our one postconventional example? The answer to this question, we believe, resides in the same principle that we used to explain the results in both the laboratory and nonlaboratory studies. That is, in cases where only one choice is consistent with principled reasoning we expect to find a relationship between moral stage and the increase in acceptance of that choice. From the principled point of view the Watergate situation represented a clear and present threat to fundamental liberties without a clearly articulated compensation in terms of maximizing other rights or extending public welfare. Therefore, the structure of highest stage reasoning should lead persons holding such reasoning to more often condemn the behavior of the Watergate participants. Lower stage subjects whose moral structure may have included a number of quasi-obligations are more likely to be in sympathy with the Watergate participants. In a survey of 370 persons (predominantly college students drawn from a variety of New England and Midwestern campuses) this prediction was borne out (Candee, 1976). In Table 7.16 we see that in fourteen of seventeen of Watergate-related situations the percentage of persons choosing the response which, prior to administration of the questionnaire, had been determined by a panel of judges to be consistent with principled reasoning increases directly with moral stage. In general, responses increase monotonically toward increased responsibility. In not all cases, however, was this choice necessarily the one which condemned the Watergate burglars. In some questions, such as number 3 which asks whether the Watergate defendants should have been allowed to conduct a public campaign for their defense (a basic right for any citizen) a greater number of Stage 5 subjects actually endorsed this right for the Watergate burglars than did Stage 4 or Stage 3 subjects.

The monotonic pattern among the choices of the public can be explained by postulating that the same quasi-obligations that we previously found to have influenced the reasoning of the Watergate participants were operative. This explanation leads to the conclusion that the Watergate participants were men of otherwise conventional honesty who, under the pressures of a political campaign, committed a series of illegal acts which they were able to excuse within the framework of conventional reasoning. Using the excerpt from Archibald Cox and the decisions of Stage 5 subjects in the public survey as data, we may further conclude that postconventional moral thought provides a "cognitive inoculation" against such pressures. Thus, the effects of higher stage reasoning in the case of Watergate seems to be consistent with effects found at My Lai and in the laboratory studies of cheating.

Conclusions

The relationship between moral thought and moral action has, over the years, been studied in two different ways. The original approach, best exemplified in the Hartshorne and May experiment, was to try to correlate the strength with which an individual held a moral value (e.g., honesty) with his or her performance of moral behavior. We began this chapter with a review of findings in this tradition. Although such research pointed to a strong situational effect, it produced little evidence to support the idea that moral behavior was determined by general moral attitudes. The reason for this failure, we believe, lies in the fact that when confronted with a real moral situation individuals do not reason in terms of abstract moral values but rather define the situation in terms of concrete rights and duties. Attitudinal phrases such as "cheating is always wrong" or "it's good to be honest," if probed further, turn out to mean cheating is always "wrong because you get caught" (Stage 1) or "it's good to be honest because nice peo-

Table 7.16. Percentage of Subjects Choosing the Rights or Responsibility Alternative on Watergate Questionnaire

Question	*Moral Stage* 2	3	4	5	X^2	*tau*
1. E. Howard Hunt sincerely believed he was helping the country. Was he right to participate in the Watergate break in? (No)	64	64	75	89	13.92[b]	.17[b]
2. Should money contributed for general use in the Nixon campaign have been given to the Watergate defendants to pay for their lawyers and feed their families? (Should not)	66	65	82	87	18.22[a]	.20[b]
3. Should the Watergate defendants have been allowed to conduct a public campaign to raise money for their defense? (Yes)	46	33	53	88	53.97[b]	.36[b]
4. Considering his duty as an officer in CRP (Committee to Reelect the President) should Magruder have admitted the burglars were hired by CRP, or tried to cover up? (Admitted)	40	53	77	94	46.43[b]	.36[b]
5. Herbert Kalmbach asked his superior, "Is this a proper assignment and am I to go through with it?" He was told it was. It later turns out that Kalmbach was collecting hush money, would you consider him responsible? (Yes)	19	26	34	62	27.27[a]	.25[a]
6. If the money was used as hush money, would you consider Kalmbach guilty of a crime? (Yes)	19	33	40	54	12.08[a]	.18[b]
7. Daniel Ellsberg stole top-secret papers that belonged to the Pentagon because they contained information about the Vietnam War that he felt the public should know. Was Ellsberg right to steal the Pentagon Papers? (Yes)	16	21	43	54	30.16[b]	.29[b]
8. Ellsberg stole the Pentagon Papers; Hunt and Liddy stole from Ellsberg's psychiatrist. Were the two crimes basically the same or different? (Different)	20	36	64	83	28.55[b]	.44[b]

9. If impeachment alone were held today, based on what you know at this time, would you be for or against impeachment? (For)	41	65	84	98	43.93[b]	.33[b]
10. If the President were already impeached and a vote were held today on removing him from office, would you be for or against removal? (For)	30	60	78	96	43.18[b]	.34[b]
11. John Caulfield was the man who delivered the hush money to the Watergate burglars. Caulfield knew the purpose of the money but had been told by John Dean that instructions to deliver the funds had come "from the Oval Office." Was Caulfield right to have delivered the money? (No)	60	83	85	100	7.87[a]	.11[a]
12. Was it permissible to have a nurse take files from Ellsberg's psychiatrist to obtain more information on his theft of the Pentagon Papers? (No)	69	89	94	98	20.35[b]	.12[b]
13. John Ehrlichman stated that taking such files is common when investigating a political suspect. Was it permissible? (No)	56	80	88	98	26.26[b]	.19[b]
14. John Ehrlichman was in part responsible for preventing leaks of military secrets. Was he right to investigate Ellsberg concerning the Pentagon Papers? (Yes)	92	86	79	85	3.17	.04
15. Was Hunt and Liddy's break-in at Ellsberg's psychiatrist's justified? (No)	87	93	95	98	4.58	.05
16. Was Ehrlichman, who had hired Hunt and Liddy, responsible for their exploits? (Yes)	72	78	76	86	2.87	.04
N at Stage	(25)	(171)	(93)	(61)		

NOTE: Entries are percentage of subjects at each stage choosing the response in parentheses. Moral stage defined as highest stage at which subject gave 25% of his/her responses on Moral Judgment Interview.

Questions 1, 2, 4, 5, 12–16 shortened for table. Method of Scoring: 1976 standard issue scoring.

SOURCE: Candee, 1976.

[a]p <.05.

[b]p <.001.

ple are honest" (Stage 3). Not surprisingly, then, a Stage 1 subject may cheat when there is no punishment or a Stage 3 subject may cheat when other nice people are cheating. Implicit in the Stage 3 definition of "good" is a stereotypical conception of "what most people do" and what "most people expect" which is much more important in defining the situational conditions of cheating or not cheating than is variation in the intensity of the statement about the value of honesty.

The observed relationship between moral judgment stage and action indicates that there is often a relationship between the way in which subjects define rights and duties in hypothetical verbal situations and the ways in which they define them in actual ones. That relationship is depicted in the model of moral judgment and moral action developed earlier. Readers may wish to refer to Figure 7.2 (p. 537). The model covers four phases of the judgment-action process, a phase of interpretation of the moral problem, a phase of deontic choice, and a follow-through phase consisting of both moral judgments and nonmoral skills. These phases parallel Rest's four-component model (Rest, 1983) and are consistent with Blasi's model of the moral self (Blasi, 1980). However, in contrast to these theorists, we have limited our model to features whose empirical relationship to moral stages have been shown.

The model in Figure 7.2 contains four moral determinants, two general and two specific. The general determinants include moral stage and moral substage. Stages and substages also lead to determinants that are more specific to particular situations. These are deontic judgments (What is right?) and judgments of responsibility (Is one responsible for acting upon what is right?). A review of selected studies supports our proposition that in situations where there is behavioral agreement at Stage 5 (defined as 75 percent of such subjects performing the same behavior) there is a monotonic relationship between that behavior and stages of moral reasoning. At each higher stage a greater proportion of subjects performed the Stage 5 action.

From the viewpoint of deontic choice, moral situations fall into two types. The first type is consensual. Those are situations in which there is widespread agreement that a behavior, such as cheating, is wrong. In those situations it appears that the monotonic relationship is due to persons at each higher stage more often making the judgment that they are responsible for carrying out that norm.

In the second type of situation there is no general consensus. If in one of the situations Stage 5 subjects tend to agree on what is right then we find a monotonic increase in subjects at lower stages also agreeing that the choice is right. Therefore, the monotonic pattern in cases such as the FSM are due to both an increase in the likelihood of subjects at each higher stage judging a given action to be right and in the increasing likelihood of subjects at each higher stage judging that they are responsible for carrying out the right action. Also as hypothesized, in those studies where we were able to measure moral substage, we found that the behavior of subjects at substage B resembled the behavior of Stage 5 subjects in comparison to subjects at the corresponding substage A.

We have seen, then, that under the conditions described above subjects at each higher stage are more likely to perform the Stage 5 behavior. On what basis, though, can we call this behavior moral? Earlier in the chapter we outlined two approaches to defining moral action. The first approach, which we call the personal consistency or "personal responsibility" approach, defines moral action as any action which is consistent with what the actor judges as being right. By this criterion we find that higher stage subjects are increasingly more moral. In every study where deontic choice and action were measured independently (i.e., FSM and McNamee) we found that persons at each higher moral stage carried out their deontic choice increasingly more often. Other studies, such as Krebs and Rosenwald, might also be included here if we assume that accepting payment for the future completion of questionnaires constituted a deontic judgment that such behavior was right. Even in the cheating situations, it may be assumed that the act of noncheating was judged to be right, thus indicating more consistency with that choice at higher stages. In short, among the studies reviewed here there were none in which increasing consistency between deontic choice and action was not found.

The second approach to defining moral action is philosophically more complex. This approach, which we call "universal right," says that we can define the more moral action in some universal or "objective" sense. In this view, a moral action is one which would be arrived at by the application of a valid ethical principle. The two major ethical principles are those of teleology (as exemplified by utilitarianism) and deontology (as exemplified by Kant's categorical imperative). In cases where the application of both ethical principles leads to the same deontic choice, that choice can be considered the more moral. Ideally, to perform this procedure one would have to systematically apply various principles and compare the resulting decisions. We have used this approach to interpret the results of those studies where there is agreement on the moral action by only Stage 5 subjects. Since such subjects evidence a principled form of reasoning, their decisions can be seen as those derivable from formal principles. We do not know which principles each Stage 5 reasoner used merely by knowing his or her stage score. One Stage 5 subject may have used a version of Mill's utilitarianism, another may have used a version of Kant's or Rawls's theory of justice. However, if despite these potential content differences we find, in a particular situation, that a consensus exists among Stage 5 subjects on either the same deontic choice or on the same behavior then we may consider that action to be the more moral in a universal sense. If we were to put that action to the test we would expect to find that it protects rights and extends welfare more than the competing action would. It is in this sense that we may call the Stage 5 (or Stage 4B) behavior of quitting the Milgram experiment, helping in the McNamee case, returning Krebs and Rosenwald's questionnaires, remaining honest in the cheating experiments, and sitting in at Berkeley to be moral actions.

In addition to the moral determinants of action depicted in Figure 7.2 there is a nonmoral component, ego controls like attention, intelligence, and delay of gratification, which enable the subject to carry out what he or she judges to be right. Ego controls, along with the distinctly moral judgments of responsibility and obligation constitute a psychological analogue to what philosopher-psychologists have called moral will.

Finally, we should remind the reader that we do not expect to find a relationship between moral stage and moral action in every situation. In situations where there is no deontic agreement at Stage 5 or, alternatively, where moral principles do not lead to a single "more moral solution," we do not expect to find a monotonic stage to action relationship. If neither action is clearly preferable from a principled point of view, then we should not expect the development of morally principled reasoning to increasingly favor one alternative over the other. Situations of this type may include whether to allow ROTC on college campuses or whether to have an abortion. In these cases both a consideration of rights and of welfare do not yield clear solutions, largely because of disagreements about the facts. In contrast, the situations in which moral behavior has been studied do have a solution in terms of maximal consideration of the rights and/or welfare of those involved. A specific method to predict which situations will be consensual at Stage 5 and which will not is yet to be established. However, once it is known that Stage 5 subjects do agree in a particular situation, then a monotonic relationship between moral stage, moral substage, and the Stage 5 behavior is found.

In focusing upon factors of moral judgment and will in interpreting studies of moral behavior, we have not been attempting to explain all the variation in morally relevant behaviors. It is obvious that a multitude of variables in the social situation or in the individual's personality have an influence on such behaviors. As we noted in our philosophic introduction, the purpose of this chapter has been to develop a model of the distinctively moral features of social action which may define a model of moral action that meets some philosophic criteria for morally worthy action and that may help guide approaches to moral education. For these purposes the study of nonmoral, or "other," variables influencing moral behavior has been of less significance to us. Given this qualification, our model succeeds in explaining a very significant portion of the behavioral variance in the studies we have reviewed.

A further important qualification must be made about the studies we have reviewed and about the model we have suggested. All of the studies reviewed have been conducted in the United States, so that their findings cannot be said to have cross-cultural universality. Future research should address some of the issues raised in this chapter just as the cross-cultural research reported in Chapters 8 and 9 addressed some of the issues concerning the longitudinal validity and universality of the stages of moral judgment themselves. It seems likely that the content of moral choice and the relationship between stage structure and content may vary from one culture to another. We would expect, however, that the monotonic increase in judgments of responsibility and resulting actions in increasing accordance with deontic choice would be found cross-culturally. Some very limited evidence from Finland, Israel, and America suggests that there is Stage 5 consensus across some cultures in dilemmas like the Heinz dilemma. The notion that there is some culturally universal content of just action requires far more evidence than we have been able to offer in this chapter.

8. Cultural Universality of Moral Judgment Stages: A Longitudinal Study in Turkey

with MORDECAI NISAN

BASIC ASSUMPTIONS of cognitive-developmental approaches lead to the proposition that both stages and sequence in the development of moral reasoning are universal, or culturally invariant. According to cognitive-developmental theorists (Chapter 1; Piaget, 1948), moral judgment represents underlying thought organization rather than specific responses; its development results from a process of interaction between organismic structuring tendencies and universal features of social experience, rather than from "transmission" through genetics or direct shaping; and the direction of development is toward greater equilibration in the organism-environment interaction and reciprocity between the self and other (Colby, Kohlberg, Gibbs, and Lieberman, 1983). These features of the development of moral judgment lead to a culturally invariant sequence of stages, or hierarchical organizations, each more differentiated and integrated, and thus more equilibrated, than its predecessor. (Volume I, Chapter 2). While the specific content of moral judgment may vary among cultures, the basic structures are said to be universal. The Kohlberg description of the stages is an attempt to expose such structures.

The hierarchical organization attributed to the stages implies that the individual should proceed through them in an invariant order. Evidence for this claim is provided by cross-sectional (Kohlberg, 1963b; Rest, Davison, and Robbins, 1978), longitudinal (Kohlberg, 1973a; Kuhn, 1976; Rest et al., 1978), and experimental (Rest, Turiel, and Kohlberg, 1969; Turiel, 1966) studies with U.S. subjects. Cross-sectional studies in Kenya (Edwards, 1975), Honduras (Gorsuch and Barnes, 1973), the Bahamas (White, 1975), India (Parikh, 1980), and New Zealand (Moir, 1974) provide support for the universality claim. However, universality is properly tested by longitudinal studies of individuals in different cultures. In one such short-term longitudinal study, White, Bushnell, and Regnemer (1978) assessed the level of moral judgment in Bahamian pupils over two or three consecutive years. Their results support the hypothesis that moral judgment advances with age (at least through the first three stages). However, their analysis is limited to group means. They do not examine whether all observed individuals do indeed develop in the sequence delineated by the theory. Turiel, Edwards, and Kohlberg (1978) did examine this point. Ours was a longitudinal and cross-sectional analysis of moral judgment among village and city subjects in Turkey. The sequential advance of each individual anticipated by the Kohlberg theory was indeed found in this sample. The results also indicated that the rate of development was slower among village than among city subjects.

The first aim of the present study is to examine further the universality claim by broadening and elaborating the study of Turiel et al. Included are data collected in 1976, providing more longitudinal data on more subjects. We now have subjects who were interviewed four times, into their twenties. More subjects were also added to the cross-sectional study in the oldest age group. The invariant sequence hypothesis can thus be examined more adequately and for more mature subjects. The broadening of age range is of special interest in light of results from the United States which show that moral development continues into the third decade of life. We would like to see whether this holds true for the Turkish subjects, and also whether there is a ceiling in moral development not passed by our oldest village subjects, as is the case in at least one traditional society (Edwards, 1975).

Furthermore, all the material used in this study (i.e., both earlier and recent interviews) was scored according to the new scoring manual (Colby and Kohlberg, 1984, in press). This manual was constructed from a reanalysis of a great deal of empirical data and presents a more refined definition of the stages as well as a more reliable scoring system (Colby, 1978). By requiring the scorer to match subjects' statements with detailed criterion judgments, the new scoring system would appear to reduce the subjectivity of the scoring process. This scoring method seems especially valuable in a cross-cultural study, where interpretations of the material are more prone to personal bias.

Method*

Subjects

Data were collected from male subjects in three locations in Turkey: a rural village (population 1,580 in 1960); a seaport provincial capital (population 520,000); and the national capital (population over one million). Subjects from the village were boys attending the local school, young workers, and young men who had recently returned from serving in the Turkish army. These subjects represent a fairly traditional society according to the criteria used by Lerner (1958) in dealing with Turkish society. Subjects from the cities were elementary school, high school, and college students or young workers. All city subjects analyzed in the present study were middle class (judged by parental occupation).

Interviewing took place in 1964, 1966, 1970, and 1976. In 1964, twenty-three village subjects, aged 10–17 years, were tested. In 1966, fifteen of these subjects were retested and ten village subjects and twenty-six urban subjects were added to the sample. In 1970, six of the village subjects were retested and fifteen college students aged 18–25 were interviewed. In 1976, nine of the village subjects and five of the city subjects were retested. Thus some of the subjects were interviewed only once, while others were interviewed two, three, or four times. All the subjects are included in the cross-sectional study; only those interviewed two or more times are included in the longitudinal study. The number of subjects in the longitudinal and cross-sectional studies, by age and social group, is presented in Tables 8.1 and 8.2. A complete picture of the longitudinal sample is given in Table 8.4.

Moral Judgment Interview and Scoring

Each subject was given an individual oral interview, including (each year) the same six hypothetical moral dilemmas and a standard set of probing questions. These dilemmas were revised versions of Kohlberg's standard stories adapted to make them more suitable for the Turkish setting. An example of one such dilemma is presented in Table 8.3. In 1964 and 1966, the interviews were administered through an interpreter. In 1970 and 1976, the inter-

* Parts of this section are taken from Turiel et al. (1978). See that source for more details.

Table 8.1. Number of Subjects in the Longitudinal Study by Year and Age at Testing

Year of Testing	*Age at Testing*				
	10–12 Years	*13–15 Years*	*16–18 Years*	*19–23 Years*	*24–28 Years*
1964 . . .	7	5	3	. . .	. . .
1966 . . .	7	9	6	2	. . .
1970 . . .	. . .	. . .	3	3	. . .
1976 . . .	. . .	. . .	. . .	9	5

views were given by the same Turkish-speaking graduate student, attending a university in the United States, who had been trained in the technique of moral judgment interviewing.

For the purpose of this study, all the interviews were organized by dilemmas, randomized by subjects and year, and then scored using the new standard form scoring manual (Colby and Kohlberg, 1984, in press), which entails a matching of interview judgments to stage-oriented moral judgment criteria organized by moral issue (two issues per dilemma). Scoring was done by dilemma, not by protocol. Thus, one dilemma was scored for all subjects, then a second dilemma, and so on. Scorers were blind to the identity, age, and social group of respondents. In addition to moral stage, the criterion judgment also indicates the mode of moral justification. For each subject, percent usage of each of five stages of moral judgment was then computed as a function of all scored judgments. The subject then received a stage score which could be a single stage (if only one stage had more than 20 percent of his

Table 8.2. Number of Subjects in the Cross-sectional Study By Age and Social Group

Social Group	*Age*				*Total*
	10–12 Years	*13–15 Years*	*16–18 Years*	*19–28 Years*	
Village . . .	17	14	16	16	63
City . . .	11	9	6	20	46

NOTE: Longitudinal subjects are represented more than once.

Table 8.3. An Example of a Dilemma Used in the Study

Dilemma III. Equivalent to Kohlberg's (1958) "Heinz Dilemma"

A man and wife have just migrated from the high mountains. They started to farm, but there was no rain and no crops grew. No one had enough food. The wife became sick from having little food and could only sleep. Finally, she was close to dying from having no food. The husband could not get any work and the wife could not move to another town. There was only one grocery store in the village, and the storekeeper charged a very high price for the food because there was no other store and people had no place else to go to buy food. The husband asked the storekeeper for some food for his wife, and said he would pay for it later. The storekeeper said, "No, I won't give you any food unless you pay first." The husband went to all the people in the village to ask for food, but no one had food to spare. So he got desperate and broke into the store to steal food for his wife.

1. Should the husband have done that? Why?
2. Is it a husband's duty to steal the food for his wife if he can get it no other way?
3. Did the storekeeper have the right to charge that much?

3*a*. (If the subject thought he should steal the food:)
Why is it all right to steal if it is to save a life?

4. If the husband does not feel very close or affectionate to his wife, should he still steal the food?

4*a*. (If the subject thought the husband should not steal the food:)
Would you steal the food to save your wife's life?

5. Suppose it wasn't his wife who was starving but it was his best friend. His friend didn't have any money and there was no one in his family willing to steal the food. Should he steal the food for his friend in that case? Why?

5*a*. If you were dying of starvation but were strong enough to steal, would you steal the food to save your own life?

6. (Everyone:)
The husband broke into the store and stole the food and gave it to his wife. He was caught and brought before the judge. Should the judge send him to jail for stealing or should he let him go free?

judgments) or a mixed stage, indicating his dominant stage and secondary stage (when more than 20 percent of his judgments fell in this stage).*

Thirty protocols, randomly selected, were scored by another trained scorer: For twenty-three protocols (78 percent) there was complete agreement for the stage score, while for seven protocols there was a discrepancy in a half stage (e.g., 2[3] and 3[2]). In no

* Thus, in principle one could obtain a score indicating a mixture of more than two stages, and these could be far apart, e.g., 1(3) (5). This never happened in the present sample, where all subjects were either in one stage or in a mixture of two adjacent stages.

case was there a larger discrepancy. For all the protocols there was an agreement for the substage. The correlation between the MMS (Moral Maturity Score) given by the two scorers was .83. Internal consistency was calculated over the scores received by the individual on the six dilemmas. The obtained Cronbach alpha figure was .72.

Results

Stage of Moral Judgment

Table 8.4 presents the stages and MMS of subjects in the longitudinal study at each testing point. Each row presents one subject. The table allows us to follow the development of an individual's moral judgment at two, three, or four points in time, where the range of ages represented is 10–28 years. The table shows a clear sequence of advance in moral judgment: out of thirty five changes, only four, or 11.4 percent, go against our prediction, a distribution whose chance probability is only .001 (by sign test, Siegel, 1956). In no case do we find the skipping of a stage.

Table 8.5 presents the distribution of subjects in the cross-sectional study according to stage, by age and social group. Subjects with a mixed score (i.e., those who had more than 20 percent of their responses in each of two stages) were combined into one mixed-stage category, which does not distinguish between dominant and secondary stages (i.e., stages 2[3] and 3[2] appear under the same category of 2/3). Table 8.6 presents means and standard deviations of MMS according to age and social group. The MMS data were subjected to analysis of variance by age (four groups) and social group. The analysis showed a strong effect of age, $F(3,101) = 48.1$, and of social group, $F(1,101) = 26.7$, both significant at .001 level, and no significant interaction. Further analysis (*posthoc t* tests) revealed that all age-group differences in each social group were significant at the .05 level.

An examination of Tables 8.5 and 8.6 suggests the following points: (1) In both village and city groups, the findings of the cross-sectional study are consistent with those of the longitudinal study. The results show a sequential advance with age through the stages of moral judgment. The correlation between MMS and age is .71 ($N = 109$). In no case do we find a regression in MMS mean of a group with advancing age. (2) The data show that the development of moral judgment continues after the age of 18 in both village and

Table 8.4. Moral Stage and Moral Maturity Score (MMS) for Longitudinal Subjects

	Age Groups									
	10–11 Years		*12–13 Years*		*14–15 Years*		*16–17 Years*		*18–19 Years*	
Subject	*Stage*	*MMS*	*Stage*	*MMS*	*Stage*	*MMS*	*Stage*	*MMS*	*Stage*	*MMS*
1	1	118	1(3)	186	...	...	...	...	...	...
2	2(1)	150	2(3)	224	...	...	2(3)	239	...	...
3	1(2)	133	2	178	...	...	3(1)	229	...	...
4	...	...	1(2)	158	2(1)	177	...	...	3(2)	263
5	...	...	2(1)	192	2(3)	198	...	...	3(2)	247
6	...	...	...	...	2(3)	207	2(3)	208	...	...
7	...	...	...	...	...	...	3(2)	216	2(3)	243
8	...	...	...	...	...	...	2	192	2	196
9	1(2)	124	2	200	...	...	...	...	...	...
10	1(2)	146	2	209	...	...	...	...	...	...
11	...	...	1(2)	160	2	203	...	...	...	...
12	...	...	2(1)	176	2(3)	247	...	...	...	...
13	...	...	2(1)	188	1(2)	150	...	...	...	...
14	...	...	2	216	2(3)	207	...	...	...	...
15	...	...	...	...	...	...	2	217	2(1)	198
16	1(2)	153	...	...	...	...	...	...	...	...
17	1(2)	172	...	...	...	...	...	...	...	...
18	2	183	...	...	...	...	...	...	...	...
19	2	191	...	...	...	...	...	...	...	...
20	...	...	3(2)	259	...	...	...	...	...	...
21	...	...	3(2)	277	...	...	...	...	...	...
22	...	...	...	...	...	...	2(3)	230	...	...
23	...	...	...	...	...	...	...	...	...	...

Subject	Age Groups							
	20–21 Years		22–23 Years		24–25 Years		26–28 Years	
	Stage	*MMS*	*Stage*	*MMS*	*Stage*	*MMS*	*Stage*	*MMS*
1	...	...	2(3)	218	...	...	...	...
2	...	...	3	281	...	...	...	...
3	...	...	3	296	...	...	...	...
4	...	...	...	...	3	294	...	...
5	...	...	...	...	...	...	...	...
6	...	...	...	...	...	...	3(2)	283
7	...	...	3	311	...	...	4(3)	365
8	...	...	...	...	...	...	3	261
9	...	...	...	...	...	...	...	...
10	...	...	...	...	...	...	...	...
11	...	...	...	...	...	...	...	...
12	...	...	...	...	...	...	...	...
13	...	...	...	...	...	...	...	...
14	...	...	...	...	...	...	...	...
15	...	...	...	...	...	...	...	...
16	4(3)	340	...	...	...	...	...	...
17	4(3)	347	...	...	...	...	...	...
18	2(3)	231	...	...	...	...	...	...
19	4(3)	353	...	...	...	...	...	...
20	...	...	4(5)	434	...	...	...	...
21	...	...	3(4)	367	...	...	...	...
22	...	...	...	...	...	...	2(3)	241
23	3(2)	218	3	296	...	...	...	...

Table 8.5. Number of Subjects in Various Stages by Age and Social Group

Age and Social Group	Stage 1	1/2	2	2/3	3	3/4	4	4/5	Total
10–12 years:									
Village	1	12	3	1	...	...	...	...	17
City	...	4	2	4	1	...	...	...	11
13–15 years:									
Village	...	5	3	6	...	...	...	...	14
City	...	1	...	8	...	...	...	...	9
16–18 years:									
Village	...	2	2	12	...	...	...	...	16
City	...	...	...	4	1	1	...	...	6
19 + years:									
Village	...	...	...	5	9	2	...	...	16
City	...	...	...	4	7	8	...	1	20

city subjects. This result is similar to findings in the United States, which show that moral development continues at least into the third decade of life (Kohlberg, 1973a). This result is of special interest for the village population in light of the following points. (3) We find that the rate of moral judgment development is slower in the village than in the city, and that this is also true for our oldest subjects. The differences between village and city subjects are statistically significant for each of the four age groups (significance is at the .01 level by *posthoc t* test in all four cases). (4) We find no subject older than 15 in the city or 18 in the village within a pure preconventional stage (i.e., Stages 1 and 2), although even in the oldest age group sampled we do find subjects in a mixed Stage 2/3. (5) Among the village subjects there is an indication of stabilization at Stage 3. Only two out of sixteen (12.5 percent) in the oldest age group show any sign of Stage 4 development, as compared to nine out of twenty (45 percent) city subjects of this age. The impression that village subjects stabilized at Stage 3 is strengthened by the tendency noted in point 6. (6) Table 8.4 shows that, in general, subjects tend to show a mixed rather than a pure stage. However, this tendency is weaker after the age of 18, especially for our village subjects. Up to the age of 18, only thirteen out of seventy-three (17.8 percent) are in a pure stage (where a pure stage indicates that only one stage gets

Table 8.6. Means and Standard Deviation for MMS by Age and Group

Social Group	*Age* 10–12 Years	13–15 Years	16–18 Years	19+ Years
Village:				
M	167.05	202.6	228.7	279.3
SD	31.19	31.4	27.7	39.9
City:				
M	206.7	243.3	274.8	312.6
SD	51.4	32.9	34.3	41.0
t value	2.549*	2.979*	3.266*	2.457*

*$p < .01$.

more than 20 percent of the scored responses of the subject), while after this age we find nine out of sixteen (56.3 percent) village subjects and seven out of twenty (35 percent) city subjects showing pure Stage 3 responses. The difference between percentage of subjects of pure stage in the 10–18-year-old group and in the older age group is statistically significant, $x^2 = 7.18, p < .01$. The consistency in the moral reasoning of the older subjects, especially those from the village, suggests a tendency to stabilize, at least temporarily, at this stage of reasoning. Is it then the case that the village people tend to remain in Stage 3, as do Edwards's (1975) Kenyan subjects? No decisive answer is possible here without further follow-up of the village subjects.

Discussion

Universality in Development of Moral Judgment

The first aim of this study was to examine whether the claim of universal structures in moral reasoning, which grew mainly out of research in the United States, would find support in a different culture. Our Turkish village subjects represent a traditional culture quite distinct from the Western urban culture which characterized the subjects of the Kohlberg longitudinal study. Two aspects of the claim of universality are that moral responses of individuals in any culture fit the structures I have suggested (i.e., are classifiable in one of my stages) and that the stage sequence is constant across cultures. A longitudinal study is essential in examining this second element.

The present study has found support for both aspects of the claim, support which should be seen as only a single step in a necessarily much large body of research in different cultures. The longitudinal study presents a consistent picture of sequential advance in the stages of moral development up to Stage 4, as well as in the quantitative score of MMS. This picture was supported in the cross-sectional study both in the village and in the city. It should be mentioned, however, that the sequence observed in this study is limited to the first four stages in my scheme with the exception of one city-bred youth.

Turning to the fitting of the stages to the Turkish data, it seems quite remarkable that the scorers had no difficulty and achieved satisfactory agreement analyzing the Turkish responses according to the moral stages, using a manual which requires a matching of responses. There were differences between Turkish and American responses, as well as between city and village. However, these differences did not interfere with the identification of basic structures which framed the responses. The scorers generally felt the match between actual responses and criterion judgments in the manual to be satisfactory and not forced.

One may argue that this apparent ease in scoring the Turkish data results from an inevitable overlaying of preconceptions on the data, leading to biased interpretation of the responses. This argument is somewhat weakened both by the relatively high reliability between judges and by the observed sequence in development. However, a more important—although far from conclusive—test of this argument would be the judgment of a sensitive and open person who is aware of the possibility of bias (Piaget, 1929). The scorer in this study was aware of the possibility of bias, and sought for cross-cultural variance in addition to searching for universality. Our analysis rests, not on one standard and mechanical response, but on a multitude of judgments generated by several moral dilemmas, each possessing a number of questions. This seems to add to the credibility of the scoring. Yet there is no doubt that more research with maximal openness to the possibility of bias is needed (Price-Williams, 1975).

A related issue concerns the representativeness of our data. Do the dilemmas presented to the subjects constitute true moral issues in their lives? Do their responses to these dilemmas represent genuine thinking in these domains rather than "playing the researcher's game"? The best we can do in regard to these basic problems of cross-cultural research is to examine the dilemmas and the responses from this viewpoint, using relevant ethnographic material (Cole, Gay, Glick, and Sharp, 1971). Our impression is that the dilemmas are representative. The least we can say is that the Turkish responses were given with an appropriate sense of reality and involvement. Again, more research and further examination of these issues are clearly needed.

The universality claim may have another ramification to which this study does not relate. A strong claim of universality would imply that the structures I have described exhaust more or less the whole domain of morality in every culture. Even if one assumes a degree of success in representing the moral domain of one's own culture, such an assumption does not seem as simple for other cultures. It is possible that in other cultures, principles are held which are distinct from ours, and moral reasoning is used that does not fit the structures I have described.

The Rate of Development and Cultural Variation

The universality claim allows for the possibility of differences in the rate and end point of development. Such differences are indeed revealed in our study. The rate of development is slower among village that among city subjects. Our findings do indicate that after the age of 16, all village subjects develop beyond the preconventional level and show Stage 3 judgment (or a mixture of Stages 2 and 3). At the same time, they show scarcely any sign of development beyond Stage 3. Clearly, the data cannot show whether village subjects will adopt Stage 4 judgment in the future. However, the high frequency of a pure Stage 3 and the almost complete lack of Stage 4 among the oldest subjects indicate that Stage 3 may be the stage in which the judgment of village subjects is stabilized, later development being mainly in a further decline of Stage 2 judgments. This coincides with the finding of Stage 3 as the final point of development in the traditional culture studied by Edwards (1975) and supports her suggestion that Stage 3 is a necessary and sufficient level of functioning in societies having a social order based on face-to-face relationships and a high level of normative consensus. These conditions do not necessitate differentiation and integration beyond Stage 3. Thus we have here an equivalent—in the moral domain—of what Berry (1971) has called ecological functionalism.

9. Cultural Universality of Moral Judgment Stages: A Longitudinal Study in Israel

with JOHN SNAREY and JOSEPH REIMER

Introduction

This chapter presents the results of a longitudinal study of moral development among Israeli adolescents. The research objectives were to evaluate the cultural universality of the Kohlberg theory of moral development from the cross-cultural perspective of an Israeli kibbutz and to gain an understanding of the cultural uniqueness of kibbutz social-moral reasoning from the perspective of that theory.

The data presented, based on a sample of ninety-two kibbutz-born and Middle Eastern Israeli adolescents, is able to address these objectives since it is the largest and longest longitudinal study of moral reasoning to date, in contrast to most previous cross-cultural studies of moral development, which have been cross-sectional. These studies have been previously reviewed by Edwards (1981, 1982) and Snarey (1982). The sample also includes males and females in contrast to my original longitudinal study in the United States, which included only male subjects (Kohlberg, 1958; Colby and Kohlberg, 1984, in press; and Chapter 5) and in contrast to my longitudinal study in Turkey with Nisan (Chapter 8) which again included only males (Turiel, Edwards, and Kohlberg, 1978). Finally, the present study also attempts to replicate many of the same analyses that were performed in the United States and in Turkey, the only two previous longitudinal studies that have used the standardized scoring system (Colby and Kohlberg, 1984, in press). This will enable us to make specific comparisons in order to clarify the cross-cultural validity of my model and method.

Research Questions

This study considers six specific research questions. The first three apply conventional psychological indicators of reliability and validity to my theory. To what degree is the moral development of kibbutzniks, as measured by my model and method, like that of all other people? The second three apply anthropological methods to my theory. To what degree is the moral reasoning of kibbutzniks different from that of the people from other cultures?

Developmental Questions

Stage sequence

The invariant-sequence assumption of my moral development theory should be supported by the combined results of the blind-scored longitudinal data. Stage change should be upward and sequential, and stage regressions should not be found beyond the level explainable by scoring error (cf. Kurtines and Grief, 1974; Broughton, 1978b; Chapter 5).

Structural wholeness

Structural wholeness is a critical empirical criterion of construct validity. The internal consistency of the model and measure was previously established for subjects in the United States, using the standardized scoring manual (Chapter 5; Colby and Kohlberg, 1984, in press). A replication of their analyses on the kibbutz longitudinal data should yield similar findings.

Age norms and stages

Moral judgment can be expected to be positively correlated with age, as developmental theory suggests and previous research has found. The age norms among kibbutz subjects will also be compared with the findings from previous research.

Cultural Questions

Culturally defined sex differences

Moral development among kibbutzniks should not yield sex differences. Structural-developmental theory's claim to universality is not consistent with inherent sex differences in the structure of moral reasoning. From the anthropological perspective, however, the general equality of sex roles in the community's socialization process also suggests that sex differences in the level of moral development should not be expected among kibbutz subjects. That is, while the issue of sex difference in moral judgment is a topic of current debate (Gilligan, 1977, 1982), we would argue that sex differences will not be found unless culturally defined sex roles assign different educational and social rights to males and females. Since kibbutz ideology stresses equality of sex roles, at least as an ideal, we would anticipate that there would not be sex differences in moral development among kibbutzniks.

Culturally defined moral issues

There may be culturally based differences in choices that subjects make regarding what issue or content within a dilemma they will consider the most important. Each of the dilemmas requires the subject to make a content choice between two moral issues, for example, to steal or not to steal the drug. From an ethnographic perspective, one might expect Middle Eastern Youth Aliyah students to more commonly favor particular kinds of action (such as upholding the law and authority), which reflect the content of moral reasoning stressed in their culture and families, while kibbutz-born subjects might be expected to more commonly select other choices (e.g., upholding conscience, life, contract). This difference between the two groups, if it exists, would also be expected to decrease as Youth Aliyah students spend more time on the kibbutz.

Culturally defined moral structures

Another aspect of the cultural uniqueness question, aside from content differences, is the possibility that the scoring manual simply misses or misunderstands particular structures of moral reasoning because of cultural differences between subject and theoretician (cf. Bloom, 1977; Simpson, 1974). We assessed the cultural uniqueness of stage formulations by examining interview material that the scorers indicated was difficult to score. This material was analyzed for patterns that relate to kibbutz norms and values.

Method

Samples

Kibbutzim are intentionally created collective communities in Israel characterized by communal child rearing, collective economic production, and direct participatory democracy. The kibbutz under study, which we will call Ramat Yedidim, was founded in 1949 in the northern Galilean hills by a group of young Jewish men and women who had grown up in the Young Guard (Hashomer Hatzair) Youth Movement.

Kibbutz Ramat Yedidim's educational system, in general, is typical of the approach of other kibbutzim within the National Kibbutz Federation (Kibbutz Artzi), the Federation most loyal to the traditional approach to structuring a kibbutz learning environment. Small age-graded peer groups (*kvutzot*) live together in their own houses from infancy until 18, when they enter the army. Each of these cohorts is given a name, which serves some of the same identification functions as a family surname in the United States, although they also have family surnames. Each cohort of children has one or more full-time teachers who guide their formal education and also a house-parent or caretaker (*metapelet*) who is responsible for directing and socializing the children in the communal living and work activities of the children's house. Since, to a limited degree, their peers are experienced as their family and their educators as parental figures, there is an unusual unity to their educational, work, and social experience. Kibbutz Ramat Yedidim has, however, modified an element of the traditional kibbutz movement's approach to educating adolescents in that they fully integrate city-born youth into the kibbutz educational system. Nearly all of these youth are so-called Middle Eastern Jews (i.e., their parents immigrated to Israel from the Arab countries) and they also come from economically disadvantaged backgrounds. A group of Middle Eastern 12- to 13-year-olds are brought to the kibbutz, through the services of the Youth Aliyah organization, and are fully integrated with a parallel cohort of kibbutz-born youth. This new cohort of kibbutz-born and city-born youth are educated together and live together until early adulthood (cf. Snarey, 1982; Reimer, 1977; Kohlberg 1971a).

The ninety-two adolescents in this study are divided into four subsamples, each of which corresponds to a kibbutz cohort. Each subsample of kibbutz-educated students includes both kibbutz-born and city-born adolescents. The subjects in all four subsamples were residing at Kibbutz Ramat Yedidim, with the following two exceptions; subsample I was supplemented with kibbutz-born subjects from Kibbutz F and with two groups of city-born and city-educated youth; subsample II was supplemented with a group of city-born, kibbutz-educated youth from Kibbutz M.

Table 9.1. Sample Description

Cohort Numbers	*Cohort Names*	*Place of Birth*	*Place of Residence*	*Background Data at First Interview*				
				Age	*Grade*	*Males*	*Females*	*N*
I A	Cyclamen Youth Aliyah	City	Kibbutz RY	15–17	10	10	0	10
I B	Federation Kibbutz-born	Kibbutz F	Kibbutz F	15–17	10	9	0	9
I C	Middle Class Academic Students	City	City	15–17	10	9	0	9
I D	Lower Class Vocational Students	City	City	15–17	10	10	0	10
II A	Sparrow Kibbutz-born	Kibbutz RY	Kibbutz RY	13–15	8	4	3	7
II B	Sparrow Youth Aliyah	City	Kibbutz RY	13–15	8	4	4	8
II C	Gazelle Youth Aliyah	City	Kibbutz M	13–15	8	6	5	11
III A	Crane Kibbutz-born	Kibbutz RY	Kibbutz RY	12–13	7	6	2	8
III B	Crane Youth Aliyah	City	Kibbutz RY	12–13	7	8	3	11
IV A	Turtle Dove Kibbutz-born	Kibbutz RY	Kibbutz RY	13–15	8	2	3	5
IV B	Turtle Dove Youth Aliyah	City	Kibbutz RY	13–15	8	1	3	4
Totals						69	23	92

Research Instrument

The Kohlberg moral judgment interview, Form A, was used to collect the longitudinal data on moral development. The three dilemmas in Form A are III, the classic Heinz dilemma, involving a husband's conflict between the issues of life versus law; III′, the Brown dilemma, involving a court judge's conflict between conscience versus punishment; and I, the Joe dilemma, involving a father-son conflict between contract and authority. Each dilemma is followed by nine to twelve standardized probe questions designed to clarify the reasons "why" a subject has made a particular moral judgment.

The dilemmas and probe questions were translated into Hebrew and were also modified slightly for use with kibbutz subjects, for example, U.S. dollars became Israeli pounds, Heinz became Moshe, and so forth.

Data Collection Procedure

The subjects were interviewed individually in Hebrew. Each interview was conducted privately, tape-recorded, and later transcribed. Moral judgment interviews were collected from the entire cohort shortly after a group of Youth Aliyah students arrived at Kibbutz Ramat Yedidim or shortly after the Youth Aliyah group was integrated with the parallel group of kibbutz-born subjects. All subjects in a particular subsample were then reinterviewed one or two years later and again five years later. For some kibbutz cohorts a city-residing comparison group was also interviewed. The interview schedule, according to both sample subgroups and frequency of interview, is presented in Table 9.2. The frequency of the longitudinal follow-up interviews may be summarized as follows: thirty two subjects were interviewed three times each for a total of 96 interviews, thirty two subjects were interviewed two times for a total of 64 interviews, and twenty eight subjects were interviewed only once. Thus, taken together, there was a total of 188 interviews from ninety two subjects.

Scoring and Analysis

Moral judgment interviews

Moral development interviews were scored using the new standard issue scoring manual (Colby and Kohlberg, 1984, in press). This standardized scoring method yielded two indices of moral

Table 9.2. Schedule of Interviews

Cohort Numbers	Cohort Names	Time I N	Time I Ages	Time II N	Time II Ages	Time III N	Time III Ages	Time IV N	Time IV Ages	Time V N	Time V Ages	Total Interviews Per Cohort
I A	Cyclamen Youth Aliyah	10	(15–17)	6	(17–19)					6	(24–26)	22
I B	Federation Kibbutz-born	9	(15–17)							4	(24–26)	13
I C	Middle Class Academic Students	9	(15–17)									9
I D	Working Class Vocational Students	10	(15–17)									10
II A	Sparrow Kibbutz-born			7	(13–15)			7	(15–17)	7	(20–22)	21
II B	Sparrow Youth Aliyah			8	(13–15)			8	(15–17)	8	(20–22)	24
II C	Gazelle Youth Aliyah			11	(13–15)			11	(15–17)			22
III A	Crane Kibbutz-born					8	(12–13)			8	(18–19)	16
III B	Crane Youth Aliyah					11	(12–13)	11	(13–14)	11	(18–19)	33
IV A	Turtle Dove Kibbutz-born							5	(13–15)	5	(18–20)	10
IV B	Turtle Dove Youth Aliyah							4	13–15)	4	(18–20)	8
Total Interviews Per Year		38		32		19		46		53		188

development: a global stage score and a moral maturity score. The global stage score is a categorical stage assessment that was calculated on a nine-point scale (1,1/2, 2, . . . 5). The moral maturity score is a continuous stage assessment that can range from 100 to 500.

To assign each of the 188 interviews in this study a global stage score and a moral maturity score, they were divided and distributed randomly to three expert scorers, one of whom was a coauthor of the scoring manual. All interviews were scored blind from English transcripts, that is, without knowing the subject's name, age, sex, cohort membership, time of testing, or scores assigned to other interviews. To assess interrater reliability, twenty interviews were selected randomly and scored independently by all three scorers. Comparing the level of agreement between the global stage scores, we found that in 65–70 percent of the cases an interview received the exact same score from any two scorers. In 95 percent of the cases the interview received the exact same score or within one half of a stage score from all three scorers. The mean reliability between all three scorers was estimated to be .89 for the categorical global stage scores and .91 for the continuous moral maturity scores, using Cronbach's alpha. To assess the translation reliability, seven interviews were also randomly selected for independent scoring in Hebrew by a bilingual scorer. Comparing the level of agreement on a nine-point scale between the global stage score assigned to the untranslated interview and the score assigned to the translated version, we found that in 57 percent of the cases an interview received the exact same score and 100 percent received the exact same or within one half of a stage score. The interrater correlation was .84 for the global stage scores and .93 for continuous scores. Translating the interviews, therefore, did not significantly alter the scoring reliability.

Findings and Analysis

Developmental Findings

The findings from the four samples will be combined in order to evaluate the degree to which they support the three developmental questions regarding the basic theoretical assumptions of my developmental model and the reliability of the new scoring method. The results will also be compared with findings from the only two previous longitudinal moral development studies—one in the

United States and one in Turkey—that have used the standardized scoring manual.

Developmental sequence and regressions

According to my theory, developmental sequence or stage change should be consecutive and upward, that is, without regressions or omissions. The actual interview scores for each of the sixty-four longitudinal subjects in this study are presented in Table 9.3. Then Table 9.4 summarizes the types of stage change that occurred in the interval from time n to time $n + 1$.

As Table 9.3 indicates and Table 9.4 summarizes, small amounts of regression occurred in six out of ninety-six longitudinal interviews (6.3 percent) using the customary nine-point scale, and regressions occurred in seven out of ninety-six cases using the most differentiated thirteen-point scale. To evaluate this finding, previous test-retest reliability data can be used as an estimate of the number of such deviations that can be attributed to measurement error. In Chapter 5 I reported test-retest error for the Form A interview to be 19 percent. I also reported that the longitudinal regressions in the United States were 5 percent for the Form A interview using the nine-point scale and 7 percent using the thirteen-point scale and thus we conclude that since the test-retest reversals are well over twice as great as the longitudinal reversals, it seems reasonable to attribute the violations of longitudinal sequence to measurement error. One might add, of course, that some of the nonreversals might also be due to measurement error, but it still seems reasonable to conclude that the assumptions regarding developmental sequence and regressions are supported by the kibbutz findings, since the percentage of violations of the longitudinal sequence in this kibbutz longitudinal study was nearly identical to the finding in the United States longitudinal study. This conclusion is also supported by the fact that in no case did a longitudinal subject skip a stage. Each subject reached his or her highest stage at the last interview time by going through each of the preceding intermediate stages between the first and last interview stage scores.

Structural wholeness

I have suggested that, in addition to invariant sequence, the most critical empirical criterion of construct validity is "structural wholeness," or internal consistency. This refers to the generality

Table 9.3. Longitudinal Sequence

Subject ID* and Testing Time	Moral Development Scores: Global Stage	Moral Development Scores: Maturity Scale
IA. Cyclamen Cohort—Youth Aliyah Subjects at Kibbutz Ramat Yedidim		
01-1	3/4	352
01-2	3/4	350
01-5	4/5	429
03-1	3/4	338
03-2	3/4	332
03-5	3/4	350
05-1	2/3	266
05-2	3/4(2)[b]	316
05-5	4/5	437
07-1	2/3	246
07-2	3	302
07-5	3/4	355
09-1	3	310
09-2	3	300
09-5	3/4	338
10-1	3	300
10-2	2/3[x]	280
10-5	3/4	326
IB. Federation Cohort—Kibbutz-born Subjects at Other Kibbutzim		
11-1	3	290
11-5	4	377
13-1	3	320
13-5	4	415
14-1	3/4(2)[b]	350
14-5	3/4	367
16-1	3	314
16-5	3/4	373

Table 9.3—Continued

Subject ID* and Testing Time	Moral Development Scores: Global Stage	Maturity Scale
IIA. Sparrow Cohort—Kibbutz-born Subjects at Kibbutz Ramat Yedidim		
39-2	2/3	256
39-4	3	315
39-5	3/4	343
40-2	3	322
40-4	3/4	350
40-5	4	396
41-2	3[x]	320
41-4	3/4	341
41-5	3/4	332
42-2	3/4	335
42-4	3/4	341
42-5	3/4	350
43-2	3/4	327
43-4	3[x]	318
43-5	4	400
44-2	3/4	325
44-4	3/4	340
44-5	3/4	350
45-2	3	300
45-4	3/4	327
45-5	3/4	334
IIB. Sparrow Cohort—Youth Aliyah Subjects at Kibbutz Ramat Yedidim		
46-2	3	283
46-4	3/4	336
46-5	3/4(5)[b]	350
47-2	2	200
47-4	2/3(4)[b]	245
47-5	3	300

Table 9.3—**Continued**

Subject ID and Testing Time*	*Moral Development Scores*	
	Global Stage	*Maturity Scale*
48-2	2/3	253
48-4	3	310
48-5	3/4	357
49-2	2/3	263
49-4	3	315
49-5	4	423
50-2	2	190
50-4	3	316
50-5	3	316
51-2	2/3	272
51-4	3	300
51-5	3/4	323
52-2	2/3(4)[b]	283
52-4	3	296
52-5	3/4	346
53-2	2/3	250
53-4	3	300
53-5	3/4	362
IIC. Gazelle Cohort—Youth Aliyah Subjects at Kibbutz M		
54-2	2/3	255
54-4	3	300
55-2	3	300
55-4	3	300
56-2	3	311
56-4	3	300
57-2	3/4	340
57-4	3[x]	300
58-2	2/3	250
58-4	3	282
59-2	3	307
59-4	3/4	338

Table 9.3—Continued

Subject ID* and Testing Time	Moral Development Scores: Global Stage	Maturity Scale
60-2	2/3	250
60-4	3	300
61-2	3	300
61-4	3	300
62-2	3	300
62-4	3	310
63-2	3	300
63-4	3	318
64-2	3	300
64-4	3	311
IIIA. Crane Cohort—Kibbutz-born Subjects at Kibbutz Ramat Yedidim		
65-3	3	286
65-5	3/4	335
66-3	3	306
66-5	3/4	347
67-3	2/3(4)[b]	276
67-5	3/4	326
68-3	2/3	263
68-5	3/4	325
69-3	3	300
69-5	4	380
70-3	3	285
70-5	4	382
71-3	2/3	230
71-5	3/4	350
72-3	3	300
72-5	3/4	366
IIIB. Crane Cohort—Youth Aliyah Subjects at Kibbutz Ramat Yedidim		
73-3	2/3	244

Table 9.3—Continued

*Subject ID** *and* *Testing Time*	*Moral Development Scores* *Global* *Stage*	*Maturity* *Scale*
73-4	2/3	254
73-5	3/4	332
74-3	2/3	250
74-4	2/3(4)[b]	278
74-5	3/4	336
76-3	2/3	277
76-4	2/3	266
76-5	3/4(2)[b]	319
77-3	2/3	263
77-4	3	280
77-5	4	386
78-3	2/3(4)[b]	267
78-4	3	283
78-5	3/4	331
79-3	3/4	356
79-4	3[x]	300
79-5	3/4	379
80-3	2/3	253
80-4	2/3	270
80-5	4	392
81-3	3	281
81-4	2/3[x]	269
81-5	3/4	333
85-3	2/3	256
85-4	2/3	272
85-5	3/4	370
87-3	3	293
87-4	2/3[x]	264
87-5	3/4(5)[b]	380
88-3	3	311
88-4	3	271
88-5	3/4	340

Table 9.3—Continued

Subject ID* and Testing Time	Moral Development Scores	
	Global Stage	Maturity Scale
IVA. Turtle Dove Cohort—Kibbutz-born Subjects at Kibbutz Ramat Yedidim		
89-4	3	306
89-5	3/4	373
90-4	3	318
90-5	4	404
91-4	3/4	346
91-5	3/4	371
92-4	3/4	350
92-5	4/5	436
93-4	3	286
93-5	3/4	350
IVB. Turtle Dove Cohort—Youth Aliyah Subjects at Kibbutz Ramat Yedidim		
95-4	2/3	263
95-5	3/4	350
96-4	3	293
96-5	3/4	357
97-4	3	234
97-5	3/4	359
99-4	3	304
99-5	3	311

[x]Indicates a stage score reversal.

*The gaps in the subject ID numbers refer to cross-sectional subjects who have not been included in this longitudinal report.

[b]Represents 10 percent or more usage of a third stage.

of stage usage across moral issues and dilemmas within the interview. If stages are to be understood as structural wholes, a subject's stage should be consistent over various moral issue and dilemmas. A series of analyses were conducted to evaluate this claim.

Table 9.4. Summary of Longitudinal Sequence

Type of Stage Change	*Frequency*	*Percentage*
Stage Progression		
2 to 2/3	1	
2 to 3	1	
2/3 to 3	13	
2/3 to 3/4	12	
2/3 to 4	1	
3 to 3/4	23	
3 to 4	8	
3/4 to 4	1	
3/4 to 4/5	3	65.6%
No Stage Change		
2/3 to 2/3	5	
3 to 3	10	
3/4 to 3/4	12	28.1%
Stage Regression		
3 to 2/3	3	
3/4 to 3	3	6.3%
Total	96	100. %

One indication that a stage forms a structured whole would be the degree to which any particular individual reasoned at the same stage or two adjacent stages at any one interview time. The 160 interviews presented in Table 9.3 indicate that in 150 (94 percent) of the cases all reasoning was at one major stage or in two adjacent stages, and 10 (6 percent) of the interviews included reasoning at three adjacent stages. In no case was a subject reasoning at nonadjacent stages. The interviews that show reasoning at three adjacent stages were identified using a 10 percent error boundary (see Colby and Kohlberg, 1984, in press). The 6 percent showing usage of three stages found in this longitudinal study is comparable to the U.S. longitudinal study, in which 9 percent of the interviews exhibited reasoning at three adjacent stages.

Another procedure for evaluating the structural-wholeness claim is to examine the correlations among the stage scores for each of the six issues that make up the global or overall interview score. A correlation matrix for the entire sample is presented in Table 9.5. Consistent with my assumptions, the correlations were all positive, significant, and moderately high (.74 to .42). If the structural-wholeness hypothesis is correct, one would also expect to find one major factor, not several factors, accounting for the major portion of the variability. The factor loadings and principal components analysis for three age groupings (12–15, 16–19, 20–26) on all six moral issues were thus examined. The first factor accounts for 79 percent to 100 percent of the variance, with eigenvalues of 3.49, 2.88, and 2.74. The second factor's eigenvalue is always less than one for each age group and for the sample as a whole. Nevertheless, to consider the possibility of a multifactoral solution, the factors were rotated. Again, using a varimax (orthagonal) rotated factor matrix, no underlying consistent pattern is interpretable across the factors. Thus, in summary, the eigenvalue and proportion of variance were predominately accounted for by only one general factor, and rotation of multiple factors did not yield any consistent pattern across the factors. The structural-wholeness hypothesis, therefore, cannot be rejected; the findings suggest that there is a general dimension of moral reasoning that is not issue specific. These findings are also clearer than those from the U.S. study in which the second eigenvalue was greater than 1 (1.05 to 2.05) for similar age groups.

Age norms and moral stage

Moral development would be expected to show a clear relationship with age. The actual relationship between age and moral stage can be summarized by observing the mean and range of stages for each age. Stage 2/3 was the lowest commonly assigned

***Table 9.5.* Correlations Among Six Moral Issues in Form A Interview for Total Sample**

	Law	*Conscience*	*Punishment*	*Contract*	*Authority*
Life	0.7191[a]	0.6509[a]	0.4757[a]	0.4977[a]	0.4228[a]
Law		0.7458[a]	0.7022[a]	0.5158[a]	0.4578[a]
Conscience			0.6312[a]	0.4687[a]	0.5259[a]
Punishment				0.4681[a]	0.4803[a]
Contract					0.4942[a]

a. Significance level is $p<.001$.

stage, 61 percent of the subjects at age 12 were assigned this stage. No one aged 18 or over scored at Stage 2/3. Stage 3 was the modal stage for ages 13–14 and 15–17. No one in the 13–17 age group scored higher than Stage 3/4. Stage 3/4 was assigned to 62 (33 percent) of the interviews and was the modal stage for the 18–26 age groups. Stage 4 was assigned to 10 (5 percent) of the interviews; it did not appear until the 18–19 age group, at which time 14.3 percent of this cohort was assigned Stage 4. Stage 4/5 also appears for the first time in the 18–19 age group, but it does not become common until the 24–26 age group. Stages 4/5 and 5 thus appear to be confirmed as stages of adulthood and not of adolescence.

In sum, the mean moral maturity scores gradually and consistently increased from 278 at age 12 to 377 at ages 24–26. A regression analysis indicated that age accounts for 40 percent of the variance in moral maturity scores.

As Table 9.6 indicates, the Israeli age norms compare quite favorably with the findings from the two previous longitudinal studies that have used the standardized scoring system. Colby and I found that the scores on the Form A interview in the United States ranged from Stage 1 to Stage 4/5 between ages 10 and 26, and Nisan and I also found that in Turkey the scores ranged from Stages 1 to 4/5 between ages 10 and 28; the Israeli scores are somewhat similar; they ranged from Stage 2 to Stage 4/5 between ages 12 and 26, but there were no scores at Stages 1 or 1/2. The kibbutz mean stage scores at *all* ages were consistently higher than the mean stage scores in the United States or in Turkey. Stage 2/3, for instance, disappeared on the kibbutz by age 16, whereas it continued to be present until age 24 in the United States and until age 26 in Turkey. On the other hand, global Stage 4/5 was first exhibited in the kibbutz sample at age 18, but in the United States Stage 4/5 was first present at age 24; the one subject in the Turkish sample who scored at Stage 4/5 was age 23.

Another dimension of the relationship between age and stage is the stability of individual differences, that is, the relationship between a subject's score at one age with the same subject's score at a later age. The correlations among moral maturity scores for the different ages were thus examined. The correlations between moral maturity scores at one age with scores at a later age were positive but not always high or significant. The highest correlation was between scores at ages 15–17 and scores at the adjoining 18–

Table 9.6. **Percentage of Subjects in Each Age Group at Each Stage by Nation**

			Global Moral Stages								
Ages	*Country*	*N*	*1*	*1/2*	*2*	*2/3*	*3*	*3/4*	*4*	*4/5*	*Mean*
12	Israel	18				61.1	33.3	5.6			278
10	U.S.	21	5.3	26.3	42.1	15.8	10.5				204
10–12	Turkey	28	3.5	57.1	17.9	17.9	3.5				183
13–14	Israel	40			2.5	32.5	55.0	10.0			288
13–14	U.S.	37		11.1	8.3	58.3	16.7	2.8			249
13–15	Turkey	23		26.1	13.0	60.2					219
15–17	Israel	70			1.4	17.1	57.1	24.3			303
16–18	U.S.	46		2.3	4.5	22.7	31.8	36.4			299
16–18	Turkey	22		9.1	9.1	72.7	4.5	4.5			241
18–23	Israel	50					14.0	68.0	16.0	2.0	348
20–22	U.S.	33				6.5	25.8	54.8	9.7	3.2	335
19–28	Turkey	36				25.0	44.4	27.8	0.0	2.8	298
24–26	Israel	10						50.0	30.0	20.0	377
24–26	U.S.	25				4.3	17.4	43.5	21.7	13.0	365
28–30	U.S.	38					21.6	48.6	16.2	13.5	362
32–33	U.S.	23					4.5	68.2	18.2	9.1	366
36	U.S.	9						77.8	11.1	11.1	374

NOTE: The three samples are equivalent in that each includes an approximately equal number of lower and middle class subjects.

19 age range (.75 $p < .05$), but scores at ages 13–14 were the best general predictors of scores in later adolescence and early adulthood (.48 with scores at ages 15–17, .49 with scores at ages 18–19, and .56 with scores at ages 20–23). The Kohlberg and Colby longitudinal study in the United States also found that scores at ages 13–14 were better predictors of later stages, presumably because this age represents a period of stabilization after entering adolescence. Scores at age 12 may be poor predictors because some individuals who will reach formal operations in cognitive development have not yet done so, and cognitive development is a necessary prerequistie for moral development. The correlations reported by Colby and I between scores at age 13–14 with later ages were generally higher than was found in this present study: .70 with scores at ages 16–18, .46 at ages 20–22, .70 at ages 24–26, and .67 at ages 28–30.

Cultural Findings

The findings reported in the previous section supported the developmental assumptions underlying the Kohlberg theory of moral development. While these data have lent support to arguments for the cross-cultural universality of my model as well as my method of studying moral judgment, they have not spoken to the cross-cultural uniqueness of moral reasoning among kibbutzniks. This section will focus on the cultural content of moral reasoning and the ways in which the cultural characteristics of kibbutz moral reasoning may be unique.

Culturally defined sex differences

One assumption of structural development theory is that there will not be sex differences in the *structure* of moral reasoning. Yet some researchers, notably Carol Gilligan, have argued that there are sex differences in moral judgment (1977, 1982). Table 9.7 presents a cross-tabulation of sex by global stage for all cohorts that included *both* male and female subjects (i.e., samples 2, 3, and 4). The association between sex and moral stage scores is weak (Cramer's V = .19) and not significant ($X^2 = 4.65$, $df = 3$, $p =$ NS).

The relationship between sex and specific moral stages can be further examined by considering the percentage of reasoning at each stage for males and females. This information is presented in Table 9.8. Sex and stage usage are cross-tabulated for each stage. The strength of the association between sex and percentage using

Table 9.7. Cross-Tabulation of Sex by Global Stage Scores

Sex		Global Stage Scores 2,2/3	3	3/4	4,4/5	N
Males	n	21	25	25	7	78
	%	26.9	32.0	32.0	8.9	
Females	n	9	25	20	2	56
	%	16.0	44.6	35.7	3.5	

NOTE: $X^2=4.65$, $df=3$, $p=$NS, V=.19.

a particular stage is always weak (V ranged from .16 to .25), and the sexes do not differ significantly in the percentages with which they use any of the stages.

In sum, there were no significant sex differences in moral judgment between male and female subjects. Controlling for cultural background, stage usage, and interview time also did not reveal any significant differences.

Culturally Defined Postconventional Morality

One aspect of the cultural-uniqueness question can be assessed by examining the interview material which the scorers considered to be difficult to evaluate in terms of stage structure. That is, the present scoring system requires the matching of interview judgments with scoring manual judgments or examples, but occasionally the reason a subject gives for prescribing a particular moral action cannot be matched with a structural example in the scoring manual. Under these circumstances the scorer assigns a "guess" score to the judgment and it is included, but weighted less, in the scoring algorithm. Such difficult material, especially within cross-cultural interviews, may indicate aspects of moral reasoning that the stage model and scoring manual miss or misunderstand because they were created from interviews collected in the United States. That possibility was explored by clinically examining each judgment to which the scorers had given a guess score (cf. Price-Williams, 1975).

Systematic examination of the guess-scored material at the conventional stages did not reveal any new or unique structures of reasoning, but the higher stage judgments that were difficult to score did appear to be culturally patterned. Kibbutzniks typically brought much more of a communal emphasis to solving the dilem-

***Table 9.8.* Cross-Tabulation of Sex with Percentage of Stage Usage at Each Stage**

Stage and Sex		*Stage Usage in Percent*					*Chi-square p value*
		0%	*4–24%*	*25–49%*	*50–74%*	*75–100%*	
Stage One							
Males	*n*	76	2	0	0	0	
	%	97.4	2.5				
Females	*n*	54	2	0	0	0	
	%	96.4	3.5				NS
Stage Two							
Males	*n*	47	11	15	4	1	
	%	60.2	14.1	19.2	5.1	1.2	
Females	*n*	40	7	5	4	0	
	%	71.4	12.5	8.9	7.1		NS
Stage Three							
Males	*n*	2	6	11	34	25	
	%	2.5	7.6	14.1	43.5	32.0	
Females	*n*	1	2	8	19	26	
	%	1.7	3.5	14.2	33.9	46.4	NS
Stage Four							
Males	*n*	31	15	17	9	6	
	%	39.7	19.2	21.7	11.5	7.6	
Females	*n*	21	14	8	13	0	
	%	37.5	25.0	14.2	23.2		NS
Stage Five							
Males	*n*	74	4	0	0	0	
	%	94.8	5.1				
Females	*n*	52	3	1	0	0	
	%	92.8	5.3	1.7			NS

NOTE: N = 134; male $n = 78$, female $n = 56$. Percentages refer to rows.

mas than did North Americans, and they expressed a much greater investment in the preservation and maintenance of their society. They also used the concept of a "kibbutz" as a moral justification in a way that seemed to suggest a conventionalization or cultural legitimization of postconventional principles. In particular, some judgments that were scored as guess score 4 or guess score 4/5 could be understood as higher stage judgments from a kibbutz perspective. To illustrate this thesis the following example is given from an interview with a 19-year-old female:

Q.—It is against the law for Moshe to steal the drug. Does that make it morally wrong?
A.—It will be illegal or against the formal law, but not against the law which is the moral law. Again, if we were in a utopian society, my hierarchy of values, and the hierarchy of others through consensus, would be actualized.

Q.—What are those values?
A.—Socialism! But don't ask me to explain it.

Q.—What is wrong with a nonsocialistic society that makes it unjust?
A.—In a utopia there will be all the things I believe in. There would not be murder, robbery, and everyone will be equal. In this society, the greatest value, the value of life, is perfectly held. Disvaluing life is forbidden. It is like our dream, our ideal. In one way it is ridiculous since this utopia will never be achieved, of course. You can even observe children in the kindergarten; they can be very nasty and cruel to each other.

Q.—Should people still do everything they can to obey the law in an imperfect world?
A.—Yes, unless it will endanger or hurt another important value. . . . But generally speaking, people should obey the law. The law was created in order to protect . . . from killing, robbery, and other unjust uses of power. . . . I believe everyone has the right to self-growth and the right to reach happiness. . . . People are not born equally genetically, and it is not fair that one who is stronger physically should reach his happiness by whatever means at the expense of one who is weaker, because the right to happiness is a basic human right of every person and equal to all. A nonkibbutz society that is based on power negates the right and possibility of those who are weaker to get their happiness. . . .

Q.—So should people who break the law be punished?
A.—From the point of view of society, yes, but it is too general. [One] has to take into consideration both sides which means the conscience law behind the formal legal law. It is an infinite cycle between these . . . it is a paradox for you have to sometimes break the formal law that was designed to protect the law behind the law.

In a similar vein, a 26-year-old male answered the same question as follows:

Q.—Should people try to do everything they can to obey the law?
A.—In principle, yes. It is impossible to have any kind of state, country, society, without laws. [Otherwise], it will be complete anarchy and those who have the power will dominate the weaker.

Q.—Why is that wrong?
A.—I am strong. [Laughter.] But really, you can see in totalitarian societies today in contrast to, for example, the kibbutz. You damage the principle of democracy and most importantly, you destroy the principle of equality. Which is why I [have chosen to] live on a kibbutz.

In scoring these excerpts as *guess* Stage 4 or 4/5, the scorer made two judgments: (1) there was not a clear match example in the scoring manual by which to evaluate these judgments, and (2) clinically, these statements seem to be at least Stage 4, but they do not seem to be fully postconventional Stage 5 judgments. Since the subjects do appear to be arguing for the maintenance of the social system, it seems reasonable, in the absence of material in the scoring manual, that these excerpts were so scored. Yet, one could also argue that there is a sense in which the systems perspective common to the subjects seems to be based on moral principles which are prior to or should serve as the foundation of society or of a particular kind of society—the kibbutz. One notes that the kibbutz functions for the subjects as an imperfect embodiment of a more utopian ideal. In raising the "kibbutz" as a moral argument, it is not clear to North Americans that the kibbutzniks are making claims for the protection of human rights and the furtherance of social equality. Yet, for some young adult kibbutzniks, the very concept of "kibbutz" is based on the idea of a commitment, a social contract, between all the members, who share a consensus regarding the equal social rights and the equal democratic participation responsibilities of all persons. Allusions to the system falling apart or becoming dysfunctional may also not necessarily be simply conventional Stage 4 judgments *if* the reason they are protecting the social system is because it is based on the principles of democracy, equality, and individual human worth. To use the kibbutz as a *moral* justification is to appeal to these principles if this is what "kibbutz" means to them. That is, the kibbutz is seen by some subjects as a principled society and this conventionalization of the postconventional creates a scoring problem (cf. Cole et al., 1971). The clear recognition in the first excerpt, however, that the kibbutz does not fully meet these ideals, is a critical feature that points to the autonomous use of principles that are prior to kibbutz society. This interpretation also gives a different meaning to the so-called conformity of kibbutz youth observed by Bettelheim and Spiro. Our previous review of this literature (Snarey and Blasi, 1980) suggested that kibbutz youth were not more conforming but that more of them are enabled to reach the conventional stages of moral development earlier than nonkibbutz youth. The kibbutz conventionalization of postconventional moral principles may suggest further that the moral conventions to which they are "conforming"are themselves simply more intuitive and less clearly articulated forms of postconventional principles.

In summary, we have argued that some higher stage judgments may have been mistakenly scored as primarily Stage 4 because the scoring manual does not fully capture the cultural uniqueness of postconventional reasoning on the kibbutz. A more culturally sensitive scoring of the excerpts presented above would thus have assigned a score of Stage 5. Such a culturally sensitive scoring would not, however, have drastically increased the number of Stage 5 interviews in the sample. While the current stage distribution included three young adults who scored at Stage 4/5, the above considerations would have increased the number to five interviews scored as fully Stage 5.

Summary Conclusion

The moral development of 92 adolescents in Israel was studied with the aims of evaluating the cross-cultural validity of my claim to universality in the development of moral judgment. The research questions focused both on the degree to which the moral development of kibbutzniks is like that of all other people and on possible culturally defined variations in moral development between kibbutz and nonkibbutz populations.

Developmental Universality of Moral Judgment

The longitudinal findings indicated that stage change was consecutive, gradual, and upward. The number of stage regressions was not higher than one would expect due to scoring error and in no case did a subject skip a stage. The Colby and Kohlberg analyses regarding structural wholeness and internal consistency were also replicated. The 188 interview profiles indicated that in 83 percent of the cases all reasoning was at one major stage or in transition between two adjacent stages.The correlations among the stage scores for each of the six moral issues within each interview were all positive, significant, and moderately high. Finally, the eigenvalue and proportion of variance were predominantely accounted for by only one general factor.

Age showed a clear relationship with stage and accounted for 40 percent of the variance in moral maturity scores. The age norms compare favorably with the findings from the two previous longitudinal studies that have used the standardized scoring system. The range of stages is from 2 to 4/5, compared to a range of 1 to 4/5 in the United States and Turkey. Furthermore, the kibbutz mean stage scores at all ages are consistently higher than the mean stage scores in the United States and Turkey. This distribution of the kibbutz stage scores is also impressive when one considers that previous research has found that children in rural communities generally progress more slowly, not faster, than city children (Turiel, 1969, p. 125; Edwards, 1975). Yet in all studies to date, Stages 4/5 and 5 have been relatively rare: eight subjects in the United States, Chapter 5, eighteen kibbutz founders in Israel (Snarey, 1982), one subject in Turkey (Chapter 8), and three kibbutz youth in the present study.

Regarding the stability of individual differences, Colby and I had found that scores at ages 13–14 were the best predictors of later stages. The finding from the United States was replicated in Israel, although the correlations between scores at age 13–14 with later scores were generally lower in this present study than they had been in the United States.

Culturally unique aspects of postconventional reasoning were revealed by an analysis of interview material that the scorers had labeled as difficult to score. It was found that the kibbutz was seen by some subjects as a principled society, and this conventionalization of the postconventional created problems in scoring such that five interviews evaluated under the blind scoring procedure were scored as Stage 4 or 4/5, whereas a culturally sensitive blind-scoring placed them at Stage 5. The kibbutzniks' communal emphasis and greater investment in the preservation and maintenance of their society obscured their autonomous use of moral principles when considered strictly from the perspective of the standard issue scoring manual. This suggests that perhaps one of the most important cultural implications of this present study is that the scoring manual needs to be fleshed out with culturally indigenous examples of reasoning at the higher stages if it is to avoid missing or misunderstanding the reasoning of subjects from a different cultural background than that of the subjects on which the manual was based. This finding also underscores the importance of the researcher being thoroughly immersed in the culture of the population under study.

In conclusion, the Kohlberg model and method have fared well in that the kibbutz findings are consistent with a structural model of moral development. The data, however, also revealed some degree of cultural uniqueness in the moral judgments of kibbutzniks. These findings should be seen, of course, as only one part of a broader investigation of the universality claim of my theory within diverse cultural settings.

Appendix A: The Six Stages of Justice Judgment

In Chapter 2, we gave a detailed account of the moral stages in terms of the underlying sociomoral perspectives of each stage. Table 2.1 summarized this characterization in terms of "What Is Right," "Reasons for Doing Right," and "Social Perspective of the Stages." There is a relation between general social perspective-taking levels as described by Selman (1980) and moral perspective-taking, which we have interpreted as one in which a social perspective level is necessary but not sufficient for a moral perspective level. Moral perspectives are perspectives on social values, not social facts, and are perspectives upon the desirable and not just the desired. Stages of moral judgment are structures of thinking about *prescription,* about rules or principles obliging one to act because the action is seen as morally right. The mode of judgments stressed in our dilemma interviews is "deontic"; they not only refer to the twelve basic moral norms but stress the modal elements of "rightness, "rights," and "obligations." Rights and obligations at higher stages are correlative to one another: obligations entail respect for persons and rights. These justice modes of judgment are in turn justified by the value elements of impartial order, maximum welfare (each person is considered to count as one), social harmony, and fairness (as reciprocity and prescriptive role-taking).

Our moral dilemmas address three problems of justice that have been identified in Aristotle's *Nicomachean Ethics.* The first problem is one of distributive justice; that is, the way in which society or a third party distributes "honor, wealth, and other desirable assets of the community" (Aristotle, *Ethics,* 1130b). This is done in terms of such operations as equality, desert, or merit (i.e., reciprocity defined in terms of proportionality), and finally, equity in light of need or extenuating circumstance. The second type of justice problem is

---

Sections of this appendix are adapted from Levine, C., and DeVos, E., "The Form-Content Distinction and Kohlberg's Theory of Moral Development," unpublished manuscript, 1983. This appendix is revised from that of Volume I which appears in this volume as Table 2.1 in chapter 2.

commutative justice, which focuses upon voluntary agreement, contract, and equal exchange. A third and closely related type of justice problem is the problem of corrective justice, which supplies corrective principle in private transactions which have been unequal or unfair and require restitution or compensation. In addition, corrective justice deals with crimes or torts violating the rights of an involuntary participant and in this sense requires restitution or retribution.

There is a fourth type of justice problem which is not independent of the three already mentioned. It is the problem of procedural justice, an aspect of justice which must be addressed in problems of distributive, commutative, and corrective justice. This problem of procedural justice, a concern more clearly distinguishable in high moral stage judgments, often represents the considerations which moral philosophers treat as validity checks on moral reasoning. These "checks" are derived from a concern for balancing perspectives or making one's judgments reversible (i.e., employing the golden rule) and from a concern for making one's judgments universalizable (i.e., employing Kant's categorical imperative). The reversibility check asks, Would you judge this action as fair if you were in the other person's shoes? The universalizability check asks, Would you judge this action right if everyone were to do it? Procedural justice, which involves a special set of considerations at lower stages, becomes a solution to substantive justice problems of distribution and correction at Stage 6, where universalizability and reversibility constitute self-conscious validity checks on one's reasoning.

Before proceeding to our descriptions of the six stages, we wish to make a few comments about justice operations and that we understand them as developing into a grouped structure, in the Piagetian sense, by Stage 6.

In Chapter 3 we pointed out that there were four orientations to the justice problems reviewed above—that is, the norm-maintaining, utilitarian, perfectionistic, and fairness orientations. We also pointed out that justice operations were explicitly used in the fairness orientation, where they defined elements of fairness such as reciprocity, equality, equity, balancing perspectives, and so on. In contrast, we suggested that the justice operations were implicit in the use of elements of the other three justice orientations. Our stage descriptions will, accordingly, focus more directly on the fairness orientation, where the use of the justice operations is most clearly visible.

For us the justice operation of equality can be defined as (*a*) identical quantities of goods for all, or for all relevant, persons and/or (*b*) equal consideration of competing claims prior to distribution or adjudication and/or (*c*) assertion that all persons are equal as a justification for (*a*) and (*b*) (i.e., since all are of equal moral worth, then . . .). We define equity as an operation of compensation on equality; that is "shades of inequality." For example, an equity operation constructs a notion of unequal distribution in order to compensate for inequalities that may have existed prior to the situation or that are due to special circumstances within the situation. A contemporary example of the equity operation is the justification of "reverse discrimination" with regard to affirmative action policy. We define a third justice operation, reciprocity, as an operation of distribution by exchange. Of course, what is considered just reciprocity varies by stage. However, in general terms reciprocity is an operation which exchanges merit or "just deserts," reward, or punishment in return for effort, virtue, talent, or deviance. At lower stages what is considered reciprocal and equal is often hard to distinguish since reciprocity implies some notion of equality in exchange. At Stage 6, however, reciprocity is distinguished from and derived from an explicit concern for equality or equity. Our fourth justice operation is prescriptive role-taking or balancing perspectives, an operation closely tied to the problem of procedural justice. At higher stages, prescriptive role-taking stems from the realization that one must (*a*) take into account the perspectives of others and (*b*) imaginatively change positions with others in such a way that one is satisfied with the outcome of the dilemma regardless of who one is (i.e., moral musical chairs or the validity check of reversibility mentioned already). At lower moral stages prescriptive role-taking is often closely tied to the other justice operations as well as to the respondent's sense of moral norms. For example, a question regarding upholding the norm of property is answered with the response: How would you feel if someone stole from you? While one can detect a prescriptive role-taking operation in a response such as this, it clearly does not take the form of a self-conscious validity check on justice reasoning as it does at Stage 6. The final operation which we identify is the operation of universalizability. This operation is closely tied to the operations of equality and equity, and it is expressed by the appeal, Is it right for anyone to do *X*? This statement implies a concern for equality and equity, and at the principled stages it is explicitly expressed as a self-conscious validity check on the conceptions of equality and equity which one has employed in moral reasoning.

We now offer the following stage descriptions. Each moral stage is reviewed by discussing stage-specific sociomoral perspectives on norms in general and upon the justice operations of equality, equity, reciprocity, prescriptive role-taking, and universalizability. Each stage description is then completed with examples of justice operations applied to the three justice problems of distributive, commutative, and corrective justice.

Stage 1: Heteronomous Morality

The perspective at Stage 1 is that of naive *moral realism.* That is, the moral significance of an action, its goodness or badness, is seen as a real, inherent, and unchanging quality of the act, just as color and mass are seen as inherent qualities of objects. This realism is reflected by an assumption that moral judgments are self-evident, requiring little or no justification beyond assigning labels or citing rules. For example, telling on your brother is wrong because it is "tattling," breaking into the druggist's store is wrong because "you're not supposed to steal." Punishment is seen as important in that it is identified with a bad action rather than because the actor is attempting pragmatically to avoid negative consequences to him- or herself. Likewise, there is an absence of mediating concepts, such as deservingness or intentionality, through which the particular circumstances of the case alter its moral significance. Thus, moral rules and labels are applied in a literal, absolute manner and both distributive and retributive justice are characterized by strict equality rather than equity. Characteristics of persons that determine their authority, power, or moral worth tend to be physicalistic or categorical. For example, the father is the boss because he's bigger. You should steal to save a life if it is that of Betsy Ross, who made the flag. The perspective of moral realism represents a failure to differentiate multiple perspectives on dilemmas. This means that authority and subordinate, self and other, and other individuals in conflict or disagreement are assumed to share a single perception of the situation and of the morally appropriate response to it. Morality at Stage 1 is heteronomous in the Piagetian sense; that is, what makes something wrong is defined by the authority rather than by cooperation among equals.

Norms and Justice Operations

At Stage 1 *norms* are concrete rules which are not identified with the psychological perspective of, or expectations of, any individuals, including the self. Instead, norms are perceived categories of right and wrong behavior. These categories define types of actions and types of persons (e.g., thieves, good sons, important persons, etc.). *Equality* at Stage 1 is a notion of distribution by strict equalization to those who are classified within any one category of actor or person. Unequal distribution can be acceptable if to persons of a less valued category. *Reciprocity* is a notion of "exchange" of goods or actions without regard for the psychological valuing of goods or actions by self or other. This exchange is balanced in terms of the idea of "same for same" (i.e., Eskimos kill seals so seals should kill Eskimos). The operations of *equity* and *prescriptive role-taking* are absent at Stage 1 because of the egocentric, heteronomous nature of this stage of reasoning. Finally, at Stage 1 *universalizability* exists in the sense that a rule or norm is generalized and admits of no exceptions, with the possible exception of authorities who create and enforce the rule or norm. In formal terms, Stage 1 reasoning is characterized by the uncoordinated use of equality and reciprocity.

Distributive justice is guided by strict equality, and special considerations of need or deservingness are not taken into account. In cases where an authority is involved, distributive justice is guided by heteronomous obedience to or respect for authority. This is illustrated by the following response to Dilemma I (see appendix B for dilemmas and questions):

Q.—Should Joe refuse to give his father the money?
A.—If his father told him to save the money up, I'd give it to him, because he's older than you and he's your father. Because he's older than him.

Corrective justice tends to be retributive and based on strict reciprocity. For example, "The doctor should be given the death penalty (if he performs the mercy killing)—he killed the woman so they should kill him." Again, moderating circumstances such as intention are not incorporated. Also characteristic of Stage 1 is the notion of immanent justice—that punishment necessarily follows as an automatic consequence of transgression. For example:

Q.—Why is it important to keep a promise?
A.—If you don't then you're a liar. You're not supposed to lie because you'll get pimples on your tongue.

Commutative justice, as already illustrated, is a matter of following externally defined rules: "You should keep a promise because if you don't, you're a liar." Avoidance of the punishment that would inevitably follow transgression is another reason to follow promise-keeping rules (as is also the case with other rules).

Stage 2: Individualistic, Instrumental Morality

Stage 2 is characterized by a concrete individualistic perspective. There is an awareness that each person has his or her own interests to pursue and that these may conflict. A moral relativity develops out of the understanding that different persons can have different, yet equally valid, justifications for their claims to justice. That is, there is a recognition of more than one perspective on a situation and a respect for the moral legitimacy of pursuing one's own interests. The morally right is relative to the particular situation and to the actor's perspective on the situation. Since each person's primary aim is to pursue his or her own interests, the perspective at Stage 2 is pragmatic—to maximize satisfaction of one's needs and desires while minimizing negative consequences to the self. The assumption that the other is also operating from this premise leads to an emphasis on instrumental exchange as a mechanism through which individuals can coordinate their actions for mutual benefit. Thus, the moral realism of Stage 1 is no longer in evidence. An important limitation of Stage 2 is that it fails to provide a means for deciding among conflicting claims, ordering or setting priorities on conflicting needs and interests.

Norms and Justice Operations

At Stage 2 *norms* are psychological expectations of individual selves. They are standards for regulating action which are thought to be satisfying to the needs or interests of individual selves. At this stage norms have no fixed values except insofar as they allow individuals to have expectations of one another which maintain a balance through exchange. The Stage 2 operation of *equality* recognizes the category "persons" as all individuals, including the self, who have needs, desires, and so on that can be satisfied through one's own action and through the exchange of goods and actions with others. Categories of good and bad actions or actors have no interent value at this stage except insofar as they represent an expectation of right that an individual would hold psychologically in terms of his or her interests or needs. The operation of *reciprocity* in this context defines a notion of concrete exchange of equal values or goods in serving the needs of self and other. The operations of equality and reciprocity are coordinated at Stage 2, as they are not at Stage 1. For example, at this stage one can reason that "Joe should refuse to give his father the money because he worked for it and earned it, and if his father wants money, then he should earn it himself." The Stage 2 operation of *equity* compensates by focusing on the needs, not the intentions, of actors. For example, it can be fair for the poor to steal because they *need* the food. The operation of *prescriptive role-taking* at this stage acknowledges the fact that the self would have needs as others do (e.g., "If I were Heinz and needed the drug for my wife as he did, then I'd steal it"). While perspectives are balanced at this stage in the sense that self can understand the needs and actions of the other, they are not balanced in the sense of taking into account conflicts between perspectives. At Stage 2 the operation of *universalizability* is expressed in terms of a concern for limiting deviation from norms by naturally self-interested persons. Thus, it is a concern that if deviation from norms is allowed for one, then there could be deviation by many, and this could produce a state of affairs which would interfere with what is considered the fair pursuit of self-interest and fair exchange. An example of this type of concern can be seen in the following Stage 2 response: "The judge should punish Heinz, because if he doesn't others may try to get away with stealing."

Distributive justice involves coordinating considerations of equality and reciprocity, so that judgments take into account the claims of various persons and the demands of the specific situation. In addition to equality and reciprocity Stage 2 can use an equity operation to consider individual needs or intentions in the light of special or extenuating circumstances. The Stage 2 conception of equity is based on the reasonable pursuit of individual needs and interests, whereas at Stage 3, equity operations consider shared social norms as the basis of distribution.

The coordination of reciprocity with equality in distributive justice at Stage 2 is illustrated by the following response to Dilemma I:

Q.—Should Joe refuse to give his father the money?

A.—He shouldn't give him the money, because he saved it and should use it however he wants. If his father wants to go fishing he should make his own money.

In this judgment, the reciprocal relation between working for money and being able to spend it is seen as applying equally to both father and son.

Corrective justice at Stage 2 can involve reference to individual needs or intentions as the basis for equity. For example, "The doctor should not be given the death penalty for mercy-killing the woman, because she wanted to die, and he was just trying to put her out of her pain." This represents the beginning of a recognition that one person can see the other's point of view and modify his or her own action in response. Another example is the following: "The judge shouldn't punish the doctor, because the judge would think that if it was him who was sick he would want the doctor to kill him too."

Commutative justice at Stage 2 is based on instrumental exchange which serves to coordinate in a simple way the needs and interest of individuals. For example, it is seen as important to keep promises to ensure that others will keep their promises to you and do nice things for you, or it is important in order to keep them from getting mad at you.

Stage 3: Interpersonally Normative Morality

At Stage 3 the separate perspectives of individuals are coordinated into a third person perspective, that of mutually trusting relationships among people, which is embodied in a set of shared moral norms according to which people are expected to live. These moral norms and expectations transcend or are generalized across particular persons and situations. Stage 3 norms can be distinguished from Stage 1 rules in that norms represent an integration of perspectives that have been recognized as separate, a coming to general social agreement on what constitutes a good role occupant, whereas the orientation to rules at Stage 1 represents a failure to differentiate individual perspectives. The primacy of shared norms at Stage 3 entails an emphasis on being a good, altruistic, or prosocial role occupant and on good or bad motives as indicative of general personal morality. This recognition of the importance of motives also distinguishes Stage 3 norms from Stage 1 rules. As a result of the socially shared perspective, the individual at Stage 3 is particularly concerned with maintaining interpersonal trust and social approval.

The justice operations of Stage 3 are most clearly represented in golden rule role-taking—Do unto others as you would have others do unto you. Logically, this involves the coordination of the inverse and reciprocal operations. It involves a second-order operation whereby a Stage 2 reciprocal exchange is subjected to evaluation by reference to a superordinate or shared norm against which its fairness can be judged. That is, reciprocal exchanges are not necessarily fair but must be negated or affirmed in relation to standards of morally good conduct that stand outside the reciprocal exchange.

Norms and Justice Operations

At Stage 3 *norms* are understood as expectations shared by persons in relationship. The purpose of norms is to maintain relationships and the loyalty, trust, and caring between persons in the relationship or group. Such relational norms are felt as obligatory. The Stage 3 operation of *reciprocity* constructs a conception of obligation as debt; the other has given a value or something valuable to the self, and the self cannot terminate this inequality by a simple one-to-one exchange but feels a sentiment of gratitude, loyalty, or duty to reciprocate. For example, when asked, "Is it a duty for Heinz to steal?" Case 9 says: "If I was Heinz, I would have stolen the drug for my wife. You can't put a price on love, no amount of gifts make love. You can't put a price on life either." This respondent is asserting that relationships and obligation are not reducible to the Stage 2 notion of concrete equal exchange. When scored as Stage 2, Case 9 was asked, "Should Heinz steal for a friend?" He replied, "No, that's going too far. He could be in jail while his friend is alive and free. I don't think a friend would do that for him." As the example of Case 9 suggests, Stage 3 reciprocity involves the notions of obligation, debt, and gratitude which allow one to understand reciprocity as going beyond concrete notions of equal exchange to maintaining relationship, mutuality of expectations, and sentiments of gratitude and obligation. Stage 3 reciprocity can also construct an idea of exchange whereby persons who are good or have worked hard are entitled to their just deserts or rewards (e.g., Heinz should steal if he doesn't love his wife, out of gratitude or appreciation). The operation of *equality* at this stage constructs a category of persons who are to be treated equally based on the notions of "good role occupants" and "persons with good motives." The operation of *equity* at Stage 3 leads to the making of exceptions for those who deviate, based on the recognition of extenuating circumstance and upon empathy with good intentions. At this stage, the operations of reciprocity, equality, and equity can be expressed in a way that indicates that they are coordinated and linked to a prescriptive role-taking operation. The following response exemplifies this idea: "It's all right for Heinz to steal the drug because the druggist is heartless in ignoring Heinz's wife's right to live." Another example of this coordination of operations at Stage 3 can be seen in the following response: "The judge should be lenient with Heinz because he has suffered enough and didn't want to steal." The Stage 3 operation of *prescriptive role-taking* or balancing perspectives is the Golden Rule. There is a clear use of the Golden Rule for the first time at this stage. It is expressed as the idea that something is right or fair from one's point of view if one could accept it as right or fair from the other's point of view. Here the Golden Rule can be a positive prescription (e.g., "You should help someone to save their life, because if you were them you would want that to be done for you") or it can be expressed as a limiting prescription in the sense that an expectation at odds with taking the other's viewpoint is not considered to be obligating (e.g., "Joe should refuse to give his father the money because his father should not demand the money and should be concerned with how Joe feels"). An example of how the operation of *universalizability* is expressed at this stage can be seen in the following response: "All people should obey the law because without laws immoral people would cause chaos." At Stage 3 this operation of universalizability expresses a desire to limit deviation that would interfere with the actions and the realization of the intentions of morally motivated persons (i.e., those who are loyal, good, etc.). Thus, the chaos feared at Stage 3 is one that would interrupt a community of persons with good intentions.

Distributive justice at Stage 3 is based on the coordinated use of operations of equality, reciprocity, and equity. At Stage 3, the strict equality and literal reciprocity of Stage 2 is replaced and modified by reference to shared norms or motives. Thus, in addition to focusing on individual needs or interests, as at Stage 2, persons are now considered in terms of their goodness, badness, and deservingness. An example is provided by the following response to Dilemma III: "That must be a pretty terrible druggist. A druggist is like a doctor; he's supposed to save people's lives." Thus, the Stage 2 notion of reciprocity as "he made the drug so he can do what he wants with it" is negated by reference to socially shared norms of a good druggist.

Corrective justice at Stage 3 also emphasizes the relevance of motives and whether or not the transgressor is living up to a shared conception of a good person. If so, punishment is not warranted:

Q.—Should the judge sentence Heinz?
A.—The judge should see why he did it and see his past record. Let him go free and give a warning.

Q.—Why?
A.—He did it from the fondness of his heart . . . what most humans would do.

Commutative justice also involves the modification of reciprocity by reference to shared norms and deservingness. For example, while a young child might freely agree to trade his dollar for an adult's twenty-five-cent candy bar, at Stage 3 the fairness of this exchange would be denied on the ground that the adult knows better and should not take advantage of the child's ignorance. That is, at Stage 3 the adult should live up to a socially shared conception of his benevolent, protective role in relation to the child.

A similar idea is represented by the following response to Dilemma I: "Joe shouldn't give his father the money, because even though, as his parent, his father can demand the money, he shouldn't do it because that would be selfish and childish."

Stage 4: Social System Morality

At Stage 4 the individual takes the perspective of a generalized member of society. This perspective is based on a conception of the social system as a consistent set of codes and procedures that apply impartially to all members. The pursuit of individual interests is considered legitimate only when it is consistent with the maintenance of the sociomoral system as a whole. The informally shared norms of Stage 3 are systematized at Stage 4 in order to maintain impartiality and consistency. A social structure that includes formal institutions and social roles serves to mediate conflicting claims and promote the common good. That is, there is an awareness that there can be conflicts even between good role occupants. This realization makes it necessary to maintain a system of rules for resolving such conflicts. The perspective taken is generally that of a societal, legal, or religious system which has been codified into institutionalized laws and practices. Alternatively, the perspective may be that of some higher moral or religious law which is embodied in the individual's conscience and which may conflict with institutionalized law. In this case, internal conscience or moral law is equated with some system of divine or natural law. That is, moral judgments at Stage 4 are made in reference to institutions or systems—either legal and social institutions or moral and religious institutions and systems of belief.

Norms and Justice Operations

At Stage 4 *norms* promote cooperation or social contribution and act as regulations designed to avoid disagreement and disorder. *Equality* as an operation constructs the idea of "equality before the law"; that is, persons are equal in the sense that the rights and obligations of each are defined by societal standards such that each counts as a citizen. For example, it is reasoned that "you should obey a law even if you don't agree with it because a law is made by the majority of people and you have to consider what's good for the majority." Examples of the *equity* operation at Stage 4 can be seen in the following responses: "The judge should be lenient to Heinz in order to demonstrate that the law can be fair or humane." In other words, equity at this stage makes exceptions to the general application of norms on the basis of the idea that societal standards may not be sufficiently sensitive to take into account certain individual circumstances or needs. This equity operation is different from the Stage 3 notion in the sense that it is the system and not a specific other that is recognized to be the agent responsible for exception making. The operation of *reciprocity* at this stage is articulated as a "norm of reciprocity" linking the individual with the collectivity. There is a sense of duty, obligation, or debt to society incurred by the benefits received from living in or having membership in the institutions of society. Such an idea is expressed in the following response to Dilemma III: "The druggist should have used his invention to benefit society," and "it is important to save another's life because people must have some sense of responsibility for others for the sake of society." The operation of *prescriptive role-taking* at Stage 4 achieves a balanced perspective between individual actions and societal standards, an idea expressed in the following response: "Heinz should steal the drug but he should still see that it is wrong in society's eyes and that he'll have to be prepared to accept the consequences." Finally, at this stage the operation of *universalizability* constructs the idea of limiting deviation for the sake of maintaining universalized attitudes of respect for law and the integrity of societal organization. This idea is expressed in the following response: "One should obey the law because respect for the law will be destroyed if citizens feel they can break it just because they disagree with it."

Distributive justice at Stage 4 is based upon the coordinated use of the three justice operations. However, at Stage 4 these operations are modified by a concern for impartiality, respect for social institutions (such as systems of authority and private property), and considerations of social merit and contribution to society. Generally, maintaining respect for property rights as a return for investment of effort is considered to be central to social organization. On the other hand, property rights may also be seen as contingent upon demonstration of social responsibility. This is exemplified by the following response to Dilemma III:

Q.—Did the druggist have the right to charge that much?
A.—No, for him to make that much profit is ignoring his responsibility to people.

Corrective justice at Stage 4 centers on the notions of impartiality in application of the law and corrective action as protecting society through deterrence, by removing threats to society or by providing a means for the offender to "pay his or her debt to society." The importance of upholding impartiality or consistency reflects a concern about procedural justice which emerges as a central justice problem at Stage 4. This is illustrated by the following response to Dilemma III:

Q.—What would be the best reason for the judge to give him a sentence?
A.—Exceptions to the law cannot be given. This would lead to totally subjective decisions on the part of the law enforcers.

Commutative justice at Stage 4 is based on a recognition of the importance of contractual agreements for maintaining a smoothly functioning society or on the value of upholding one's moral character, integrity, or honor. For example:

Q.—Is it important to keep a promise to someone you don't know well?
A.—Yes. Perhaps even more so than keeping a promise to someone you know well. A man is often judged by his actions in such situations, and to be described as being a "man of honor" or a "man of integrity" is very fulfilling indeed.

Stage 5: Human Rights and Social Welfare Morality

The Stage 5 prior-to-society perspective is that of a rational moral agent aware of universalizable values and rights that anyone would choose to build into a moral society. The validity of actual laws and social systems can be evaluated in terms of the degree to which they preserve and protect these fundamental human rights and values. The social system is seen ideally as a contract freely entered into by each individual in order to preserve the rights and promote the welfare of all members. This is a "society-creating" rather than a "society-maintaining" perspective. Society is conceived of as based on social cooperation and agreement. Within the Stage 5 perspective, the primary focus may be either on rights or on social welfare. The former orientation emphasizes the point that some rights must be considered inviolable by the society. These rights cannot be abridged even through freely chosen contracts. Each person has an obligation to make moral choices that uphold these rights, even when they conflict with society's laws or codes. There is a concern for the protection of the rights of the minority that cannot be derived from the social system perspective of Stage 4. The social welfare orientation reflects a rule-utilitarian philosophy in which social institutions, rules, or laws are evaluated by reference to their long-term consequences for the welfare of each person or group in the society.

Norms and Justice Operations

At Stage 5 *norms* are defined as maximizing and protecting individual rights and welfare and are seen as being created among free persons through procedures of agreement. The *equality* operation at this stage recognizes the fundamental equal rights and equal worth of individuals as reflected in judgments about the ultimate value of human life and human liberty. At Stage 5 the *equity* operation reasserts equality claims when norms, laws, or procedures exist which are insensitive to, or prevent the realization of, basic human rights and respect for the value of human life. An example of such a view can be seen in the following response to Dilemma III: "It may not be wrong to break a law where the function of it was not protecting rights, but was protecting infringements on them." Unlike previous stages, where the "target" of compensation for the equity operation was some notion of equality, at Stage 5 the target becomes the norms, laws, or procedures. This shift in perspective is a function of the fact that at Stage 5 equality notions of life and liberty are fundamental assumptions in reasoning and provide for the foundation of norms, whereas at earlier stages notions of equality are derived from norms, laws, and so on and are employed to justify them. The *reciprocity* operation at this stage constructs an idea of the exchange of concrete or symbolic equivalents between freely contracting individuals. In this notion, the key idea is free agreement into contract and not just the idea of the equivalence implied in exchange. At Stage 5 the *prescriptive role-taking* operation stresses the necessity of taking into account the viewpoint of each individual involved in a social situation; that is, each is seen as, and is to be counted as, an individual. This idea is expressed in the following response to Dilemma IV: "The doctor should take the women's point of view as to whether to live or not, out of respect for her own sense of dignity and autonomy." An example of how equality, equity, and reciprocity are coordinated at Stage 5 can be seen in the following response concerning the issue of equal opportunity: "Each should have an equal chance to make their contribution to society and reap the appropriate benefits, even if they have different starting points or are disadvantaged." The operation of *universalizability* at this stage expresses a universalized regard for the value of human life and liberty. Moral norms or laws should be generalized or universalized for human beings living in any society.

The justice operations of *distributive justice* at Stage 5 are structured around respect for fundamental human rights and a rational hierarchy of rights and values, or around a process of social cooperation and agreement. The latter is exemplified in the following response to Dilemma III:

Q.—Last time we talked you mentioned something about a priori rights. . . .

A.— . . . it revolves around what I was saying just now about rights that kind of go with being a human being, but really those rights have been defined by us as people, by agreements that we have reached through some kind of social process, and so I may be kind of backing off from the concept. . . .

Corrective justice also focuses on human rights and/or social welfare, and retributive notions of punishment are given up. Capital punishment, for instance, is typically rejected as retributive. *Procedural justice,* including a concern for due process, is closely related to corrective justice at Stage 5. It is assumed that the practice of consistently applying due process will (in a reasonably just legal system) lead to more equity than will the practice of making each individual decision on an *ad hoc* basis. Corrective justice may also be oriented toward effecting social change through the judge's discretion in interpreting the law. For example, "I can see the point of the judge trying to act as a reforming force in law by handing down a sentence which is so light as to effectively say the law itself is wrongly applied here."

Commutative justice focuses on contract as a necessary form of social agreement, the foundation of human relationships. That is, making and being able to depend upon agreements is the basis for social relationships and a source of moral obligation: "Society is interrelationships with other individuals. You would have no basis for that relationship if there were no trust or acting in good faith, so to speak." As is true of distributive and corrective justice, commutative justice at Stage 5 may also focus on respect for the rights of the parties to an agreement. The importance of upholding contracts is seen as deriving from the fact that people warrant respect in their own right as individuals having intrinsic worth and dignity. Breaking an agreement is seen as a violation of the other's intrinsic dignity or value.

Stage 6: Morality of Universalizable, Reversible, and Prescriptive General Ethical Principle(s)

The sociomoral perspective of Stage 6 is that of "the moral point of view," a point of view which ideally all human beings should take toward one another as free and equal autonomous persons. This means equal consideration of the claims or points of view of each person affected by the moral decision to be made. This prescriptive role-taking is governed by procedures designed to insure fairness, impartiality, or reversibility in role-taking. Procedures of this sort are formalized in various ways. One formalization is Rawls's original position of choosing under "a veil of ignorance" in which the chooser does not know which person in a situation or society one is to be and must choose a principle or policy with which one could best live in any position including, especially, the position of the person(s) who would be most disadvantaged in the society. A second formalization is that of "moral musical chairs," a second order application of the Golden Rule. Not only is Heinz to take the point of view of the dying person, of the druggist, and of himself, but in doing so each person (druggist, dying person) is expected to take the point of view of the other in putting forward his claim and so modifying it. A third formalization is expressed through an emphasis on actual dialogue, as in what Habermas calls an ideal communication situation, the equivalent of internal dialogue as described by Kohlberg. A fourth, utilitarian, formalization by Harsanyi is that of considering preferences under the condition of having an equal probability of being any of those involved in a situation or a society. It is manifested in response to a dilemma by considering the point of view of each person involved and balancing these points of view. It is also manifested in explicit statements of the intrinsic worth, dignity, or equality of every human being, that is, in expressing the attitude of respect or care for persons as ends in themselves, not solely as means to achieving other values, no matter how lofty or desirable, such as the good of society or human survival and development. It is manifest in using the criterion of universalizability, that is, would I want anyone in my (or Heinz's) position to choose the way I do? It is manifest, fourth, in using one or more general principles to make a decision. General principles are distinct from either rules or rights, first, in being positive *pre*scriptions rather than negative *pro*scriptions (don't kill, don't steal or cheat), and second, in that they apply to all persons and situations. Respect for human dignity may imply sometimes breaking the rules or violating societally recognized rights (stealing the drug, giving a lethal dose of morphine at the request of a dying woman in pain). General principles at Stage 6 may be one or several. Single principles include the principle of justice or respect for human personality or dignity and the principle of utility or benevolence, that is, act so as to maximize the welfare of all individuals concerned, the attitude of universal human care or *agape.* Multiple principles of justice include the principle of maximum quality of life for each, maximum liberty compatible with the like liberty of others, equity or fairness in distribution of goods and respect. These principles may be expressed either in terms of the language of human rights (and reciprocal duties) or in the language of care and responsibility for human "brothers and sisters."

Operations and Principles

At Stage 6 the operations we have been discussing form a coordinated whole which constitutes a self-conscious structure for moral decision making. At Stage 5 law and moral norms are grounded on the operations of equality, equity, and so on. At Stage 6 these operations become self-conscious principles. Given this self-consciousness of moral agency and decision making, the operations of prescriptive role-taking (i.e., balancing perspectives) and universalizability become operative principles as well as being validity checks on the reasons given for upholding moral laws or norms. Stage 6 is not so much "based" on a new social perspective beyond Stage 5's notion of a prior-to-society perspective as it is on a *deliberate* use of the justice operations as principles to ensure that perspective when reasoning about moral dilemmas. These characteristics of Stage 6 reasoning require that Stage 6 raise dialogue to a principle, a principle of procedure or "moral musical chairs." Thus, while Stage 5 is grounded on the notion of fixed contract or agreement, Stage 6 is oriented to the process by which agreements or contracts are reached as well as to ensuring the fairness of the procedures which underlie such agreement. Underneath the fixed contract and agreement of Stage 5, designed to protect human rights, is the notion of the importance of maintaining human trust and community. At stage 6 the notion of trust and community becomes the precondition for dialogue, human rights, and so on. (We should note that Stage 5 has difficulty balancing the notion of fixed contract with the underlying notions of trust and community, a problem that Stage 6 resolves through the operation of dialogue, a derivative of moral musical chairs.)

Distributive Justice at Stage 6, in addition to the principle of equality, uses the principle of equity or fairness. At this stage equity does not include reference to special rewards for talent, merit, or achievement. These are largely seen as resulting from differences in genes or in educational and social opportunities which are morally arbitrary, or to unequal distribution by society. However, Stage 6 equity does include recognition of differential need, that is, the need to consider the position of the least advantaged. Where distribution of scarce basic goods must be unequal (e.g., issues of who should live in "life-boat" dilemmas) a lottery approach is preferred to favoring the strong or the more socially useful.

Corrective Justice is not retributive; while punishment through either incarceration or restitution is seen as necessary to protect the rights or welfare of potential or actual victims of crime through isolation or deterrence, it is not based upon inflicting suffering or death as "repayment" for demerit or immorality. The offender is still seen as a human being with human dignity to be respected as far as this is compatible with justice principles. For example, the actions of Heinz stealing the drug or Dr. Jefferson performing euthanasia are seen to require no punishment, but they do require one to consider issues of procedural justice.

Commutative Justice is based on the recognition of trust and mutual respect as the bases of contracts and promises. Promises are seen as the foundation of contracts. Promises presuppose and affirm a moral relationship between promisor and promisee. A violation of a promise is both a violation of trust and a violation of a relationship of mutual respect between promisor and promisee as autonomous persons of worth and dignity. It is the violation of a right awarded to the promisee in making the promise. Promises may be modified or violated only insofar as they maintain a moral relation of mutual respect or reversible role-taking; for example, one may break an appointment to serve the urgent need of a third party, a violation of promise which the promisee as a moral person would necessarily understand through ideal role-taking or "moral musical chairs." Violation of promises is not so much seen as a violation of the self's integrity (Stage 4) as it is seen as an issue of the integrity of the other and of the relationship.

Appendix B: The Nine Hypothetical Dilemmas*

ASTERISKED QUESTIONS may be eliminated if time for interviewing is limited.

Moral Judgment Interview

Form A

Dilemma III: In Europe, a woman was near death from a special kind of cancer. There was one drug that the doctors thought might save her. It was a form of radium that a druggist in the same town had recently discovered. The drug was expensive to make, but the druggist was charging ten times what the drug cost him to make. He paid $400 for the radium and charged $4,000 for a small dose of the drug. The sick woman's husband, Heinz, went to everyone he knew to borrow the money and tried every legal means, but he could only get together about $2,000, which is half of what it cost. He told the druggist that his wife was dying, and asked him to sell it cheaper or let him pay later. But the druggist said, "No, I discovered the drug and I'm going to make money from it." So, having tried every legal means, Heinz gets desperate and considers breaking into the man's store to steal the drug for his wife.

1. Should Heinz steal the drug?
1a. Why or why not?
*2. [*The following question is designed to elicit the subject's moral type and should be considered optional.*] Is it actually right or wrong for him to steal the drug?
*2a. [*The following question is designed to elicit the subject's moral type and should be considered optional.*] Why is it right or wrong?

---

* The numbering of the dilemmas reflects their placement in the original research interview (Kohlberg, 1958). Since the numbers quickly became labels denoting the particular dilemmas, they were not changed when the forms were created rearranging their order.

3. Does Heinz have a duty or obligation to steal the drug?
3a. Why or why not?
4. If Heinz doesn't love his wife, should he steal the drug for her? (*If subject favors not stealing ask:* Does it make a difference in what Heinz should do whether or not he loves his wife?)
4a. Why or why not?
5. Suppose the person dying is not his wife but a stranger. Should Heinz steal the drug for the stranger?
5a. Why or why not?
*6. (*If subject favors stealing the drug for a stranger*) Suppose it's a pet animal he loves. Should Heinz steal to save the pet animal?
*6a. Why or why not?
7. Is it important for people to do everything they can to save another's life?
7a. Why or why not?
*8. It is against the law for Heinz to steal. Does that make it morally wrong?
*8a. Why or why not?
9. In general, should people try to do everything they can to obey the law?
9a. Why or why not?
9b. How does this apply to what Heinz should do?
*10. [*The following question is designed to elicit the subject's orientation and should be considered optional.*] In thinking back over the dilemma, what would you say is the most responsible thing for Heinz to do?
*10a. Why?

[*Questions 1 and 2 of Dilemma III′ are optional. If you do not choose to use them, read Dilemma III′ and its continuation and begin with question 3.*]

Dilemma III′: Heinz did break into the store. He stole the drug and gave it to his wife. In the newspapers the next day there was an account of the robbery. Mr. Brown, a police officer who knew Heinz, read the account. He remembered seeing Heinz running away from the store and realized that it was Heinz who stole the drug. Mr. Brown wonders whether he should report that it was Heinz who stole the drug.

*1. Should Officer Brown report Heinz for stealing?
*1a. Why or why not?

*2. Suppose Officer Brown were a close friend of Heinz, should he then report him?
*2a. Why or why not?

Continuation: Officer Brown did report Heinz. Heinz was arrested and brought to court. A jury was selected. The jury's job is to find whether a person is innocent or guilty of committing a crime. The jury finds Heinz guilty. It is up to the judge to determine the sentence.

3. Should the judge give Heinz some sentence, or should he suspend the sentence and let Heinz go free?
3a. Why is that best?
4. Thinking in terms of society, should people who break the law be punished?
4a. Why or why not?
4b. How does this apply to how the judge should decide?
5. Heinz was doing what his conscience told him when he stole the drug. Should a lawbreaker be punished if he is acting out of conscience?
5a. Why or why not?
*6. [*The following question is designed to elicit the subject's orientation and should be considered optional.*] Thinking back over the dilemma, what would you say is the most responsible thing for the judge to do?
*6a. Why?

Questions 7–12 are designed to elicit the subject's theory of ethics and should be considered optional. They should not be scored for moral stage.]

*7. What does the word *conscience* mean to you, anyhow? If you were Heinz, how would your conscience enter into the decision?
*8. Heinz has to make a moral decision. Should a moral decision be based on one's feelings, or on one's thinking and reasoning about right and wrong?
*9. Is Heinz's problem a moral problem? Why or why not?
*9a. In general, what makes something a moral problem or what does the word *morality* mean to you?
*10. If Heinz is going to decide what to do by thinking about what's really right, there must be some answer, some right solution. Is there really some correct solution to moral prob-

lems like Heinz's, or when people disagree, is everybody's opinion equally right? Why?

*11. How do you know when you've come up with a good moral decision? Is there a way of thinking or a method by which one can reach a good or adequate decision?

*12. Most people believe that thinking and reasoning in science can lead to a correct answer. Is the same thing true in moral decisions or are they different?

Dilemma I: Joe is a fourteen-year-old boy who wanted to go to camp very much. His father promised him he could go if he saved up the money for it himself. So Joe worked hard at his paper route and saved up the forty dollars it cost to go to camp, and a little more besides. But just before camp was going to start, his father changed his mind. Some of his friends decided to go on a special fishing trip, and Joe's father was short of the money it would cost. So he told Joe to give him the money he had saved from the paper route. Joe didn't want to give up going to camp, so he thinks of refusing to give his father the money.

1. Should Joe refuse to give his father the money?

1a. Why or why not?

[*Questions 2 and 3 are designed to elicit the subject's moral type and should be considered optional.*]

*2. Does the father have the right to tell Joe to give him the money?

*2a. Why or why not?

*3. Does giving the money have anything to do with being a good son?

*3a. Why or why not?

*4. Is the fact that Joe earned the money himself important in this situation?

*4a. Why or why not?

5. The father promised Joe he could go to camp if he earned the money. Is the fact that the father promised the most important thing in the situation?

5a. Why or why not?

6. In general, why should a promise be kept?

7. Is it important to keep a promise to someone you don't know well and probably won't see again?

7a. Why or why not?
8. What do you think is the most important thing a father should be concerned about in his relationship to his son?
8a. Why is that the most important thing?
9. In general, what should be the authority of a father over his son?
9a. Why?
10. What do you think is the most important thing a son should be concerned about in his relationship to his father?
10a. Why is that the most important thing?
*11. [*The following question is designed to elicit the subject's orientation and should be considered optional*]. In thinking back over the dilemma, what would you say is the most responsible thing for Joe to do in this situation?
*11a. Why?

Form B

Dilemma IV: There was a woman who had very bad cancer, and there was no treatment known to medicine that would save her. Her doctor, Dr. Jefferson, knew that she had only about six months to live. She was in terrible pain, but she was so weak that a good dose of a painkiller like morphine would make her die sooner. She was delirious and almost crazy with pain, but in her calm periods she would ask Dr. Jefferson to give her enough morphine to kill her. She said she couldn't stand the pain and she was going to die in a few months anyway. Although he knows that mercy-killing is against the law, the doctor thinks about granting her request.

1. Should Dr. Jefferson give her the drug that would make her die?
1a. Why or why not?
*2. [*The following question is designed to elicit the subject's moral type and should be considered optional.*] Is it actually right or wrong for him to give the woman the drug that would make her die?
*2a. Why is it right or wrong?
3. Should the woman have the right to make the final decision?
3a. Why or why not?
*4. The woman is married. Should her husband have anything to do with the decision?

4a. Why or why not?
*5. [*The following question is designed to elicit the subject's moral type and should be considered optional.*] What should a good husband do in this situation?
*5a. Why?
6. Is there any way a person has a duty or obligation to live when he or she does not want to, when the person wants to commit suicide?
6a. Why or why not?
*7. [*The following question is designed to elicit the subject's moral type and should be considered optional.*] Does Dr. Jefferson have a duty or obligation to make the drug available to the woman?
*7a. Why or why not?
8. When a pet animal is badly wounded and will die, it is killed to put it out of its pain. Does the same thing apply here?
8a. Why or why not?
9. It is against the law for the doctor to give the woman the drug. Does that make it morally wrong?
9a. Why or why not?
10. In general, should people try to do everything they can to obey the law?
10a. Why or why not?
*10b. How does this apply to what Dr. Jefferson should do?
*11. [*The following question is designed to elicit the subject's moral orientation and should be considered optional.*] In thinking back over the dilemma, what would you say is the most responsible thing for Dr. Jefferson to do?
*11a. Why?

[*Question 1 of Dilemma IV′ is optional. If you do not choose to use it, read Dilemma IV′ and its continuation and begin with question 2.*]

Dilemma IV′: Dr. Jefferson did perform the mercy-killing by giving the woman the drug. Passing by at the time was another doctor, Dr. Rogers, who knew the situation Dr. Jefferson was in. Dr. Rogers thought of trying to stop Dr. Jefferson but the drug was already administered. Dr. Rogers wonders whether he should report Dr. Jefferson.

*1. Should Dr. Rogers report Dr. Jefferson?
*1a. Why or why not?

Continuation: Dr. Rogers did report Dr. Jefferson. Dr. Jefferson is brought to court and a jury is selected. The jury's job is to find whether a person is innocent or guilty of committing a crime. The jury finds Dr. Jefferson guilty. It is up to the judge to determine the sentence.

2. Should the judge give Dr. Jefferson some sentence, or should he suspend the sentence and let Dr. Jefferson go free?
2a. Why is that best?
3. Thinking in terms of society, should people who break the law be punished?
3a. Why or why not?
3b. How does this apply to how the judge should decide?
4. The jury finds Dr. Jefferson legally guilty of murder. Would it be wrong or right for the judge to give him the death sentence (a legally possible punishment)? Why?
5. Is it ever right to give the death sentence? Why or why not? What are the conditions under which the death sentence should be given, in your opinion? Why are these conditions important?
6. Dr. Jefferson was doing what his conscience told him when he gave the woman the drug. Should a lawbreaker be punished if he is acting out of conscience?
6a. Why or why not?
*7. [*The following question is designed to elicit the subject's moral orientation and should be considered optional.*] Thinking back over the dilemma, what would you say is the most responsible thing for the judge to do?
*7a. Why?

[*Questions 8-13 are designed to elicit the subject's theory of ethics and should be considered optional. They should not be scored for moral stage.*]

*8. What does the word *conscience* mean to you, anyhow? If you were Dr. Jefferson, how would your conscience enter into the decision?
*9. Dr. Jefferson has to make a moral decision. Should a moral decision be based on one's feelings or on one's thinking and reasoning about right and wrong?
*10. Is Dr. Jefferson's problem a moral problem? Why or why not?

*10a. In general, what makes something a moral problem, or what does the word *morality* mean to you?

*11. If Dr. Jefferson is going to decide what to do by thinking about what's really right, there must be some answer, some right solution. Is there really some correct solution to moral problems like Dr. Jefferson's, or when people disagree is everybody's opinion equally right? Why?

*12. How do you know when you've come up with a good moral decision? Is there a way of thinking or a method by which one can reach a good or adequate decision?

*13. Most people believe that thinking and reasoning in science can lead to a correct answer. Is the same thing true in moral decisions, or are they different?

Dilemma II: Judy was a twelve-year-old girl. Her mother promised her that she could go to a special rock concert coming to their town if she saved up from babysitting and lunch money to buy a ticket to the concert. She managed to save up the fifteen dollars the ticket cost plus another five dollars. But then her mother changed her mind and told Judy that she had to spend the money on new clothes for school. Judy was disappointed and decided to go to the concert anyway. She bought a ticket and told her mother that she had only been able to save five dollars. That Saturday she went to the performance and told her mother that she was spending the day with a friend. A week passed without her mother finding out. Judy then told her older sister, Louise, that she had gone to the performance and had lied to her mother about it. Louise wonders whether to tell their mother what Judy did.

1. Should Louise, the older sister, tell their mother that Judy lied about the money or should she keep quiet?

1a. Why?

*2. In wondering whether to tell, Louise thinks of the fact that Judy is her sister. Should that make a difference in Louise's decision?

*2a. Why or why not?

*3. [*The following question is designed to elicit the subject's moral type and should be considered optional.*] Does telling have anything to do with being a good daughter?

*3a. Why or why not?

*4. Is the fact that Judy earned the money herself important in this situation?
*4a. Why or why not?
5. The mother promised Judy she could go to the concert if she earned the money. Is the fact that the mother promised the most important thing in the situation?
5a. Why or why not?
6. Why in general should a promise be kept?
7. Is it important to keep a promise to someone you don't know well and probably won't see again?
7a. Why or why not?
8. What do you think is the most important thing a mother should be concerned about in her relationship to her daughter?
8a. Why is that the most important thing?
9. In general, what should be the authority of a mother over her daughter?
9a. Why?
10. What do you think is the most important thing a daughter should be concerned about in her relationship to her mother?
10a. Why is that the most important thing?

[*The following question is designed to elicit the subject's orientation and should be considered optional.*]

*11. In thinking back over the dilemma, what would you say is the most responsible thing for Louise to do in this situation?
*11a. Why?

Form C

Dilemma V: In Korea, a company of Marines was way outnumbered and was retreating before the enemy. The company had crossed a bridge over a river, but the enemy were mostly still on the other side. If someone went back to the bridge and blew it up, with the head start the rest of the men in the company would have, they could probably then escape. But the man who stayed back to blow up the bridge would not be able to escape alive. The captain himself is the man who knows best how to lead the retreat. He asks for volunteers, but no one will volunteer. If he goes himself, the men will probably not get back safely and he is the only one who knows how to lead the retreat.

1. Should the captain order a man to go on the mission or should he go himself?
1a. Why?
2. Should the captain send a man (or even use a lottery) when it means sending him to his death?
2a. Why or why not?
3. Should the captain go himself when it means that the men will probably not make it back safely?
3a. Why or why not?
4. Does the captain have the right to order a man if he thinks it's best?
4a. Why or why not?
5. Does the man who is selected have a duty or obligation to go?
5a. Why or why not?
6. What's so important about human life that makes it important to save or protect?
6a. Why is that important?
*6b. How does that apply to what the captain should do?
*7. [*The following question is designed to elicit the subject's orientation and should be considered optional.*] In thinking back over the dilemma, what would you say is the most responsible thing for the captain to do?
*7a. Why?

Dilemma VIII: In a country in Europe, a poor man named Valjean could find no work, nor could his sister and brother. Without money, he stole food and medicine that they needed. He was captured and sentenced to prison for six years. After a couple of years, he escaped from the prison and went to live in another part of the country under a new name. He saved money and slowly built up a big factory. He gave his workers the highest wages and used most of his profits to build a hospital for people who couldn't afford good medical care. Twenty years had passed when a tailor recognized the factory owner as being Valjean, the escaped convict whom the police had been looking for back in his hometown.

1. Should the tailor report Valjean to the police?
1. Why or why not?
2. Does a citizen have a duty or obligation to report an escaped convict?

2a. Why or why not?
3. Suppose Valjean were a close friend of the tailor. Should he then report Valjean?
3a. Why or why not?
4. If Valjean were reported and brought before the judge, should the judge send him back to jail or let him go free?
4a. Why?
5. Thinking in terms of society, should people who break the law be punished?
5a. Why or why not?
5b. How does this apply to what the judge should do?
6. Valjean was doing what his conscience told him to do when he stole the food and medicine. Should a lawbreaker be punished if he is acting out of conscience?
6a. Why or Why not?
*7. [*The following question is designed to elicit the subject's orientation and should be considered optional.*] In thinking back over the dilemma, what would you say is the most responsible thing for the tailor to do?
*7a. Why?

[*Questions 8–13 are designed to elicit the subject's theory of ethics and should be considered optional. They should not be scored for moral stage.*]

*8. What does the word *conscience* mean to you, anyhow? If you were Valjean, how would your conscience enter into the decision?
*9. Valjean has to make a moral decision. Should a moral decision be based on one's feelings or on one's thinking and reasoning about right and wrong?
*10. Is Valjean's problem a moral problem? Why or why not?
*10a. In general, what makes something a moral problem, or what does the word *morality* mean to you?
*11. If Valjean is going to decide what to do by thinking about what's really right, there must be some answer, some right solution. Is there really some correct solution to moral problems like Valjean's, or when people disagree is everybody's opinion equally right? Why?
*12. How do you know when you've come up with a good moral decision? Is there a way of thinking or a method by which one can reach a good or adequate decision?
*13. Most people believe that thinking and reasoning in science

can lead to a correct answer. Is the same thing true in moral decisions, or are they different?

Dilemma VII: Two young men, brothers, had got into serious trouble. They were secretly leaving town in a hurry and needed money. Karl, the older one, broke into a store and stole a thousand dollars. Bob, the younger one, went to a retired old man who was known to help people in town. He told the man that he was very sick and that he needed a thousand dollars to pay for an operation. Bob asked the old man to lend him the money and promised that he would pay him back when he recovered. Really Bob wasn't sick at all, and he had no intention of paying the man back. Although the old man didn't know Bob very well, he lent him the money. So Bob and Karl skipped town, each with a thousand dollars.

1a. Which is worse, stealing like Karl or cheating like Bob?
1a. Why is that worse?
2. What do you think is the worst thing about cheating the old man?
2a. Why is that the worst thing?
3. In general, why should a promise be kept?
4. Is it important to keep a promise to someone you don't know well or will never see again?
4a. Why or why not?
5. Why shouldn't someone steal from a store?
6. What is the value or importance of property rights?
7. Should people do everything they can to obey the law?
7a. Why or why not?
*8. [*The following question is designed to elicit the subject's orientation and should be considered optional.*] Was the old man being irresponsible by lending Bob the money?
*8a. Why or why not?

Appendix C: From Substages to Moral Types: Heteronomous and Autonomous Morality

with ANN HIGGINS, MARK TAPPAN, and DAWN SCHRADER*

Piaget's Moral Typology

Jean Piaget's (1932, 1965) *Moral Judgment of the Child* defined moral stages, not in the strict structural or "hard stage" manner of our standard scoring method, but in terms of an ideal-typological approach, an approach also used in my original (Kohlberg, 1958) definition of moral stages. In the ideal-typological approach, a cluster of chosen content themes is assumed to hold together because of an underlying postulated but not observable structure which makes one element of content compatible with the others. The two ideal types Piaget defined were the heteronomous and the autonomous types. Following Kant and, in part, Durkheim, Piaget saw morality as respect for rules and, ultimately, for the persons originating the rules. For Piaget there were two types of respect and two corresponding moral types. The first type was that of unilateral respect for parents or other authorities and the rules they prescribed (a "*sui generis* mixture of affection and fear or awe"). The second type was that of mutual respect among peers or equals and of respect for the rules that guided their interaction. Fairness in the sense of reciprocity and equality was the underlying structure of autonomous morality as conformity or obedience to authority and authority-made rule was of heteronomous morality. Piaget says, "Our earlier studies led us to the conclusion that the norms of reason, and in particular, the important norm of reciprocity, the source of the logic of relation,

---

*A lengthier elaboration of this appendix will be published in Colby and Kohlberg (1984). The authors wish to acknowledge the important contributions of Cheryl Armon, Daniel Candee, Eileen Gardner, and Ting Lei to this appendix.

can only develop in and through cooperation. Whether cooperation is an effect or a cause of reason, or both, reason requires cooperation insofar as being rational consists in 'situating oneself' so as to submit the individual to the universal. Mutual respect therefore appears to us as the necessary condition of autonomy under its double aspect, intellectual and moral. From the intellectual point of view, it frees the child from the opinions that have been imposed upon him while it favors inner consistency and reciprocal control. From the moral point of view, it replaces the norms of authority by that norm immanent in action and in consciousness themselves, the norm of reciprocity or sympathy.

"In short, whether one takes up the point of view of Durkheim or of M. Bovet, it is necessary, in order to grasp the situation, to take account of two groups of social and moral facts—constraint and unilateral respect on the one hand, cooperation and mutual respect, on the other. Such is the guiding hypothesis which will serve us in the sequel and which will lead us in examining the moral judgments of children to dissassociate from one another the two systems of totally different origin. Whether we describe the facts in the terms of social morphology or from the point of view of consciousness (and the two languages are, we repeat, parallel and not contradictory) it is impossible to reduce the effect of cooperation to those of constraint and unilateral respect" (1965, pp. 107–108).

Piaget's (1965) treatise on moral judgment stresses the domain of morality as justice. The most fundamental part of justice, he says, is distributive justice, which in the autonomous orientation is reducible to equality, equity (equal distribution according to need), and reciprocity. Piaget also studied restorative or corrective justice, which in the autonomous orientation is also directed to equality and reciprocity. Without clarifying his idea of conscience, he says, "Young children confuse what is just with what is law, law being whatever is prescribed by adult authority. Justice is identified with formulated rules, as indeed it is in the opinion of a great many adults, of all adults namely, who have not succeeded in setting autonomy of conscience above social prejudice and the written law" (1965, p. 317).

As the quotation makes clear, Piaget's ideal typology is developmental, but he assumes that many adolescents or adults may remain in the heteronomous orientation.

While Piaget's typology is age-developmental, he does not believe that his typology defines true stages. Speaking of his empirical data on children's ideas of justice, he says,

> A law of evolution emerges sufficiently clearly from all these answers. True we cannot speak of stages properly so called, because it is extremely doubtful whether every child passes successively through the four attitudes we have just described. It is greatly a question of the kind of education the child has received. (1965, p. 284)

There are three reasons why Piaget does not believe his typology defines true or "hard" stages. First, his empirical observations mix content with structure as suggested by his statement that the type of response he gets may be influenced by the kind of education the child receives. Second, he sees the two moralities as in opposition to one another, rather than the autonomous morality growing out of, and being a transformation of, the heteronomous morality. He says, "We find in the domain of justice that opposition of the two moralities to which we have so often drawn the readers attention" (1965, p. 324).

Third, the two moralities originate in two different sorts of social relationships and social experiences, those of unilateral and mutual respect. Characterizing autonomous morality as arising from solidarity between equals, he asks "whether autonomous morality could ever develop without a preliminary stage during which the child's conscience is molded by his unilateral respect for the adult? As this cannot be put to the test by experiment, it is idle to argue the point" (1965, p. 324).

Even though Piaget does not conceive his typology as defining true stages, he does think they are age-developmental. There are two reasons for this. First, as the child grows older he or she is more able to enter into peer relationships of mutual respect and solidarity which generate autonomous morality. Second heteronomous morality is less equilibrated than autonomous morality.

> But what is certain is that the moral equilibrium achieved by the complementary conceptions of heteronomous duty and of punishment so called is an unstable equilibrium, owing to the fact that it does not allow the personality to grow and expand to its full extent. [1965, p. 324]

According to Piaget, as we have noted, with age there is a gradual predominance of the autonomous type over the heteronomous type of morality rather than a qualitative transformation from one morality to the other. Stated in slightly different terms, Piaget does not think that there is an inner logic in terms of which developmental differentiation and integration lead heteronomous morality to be transformed into an autonomous morality which presupposes a prior stage of heteronomous morality.

Furthermore, according to Piaget, such a predominance of autonomous morality is dependent upon the kind of social relations or society in which the child lives. Piaget expects that in traditional or gerontocratic societies based on what Durkheim calls mechanical solidarity heteronomous morality will extend into adulthood and that it is only societies based on "organic solidarity" or cooperation and on "equalitarian democracy" and the emancipation of one generation from another that render possible in children and adolescents the development he outlined (1965, p. 325).

The Kohlberg (1958) Effort to Use the Piaget Typology to Define Stages and the Apparent Failure

My dissertation (Kohlberg, 1958) retained Piaget's ideal-typological approach to the study of moral judgment development rather than attempting to define stages by the complete separation of form or structure from content currently used and described in Chapters 3 and 5.

My methodology was originally designed to isolate Piaget's heteronomous and autonomous types. Each dilemma pitted conformity to authority or to rules against fairness as equality, reciprocity, or human rights. Dilemma choice was then thought to be one criterion of an autonomous type. Other criteria coming from Piaget's typology would include references to mutual respect, to reciprocity, to equality, and to contract or free agreement as a basis for moral obligation.

In Dilemma I (father breaking a promise to his son), one would expect an autonomous type to think Joe should refuse to give his father the money, to emphasize contract and promise and the right to reciprocal maintenance of what he worked to earn, and to discuss the father-son relationship in terms of mutual respect. In the Heinz dilemma one would expect the autonomous type to choose to steal as against obeying the law, to orient to the right to life and the mutual relationship with the dying wife, to perceive the druggist's demand as unfair, and so on. In considering Heinz's punishment, the Piagetian autonomous type would take a nonretributive stance, orienting to restitution rather than retribution, considering motives and intentions rather than only commission of the act, and so forth. As a first approximation, my dissertation (Kohlberg, 1958) saw Piaget's heteronomous type as what I called Developmental Type/Stage 1 and the autonomous type as Developmental Type/Stage 2.

These two types, however, did not appear to define two different types of social relationship or two different types of respect. Type/Stage 1 did not appear to be tied to a sense of heteronomous respect toward adults and rules grounded on a sense of reverence and awe for them but instead appeared to be tied more to a calculated deferrence to superior power and to obedience and punishment which cut across relations toward adults and toward peers.

Similarly, Type/Stage 2 did not appear to be oriented to an intrinsic feeling of mutual respect and solidarity, but instead reflected an instrumental understanding of relationships that cut across those with both adults and peers. In Chapter 2 I cited Tommy, aged 10, Type/Stage 1, responding to Dilemma II (telling a brother's confidence to a parent) by saying, "In one way it was right to tell because his father might beat him up. In another way it's wrong because his brother will beat him up if he tells." Whether peer or adult, Tommy responds to avoidance of retribution. At age 13, and Type/Stage 2, Tommy responded to the dilemma by saying, "The brother should not tell or he'll get his brother in trouble. If he wants his brother to keep quiet for him sometime, he'd better not squeal now."

While Tommy at age 13 and Type/Stage 2 is clearly more oriented to reciprocity than at Type/Stage 1, these responses do not suggest a peer system of social solidarity and mutual respect distinct from a child-adult system of intrinsic heteronomous respect expressed at Type/Stage 1.

These considerations led me (Kohlberg, 1958) to conclude that while Piaget's typology suggested some aspects or dimensions of moral judgment related to age and cognitive development, they did not define stages or even developmental types as "structured wholes" or interlocked patterns of consistency of moral judgment response. The Kohlberg (1958) ideal-typological scoring of types/stages included some "aspects" derived from Piaget's monograph, such as a focus on intentions as distinct from consequences in judging moral responsibility in the first three stages. Drawing more on J. M Baldwin (1906) than Piaget, as we discuss later, I (Kohlberg,

1958) drew up a table of similarities and differences between Piaget's heternomous and autonomous stages and the first two of my stages, reproduced as Table C.1.

Current Statements of Piaget's "Two World" Theory

An enormous amount of research has been done using Piaget's original measures or questions, measures usually requiring a child to make a dichotomous choice between a "heteronomous" response (e.g., punish more the act with quantitatively worse consequences like breaking ten cups by accident) and an "autonomous" choice (e.g., punish the act with worse intention, breaking one cup while trying to steal some jam).

This research has not supported the notion that these choices indicate qualitative "structured wholes or clusters of response" forming an invariant sequence of transformations and integration as is indicated by various reviews of this research (Kohlberg, 1964, Lickona, 1976, Kohlberg and Helkama, in preparation).

Advocates of Piaget's original theory of moral judgment such as Youniss (1980, 1981), Damon (1977), and Wright (1982, 1983) elaborate the theory at the level of theory (Wright) or use quite different research methods (Youniss and Damon).

As we discuss in more detail in a later section, Wright stresses that Piaget's typology is an affective typology, it is based on two different sentiments of obligation rooted in actual social relationships, heteronomous respect, composed of fear, affection, and a sense of superior value and power felt toward parents and teachers, and autonomous respect, composed of mutual and reciprocal feelings toward equals, friends, or peers with whom the child cooperates. According to Wright such sentiments of obligation are unlikely to be elicited by the "abstract," "cognitive" hypothetical dilemmas used by both Piaget (1965) and myself (Kohlberg, 1958).

While centering less on the affective side of Piaget's typology, Damon (1977) used real-life situations as well as hypothetical dilemmas to explain the development of levels of distributive justice for children between themselves, and the development of levels of definition of legitimacy and obedience to authorities with parents and peers. Believing these to be quite distinct domains, Youniss (1980) collected data through interviews with children and young adolescents about their relations to parents and friends, interviews

Table C.1. Piaget's Stages of Moral Development Compared with First Two Kohlberg Stages

---

Stage 1 (Heteronomous stage)

---

1. Value and conformity are *egocentric* or *syntelic* (Baldwin). (Manifested in absolutism of value or unawareness of moral perspectives.) Our interpretation similar to Piaget's.
2. Conformity is *realistic* or *projective* (Baldwin). Judgments of bad are made in terms of physical properties and consequences of action rather than in terms of the act's psychological intentions or functional appropriateness to some norm. Manifested in objective responsibility, in physicalistic definitions of lies, and in belief that punishment is a physically automatic response to deviance (immanent justice and expiative, rather than restitutive or reforming, punishment)

   Piaget: There is a confusion of rules and things. Rules are oriented to as fixed sacred things. Deviance is always wrong. Acts are evaluated in terms of the "letter of law," and in terms of consequences instead of intentions.

   Our interpretation: Objective responsibility is merely an expression of "projective" modes of value and a failure to differentiate moral good from other kinds of good. It does not imply an orientation to rules in the usual sense of a concept of a rule-orientation. We find Type 1 not oriented to rules as entities, but oriented to projectively bad acts and to obedience to persons, not rules.
3. Conformity is *heteronomous*, or based on unilateral respect or *objective necessity* (Baldwin). i.e., might makes right. Manifested in belief that obedience to adults or other power figures is right when it conflicts with other rules or welfare considerations, and in belief that punishment makes an act wrong necessarily.

   Piaget: Duty is based on a sense of heteronomous respect for adults transferred to their commands and rules. This respect, compounded of love and fear, leads to an overevaluation and sense of sacredness of authority and rules.

   Our interpretation: Adults must be seen representing something beyond themselves before they are "respected." While we find children of Type 1 oriented to obedience, we find little evidence that they respect authorities in any sense beyond recognizing that they are more powerful. Various kinds of response used by Piaget as indicating a sense of the "sacredness" of adults are interpreted as indicating cognitive naiveté, independent of emotional overevaluation. Often they indicate a lack of awareness of moral rule, against which the adult is to be measured, rather than an idealization of the adult.

Stage 2 (Autonomous stage)

---

1. Value and conformity are relativistic.
2. Conformity and punitive justice are flexible and oriented to intentions and functional needs.

Table C.1—Continued

Piaget: Rules are seen as the expression of understandable human purposes and as means to those purposes. Deviance may be justifiable in terms of an intent to conform to the "spirit" or purpose of the rule or in terms of a particular unusual situation. Acts are evaluated in terms of their intent.

Our interpretations: Rules may be seen as merely instrumental acts, as commands based on the individual needs of authority. Deviance may be justified on the basis of an act being a means to a natural end. The end is not itself evaluated in terms of its worthiness for a moral self. Rules are seen as a basis for shared action but not as a basis of shared evaluation or judgment.

3. Conformity is autonomous or based on mutual respect. Manifested in sense of the need to conform to peer-expectations, in concern about distributive equality, in the importance of exchange or reciprocity, in the notion that peer vengeance is similar to authority's punishment, and in the notion that adult punishment is not the ultimate criterion of wrong but is only a painful consequence to be considered in decision making.

Piaget: Conformity is based on empathic identification with the needs of others, shared goals, maintenance of agreement, and a concern for approval by those approved of by the self. Conformity as to the attitude of other equals.

Our interpretation: These attitudes may be invoked as a basis of conformity without any really internalized conformity, shared goals, or concern for others. There may be no differentiation between "legitimate" and other needs of self, and all may be hedonistically oriented. Needs of others empathized with is based on the degree to which the other comes within the boundaries of the self. Equality is not a norm but a fact, "I and my needs are as good as anyone else's." A seeking to maximize quantity of approval by direct instrumental techniques.

---

not specifically focused on the moral. He concludes that his data support the "two worlds" hypothesis of Piaget and of Harry Stack Sullivan (1953).

The goal of the present paper is to state and discuss a position within the structural framework which may provide some answers to critics. Throughout this paper, it is called *the two world perspective,* the two worlds being those the child shares with parents and with friends. The thesis is that parents and friends contribute equally but differently to the child's development.

For the first, the thesis begins in the premise that structures are built from *interpersonal interactions.* For the second, the thesis focuses on the *reciprocity* which is found to hold and recur across interactions. These are deceptively powerful starting points from which one can derive the two world viewpoint. Piaget, Sullivan and others suggest that there is a common, recurring form to parents' interactions with children. They describe it through the concept of *reciprocity of complement* (Hinde, 1976). To wit, the part parents play in interactions is that of leader or arbiter. This means that they tell the children what to do and not do by accepting or rejecting children's contributions to interactions. Children, in turn, have the part of learner or follower. Their role in interactions is to complete the part set forth by parents. . . .

Parents have the right to step outside the ongoing flow of behavior to make a judgment on it. They need not do this all of the time. The important element, however, is that they can do it, while children cannot. This gives the full meaning of arbiter which is found in its *unilaterality*. Were this not the case, the child would have the right to judge parents' actions. More critically, when parent and child disagreed, neither would impose a resolution, but the two would enter into negotiation. Both would be willing to give up their respective viewpoints in adjustment to the other until a common view was rendered.

What has just been described is the more apt description of interactions of peers whose general form follows the *reciprocity of symmetry* (Hinde, 1976). In this form, each peer is free to act as the other has just acted, or is expected to act subsequently. When one offers a toy, the other may offer candy. When one hits the other may retaliate. When one asserts an opinion, "This is how we should play," the other is free to present a different opinion, "No, we should play like this." In the taking of turns in interactions, peers may duplicate each other's contributions, with neither being able to step outside and take charge. Should one of the peers try to do so, the other may do the same. [1981, pp. 35–44]

Focusing specifically on Piaget's theory of moral development, Youniss in a paper "The Development of Reciprocity and Morality" (1982) makes the following points:

Piaget was concerned with the historical question of how persons were free to construct moral positions and yet able to reach positions which were truthful or valid. Like other scholars, Piaget was conscious of Kant's solution which was, in short, to endow individuals with rationality. For Kant, individuals could achieve moral principles, which were universal and valid, through reason. Piaget disagreed with this solution in a critical respect. He defined morality as respect for rules and for the persons who co-constructed the rules. As to validity, Piaget denied that reason alone could be the referent for truth. Instead, he argued that the truth of moral principles came from recourse to the interpersonal methods by which two individuals submitted their respective moral positions to one another for mutual verification.

For another example, "autonomy" was defined as the state of moral maturity, meaning that the individual took a step beyond social convention to establish a moral position which could be justified with reason.

Given recent work, it is now possible to see Piaget's 1932 study in a fresh light. It was an attempt to show how methods of interpersonal exchange of thought developed and so permitted attainment of valid moral principles. It was also an attempt to describe how different interpersonal relations were more or less conducive to development of methods of rationality and why the former were, in turn, the basis of mutual respect. This brings us to the present study, which suggests a synthesis between Piaget's developmental theory and the general position on morality taken by Habermas, Macmurray, and Ricoeur.

As Youniss points out, Piaget's basic theory is loosely compatible with Habermas's theory of communicative competence discussed in Chapter 4. Habermas's theory in turn derives from that G. H. Mead's (1934) theory of role-taking in communication. As my lengthy discussion of Mead's theory in Chapter 1, "Stage and Sequence," indicates, Mead himself stresses the role-taking and communication common to interaction with both adults and peers, though he uses examples of role-taking with peers in the "play" and the "game" stages of development of role-taking "the generalized others."

As Rawls's (1980) essay on "Kantian Constructivism in Moral Theory" and Habermas's (1982a) paper relating to his universal communication theory of justice to Kant's transcendental formalism indicate, the disparities between a Piagetian ontogenetic rational reconstruction of moral principles and a Kantian or Rawlsian moral theory are essentially different perspectives on moral principles, rather than radically different theories. (This point is elaborated in Chapter 3.) The remainder of this discussion will focus upon a construction of moral types which integrates Piagetian and Kantian concepts of autonomy.

Limits of the "Two Worlds" Hypothesis, But a Continued Return to the Piaget Typology

Earlier, we discussed the fact that my original study (Kohlberg, 1958) did not seem to support the idea that there was one set of stages or types of moral obligations for relating to adults and another for peers. We quoted Tommy who oriented to both the father and the brother in Dilemma II at a heteronomous Stage 1 level and longitudinally moved to a Stage 2 level of reasoning and instrumental obligation to both parents and peers.

Stated in our terms we found the Kohlberg moral stages cutting across adult authority and peer dilemmas and issues. As Chapter 5 shows, the recent standard issue scoring system indicates that our moral stages crosscut issues and dilemmas of parental or adult authority and peer relations and affiliation as indicated by the existence of a single general stage factor in a factor analysis by issue and dilemma as well as by other statistical techniques (Colby, Kohlberg, et al., 1983).

Similar structural generality of level across parent-child, friendship, and peer group status is reported by Selman (1980). Selman describes four levels of stages of both describing and prescribing parent-child relations, four parallel levels for friendship relations, and four parallel levels of peer group relations. The four levels of each type of relation are derived from four underlying structural levels of social perspective taking, originally abstracted by Selman (1971) from the moral judgment stages. Selman reports correlations between level of conception of the individual person, of peer group, and of friendship in the .80s. Correlations with conception of parent-child relations were similar (Bruss-Saunders, 1979).

In summary, our own longitudinal research and that of others does not support the thesis that the Piaget heteronomy-autonomy developmental typology defines clear or "hard" stages detectable in hypothetical dilemmas. The research also does not suggest that there are different structural stages in the adult-child and the peer worlds, at least as detectable by hypothetical dilemmas and reflective interviews like Selman's.

Two sets of data, however, suggested the need to continue to attempt to develop a heteronomous-autonomous developmental typology. The first, discussed in Chapter 6, was the fact that some of our longitudinal subjects who were more autonomous and apparently postconventional later went through a relativistic skeptical or egoistic phase before actually attaining postconventional autonomy in moral judgment. This led us to a preliminary definition of a B "substage" at conventional Stages 3 and 4 as discussed in Chapters 2 and 6. The second impetus was that college students originally scored as Stage 5 and Stage 6 in the Kohlberg (1958) system acted more autonomously or justly in the Milgram situation and the Berkeley Free Speech Movement, as reported in Chapter 1, "Stage and Sequence," written in 1969. In Chapter 7 we construe the relationship as often representing the actions of students at Stages 3B and 4B. These data led us to develop a second formulation of the Piagetian developmental typology: "substages."

The Kohlberg (1976) Formulation of Substages

In Chapter 2, "Moral Stages and Moralization" (1976), a more "structuralist" and less ideal typological concept of "substage" was presented, one not closely tied to Piaget's (1965) own original formulation of the heteronomy-autonomy dichotonomy, but more tied to the notion that after entry into a new stage, there would be an increase in reversibility and equilibration (substage B). This is what the term *substage* would strictly imply.

In Chapter 2, a "strong substage" notion was hypothesized; that is, that an individual would enter Stage 3 as a "substage" A, move on to "substage" B within the same stage, then move on to 4A, and then to 4B. However, this hypothesis suggested that skipping of the A "substage" (or the B "substage") might be found in the three-year intervals of our longitudinal study if there was a total stage change in that period.

Chapter 2 also suggested that the method used to define "substage" would come from value elements presented in Table 5.3 in Chapter 5. These elements of moral value form the orientations discussed in Chapter 2, for example:

1. The Normative Order Orientation
2. The Utility Consequences Orientation
3. The Justice or Fairness Orientation
4. The Ideal-Self, Conscience and Harmony, or Perfectionist Orientation

These four orientations came from philosophic classification of types of moral theory, a philosophic ("structuralist") conception of types of moral value, rather than directly from Piaget's theory or typology. The categories of "Fairness" and "Ideal Self" or "Perfectionist" orientations together define "substage" B, defined as 51 percent or more usage of elements from these orientations as being "substage" B.

The longitudinal results on our American cases did not support this "substage" analysis. There was a shift to increased usage of the B "substage" with age. There was not, however, sequential "substage" change, a movement from 3A to 3B to 4A and to 4B. A number of subjects moved from B to A within the same stage, for example, from 3B at Time n to 3A at Time 4n+1.

The failure of this conception of "substages" led us to return to the original Piagetian heteronomous-autonomous developmental typology which is the focus of the discussion in this appendix. To more accurately reflect our thinking, we have called the two poles of this typology Type A, heteronomous morality, and Type B, autonomous morality. The reconstruction of this developmental typology led us back to the two original theoretical inspirations of the Kohlberg (1958) scheme: Piaget and Baldwin (1906). Underlying both is Kant's theory of moral autonomy.

The Kohlberg Reconstruction of Piaget's Developmental Typology

After a series of preliminary efforts to define a developmental typology of A and B "substages" as described above and briefly discussed in Chapter 2 (first published in 1976) and Chapter 6 (an earlier version of which was published in 1973), in 1980 we began serious work on reconstructing a Piagetian typology to apply to our hypothetical dilemmas. In Chapter 6, "Continuities Revisited—Again," we emphasized that the reasoning we originally thought to be postconventional later eroded in the college relativistic years, and we were, therefore, led to define autonomous "substages" at the conventional stages (Stages 3B and 4B). In Chapter 7, "Relationship of Judgment to Action," we found these "substages" necessary to account for autonomous action in those who had not reached postconventional or principled reasoning. In addition to the potential usefulness of a Piagetian typology to relate judgment to action, we thought it would be useful in the way in which Piaget originally intended, as an index of the type of social relationships in which the individual was imbedded, those of hierarchical authority or those of egalitarian cooperation and solidarity. We expected these to vary by culture, class, and peer-group participation independent of stage.

Accordingly, we constructed a manual for scoring moral types for Forms A and B. The technical details of this scoring system are presented elsewhere (Tappan, Kohlberg, Schrader, and Higgins, 1984). The criteria for Type B taken from Piaget's monograph, first presented in a slightly different form in Chapter 3, are reproduced here as Table C.2.

As can be seen, Table C.2 is not strictly addressed to reasons why a given action is right, the focus of our moral stages, but rather focuses on what is considered to be right or obligatory. This

Table C.2. "Piagetian" Criteria for Type B (Form A)

1. *Choice:* Chooses as right the action opposed to rules and authority and in line with human rights, welfare, and reciprocal justice.
2. *Autonomy:* The response to the dilemma must reflect an understanding that the actor in question is an autonomous moral agent, and hence must make moral judgments and decide on a moral course of action without determination by external sources of power or authority, using a rational and logical method of decision making.
3. *Mutual Respect:* This criterion reflects the understanding that the actors in the dilemma should have relations of mutual respect or solidarity with one another. As such, in Dilemma III, Heinz must be understood to have a relation of mutual respect or solidarity with his wife and friend and in Dilemma I, Joe and his father must have respect for each other.
4. *Reversibility:* The most important criterion from the Piagetian perspective (but also the most difficult one to indentify in an interview) is reversibility. It is understood to be present when the judgments made in response to the dilemma consider the interests and points of view of other actors involved, such that it is clear that the subject can view the problem from the perspective of other actors involved in the situation. The subject makes a decision with some awareness that he or she could logically trade places with other actors in the dilemma. As an example, in Dilemma I, a "good son" is not seen as having to obey the father, since the expectations of the father are not those which a "good father" would have, that is, the role of "good father" is defined by the respondent putting himself in the father's place and expecting the father to be able to put himself in the son's place. Reversibility is a mutual perspective taking or mutual use of the Golden Rule. For Piaget, *logical* operations are equilibrated when they are reversible; hence, a formal criterion for equilibrated *moral* judgments, that is, type B judgments, must be a correlative form of reversibility.
5. *Constructivism:* This criterion reflects the subject's awareness that the rules, laws, and role-prescriptions used to guide and frame moral decision making are *actively constructed* by human beings, in the context of a social system of cooperation for human welfare and justice. In other words, all of society (however "society" is interpreted by the subject), including its institutions, rules, and laws, is understood to be derived from communication and cooperation between and among persons. (Note: This notion of constructivism is understood to refer only to the subject's *normative ethical judgments,* and not to his or her *metaethical judgments.*)

is most evident in the choice being one of the five criteria which must be passed for assignment of Type B to each dilemma. Being autonomous as a criterion is not an answer to a why question. It is inferred from the respondents' decisions about what the husband or the judge or the son consider in coming to a decision, for example, the judge's consideration of law or authority, on one side, and a freedom to consider what is a just balancing of legal precedent with Heinz's moral motivation, on the other. It is typically not the same as a stage-scorable specific reason why the choice is not to punish Heinz. Similarly, a relation of son and father or husband and wife can be described as involving mutual respect and solidarity, independent of stageable reasons for the right choice. As an example, a subject tells us on Dilemma I, "If I were the father I would want my son to act in a way that I would be proud of him and try to set examples so he can grow up in the same way. In the son it works the same way, respect, mutual respect for one another."

This response also implicitly exemplifies the criterion of reversibility or role-exchange, imaginatively assuming the father's role as a good father in defining the son's role. Another example of reversibility is given by another subject. Asked, "Does giving the money have anything to do with being a good son?" the subject answers, "No, a good son is obedient but when the parent is wrong in the first place, I don't think the son should have to obey him." In this case, definitions of the good son and good father roles are reversible or reciprocal to one another. The stages of these response are not the same, however, the first being Stage 4, Type B, and the latter being Stage 3, Type B.

Constructivism, another type B criterion, is reflected in the subject's understanding of what the law is. For instance, in Dilemma III (stealing the drug), the subject may assume that the law will be flexible or "merciful" to Heinz so that law breaking need not be a primary consideration for Heinz. Or in III′ (the judge sentencing Heinz), a subject says, "I think basically the law is an attempt to maintain equality or restore it," clearly passing the criterion of constructivism as well as implicitly passing criteria of mutual respect (between legal authorities and subjects) and reversibility (between the role of judge and defendant or between all persons).

A Clinical Example of an Autonomous Type B: Case 18

As noted, my (Kohlberg 1958) cross-sectional study of moral development attempted to retain the Piagetian developmental-typological concept of autonomy. The 1958 study attempted to obtain "behavioral" measures of autonomy, as well as looking at responses to hypothetical dilemmas. To do so, two procedures were employed. The first was to have the interviewer, an adult authority, put pressure on the student to change his mind about the content of his choice on three of the nine dilemmas. Two levels of pressure were used. On the Heinz dilemma (III), for instance, if the student said that Heinz was right to steal the drug, the interviewer said, "A lot of people don't really think that Heinz should steal the drug, though maybe some people would. He might end up being killed and lose a life instead of saving it, do you agree with that?" If the student did not agree, a second level of pressure was used. On the Heinz dilemma, the interviewer said, "A lot of people think that Heinz shouldn't do it because the drug was scarce and other people needed it as much as Heinz's wife. So Heinz was taking the drug from someone who could honestly buy it. Would you agree that Heinz shouldn't have stolen it?"

Case 18, age 10, did not change his mind or agree on either set of pressure probes. In addition to autonomy from adult authority, our Piagetian conception of autonomy in Kohlberg (1958) implied that the student should also resist a Durkheimtype authority of the group majority. Accordingly, I used in Kohlberg (1958) a "revealed difference technique" to create a moral opinion analogy to the Asch (1952) group conformity study of judgments of length of lines (later studied in relation to moral stage by Saltzstein, Diamond, and Belenkey [1972], who found Stage 3 subjects most likely to agree or yield to the group majority in the Asch situation).

Although Stage 3 at age 10, Case 18 passed this "revealed differences" or group majority pressure with autonomous flying colors. Confronted with two of his classmates who thought stealing wrong, he emerged with his sense of the rightness of stealing unchanged.

Case 18 displayed this same sense of autonomy in his own family milieu. On Dilemma VII (which is worse, stealing or cheating?), he was pressured by the interviewer to agree that stealing was worse (Kohlberg, 1958, p. 306). Told, "The law makes it worse to steal, they give a worse sentence; don't you agree that made it worse to steal," he replied, "Well, the man who loaned the money was planning on getting the money back and if he didn't he'd have to turn other people down. And to himself he would probably think it was pretty bad, worse than stealing." Further pressured by the interviewer, who said, "The country could get along without loans better than stealing; wouldn't you agree that makes it worse to steal," he replied, "To the country it would be worse to steal but to *the man in Joe's conscience,* your own conscience, you should go by that because you know when you lie you feel bad and you want to go back and tell the truth and otherwise you feel worse."

Case 18's reference to conscience as "the man in Joe's conscience" immediately suggests the hypothesis of both Freud and J. M. Baldwin (1906) that conscience is the internalization of the father's authority. In terms of autonomy this raises the next question, Was Case 18 autonomous with regard to his father's authority? Some days after interviewing Case 18 about Dilemma VII (cheating versus stealing) I asked Case 18 whether he had talked to his family about the moral interviews. He said, "Yes, when my father was saying goodnight to me I told him about the story about cheating and stealing. I told him I thought cheating was worse. He told me he thought stealing was worse because it was worse according to the law. But I told him it might be worse in the lawbook but I thought cheating was worse in God's book." I asked, "What did your father say to that?" and Case 18 answered, "He said it was late and he turned off the light." From this I inferred that Case 18 was autonomous and that his family milieu was one of some acceptance of autonomy and mutual respect. His father tacitly recognized and accepted an equal in moral discussion.

It should also be noted that Case 18's peer group milieu was also consistent with his autonomous orientation, he was among the sociometrically best integrated students in his classroom peer group by my (Kohlberg, 1958) measure of peer group integration.

Case 18 in our current scoring system was Stage 3 at age 10 and when last interviewed was Stage 4 at age 29. He was the only 10-year-old in our American longitudinal study to be scored Type B at age 10, and he remained Type B through all interviews through his last interview at age 29. Thus his moral type remained equilibrated, though his stage did not. We may conclude this portion of our discussion of moral type by noting the analogy of Case 18's behavioral autonomy as Type B to Piaget's conception of equilibration. For researchers into Piaget's cognitive stages, one of the most striking phenomena is the "autonomy" of a child who has attained an equilibrated invariant operational structure, for instance of conservation. Studies by Smedslund (1968) and others indicate that the preconserving child can easily be induced by an experimenter to make either conserving or nonconserving responses, but that the "truly" concrete-operational conserver will resist all pressure and suggestion to agree with a nonconserving response.

The Kohlberg (1958) Postconventional Typology as Based on J. M. Baldwin and on Kant and Redefined as Type B.

In Chapter 6, "Continuities and Discontinuities Revisited—Again," we report how high-school age subjects who originally had been scored as approximating the ideal types of Stages 5 and 6 became relativistic, which led us to redefine the postconventional stages in more structural terms. These more structural or hard stages cannot be dissolved by relativistic questioning nor become disequilibrated as could the earlier 1958 stages.

The fact of relativism also led us to redefine the typological concept of autonomy which exists at the conventional stages as well as at the postconventional stages. At the conventional stages, Stages 3 and 4, the autonomous types became represented as Type B.

While responses to our hypothetical moral dilemmas could loosely be classified as being of the heteronomous or autonomous types, the Piagetian typology did not do justice to age-developmental qualitative differences which I thought necessary to define stages. Piaget's typology did not seem to do justice to the obvious developmental differences that divided what I called the preconventional, conventional, and postconventional (or principled) levels. Ultimately the definition and description of moral stages discarded the ideal typological method and in standard issue scoring made a strict distinction between structure and content to define invariantly sequential and holistic hard stages. In the 1958 thesis, however, I retained the ideal-typological method which does not clearly separate structure and content.

In developing the 1958 ideal typical stages, I made heavy usage of James Mark Baldwin's (1906) conceptions of the development of the ideal self or conscience, particularly in order to define what I thought to be a postconventional level of morality.

In Chapter 1, "Stage and Sequence," I briefly summarized Baldwin's (1906) theory of the social self as arising out of imitation, and resulting reciprocal relationship between the self and the other, originally a bipolar self that was alternately imitative or accommodative to the other as model, and dominating or assimulative and "showing off" as a model to another. This premoral bipolar self became an ideal or moral self with the recognition that there were rules or norms which the model or authority, for example, the father, obeyed or accommodated to whether he was the dominating partner in the bipolar self-other relationship or not. At this point the child understood that there were rules and norms to which everyone in the family group (or everyone in general) had to conform. The self that was to morally conform to such norms is an ideal self, an imaginative self that the child was to become and one which the parent only imperfectly represented or modeled. Baldwin's theory of the origins of the social and the moral, or ideal, self is discussed at length elsewhere (Kohlberg, 1982b; Hart and Kohlberg, 1985).

Baldwin, then, sees the equality in the bipolar self-other relationship as arising not through peer interaction but through the subordination of both self and other to the ideal self or conscience. Such a conception was suggested by Case 18, who talked about "the man in Joe's conscience, your own conscience, you should go by that" in explaining why cheating was worse than stealing (Dilemma VII).

Case 18, aged 10, was interviewed on the kinds of persons or roles he would like to be—an ideal self interview. In it he went on to illustrate both his sense of his father as a moral model and a differentiation of his own moral self from explicit copying or obedience to his father (Kohlberg, 1958, pp. 302–303). Asked why he wanted to be "a good father," a chosen ideal self role, he responded, "Like every year you need good educated kids and you can't get all your experience in school, you get some from experience and your father has had experience and he knows what's what." Asked about "being someone who makes his family proud" he responded, "You don't have to be any hot shot to make your family proud. Just be a good boy and they aren't going to feel any different about you. It's nice but it's not real important."

Asked about "someone who takes after your father" he responded, "Well, it's nice but you shouldn't take after somebody unless they are real good. You should have your own mind and your own feelings, and if you act exactly like your father, you just sort of get the habit of following other people. They might be doing something bad."

As mentioned earlier, Case 18 was scored 3B at this time of interviewing. It is easy to understand why I described Stage 3 as the "good-boy stage" in terms of such material (Kohlberg, 1958). It is evident also that Case 18's autonomy or Type B orientation differentiated the ideal self, conscience, or being a good person from actually imitating or copying his father or other people in general, and was, rather, based on being a nonfollowing "good person."

In Kohlberg (1958) and Kohlberg (1982b), following Baldwin, I point to ideal self morality, particularly at Stage 3B, as representing the first genuine "categorical imperative," to use Kant's term.

In Chapter 1, "Stage and Sequence," I briefly elaborate Baldwin's (1911) theory of stages of intellectual and epistemological development recently empirically elaborated by Broughton (1982b).

Foreshadowing and influencing Piaget, Baldwin's theory of genetic logic postulated an original adualism of subjective and objective and a successive set of differentiations of the subjective and objective, first differentiating the real-unreal distinction; next, the internal-external distinction; next, the distinction between mental and physical; and last, the distinction between the subjective "transcendental" self as experiencer and the objective self as the valued knowledge content of experience.

Baldwin (1911) has a parallel series of moral stages summarized in Table C.3.

In Kohlberg (1958), Baldwin's threefold typology was partly taken as defining the first three stages. In Chapter 2, I cited 9-year-old Tommy's Stage 1 response to the Heinz dilemma with its confusion of the value of human lives with their importance and the value of furniture as illustrating Stage 1's adualistic, syntelic, or projective characteristics of Baldwin's Level I as these are summarized in Table C.3.

The first level of evaluation by the young child is reflection of a multiplicity of concrete characteristics. In the first place, projective valuing leads to a confusion of the perceptual or physical qualities of an act or object with its value, whether this value is instrumental (technical, economic, or egoistic) or moral. The moral and the instrumental goodness or badness of a person are not only confused with each other but with physical-perceptual qualities like clean-dirty, pretty-ugly, and so on. The value of an act is judged in terms of its manifest physical consequences rather than in terms of its purpose or its conformity to standards. Physical similarity between two objects implies that both have similar moral value, so that value judgments are justified on grounds of value-irrelevant similarity.

The dualistic Level II nature of moral Stage 2 is quite obvious.

Table C.3. **Baldwin's Ethical Stages**

I. Objective or Adualistic Stage

1. Value is *syntelic.* Failure to localize or distinguish for whom a bad event is bad. The value of an event to another person is shared by the self without basis, or the evaluation of the event by the self is believed to be held by others without basis.

2. Value is *projective.* Failure to see the value of an event as a means to an end, on which its value is strictly contingent, or as an expression of a purpose which defines its value. Value of an act is dependent on its consequences and on irrelevant perceptual similarities to other valued acts. There is a general failure to differentiate good and right from other meanings of good and right.

3. Duty is perceived as based on *objective* or external necessity. Duty or right action is identified with that which the self "has to do" or is compelled to do by external forces, authority, and sanctions.

II. Dualistic, Prudential, or Intellectual Stage

1. Value is *relativistic.* Judgments of right and good are relative to self-interest, and judgments may be seen as conflicting where interests conflict.

2. Value is *instrumental* and based on need. The value of an object or act is based on its relation to an actual need or end involved in the particular situation.

3. Duty is perceived as a *hypothetical* imperative. Direction of action is not by compelling prescription or external pressure but is advisory and contingent on needs or motives of the actor.

III. Ethical or Ideal Stage

1. Value is public or *synnomic.* The moral value accorded by the self to the event is that which it is believed could be accorded to it by anyone. At the same time this value which the public could hold is a value based on the self's own legitimate perspective in the situation. The value is not the opinion poll value but the value which the self perceives when taking the role of "any rational person" in the society, or which we think society ought to take.

2. Value is ideal and objective. Events are valued not in terms of ideal desires which the self *does* have, but in terms of ideal desires which the self *should* have. It is felt that objects or events *should* be valued in certain ways, that value requires an effort of judgment and appreciation.

When Tommy moved to Stage 2, he replied to the euthanasia Dilemma (IV) by saying: "If she wanted to, she could, but her husband probably wouldn't want it. If a pet dies you can always get another one. Well, if he married someone else, he wouldn't have a wife just the same as he had."

The naiveté of Tommy's Stage 2 purely instrumental approach to moral value suggests the need for a third level, Baldwin's *ethical* or *ideal* stage of moral evaluation. In the ethical stage intrinsic values are, for example, values or purposes which are *desirable* rather than simply *desired.* The term *ideal* implies a differentiation between the desires people *do* have and the desires they *should* have. At the ethical level, one has an ideal self in the sense of wishing to possess ethically good motives or ends.

This third level is partly present at Stage 3, as our discussion of Case 18's ideal self interview indicated. It is, however, not clear in all Stage 3 persons but only in those we call Type B. Stage 3 Type A confuses the ideal self and the moral "ought" with what is generally done, and expected of or by, most people or most boys (or girls); it is conformist, not autonomous.

A second case, Case 37, discussed as an adult in Chapter 6, "Continuities and Discontinuities Revisited—Again," is also illustrative of Baldwin's concept of the ideal self of moral obligation when first interviewed at age 13, when he was scored Stage 3 Type B.

I quoted (Kohlberg, 1958) Case 37, age 13, in his response to Dilemma IV (the euthanasia dilemma), involving a conflict between rules against murder on the one side and sympathy for suffering on the other.

> If I was a doctor, I just wouldn't like to kill people, but in a way he'd be doing her a favor. These are murder. I really don't know, but I can't see anybody being killed . . . I don't think a person should be killed like an animal. It wouldn't be any compliment to that person, but then she wanted it. I'm trying to put myself in the shoes of the doctor and I don't think anyone can imagine the pain. If it were absolutely necessary, if they were sure she would die and she were out of her mind, they would do it in a painless way.

Case 37 cannot simply sympathize with the woman and let his sympathy determine his choice. Neither can he simply determine his action with a habitual self of natural reluctance to kill or of conformity to definite prescribed rule. There is, rather, a struggle to decide rightly, to anticipate what an ideal self, an all-wise and ethical self, would choose. The appeal is to a general self, to a reorganizing perspective, which is the same for himself and for the doctor. Though general, it is neither simply a socially accepted rule of society nor a simple habit. The boy has perhaps never before questioned the habitual view or social rule that killing is wrong. It is not simply spontaneous sympathy, however, but his moral set, his ideal self, which requires the examination of the merit of the claim of the individual woman in the individual situation.

I (1958, 1982b) used Baldwin's third structural stage not only to characterize Stage 3 as the first truly moral stage but to characterize postconventional morality, especially a Stage 6 of principled conscience. Baldwin's notion of the morally autonomous type is much more Kantian than is Piaget's notion. Baldwin stresses the Kantian sense of prescriptive duty, opposing the categorical imperative of the fully moral to the hypothetical imperative of Stage 2, "If you want this to happen, then do this." Baldwin also stresses the universality or universalizability central to Kant. He points out how the ethical level may have the universality not of conventionally agreed upon shared rules but of the postconventional and autonomous or self-created judgment of principle.

> As to the second form of universality—giving a rule on which all act—this also does not alone exhaust the sort of sanction which rules have. We can imagine a form of society built on the basis of a system of conventional social rules which each citizen is always to observe. This would be strictly social sanction; the rules would be civil; they might be compulsory, but they need not be ethical. The society would lack just the one thing which we have found essential to human society considered as a progressive organization, the element omitted by the traditional theories of human society which liken convention and conformity to convenience and utility. This lack of principle of growth, the give-and-take of personal influence between the man and the group . . . in the individual is what we mean by his ethical growth. . . . And as in the individual . . . so in society ethical sanctions supersede those of intelligence, convention, and suggestion. . . . If we bring this finally under the question of rule, we reach a last possibility: *that in the ethical realm the individual rules himself by rules which are in advance of those which society prescribes, and also exacts them.* [1906, pp. 559–567]

For Piaget, a postconventional principle's affective source is still respect for other (heteronomous or mutual respect). For Baldwin, the germ of postconventionality lies in the origin of morality as social but ideal, the progressive differentiation of the ideal from its embodiment in concrete persons.

Piaget's theoretical account of the genesis of autonomy, then, differs in significant ways from Baldwin's and ultimately from Kant's notion of autonomy, which is that of generalized and universalizable self-legislation of duties which are taken to be intrinsically obligating. Kant's test of universalizability coheres in Baldwin's notion of the synnomic. The Kantian conception of autonomy seems to overlap to a large extent with that of Baldwin, as well as Piaget. In the Heinz dilemma (III), one would expect a general, intrinsic, and universal obligation of conscience toward life; in Joe and his father (Dilemma I), an obligation toward promise keeping, and in punishing Heinz (Dilemma III′), a judgment that Heinz had acted with goodwill and so need not be punished.

Drawing on Baldwin, Kant, and Hare (1952), I tried to sketch out an autonomous ideal type for rating each dilemma (Kohlberg, 1958). For the Heinz dilemma, considering Stage 6 as the most autonomous, for instance, the rating schema was as follows:

Choice: Though the act is legally wrong it is justified as right to the rational and moral actor under the circumstances.
Value: Emphasis on the value of life.
Roles: If necessary would do it for a friend or acquaintance.
Justice: No justice on the druggist's side in a case of life, a case that the druggist is violating the right to life.

Again looking at the Heinz dilemma, the Stage 5 rating schema was the following:

Choice: The conflict is between the legal judgment and what the rational individual is justified in doing. Though "wrong" legally, tendency to say should steal.
Value: The end, value life, does not completely justify the means.
Roles: Duty to wife is within and limited by the general legal framework. A rational and natural person would prefer stealing and jail to the loss of his wife.
Justice: Druggist still has his legal rights, regardless of his unfairness. The unfairness of the druggist is irrelevant to the legal and rational decision, though it is perceived.

This Kohlberg (1958), Baldwin, or Kantian construction of postconventional morality has led us in our type project starting in 1980 to develop "Kantian" or "Baldwin" criteria of ideal types A and B as well as Piagetian ones. The Kantian criteria are more immediately applicable to Dilemma III (Heinz) involving a conflict between two general sociomoral norms, the Piagetian, to Dilemma I (Joe and his father) a dilemma of interpersonal relations between the generations. The "Kantian" criteria of Type B are presented in Table C.4.

In considering these criteria, it is important to see the relation between Kant's formalism and that of Piaget. Kant's concept of autonomy is, first, that of the autonomy of moral norms and principles and duties as distinct from nonmoral values of a more factual sort which are more descriptive and consequentialist than prescriptive, and more pragmatic or aesthetic than purely moral. Second, it is the autonomy of the moral personality as the object of moral respect, "treat each person as an end in him- or herself, not merely as a means." This implies intrinsic value to a person's life in Dilemma IV and Dilemma III or to promise keeping in Dilemma I. Third, it is the autonomy of universality and universalizability. In Baldwin's genetic psychology, postconventional autonomy arises through the effort to generalize and universalize more specific or special conventional rules. In our account of the development of postconventional moral principles in Chapter 6, "Continuities and Discontinuities Revisited—Again," we stressed the move from a questioning of culturally and religiously local and situation specific rules, like the Ten Commandments, to culturally universal general and formal principles like the Golden Rule of reversibility or the Kantian categorical imperative of universalizability itself. The meaning of Kantian generalization and universalization in moral reasoning and the related distinction between rules and principles is clearly spelled out in Singer's (1971) "Generalization in Ethics." The close relationship between "Kantian" universalizability and "Piagetian" reversibility in the moral point of view is clearly brought out in the writings of Hare (1963, 1981), Rawls (1980), and other moral philosophers and is also elaborated in Volume I, Chapter 5, "Justice as Reversibility." Here we need note that to universalize a norm or obligation is to make it reversible. It is giving oneself an obligation one wishes all others to adhere to. In so doing it implies reversibility or interchangeability between one's own point of view, what one expects of oneself, what one expects of others, and what expectations of others one will accept for oneself. Whether reversibility is genetically prior to universalizability or universalizability prior to reversibility is a center of debate between J. M. Baldwin and Piaget, a debate we shall not enter into here.

Table C.4. **"Kantian" Criteria for Type B (Form A)**

1. *Choice:* The subject must choose the more "just" course of action or solution to the dilemma (i.e., the choice which is empirically agreed upon by subjects at Stage 5). In the Heinz dilemma (III), the choice is to steal the drug; in the Officer Brown dilemma (III′), the choice is to set Heinz free or to put him on probation; and in the Joe dilemma (I), the choice is to refuse to give the father the money.

2. *Hierarchy:* Reflects the second formulation of the categorical imperative: "Treat persons never simply as means, but always at the same time as ends." As such, the right to life, the value of acting on one's conscience, and the importance of promise keeping or of respecting earned property (understood to be the only considerations that insure that persons are treated as ends) are all placed above any other considerations in the resolution of the respective dilemmas in Form A (III, III′, and I).

3. *Intrinsicalness:* The intrinsic moral worth of persons, or an intrinsic respect for persons and personality (including personal autonomy), is recognized and upheld in the course of resolving the dilemma. This may be reflected in responses that refer to the intrinsic value of life, the intrinsic rights that all human beings possess, the intrinsic value of persons and personality in general, or the intrinsic value of promises as a means to insure respect for persons and personality.

4. *Prescriptivity:* The categorical imperative also implies a categorical moral "ought" that prescribes a certain set of moral actions (e.g., saving a life or keeping a promise) regardless of the inclinations of the actor or of various pragmatic considerations. As such, the categorical imperative is distinguished from a hypothetical imperative, which is not prescriptive, and thus takes a simple "if–then" form.

5a. *Universality:* Reflects the third formulation of the categorical imperative: "Act so that your will can regard itself at the same time as making universal law through its maxim." Universality implies that the particular set of actions that have been prescribed in the course of resolving the dilemma must apply *universally* to any and all human beings. As such, human beings are understood to be universal moral objects, and the corresponding universal moral judgment takes the following form: You should act this way (do *X*) toward any and all human beings.

Table C.4—Continued

5b. *Universalizability:* Reflects the most crucial of the tests implied by the first formulation of the categorical imperative: "Act as if the maxim of your action were to become through your will a universal law of nature." Universalizability implies that the particular set of actions that have been prescribed for the actor in the dilemma must be such that they apply to any and all other *actors in similar situations or circumstances.* As such, a universalizable moral judgment implies a universal moral agent, and the judgment takes the following form: All agents in *A*'s position should act this way (do *X*).

At Stage 6, reversibility represents universal ideal role-taking, "moral musical chairs," or dialogues and agreement between persons conceived as free and equal in discourse and contract. But at the conventional stages, both universality and reversibility are immanent norms of justice or impartiality and lead to autonomy with regard to nonuniversal (or general) and nonreversible rules or demands of authority in Type B judgments.

The Theoretical Meaning of the Moral Typology as Related to Wright's Interpretation of Piaget—Judgment and Action

In two recent papers Wright (1982, 1983) elaborates the meaning and current value of Piaget's typology given the more recent work by myself and other researchers using the Kohlberg stages. Wright takes for granted the fact that the Kohlberg stages correspond much better to what in Chapter 3 are called hard stages than does the Piaget typology. He is aware of the limits of the Piaget typology from a purely structural stage viewpoint, limitations elaborated in Kohlberg (1958, 1964) and in Kohlberg and Helkama (in preparation). However, he argues that the Kohlberg stages do not assess certain important aspects of moral judgment stressed in Piaget's theory. He points out that the Kohlberg stages are defined as kinds of reasoning about hypothetical dilemma action. Statements of obligation or rightness made in response to these dilemmas, Wright claims, involve deductive reasoning from the general norms and elements of the child's stage structure. In contrast, Wright asserts, Piaget's theory, if not his empirical data, is much more centrally directed to the child's sense of practical obligations and the social sentiment of respect from which it derives, this is to say, a child's sense of obligation to social others to whom he is related in real-life situations of choice. Wright, then, claims that Piaget's theory focuses squarely on the "practical" morality of the child, whereas my stages are stages in the child's "theoretical" morality. While we would not accept the notion that our stages are stages merely of "theoretical" morality, it is true that Piaget's central interest was in the child's sense of obligation in real situations and the qualitative types of such obligations, rather than the moral reasoning of the child.

Given this interpretation of Piaget, the Piagetian typology can be seen as providing additional insight to two aspects of the child's morality not completely represented by our stages. First, Wright claims that Piaget's typology provides a more significant account of the relation of moral judgment to action. In Chapter 7 we noted this contribution in part by demonstrating the relationship that "substage" B in the judgment-action studies adds a great deal to the prediction of action for the conventional stages. The studies showed a monotonic increase of just action by stage with a large majority of Stage 5 subjects and of "substage" B, Stages 3 and 4, subjects engaging in the right action.

More fundamentally, Wright's critique contends that our hypothetical dilemmas are "theoretical," whereas Piaget's typology is "practical." The fact that an autonomous orientation to our hypothetical dilemmas, as well as stage on the dilemmas, predicts to moral action seems to us to refute Wright's claim that our own approach is only directed toward "theoretical morality."

The Theoretical Meaning of the Moral Typology: Types of Social Relations

The heteronomous type of moral obligation is Piaget's ideal type relationship of unilateral respect in which greater power and value is attributed to an elder or authority figure or to a group felt as a Durkheimian collectivity. Corresponding to the autonomous type of moral duty is Piaget's ideal type interrelationship of mutual respect and cooperation in which power and value are attributed to each person on the basis of equality and reciprocity. This leads us to expect differences in type in differing social environments. In our American data we find significant differences, as Piaget would have us expect, between children and adolescents integrated into their peer group, as assessed by a sociometric test, as compared to those isolated from the peer group. The integrated children and adolescents were more likely than the isolated ones to be Type B.

A second expectation is that subjects of higher socioeconomic status are more likely to be Type B than working class subjects. This hypothesis derives from the extensive work of Kohn (1977) showing that fathers of higher socioeconomic status value autonomy in their children more highly than do working class fathers, in part due to the greater autonomy they experience in their own jobs. Out data suggest that adolescents of upper middle and middle class origins are more likely to be Type B than working class adolescents in an American sample.

Third, and most important, we would expect cultural differences in the balance of relations of unilateral and mutual respect. As an example, Lei (1983) found his Taiwanese sample to be less frequently Type B than our American sample across the same age groups. At the conventional stages (Stages 3, 3/4, and 4) there was a statistically significantly greater frequency of Type B in the American sample than in the Taiwanese sample; the mean percentage of American Type B conventional subjects is 56 percent and for the Taiwanese subjects only 15 percent. This was not solely due to a greater orientation to filial piety or obedience to the father on Dilemma I; a lower frequency of Type B was found on the other dilemmas as well. As might be expected, however, the differences were most marked for Dilemma I, the father-son dilemma.

The cultural differences in moral type between Taiwan and America found by Lei are not due to any difference in moral stage, as the Taiwanese sample average at each age was slightly higher than the American sample at similar ages. Analyses from a comparison of a longitudinal Israeli kibbutz sample with our American longitudinal sample, the study reported in Chapter 9, indicates that the Israeli subjects were more likely than the American subjects to be Type B. Finally Turkish village subjects (reported in Chapter 8) were most likely to remain Type A.

Considering these four studies, one would expect the greatest equality and mutuality of relationships in the kibbutz, which stresses equality in its ideology and in its patterns of education and child care. One would expect the United States to be intermediate in this regard, since there is emphasis upon democracy and cooperation in the American ideology of education and child rearing compared to Taiwanese ideology. Finally Turkish village cultures are probably the most likely to retain what Piaget calls a "gerontocratic" social structure.

Types A and B and Longitudinal Change

While our American longitudinal data did not fit the notion of substages as described in Chapter 2, they do fit Piaget's notion of a heteronomous-autonomous developmental typology. Piaget, as quoted earlier, implied that some persons might remain heteronomous all their lives. In fact, in our sample using Form A, 38 percent of our subjects fit this pattern, starting at heteronomous Type A and remaining Type A at all subsequent times of testing. Very few of our subjects were autonomous Type B at first testing. The 5 percent who were remained autonomous Type B throughout. A common pattern was for subjects to start as Type A then make a shift to Type B and remain Type B at all subsequent testings. This group comprised 33 percent of the entire sample. The remaining one-fourth (24 percent) of the subjects had no particular pattern.

In the 242 observation points or comparisons of two adjacent times of testing on Form A, only 6 percent involved "regression," that is, movement from Type B to Type A. This percentage of "regression" is less than that found for either interrater or one-month test-retest agreement scores on moral type, which are 90 percent in agreement. These findings are reminiscent of the findings of 7 percent regression in stage attributable to measurement error (see Chapter 5 and Colby and Kohlberg, 1984).

In our sample using Form B, 54 percent of our subjects remained heteronomous at subsequent test times, and none of our subjects were autonomous Type B at the first time of testing. Twenty three percent of the sample made a one-time shift from Type A to Type B, while 23 percent of the subjects had no particular pattern.

In addition, only 4 percent of the 230 observations involved "regression," a percentage that is again less than that due to measurement error. Across the two forms, there was 75 percent consistency of scores and patterns of moral types.

Similar longitudinal findings were found cross-culturally in Turkey and Israel (Tappan, Kohlberg, et al., 1984 in press).

It should be noted that our concept and measure of heteronomous and autonomous types are methodologically fairly rough.

The types are ideal types mixing structure and content and showing considerable variation from one dilemma to another, unlike the consistency or "structured whole" quality of the moral stages. Given the mixture of structure and content, the scoring algorithm for assignment of an overall Type A or Type B score for a subject across the three dilemmas on a form has been somewhat arbitrary. We have used a two-out-of-three rule for type assignment; a subject is assigned to Type B only if on at least two of the three dilemmas on a form the criteria for Type B are passed. Other cases are assigned to Type A.

Conclusions

In conclusion, we have redefined our search for "substages" to a concern for heteronomous and autonomous ideal types, linked to development but without "hard stage," or structural, definitions or implications. We have drawn our conception of the developmental types not only from Piaget but also from Baldwin and Kant. A few tentative findings arising from research with these types are consistent with the Piagetian "two worlds" hypothesis. These findings, such as the cross-cultural differences, suggest that developing persons are more likely to show the autonomous type orientation in a more egalitarian or democratic sociocultural environment. Our discussion of Baldwin, however, suggests other aspects of experience leading to the autonomous type orientation, experiences of the formation of an ideal self or conscience which is generalized and universalized within the context of an idealization of admired authorities and rules, as seemed to be done by Case 18.

Without attempting to draw firm theoretical conclusions as to the nature of experience leading to the development of the autonomous Type B, our research suggests that it may relate to different kinds of social and familial environments.

The importance of our typology for understanding the differential influence of various environments will be explored in Volume III in chapters comparing students in Just Community alternative high schools with those from regular high schools.

The importance of our typology for understanding moral action was demonstrated in Chapter 7. Its implications for moral action will be further analyzed in Volume III in discussions of the influence of educational environments on student behavior.

Finally, there is a further question of psychology and philosophy about the domains to which a typology of heteronomous and autonomous morality may be usefully applied. The domain from which we have developed our specific typology (Type A and Type B) is the domain of the deontic right or justice. Usually distinguished from this domain is the domain of the good as one of aspiration toward a good life or toward being a good or virtuous person. Whether a typology of heteronomy and autonomy is applicable to domains of the good is an open and unstudied question.

References

Adams, J. S. "Toward an Understanding of Inequity." *Journal of Abnormal and Social Psychology 67* (1963):422–436.

Ainsworth, M. D. "Development of Infant-Mother Interaction Among the Ganda." In B. Foss, ed., *Determinants of Infant Behavior,* vol. 2. London: Methuen, 1963.

Ainsworth, M. D. "Patterns of Attachment Behavior Shown by the Infant in Interaction with his Mother." *Merrill-Palmer Quarterly 10* (1964):51–58.

Allinsmith, W. "Moral Standards: II. The Learning of Moral Standards." In D. R. Miller and G. E. Swandon, *Inner Conflict and Defense.* New York: Holt, 1960.

Ammons, R., and Ammons, H. "Parent Preference in Young Children's Doll-Play Interviews." *Journal of Abnormal and Social Psychology 44* (1949):490–505.

Anderson, J. "Development." In D. Harris, ed., *The Concept of Development.* Minneapolis: University of Minnesota Press, 1957.

Anderson, J. "The Prediction of Adjustment over Time." In I. Iscoe and H. Stevenson, eds., *Personality Development in Children.* Austin: University of Texas Press, 1960.

Angrilli, A. F. "The Psychosexual Identification of Preschool Boys." *Journal of Genetic Psychology 97* (1960):329–340.

Aristotle. *The Ethics of Aristotle.* New York: Carlton House, n.d.

Armon, C. "Ethical Reasoning in Adulthood: A Structural Analysis of Postconventional Thought." In M. Commons, F. Richards, and C. Armon, eds., *Beyond Formal Operations: Late Adolescent and Adult Cognitive Development.* New York: Praeger, 1984a.

Armon, C. "Ideals of the Good Life and Moral Judgment: Ethical Reasoning Across the Life Span." In M. Commons, F. Richards, and C. Armon, eds., *Beyond Formal Operations: Late Adolescent and Adult Cognitive Development.* New York: Praeger, 1984b.

Aron, R. "Moral Education: The Formalist Tradition and the Deweyite Alternative?" In B. Munsey, ed., *Moral Development, Moral Education and Kohlberg.* Birmingham, Ala.: Religious Education Press, 1980.

Aronfreed, J. "The Nature, Variety, and Social Patterning of Moral Responses to Transgression." *Journal of Abnormal and Social Psychology 63* (1961):223–241.

Aronfreed, J. "Concept and Conscience: The Experimental Study of Internalization." Unpublished manuscript, 1966.

Aronfreed, J. *Conduct and Conscience: The Socialization of Internalized Control Over Behavior.* New York: Academic Press, 1968.

Aronfreed, J. "The Concept of Internalization." In D. A. Goslin, ed., *Handbook of Socialization Theory and Research.* Chicago: Rand McNally, 1969.

Asch, S. E. *Social Psychology.* Englewood Cliffs, N.J.: Prentice-Hall, 1952.

Ausubel, D. P. *Ego Development and the Personality Disorders.* New York: Grune & Stratton, 1952.
Ausubel, D. P. "Perceived Parent Attitudes as Determinants of Children's Ego Structure." *Child Development 25* (1954):173–183.
Ausubel, D. P. *Theory and Problems of Child Development.* New York: Grune & Stratton, 1957.
Ayer, A. J. *Language Truth and Logic.* London: Gollancz, 1936.
Azrin, N., and Lindsley, O. R. "The Reinforcement of Cooperation Between Children." *Journal of Abnormal and Social Psychology 52* (1956):100–102.
Baer, D.; Peterson, R.; and Sherman, J. "The Development of Generalized Imitation by Programming Similarity Between Child and Model as Discriminative for Reinforcement." *Journal of Experimental Analysis of Behavior 10* (1967):405–416.
Baier, K. *The Moral Point of View: A Rational Basis of Ethics.* Rev. ed. New York: Random House, 1965.
Bakken, L. "Moral Judgment in Adults: Its Relationship to Age, Sex, and Education." Unpublished doctoral dissertation, Boston University, 1983.
Baldwin, A. L. "Cognitive Theory," In D. A. Goslin, ed., *Handbook of Socialization Theory and Research.* Chicago: Rand McNally, 1969.
Baldwin, J. M. *Mental Development in the Child and the Race.* New York: Macmillan, 1895.
Baldwin, J. M. *Social and Ethical Interpretations in Mental Development.* New York: Macmillan, 1906.
Baldwin, J. M. *Thoughts and Things, or Genetic Logic,* 3 vols. New York: Macmillan, 1906–11.
Baldwin, J. M. *Genetic Theory of Reality,* New York: Putnam, 1915.
Bandura, A. "Social-Learning Theory of Identificatory Processes." In D. A. Goslin, ed., *Handbook of Socialization Theory and Research.* Chicago: Rand McNally, 1969.
Bandura, A., and Walters, R. H. *Adolescent Aggression.* New York: Ronald, 1959.
Bandura, A., and Huston, A. C. "Identification as a Process of Incidental Learning." *Journal of Abnormal and Social Psychology 63* (1961):311–319.
Bandura, A., and MacDonald, F. "The Influence of Social Reinforcement and the Behavior of Models in Shaping Children's Moral Judgment." *Journal of Abnormal and Social Psychology 67* (1963):274–281.
Bandura, A., and Kupers, C. "Transmission of Patterns of Self-Reinforcement Through Modeling." *Journal of Abnormal and Social Psychology 69* (1964):1–9.
Bandura, A., and Whalen, C. "The Influence of Antecedent Reinforcement and Divergent Modeling Cues on Patterns of Self-Reward." *Journal of Personality and Social Psychology 3* (1966): 373–382.
Bandura, A.; Grusic, J.; and Menlove, F. "Some Social Determinants of Self-Monitoring Systems." *Journal of Personality and Social Psychology 5* (1967):449–455.
Bandura, A.; Ross, D.; and Ross, S. "Transmission of Aggression Through Imitation of Aggressive Models." *Journal of Abnormal and Social Psychology 66* (1963a):3–11.

Bandura, A.; Ross, D.; and Ross, S. "A Comparative Test of the Status Envy, Social Power and Secondary Reinforcement Theories of Identificatory Learning." *Journal of Abnormal and Social Psychology 67* (1963b):527–534.

Bandura, A.; Ross, D.; and Ross, S. "Vicarious Reinforcement and Imitative Learning." *Journal of Abnormal and Social Psychology 67* (1963c):601–607.

Barclay, A., and Cusumano, D. "Effects of Father Absence upon Field-Dependent Behavior." Paper delivered at the meeting of the American Psychological Association, September, 1965.

Barrett, D. E. and Yarrow, M. R. "Prosocial Behavior, Social Inferential Ability and Assertiveness in Children." *Child Development 48* (1977):475–481.

Bar-Yam, M.; Kohlberg, L.; and Naame, A. "Moral Reasoning of Students in Different Cultural, Social and Educational Settings." *American Journal of Education 88* (1980):345–362.

Becker, H. *Outsiders: Studies in the Sociology of Deviance.* New York: Free Press, 1963.

Becker, W. "Consequences of Different Kinds of Parental Discipline." In M. Hoffman and L. Hoffman, Eds., *Review of Child Development Research,* vol. 1. New York: Russell Sage Foundation, 1964.

Berkowitz, L. *Development of Motives and Values in a Child.* New York: Basic Books, 1964.

Berkowitz, L., and Daniels, L. R. "Responsibility and Dependency." *Journal of Abnormal and Social Psychology 66* (1963):429–436.

Berlyne, D. *Conflict Arousal and Curiosity.* New York: McGraw-Hill, 1961.

Berlyne, D. *Structure and Direction in Thinking.* New York: Wiley, 1965.

Berry, J. "Ecological and Cultural Factors in Spatial Perceptual Development." *Canadian Journal of Behavioral Science 3* (1971):324–336.

Blasi, A. "Bridging Moral Cognition and Moral Action: A Critical Review of the Literature." *Psychological Bulletin 88* (1980):1–45.

Blasi, A. "Autonomy and Obedience in Children's Moral Judgment." Unpublished manuscript, University of Massachusetts at Boston, 1982.

Blasi, A. "Bridging Moral Cognition and Action, A Theoretical View." *Developmental Review 3*(1983):178–210..

Blatt, M. "The Effects of Classroom Discussion Programs upon Children's Level of Moral Judgment." Unpublished Ph.D. dissertation, University of Chicago, 1969.

Blatt, M., and Kohlberg, L. "The Effects of Classroom Moral Discussion upon Children's Moral Judgment. *Journal of Moral Education 4* (1975):129–161.

Bloom, A. H. "Two Dimensions of Moral Reasoning: Social Principledness and Social Humanism in Cross-Cultural Perspective." *Journal of Social Psychology 101(1)* (1977):29–44.

Bowers, W. J. "Student Dishonesty and Its Control in College." Cooperative Research Project No. OE 1672. Unpublished manuscript, Columbia University Bureau of Applied Social Research, 1964.

Bowlby, J. "The Nature of the Child's Tie to His Mother." *International Journal of Psychoanalysis 39* (1958):350–373.

Boyd, D. "The Rawls Connection." In B. Munsey, ed., *Moral Development, Moral Education and Kohlberg.* Birmingham, Ala.: Religious Education Press, 1980.

Brandt, R. B. *Value and Obligation: Systematic Readings in Ethics.* New York: Harcourt, 1961.

Branstetter, E. "Separation Reactions in Hospitalized Children with and without Substitute Mothers." Unpublished Ph.D. dissertation, University of Chicago, 1969.

Brim, O. G., Jr. "Family Structures and Sex-Role Learning by Children." *Sociometry 21* (1958):1–6

Bronfenbrenner, U. "The Role of Age, Sex, Class, and Culture in Studies of Moral Development." *Religious Education* 57 (1962): 3–17.

Brotemarkle, R. A. "A Comparison Test for Investigating the Ideational Content of the Moral Concepts." *Journal of Applied Psychology 6* (1922):235–242.

Broughton, J. M. "The Development of Concepts of Self, Mind, Reality, and Knowledge." In W. Damon, ed., *New Directions for Child Development: Social Cognition.* San Francisco: Jossey-Bass, 1978a.

Broughton, J. M. "The Cognitive-Developmental Approach to Morality: A Reply to Kurtines and Grief." *Journal of Moral Education 7(2)* (1978b):81–96.

Broughton, J. M. "The Development of the Child's Epistemology in Metaphysics Through Adolescence and Youth." In J. M. Broughton, D. J. Freeman-Moir, eds., *The Cognitive-Developmental Psychology of James Mark Baldwin.* Norwood, N.J.: Ablex, 1982a.

Broughton, J. M. "Genetic Logic and the Developmental Psychology of Philosophical Concepts." In J. M. Broughton and D. J. Freeman-Moir, eds., *The Cognitive Developmental Psychology of James Mark Baldwin.* Norwood, N.J.:Ablex, 1982b.

Broughton, J. M., and Zahaykevich, M. "Review of J. Loevinger's *Ego Development: Conceptions and Theories.*" *Telos 32* (1977):246–253.

Brown, D. G. "Sex-Role Preference in Young Children." *Psychological Monographs 70* (1956):no. 14.

Brown, R., and Herrnstein, R. "Moral Reasoning and Conduct." In *Psychology,* pp. 289–340. Boston: Little, Brown and Company, 1975.

Bruss-Saunders, E. "Children's Thought About Parents: A Developmental Study." Unpublished doctoral dissertation, Harvard Graduate School of Education, 1979.

Bull, N. J. *Moral Education.* London: Routledge, 1969.

Burton, R. V. "Generality of Honesty Reconsidered." *Psychological Review 70* (1963):481–499.

Burton, R. V.; Maccoby, E.; and Allinsmith, W. "Antecedents of Resistance to Temptation in Four-Year-Old Children." *Child Development 22* (1961):689–710.

Calley, W., with Sack, J. *Lieutenant Calley: His Own Story.* New York: Viking Press, 1975.

Candee, D. "The Psychology of Watergate." *Journal of Social Issues 31* (1975):No. 2.

Candee, D. "Structure and Choice in Moral Reasoning." *Journal of Personality and Social Psychology 34* (1976):1293–1301.

Candee, D., and Kohlberg, L. "Moral Judgment and Moral Action: A Reanalysis of Haan, Smith and Block's FSM Study." In L. Kohlberg and D. Candee, eds., *Research in Moral Development.* Cambridge, Mass.: Harvard University Press, (in preparation).

Candee, D., and Kohlberg, L. "Moral Reasoning and Obedience to Authority." In L. Kohlberg, and D. Candee, eds., *Research in Moral Development.* Cambridge, Mass.: Harvard University Press, in preparation.

Carter, R. E. "What is Lawrence Kohlberg Doing?" *Journal of Moral Education 9* (1980):2.

Casler, L. "Maternal Deprivation: A Critical Review of the Literature." Monograph of the Society for Research in Child Development, vol. *26*, no. 26, 1961.

Cattell, R. B. *Personality and Motivation: Structure and Measurement.* Yonkers, New York: World Book, 1957.

Child, I. "Socialization." In G. Lindzey, ed., *Handbook of Social Psychology.* Cambridge, Mass.: Addison-Wesley, 1954.

Chomsky, N. "Language and the Mind." *Psychology Today 1(9)* (1968):48–51, 66–68.

Cistone, D. F. "Levels of Moral Reasoning Compared with Demographic Data Among Teachers, Administrators, and Pupil Personnel Employees Enrolled in Graduate Schools." Ph.D. dissertation, University of Southern California, 1980. *Dissertation Abstracts International 41* (1980):236A.

Colby, A. "Logical Operational Limitations on the Development of Moral Judgment." Unpublished Ph.D. dissertation, Columbia University, 1972.

Colby, A. "Evolution of a Moral-Developmental Theory." In W. Damon, ed., *New Directions for Child Development: Moral Development.* San Francisco: Jossey-Bass, 1978.

Colby, A., and Kohlberg, L. "The Relation Between Logical and Moral Development." in L. Kohlberg and D. Candee, eds., *Research in Moral Development.* Cambridge, Mass.: Harvard University Press, in preparation.

Colby, A., and Kohlberg, L. *The Measurement of Moral Judgment,* vols. I and II. New York: Cambridge University Press, 1984, in press.

Colby, A.; Kohlberg, L.; Gibbs, J.; and Lieberman, M. "A Longitudinal Study of Moral Judgment." Monograph of the Society for Research in Child Development, vol. 48, no. 4, 1983.

Colby, A.; Kohlberg, L.; Fenton, E.; Speicher-Dubin, B.; and Lieberman, M. "Secondary School Moral Discussion Programmes Led by Social Studies Teachers." *Journal of Moral Education 6* (1977):2.

Cole, M.; Gay, J.; Glick, J.; and Sharp, D. *The Cultural Context of Learning and Thinking.* New York: Basic Books,, 1971.

Collins, W. A. "Effect of Temporal Separation Between Motivation, Aggression, and Consequences: A Developmental Study." *Developmental Psychology 8(2)* (1973):215–221.

Cowen, P.; Langer, J.; Heavenrich, J.; and Nathanson, M. "Has Social

Learning Theory Refuted Piaget's Theory of Moral Development?" Unpublished manuscript, 1968.

Cox, A. "Ends." *The New York Times Magazine,* May 19, 1974.

Crowley, P. M. "Effect of Training upon Objectivity of Moral Judgment in Grade-School Children." *Journal of Personality and Social Psychology 8* (1968):228–233.

Damon, W. *The Social World of the Child.* San Francisco: Jossey-Bass, 1977.

Danziger, K. "The Development of Children's Economic Concepts." *Journal of Genetic Psychology 47* (1958):231–240.

Darley, J. M., and Latane, B. "Bystander Intervention in Emergencies: Diffusion of Responsibility." *Journal of Personality and Social Psychology 10* (1968):202–214.

Decarie, T. G. *Intelligence and Affectivity in Early Childhood.* New York: International Universities Press, 1965.

Dennis, W., and Najarian, P. "Infant Development Under Environmental Handicap." *Psychological Monographics* (1957):*71* No. 7 (Whole No. 436).

DeVries, R. "The Development of Role-Taking as Reflected by Behavior of Bright, Average, and Retarded Children in a Social Guessing Game." *Child Development 41* (1970):759–770.

Dewey, J. "Experience and Conduct." In C. Murchison, ed., *Psychologies of 1930.* Worcester, Mass.: Clark University Press, 1930.

Dewey, J. "On Education: Selected Writing." Edited by R. D. Archambault. New York: Modern Library, republished 1964.

Dewey, J., and Tufts, J. H. *Ethics.* New York: Holt, 1932.

Dilthey, W. "Aufbau der geschichtlichen Welt in den Geisteswissenschaften." In *Gesammelte Schriften,* vol. 7. Göttingen: Vandenhoeck & Ruprecht, 1913, republished 1967.

Dixon, J. C. "Development of Self-Recognition." *Journal of Genetic Psychology 91* (1957):251–256.

Durkheim, E. *Sociology and Philosophy.* Glencoe, Ill.: Free Press, 1953. Written between 1898 and 1911. First published posthumously in French.

Durkheim, E. *Moral Education: A Study in the Theory and Application of the Sociology of Education.* New York: Free Press, 1961.

Dworkin, R. "The Original Position." In N. Daniels, ed., *Reading Rawls.* New York: Basic Books, 1976.

Dworkin, R. *Taking Rights Seriously.* Cambridge, Mass.: Harvard University Press, 1977.

Edwards, C. P. "The Effect of Experience On Moral Development: Results from Kenya." Ph.D. dissertation, Harvard University, 1974. Ann Arbor, Mich.: University Microfilms, 1975a, 75–16860.

Edwards, C. P. "Society Complexity and Moral Development: A Kenyan Study." *Ethos 3* (1975b):505–527.

Edwards, C. P. "The Comparative Study of the Development of Moral Judgment and Reasoning." In R. H. Munroe, R. L. Munroe, and B. B. Whiting, eds., *Handbook of Cross-Cultural Human Development.* New York: Garland Press, 1981.

Edwards, C. P. "Moral Development in Comparative Cultural Perspective." In D. Wagner and H. Stevenson, eds., *Cultural Perspectives on Child Development.* San Francisco: Freeman, 1982.

Ellinwood, C. "Structural Development in the Expression of Emotion by Children." Unpublished Ph.D. dissertation, University of Chicago, 1969.

Emmerich, W. "Family Role Concepts of Children Ages Six to Ten." *Child Development 32* (1961):609–624.

Emmerich, W. "Continuity and Stability in Early Social Development." *Child Development 35* (1964):311–333.

Emmerich, W., and Kohlberg, L. "Imitation and Attention-Seeking in Young Children Under Condition of Nurturance, Frustration, and Conflict." Unpublished mimeographed paper, University of Chicago, 1953.

Erdynast, A. "Improving the Adequacy of Moral Reasoning: An Exploratory Study with Executives and Philosophy Students." Unpublished PhD. dissertation, Harvard University, 1973.

Erdynast, A.; Armon, C., and Nelson, J. "Cognitive-Developmental Conceptions of the True and the Beautiful." *Proceedings of the 8th Annual Conference of Piaget and the Helping Professions.* Los Angeles: University of California Press, 1978.

Erikson, V. L. "The Case Study Method in the Evaluation of Developmental Programs." In L. Kuhmerker, M. Mentkowski and V. L. Erickson, eds., *Evaluating Moral Development.* New York: Character Research Press, 1980.

Erikson, E. H. "Identity and the Lifecycle." Monograph, *Psychological Issues* vol 1, no. 1. New York: International Universities Press, 1959.

Erikson, E. H. *Childhood and Society.* New York: Norton, 1963 (originally published 1950).

Erikson, E. H. *Insight and Responsibility: Lectures on the Ethical Implications of Psychoanalytic Insight.* New York: Norton, 1964.

Erikson, E. H. *Toys and Reason: Stages in the Revitalization of Experience.* New York: Norton, 1977.

Fernald, G. G. "The Defective Delinquent Differentiating Tests." *American Journal of Insanity 68* (1912):523–594,

Fishbein, M. "Attitudes and Prediction of Behavior." In M. Fishbein, ed., *Readings in Attitude Theory and Measurement.* New York: Wiley, 1967.

Fishkin, J. *Beyond Subjective Morality.* New Haven: Yale University Press, 1983.

Flavell, J. H. *Cognitive Development.* Englewood Cliffs, N.J.: Prentice-Hall, 1977.

Flugel, J. C. *Man, Morals, and Society: A Psychoanalytic Study.* New York: International Universities, 1955.

Fowler, J. *Stages of Faith: The Psychology of Human Development and the Quest for Meaning.* San Francisco: Harper & Row, 1981.

Fowler, J., and Vergote, A., eds. *Toward Moral and Religious Maturity.* Morristown, N.J.: Silver-Burdett, 1980.

Frankena, W. K. *Ethics.* Englewood, N.J.: Prentice-Hall, 1973.

Freedman, J. L. "Long-Term Behaviorial Effects of Cognitive Dissonance." *Journal of Experimental Social Psychology 1* (1965):145–155.

Freud, A. *The Ego and the Mechanisms of Defense.* New York: International Universities Press, 1946.

Freud, A., and Dann, S. "An Experiment in Group Upbringing." In R. Eissler et al., eds., *The Psychoanalytic Study of the Child,* vol. 6. New York: International Universities Press, 1951.

Freud, S. "The Ego and the Id." In Sigmund Freud, *The Standard Edition of the Complete Psychological Works of Sigmund Freud,* vol. 19, pp. 12–63. London: Hogarth; New York: Macmillan, 1961 (first published as *Das Ich und das Es,* 1923).

Freud, S. "The Resistances to Psycho-Analysis." In Sigmund Freud, *The Standard Edition of the Complete Psychological Works of Sigmund Freud,* vol. 19, pp. 213–222. London: Hogarth; New York: Macmillan, 1961 (first published in 1925).

Freud, S. "Some Psychological Consequences of the Anatomical Distinction Between the Sexes." *International Journal of Psychoanalysis 8* (1927):133–142.

Freud, S. *Civilization and Its Discontents.* Garden City, N.Y.: Doubleday, 1958 (first published as *Das Unbehagern in de Kultur,* 1930).

Freud, S. *The Basic Writings of Sigmund Freud.* New York: Modern Library, 1938.

Fromm, E. *Man for Himself: An Inquiry into the Psychology of Ethics.* Greenwich, Conn.: Fawcett, 1947. New York: Rinehart, 1955.

Gadamar, H. G. *Truth and Method.* New York, 1975 (translation of *Wahrheit und Methode.* Tübingen, 1965).

Galon, D. "The Moral Process, Lawrence Kohlberg's Psychology and Bernard Lonergan's Philosophy." Unpublished Ph.D. dissertation, University of Toronto, 1980.

Garwood, S. C.; Levine, D. W.; and Ewing, L. "Effect of Protagonist's Sex on Assessing Gender Differences in Moral Reasoning." *Developmental Psychology 16* (1980):677–681.

Gesell, A. "The Ontogenesis of Infant Behavior." In L. Carmichael, ed., *Manual of Child Psychology.* New York: Wiley, 1954.

Gewirth, A. *Reason and Morality.* Chicago: University of Chicago Press, 1978.

Gewirtz, J. L. "Mechanisms of Social Learning: Some Roles of Stimulation and Behavior in Early Human Development." In D. A. Goslin, ed., *Handbook of Socialization Theory and Research.* Chicago: Rand McNally, 1969.

Gibbs, J. C. "Kohlberg's Stages of Moral Judgment: A Constructive Critique." *Harvard Educational Review 47* (1977):43–61.

Gibbs, J. C. "Kohlberg's Moral Stage Theory: A Piagetian Revision." *Human Development 22* (1979a):89–112.

Gibbs, J. C. "The Meaning of Ecologically Oriented Inquiry in Contemporary Psychology." *American Psychologist 34* (1979b):127–140.

Gibbs, J. C., and Widaman, K. *Social Intelligence: Measuring the Development of Sociomoral Reflection.* Englewood Cliffs, N.J.: Prentice-Hall, 1982.

Gibbs, J. C.; Arnold, K. D.; and Burkhart, J. E. "Sex Differences in the Expression of Moral Judgment." Unpublished manuscript, Ohio State University, 1982.

Gilligan, C. "In a Different Voice: Women's Conceptions of the Self and of Morality." *Harvard Educational Review 47* (1977):481–517.

Gilligan, C. *In a Different Voice: Psychological Theory and Women's Development.* Cambridge, Mass.: Harvard University Press, 1982.
Gilligan, C., and Belenky, M. "A Naturalistic Study of Abortion Decisions." In R. Selman and R. Yando, eds., *Clinical Developmental Psychology.* San Francisco: Jossey-Bass, 1980.
Gilligan, C., and Murphy, J. M. "Development from Adolescence to Adulthood: The Philosopher and the 'Dilemma of the Fact.' " In D. Kuhn, ed., *Intellectual Development Beyond Childhood.* San Francisco: Jossey-Bass, 1979.
Gilligan, C.; Kohlberg, L.; Lerner, J.; and Belenky, M. "Moral Reasoning About Sexual Dilemmas: A Developmental Approach." Technical Report of the Commission on Obscenity and Pornography, vol. 1 (no. 52560010), Washington, D.C.: U. S. Government Printing Office, 1971.
Gilligan, C.; Langsdale, S.; Lyons, N.; and Murphy, J. M. "Contributions of Women's Thinking to Developmental Theory: The Elimination of Sex Bias in Moral Development Theory and Research." Final Report to National Institute of Education, 1982.
Gilligan, J. "Beyond Morality: Psychoanalytic Reflections on Shame, Guilt and Love." .In T. Lickona, ed., *Moral Development and Behavior.* New York: Holt, Rinehart & Winston, 1976.
Gilmore, B. "Toward an Understanding of Imitation." Unpublished manuscript, Waterloo University, 1967.
Glueck, S., and Glueck, E. *Unraveling Juvenile Delinquency.* New York: Commonwealth Fund, 1950.
Gorsuch, H. L., and Barnes, M. L. "Stages of Ethical Reasoning and Moral Norms of Carib Youths. *Journal of Cross-Cultural Psychology 4* (1973):283–301.
Gottesman, I. "Heritability of Personality: A Demonstration." *Psychological Monographs* 77 (1963):No. 9.
Gouldner, A. W. "The Norm of Reciprocity." *American Sociological Review 25,* (1960):165–167.
Green, B. "A Method of Scalogram Analysis Using Summary Statistics." *Psychometrika 21* (1956):79–88.
Grim, P.; Kohlberg, L.; and White, S. "Some Relationships Between Conscience and Attentional Processes." *Journal of Personality and Social Psychology 8* (1968):239–253.
Grimley, L. "A Cross-Cultural Study of Moral Judgment Development in India, Japan and Zambia." Unpublished Ph.D. dissertation, Kent State University, Ohio, 1973.
Grinder, R. E. "New Techniques for Research in Children's Concepts of Justice." *Child Development 32* (1961):679–683.
Grinder, R. E. "Parental Child-Rearing Practices, Conscience and Resistence to Temptation of Sixth Grade Children." *Child Development 33* (1962):802–820.
Grinder, R. E. "Relations Between Behavioral and Cognitive Dimensions of Conscience in Middle Childhood." *Child Development 35* (1964):881–893.
Guttman, L. "The Basis of Scalogram Analysis." In S. A. Stougger, et al.,

Measurement and Prediction. Princeton: Princeton University Press, 1954.

Haan, N. *Coping and Defending: Processes of Self-Environment Organization.* New York: Academic Press, 1977.

Haan, N.; Langer, J.; and Kohlberg, L. "Family Patterns of Moral Reasoning." *Child Development 47* (1976):1204–1206.

Haan, N.; Smith, B.; and Block, J. "The Moral Reasoning of Young Adults." *Journal of Personality and Social Psychology 10* (1968):183–201.

Haan, N.; Bellah, R.; Rabinow, P.; and Sullivan, W. *Social Science as Moral Inquiry.* Columbia University Press, 1983.

Habermas, J. *Communication and the Evolution of Society.* T. McCarthy, trans. Boston: Beacon Press, 1979.

Habermas, J. "A Universal Ethic of Communication and Problems of Ethical Relativity and Skepticism." Paper given at the International Symposium on Moral Education, Fribourg University, Switzerland, 1982a.

Habermas, J. "A Communicative Approach to Moral Theory." Paper presented at the International Conference of Moral Education, Fribourg, 1982b. To be published in M. Berkowitz and F. Oser, eds., *Moral Education: International Perspective.* Hillside, N.J.: Ehrlbaum Assoc, in preparation.

Habermas, J. "Interpretive Social Science vs. Hermeneuticism." In N. Haan, R. Ballah, P. Rabinow, and W. Sullivan, eds., *Social Science as Moral Inquiry.* New York: Columbia University Press, 1983.

Hammer, R. *Court-Martial of Lieutenant Calley.* New York: Coward, McCann & Geoghegan, 1975.

Hare, R. M. *The Language of Morals.* New York: Oxford University Press, 1952.

Hare, R. M. *Freedom and Reason.* New York: Oxford University Press, 1963.

Hare, R. M. *Moral Thinking.* Oxford: Clarendon Press, 1981.

Hare, R. M. "Ethical Theory and Utilitarianism." In A. Sen and B. Williams, eds., *Utilitarianism and Beyond.* Cambridge: Cambridge University Press, 1982.

Harlow, H. "Love in Infant Monkeys." *Scientific American 200* (1959):68–74

Harlow, H., and Harlow, M. "Social Deprivation in Monkeys." *Scientific American 207* (1962):136–146.

Harman, G. *The Nature of Morality: An Introduction to Ethics.* New York: Oxford University Press, 1977.

Harsanyi, J. C. "Morality and the Theory of Rational Behavior." In A. Sen and B. Williams, eds., *Utilitarianism and Beyond.* Cambridge: Cambridge University Press, 1982.

Hart, D., and Kohlberg, L. "Theories of the Social Self of J. M. Baldwin and G. H. Mead." In L. Kohlberg, *Child Psychology and Childhood Education.* New York: Longman Press, 1985, in press.

Hartshorne, H., and May M. A. *Studies in the Nature of Character.* Columbia University Teachers College. Vol. 1: *Studies in Deceit.* Vol. 2: *Studies in Service and Self-Control.* Vol. 3: *Studies in Organization of Character.* New York: Macmillan, 1928–30.

Hartup, W. W. "Some Correlates of Parental Imitation in Young Children. *Child Development 33* (1962):85–97.

Harvey, O. J.; Hunt, D.; and Schroeder, D. *Conceptual Systems.* New York: Wiley, 1961.

Helkama, K. "The Development of the Attribution of Responsibility: A Critical Survey of Empirical Research and a Theoretical Outline." *Research Reports of the Department of Social Psychology,* University of Helsinki, *3,* 1979.

Hersh, S. *My Lai 4.* New York: Vintage, 1975.

Hetherington, E. M. "A Developmental Study of the Effects of Sex of the Dominant Parent on Sex-Role Preference, Identification and Imitation in Children." *Journal of Personality and Social Psychology 2* (1965):143–153.

Hetherington, E. M., and Frankie, G. "Effects of Parental Dominance, Warmth, and Conflict on Imitation in Children." *Journal of Personality and Social Psychology 6* (1967):119–125.

Hickey, J., and Scharf, P. *Toward a Just Correctional System.* San Francisco: Jossey-Bass, 1980.

Higgins, A. "Research and Measurement Issues in Moral Education Interventions." In R. L. Mosher, ed., *Moral Education: A First Generation of Research and Development.* New York: Praeger, 1980.

Higgins, A.; Power, C.; and Kohlberg, L. "The Relationship of Moral Atmosphere to Judgments of Responsibility." In W. Kurtines and J. Gewirtz, eds., *Morality, Moral Behavior and Moral Development.* New York: Wiley Interscience, 1984.

Hobhouse, J. T. *Morals in Evolution: A Study in Comparative Ethics.* New York: Holt, 1923 (originally published in 1906).

Hoffman, M. L. "Moral Development." In P. Mussen, ed., *Manual of Child Psychology.* New York: Wiley, 1969.

Hoffman, M. L. "Conscience, Personality and Socialization Techniques." *Human Development 13* (1970):90–126.

Hoffman, M. L. "Developmental Synthesis of Affect and Cognition and Its Implications for Altruistic Motivation." *Developmental Psychology 11* (1975):607–622.

Hoffman, M. L. "Empathy, Role-Taking, Guilt, and Development of Altruistic Motives." In T. Lickona, ed., *Moral Development and Behavior: Theory, Research and Social Issues.* New York: Holt, Rinehart & Winston, 1976.

Hoffman, M. L. "Development of Moral Thought, Feeling, and Behavior." *American Psychologist 34* (1979):958–966.

Hoffman, M. L., and Saltzstein, H. "Parent Discipline and the Child's Moral Development." *Journal of Personality and Social Psychology 5* (1967):45–57.

Holstein, C. "Parental Determinants of the Development of Moral Judgment." Unpublished Ph.D. dissertation, University of California, Berkeley. 1968.

Holstein, C. "The Relation of Children's Moral Judgment Level to That of Their Parents and to Communications Patterns in the Family." In R. C. Smart and M. S. Smart, eds., *Readings in Child Development and Relationships.* New York: Macmillan, 1972.

Holstein, C. "Development of Moral Judgment: A Longitudinal Study of

Males and Females." *Child Development 47* (1976):51–61.
Horton, R. "African Traditional Thought and Western Science." *Africa 37* (1967):50–71, 155–187.
Hull, C. *Principles of Behavior.* New York: Appleton-Century, 1943.
Hume, D. *An Enquiry into the Principles of Morals.* Chicago: Open Court Publishing, 1930.
Hunt, J. McV. *Intelligence and Experience.* New York: Ronald Press, 1961.
Hunt, J. McV. "Motivation Inherent in Information Processing and Action." In O. J. Harvey, ed., *Interaction.* New York: Ronald, 1963.
Hunt, J. McV., and Uzgiris, I. "An Ordinal Scale of Infant Development." Unpublished manuscript, University of Illinois, Urbana. 1967.
Inhelder, B., and Piaget, J. *The Growth of Logical Thinking from Childhood to Adolescence.* New York: Basic Books, 1958.
James, W. *Principles of Psychology.* New York: Holt, 1890.
James, W. *Varieties of Religious Experience.* New York, Modern Library, 1902.
Jennings, W., and Kohlberg, L. "Effects of Just Community Programs on the Moral Development of Youthful Offenders." *Journal of Moral Education 12* (1983):no. 1.
Kagan, J. "The Concept of Identification." *Psychological Review 65* (1958):296–305.
Kagan, J. "The Many Faces of Response." *Psychology Today 1* (1968):22–27.
Kagan, J. *Change and Continuity in Infancy.* New York: Wiley, 1971.
Kagan, J., and Moss, H. *Birth to Maturity.* New York: Wiley, 1962.
Kant, I. *Fundamental Principles of the Metaphysics of Morals.* New York: Liberal Arts Press, 1949.
Kaplan, B. "The Study of Language in Psychiatry." In S. Arieti, ed., *American Handbook of Psychiatry,* vol. 3. New York: Basic Books, 1966.
Keasey, C. B. "The Lack of Sex Differences in the Moral Judgment of Preadolescents." *Journal of Social Psychology 86* (1972):157–158.
Kegan, R. "A NeoPiagetian Approach to Object Relations." In B. Lee and G. Noam, eds., *The Self: Psychology, Psychoanalysis and Anthropology.* New York: Plenum, 1981.
Kessen, W., ed. *The Child.* New York: Wiley, 1965.
Kinsey, A., et al. *Sexual Behavior in the Human Female.* Philadelphia: Saunders, 1953.
Kleinberger, A. F. "The Proper Object of Moral Judgment and of Moral Education." *Journal of Moral Education 11* (1982):147–158.
Kohlberg, L. "The Development of Modes of Moral Thinking and Choice in the Years Ten to Sixteen." Unpublished Ph.D. dissertation, University of Chicago, 1958.
Kohlberg, L. "Moral Development and Identification." In H. Stevenson, ed., *Child psychology, 62nd Yearbook of the National Society for the Study of Education.* Chicago: University of Chicago Press, 1963a.
Kohlberg, L. "The Development of Children's Orientations Toward a Moral Order: 1. Sequence in the Development of Moral Thought." *Vita Humana 6* (1963b):11–33.
Kohlberg, L. "Stages in Conceptions of the Physical and Social World." Unpublished monograph, 1963c.
Kohlberg, L. "The Development of Moral Character and Ideology." In M.

L. Hoffman, ed., *Review of Child Development Research,* vol. 1. New York: Russell Sage Foundation, 1964.

Kohlberg, L. "Psychosexual Development, a Cognitive-Developmental Approach." Unpublished mimeographed manuscript, University of Chicago, 1965.

Kohlberg, L. "Cognitive Stages and Preschool Education." *Human Development 9* (1966a):5–17.

Kohlberg, L. "A Cognitive Developmental Analysis of Children's Sex-Role Concepts and Attitudes." In E. Maccoby, ed., *The Development of Sex Differences.* Stanford, Calif.: Stanford University Press, 1966b.

Kohlberg, L. "Moral Education in the School." *School Review 74* (1966c):1–30.

Kohlberg, L. "Moral and Religious Education and the Public Schools: A Developmental View." In T., Sizer, ed., *Religion and Public Education.* Boston: Houghton Mifflin, 1967.

Kohlberg, L. "Early Education: A Cognitive-Developmental Approach." *Child Development 39* (1968):1013–1062.

Kohlberg, L. "Stage and Sequence: The Cognitive-Developmental Approach to Socialization." In D. A. Goslin, ed., *Handbook of Socialization Theory and Research.* Chicago, Ill.: Rand McNally, 1969.

Kohlberg, L. "Cognitive-Developmental Theory and the Practice of Collective Moral Education." In M. Wolins and M. Gottesman, ed., *Group Care: An Israeli Approach.* New York: Gordon & Breach, 1971a.

Kohlberg, L. "From *Is* to *Ought*: How to Commit the Naturalistic Fallacy and Get Away with It in the Study of Moral Development." In T. Mischel, ed., *Cognitive Development and Epistemology.* New York: Academic Press, 1971b.

Kohlberg, L. "Continuities in Childhood and Adult Moral Development Revisited." In P. B. Baltes and K. W. Schaie, eds., *Life-span Developmental Psychology: Personality and Socialization.* New York and London: Academic Press, 1973a.

Kohlberg, L. "The Claim to Moral Adequacy of a Highest Stage of Moral Judgment." *Journal of Philosophy 70* (1973b):630–646.

Kohlberg, L."Moral Stages and Moralization: The Cognitive-Developmental Approach." In T. Lickona, ed., *Moral Development and Behavior: Theory, Research, and Social Issues.* New York: Holt, Rinehart & Winston, 1976.

Kohlberg, L. "Forward." In J. Rest, *Development in Judging Moral Issues.* Minneapolis: University of Minnesota Press, 1979.

Kohlberg, L. *Essays in Moral Development. Volume I: The Philosophy of Moral Development.* New York: Harper & Row, 1981a.

Kohlberg, L. "The Meaning and Measurement of Moral Development." *The Heinz Werner Lecture Series,* vol. 13 (1979) Clark University Press, Worcester, Mass, 1981b.

Kohlberg, L. "The Just Community Approach to Moral Education in Theory and in Practice." Paper presented at Fribourg University, Switzerland, 1982a. To appear In F. Oser and M. Berkowitz, eds., *Moral Education, International Perspective.* Hillside, N.J.: Ehrlbaum Assoc., in preparation.

Kohlberg, L. "Moral Development." In *The Cognitive Developmental Psychology of James Mark Baldwin.* In J. M. Broughton and D. J. Freeman-Moir, eds. Norwood, N.J.: Ablex, 1982b.

Kohlberg, L. "Moral Development Does Not Mean Liberalism as Destiny: A Reply to R. Schweder." *Contemporary Psychology* 27(1982c):935–940.

Kohlberg, L. "Foreword." In J. C. Gibbs and K. Widaman, *Social Intelligence.* Englewood Cliffs, N.J.: 1982d.

Kohlberg, L. *Ethical Stages: Moral Development Through the Life Cycle.* San Francisco: Harper & Row, 1985, in press.

Kohlberg, L. *Child Psychology and Childhood Education: A Structural Developmental View.* New York: Longman Press, 1985, in press.

Kohlberg, L., and Candee, D. "The Relation of Moral Judgment to Moral Action." In W. Kurtines and J. Gerwitz, eds., *Morality, Moral Behavior and Moral Development.* New York: Wiley Interscience, 1984.

Kohlberg, L., and DeVries, R. "Relations Between Piaget and Psychometric Assessments of Intelligence." Paper presented at the Conference on the Natural Curriculum, Urbana, Ill.: 1969.

Kohlberg, L., and Gilligan, C. "The Adolescent as a Philosopher: The Discovery of the Self in a Post-Conventional World." *Daedalus 100* (1971):1051–1086.

Kohlberg, L., and Helkama, K. "Research on Piaget's Theory of Moral Judgment." In L. Kohlberg and D. Candee, eds., *Research in Moral Development.* Cambridge, Mass.: Harvard University Press, in preparation.

Kohlberg, L., and Kramer, R. "Continuities and Discontinuities in Childhood and Adult Moral Development." *Human Development 12* (1969):93–120.

Kohlberg, L., and Turiel, E. "Moral Development and Moral Education." In G. S. Lesser, ed., *Psychology and Educational Practice.* Glenview, Ill.: Scott, Foresman, 1971.

Kohlberg, L., and Zigler, E. "The Impact of Cognitive Maturity on Sex-Role Attitudes in the Years Four to Eight." *Genetic Psychology Monographs 75* (1967):89–165.

Kohlberg, L., and Candee, D., eds., *Research in Moral Development.* Cambridge, Mass.: Harvard University Press, in preparation.

Kohlberg, L.; Hickey, J.; and Scharf, P. "The Justice Structure of the Prison: A Theory and Intervention." *The Prison Journal 51* (1972):3–14.

Kohlberg, L.; Lacrosse, J.; and Ricks, D. "The Predictability of Adult Mental Health from Childhood Behavior." In B. Wolman, ed., *Handbook of Child Psychopathology.* New York: McGraw-Hill, 1970.

Kohlberg, L.; Slaby, R.; and Uhlian, D. "Psychosexual Development. I. L. Kohlberg, *Child Psychology and Childhood Edition.* New York; Longman Press, 1985, in press.

Kohlberg, L.; Yaeger, J.; and Hjertholm, E. "The Development of Private Speech: Four Studies and a Review of Theory." *Child Development 39* (1968):691–736.

Kohn, M. *Class and Conformity: A Study in Values.* 2nd ed. Chicago: University of Chicago Press, 1977.

Kohn, N. "Performance of Negro Children of Varying Social Class Background on Piagetian Tasks." Unpublished Ph.D. dissertation, University of Chicago, 1969.

Kohs, S. C. "An Ethical Discriminations Test." *Journal of Delinquency 7* (1922):1–15.

Kramer, R. "Moral Development in Young Adulthood." Unpublished Ph.D. dissertation, University of Chicago, 1968.

Krebs, D., and Rosenward, A. "Moral Reasoning and Moral Behavior in Conventional Adults." *Merrill-Palmer Quarterly 23* (1977):79–84.

Krebs, R. "Some Relationships Between Moral Judgment, Attention and Resistance to Temptation." Unpublished Ph.D. dissertation, University of Chicago, 1967.

Krebs, R., and Kohlberg, L. "Moral Judgment and Ego Controls as Determinants of Resistance to Cheating." In L. Kohlberg and D. Candee, eds., *Research in Moral Development.* Cambridge, Mass.: Harvard University Press, in preparation.

Krogh, E. Statement, *New York Times,* January 25, 1974, p. 16.

Kuhn, D. "Short-Term Longitudinal Evidence for the Sequentiality of Kohlberg's Early Stages of Moral Judgment." *Developmental Psychology 12* (1976):162–166.

Kuhn, D., and Langer, J. "Cognitive-Developmental Determinants of Imitation." Unpublished manuscript, 1968.

Kuhn, D.; Langer, J.; Kohlberg, L.; and Haan, N. "The Development of Formal Operations in Logical and Moral Judgment." *Genetic Psychology Monographs 95* (1977):97–188.

Kuhn, T. S. *The Structure of Scientific Revolutions.* 2nd ed. Chicago: University of Chicago Press, 1970.

Kurdek, L. A. "Perspective Taking as the Cognitive Basis of Children's Moral Development: A Review of the Literature." *Merrill-Palmer Quarterly 24* (1978):3–28.

Kurtines, W., and Grief, E. B. "The Development of Moral Thought: Review and Evaluation of Kohlberg's Approach." *Psychological Bulletin 81* (1974):453–470.

Kusatsu, O. "Ego Development and Socio-Cultural Process in Japan." *Journal of Economics Tokyo 3* (1973):41–128.

LaCrosse, J., and Kohlberg, L. "The Predictability of Adult Mental Health from Childhood Behavior and Status." In B. Wolman, ed, *Handbook of Psychopathology.* New York: McGraw-Hill, 1969.

Lakatos, I. *The Methodology of Scientific Research Programs.* In J. Worral and G. Currie, eds. Cambridge: Cambridge University Press, 1978.

Lambert, H. V. "A Comparison of Jane Loevinger's Theory of Ego Development and Lawrence Kohlberg's Theory of Moral Development." Unpublished Ph.D. dissertation, University of Chicago, 1972.

Langer, J. "Disequilibrium as a Source of Cognitive Development." Paper presented at the meeting of the Society for Research in Child Development. New York, 1967.

Lapsley, D., and Serlin, R. "On the Alleged Degeneration of the Kohlbergian Research Program." Paper presented at the 1983 Society for Research in Child Development. Obtainable from D. Lapsley, Department of Educational Psychology, University of Wisconsin, Madison, Wis. 53706.

Lasker, H. M. "Stage Specific Reactions to Ego Development Training." In "Formative Research in Ego Stage Change." Study No. 3, Humanas Foundation, Willemstad, Curaçao, 1974a.

Lasker, H. M. "Self-Reported Change Manual." In "Formative Research in Ego Stage Change." Study No. 4, Humanas Foundation, Willemstad, Curaçao, 1974b.

Lasker, H. M. "Interim Summative Evaluation Report. An Initial Assessment of the Shell/Humanas OD Program." Cambridge, Mass.; Harvard University Press, 1977.

Latene, B., and Darley, J. "Group Inhibition of Bystander Intervention." *Journal of Personality and Social Psychology 10* (1968):215–221.

Leahy, R. L. "Parental Practices and the Development of Moral Judgment and Self-Image disparity During Adolescence." *Developmental Psychology 17* (1981):580–594.

Leeds, R. "Altruism and the Norm of Giving." *Merrill-Palmer Quarterly 9* (1963):229–240.

Lehrer, L. "Sex Differences in Moral Behavior and Attitudes." Unpublished Ph.D. dissertation, University of Chicago, 1967.

Lei, T. "Toward a Little But Special Light of the Universality of Moral Judgment Development: A Study of Moral Stage and Moral Type in a Taiwanese Sample." Unpublished qualifying paper, Harvard Graduate School of Education, 1983.

Lei, T., and Cheng, S. W. "An Empirical Study of Kohlberg's Theory and Moral Judgment in Chinese Society." Unpublished manuscript, Harvard University, 1982.

Leming, J. S. "Curricular Effectiveness in Moral/Values Education: A Review of Research. *Journal of Moral Education 10* (1981): 147–164.

Lerner, D. *The Passing of Traditional Society.* Glencoe, Ill.: Free Press, 1958.

Levine, C. G. "Role-Taking Standpoint and Adolescent Usage of Kohlberg's Conventional Stages of Moral Reasoning." *Journal of Personality and Social Psychology 34* (1976):41–46.

Levine, C. G. "Stage Acquisition and Stage Use: An Appraisal of Stage Displacement Explanations of Variation in Moral Reasoning." *Human Development 22* (1979):145–164.

Levinson, D. J. *The Seasons of a Man's Life.* New York: Ballantine Books, 1978.

Lickona, T., ed. *Moral Development and Behavior: Theory, Research and Social Issues.* New York: Holt, Rinehart, & Winston, 1976.

Limoges, J. "French Translation of the Sentence Completion Test." Unpublished manuscript, University of Sherbrooke, Quebec, Canada, 1978.

Lippett, R., and White, R. "The Effects of Social Climates." In R. Barker, J. Kounin, and H. Wright, eds., *Child Behavior and Development.* New York: McGraw-Hill, 1943.

Locke, D. "Doing What Comes Morally." *Human Development 26* (1983): 11–25.

Lockwood, A. "The Effects of Values Clarification and Moral Development Curricula on School-Age Subjects: A Critical Review of Recent Research." *Review of Educational Research, 48* (1978): 325–64.

Loevinger, J. "The Meaning and Measurement of Ego Development." *American Psychologist 21* (1969):195–217.

Loevinger, J. *Ego Development. Conceptions and Theories.* San Francisco: Jossey-Bass, 1976.

Loevinger, J. "Scientific Ways in the Study of Ego Development." *Heinz Werner Lecture Series,* vol. 12., 1978. Worcester, Mass.: Clark University Press, 1979.

Loevinger, J. "On the Self and Predicting Behavior." Unpublished paper, Washington University, 1982.

Loevinger, J, and Wessler, R. *Measuring Ego Development, Vol. I: Construction and Use of a Sentence Completion Test.* San Francisco: Jossey-Bass, 1970.

Loevinger, J.; Wessler, R.; and Redmore, C. *Measuring Ego Development, Vol. II: Scoring Manual for Women and Girls.* San Francisco: Jossey-Bass, 1970.

Lorenz, K. *Evolution and the Modification of Behavior.* Chicago: University of Chicago Press, 1965.

Lovaas, O. I. "A Program for the Establishment of Speech in Psychotic Children." In J. Wing, ed., *Childhood Autism.* Oxford: Pergamon Press, 1967.

Lyons, N. "Considering Justice and Care: Manual for Coding Real-Life Moral Dilemmas." Unpublished manuscript. Harvard University, 1981.

Lyons, N. "Conceptions of Self and Morality and Modes of Moral Choice: Identifying Justice and Care in Judgments of Actual Moral Dilemmas." Unpublished Ph.D. dissertation, Harvard University, 1982.

Maccoby, E. "Role-Taking in Childhood and Its Consequences for Early Learning." *Child Development 30* (1959a):239–252.

Maccoby, E. "The Generality of Moral Behavior." Paper presented at American Psychological Association, Cincinnati, Ohio 1959b.

Maccoby, E. "Social Attachment." In P. Mussen, ed., *Manual of Child Psychology.* New York: Wiley, 1969.

MacFarlane, J.; Allen, L.; and Honzik, N. *A Developmental Study of Behavior Problems of Normal Children Between 21 months and Four Years.* Berkeley: University California Press, 1954.

MacIntyre. A. *After Virtue.* Notre Dame, Ind.: University of Notre Dame Press, 1982.

MacKinnon, D. W. "Violation of Prohibitions." In H. A. Murray, ed., *Explorations in Personality.* New York: Oxford University Press, 1938.

Marcia, J. E. "Development and Validation of Ego Identity Status." *Journal of Personality and Social Psychology 3* (1966):551–558.

Mays, W. "Piaget's Sociological Theory." In S. Modgil and C. Modgil, eds., *Jean Piaget: Consensus and Controversy.* New York: Praeger, 1982.

McCarthy, T. *The Critical Theory of Jurgen Habermas.* Cambridge, Mass.: MIT Press, 1978.

McCord, J.; McCord, J.; and Thurber, E. "Some Effects of Paternal Absence on Male Children." *Journal of Abnormal and Social Psychology 64* (1962):361–369.

McDougall, W. *An Introduction to Social Psychology.* London: Methuen, 1908.

McGrath, M. C. "A Study of the Moral Development of Children." *Psychology Monographs, 32* (1923): no. 14.

McNamee, S. "Moral Behavior, Moral Development and Motivation." *Journal of Moral Education,* 7 (1978):27–31.

Mead, G. H. *Mind, Self and Society.* Chicago: University of Chicago Press, 1934.

Milgram, S. "Behavioral Study of Obedience." *Journal of Abnormal and Social Psychology, 67* (1963):371–378.

Milgram, S. *Obedience to Authority: Experimental View.* New York: Harper & Row, 1974.

Mill, J. S. (1861) *Utilitarianism.* Indianapolis: Bobbs-Merrill, 1957.

Miller, D. R. "Psychoanalytic Theory of Development." In D. A. Goslin, ed., *Handbook of Socialization Theory and Research.* Chicago: Rand McNally, 1969.

Miller, D., and Swanson, G. *Inner Conflict and Defense.* New York: Holt, Rinehart & Winston, 1960.

Miller, N., and Dollard, J. *Social Learning and Imitation.* New Haven: Yale University Press, 1941.

Moir, J. "Egocentrism and the Emergence of Conventional Morality in Preadolescent Girls." *Child Development 45* (1974):299–304.

Money, J.; Hampson, J.; and Hampson, J. "Imprinting and the Establishment of Gender Role." *Archeological Neurological Psychiatry* 77 (1957).

Morgan, G., and Ricciutti, H. "Infant's Responses to Shapes During the First Year." In B. M. Foss, ed., *Determinants of Infant Behavior,* vol. 4, London: Methuen, 1968.

Munsey, B. "Cognitive Developmental Theory and Moral Development: Metaethical Issues." In B. Munsey, ed., *Moral Development: Moral Education and Kohlberg.* Birmingham, Ala.: Religious Education Press, 1980.

Murphy, J. M., and Gilligan, C. "Moral Development in Late Adolescence and Adulthood: A Critique and Reconstruction of Kohlberg's Theory." *Human Development 23* (1980):77–104.

Mussen, P., and Eisenberg-Berg, N. *The Roots of Caring, Sharing and Helping.* San Francisco: Freeman, 1977.

Mussen, P., and Rutherford, E. "Parent-Child Relations and Parental Personality in Relation to Young Children's Sex-Role Preferences." *Child Development 34* (1963):589–607.

Nisan, M., and Kohlberg, L. "Universality and Cross-Cultural Variation in Moral Development: A Longitudinal and Cross-Sectional Study in Turkey. *Child Development 53* (1982):865–876.

Nunner-Winkler, G. "Two Moralities? A Critical Discussion of an Ethic of Care and Responsibility Versus an Ethic of Rights and Justice." In W. Kurtines and J. Gewirtz, eds., *Morality, Moral Behavior and Moral Development.* New York: Wiley Interscience, 1984.

Parikh, B. "Moral Judgment Development and Its Relation to Family Environmental Factors in Indian and American Families." *Child Development 51* (1980):1030–1039.

Parsons, T., and Bales, R. F. *Family, Socialization and Interaction Process.* Glencoe, Ill.: Free Press, 1955.

Parten, M., and Newhall, S. M. "The Development of Social Behavior in

Children." In R. Barker, J. Kounin, and H. Wright, eds., *Child Behavior and Development.* New York: McGraw-Hill, 1943.

Pavlov, I. P. *Lectures on Conditional Reflexes.* New York: Liveright, 1928.

Peck, R. F., and Havighurst, R. J. *The Psychology of Character Development.* New York: Wiley, 1960.

Perry, W. G., Jr. *Forms of Intellectual and Ethical Development in the College Years.* New York: Holt, Rinehart & Winston, 1968.

Peters, R. S. *Ethics and Education.* Chicago: Scott, Foresman, 1968.

Peters, R. S. "Moral Development: A Plea for Pluralism." In T. Mischel, ed., *Cognitive Development and Epistemology.* New York: Academic Press, 1971.

Phillips, D., and Nicolayev, J. "Kohlbergian Moral Development: A Progressing or Degenerating Research Program." *Educational Theory, 28* (1978):286–301.

Piaget, J. *The Child's Conception of the World.* London: Routledge & Kegan Paul, 1929.

Piaget, J. *The Psychology of Intelligence.* London: Routledge & Kegan Paul, 1947.

Piaget, J. *The Moral Judgment of the Child.* Glencoe, Ill.: Free Press, 1948, 1965 (originally published in 1932).

Piaget, J. *Introduction à epistemologie genetique, Volume III.* Paris: P.U.F., 1950.

Piaget, J. *Play, Dreams, and Imitation in Childhood.* New York: Norton, 1951.

Piaget, J. *Les relations entre l'affectivitie et l'intelligence dans le development mental de l'enfant.* Le course de Sorbonne psychologie. Paris: Centre de Documentation Universitaire, 1952a. (Mimeographed.)

Piaget, J. *The Origins of Intelligence in Children.* New York: International Universities Press, 1952b.

Piaget, J. *The Construction of Reality in the Child.* New York: Basic Books, 1954.

Piaget, J. "The General Problems of the Psychobiological Development of the Child." In J. M. Tanner and B. Inhelder, eds., *Discussions on Child Development: Proceedings of the World Health Organization Study Group on the Psychobiological Development of the Child,* vol. 4. New York: International Universities Press, 1960.

Piaget, J. "Cognitive Development in Children." In R. Ripple and V. Rockcastle, eds., *Piaget Rediscovered: A Report on Cognitive Studies in Curriculum Development.* Ithaca, N.Y.: Cornell University School of Education, 1964.

Piaget, J. *Six Psychological Studies.* New York: Random House, 1967.

Piaget, J. *On the Development of Memory and Identity.* Worcester, Mass.: Clark University Press, 1968.

Piaget, J. *Structuralism.* New York: Basic Books, 1970.

Piaget, J. "Intellectual Evolution from Adolescence to Adulthood." *Human Development 15* (1972):1–12.

Piaget, J. *The Child and Reality.* New York: Grossman, 1973.

Piaget, J. "Piaget's Theory." In P. H. Mussen, ed., *Handbook of Child Psychology,* vol. 1 (4th ed.). New York: John Wiley, 1983.

Piaget, J., and Inhelder, B. *The Early Growth of Logic.* New York: Norton 1969a.

Piaget, J., and Inhelder, B. *The Psychology of the Child.* New York: Basic Books, 1969b.

Pinard, A., and Laurendeau, M. *Causal Thinking in Children.* New York: International Universities Press, 1964.

Pittel, S. M., and Mendelson, G. A. "Measurement of Moral Values: A Review and Critique." *Psychological Bulletin* (1966):22–35.

Plato, *Laches.*

Power, C. "The Moral Atmosphere of a Just Community High School: A Four Year Longitudinal Study." Unpublished doctoral dissertation, Harvard Graduate School of Education, 1979.

Power, C. and Kohlberg, L. "Faith, Morality and Ego-Development." In J. Fowler and A. Vergote, eds., *Toward Moral and Religious Maturity.* Morristown, N.J.: Silver-Burdett, 1980.

Power, C., and Reimer, J. "Moral Atmosphere: An Educational Bridge Between Moral Judgment and Action." In W. Damon, ed., *New Directions for Child Development: Moral Development 2* (1978).

Powers, S. "Family Interaction and Parental Moral Judgment as a Context for Adolescent Moral Development: A Study of Patient and Non-Patient Adolescents." Unpublished doctoral dissertation. Harvard Graduate School of Education, 1982.

Pratt, M., Golding, G., and Hunter, W. "Aging as Ripening: Character and Consistency of Moral Judgment in Young, Mature, and Older Adults." *Human Development, 26* (1983):277–288.

Pressey, S. L., and Pressey, L. A. "Cross-Out Tests: With Suggestions as to a Group Scale of the Emotions." *Journal of Applied Psychology 3* (1919):138–150.

Price-Williams, D. R. *Explorations in Cross-Cultural Psychology.* San Francisco: Chandler & Sharp, 1975.

Puka, W. "A Kohlbergian reply." In D. Cochrane, C. Hamm, and A. Kazepides, eds., *The Domain of Moral Education.* New York: Paulist Press, 1979.

Rawls, J. *A Theory of Justice.* Cambridge, Mass.: Harvard University Press, 1971.

Rawls, J. "Kantian Constructivism in Moral Theory." *Journal of Philosophy 87* (1980):515–572.

Reimer, J. "A Study in the Moral Development of Kibbutz Adolescents." Unpublished doctoral dissertation, Harvard Graduate School of Education, 1977.

Rest, J. "Developmental Hierarchy in Preference and Comprehension of Moral Judgment." Unpublished Ph.D. dissertation, University of Chicago, 1968.

Rest, J. "The Hierarchical Nature of Moral Judgment." *Journal of Personality 41* (1973):86–109.

Rest, J. "New Approaches in the Assessment of Moral Judgment." In T. Lickona, ed., *Moral Development and Behavior: Theory, Research, and Social Issues.* New York: Holt, Rinehart and Winston, 1976.

Rest, J. *Development in Judging Moral Issues.* Minneapolis: University of Minnesota Press, 1979.

Rest, J. "Morality." In J. H. Flavell and E. Markman, eds., *Manual of Child*

Psychology. 4th ed. *volume 3: Cognitive Development*. New York: Wiley 1983.

Rest, J. "Major Component Processes in the Production of Moral Behavior." In W. Kurtines and J Gewirtz, eds., *Morality, Moral Behavior and Moral Development*. New York: Wiley Interscience, 1984.

Rest, J.; Davison, M. L.; and Robbins, S. "Age Trends in Judging Moral Issues: A Review of Cross-Sectional, Longitudinal and Sequential Studies of the Defining Issues Test." *Child Development 49* (1978):263–279.

Rest, J.; Turiel, E.; and Kohlberg, L. "Level of Moral Development as a Determinant of Preference and Comprehension of Moral Judgments Made by Others." *Journal of Personality 37* (1969):225–252.

Ricciutti, H. "Social and Emotional Behavior in Infancy: Some Developmental Issues and Problems." *Merrill-Palmer Quarterly 14* (1968):82–100.

Riegel, K. "Dialectic Operations: The Final Period of Cognitive Development." *Human Development 16* (1973):346-370.

Riesen, A., and Kinder, E. *The Postural Development of Infant Chimpanzees*. New Haven: Yale University Press, 1952.

Riesman, D. *The Lonely Crowd*. New Haven: Yale University Press, 1950.

Rosenhan, D. L.; Underwood, B., and Moore, B. "Affect Moderates Self-Gratification and Altruism." *Journal of Personality and Social Psychology 30* (1974):546–552.

Ruma, E., and Mosher, P. "Relationship Between Moral Judgment and Guilt in Delinquent Boys." *Journal of Abnormal Psychology 72* (1967):122–127.

Rushton, J. P. "Altruism in Society: A Social Learning Perspective." *Ethics 92* (1982):425–447.

Saltzstein, H. D.; Diamond, R. M.; and Belenky, M. "Moral Judgment Level and Conformity Behavior." *Developmental Psychology* 7 (1972):327–336.

Sarnoff, I. "Identification with the Aggressor: Some Personality Correlates of Anti-Semitism Among Jews." *Journal of Personality 20* (1951):199–218.

Schachter, S. "The Interaction of Cognitive and Physiological Determinants of Emotional State." In L. Berkowitz, ed., *Advances in Social Psychology*, Vol. I. New York: Academic Press, 1964.

Schaffer, H. R. "The Onset of Fear of Stranger and the Incongruity Hypothesis." *Journal of Child Psychology and Psychiatry* 7 (1966):95–106.

Schaffer, H. R., and Emerson, P. E. "The Development of Social Attachment in Infancy." Monograph of the Society for Research in Child Development, vol. 29, 1964.

Scheffler, R. "The Development of Children's Orientations to Fantasy in the Years 5 to 7." Unpublished Ph.D. dissertation, Harvard University, 1971.

Schwartz, S. H. "Normative Influences on Altruism." In L. Berkowitz, ed., *Advances in Experimental Social Psychology*, Vol. 10. New York: Academic Press, 1977.

Schwartz, S. H.; Feldman, R.; Brown, M.; and Heingartner, A. "Some Personality Correlates of Conduct in Two Situations of Moral Conflict." *Journal of Personality 37* (1969).

Sears, R. R. "Identification as a Form of Behavior Development." In D. B. Harris, ed., *The Concept of Development.* Minneapolis: University of Minnesota Press, 1957.

Sears, R. R. "The Growth of Conscience." In I. Iscoe and H. W. Stevenson, eds., *Personality Development in Children.* Austin: University of Texas Press, 1960.

Sears, R. R. "Relations of Early Socialization Experience to Aggression in Middle Childhood." *Journal of Abnormal and Social Psychology 63* (1961):466–493.

Sears, R. R.; Rau, L.; and Alpert, R. *Identification and Child-Rearing.* Stanford, Calif.: Stanford University Press, 1965.

Sears, R. R.; Maccoby, E. E.; and Levine, H. *Patterns of Child Rearing.* Evanston, Ill.: Row, Peterson, 1957.

Selman, R. L. "The Relation of Role Taking to the Development of Moral Judgment in Children." *Child Development 42*(1971):79–91.

Selman, R. L. *The Growth of Interpersonal Understanding.* New York: Academic Press, 1980.

Selman, R., and Jaquette, D. "Stability and Oscillation in Interpersonal Awareness." In C. Keasey, ed., *Nebraska Symposium on Motivation,* vol. 25. Lincoln, Neb.: University of Nebraska Press, 1977.

Selman, R. L. "The Development of Social-Cognitive Understanding: A Guide to Education and Clinical Practice." In T. Lickona, ed., *Moral Development and Behavior: Theory, Research, and Social Issues.* New York: Holt, Rinehart and Winston, 1976.

Shantz, C. "The Development of Social Cognition." In E. M. Hetherington, ed., *Review of Child Development Research,* vol. 5. Chicago: University of Chicago Press, 1975.

Shawver, J. "Character and Ethics: An Epistemological Inquiry of Lawrence Kohlberg's Cognitive Theory of Moral Development." Unpublished Ph.D. dissertation, McGill University, 1979.

Shirley, M. *The First Two Years.* 2 vols. Minneapolis: University of Minnesota Press, 1933.

Shweder, R. "Review of Lawrence Kohlberg's *Essays on Moral Development,* Volume I: *The Philosophy of Moral Development.*" *Contemporary Psychology* (June 1982):421–424.

Sidgwick, H. *Methods of Ethics.* London: Macmillan, 1887.

Siegel, S. *Nonparametric Statistics.* New York: McGraw-Hill, 1956.

Sigel, I., and Hooper, F., eds. *Logical Thinking in Children: Research Based on Piaget's Theory.* New York: Holt, Rinehart and Winston, 1968.

Simpson, A., and Graham, D. "The Development of Moral Judgment, Emotion and Behavior in British Adolescents." In L. Kohlberg and D. Candee, eds., *Research in Moral Development.* Cambridge, Mass.: Harvard University Press, in preparation.

Simpson, E. L. "Moral Development Research: A Case Study of Scientific Cultural Bias." *Human Development 17* (1974):81–106.

Singer, M. G. *Generalization in Ethics.* New York: Atheneum, 1971.

Skinner, B. F. *Beyond Freedom and Dignity.* New York: Knopf, 1971.

Smedslund, J. "The Acquisition of Conservation of Substance and Weight in Children, III: Extinction of Conservation of Weight Acquired Normally by means of Empirical Control as a Balance." *Scandinavian Journal of Psychology 2* (1961):85–97 (reprinted in Sigel and Hooper, 1968).

Smith, A. *Theory of Moral Sentiments.* In *Smith's Moral and Political Philosophy.* New York: Hafner, 1948.

Snarey, J. R. "The Social and Moral Development of Kibbutz Founders and Sabras: A Cross-Sectional and Longitudinal Study." Unpublished doctoral dissertation, Harvard Graduate School of Education, 1982.

Snarey, J. R., and Blasi, A. "Ego Development Among Adult Kibbutzniks: A Cross-Cultural Application of Loevinger's Theory." *Genetic Psychological Monographs 102* (1980):117-157.

Snarey, J. R.; Reimer, J.; and Kohlberg, L. "The Sociomoral Development of Kibbutz Adolescents: A Longitudinal Cross-Cultural Study." *Developmental Psychology,* in press.

Snarey, J. R.; Kohlberg, L.; and Noam, G. "Ego Development and Education: A Structural Perspective." *Developmental Review 3* (1983):303–338.

Solomon, R., and Coles, R. "A Case of Failure of Generalization of Imitation Learning Across Drives and Across Situations." *Journal of Abnormal and Social Psychology 49* (1954):7–13.

Speicher-Dubin, B. "Parent Moral Judgment, Child Moral Judgment and Family Interaction: A Correlational Study." Unpublished doctoral dissertation, Harvard Graduate School of Education, 1982.

Spinoza, B. *Ethics.* London: Hafner Press, 1949.

Staub, E. "Helping a Distressed Person: Social, Personality, and Stimulus Determinants." In L. Berkowitz, ed., *Advances in Experimental and Social Psychology,* vol. 7. New York: Academic Press, 1974.

Stevenson, C. L. *Facts and Value.* New Haven: Yale University Press, 1963.

Stevenson, H. "Social Reinforcement of Children's Behavior." In C. Spiker, ed., *Advances in Child Development,* vol. 2. New York: Academic Press, 1965.

Stotland, E.; Zander, A.; and Natsoulas, T. "Generalization of Interpersonal Similarity." *Journal of Abnormal and Social Psychology 62* (1961):250–258.

Strauss, A. "The Learning of Social Roles and Rules as Twin Processes." *Child Development 25* (1954):192–208.

Sullivan, C.; Grant, M. Q.; and Grant, J. D. "The Development of Interpersonal Maturity: Application to Delinquency." *Psychiatry 20* (1957):373–385.

Sullivan, E. V. "A Study of Kohlberg's Structural Theory of Moral Development: A Critique of Liberal Social Science Ideology." *Human Development 20* (1977):352–376.

Sullivan, E. V.; McCullough, G.; and Stager, M. "A Developmental Study of the Relationship Between Conceptual Ego and Moral Development." *Child Development 35* (1964):231–242.

Sullivan, H. S. *An Interpersonal Theory of Psychiatry.* New York: Norton, 1953.

Tappan, M.; Kohlberg, L.; Schrader, D.; and Higgins, A. "Assessing Autonomous and Heteronomous Morality: From Substages to Moral Types." In A. Colby and L. Kohlberg, *The Measurement of Moral Judgment.* New York: Cambridge University Press, 1984 in press.

Terman, L. M., and Miles, C. C. *Sex and Personality Studies in Masculinity and Femininity.* New York: McGraw-Hill, 1936.

Thrower, J. S. "Effects of Orphanage and Foster Home Care on Development of Moral Judgment." In L. Kohlberg and D. Candee, eds., *Research in Moral Development.* Cambridge, Mass.: Harvard University Press, in preparation.

Turiel, E. "An Experimental Test of the Sequentiality of Developmental Stages in the Child's Moral Judgment." *Journal of Personality and Social Psychology 3* (1966):611–618.

Turiel, E. "Developmental Processes in the Child's Moral Thinking." In P. Mussen, J. Langer, and M. Covington, eds., *New Directions in Developmental Psychology.* New York: Holt, Rinehart & Winston, 1969.

Turiel, E. "Conflict and Transition in Adolescent Moral Development." *Child Development 45* (1974):14–29.

Turiel, E. "Conflict and Transition in Adolescent Moral Development II: The Resolution of Disequilibrium Through Structural Reorganization." *Child Development 48* (1977):634–637.

Turiel, E. *Moral Development and Socialization.* Edited by M. Windmiller, N. Lambert, and E. Turiel. Boston: Allyn and Bacon, 1980.

Turiel, E., and Guinsburg, G. "The Cognitive Conditions for Imitation Without Reinforcement." Unpublished manuscript, 1968.

Turiel, E.; Edwards, C. P.; and Kohlberg, L. "Moral Development in Turkish Children, Adolescents and Young Adults." *Journal of Cross-Cultural Psychology 9* (1978):75–85.

Turnure, J., and Zigler, E. "Outer Directedness in the Problem Solving of Normal and Retarded Children." *Journal of Abnormal and Social Psychology 69* (1964):427–436.

Valentine, C. W. *The Psychology of Early Childhood.* London: Methuen, 1942.

Van den Daele, L. "A Developmental Study of Ego-Ideals." *Genetic Mongraphs, 78* (1968):191–256.

VanManen, G. "An Interpersonal Theory of Deviance: A Test of General Theory." Unpublished Ph.D. dissertation, University of Chicago, 1967.

Vetter, M. "Dimensionen des Selbskonzeptes und der Ich-Entwicklung." Unpublished master's thesis. Johannes-Gutenberg Universität, Mainz, Germany, 1978.

Walker, L. J. "Cognitive and Perspective-Taking Prerequisites for Moral Development." *Child Development, 51* (1980):131–140.

Walker, L. J. "Sex Differences in the Development of Moral Reasoning: A Critical Review of the Literature." Paper presented at Canadian Psychological Association, Montreal, June 1982.

Walker, L. J. "The Sequentiality of Kohlberg's Stages of Moral Development." *Child Development,* in press.

Walker, L., and Richards, B. S. "Stimulating Transitions in Moral Reasoning as a Function of Stage of Cognitive Development." *Developmental Psychology, 15* (1979):95–103.

Walster, E.; Berscheid, E.; and Walster, G. W. "New Directions in Equity Research." *Journal of Personality and Social Psychology 25* (1973): 151–176.

Warden, C., and Jackson, T. "Imitative Behavior in the Rhesus Monkey." *Journal of Genetic Psychology 46* (1935):103–125.

The Watergate Hearing. New York: Viking Press, 1973.

Weber, C. O. "Moral Judgment in Female Delinquents." *Journal of Applied Psychology 10*(1929):89–91.

Weber, M. "Politics as a Vocation." In H. H. Gerth and C. W. Mills, eds., *From Max Weber: Essays in Sociology.* New York: Oxford University Press, 1946.

Weber, M. *The Methodology of the Social Sciences.* New York: Free Press, 1949.

Weisbroth, S. P. "Moral Judgment, Sex and Parental Identification of Adults." *Developmental Psychology 2* (1970):396–402.

Werner, H. *The Comparative Psychology of Mental Development.* Chicago: Wilcox & Follett, 1948.

White, R. "Motivation Reconsidered: The Concept of Competence." *Psychological Review 66* (1959):297–333.

White, R. "Ego and Reality in Psychoanalytic Theory." *Psychological Issues,* vol. 3, no. 3. New York: International Universities Press, 1963.

White, C. B. "Moral Development in Bahamian School Children: A Cultural Examination of Kohlberg's Stages of Moral Reasoning." *Developmental Psychology 11* (1975):535–536.

White, C. B.; Bushnell, N.; and Regnemer, J. L. "Moral Development in Bahamian School Children: A 3-Year Examination of Kohlberg's Stages of Moral Development." *Developmental Psychology 14* (1978):58–65.

White, S. H. "Some General Outlines of the Matrix of Developmental Changes Between Five to Seven Years." *Bulletin of the Orton Society 20* (1970):41–57.

Whitely, J. M., et. al., *Character Development in College Students,* vol. 1. Schenectady, N.Y.: Character Research Press, 1982.

Whiting, J.W.M. "Resource Mediation and Learning by Identification." In I. Iscoe and H. W. Stevenson, ed., *Personality Development in Children.* Austin, Tex.: University of Texas Press, 1960.

Whiting, J.W.M. "The Concept of Identification." Paper delivered at the meeting of the Society for Research in Child Development, New York, 1967.

Whiting, J.W.M. and Child, I. L. *Child Training and Personality: A Cross-Cultural Study.* New Haven: Yale University Press, 1953.

Wilson, J. "An Experimental Investigation of the Development of Smiling." Unpublished Ph.D. disseration, University of Chicago, 1962.

Wilson, J. *The Assessment of Morality.* Slough: N.E.E.R., 1973.

Witkin, H. A. "Social Influences in the Development of Cognitive Syle." In D. A. Goslin, ed., *Handbook of Socialization Theory and Research.* Chicago: Rand McNally, 1969.

Wolff, P. H. "The Development of Attention in Young Infants." New York Academy of Sciences, *Transactions 118* (1965):783–866.

Wright, D. "Piaget's Theory of Moral Development." In S. Modgil and C. Modgil, eds., *Jean Piaget: Consensus and Controversy.* New York: Praeger, 1982.

Wright, D. "The Moral Judgment of the Child Revisited." In H. Weinrich-Haste and D. Locke, eds. *Morality in the Making.* New York: Wiley, 1983.

Yarrow, L. J. "Separation from Parents During Early Childhood." In M. L. Hoffman and L. W. Hoffman, eds., *Review of Child Development Research.* New York: Russell Sage Foundation, 1964.

Youniss, J. *Parents and Peers in Social Development: A Sullivan–Piaget Perspective.* Chicago: University of Chicago Press, 1980.

Youniss, J. "Friendship and Development." *Social Thought* 7(1981):35–46.

Youniss, J. "Why Persons Communicate on Moral Matters: A Response to Schweder." *Merrill Palmer Quarterly 28*(1982):71–77.

Zimbardo, P. G. "The Human Choice: Individualization, Reason and Order Versus Deindividualization, Impulse and Chaos." In W. J. Arnold and D. Levine, ed., *Nebraska Symposium on Motivation,* no. 17, pp. 237–307.

Bibliography of Writings by Lawrence Kohlberg

Kohlberg, L. "Bed for Bananas" in *The Menorah Journal,* Vol. IIIVI, #4, Autumn 1948, pp. 285–399.

Kohlberg, L. "The Development of Modes of Thinking and Choices in Years 10 to 16." Ph.D. dissertation, University of Chicago, 1958.

Kohlberg, L. "The Development of Children's Orientations Toward a Moral Order: Sequence in the Development of Moral Thought." *Vita Humana 6* (1963a):11–33.

Kohlberg, L. "Moral Development and Identification." In H. Stevenson, ed., *Child Psychology.* 62nd Yearbook of the National Society for the Study of Education, Part I. Chicago: University of Chicago Press, 1963b.

Kohlberg, L. "Psychological Analysis and Literary Form: A Study of the Doubles in Dostoevsky." *Daedalus 92* (1963c):345–363.

Kohlberg, L. "The Development of Moral Character and Ideology." In M. L. Hoffman and L. W. Hoffman, eds., *Review of Child Developmental Research,* Vol 1. New York: Russell Sage, 1964.

Kohlberg, L. "A Cognitive-Developmental Analysis of Children's Sex-Role Attitudes." In E. Maccoby, ed., *The Development of Sex Differences.* Stanford, Calif.: Stanford University Press, 1966a.

Kohlberg, L. "Cognitive Stages and Preschool Education." *Human Development 9* (1966b):5–17.

Kohlberg, L. "Moral Education in the School." *School Review 74* (1966c):1–30.

Kohlberg, L. "Moral and Religious Education, and the Public Schools: A Developmental View." In T. Sizer, ed., *Religion and Public Education.* Boston: Houghton Mifflin, 1967.

Kohlberg, L., and Zigler, E. "The Impact of Cognitive Maturity upon the Development of Sex-Role Attitudes in the Years Four to Eight." *Genetic Psychology Monographs 75* (1967):89–165.

Kohlberg, L. "The Child as a Moral Philosopher." *Psychology Today 7* (1968a):25–30.

Kohlberg, L. "Early Education: A Cognitive-Developmental View." *Child Development 39* (1968b):1013–1062.

Kohlberg, L. "Montessori with the Culturally Disadvantaged: A Cognitive-Developmental Interpretation." In R. Hess and R. Bear, eds., *The Challenge of Early Education: Current Theory, Research and Action.* Chicago: Aldine Press, 1968c.

Kohlberg, L. "Moral Development." In *International Encyclopedia of the Social Sciences.* New York: Crowell, Collier and Macmillan, 1968d.

Kohlberg, L. "Stages in Moral Growth." *International Journal of Religious Education 44* (1968e):8–9.

Grim, P. F., Kohlberg, L., and White, S. H. "Some Relationships Between Conscience and Attentional Processes." *Journal of Personality and Social Psychology* (1968):239–252.

Kohlberg, L., Hjertholm, E., and Yaeger, J. "Private Speech: Four Studies and a Review of Theories." *Child Development 39* (1968): 691–736.

Kohlberg, L. "Stage and Sequence: The Cognitive-Developmental Approach to Socialization." In D. A. Goslin, ed., *Handbook of Socialization Theory and Research.* Chicago: Rand McNally, 1969.

Kohlberg, L., and DeVries, R. "Concept Measurement Kit: Conservation: Review." *Journal of Educational Measurement 6* (1969):263–266.

Kohlberg, L., and Kramer, R. "Continuities and Discontinuities in Children and Adult Moral Development." *Human Development 12* (1969):93–120.

Rest, J., Turiel, E., and Kohlberg, L. "Level of Moral Development as a Determinant of Preference and Comprehension of Moral Judgments Made by Others." *Journal of Personality 37* (1969):225–252.

Kohlberg, L. "Development of Moral Character." In *Developmental Psychology.* Del Mar, Calif.: CRM Books, 1970a.

Kohlberg, L. "Education for Justice: A Modern Statement of the Platonic View." In T. Sizer, ed., *Moral Education: Five Lectures.* Cambridge, Mass.: Harvard University Press, 1970b.

Kohlberg, L. "The Moral Atmosphere of the School." In N. Overley, ed., *The Unstudied Curriculum: Its Impact on Children.* Monograph of the Association for Supervision and Curriculum Development. Washington, D.C.: 1970c.

Kohlberg, L. "Moral Development and the Education of Adolescents." In R. F. Purnell, ed., *Adolescents and the American High School.* New York: Holt, Rinehart and Winston, 1970d.

Kohlberg, L. "Reply to Bereiter's Statement on Kohlberg's Cognitive-Developmental View." *Interchange 1* (1970e):40–48.

Kohlberg, L., LaCrosse, J., and Ricks, D. "The Predictability of Adult Mental Health from Childhood Behavior." In B. Wolman, ed., *Handbook of Child Psychopathology.* New York: McGraw-Hill, 1970.

Kohlberg, L. "Cognitive-Developmental Theory and the Practice of Collective Moral Education." In M. Wolins and M. Gottesman, eds., *Group Care: An Israeli Approach: The Education Path of Youth Aliyah.* New York: Gordon & Breach, 1971a.

Kohlberg, L. "From *Is* to *Ought:* How to Commit the Naturalistic Fallacy and Get Away with It in the Study of Moral Development." In T. Mischel, ed., *Cognitive Development and Epistemology.* New York: Academic Press, 1971b.

Kohlberg, L. "Indoctrination Versus Relativity in Value Education." *Zygon 6* (1971c):285–310.

Kohlberg, L. "Moral Education, Psychological View of." *International Encyclopedia of Education.* Vol. 6. New York: Macmillan and Free Press, 1971d.

Kohlberg, L. "Stages of Moral Development as a Basis for Moral Education." In C. Beck, B. Crittendon, and E. Sullivan, eds., *Moral Education: Interdisciplinary Approaches.* Toronto: University of Toronto Press, 1971e.

Kohlberg, L., and Gilligan, C. "The Adolescent as a Philosopher: The Discovery of the Self in a Post-Conventional World." *Daedalus 100* (1971):1051–1086.

Kohlberg, L., and Turiel, E. "Moral Development and Moral Education." In G. Lesser, ed., *Psychology and Educational Practice.* Chicago: Scott Foresman, 1971.

Gilligan, C., Kohlberg, L., Lerner, J., and Belenky, M. "Moral Reasoning About Sexual Dilemmas." Technical Report of the Commission on Obscenity and Pornography, Vol. 1 (No. 52560010). Washington, D.C.: U.S. Government Printing Office, 1971.

Tapp, J. and Kohlberg, L. "Developing senses of law and legal justice." *Journal of Social Issues 27,* no. 2 (1971):65–91. Also in Tapp and Levine, eds., *Law, Justice and the Individual in Society: Psychological and Legal Issues.* Holt, Rinehart and Winston, 1977.

Kohlberg, L. "The Cognitive-Developmental Approach to Moral Education." *Humanist 32* (1972a):13–16.

Kohlberg, L. "The Concepts of Developmental Psychology as the Central Guide to Education: Examples from Cognitive, Moral, and Psychological Education." In M. C. Reynolds, ed., *Psychology and the Process of Schooling in the Next Decade: Alternative Conceptions.* Minneapolis: University of Minnesota Press, 1972b.

Kohlberg, L., and Mayer, R. "Development as the Aim of Education." *Harvard Educational Review 42* (1972):449–496.

Kohlberg, L., and Selman, R. L. "Preparing School Personnel Relative to Values: A Look at Moral Education in the School." Washington, D.C.: ERIC Clearinghouse on Teacher Education, 1972.

Kohlberg, L., and Whitten, P. "Understanding the Hidden Curriculum." *Learning Magazine 1* (1972):2.

Kohlberg, L., Hickey, J., and Scharf, P. "The Justice Structure of the Prison: A Theory and Intervention." *Prison Journal 51* (1972):3–14.

Kohlberg, L. "The Claim to Moral Adequacy of a Highest Stage of Moral Judgment." *Journal of Philosophy 70* (1973a):630–646.

Kohlberg, L. "Continuities in Childhood and Adult Moral Development Revisited." In P. B. Baltes and K. W. Schaie, eds., *Life-Span Developmental Psychology: Personality and Socialization.* New York Academic Press, 1973b.

Kohlberg, L. "Contributions of Developmental Psychology to Education: Examples from Moral Education." *Educational Psychologist 10* (1973c):2–14.

Kohlberg, L. "Moral Development and the New Social Studies." *Social Education 37* (1973d):369–375.

Kohlberg, L. "Moral Psychology and the Study of Tragedy." In S. Weintraub and P. Young, eds., *Directions in Literary Criticism: Contemporary Approaches to Literature.* University Park: Pennsylvania State University Press, 1973e.

Kohlberg, L. "Stages and Aging in Moral Development: Some Speculations." *Gerontologist 13* (1973f):497–502.

Kohlberg, L., and Boyd, D. "The *Is-Ought* Problem: A Developmental Perspective." *Zygon 8* (1973):358–371.

Kohlberg, L. "Comments on the Dilemma of Obedience." *Phi Delta Kappan 55* (1974a):607.

Kohlberg, L. "Discussion: Developmental Gains in Moral Judgment." *American Journal of Mental Deficiency 79* (1974b):142–144.

Kohlberg, L. "Education, Moral Development and Faith." *Journal of Moral Education 4* (1974c):5–16.

Kohlberg, L. "The Cognitive-Development Approach to Moral Education." *Phi Delta Kappan 61* (1975a):670–677. Also in D. Purpel and K. Ryan, eds., *Moral Education: It Comes with the Territory.* Berkeley, Calif.: McCutchan, 1976.

Kohlberg, L. "Counseling and Counselor Education: A Developmental Approach." *Counselor Education and Supervision 14* (1975b): 250–256.

Kohlberg, L. "Moral Education for a Society in Moral Transition." *Educational Leadership 33* (1975c):46–54.

Kohlberg, L. "The Relationship of Moral Education to the Broader Field of Values Education." In J. R. Meyer, B. Burnham, and J. Cholvat, eds., *Values Education: Theory, Practice, Problems, Prospects.* Waterloo, Ontario: Wilfred Laurier University Press, 1975d.

Blatt, M. M., and Kohlberg, L. "The Effects of Classroom Moral Discussion upon Children's Level of Moral Judgment." *Journal of Moral Education 4* (1975):129–161.

Kohlberg, L., and Colby, A. "Moral Development and Moral Education." In G. Steiner, ed., *Psychology in the Twentieth Century.* Zurich: Kindler Verlag, 1975.

Kohlberg, L., and Elfenbein, D. "The Development of Moral Judgments Concerning Capital Punishment." *American Journal of Orthopsychiatry 45* (1975):614–640. Also in H. A. Bedau and C. M. Pierce, eds., *Capital Punishment in the United States.* New York: A.M.S. Press, 1976.

Kohlberg, L., Kauffman, K., Hickey, J., and Scharf, P. *Corrections Manual,* Parts I and II. Cambridge, Mass: Moral Education Research Foundation, 1975.

Kohlberg, L., Kauffman, K., Scharf, P., and Hickey, J. "The Just Community Approach to Corrections: A Theory." *Journal of Moral Education 4,* (1975):243–260.

Kohlberg, L. "Moral Stages and Moralization: The Cognitive-Developmental Approach." In T. Lickona, ed., *Moral Development and Behavior: Theory, Research and Social Issues.* New York: Holt, Rinehart and Winston, 1976a.

Kohlberg, L. "The Quest for Justice in 200 Years of American History and in Contemporary American Education." *Contemporary Education 48* (1976b):5–16.

Kohlberg, L. "This Special Section in Perspective." In E. Fenton, ed., *Social Education 40* (1976c):213–215.

Gibbs, J., Kohlberg, L., Colby, A., and Speicher-Dubin, B. "The Domain and Development of Moral Judgment: A Theory and a Method of Assessment." In J. Meyer, ed., *Reflections on Values Education.* Waterloo,

Ontario: Wilfrid Laurier University Press, 1976.

Haan, N., Langer, J., and Kohlberg, L. "Family Patterns of Moral Reasoning." *Child Development 47* (1976):1204–1206.

Kohlberg, L. "The Implications of Moral Stages for Adult Education." *Religious Education 72* (1977a):183–201.

Kohlberg, L. "Moral Development, Ego Development and Psychoeducational Practice." *Pupil Personnel Services Journal 6* (1977b):25–40.

DeVries, R., and Kohlberg, L. "Relations Between Piaget and Psychometric Assessments of Intelligence." In L. Katz, ed., *Current Topics in Early Childhood Education,* Vol. 1. Norwood, N.J.: Ablex, 1977.

Kohlberg, L., and Hersh, R. H. "Moral Development: A Review of the Theory." *Theory into Practice 16* (1977):53–59.

Kuhn, D., Langer, J., Kohlberg, L., and Haan, N. "The Development of Formal Operations in Logical and Moral Judgment." *Genetic Psychology Monographs 95* (1977):97–188.

Colby, A., Kohlberg, L., Fenton, E., Speicher-Dubin, B., and Lieberman, M. "Secondary School Moral Discussion Programmes Led by Social Studies Teachers." *Journal of Moral Education 6* (1977):90–111.

Gilligan, C. and Kohlberg, L. "From adolescence to adulthood: the recovery of reality in a postconventional world." Proceedings of the Piaget Society, 1973. In M. Appeal and B. Preseissen eds., *Topics in Cognitive Development.* N.Y.: Plenum Press, 1977.

Kohlberg, L. "The Cognitive-Developmental Approach to Behavior Disorders: A Study of the Development of Moral Reasoning in Delinquents." In G. Serban, ed., *Cognitive Defects in the Development of Mental Illness.* New York: Brunner-Mazel, 1978a.

Kohlberg, L. Foreword to *Kohlberg's Theory of Moral Education in Practice.* by R. Hersh, D. Paolitto, and J. Reimer. New York: Longman Press, 1978b.

Kohlberg, L. "Moral Development." *Synthesis: The Realization of the Self, 5* (1978c).

Kohlberg, L. "Moral Education Reappraised." *Humanist 38* (1978d):13–15.

Kohlberg, L. *Preface to New Directions in Child Development.* Vol. 1, No. 2: "Moral Development," ed. W. Damon. San Francisco: Jossey-Bass, 1978e.

Kohlberg, L. Preface to *Readings in Moral Education,* ed. P. Scharf. Minneapolis: Winston Press, 1978f.

Kohlberg, L., Wasserman, E., and Richardson, N. "Die Gerechte Schul-Kooperative: Ihre Theorie und das Experiment der Cambridge Cluster School." In G. Portel, ed., *Socialisation und Moral: Neuere Ansatze zur Moralishen Entwicklung und Erziehung.* Wienheim, Basel: Beltz Verlag, 1978.

Turiel, E., Edwards, C. P., and Kohlberg, L. "A Cross-Cultural Study of Moral Development in Turkey and the United States." *Journal of Cross-Cultural Psychology 9* (1978):75–87.

Kohlberg, L. Foreword to *Developments in Judging Moral Issues,* by James Rest. Minneapolis: University of Minnesota Press, 1979a.

Kohlberg, L. "From Athens to Watergate: Moral Education in a Just Society." *Curriculm Review 18* (1979b):8–11.

Kohlberg, L. "Justice as Reversibility." In P. Laslett and J. Fishkin, eds., *Philosophy, Politics and Society.* Fifth Series. Oxford: Blackwell, 1979c.

Kohlberg, L. "The Relations Between Piagetian Theory and Educational Practice: Perspectives from Moral Education." In *Piagetian Theory and the Helping Professions, Eighth Annual Conference.* Los Angeles: University of Southern California Press, 1979d.

Kohlberg, L. "The Young Child as a Philosopher: Moral Development and the Dilemmas of Moral Education. In M. Wolman, ed., *Taking Early Childhood Seriously: The Evangeline Burgess Memorial Lectures.* Pasadena, Calif: Pacific Oaks, 1979e.

Kohlberg, L. "The Future of Liberalism as the Dominant Ideology of the West." In R. Wilson and G. Schochet, eds., *Moral Development and Politics.* New York: Praeger, 1980a.

Kohlberg, L. "High School Democracy and Educating for a Just Society." In R. Mosher, ed., *Moral Education: A First Generation of Research.* New York: Praeger, 1980b.

Kohlberg, L. "The Meaning and Measurement of Moral Development." Heinz Werner Lecture. Worcester, Mass: Clark University Press, 1980c.

Kohlberg, L. "Moral Education: A Response to Thomas Sobol." In *Educational Leadership 38,* no. 1 (1980d).

DeVries, R., and Kohlberg, L. "Don't Throw Out the Piagetian Baby with the Psychometric Bath: Reply to Humphreys and Parsons." *Intelligence 4* (1980):175–177.

Power, F. C. and Kohlberg, L. "Religion, Morality, and Ego Development." In J. Fowler and A. Vergote, eds., *Toward Moral and Religious Maturity.* Morristown, N.J.: Silver-Burdett, 1980.

Kohlberg, L., and Wasserman, E. "The Cognitive-Developmental Approach and the Practicing Counselor: An Opportunity for Counselors to Rethink Their Roles." *Personnel and Guidance Journal* (May 1980):559–565.

Bar-Yam, M., Kohlberg, L., and Naame, A. "Moral Reasoning of Students in Different Cultural, Social, and Educational Settings." *American Journal of Education 88* (1980):345–362.

Kohlberg, L. *Essays in Moral Development.* Vol. 1: *The Philosophy of Moral Development.* San Francisco: Harper & Row, 1981.

Kohlberg, L., and Power, C. "Moral Development, Religious Development, and the Question of a Seventh Stage." *Zygon 16,* no. 1 (1981).

Kohlberg, L. "Moral Development." In J. M. Broughton and D. J. Freeman Moir, eds., *The Cognitive-Developmental Psychology of James Mark Baldwin: Current Theory and Research in Genetic Epistemology,* Norwood, N.J.: Ablex, 1982a.

Nisan, M. and Kohlberg, L. "Universality and Variation in Moral Judgment: A Longitudinal & Cross-Sectional Study in Turkey." *Child Development 53,* (1982):865–876.

Kohlberg, L. "Moral Development Does Not Mean Liberalism as Destiny: A Reply to R. Shweder." *Contemporary Psychology 27,* (1982b):935–940.

Kohlberg, L. "Reply to Owen Flanagan." *Ethics 92,* (April 1982):513–528.

Higgins, A. and Kohlberg, L. "Perspectives on the International Symposium on Socio-Moral Education at Fribourg, Switzerland." *Moral Education Forum 7,* no. 4 (1982).

Jennings, W. and Kohlberg, L. "Effects of Just Community Program on the Moral Level and Institutional Perceptions of Youthful Offenders." *Journal of Moral Education 12,* no. 1, (1983).

Jennings, W., Kilkenny, R. and Kohlberg, L. "Moral Development Theory and Practice for Youthful and Adult Offenders." In Wm. S. Laufer and James Day, eds., *Personality, Theory, Moral Development and Criminal Behavior.* Lexington, MA: Lexington Books, 1983.

Colby, A., Kohlberg, L. Gibbs, J. and Lieberman, M. "A Longitudinal Study of Moral Judgment," *A Monograph for the Society of Research in Child Development 48,* no. 4. Chicago: The University Chicago Press, 1983.

Noam, G., Kohlberg, L. and Snarey, J. "Steps Toward a Model of the Self." In B. Lee and G. Noam, eds., *Developmental Approaches to the Self.* New York: Plenum Press, 1983.

Snarey, J., Kohlberg, L., and Noam, G. "Ego Development in Perspective: Structural Stage, Functional Phase & Cultural Age-Period Models." *Developmental Review 3,* no. 3 (1983).

Candee, D. and Kohlberg, L. "Relationship of Moral Judgment to Moral Action."

Higgins, A., Power, C. and Kohlberg, L. "The Relationship of Moral Atmosphere to Judgments of Responsibility."

Colby, A., and Kohlberg, L. "Invariant Sequence and Internal Consistency in Moral Judgment Stage."

All three papers presented at Florida International University Conference on Morality and Moral Education, Miami Beach, Florida, December 1981 and in W. Kurtines and J. Gewirtz, eds., *Morality, Moral Behavior and Moral Development: Basic Issues in Theory and Research.* New York: Wiley Interscience, 1984.

Kohlberg, L., Levine, C. and Hewer, A. "Moral Stages: A Current Formulation and A Response to Critics." *Contributions to Human Development 10.* Basel: S. Karger, 1983.

Colby, A. and Kohlberg, L. "The Measurement of Moral Judgment." Volumes I and II. New York: Cambridge University Press, 1984, in press.

Kohlberg, L., and Armon, C. "Three Types of Stage Models Used in the Study of Adult Development." In M. L. Commons, F. A. Richards and C. Armon, eds., *Beyond Formal Operations: Late Adolescent and Adult Cognitive Development.* New York: Praeger Press, 1983.

Power, C., Kohlberg, L., and Higgins, A. "Democratic Moral Education in the Large, Urban Public High School." Paper presented at Fribourg, Switzerland Conference, 1982. In F. Oser and M. Berkowitz, eds., *Moral Education: International Perspectives.* Hillside, N.J.: Ehrlbaum Assoc., in preparation.

Snarey, J., Reimer, J, and Kohlberg, L. "The Development of Social-Moral Reasoning Among Kibbutz Adolescents: A Longitudinal Cross-Cultural Study." *Developmental Psychology,* in press.

Kohlberg, L. *Essays in Moral Development.* Volume II: *The Psychology of Moral Development.* San Francisco: Harper & Row, 1984.

Index